# Continuity, Influences and Integration in Scottish Legal History

EDINBURGH STUDIES IN LAW

*Series Editor*
Alexandra Braun, University of Edinburgh

*Editorial Board*
George Gretton, University of Edinburgh
John Lovett, Loyola University
Hector MacQueen, University of Edinburgh
Elspeth Reid, University of Edinburgh
Kenneth Reid, University of Edinburgh
Lionel Smith, McGill University
Anna Veneziano, Universities of Teramo and UNIDROIT
Neil Walker, University of Edinburgh
Reinhard Zimmermann, Max Planck Institute for Comparative and International Private Law in Hamburg

*Volumes in the series*:

Hector L MacQueen (ed), *Continuity, Influences and Integration in Scottish Legal History: Select Essays of David Sellar* (2022)

Guido Rossi (ed), *Authorities in Early Modern Law Courts* (2021)

John W Cairns, *Enlightenment, Legal Education, and Critique: Selected Essays on the History of Scots Law, Volume 2* (2015)

John W Cairns, *Law, Lawyers, and Humanism: Selected Essays on the History of Scots Law, Volume 1* (2015)

Paul J du Plessis and John W Cairns (eds), *Reassessing Legal Humanism and its Claims: Petere Fontes?* (2015)

Remus Valsan (ed), *Trusts and Patrimonies* (2015)

Eric Descheemaeker (ed), *The Consequences of Possession* (2014)

Neil Walker (ed), *MacCormick's Scotland* (2012)

Elaine E Sutherland, Kay E Goodall, Gavin F M Little and Fraser P Davidson (eds), *Law Making and the Scottish Parliament* (2011)

J W Cairns and Paul du Plessis (eds), *The Creation of the* Ius Commune: *From* Casus *to* Regula (2010)

James Chalmers, Lindsay Farmer and Fiona Leverick (eds), *Essays in Criminal Law in Honour of Sir Gerald Gordon* (2010)

Vernon Valentine Palmer and Elspeth Christie Reid (eds), *Mixed Jurisdictions Compared: Private Law in Louisiana and Scotland* (2009)

John W Cairns and Paul du Plessis (eds), *Beyond Dogmatics: Law and Society in the Roman World* (2007)

William M Gordon, *Roman Law, Scots Law and Legal History* (2007)

Kenneth G C Reid, Marius J de Waal and Reinhard Zimmermann (eds), *Exploring the Law of Succession: Studies National, Historical and Comparative* (2007)

Hector MacQueen and Reinhard Zimmermann (eds), *European Contract Law: Scots and South African Perspectives* (2006)

Elspeth Reid and David L Carey Miller (eds), *A Mixed Legal System in Transition: T B Smith and the Progress of Scots Law* (2005)

https://edinburghuniversitypress.com/series/esil

EDINBURGH STUDIES IN LAW
VOLUME 17

# Continuity, Influences and Integration in Scottish Legal History
## Select Essays of David Sellar

*Edited by*
Hector L MacQueen

**EDINBURGH**
University Press

Edinburgh University Press is one of the leading university presses in the UK. We publish academic books and journals in our selected subject areas across the humanities and social sciences, combining cutting-edge scholarship with high editorial and production values to produce academic works of lasting importance. For more information visit our website: edinburghuniversitypress.com

© David Sellar, 2023
© editorial matter and organization The Edinburgh Law Review Trust, 2022, 2023

Edinburgh University Press Ltd
The Tun – Holyrood Road
12(2f) Jackson's Entry
Edinburgh EH8 8PJ

First published in hardback by Edinburgh University Press 2022

Typeset in New Caledonia by
Cheshire Typesetting Ltd, Cuddington, Cheshire

A CIP record for this book is available from the British Library

ISBN 978 1 4744 8876 1 (hardback)
ISBN 978 1 4744 8877 8 (paperback)
ISBN 978 1 4744 8878 5 (webready PDF)
ISBN 978 1 4744 8879 2 (epub)

The right of David Sellar to be identified as the author of this work has been asserted in accordance with the Copyright, Designs and Patents Act 1988, and the Copyright and Related Rights Regulations 2003 (SI No. 2498).

The right of The Edinburgh Law Review Trust to be identified as the editor of this work has been asserted in accordance with the Copyright, Designs and Patents Act 1988, and the Copyright and Related Rights Regulations 2003 (SI No. 2498).

# Contents

| | | |
|---|---|---|
| | List of Figures | vi |
| | List of Abbreviations | vii |
| | Acknowledgements | xi |
| | Table of Statutes | xii |
| | Table of Cases | xviii |
| | Introduction: David Sellar, Legal Historian<br>H L MacQueen | 1 |
| 1 | The Continuity of Scottish Legal History: An Overview | 15 |
| 2 | Celtic Law and Scots Law: Survival and Integration | 53 |
| 3 | Marriage, Divorce and Concubinage in Gaelic Scotland | 84 |
| 4 | The Lyon and the *Seanchaidh* | 107 |
| 5 | Birlaw Courts and Birleymen | 123 |
| 6 | English Law as a Source of Stair's *Institutions* | 142 |
| 7 | The Resilience of the Scottish Common Law | 156 |
| 8 | Scots Law: Mixed from the Very Beginning? A Tale of Two Receptions | 173 |
| 9 | Marriage by Cohabitation with Habit and Repute: Review and Requiem? | 191 |
| 10 | Marriage, Divorce and the Forbidden Degrees: Canon Law and Scots Law | 216 |
| 11 | Forethocht Felony, Malice Aforethought and the Classification of Homicide | 239 |
| 12 | Juridical Acts Made in Contemplation of Death | 263 |
| 13 | Succession Law | 279 |
| 14 | Courtesy, Battle and the Brieve of Right, 1368 | 297 |
| 15 | Promise | 311 |
| 16 | Presumptions | 346 |
| | Index | 373 |

# Figures

| | | |
|---|---|---|
| Figure 2.1 | The toiseachdeor. From Peter G B McNeill and Hector L MacQueen, *An Atlas of Scottish History to 1707* (Edinburgh: The Scottish Medievalists and Department of Geography, University of Edinburgh, 1996), p 212. Reproduced with permission of the Trustees of the Scottish Medievalists: The Society for Scottish Medieval and Renaissance Studies. | 66 |
| Figure 4.1 | Inauguration of Alexander III, from Bower's Scotichronicon, courtesy of the Master and Fellows of Corpus Christi College, Cambridge | 112 |
| Figure 4.2 | Seal of Scone Abbey around 1250, showing the inauguration of Alexander III, courtesy of Lord Lyon King of Arms/Crown Copyright: RCAHMS | 113 |
| Figure 14.1 | Courtesy 1368 | 299 |
| Figure 14.2 | Courtesy 1437 | 310 |

# Abbreviations

| | |
|---|---|
| APS | T Thomson and C Innes (eds), *Acts of the Parliaments of Scotland* (12 vols, 1814–1875) |
| Balfour, *Practicks* | P G B McNeill (ed), *The Practicks of Sir James Balfour of Pittendreich* (Stair Society vols 21 and 22, 1962–1963) |
| Bankton, *Inst* | A McDouall, Lord Bankton, *An Institute of the Laws of Scotland* (3 vols, 1751–1753; reprinted with an introduction by W M Gordon, Stair Society vols 41–43, 1993–1995) |
| Barrow, "Justiciar" | G W S Barrow, "The Scottish justiciar in the twelfth and thirteenth centuries", 1971 *JR* 97, reprinted in G W S Barrow, *The Kingdom of the Scots* (2nd edn, 2003) ch 3 |
| Bracton | G E Woodbine and S E Thorne (eds), *Bracton's De Legibus et Consuetudinibus Angliae* (4 vols, 1968–1977) |
| Chron Fordun | W F Skene (ed), *Johannis de Fordun Chronica Gentis Scotorum* (2 vols, 1871–1872) |
| Craig, *De Unione* | T Craig, *De Unione Regnorum Britanniae Tractatus, ed and trans C S Terry* (SHS, 1909) |
| Craig, *JF* | J Baillie (ed), *D. Thomae Cragii de Riccarton, Jus Feudale Tribus Libris Comprehensum* (1732); Lord Clyde (trans), *The Jus Feudale by Sir Thomas Craig of Riccarton* (1933); L Dodd (ed), *Jus Feudale Tribus Libris Comprehensum by Sir Thomas Craig of Riccartoun Book I* (Stair Society vol 64, 2017) |
| Edin LR | *Edinburgh Law Review* |
| Erskine, *Inst* | J Erskine, *An Institute of the Law of Scotland* (1st edn, 1773; 8th edn, 1871) |
| Erskine, *Prins* | J Erskine, *Principles of the Law of Scotland* (1st edn, 1754; 21st edn, 1911) |
| Glanvill | G D G Hall (ed), *Tractatus de Legibus et* |

|  |  |
|---|---|
|  | *Consuetudinbus Angliae qui Glanvilla Vocatur* (1965) |
| Hope, *Practicks* | J A Clyde (ed), *Hope's Major Practicks 1608–1633* (SS vols 3 and 4, 1937–1938) |
| Hume, *Commentaries* | D Hume, *Commentaries on the Law of Scotland respecting Crimes* (1st edn, 1797; 4th edn, 1844) |
| Hume, *Lectures* | G C H Paton (ed), *Baron David Hume's Lectures 1786–1822* (6 vols, Stair Society, vols 5, 13, 15, 17–19, 1939–1958) |
| ISLH | G C H Paton (ed), *An Introduction to Scottish Legal History* (SS vol 20, 1958) |
| JLH | *Journal of Legal History* |
| JR | *Juridical Review* |
| *Justiciary Cases* | I: S A Gillon (ed), *Justiciary Cases 1624–1650 vol 1* (SS vol 16, 1953) |
|  | II: J Irvine Smith (ed), *Selected Justiciary Cases, 1624–1650, volume 2* (SS vol 27, 1972) |
|  | III: J Irvine Smith (ed), *Justiciary Cases 1624–1650 vol 3* (SS vol 28, 1974) |
| *Justiciary Records* | I: W G Scott-Moncrieff (ed), *Records of the Proceedings of the Justiciary Court, Edinburgh, 1661–1678, volume 1* (SHS, 1905) |
|  | II: W G Scott-Moncrieff (ed), *Records of the Proceedings of the Justiciary Court, Edinburgh, 1661–1678, volume 2* (SHS, 1905) |
| LMS | A Taylor (ed), *The Laws of Medieval Scotland: Legal Compilations from the Thirteenth and Fourteenth Centuries* (Stair Society vol 66, 2019) |
| LQR | *Law Quarterly Review* |
| Mackenzie, *Inst* | G Mackenzie, *Institutions of the Law of Scotland* (1st edn, 1684; 8th edn, 1758) |
| Mackenzie, *Matters Criminal* | O F Robinson (ed), *The Laws and Customs of Scotland in Matters Criminal by Sir George Mackenzie* (Stair Society vol 59, 2012) |
| Mich LR | *Michigan Law Review* |
| MLR | *Modern Law Review* |
| Mor | W M Morison (ed), *Decisions of the Court of Session . . . Digested under Proper Heads in the Form of a Dictionary* (1801–1804) |

|  |  |
|---|---|
| NLS | National Library of Scotland |
| NRS | National Records of Scotland |
| Pollock & Maitland | F Pollock and F W Maitland, *History of English Law* (2nd edn, 1898; reprinted 1968, with an introduction by S F C Milsom) |
| *RM (APS)* | T Thomson (ed), "Regiam Majestatem", *APS*, vol 1, at 597–641 |
| *RM (Cooper)* | Lord Cooper (ed), *Regiam Majestatem and Quoniam Attachiamenta* (Stair Society vol 11, 1947) |
| *RMS* | J M Thomson and others (eds), *Registrum Magni Sigilli Regum Scotorum* (1882–1914) |
| *RPS* | K M Brown and others (eds), *Records of the Parliaments of Scotland to 1707* |
| *RRS* | *Regesta Regum Scottorum*: vol 1: *The Acts of Malcolm IV 1153–1165* (ed G W S Barrow, 1960); vol 2: *The Acts of William I 1165–1214* (ed G W S Barrow, 1971); vol 5: *The Acts of Robert I 1306–1329* (ed A A M Duncan, 1988); vol 6: *The Acts of David II 1329–1371* (ed B Webster, 1982). |
| *RSS* | M Livingstone and others (eds), *Registrum Secreti Sigilli Regum Scotorum* (1908–) |
| *Scottish Formularies* | A A M Duncan (ed), *Scottish Formularies* (SS vol 58, 2011) |
| Sellar, "Common law" | W D H Sellar, "The common law of Scotland and the common law of England", in R R Davies (ed), *The British Isles 1100–1500: Comparisons, Contrasts and Connections* (1988) 82 |
| Sellar, "Custom" | W D H Sellar, "Custom as a source of law", *SME* vol 22 (1987) paras 355–393 |
| *SHR* | *Scottish Historical Review* |
| SHS | Scottish History Society |
| Skene, *DVS* | Sir J Skene, *De Verborum Significatione: The Exposition of the Terms and Difficil Wordes, conteined in the Foure Buikes of Regiam Majestatem etc* (1597, reprinted 2006) |

| | |
|---|---|
| Skene, *RM (Latin)* | Sir J Skene, *Regiam Majestatem Scotiae Veteres et Constitutiones* (1609) |
| Skene, *RM (Scots)* | Sir J Skene, *Regiam Majestatem: The Auld Lawes and Consitutions of Scotland* (1609) |
| *SLSL* | H McKechnie (ed), *The Sources and Literature of Scots Law* (SS vol 1, 1936) |
| Smith, *Short Commentary* | T B Smith, *A Short Commentary on the Laws of Scotland* (1962) |
| Spotiswoode, *Practicks* | R Spotiswoode, *Practicks of the Law of Scotland*, 1706) |
| SS | Stair Society |
| Stair, *Inst* | J Dalrymple, Viscount Stair, *Institutions of the Laws of Scotland* (1st edn 1681; 6th edn by D M Walker, 1981) |
| *SME* | T B Smith and others (eds), *The Laws of Scotland: Stair Memorial Encyclopaedia* (1987–) |

# Acknowledgements

In preparing this collection for publication I have received much appreciated help and support from David Sellar's family (especially his widow Sue and son Gavin), as well as from friends and colleagues of Sellar and myself; in particular Gillian Black, Alexandra Braun, Dauvit Broun, John Cairns, James Chalmers, Alex Maxwell Findlater, Mark Godfrey, Greg Gordon, Michael Jones and Elaine Sutherland. My Honours classes in "Lords and Vassals in Medieval Scotland" 2017–2020 helped me get back up to speed on medieval legal history after eight years at the Scottish Law Commission. I am grateful to them all. I must also thank the first publishers of the works collected here for enabling them to be re-published: the Saltire Society, the Stair Society, the School of Scottish Studies in the University of Edinburgh, the Gaelic Society of Inverness, Edinburgh University Press, the Jean Bodin Society (Brussels), Duncker & Humblot (Berlin), Oxford University Press, the Edinburgh Law Review Trust and the board of the Edinburgh Studies in Law, in whose series this volume now takes its place. The place of first publication for each chapter is given in an opening asterisked footnote.

Hector L MacQueen<br>
Edinburgh, 1 March 2021

# Table of Statutes

APS vol 1 424 (Crown Entail Act 1284) ................................................... 274
RPS 1318/4 (Common Law and Justice Act 1318) ................................. 158
RPS 1318/25 (Brieve of Recognition Amendment Act 1318) ................ 306
RPS 1318/29 (Defence of the Realm Act 1318) ........................................ 78
RPS 1318/30 (Crown Entail Act 1318) .................................................. 274
RPS 1370/2/12 (Remissions for Murder Abolition Act 1370) ............................................................................. 245, 249–50, 255
RPS 1370/2/36 (Remissions for Homicide Act 1370) .......... 245, 249–50, 255
RPS 1372/3/9 (Homicide Chaudmella Act 1372) ..... 245, 245–6, 247, 249–50
RPS 1372/3/7 (Girth and Forethought Felony Act 1372) .... 245, 247, 249–50
RPS 1373/3 (Crown Entail Act 1373) .................................................... 274
RPS 1399/1/2 (Royal Officers Act 1399) ............................................... 158
RPS 1424/15 (Royal Mines Act 1424 (c 13)) ......................................... 3, 38
RPS 1426/6 (Law of the Land Act 1426) ...................................... 158–9, 188
RPS 1426/10 (Forethought Felony Act 1426) ...................................... 246–7
RPS 1426/13 (Statute Law Revision Act 1426) ...................................... 305
RPS 1426/25 (Sessions Act 1426) ............................................................ 33
RPS 1427/7/6 (Spiritual Courts Procedure Act 1427) ............................ 305
RPS 1428/3/3 (Members of Parliament Act 1428) ................................. 180
RPS 1430/5 (Brieves Act 1430) .............................................................. 305
RPS 1432/3/6 (Murder Act 1432) ............................................................ 69
RPS 1450/1/16–17 (Leases Act 1449) ....................................................... 38
RPS 1456/4 (Defence of the Realm Act 1456) .................................... 78, 79
RPS 1469/18 (Prescription Act 1469 (c 28)) ........................................... 37
RPS 1469/20 (Notaries Act 1469) ...................................................... 159–60
RPS 1469/25 (Murder Act 1469) .................................................... 247, 257
RPS 1471/8/26 (Brieves Act 1471) ......................................................... 305
RPS A1474/5/9 (Prescription Act 1474 (c 54)) ........................................ 37
RPS 1481/4/4 (Defence of the Realm Act 1481) ................................. 78, 79
RPS 1484/2/30 (Defence of the Realm Act 1484) ............................... 78, 79
RPS 1504/3/42 (Terce Act 1504) ................. 165, 191, 191–5, 197, 347–8, 367
RPS A1504/3/124 (Law of the Land Act 1504) ............... 97, 158, 159, 188
RPS A1504/3/140 (Brieves of Inquest Act 1504) ................................... 305

*RPS* 1532/6 (College of Justice Act 1532 (c 36))..............................33, 33–4
*RPS* 1540/12/92 (Subscription of Deeds Act 1540) ...................................37
*RPS* A1555/6/22 (Sasines Act 1555 (c 46))..............................................179
*RPS* A1557/12/5 (Exceptions Act 1555) ..................................................305
*RPS* A1560/8/4 (Papal Jurisdiction Act 1560) ...............................7, 29, 217
*RPS* A1563/6/10 (Adultery Act 1563)......................................................228
*RPS* 1567/12/54 (Law Commission Act 1567) .......................................187
*RPS* A1567/12/14 (Incest Act) ............................30, 37, 179, 233–4, 237, 238
*RPS* A1567/12/15 (Marriage Act 1567) ...............37, 179, 233, 234, 237, 238
10/31, 10/32, 10/33
*RPS* 1573/4/2 (Divorce for Desertion Act 1573).............................4, 229–30
*RPS* A1575/3/5 (Beggars and Provision for the Poor Act 1575)...............178
*RPS* 1579/10/33 (Subscription of Deeds Act 1579 (c 80)).........................37
*RPS* 1579/10/36 (Prescription Act 1579 (c 83)) ........................................37
*RPS* 1584/5/10 (Unlawful Jurisdictions Act 1584) ...................................188
*RPS* 1587/7/67 (Justice Ayres Act 1587)..................................................351

*RPS* 1587/7/143 (Barons in Parliament Act 1587) ....................................180
*RPS* 1592/4/86 (Commissariot Act 1592) .................................................325
*RPS* A1596/5/3 (Proclamation against the Rebels in the Isles Act 1596) ........................................................................................................78
*RPS* 1599/7/6 (Sasine Registration Act 1599) ..........................................179
*RPS* 1600/11/42 (Marriage of Adulterers Act 1600) .................................229
*RPS* 1600/11/49 (Sasines Act 1600) .........................................................179
*RPS* 1609/4/20 (Commissariots Act 1609)..................................165, 218, 325
*RPS* 1612/10/10 (Hornings in Case of Murder Act 1612) ........................273
*RPS* 1617/5/30 (Registration Act 1617 (c 16))...............................3, 38, 179
*RPS* 1617/5/35 (Cawps Act 1617 (c 21))..................................................264
*RPS* 1621/6/30 (Bankruptcy Act 1621 (c 18))...........37–8, 151, 347–8, 367–8
*RPS* 1649/1/118 (Casual Homicide Act 1649)........251, 252–3, 254, 255, 257
*RPS* 1649/5/219 (Incest Act 1649)........................................................236–7
*RPS* 1661/1/265 (Homicide Act 1661).....................................................252
*RPS* 1661/1/302 (Clandestine Marriages Act 1661)..................................219
*RPS* 1681/7/27 (Subscription of Deeds Act 1681 (c 5))............................37
*RPS* 1685/4/16 (Supply Act 1685).............................................................78
*RPS* 1685/4/49 (Entail Act 1685 (c 26))............................................269, 278
*RPS* 1686/4/37 (Winter Herding Act 1686)..............................................138
*RPS* 1689/3/108 (Claim of Right Act 1689)................................................80
*RPS* 1689/6/41 (Defence of the Realm Act 1689).................................78, 79

*RPS* 1690/4/33 (Confession of Faith Act 1690)..........................................237
*RPS* 1690/4/111 (Child Murder Act 1690)................................................368
*RPS* 1695/5/156 (Runrig Lands Act 1695 (c 36))........................................138
*RPS* 1695/5/204 (Division of Commonties Act 1695 (c 69))......................138
*RPS* 1696/9/56 (Deathbed Act 1696)..........................................277, 282, 370
*RPS* 1696/9/57 (Bankruptcy Act 1696 (c 5))...........................................37–8
*RPS* 1696/9/143 (Blank Bonds and Trusts Act 1696 (c 25))................37, 275
*RPS* 1698/7/113 (Clandestine Marriages Act 1698)..................................219
*RPS* 1701/10/234 (Criminal Procedure Act 1701 (c 6))................................42
*RPS* 1704/7/68 (Security of the Kingdom Act 1704).............................78–9
*RPS* 1706/10/257 (Union with England Act 1706).........2, 43–4, 52, 160, 263
    Article II .................................................................................................274
    Article XIX................................................................................................43
    Article XXV..........................................................................................43–4

## Pre-1707 English Acts
1535  Statute of Enrolments (27 Hen VIII, c 16)....................................179
1540  Marriage Act (32 Hen 8, c 38).........................................179, 233, 234
1572  Vagabonds Act 1572 (14 Eliz c 5) ......................................................178
1701  Act of Settlement (12 & 13 Will III c 2)..........................................274

## Acts of the UK and Scottish Parliaments
1746  Heritable Jurisdictions Act (20 Geo 2, c 43) ....................10, 44–5, 138
1753  Act for the Better Preventing of Clandestine Marriages (26 Geo
        2, c 33) ............................................................................219, 220, 225
1770  Entail Improvement Act (Montgomery Act) (10 Geo 3, c 51)........278
1800  Accumulations Act (39 & 40 Geo 3, c 98)........................................272
1819  Appeal of Murder Act (59 Geo 3, c 46)............................................309
1835  Marriage Act (5 & 6 Will 4, c 54)......................................................226
1836  Bastards (Scotland) Act (6 & 7 Will 4, c 22)............................277, 278
1845  Lands Clauses Consolidation Act (8 & 9 Vict, c 18) .........................49
        Lands Clauses Consolidation (Scotland) Act (8 & 9 Vict, c 19) ........49
1848  Entail Amendment Act (Rutherfurd Act) (11 & 12 Vict, c 36)
        s 48 ..................................................................................................272, 278
1855  Moveable Succession (Scotland) Act (18 Vict, c 22).......................278
        Intestate Moveable Succession (Scotland) Act (18 & 19 Vict, c 23)
            s 1....................................................................................................288
            s 5....................................................................................................287
1856  Marriage (Scotland) Act (19 & 20 Vict, c 96).................................221

| | |
|---|---|
| 1857 Matrimonial Causes Act (20 & 21 Vict, c 85) | 231 |
| 1868 Entail Amendment (Scotland) Act (31 & 32 Vict, c 84) s 17 | 272 |
| Titles to Land Consolidation (Scotland) Act (31 & 32 Vict, c 101) | 278 |
| s 20 | 267, 271, 276 |
| 1871 Law of Deathbed Abolition (Scotland) Act (34 & 35 Vict, c 81) | 162, 277, 278, 282, 370 |
| 1873 Supreme Court of Judicature Act (36 & 37 Vict, c 66) | 34 |
| 1874 Conveyancing (Scotland) Act (37 & 38 Vict, c 94) | 278 |
| s 9 | 284 |
| s 27 | 275 |
| s 37 | 163, 284 |
| 1875 Supreme Court of Judicature Act (38 & 39 Vict, c 77) | 34 |
| 1876 Appellate Jurisdiction Act (39 & 40 Vict, c 59) | 49 |
| 1878 Dentists Act (41 & 42 Vict, c 33) | 44 |
| Marriage Notice (Scotland) Act (41 & 42 Vict, c 43) | 4 |
| 1881 Married Women's Property (Scotland) Act (44 & 45 Vict, c 21) | 271–2, 278 |
| s 6 | 271–2, 290 |
| s 7 | 272 |
| Presumption of Life Limitation (Scotland) Act (44 & 45 Vict, c 47) | 367 |
| 1886 Crofters Holdings (Scotland) Act (49 & 50 Vict, c 29) | 53 |
| 1887 Criminal Procedure (Scotland) Act (50 & 51 Vict, c 35) | |
| s 43 | 42 |
| s 56 | 237 |
| 1903 Licensing (Scotland) Act (3 Edw 7, c 25) | 227 |
| 1906 Statute Law Revision (Scotland) Act (6 Edw 7, c 38) | 79 |
| 1907 Deceased Wife's Sister's Marriage Act (7 Edw 7, c 47) | 238 |
| 1908 Punishment of Incest Act (8 Edw 7, c 45) | 233 |
| 1911 Intestate Husband's Estate (Scotland) Act (1 & 2 Geo 5, c 10) | 292 |
| 1914 Entail (Scotland) Act (4 & 5 Geo 5, c 43) | 269, 278 |
| 1919 Intestate Husband's Estate (Scotland) Act (9 & 10 Geo 5, c 9) | 292 |
| Intestate Moveable Succession (Scotland) Act (9 & 10 Geo 5, c 61) | 287 |
| 1921 Trusts (Scotland) Act (11 & 12 Geo 5, c 58) s 9 | 272 |
| 1923 Matrimonial Causes Act (13 & 14 Geo 5, c 19) | 232 |
| 1925 Administration of Estates Act (15 & 16 Geo 5, c 23) | 280 |
| 1929 Age of Marriage Act (19 & 20 Geo 5, c 36) | 209, 221 |

1930 Adoption of Children (Scotland) Act (20 & 21 Geo 5, c 37) ............293
1937 Matrimonial Causes Act (1 Edw 8 & 1 Geo 6, c 57)......................232
1938 Divorce (Scotland) Act (1 & 2 Geo 5, c 50) .................................4, 230
1939 Marriage (Scotland) Act (2 & 3 Geo 6, c 34) ......4, 30, 86, 203–7, 209,
                 212, 213, 223, 224, 225
  s 1..................................................................................................225
  s 5...................................................................................203, 223, 366
1949 Criminal Justice (Scotland) Act (12, 13 & 14 Geo 6, c 94)
  s 15(2) ............................................................................................273
1959 Intestate Husband's Estate (Scotland) Act (7 & 8 Eliz 2, c 21).......292
1964 Succession (Scotland) Act (c 41)....4, 26, 163, 178, 263, 267, 270, 272,
              278, 279, 285, 290, 292–3, 349
  s 10........................................................................................285, 286
  s 23..................................................................................................293
  s 31.........................................................................................296, 367
  s 37(1) ............................................................................................270
  Statute Law Revision (Scotland) Act (c 80).............................219, 229
1968 Law Reform (Miscellaneous Provisions) (Scotland) Act (c 70)
  s 2..................................................................................................293
1969 Age of Majority (Scotland) Act (c 39)..............................................277
1973 Prescription and Limitation (Scotland) Act (c 52)...........................37
1974 Land Tenure Reform (Scotland) Act (c 38) ........................................5
  Consumer Credit Act (c 39)..............................................................50
1975 Criminal Procedure (Scotland) Act (c 21) s 101 .................................42
1976 Damages (Scotland) Act (c 13)..........................................................68
  s 6..................................................................................................244
  s 8..................................................................................................117
  Divorce (Scotland) Act (c 39) ....................................................5, 227
  s 9..................................................................................................228
1977 Marriage (Scotland) Act (c 15) ................................5, 37, 179, 234, 238
  s 1..................................................................................................221
  s 5(4) ..............................................................................................221
  Presumption of Death (Scotland) Act (c 27)............................214, 367
1979 Land Registration (Scotland) Act (c 33)..............................................5
1985 Bankruptcy (Scotland) Act (c 66) ..............................................38, 368
  s 34..................................................................................................368
  s 75(2) ............................................................................................368
1986 Law Reform (Parent and Child) (Scotland) Act (c 9)......................277
  s 5..................................................................................................369

        s 9(1)(c) ............................................................................................... 270
        Incest and Related Offences (Scotland) Act (c 36) ......... 37–8, 179, 238
1991  Age of Legal Capacity (Scotland) Act (c 50) ............................ 221, 277
1995  Requirements of Writing (Scotland) Act (c 7) ........... 37, 275, 311, 315,
                                                                                                    330, 340, 341–5
        s 1 ...................................................................................................... 342–3
        s 1(3), (4) .......................................................................................... 345
        Criminal Law (Consolidation) (Scotland) Act (c 39) ss 1, 2 and 4 .... 38
        Criminal Procedure (Scotland) Act (c 46) s 65 .................................. 42
2000  Abolition of Feudal Tenure etc (Scotland) Act (asp 5) ...... 5, 6, 25, 270
2004  Criminal Procedure (Amendment) (Scotland) Act (asp 5) s 6 .......... 42
2006  Family Law (Scotland) Act (asp 2) s 3 .................................. 5, 215, 224
2010  Criminal Justice and Licensing (Scotland) Act (asp 13) Sch 7
        para 15 ................................................................................................ 38
2012  Land Registration etc (Scotland) Act (asp 5) ........................................ 5
2016  Criminal Justice (Scotland) Act (asp 1) s 79 ...................................... 42
        Succession (Scotland) Act (asp 7) ....................................... 4, 278, 292
            s 6 ............................................................................... 183, 276, 295
            s 9 ............................................................................... 296, 349, 367
            s 10 .................................................................................................. 349
            s 25(1) ....................................................................... 183, 274, 295
            s 29 ............................................................................. 183, 276, 295
        Bankruptcy (Scotland) Act (asp 21) .................................................. 38
            s 98 .................................................................................................. 368

## Pre-1800 Irish Acts
1745  Marriage Annulment Act (19 Geo II, c 13) s 1 .............................. 225

## ACTS OF SEDERUNT
1592  Act of Sederunt ............................................ 317, 321–2, 325, 326, 332
1692  Act of Sederunt ................................................................................ 370

# Table of Cases

AB v CD 1957 SC 415 (see also *Woodward v Woodward*) ....... 209, 213, 214
*Auchmoutie v Hay* (1609) Mor 12126, sub nom *Auchmoutie v Laird of Mainehay* (1609) Haddington's Decisions, NLS, Adv MS 24.2.2, no 1657 ................................................................................................. 316, 321
*Adam's Executrix v Maxwell* 1921 SC 418 ................................................. 288
*Aitken's Trustees v Aitken* 1927 SC 374 ..................................................... 268
*Annan v Annan* 1948 SC 532 ....................................................................... 228
*Anstruther v Anstruther* (1836) 14 S 272 .................................... 284, 286–7
*Ashford v Thornton* (1818) 1 B & Ald 405 ................................................. 309
*Auchinleck v Gordon* (1580) Mor 12382 ..................................................... 314
*Barclay v Blackhall* (1542) Balfour, *Practicks*, 29 .................................... 323
*Bartonshill Coal Company v Reid* (1858) 3 Macq 266 ......................... 49–50
*Bathgate v Rosie* 1976 SLT (Sh Ct) 16 .............................................. 340, 341
*Bikartoune (William)* (1581) Pitcairn, *Criminal Trials*, vol 1, part 2, 93–99 ................................................................................................................ 250
*Blak v Robertsone* (1516–20) *Liber Officialis Sancti Andree* (1845) 14 ................................................................................................................ 196–7
*Buccleugh, Duke and Duchess of v Marquess of Tweeddale* (1677) Mor 2369 ................................................................................................................ 295
*Cadder v Her Majesty's Advocate* 2011 SC (UKSC) 13 .............................. 51
*Campbell v Campbell* (1866) 4 M 867 .................... 202, 203, 205, 206, 229
*Campbell v Campbell* (1867) 5 M (HL) 115 ................. 197, 202–3, 210, 229
*Carlill v Carbolic Smoke Ball Co* [1893] 1 QB 256 ............................... 337–9
*Carnegie (Lady) v Cranburn (Lord)* (1663) Mor 10375 ........................... 152
*Chisholm v Chisholm* 1949 SC 434 ............................................................. 275
*Clackmannan (Laird of) v Sir William Nisbet* (1624), Spotiswoode, *Practicks* (1706) 248 ............................................................................ 321, 326
*Clinton v Trefusis* (1869) 8 M 370 ............................................................... 286
*Colville's JF v Nicoll* 1914 SC 62 ................................................................. 288
*Cuninghame v Cuninghame* (1770) Mor 14875 ........................................ 286
*Dalmahoy or Ralstoun v Mason* (1674) *Justiciary Records* II 278 ............ 253
*Davis v Sutherland's Executrix*, 20 December 1989, 1990 GWD 8-433 ................................................................................................................. 211

*De Warenne (John) v De la Zouche (Alan)* (1270) ..................... 241, 242, 256
*Deuchar v Brown* (1672) Mor 12386 ........................... 314–15, 321, 326
*Donnelly v Donnelly's Executor* 1992 SLT 13 ..................... 211–12, 213, 224
*Douglas of Drumlanrig (William)* (1512) Pitcairn, *Criminal Trials*, vol 1, part 1, 79 ................................................................................ 250
*DPP v Smith* [1961] AC 290 ............................................................ 239
*Drummond's JF v HM Advocate* 1944 SC 298 ............................. 295–6
*Drury v HM Advocate* 2001 SLT 1013 ............................................ 262
*Duthie v Keir's Executor* 1930 SC 645 .............................................. 273
*Edmonston v Edmonston* (1861) 23 D 995 .................................... 315
*Elder v M'Lean* (1829) 8 S 56 ...................................... 208, 211, 213
*Farquhar* (1753) Mor 4669 .............................................................. 273
*Farquharson (Captain Alwyne) of Invercauld* 1950 SLT (Lyon Ct) 13....264
*Ferguson v Paterson* (1748) Mor 8440 ..................................... 329, 336
*Fergusone (William)* (1562) Pitcairn, *Criminal Trials*, vol 1, part 1, 425 ................................................................................................ 250
*Fotheringham of Pourie v Heir of Hunter of Burnside* (1708) Mor 12414 .............................................................................................. 315
*George Heriot's Trust, Governors of v Caledonian Railway Company* 1915 SC (HL) 52 .............................................................................. 49
*Gibson's Trustees* 1933 SC 190 ........................................................ 34
*Glasgow Corporation v Central Land Board* 1956 SC (HL) 1 ............. 79
*Glasgow Corporation v Lord Advocate* 1959 SC 203 ...................... 190
*Hamilton v Wylie* (1827) 5 S 716 .......................................... 199, 237
*Hawick Heritable Investment Bank v Huggan* (1902) 5 F 75 ........... 315
*Hill v Hill*, 15 July 1986 (unreported) ............................................ 211
*Hopkinson (George) v Napier & Son* 1953 SC 139 ........................ 366
*Hunter v General Accident Co* 1909 SC (HL) 30 ..................... 338, 341
*Hunter v Hunter* (1904) 7 F 136 .................................................... 338
*Hodge v Fraser* (1740) Mor 3119 .................................................. 295
*Imre v Mitchell* 1958 SC 439 ........................................................ 369
*Irvine v Ker* (1695) ............................................................... 199, 229
*Irvings v Bell* (1646) *Justiciary Cases* III 583 ............................ 251–2
*Jack v Jack* 1962 SC 24 ................................................................. 227
*Johnesoune v Eldare* (1522) *Liber Officialis Sancti Andree* (1845) 21 ..... 197
*Kamperman v MacIver*, 20 March 1992, 1992 GWD 15–893; rev'd 1994 SC 230 ............................................................................ 197, 212
*Kelly v Kelly* (1861) 23 D 703 ....................................................... 275
*Kerr v Martin* (1840) 2 D 752 ....................................................... 293

*Kilbocho v Kilbocho* (1665) Mor 3058................................................................150
*Kininmonth v Spens* (1458?) Balfour, *Practicks*, 511....................................76
*Kintore v Sinclair* (1623) Mor 9425.................................................321, 326
*Kirkpatrick v Kirkpatrick's Trustees* (1874) 1 R (HL) 37..........................275
*Knox (Jean)* (1646) *Justiciary Cases* III 690.............................30, 235, 237
*Lapsley v Grierson* (1848) 8 D 34 .......................................................204
*Law v Newnes* (1894) 21 R 1027 .......................................................338
*Law Hospital NHS Trust v Lord Advocate* 1996 SC 301 ..........................27
*Lecprevik (Alexander)* (1509) Pitcairn, *Criminal Trials*, vol 1, part 1,
 62 ........................................................................................................250
*Lindsay's Executor v Forsyth* 1940 SC 568..........................................268
*Lord Advocate v Balfour* 1907 SC 1360................................................32
*Lord Advocate v University of Aberdeen and Budge* 1963 SC
 533 .................................................................................4, 27, 32
*Low v Gorman* 1970 SLT 356......................................................209–10, 210
*M'Beath's Trs v M'Beath* 1935 SC 471 ...............................................275
*M'Caig v University of Glasgow* 1907 SC 231 ....................................268
*M'Caig's Trs v Lismore United Free Kirk Session* 1915 SC 426........268, 276
*MacCormick v Lord Advocate* 1953 SC 396........................................44, 79
*MacDonald (Charles)* (1867) 5 Irv 525 ................................................255
*Macfarlane v Johnston* (1864) 2 M 1210.......................................329, 337
*MacGillivray v Souter* (1862) 24 D 759............................................74, 269
*M'Kendrick v Sinclair* 1972 SC (HL) 25................55, 68, 117, 164, 244, 309
*Mackenzie v Scott* 1980 SLT (Notes) 9..............................................210
*Mackie v Mackie* 1917 SC 276 ..........................................199, 223, 366
*McKowloche (Patrik)* (1497) Pitcairn, *Criminal Trials*, vol 1, part 1, 99 ..250
*Maclean of Ardgour v Maclean* 1941 SC 613.....................................264
*Macrae* (1836) 15 S 54 ..........................................................................273
*Manderstoune (Robert)* (1530) Pitcairn, *Criminal Trials*, vol 1, part 1,
 151 ........................................................................................................250
*Marshall & M'Kell v Blackwood of Pitreavie* (1747) Elchies, "Sale",
 no 6 .........................................................................................335–6, 340
*Mathiesone v Anderson* (1640) *Justiciary Cases* II 395..........................132
*Maxwell v Gordon* (1775) Hailes' Decisions 624....................................31
*Meeres v Dowell's Executor* 1923 SLT 184...........................................271
*Millar v Mitchell, Cadell and Co* (1860) 22 D 833 .............359, 359–60, 360
*Millar v Tremamondo* (1771) Mor 12395; Hailes' Decisions 409 .............315
*Morgan Guaranty Trust Co of New York v Lothian Regional Council*
 1995 SC 151........................................................................................190

*Morris v Riddick* (1867) 5 M 1036 .................................................... 183, 274
*Morton's Trustees v Aged Christian Friend Society* (1899) 2 F 82 ........... 337
*Mullen v Mullen* 1991 SLT 205 ........................................... 211, 213, 214, 224
*Munro-Lucas-Tooth* 1965 SLT (Lyon Court) 2 ......................................... 269
*Mures of Auchindrain* (1611) Pitcairn, *Criminal Trials*, vol 3, 143, 182 ................................................................................................................ 371
*Nicol v Bell* 1954 SLT 314 ............................................................. 207–9, 213
*Nisbet's Trustees v Nisbet* (1871) 9 M 937 ............................................... 277
*Paterson (A & G) v Highland Railway Co* 1927 SC (HL) 32 ........ 338–9, 339
*Pennycook v Grinton* (1752) Mor 12677 ........................................... 199, 223
*Petrie v Airlie (Earl of)* (1834) 13 S 68 .................................. 336–7, 338, 339
*Petto v HM Advocate* 2012 JC 105 .......................................................... 262
*Pringle of Stichill, Baronetcy of* 2016 SC (PC) 1 ....................................... 270
*R v Hancock and Shankland* [1986] AC 455 .............................................. 239
*R v Hyam* [1975] AC 55 ............................................................................ 239
*R v Millis* (1844) 10 Cl & Fin 534 ............................................................. 220
*R v Moloney* [1985] AC 905 ...................................................................... 239
*R(G) 2/82* ................................................................................................. 212
*R(G) 4/84* ................................................................................................. 212
*R(G) 5/83* .......................................................................................... 212, 213
*Reid (James)* (1539) Pitcairn, *Criminal Trials*, vol 1, part 1, 220 ............... 250
*Reoch v Young* (1712) Mor 9439 ..................................... 329, 335, 340, 341
*Riddell v Riddell* 1952 SC 475 ................................................................. 228
*Saxby v Saxby's Executors* 1952 SC 352 ................................................... 273
*Scruton v Gray* (1772) Hailes' Decisions 499 ........................................... 219
*Sharp v Sharp* (1631) Mor 4299, 15562 ................................... 317, 321, 326
*Shaw v Henderson* 1982 SLT 211 ...................................... 210–11, 212, 213
*Shetland Salmon Farmers Association v Crown Estate Commissioners* 1991 SLT 166 ............................................................................................ 32
*Smeaton (Andrew)* (1636) *Justiciary Cases* I 264 .................................... 371
*Smith v Lerwick Harbour Trustees* (1903) 5 F 680 .................................... 32
*Smith v Oliver* 1911 SC 103 .................................................................... 315
*Stone v Macdonald* 1979 SC 363 ............................................................. 340
*Strathclyde Police, Chief Constable of v Sharp* 2002 SLT (Sh Ct) 95 ....... 366
*Stuart v Stuart* 1942 SC 510 .................................................................... 295
*Sturzenegger Petitioner (No 2)* 2015 SLT (Lyon Ct) 2 ................................ 13
*Tayt (William)* (1493) Pitcairn, *Criminal Trials*, vol 1, part 1, 17 ............. 250
*Thomson v Thomson* 1908 SC 179 .......................................................... 228
*Turnbull v Forrest* (1520–22) *Liber Officialis Sancti Andree* (1845) 19 ... 196

*Walker v M'Adam* (1813) 5 Pat 675 ................................................................... 199, 222
*Walker v Walkers Trs* 1917 SC 46 ............................................................................. 284
*Wallace v Fife Coal Company* 1909 SC 682 ........................ 210, 210–11, 212
*Weir (John)* (1629) *Justiciary Cases* I 121 ............................................. 30, 235
*Whytlaw v Ker* (1598) 1 Riddell, *Inquiries into the Law and Practice of Scottish Peerages* 392 .................................................................................. 229
*Wigton (Earl of) v Lindsay (Lady Margaret)* (1708) (SS vol 6, 1940 at 45) ............................................................................................................................ 369
*Wing v Taylor* (1861) 2 Sw & Tr 278 ....................................................................... 237
*Wood v Moncur* (1591) Mor 7719 ................................................................. 316, 321
*Woodward v Woodward* 1958 SLT 213 (see also *AB v CD*) ..................... 209
*Yelverton v Yelverton* (1864) 4 MacQueen 743; (1864) 2 M (HL) 49; (1862) 1 M 161 ............................................................................... 221, 224–5, 225

# Introduction:
# David Sellar, Legal Historian

David Sellar (1941–2019) was a pioneering historian of Scots law who convincingly and conclusively rejected previous interpretations of the subject as a series of false starts and rejected experiments.[1] He emphasised instead the continuity of legal development in Scotland, with change a process of integration of external influences with indigenous customs from very early times on. Thus, down to the present Scots law embraces Celtic and other customary elements reaching far back into its past, while also having been open to innovation from the developing Canon, Civil, Feudal and English Common law since the middle ages. This too has left deep marks upon the law's character as a "mixed legal system".

Sellar's approach, articulated mainly through essays published in diverse places over four decades, has had significant influence upon general understanding of legal history in Scotland as well as leading to appreciation elsewhere of its comparative significance. Gathering his major essays together in this single collection demonstrates the scope and reach of Sellar's overall contribution; it is perhaps an approximation to the monograph that he was not spared to write. What distinguishes the contribution from others in the field is the perspective that Sellar himself brought to bear, which was one no other writer in the field could achieve, especially in relation to Celtic and Canon law.

The book opens with Sellar's most general treatment of Scottish legal development from the period before 1100 down to the near present.[2] Although this essay was jointly published by the Saltire and Stair Societies in 1991, and he did much subsequent further research, it remains the best introduction to the ways in which Sellar saw his contribution as differing from those who had gone before him, as well as providing an overview

---

1 A memoir by the present writer privately printed in 2020 appears in revised form as "William David Hamilton Sellar MVO, BA, LLB, LLD, FRHistS, FSA(Scot): a memoir" (2021) 150 *Proceedings of the Society of Antiquaries* 187. See also A Maxwell Findlater, "Memoir of David Sellar umquhile Lord Lyon King of Arms" (2021) 44 *The Double Tressure* 61.
2 Chapter 1 below.

against which the subsequent chapters may be set. Inevitably over the last thirty years there has been a great deal of writing in all the areas addressed by Sellar, including his own. Rather than attempt a summary update in this introduction, I have chosen instead to use the footnotes to the first chapter to help guide the reader to that newer material by others. None of it, I believe, undermines Sellar's general thesis of continuity, while much of it gives that thesis at least mute support. In a few places I have updated the text itself to avoid now anachronistic references. I have followed a similar approach in the other chapters, although not to the same extent as in the opening chapter.

The introductory chapter formed part of the matter with which a Saltire Society pamphlet on the Scottish Legal System, written in 1949 by Lord President Cooper (1892–1955), was itself updated. Cooper's writings in the 1940s had established the prevailing orthodoxy on the general development of Scots law from the middle ages on when Sellar began his own researches at the end of the 1960s. Cooper's reiterated view was that the story of Scots law was one of "false starts and rejected experiments",[3] ending only with the 1681 publication of the seminal *Institutions* of James Dalrymple, Viscount Stair (1619–1695). The book came in the nick of time to save at least Scots private law from the fate of absorption into English law after the Anglo-Scottish Union of 1707. Borrowing from England had been the false start and the rejected experiment of the "Scoto-Norman" period before 1300; there had then followed a "Dark Age" for the system.[4] From this it began to be rescued by the development of a central court (the Court of Session) in the sixteenth century, the emergence of a legal profession around that court, and (resulting in part from the education of many members of that profession in the law schools of continental Europe) a reception of the learned Roman law as taught in the universities. The end result, systematised by Stair in particular, was something quite distinct from English law, and it was expressly preserved by the Treaty and Acts of Union in 1707, along with a separate legal system within the newly united kingdom of Great Britain.

Before turning to the detail of how Sellar challenged this view of Scottish legal history, it is worth reflecting on the system as it stood when a young

---

3 Lord Cooper, *The Scottish Legal Tradition* (Saltire Society, 1949) at 8. See also for the same phrase his *Select Scottish Cases of the Thirteenth Century* (1944) at lxi and "From David I to Bruce, 1124–1329, the Scoto-Norman law", in *ISLH* 3 at 3.

4 Cooper's line here received influential support from the medievalist historian W C Dickinson: "The administration of justice in medieval Scotland" (1951–2) 34 *Aberdeen University Review* 338.

Oxford historian entered its study at Edinburgh in 1962 before proceeding in 1964 to a legal apprenticeship with the city firm of Shepherd & Wedderburn WS. Academically, he was pursuing a long-established route into the Scottish legal profession whereby an initial Arts degree was followed by an "accelerated" LLB taken over two years. A full-time, entirely undergraduate LLB programme had been introduced only the previous year. T B Smith, Edinburgh's Professor of Civil Law, had just published *A Short Commentary on the Law of Scotland* in order to ensure that the increasing numbers of law students had an up-to-date textbook. In many key respects the system described by Smith must have appeared an antiquated one to most students. But that might increase its interest for a historian, especially as it did not fit the idea (re-articulated in Smith's opening chapter) of a system that had from time to time rejected its past wholesale and begun afresh.

While statute and judicial decisions were the main sources of Scots as English law, there was also dependence for the unenacted common law upon a group of writers (described as "institutional") who had worked in the seventeenth, eighteenth and early nineteenth centuries. Stair was pre-eminent among them but other important writers were John Erskine (1695–1768) and George Joseph Bell (1770–1843). Relevant legislation included many Acts of the pre-1707 Scottish Parliament, the earliest being the Royal Mines Act 1424.[5] The significance of Roman law as a further source was apparent from its successful study being a requirement for entry to the Scottish bar (the Faculty of Advocates). Land law and conveyancing were firmly based upon a feudal system of tenure established in Scotland since the twelfth century, and its lynchpin was the Register of Sasines (i.e. of the giving of lawful possession, not title) first set up by statute in 1617.[6] The law of succession distinguished as it had done since medieval times between heritable and moveable property, with the rules on the former (land, or heritage) depending still on the entitlement of the heir-at-law who succeeded to land by right of primogeniture with males preferred to females. If the deceased was survived by daughters only, they shared the property as "heirs-portioner". A widow had a lifetime "terce" (third) of her late husband's heritage, while a widower had a similarly lifetime right ("courtesy") to the whole of his deceased wife's lands provided that a child had been born of their marriage and heard to cry.

5 *RPS* 1424/15.
6 *RPS* 1617/5/30.

In moveable succession there was freedom of testation but subject amongst other things to the "legal rights" of surviving spouses and legitimate children of the marriage; while these now had names derived from Roman law (*jus relicti, jus relictae, legitim*), it was arguable that their origins lay in customary law. Formalities of marriage beyond parties' mutual consent, either before a minister of religion or in a civil ceremony, had been introduced by statute only in 1878 and 1939 respectively.[7] The latter legislation had also abolished the "irregular" forms of marriage by present consent (*per verba de presenti*) and by promise of marriage followed by copulation (*per verba de futuro subsequente copula*) but marriage by cohabitation with habit and repute had survived. Although divorce was mostly based upon matrimonial faults specified in an Act of 1938, one (adultery) originated in the unlegislated post-Reformation law of the kirk sessions, while another (desertion) had first been provided for in a statute of 1573.[8] Substantive criminal law and the law of obligations (i.e. contract, delict and unjustified enrichment) depended upon the common law rather than legislation. A further historical element in the legal landscape emerged during Sellar's LLB studies with the 1963 Court of Session decision about the St Ninian's Isle Treasure found in Shetland in the 1950s. There much ink was spilled on the question of the continuing applicability or not of the Norse Udal law, which had certainly been the law in force in Orkney as well as Shetland before the islands were impignorated to the Scottish Crown in 1469.[9]

The view from 1962 has been highlighted here because the statutory transformation of the law over the ensuing fifty years does mean that what preceded it has largely slipped from the collective minds of current academic as well as practising lawyers. Others may simply be unaware of the extent to which the law changed in many of its fundamentals from the 1960s on. The Succession (Scotland) Act 1964, which came into force just as Sellar completed his LLB, can be seen now as the beginning of the process.[10] The feudal content of land law was first diluted in the 1970s and then abolished

---

7 Marriage Notice (Scotland) Act 1878; Marriage (Scotland) Act 1939.
8 Divorce (Scotland) Act 1938; RPS 1573/4/2. It is worth noting that Cooper was responsible as Lord Advocate for both the 1938 and 1939 Acts: see further H L MacQueen, "Legal nationalism: the case of Lord Cooper", in N M Dawson (ed), *Reflections on Law and History: Irish Legal History Society Discourses and Other Papers, 2000–2005* (2006) 83 at 93.
9 *Lord Advocate v University of Aberdeen and Budge* 1963 SC 533. For T B Smith's significant role in this case, see D L Carey Miller, "St Ninian's Isle Treasure: Lord Advocate v University of Aberdeen and Budge", in J P Grant and E E Sutherland (eds), *Scots Law Tales* (2010) ch 7.
10 The 1964 Act came into force on 10 June that year. Note also the Succession (Scotland) Act 2016.

altogether at the start of the twenty-first century.[11] The Register of Sasines was likewise gradually replaced by a register of title (the Land Register) from 1979 and is expected to close for new registrations in 2024.[12] Divorce and marriage laws were comprehensively overhauled in the 1970s, although marriage by cohabitation with habit and repute was not abolished until 2006.[13] This background of large-scale reform over the course of Sellar's career entailed a major shift of interest in what was antiquated but still current law to make it decisively part of legal history only. In some ways, this is a loss for the subject, because it means that the practitioner has ever less reason to know and engage with older law while the study of legal history becomes more and more the province of specialists in the field.[14] Sellar was perhaps the last figure who could knowledgeably straddle that divide, at least in the areas of it which interested him.

Like Cooper before him, however, Sellar was most interested by the medieval period of Scots law. In part this sprang from his other central research interest, Highland and islands history and genealogy, and that clearly informed the fresh contribution that he was able to make to Scottish legal history.[15] Where Cooper had (despite his own maternal ancestry) simply passed over any Highland and islands dimension to legal development,[16] Sellar dug deep, not only into the Celtic law of the Highlands and the western isles,[17] but also the Udal law of Orkney and Shetland.[18] He was able to show that in at least some aspects these continued to form part of current Scots law and must therefore have had a continuous history despite sitting

---

11 Land Tenure Reform (Scotland) Act 1974; Abolition of Feudal Tenure etc (Scotland) Act 2000.
12 Land Registration (Scotland) Act 1979; Land Registration etc (Scotland) Act 2012.
13 Divorce (Scotland) Act 1976; Marriage (Scotland) Act 1977; Family Law (Scotland) Act 2006 s 3.
14 Although judges (notably sheriffs) and members of the bar have continued to make a significant contribution to legal-historical literature, in modern times very few solicitors in private practice have matched the work in previous generations of such as David Murray (1842–1928), George Neilson (1858–1923), John Cameron (1883–1950) and David Baird Smith (1877–1951). See further T H Drysdale, "The Stair Society – the middle years", in H L MacQueen (ed), *Miscellany VI* (SS vol 54, 2009) 283 at 292–295.
15 Note, for example, such early contributions as "Early Maclean marriages: dispensations" (1978) 6 *Notes and Queries of the Society of West Highland and Island Historical Research* 18; "Barony jurisdiction in the highlands" (1981) 16 *Notes and Queries of the Society of West Highland and Island Historical Research* 22.
16 Cooper's mother Margaret Mackay came from Dunnet in Caithness; his own middle name was Mackay; and his peerage title was Baron Cooper of Culross of Dunnet in the County of Caithness. Cooper's father came from Dollar, Clackmannanshire. Cooper, *Scottish Legal Tradition* (n 3) at 4 offers a few desultory remarks about pre-1124 legal development, very similar to those made in Cooper, *Cases* (n 3) at lx.
17 Chapters 2 and 3 below.
18 See references in ch 1 below (text accompanying nn 50–52).

alongside the other strands of influence identified by Cooper. A key example of an institution reaching far back into the Celtic past, dealt with in what was his last major paper, was Lord Lyon King of Arms,[19] which office Sellar himself held with distinction from 2008 to 2014. Another example, although one that had apparently disappeared in the course of the nineteenth century, was the birlaw, where Norse influence, probably mediated through the English Danelaw rather than the northern isles, was crucial in the development of a long-lasting customary form of local dispute settlement.[20]

Sellar agreed with Cooper in seeing the twelfth- and thirteenth-century expansion of Scottish royal justice as heavily influenced by the contemporary growth of English royal justice to become the enduring institution of the Common Law. But, helped by studies of specific topics by Harding, Barrow and others written in the decade and a half following Cooper's death,[21] Sellar saw royal justice as much more significant in its own right than Cooper had allowed, and he differed from Cooper in seeing that English influence not being cut off by the Wars of Independence between 1296 and the mid-fourteenth century.[22] The institutions of the Scottish common law such as the itinerant justiciar and the locally based sheriff established over the previous 200 years continued to operate along with the feudal structure of land law (including succession to land) which also took shape in Scotland the century after the Norman conquest of England in 1066. There was of course further development as well as continuity in these aspects of the system, with the justiciar becoming the modern Lord Justice General at the head of the High Court of Justiciary in the seventeenth century and the law's feudal aspects being continuously adjusted and reformed until brought to an end by the Abolition of Feudal Tenure etc (Scotland) Act 2000.[23]

Sellar contended in 1981 that this continuing English influence could also be detected in Stair's *Institutions*, in particular in the "ancient and immemorial customs" of the law of succession to land, which were derived from the

---

19 See ch 4 below.
20 See ch 5 below.
21 See in particular A E Anton, "Medieval Scots executors and the courts spiritual" (1955) 67 JR 129; H McKechnie, *Judicial Process upon Brieves, 1219–1532* (David Murray Lecture, Glasgow University, 1956); A A M Duncan, "Regiam Majestatem: a reconsideration", 1961 JR 199; A Harding, "The medieval brieves of protection and the development of the common law", 1966 JR 115; I D Willock, *The Origins and Development of the Jury in Scotland* (SS vol 23, 1966); P Stein, "Roman law in medieval Scotland", *Ius Romanum Medii Aevi*, pars V, 13b (1968) 1, reprinted in P G Stein, *The Character and Influence of the Roman Civil Law: Historical Essays* (1988) ch 18; Barrow, "Justiciar".
22 For a further illustration, see ch 14 below.
23 See chs 7 and 8 below.

Common law of Anglo-Norman England.[24] Stair had further pointed out that Scotland, like England, regarded ancient custom as its common law, "anterior to any statute and not comprehended in any, as being more solemn and sure than those are."[25] Also similar to English practice was Stair's use of court decisions as recent custom and a source of law.[26] "In a sense," Sellar wrote in a later contribution not included in this collection, "the story of custom as a source is the story of the common law of Scotland itself."[27]

The theme of English influence and the customary basis of Scots law was developed even more strongly in a 1988 paper entitled "The Common Law of Scotland and the Common Law of England".[28] Only in the sixteenth century had the two systems begun to move significantly apart, with the establishment of the Court of Session as a College of Justice in 1532 being a critical event in that process.[29] Sellar saw this as a deliberate breach in continuity with the medieval court structure, with the Session acquiring a jurisdiction in land questions it had previously lacked and in the process ensuring that, unlike England, law and equity were administered together in a powerful central court.[30]

Another starting point on which Sellar made common ground with Cooper was the importance for Scotland of the development of the law of the western Church – Canon law – from the twelfth century on. But while Cooper left unclear how he saw the Canon law influence after the thirteenth century, Sellar developed a series of powerful studies which demonstrated not only continued significance in the later middle ages but also continuing effect despite the statutory abolition of papal jurisdiction at the Scottish Reformation in 1560.[31] Before then, and from the twelfth century on, there were separate jurisdictions operating in parallel in secular and ecclesiastical matters which, however, touched upon each other's sphere at many crucial points. Thus what had originally been Canon law administered in the Church

24 See ch 6 below.
25 Stair, *Inst*, 1.1.16 (1981 edn, at 87).
26 For "frequent agreeing decisions" as "recent customs", see Stair, *Inst*, 1.1.16 (1981 edn, at 88).
27 Sellar, "Custom", at para 355.
28 Sellar, "Common law", is reluctantly not included in the present collection because most of its ideas were developed in greater depth in subsequent publications which have been included, notably chs 7, 8 and 11–13 below. Chapter 8 includes some material about the history of the Register of Sasines from the 1988 paper to which Sellar referred as an example in his later text but without the same level of detail as in the earlier work.
29 This departed from the conclusions of R K Hannay, *The College of Justice* (1933) and A A M Duncan, "The central courts before 1532", in *ISLH* 321.
30 See ch 1 below (text accompanying nn 53–62).
31 *RPS* A1560/8/4.

courts became entwined with and in effect part of the Scots common law administered in the secular courts, notably the law of marriage and moveable succession.[32] Moreover, even before the Reformation, Canon law had influenced the secular criminal law into recognition of different degrees of culpability for homicide, based on the blameworthiness of the accused's conduct; and that continued into the eighteenth century when, perhaps, the language more than the substance of the law changed in response to increasingly anglicised modes of speech and writing.[33]

Cooper wrote that during his "Dark Age" period "the French alliance and the steady pressure of Continental influences bore fruit in the gradual incorporation into Scots Law of a great mass of the Roman law as taught by the French and Dutch civilians."[34] Sellar was notably less sweeping in his assessment of the influence of Roman or Civilian law upon the development of Scots law. He drew particular attention to the views of sixteenth- and seventeenth-century writers such as Thomas Craig (1538–1608) and Stair, for whom in the hierarchy of legal sources of their time Roman law ranked after Canon law, with native written and customary law ranking above both. Roman law was not a direct source but rather a point of comparison, accepted not by reason of any innate authority, but for the good sense and equity of its solutions as evidence of the requirements of natural law.[35] It could also influence the terminology of the law, as for example in converting the vernacular "widow's and bairns' parts" of moveable succession to *jus relictae* and *legitim*, or inaptly applying the Roman *pollicitatio* to the concept of unilateral promise.[36] This process could further be used to disguise what was really Canon law influence, as in the law of persons, or "the pressing of feudal wine into Roman bottles", as in the case of servitudes.[37] The reception of Roman law was thus far from covering the whole of Scots law.

Sellar was, however, equally far from denying Civilian influence altogether. He saw its importance in providing the law with overall structure and intellectual coherence.[38] He accepted that the law of moveable property had

32 See chs 9, 10, 12 and 13 below.
33 See ch 11 below.
34 Cooper, *Scottish Legal Tradition* (n 1) at 8.
35 See especially chs 1 (text accompanying nn 87 and 88), 7 (text accompanying nn 51–52, 69–73) and 8 (text accompanying nn 48–70).
36 See chs 12 (text accompanying nn 12, 33–35, 46–47), 13 (text accompanying n 66) and 15 (text accompanying nn 43, 77–91).
37 See ch 1 text after n 67. The metaphor in the text above comes from C D'O Farran, *The Principles of Scots and English Land Law* (1958) at 89. It was often mentioned in our private discussions of Scottish legal history but I cannot trace it being quoted anywhere in Sellar's writings.
38 See ch 8 (text accompanying nn 63–67).

been strongly influenced by Roman law, as also the use of the *conditiones sine liberis* and the concept of *donatio mortis causa* in moveable succession.[39] The unique Scots law on the general enforceability of unilateral promises stemmed from Stair's engagement with the Civilian legal thinking of his time.[40] The chapter on the law of presumptions is another illustration of the persistence of Civilian influence almost down to the present.[41] But these examples also show, in Sellar's view, that acceptance of the specifics of Roman law was far from total or complete, even in the most affected areas. Instead, Roman law, in particular as it had come to be interpreted and applied in the European *jus commune* from the middle ages on, provided a platform upon which the Scottish common law could continue to build through native juristic writings and court decisions. In three joint papers which Sellar and I contributed to the Gerda Henkel Stiftung series, Comparative Studies in Continental and Anglo-American Legal History, but which are not included in this collection, we showed this process ongoing down at least to the nineteenth century in the development of the Scots law on unjust enrichment (as Sellar preferred to call it), liability for negligence, and *jus quaesitum tertio* (third party rights in contract).[42] I think that in the light of that work, and also the contributions of John Cairns in particular, he might have wished to reconsider the statement made in the Saltire/Stair Societies overview in 1991, that "The achievements of the Enlightenment belong more to the history of ideas than to the history of Scots law."[43]

All these publications nonetheless presented a challenge, not only to Lord Cooper's false starts and rejected experiments, but also to the view (widely held when Sellar began his academic career in 1969) that by 1707 Scots law was essentially a Civilian system of law which began to be overlaid with English law only as a result of the Anglo-Scottish Union in 1707.[44] All the chapters in the present collection bring out the way in which Scots law before and after 1707 was (and is) actually the product of a variety of

---

39 See chs 8 (text accompanying n 51), 12 (text accompanying n 53) and 13 (text accompanying nn 91 and 92).
40 See ch 15 below.
41 See ch 16 below.
42 "Unjust enrichment in Scots law", in E J H Schrage (ed), *Unjust Enrichment: The Comparative Legal History of the Law of Restitution* (1995) 289; "History of negligence in Scots law", in E J H Schrage (ed), *Negligence: The Comparative Legal History of the Law of Torts* (2001) 273; "Scots law: ius quaesitum tertio, promise and irrevocability", in E J H Schrage (ed), *Ius Quaesitum Tertio* (2008) 357. Sellar's interest in the work of Lord Kames (1696–1782) is better evidenced in these articles than has been possible in the present collection.
43 See ch 1 below, text accompanying n 103.
44 See, for example, T B Smith, *A Short Commentary on the Law of Scotland* (1962) ch 1.

influences ranging from the indigenous and customary to the international and intellectually sophisticated Canon and Civilian systems, with much ranged in between. The law's history is one of continuity, with change being the product of openness to new, mostly external influences which were then integrated with and developed within an existing institutional and (increasingly) intellectual structure.

Understandably, given the thesis Sellar was trying to establish, he did not much explore what laid law in Scotland open to these external influences in the middle ages. Some of it was political, in particular the inevitably close links with England down to 1707 and beyond, whether relations between the two kingdoms were peaceful or hostile. Insofar as it was not also political, the position of the Church and its law stemmed from the spiritual authority that would remain largely unchallenged until overthrown by the Reformation in 1560. The Church also explained the initial influence of the Roman Civil law, which however gained further momentum from the sixteenth-century establishment of a secular central court to meet the demands of litigants dissatisfied with the de-centralised medieval system. The court's bench was staffed substantially by ecclesiastics and a lay profession grew around it, many university-educated in the learned laws. The Reformation removed papal jurisdiction but did not deprive either the Canon or the Civil law of influence in the continuing development of the law; indeed, with the latter, rather the reverse. The brilliant juristic work of Craig and Stair consolidated the law while at the same time further shaping and elaborating its form and substance.

Each of the chapters after the first is an in-depth study of its topic which at the same time, and in Sellar's characteristically fluent and readable style, brings out well its relationship with the more general picture set out in the opening chapter (and in this editorial introduction). What is omitted is what Sellar himself did not cover in his writings. There are hints, however, of topics that Sellar would have wished to take further: perhaps most notably the franchise (i.e. non-royal) jurisdictions of barony and regality which Cooper had suggested were principal contributors to what he perceived as the failure to achieve a common law in the later middle ages. Sellar, on the other hand, noted that they had survived until statutory abolition following upon the Jacobite rising of 1745 and that their holders generally did so by virtue of hereditary royal grants.[45] He would thus have agreed with recent

---

45 See ch 1 text accompanying n 31. Abolition was effected by the Heritable Jurisdictions Act 1746 (see ch 1 text accompanying n 100).

arguments that a distinctive characteristic of the medieval Scottish common law (in particular, in contrast with the English common law) lay in its combining royal and aristocratic jurisdiction rather than the first overpowering the latter by the end of the thirteenth century.[46] But he also speculated that the aristocratic jurisdictions had roots lying further back in the Celtic past. In support of this argument, he offered their procedure of "repledging" with its persistent Gaelic term of *cúlráith* for the security a lord had to leave with the court from which he recovered his man or vassal accused of crime, in order to perform justice upon him in his own court. Further there was also the possibility of repledging members of a whole clan or kindred, as in the laws of "Kynmaccaroun" and "Clan MacDuff" vouched for by later medieval sources.[47]

This possible reconfiguring of earlier lordly jurisdictions probably began in the twelfth century and Sellar would certainly have associated that with the Anglo-Norman feudalisation which had been identified as a central feature of the period by one of his scholarly heroes, Geoffrey Barrow (1924–2013).[48] Sellar also suggested that this process was facilitated by pre-existing structures of landholding such that even before the Scottish kings began granting lands in feudal form "Scottish society in the eleventh century, like contemporary Irish society, was moving in the direction of feudalism."[49] Since Barrow's death, there has been a reaction against his model of Anglo-Norman feudalisation in the twelfth century;[50] but, as we have seen, for Sellar as a lawyer feudalism was still in his own time a living legal phenomenon in Scottish landholding, with forms of documentation in which continuity with twelfth-century royal grants was readily recognisable. For a historian of law, feudalism lent critical support to the basic continuity thesis, reinforced, therefore, rather than reinvented in the centrally important work of Craig on the subject at the turn of the sixteenth and seventeenth centuries.

Re-reading half a century of scholarly work has reminded me not only of Sellar's considerable intellectual powers, but also of his ability to write with ease and fluency on the most rebarbative of subjects, including a gift for adding into the mix telling stories from his many encounters in the field

---

46 The argument is strongly advanced in A Taylor, *The Shape of the State in Medieval Scotland 1124–1290* (2016).
47 See ch 2 text accompanying nn 104–116.
48 Other such heroes identifiable from Sellar's writings include Cosmo Innes (1798–1874), F W Maitland (1850–1906), George Neilson (above n 14) and A A M Duncan (1926–2017).
49 See ch 2 text between nn 37 and 38.
50 See e.g. Taylor, *State* (n 46) at 176–184; R D Oram, *David I King of Scots 1124–1153* (2020) chs 9 and 10.

from his time in the Scottish Land Court (1967–1969). His technique as a legal historian was not based upon archival research (medieval Scots law has left almost nothing in the way of archives) or upon close examination of the manuscripts lying behind printed sources such as the Acts of the pre-1707 Scottish Parliament or the editions of *Regiam Majestatem* and other medieval works. Instead, he worked with these available sources and with the later expositions of their content by Sir John Skene (c1543–1617), Craig and Stair, tying that in with supporting evidence from other medieval sources. Bearing in mind the background of the law which he studied and trained for in the early 1960s, Sellar used Maitland's approach: "the retrogressive method 'from the known to the unknown' . . . A result is given to us: the problem is to find cause and process."[51] The subtitle of his 1985 O'Donnell lecture on Celtic law – Survival and Integration – is indicative: the survival of Celtic elements in the law meant that there must be a pre-history to be deduced from these remains as well as a process by which they were integrated in the mainstream of legal development.[52]

Sellar also drew extensively on comparative evidence to help make sense of the Scottish material. This was most obviously true of his work on Celtic law, where Ireland and to a lesser extent Wales provided rich comparisons with which the much thinner and more scattered Scottish evidence could be persuasively pulled together. But English law was also an obvious point of reference, given Sellar's argument about its primary influence on the development of the Scottish common law from the twelfth century on. The general European context for the Canon and the Civil law, too, was an important tool with which to interpret and understand the Scottish sources. The comparative material also raised important questions about the gaps in those Scottish sources: why no surviving treatises on Celtic law to compare with the many to be found in Ireland and Wales, for example, or why so little in the way of archives in which to trace the actualities of practice in the courts before 1500?

Although Sellar liked to joke that he had begun his professional life in a court for crofters and was finishing it in a court for chiefs, appointment as Lord Lyon in 2008 did not quite bring his scholarly career to an end. He developed previously half-formed thoughts into the powerful study of Lyon's origins included, as already mentioned, in the present collection. Issues also arose in the Lyon Court which brought his legal-historical scholarship into

---

51 F W Maitland, *Domesday Book and Beyond* (1897), preface.
52 See ch 2 below.

play. For example, in 2010 Lyon Sellar refused the petition of Willi Ernst Sturzenegger of Arran to be recognised as "Feudal Earl of Arran" (given that there is already an Earl of Arran, one of the subsidiary titles of the Duke of Hamilton). The Lyon's Note in explanation of his decision discusses the history of the Scottish peerage styles and the meaning of "baron" and "barony" in Scots law, to draw the conclusion that prefixing those or any other title of dignity with words like "feudal" or "territorial" is legally meaningless.[53]

Sellar's appointment as Lyon did, however, prevent him taking into account a number of monographs, editions, collections and articles published around or after that point in time. Some of the most significant are listed in the footnote below; two (which are asterisked) began as PhD theses supervised by Sellar.[54] As already mentioned, I have attempted to point the reader to these works by adding appropriate references to Sellar's footnotes and, very occasionally, adjusting his text accordingly.

A number of the sources to which Sellar regularly referred have appeared in new editions since the first publication of the articles, and wherever possible I have attempted to give the most recent version. This applies, for example, to using the online *Records of the Parliaments of Scotland* (*RPS*) rather than the nineteenth-century *Acts of the Parliaments of Scotland* (*APS*).[55] *RPS* begins, however, in 1235, and for earlier legal material (or at least material purporting to be earlier) I have cited Alice Taylor's *Laws of Medieval Scotland* (*LMS*) published by the Stair Society in 2019.[56] The Society has also begun a new edition and translation of Craig's *Jus Feudale* by Leslie Dodd, of which however only the first of the three books has so far been published.[57] That was fortunately the book to which Sellar referred

---

53 *Sturzenegger Petitioner (No 2)* 2015 SLT (Lyon Ct) 2. The note is also available on the Lyon Court website: https://www.courtofthelordlyon.scot/index_htm_files/ARRAN.PDF.
54 °J Finlay, *Men of Law in Pre-Reformation Scotland* (2000); J D Ford, *Law and Opinion in Scotland in the Seventeenth Century* (2007); °A M Godfrey, *Civil Justice in Renaissance Scotland: The Origins of a Central Court* (2009); J Finlay, *The Community of the College of Justice: Edinburgh and the Court of Session, 1687–1808* (2012); J W Cairns, *Law, Lawyers and Humanism: Selected Essays on the History of Scots Law volume 1* and *Enlightenment, Legal Education, and Critique: Selected Essays on the History of Scots Law volume 2* (both 2015); J Finlay, *Legal Practice in Eighteenth-Century Scotland* (2015); A Rahmatian, *Lord Kames: Legal and Social Theorist* (2015); Taylor, *State* (above, n 46); A R C Simpson and A L M Wilson, *Scottish Legal History: Volume One 1000–1707* (2017).
55 K M Brown and others (eds), *Records of the Parliaments of Scotland to 1707*, accessible at https://www.rps.ac.uk/.
56 A Taylor (ed), *The Laws of Medieval Scotland: Legal Compilations from the Thirteenth and Fourteenth Centuries* (SS vol 66, 2019). This largely (but not completely) supersedes the first volume of *APS* insofar as it was not already superseded by *RPS*.
57 L Dodd (ed), *Jus Feudale Tribus Libris Comprehensum by Thomas Craig of Riccarton, Book I* (SS vol 64, 2017).

most often in his own writings; however, his citations of the two other books continue to be to the 3rd edition of 1732 by James Baillie and the translation by Lord Clyde published in 1933 unless otherwise indicated. Lord Cooper's *Register of Brieves* (1946) has been replaced by A A M Duncan's *Scottish Formularies*, also published by the Stair Society in 2011.[58] Finally, the Society published in 2012 Olivia Robinson's edition of Sir George Mackenzie's *Matters Criminal* (first published 1678), a work to which Sellar also made fairly frequent reference.

It is understood that a new edition of the fourteenth-century treatise of the Scottish common law *Regiam Majestatem* is under preparation by John Reuben Davies and Alice Taylor for the Stair Society. That may go some way to resolving some issues about that enigmatic work to which Sellar referred in his Saltire/Stair Societies essay.[59] Meantime, I have *faute de mieux* ensured that references to *Regiam* are to both the existing editions (one by Thomas Thomson and Cosmo Innes in the first volume of *APS*,[60] the other Lord Cooper's for the Stair Society[61]), although neither is satisfactory.

---

58 A A M Duncan (ed), *Scottish Formularies* (SS vol 58, 2011); Lord Cooper (ed), *The Register of Brieves as contained in the Ayr MS, the Bute MS and Quoniam Attachiamenta* (SS vol 10, 1946).
59 See ch 1, text accompanying n 33.
60 *APS*, vol 1, at 597–641.
61 Lord Cooper (ed), *Regiam Majestatem and Quoniam Attachiamenta based on the Text of Sir John Skene* (SS vol 11, 1947). Sir John Skene published a Latin and a Scots version of the text in 1609. Cooper's edition of *Quoniam* has been superseded by T D Fergus (ed), *Quoniam Attachiamenta* (SS vol 44, 1996).

# 1 The Continuity of Scottish Legal History: An Overview*

## A. INTRODUCTION

Two features particularly distinguish the history of Scots law when set beside that of other legal systems. The first is the great antiquity of the Scottish legal system, and the corresponding measure of continuity which can be traced from the earliest times of which there is any record right down to the present day. This is a characteristic which Scots law shares with English law, but in which it differs from the major systems of the Continent. In France and Germany, for example, the course of the law has been broken more than once by revolution. In addition, in each country the adoption of a written code – in France, the *Code Napoléon* of 1804, and in Germany, the BGB, or *Bürgerliches Gesetzbuch* of 1900 – marked a break with the past of a different kind. In England and Scotland, by contrast, apart from the brief period of Commonwealth and Protectorate in the mid-seventeenth century, there has been no revolution, nor has a written code of law been adopted to mark a new departure. In England there was a significant break in 1066, separating the Anglo-Saxon from the Anglo-Norman. In Scotland, however, there was no corresponding break between the Celtic past and Scoto-Norman feudalism. The history of Scots law, then, is one of great antiquity and continuity.

The second distinguishing feature is the ambivalent position which Scots law has long enjoyed between the two great legal traditions which have shaped the Western legal inheritance: on the one hand, the English (or Anglo-American) Common law, and on the other, the Civilian (or Romano-Germanic) legal tradition of the Continent. The Common law has evolved continuously since its early beginnings in the king's courts of twelfth- and thirteenth-century England, and has steered a course independent to a surprising degree of outside legal influence. The Civilian tradition looks back

---

* Originally published as "A Historical Perspective", in M C Meston, W D H Sellar and Lord Cooper, *The Scottish Legal Tradition* (Saltire and Stair Societies, 1991) 29–64.

to the Emperor Justinian's great codification of Roman law in sixth-century Byzantium, the *Corpus Iuris Civilis*. In this tradition belong most, if not all modern European systems of law in the west, with the partial exception of Scandinavia. Scots law is unique in the extent to which it has drawn on and been influenced by both these great traditions throughout most of its long history.

This view of Scottish legal history, it must be admitted, differs sharply from that put forward by Lord Cooper in 1949 in his celebrated *Scottish Legal Tradition*. This is particularly true of the emphasis on continuity. Cooper wrote, indeed, that "Scots Law is in a special sense the mirror of Scotland's history and traditions . . . and just as truly a part of our national inheritance as our language or literature or religion";[1] but he also wrote, "There is a sense in which it is true to say that Scots Law has no history; for the continuity of its growth has been repeatedly interrupted and its story is a record of false starts and rejected experiments."[2] The latter comment is quite misleading. Cooper sought to emphasise, in particular, the break in legal development caused by the Wars of Independence with England at the turn of the thirteenth and fourteenth centuries, and the fresh start signalled by the later "Reception" of Roman law. In both cases, however, he exaggerated the element of change and underplayed the element of continuity.

The second main point of difference with Cooper is related to the first. Cooper, like the present writer, was concerned to emphasise the unique position of Scots law lying midway between the two great streams of European legal thought. He represented Scots law in the twelfth and thirteenth centuries as being greatly influenced by the nascent English Common law, as indeed it was. But he suggested that the Wars of Independence caused a complete break with the past, and that the English Common law did not again influence the course of Scots law to any significant extent until after the Union of 1707. It is the writer's belief that Cooper underestimated the importance of the foundation laid in the twelfth and thirteenth centuries as a basis for the future development of Scots law, and also the continuing, although admittedly reduced, role of the English Common law as a direct source of influence on Scots law between the Wars of Independence and the Union of 1707. Scots law has always been more of a hybrid than Cooper was prepared to admit, and the influence of the Civil or Roman law on Scots law

---

1 T M Cooper, *The Scottish Legal Tradition* (Saltire Society, 1949) at 5.
2 T M Cooper, *Select Scottish Cases of the Thirteenth Century* (1944) at lxi.

has never operated in a context unaffected by the countervailing influence of the English Common law.[3]

## B. CELTS AND SAXONS

The sources for the political history of Scotland before 1100 are sparse and difficult to interpret, and the sources for law and legal institutions doubly so. Nevertheless, it is clear that although a distinctively Scottish common law did not emerge until the thirteenth century, some of the component parts of that system can be traced back to a far more remote past.

In the Dark Ages there were four main political groupings in what is now Scotland; the Picts, the Scots of Dalriada, the Britons of Strathclyde and the Angles of the northern tip of the Anglo-Saxon kingdom of Northumbria. In the middle of the ninth century, the Picts, already long exposed to Scots Gaelic cultural influence, came under the kingship of Kenneth mac Alpin of the Dalriadic dynasty. Kenneth and his successors forged the kingdom of Alba, or Scotia, the forerunner of the later Scottish kingdom. This kingdom was at first restricted to Scotland north of the Forth but expanded in the tenth and eleventh centuries to incorporate both the British south west and the Anglo-Saxon south east.

Something can be deduced of the law of these four peoples. The Picts, although in many ways similar to their Celtic neighbours, appear to have operated a system of royal succession without parallel in Western Europe in historic times. Kings succeeded to the throne by virtue of their maternal rather than paternal kin. Thus, typically, a king would be succeeded by his brother (the son of his mother) or by his nephew (the son of his mother's daughter) rather than by his own eldest son or by a relative on his father's

---

3 Apart from *The Scottish Legal Tradition* and *Thirteenth Century Cases* (nn 1 and 2), Lord Cooper's views on the course of Scottish legal history can be conveniently studied in his David Murray Lecture at Glasgow University, *The Dark Age of Scottish Legal History, 1350–1650* (1951), reprinted in the Rt Hon Lord Cooper of Culross, *Selected Papers 1922–1954* (1957) 219–236; in his edition of *Regiam Majestatem* (SS vol 11, 1947); and in "From David I to Bruce, 1124–1329: the Scoto-Norman law", in *ISLH* ch 1. J H Baker, *An Introduction to English Legal History* (5th edn, 2019) can be thoroughly recommended on English law, and O F Robinson, T D Fergus and W M Gordon, *An Introduction to European Legal History* (3rd edn, 2000) helps to place the history of Scots law in a European context. General accounts of Scottish legal history not following the Cooper position include J W Cairns, "Historical introduction", in K Reid and R Zimmermann (eds), *A History of Private Law in Scotland* vol 1 (2000), 14; A R C Simpson and A L M Wilson, *Scottish Legal History Volume One 1000–1707* (2017); A R C Simpson, "The Scottish common law: origins and development, ca.1124–ca.1500", in H Pihlajamaki, M Dubber and M Godfrey (eds), *Oxford Handbook of European Legal History* (2018).

side. Anthropologists are familiar with such systems of matrilineal succession; they can still be found, for example, in the Indian state of Kerala and among the Ashanti of Ghana.[4] The law of the Britons appears to have resembled that of their P-Celtic-speaking cousins, the Welsh, whose native laws were later collected and attributed to Hywel Dda, a tenth-century South Welsh king.[5] The law of the Angles in Lothian and the Borders would have been a variant of Anglo-Saxon law, preserved in the Law Codes of kings from Ethelbert of Kent (d 616) onwards, and in a number of contemporary legal documents.

The dominant influence in the early Scottish kingdom, however, was the Gaelic-speaking Scots. Here the relevant comparison is with Ireland, the original home of the Gaelic language and the Dalriadic dynasty. Although little early legal material has survived in Scotland, the Irish record is rich. The Irish law tracts, some of them committed to writing as early as the eighth century, provide a fascinating picture of the operation of law in an archaic Celtic society. Much of the law concerns honour and status, and the avoidance of blood feuds arising from death or injury. There are sections on marriage and fosterage, on hostages, guarantors and sureties. The marriage law allowed for many different types of union of varying duration, and for ready divorce. Originally, indeed, it countenanced polygamy and concubinage. The custodians of early Irish law were a highly trained professional caste of jurists, the *breitheamhan* or "brehons" – after whom these laws are sometimes referred to as the "Brehon" laws. There is every indication that the law of the Gaelic-speaking Scots, first in Dalriada, and later in Alba, was similar to that of their compatriots in Ireland.[6]

One of the few Scots Gaelic texts to survive is the *Senchus Fer nAlban*, the "Story of the Men of Scotland", compiled in the seventh century.[7] This

---

4 There is a large literature on the Picts and the hypothesis of matrilineal succession. A P Smyth launches an attack on the hypothesis in his *Warlords and Holy Men* (1984, reprinted 1989). W D H Sellar, "Warlords, holy men and matrilineal succession" (1985) 36 *Innes Review* 29 attempts to refute Smyth.
5 For medieval Welsh law see D Jenkins, *The Law of Hywel Dda* (1986); T G Watkin, *The Legal History of Wales* (2007) ch 4.
6 F Kelly, *Guide to Early Irish Law* (1988) provides an introduction to Irish law. For the law of the Gaelic-speaking Scots see, *inter alia*, W F Skene, *Celtic Scotland* 3 vols (2nd edn, 1886–1890); J Cameron, *Celtic Law* (1937); J Bannerman, "The Scots of Dalriada", in G Menzies (ed), *Who are the Scots* (1971) 66, and "The Lordship of the Isles", in J Brown (ed), *Scottish Society in the Fifteenth Century* (1977) 209 (the latter reprinted in J Bannerman, *Kinship, Church and Culture: Collected Essays and Studies* (2016) ch 6); G W S Barrow, "The lost Gaidhealteachd of medieval Scotland", in W Gillies (ed), *Gaelic and Scotland: Alba agus a 'Ghàidhlig* (1989) 67 (reprinted in G W S Barrow, *Scotland and its Neighbours in the Middle Ages* (1992)); and ch 2 below.
7 J Bannerman, *Studies in the History of Dalriada* (1974) 27 (reprinted Bannerman, *Kinship* (n 6) 27).

lists the military strength of the various divisions of Dalriada and sets out the naval service due. Another early document which concerns Scotland as well as Ireland is *Cáin Adomnain* (Adomnan's Law), a remarkable Dark Age Geneva Convention, negotiated about 697 CE by Adomnan, successor of Columba as abbot of Iona, and designed to protect women, children and non-combatants. The named guarantors of this "law" include many contemporary Irish kings and clerics, and also Brude mac Derile, king of the Picts, two kings of Dalriada, and a bishop at Rosemarkie in the Black Isle.[8] Later, in the twelfth century, with the advent of the regular written record, bishops and monastic houses made written notes or *notitiae* of earlier land grants, some of which still survive. For example, the register of the priory of St Andrews notes in Latin that Macbeth and his queen, Gruoch, had granted Kirkness by Loch Leven in Fife to the religious community, or culdees, of St Serf.[9] One set of monastic *notitiae* provides particularly valuable evidence for our understanding of pre-feudal Scottish society, for they are written in Gaelic rather than in Latin. They record early land grants to the monastery of Deer in Buchan: thus, for example,

> Comgell son of Aed gave from Orti as far as Púréne to Colum Cille and Drostán. Muiredach son of Morgann gave pett mac Garnait ["the holding of Gartnait's sons"] and *achad toche Temne* [?"the field of Teimen's inheritance/law-suit"]; and he was mormaer and he was toisech. Matain son of Cairell gave a mormaer's "portion" [*cuit*] dues in Altrie and Culi son of Batin gave a toisech's "portion" . . .[10]

## C. FOUNDATIONS

The twelfth and thirteenth centuries saw the consolidation of the kingdom of Scotland, with the exception of the islands of Orkney and Shetland, and the forging of the Scottish national identity. They also saw the emergence of a distinctively Scottish common law.

The rise of the Scottish common law requires to be set in a wider European context. From the eleventh century onwards there had been a revival of interest in legal studies throughout Europe. Towards 1100 Irnerius became the leading figure in the teaching of Roman law – that is, the law of Justinian's

---

8 M Ni Dhonnchadha, "The guarantor list of Cain Adomnain, 697" (1982) 1 *Peritia* 178. A translated edition is G Markus, *Adomnán's "Law of the Innocents": Cáin Adomnáin: a seventh century law for the protection of non-combatants* (1997).
9 *Liber Cartarum Prioratus Sancti Andree in Scotia* (Bannatyne Club, 1841) at 114; A C Lawrie (ed), *Early Scottish Charters prior to 1153* (1905), no V.
10 K H Jackson, *The Gaelic Notes in the Book of Deer* (1972) at 33–34 and passim; K Forsyth (ed), *Studies on the Book of Deer* (2008) at 122, 137 and passim.

*Corpus Iuris* – at Bologna in northern Italy. The tradition of scholarship in Roman law has been continuous from his day until the present. At much the same time, again in Italy, the great edifice of the medieval Canon law, the *Corpus Iuris Canonici*, began to take shape. The Canon law owed much to the renewed study of Roman law; so much, indeed, as to justify the adage:

> *Legista sine canonibus parum valet*
> *Canonista sine legibus nihil.*
>
> A Roman lawyer without Canon law is not worth much,
> a Canon lawyer without Roman law nothing.[11]

A third influence was Feudal law. Unlike Roman law and Canon law, Feudal law was never codified into an authoritative system, universally recognised throughout western Christendom. Feudal rules were very adaptable and could accommodate many local variations. Nevertheless, the *Libri Feudorum*, the "Books of the Feus" (c1150), of the Milanese jurist Obertus de Orto, proved widely influential, and were sometimes even regarded as a late and final addition to Justinian's *Corpus Iuris*.[12]

Everywhere in Europe the new learned law interacted with older customary law. Scotland was no exception. In Scotland, however, as already noted, the customary base was partially Celtic, rather than purely Germanic. Although the Norman Conquest of 1066 did not extend to Scotland, the feudal law and institutions which found their way into Scotland were unmistakably Anglo-Norman. In Scotland, as in England – but unlike, for example, the situation in France and Germany – the rulers of the kingdom were able to shape a law which was largely national rather than local, coterminous with the bounds of their kingdom, a *common* law. In England, this common law was developed through precedents decided in the king's courts. In Scotland, the same was probably true, although surviving records are sparse. The Anglo-American Common law tradition can be traced back to the "common law" developed by the kings of England in the twelfth and thirteenth centuries. In Scotland the term "common law", in the sense of

---

11 The maxim was derived from *Decretum Gratiani*, C7, d10. See further F Merzbacher, "Die Parömie 'legista sine canonibus parum valet, canonista sine legibus nihil'" (1967) 13 *Studia Gratiana* 273; J Gordley, *The Jurists: A Critical History* (2013) at 55–65; R H Helmholz, "Canon law and Roman law", in D Johnston (ed), *The Cambridge Companion to Roman Law* (2015) 396; K Pennington, "Legista sine canonibus parum valet, canonista sine legibus nihil" (2017) 34 *Bulletin of Medieval Canon Law* 249.

12 For the *Libri Feudorum* see, for example, O F Robinson, T D Fergus, W M Gordon. *European Legal History* (n 3) at 37–38; S Reynolds, *Fiefs and Vassals: The Medieval Evidence Reinterpreted* (1994), at 215–230 and appendix.

the king's law, common to all his kingdom, is found already in the thirteenth century and has been in use ever since. Confusingly, the medieval European Civil and Canon lawyers also referred to their law as a "common law" – *jus commune* – although here the reference was to the common learned law of western Christendom.[13]

## (1) The survival of Celtic law

It is sometimes suggested that little, if anything, survived in Scotland of the older Celtic law into the feudal and post-feudal age. This is far from true. Traces of Celtic law survived for many centuries in the mainstream of later Scots law; and some customs, at one time regulated by Celtic law, continued to be observed in the Highlands until comparatively recent times. Thus the custom of fosterage lasted in the Highlands until the eighteenth century, and was commented on by Johnson and Boswell on their famous Hebridean tour in 1773.[14] One long survival from the Celtic past was the payment of cain (*cáin*), a food render originally due to a lord in recognition of his authority. The obligation to render cain was written into many feudal charters and continued to be paid by vassals and tenants until quite modern times. Sometimes it merged with feu-duty. Cain was regularly paid in kind and is sometimes referred to in later documents as "cain fowl" or "reek hen" – a hen from every lum that reeked. As late as the nineteenth century, Lady Colquhoun of Luss kept a gauge to ensure that tenants presenting their cain of eggs did not tender any which were undersize![15]

One survival which mirrors the survival of Celtic law itself, gradually integrated until at length virtually unrecognisable, is that of the *breitheamh*, the professional judge or jurist of Celtic society. The *breitheamh* (Latin *iudex*) long survived the introduction of Scoto-Norman feudalism. He appears in the witness lists of early charters and is referred to in royal ordinances. He became, it would appear, a speaker of the customary law. Later he became

---

13 The varying ways in which the expression "common law" is used, according to context, are thoroughly confusing. In this essay, the spelling "Common law" is reserved for the English legal system and the Anglo-American Common law tradition. But the term "common law" is also used within that tradition in a technical sense to distinguish "common law" from "equity", and to distinguish both from statute. In modern Scots law, no distinction is drawn between equity and (common) law, and the expression "common law" is used in distinction to statute.
14 R W Chapman (ed), *Johnson & Boswell: A Journey to the Western Islands of Scotland; The Journal of a Tour to the Hebrides* (1924, reprinted 1978) at 122.
15 G Donaldson, *Sir William Fraser* (1985) at 26. See further ch 2 (text accompanying nn 49, 119, 121, 136, and 149).

the "doomster" of court, the man who pronounced sentence or "doom".[16] In the High Court of Justiciary, before the office of doomster was abolished in 1773, he doubled also as executioner, a situation the dramatic potential of which was fully exploited by Sir Walter Scott in *The Heart of Midlothian* (1818). After Effie Deans has been found guilty of child-murder the doomster appears to pronounce sentence. "When the doomster showed himself, a tall haggard figure arrayed in a fantastic garment of black and grey, passmented with silver lace, all fell back with a kind of instinctive horror." The doomster then gabbles the sentence of death, and finishes thus:

> "And this," said the Doomster, aggravating his harsh voice, "I pronounce for doom." He vanished when he had spoken the last emphatic word, like a foul fiend after the purpose of his visitation has been accomplished.[17]

Even after the abolition of the office of doomster, the presiding judge at a murder trial in Scotland would conclude the sentence of death with the words "which is pronounced for doom", thus linking himself, however tenuously, with the remote Celtic past.

### (2) The Lordship of the Isles

In one part of Scotland, Celtic law continued to flourish in the later Middle Ages. After sovereignty over the Hebrides had been ceded by Norway to Scotland in 1266, the MacDonald descendants of Somerled (d 1164) gradually consolidated their authority over the islands, from Islay in the south to Lewis in the north, and over much of the adjacent mainland as well. Their title in Gaelic was *Ri Innse Gall*, in Latin *Dominus Insularum* or "Lord of the Isles". The Lords of the Isles were patrons of the arts and of learning, and there is some evidence for a virtually independent legal structure, with judges or *breitheamhan* in the Gaelic tradition stationed on the larger islands, responsible to the administrative centre of the Lordship in Islay. The MacDonalds over-reached themselves, however, and in the fifteenth and sixteenth centuries their principality was destroyed and annexed to the crown.[18]

---

16 W C Dickinson (ed), *Sheriff Court Book of Fife 1523–1542* (SHS, 1928) at lxv–lxix; G W S Barrow, "The *judex*" (1966) 45 *SHR* 16, reprinted in G W S Barrow, *The Kingdom of the Scots* (2nd edn, 2003) ch 2; A Taylor, *The Shape of the State in Medieval Scotland, 1124–1290* (2016) at 114–135; and ch 2 below.
17 Sir W Scott, *The Heart of Midlothian* (first published 1818) ch 23.
18 For the Lordship of the Isles see inter alia Bannerman (n 6) and "The Lordship of the Isles: historical background", in K A Steer and J W M Bannerman (eds), *Later Medieval Monumental*

## (3) The common law of Scotland

There was, therefore, no outright rejection of Celtic law, and the common law of Scotland has, in part at least, a Celtic base. However, the overwhelming influence on the development of the common law of Scotland in the twelfth and thirteenth centuries was the Anglo-Norman law. This law was adopted or received by the kings of Scots themselves rather than imposed from without by conquest. Its influence was all pervasive in substantive law and procedure alike, and in the administration of justice. Its traces can be clearly seen in Scots law down to the present century.[19]

The main royal officer for the administration of justice at local level in Anglo-Norman England was the sheriff. The word itself – "shire-reeve" – is Anglo-Saxon, but the office was transformed under the Norman kings. The sheriff was first introduced into Scotland in the twelfth century. By the end of the thirteenth, all of Scotland had been divided into sheriffdoms. It is ironic that in England, the country of origin, the sheriff's function gradually declined and is now mainly ceremonial, whereas in Scotland, the sheriff and his court continue to be a mainspring of judicial administration.

Another import from Anglo-Norman England was the office of justiciar. The justiciar was the king's *alter ego* in matters of justice, with extensive judicial powers, especially on the criminal side. In England, the office disappeared in the thirteenth century. Not so in Scotland. At first there were several justiciars in Scotland: one for Lothian; one for Galloway; and one for *Scotia* north of Forth. The office of justiciar north of Forth may have been assimilated with an earlier Celtic office of king's *breitheamh*. Eventually there was but one justiciar for the kingdom of the Scots, and he came to be styled the "Lord Justice General". The Lord Justice General remains Scotland's senior judge, presiding today over the High Court of Justiciary.[20]

A characteristic feature of the Anglo-Norman law was procedure by writ and inquest. The king would issue a judicial writ (Latin *breve*) directing the

---

*Sculpture in the West Highlands* (1977) appendix II (reprinted in Bannerman, *Kinship* (n 6) ch 7); R W and J Munro (eds), *Acts of the Lords of the Isles 1336–1493* (SHS, 1986); and Simpson and Wilson, *Scottish Legal History* (n 3) ch 5.

19 Sellar, "Common law"; Cairns (n 3) at 18–32; Taylor, *State* (n 16) ch 5. See further chs 6–8 below; note also a controversial reassessment of the 13th-century common law by D Carpenter, "Scottish royal government in the thirteenth century from an English perspective", in M Hammond (ed), *New Perspectives on Medieval Scotland 1093–1286* (2013) 117; countered by K J Stringer, "Law, governance and jurisdiction", in K J Stringer and A J L Winchester (eds), *Northern England and Southern Scotland in the Central Middle Ages* (2017) 87.

20 Barrow, "Justiciar", should now be read in the light of Taylor, *State* (n 16) at 210–244.

sheriff or some other officer of the law to hold an inquest, or jury, of prominent local men to determine the truth of some matter. Procedure by writ and inquest was also adopted in Scotland, and became equally characteristic of the early Scottish common law. For example, in 1261 king Alexander III directed a "brieve" (as the writ was termed in later Scottish practice) to the sheriff of Forfar to make diligent and faithful inquiry by means of good and faithful men of the neighbourhood whether Margaret, Agnes, Suannoch, Christiana and Mariota, daughters of the late Simon, gatekeeper of Montrose castle, were his nearest and lawful heirs and entitled to succeed him in his office of gatekeeper and his lands of Inyaney.[21]

A record of 1428 shows the inquest being used to clarify an ancient usage with its roots in Celtic law. John of Spens, bailie of the crown lands of Glendochart in Perthshire, sitting with an inquest of fifteen, found that Finlay Dewar was the keeper of the *coigreach* of Saint Fillan – that is, of the relic containing the saint's supposed pastoral staff – and that any inhabitant of Glendochart, whose goods or cattle had been stolen, could require Finlay to follow the goods throughout Scotland wherever they might be found, on payment of four pence, or a pair of shoes, and food for one night.[22]

Procedure by writ and inquest remained an integral part of English law until the nineteenth century. In Scotland, the procedure did not last so long in regular use, being gradually replaced from the fifteenth century onwards, save in a limited number of prescribed situations.[23] The prosecution of serious crime by way of "indictment" before a jury was as distinctive a feature of Anglo-Norman criminal procedure as were the writ and inquest on the civil side Here too Scots law borrowed in the thirteenth century from Anglo-Norman law and retains to this day indictment and trial by jury in solemn criminal matters.[24]

---

21 *APS*, vol 1, at 100; and Cooper, *Cases* (n 2), no 56.
22 Royal Commission on Historical Manuscripts (London 1870–) *4th Report*, at 514a; and see, inter alia, W A Gillies, *In Famed Breadalbane* (1938 and reprint) at 64–73. The *coigreach* still exists: it was gifted to the Society of Antiquaries of Scotland in the nineteenth century, and is currently on display in the "Kingdom of the Scots" gallery at Level 1, National Museum of Scotland, Edinburgh.
23 See H L MacQueen, *Common Law and Feudal Society in Medieval Scotland* (1993, reprinted 2016); Taylor, *State* (n 16) at 297–348; Simpson and Wilson, *Scottish Legal History* (n 3) chs 2 and 3. H McKechnie's David Murray Lecture, *Judicial Process upon Brieves, 1219–1532* (Glasgow University, 1956) remains useful on the later survivals.
24 See further on the whole subject of the assize/jury/inquest I D Willock, *The Origins and Development of the Jury in Scotland* (SS vol 23, 1966) Part Three; C J Neville, *Land, Law and People in Medieval Scotland* (2010) ch 2. On criminal procedure and the law on homicide see ch 11 below.

As was to be expected of a system rooted in feudalism, the influence of the Anglo-Norman law was greatest in matters concerning land or "heritage". From the time of King David I (1124–1153), the feudal doctrine that the king was the ultimate lord (*dominus*) of all the land came gradually to prevail. All other landowners were "vassals", holding their land at one remove or another from the king. The most honourable form of tenure was military tenure, known in later Scots law as "ward holding", in which the return or *reddendo* for the land was strictly military, the service of so many knights – or, in the Gaelic west, naval, the service of a galley of so many oars. Thus William I (1165–1214) confirmed Seton, Winton and Winchburgh to Philip de Seton for the service of one knight, and David II (1329–1371) granted Assynt in Sutherland to Torquil MacLeod for the service of a galley of 20 oars.[25] Another honourable form of tenure, in which the required service was almost nominal, was known as "blench ferme". Thus the Campbells held Kilmun in Cowal for a pair of gloves to be tendered annually at the Glasgow Fair.[26] A typical blench ferme render was one penny, "if asked only" (*si petatur tantum*).

A distinctively Scottish form of tenure was "feu ferme". Here the *reddendo* was a money payment, or "feu duty", generally payable twice a year at Whitsunday (15th May) and Martinmas (11th November). Feu ferme tenure remained the basis of landownership in Scots law until the Abolition of Feudal Tenure etc (Scotland) Act 2000 came into force on 28 November 2004,[27] and the legal relationship between "vassal" and "superior" subsisted until then, even if in many cases the actual feu duty had been redeemed. Although the feudal land law was originally adopted from Anglo-Norman England, Scots and English land law were never quite identical, and moved rapidly further apart after the legislation of Edward I (1272–1307) set English law on a fresh course. In England, for example, subinfeudation – the creation of a new feudal tenure by adding a further link to the feudal chain – was prohibited by Edward I in 1290. In Scotland, subinfeudation remained competent for a further 750 years.

The law of succession to land was similar in both countries. Males were favoured to females in every degree of succession, and among males of equal degree the eldest succeeded. When succession did open to females, they shared equally. Typically, therefore, the eldest son took all. These rules

---

25  *RRS*, vol 2, nos 200, 390; *RRS*, vol 6, no 487.
26  See *RRS*, vol 6, no 293 and note at 528–529.
27  See W D H Sellar, "Farewell to feudalism", in P B Dewar (ed), *Burke's Landed Gentry volume 1: The Kingdom of Scotland* (2001) at xix–xxi.

were well established by the fourteenth century. They remained true of succession to land on intestacy in Scots law until the Succession (Scotland) Act 1964.[28] The law of courtesy, which likewise survived until 1964, and had also been adopted originally from Anglo-Norman law, was an even more remarkable survival. Courtesy was the right which a widower enjoyed to a liferent of his deceased wife's estate. It could only be enjoyed, however, if a child had been born of the marriage, quick and living, and that child had been heard to cry. The reason for these peculiar rules was already a matter for debate in England in the thirteenth century; yet they remained part of Scots law until 1964! In 1368 Sir Thomas Erskine and Sir James Douglas of Dalkeith even fought a judicial duel before the king to determine whether a child had been still born or born live and heard to cry; and whether, therefore, courtesy was exigible.[29]

By medieval European standards the English monarchy was unusually strong and became centralised remarkably early. In England, the birth of the Common law was followed shortly by the establishment in the thirteenth century of central courts of justice, distinct from Parliament, and the emergence of a lay legal profession. In Scotland, however, a specialised central court and a lay legal profession did not begin to emerge until two hundred years later.[30]

At local level the king's ordinary court was held by the sheriff, with more serious criminal business being reserved to the justiciar on his circuits (or "justice-ayres") around the country. In royal burghs the burgh courts dispensed justice on the king's behalf. However, there were also many franchise courts in Scotland – courts of barony and courts of regality – in which local landowners exercised judicial rights on a hereditary basis. In highly centralised England such franchise courts, with a few exceptions, had ceased to exist by the end of the thirteenth century. In Scotland, by contrast, the heritable jurisdictions remained until 1748. The very greatest landowners, secular and religious, held their lands in regality. This jurisdiction, as the name implies, was semi-royal, and might include all the pleas of the crown, save only treason. Barony jurisdiction was more common, and included the much prized right of "pit and gallows" (*furca et fossa*), which allowed the baron to sentence to death on his gallows tree or in his drowning pool those convicted of red-handed theft or slaughter. More typically,

---

28 See further chs 10 and 11 below.
29 See further ch 14 below.
30 On the emergence of a legal profession see Cairns (n 3) at 30–31, 47, 62–64, 68–71; J Finlay, *Men of Law in Pre-Reformation Scotland* (2000).

however, the baron court addressed itself to petty crime and to questions of good neighbourhood.[31]

The most important legal treatise to survive from the formative years of the Scottish common law is known from its opening words as *Regiam Majestatem*. Its date, its purpose and its authority as a source of Scots law have long been controversial. Much of the material in the *Regiam* is copied, with few alterations, from the English text known as *Glanvill*, from Ranulf de Glanvill's supposed authorship of *De Legibus et Consuetudinibus Angliae* (The Laws and Customs of England), which was composed at the end of the twelfth century.[32] But the *Regiam* also incorporates some later Romano-canonical material. Lord Cooper originally dated the *Regiam* to about 1230 and thought that it reflected the development of Scots law at that date. Subsequent research points to a date after – but perhaps not long after, and possibly just before – 1318, and urges caution as to how much can be deduced about the state of Scots law at any given moment from the text of *Regiam Majestatem*.[33] If the approximate date of 1318 is correct, it certainly does not suggest that there was any conscious rejection of Anglo-Norman legal influence during or after the Wars of Independence. The *Regiam* may not have been fully official, but it does not seem to have been entirely private either. Although it has sometimes been rejected by our greatest legal writers as being no part of our law, there can be little doubt that *Regiam Majestatem* has, in practice, been regarded as a valid source of Scots law for over 500 years. Even in the twentieth century it was occasionally cited in court.[34]

---

31 Dickinson, *Sheriff Court Book of Fife* (n 13), and W C Dickinson (ed), *Court Book of the Barony of Carnwath 1523–1542* (SHS, 1937) remain the standard accounts of these courts. See further A Grant, "Franchises north of the border: baronies and regalities in medieval Scotland", in M Prestwich (ed), *Liberties and Identities in the Medieval British Isles* (2008) 155. See also text accompanying n 100 below. W C Dickinson, *Early Records of the Burgh of Aberdeen 1317, 1398–1407* (SHS, 1957) is also a valuable contribution on the burgh court. For regality courts see J M Webster and A A M Duncan (eds), *Regality of Dunfermline Court Book 1531–1538* (1953); and see on early baronial jurisdiction Neville, *Land, Law and People* (n 24) ch 1.
32 See further Baker, *English Legal History* (n 3) at 185–186.
33 On the dating of *Regiam* see A A M Duncan, "*Regiam Majestatem*: a reconsideration", 1961 *JR* 199; P G Stein, "The source of the Romano-canonical part of *Regiam Majestatem*" (1969) 48 *SHR* 107; A Harding, "*Regiam Majestatem* amongst medieval law books", 1984 *JR* 97; *LMS* at 274–280.
34 *Regiam* was cited in the St Ninian's Isle Treasure case, *Lord Advocate v University of Aberdeen and Budge* 1963 SC 533 and in *Law Hospital NHS Trust v Lord Advocate* 1996 SC 301.

## (4) The Canon law

The development of the common law and of the king's courts, however, is only part of the story. In medieval Scotland, as elsewhere in western Christendom, jurisdiction was divided between secular authority and the Church. The Church looked to Rome and to the Canon law. During the twelfth and thirteenth centuries the political power of the Papacy was at its height, and the law of the Church was developed by a succession of great lawyer Popes. It was codified in the *Corpus Iuris Canonici,* the major elements in which are the *Decretum* of Gratian (c 1150), and the *Decretals* of Pope Gregory IX (1234). From the twelfth century onwards, the courts of the Church, staffed by expert clerical lawyers, and administering Canon law, existed alongside the king's courts. At diocesan level the ordinary court was the court of the Official, the ecclesiastical judge appointed by the bishop; but there might also be special "judges-delegate" appointed *ad hoc* by Rome to resolve a particular dispute.[35]

The ambit of the Canon law was remarkably wide. It included questions of marriage and legitimacy; wills, testaments and executors; and obligations fortified by oath. Some commentators have suggested that the impact of the Canon law was so marked in thirteenth-century Scotland that it completely overshadowed royal justice. Others have suggested conversely that the general Canon law was only accepted in Scotland according to equity and expediency; that Scotland, in some sense, had a Canon law of her own. Both opinions seem misconceived. Royal justice in Scotland, though not so highly centralised as in England, was far from inadequate for the country's needs.[36] As to the proposition that Scotland had a Canon law of her own, Maitland's answer to Stubbs, who asserted the same of Canon law in medieval England, seems apposite for Scotland also:

> It would have been as impossible for the courts Christian of this country to maintain . . . a schismatical law of their own as it would now be for a judge of the High Court to persistently disregard the decisions of the House of Lords: there would have been an appeal from every sentence, and reversal would have been a matter of course.[37]

---

35 Cooper, *Cases* (n 2); S Ollivant, *The Court of the Official in Pre-Reformation Scotland* (SS vol 34, 1982); P C Ferguson, *Medieval Papal Representatives in Scotland: Legates, Nuncios, and Judges-delegate, 1125–1286* (SS vol 45, 1997).
36 Barrow "Justiciar", especially at 70–76 and 108–109, is a convincing counter to views put forward earlier by Lord Cooper and Professor Peter Stein. See further Taylor, *State* (n 16) passim.
37 Pollock & Maitland, vol 2, at 373. For an assessment see C Donahue, "Roman canon law in the medieval English church: Stubbs vs Maitland re-examined" (1974) 72 *Mich LR* 647. See also

The thirteenth century did, however, mark the apogee of the power of the church. In that century judges-delegate might even determine questions touching on the ownership of land, later the most cherished preserve of the king's ordinary courts. The record of a series of litigations conducted before judges-delegate in the 1230s survives, concerning land attached to the church of Old Kilpatrick, near Dumbarton. It provides valuable evidence for the church courts in action as well as some memorable snapshots of contemporary life. The witness Alexander son of Hugh, for example, remembered seeing a man named Bede Ferdan, sixty years before or more, living on some of the disputed land, in a large house made of wattle beside the church of Kilpatrick to the east. Asked in whose name Bede possessed the land, he replied that it was in the name of the church; and that the only service required of Bede for the land was that he receive and feed all visitors to the church. A later witness, Gilbethoc, added the ominous information that Bede had been killed in defending the right and liberty of the church.[38]

The influence of the Canon law on later Scots law was long-lasting and profound. Although the authority of the Pope was rejected at the Reformation (1559–60), the authority of the Canon law continued save where expressly superseded. Thomas Craig, who practised law in the fifty years following the Reformation, noted in his *Jus Feudale* that "although we have shaken off the papal yoke, the Canon law's great authority still survives in our country, to the extent that where it deviates from the Civil law . . . we prefer the Canon law."[39]

The influence of the Canon law was most obvious in the later Scots law of marriage and legitimacy. Canon law had recognised as valid, while condemning as irregular, marriages contracted *per verba de presenti*, that is, by a simple exchange of consents in the present tense, without the requirement of any further formality or the presence of a priest; and *per verba de futuro subsequente copula*, that is, by intercourse following on a promise to marry. Such marriages – sometimes, though incorrectly, referred to as "handfast"

---

C Donahue, *Law, Marriage and Society in the Later Middle Ages* (2007) and R H Helmholz, "The medieval Canon law in Scotland: marriage and divorce", in A M Godfrey (ed), *Miscellany VIII* (2020) 95: "the existing Scottish evidence supports the conclusion that the *enforcement* of the medieval church's law of marriage and divorce did admit of significant regional variation" (at 112, emphasis supplied).

38 C Innes (ed), *Registrum Monasterii de Passelet* (Maitland Club, 1832; New Club, 1877) at 165–167; and Cooper, *Cases* (n 2) no 22. See also C Innes, *Scotch Legal Antiquities* (1872) at 214–221.

39 Craig, *JF*, 1.3.24 (Dodd translation at 83). For the abolition of papal jurisdiction see *RPS* A1560/8/4.

marriages – survived in later Scots law until the Marriage (Scotland) Act of 1939.[40] Ironically, the Roman Catholic Church had ceased to recognise them as valid in 1563, less than five years after the Scottish Reformation. The Canon law doctrine that a child, born illegitimate, might be legitimated by the subsequent marriage of its parents, so long as there had been no impediment at conception, was early accepted into the Scots common law. Indeed Robert III (1390–1406), born some years before his parents contracted a marriage valid in the eyes of the church, could hardly have succeeded otherwise.[41] English law, by contrast, did not recognise legitimation by subsequent marriage until the twentieth century.

In other areas, too, Canon law influence was pervasive. Thus, although the Incest Act of 1567 referred to the "word of God" and to Leviticus chapter 18, in practice the forbidden degrees of relationship continued to be interpreted according to the intricate rules of the medieval Canon law, save where expressly altered by statute. The consequences were dire. Whereas incest had formerly been merely an ecclesiastical offence, it became a crime after the Reformation, and a number of unfortunates were judicially executed by hanging, drowning or beheading on the most technical of grounds. In 1629, for example, John Weir was found guilty of "the filthie and detestable cryme of incest" and sentenced "to be tane to the Mercat Croce of Edinburgh and thair his heid to be strukin from his bodie." His crime? He had married the widow of his great-uncle.[42] In 1646 Jean Knox was hanged on the Castle Hill of Edinburgh because she had married John Murray when already five months pregnant to his brother William, "committing thairby nottour and manifest incest express aganis the law of Almychtie God and Actis of Parliament".[43]

The law of contract, too, was affected by the Canonists' insistence that an obligation seriously undertaken in good faith should be binding, even although there might be no reciprocal cause, consideration or *quid pro quo*. The greatest of our legal writers, Lord Stair, noted in his *Institutions* (1681) that a bare promise was binding in Scots law: "Promises now are commonly held obligatory, the canon law having taken off the exception of the civil law, *de nudo pacto*."[44] He also noted that Scots law demanded no particular form to constitute a binding contract because "following rather the canon law . . .

---

40 See further chs 9 and 10 below.
41 See S Marshall, *Illegitimacy in Medieval Scotland, 1100–1500* (2021), at 26–41, 110–116.
42 *Justiciary Cases I* at 121.
43 *Justiciary Cases III* at 690.
44 Stair, *Inst*, 1.10.4. See further ch 15 below.

every paction produceth action".⁴⁵ As a consequence the modern Scots law of contract, unlike English law, has no doctrine of consideration, and unlike some Civilian-based systems, no notion of *causa*. The eighteenth-century judge, Lord Hailes, was right to note that "the canon law is not the law of Scotland; but the law of Scotland contains much of the canon law. This is so certain, that in many cases we determine according to the canon law without knowing it."⁴⁶

The debts owed by later Scots law to the Canon law were not confined to substantive law. Scots law also owes much to the personnel and the procedure of the Canon law. One consequence of the relatively late development of a legal profession and a central court was that churchmen trained in the Canon law continued to play an important part in the administration of lay as well as ecclesiastical justice. An outstanding example is William Elphinstone (1431–1514), Bishop of Aberdeen, and Keeper of the Great Seal. His first judicial appointment was as official of Glasgow, but his later contribution to secular justice as a lord of the king's council, and as an auditor of causes and complaints (a judicial committee of Parliament) over the long space of 35 years was of crucial importance. In addition, Elphinstone, like many churchmen, had substantial judicial powers as a lord of regality in respect of the temporal possessions of his diocese.⁴⁷

The evolution of the "Romano-canonical" procedure of the developed Canon law in the twelfth and early thirteenth centuries has been described as "one of the wonders of legal history".⁴⁸ It was rational, it was written, and it advanced by orderly logical steps from proposition to proposition. Its influence on the history of Continental civil procedure can hardly be overestimated. In Scotland, too, thanks to Elphinstone and his ilk, its effects are clearly discernible in secular tribunals such as the council and the judicial committees of Parliament from at least the fifteenth century. When a supreme central court – the Court of Session – was finally established in the sixteenth century, its procedure was based on the Romano-canonical model. To this day the procedure and terminology of the Court of Session clearly proclaim their Canon law origins.⁴⁹ From the Court of Session the

---

45 Stair, *Inst*, 1.10.7.
46 *Maxwell v Gordon* (1775) Hailes' Decisions, at 624, 626.
47 There is an outstanding modern biography of Elphinstone by L J Macfarlane, *William Elphinstone and the Kingdom of Scotland: 1431–1514* (2nd edn, 1995).
48 R C van Caenegem, "History of European civil procedure", in K Zweigert and U Drobnig (eds), *International Encyclopedia of Comparative Law*, vol 16 (1973) ch 2.19.
49 Ollivant, *Official* (n 33); D Baird Smith, "Canon law", in *SLSL*, 183; and see the writings of J J Robertson: "The development of the law", in Brown (ed), *Scottish Society* (n 6) 136

new procedure spread to the sheriff court, and gradually the sheriff became more a judge in the Canon law mould and less the chairman of a group of feudal landowners.

### (5) Udal law

In 1468 and 1469 Scotland received first Orkney and then Shetland as pledges for the dowry of Margaret, princess of Norway and Denmark, and queen of James III. The pledge was never redeemed, and the United Kingdom now exercises full sovereignty over the northern isles. However, some traces of the islands' former law, based on the Gulathing Code of the Norwegian king Magnus "the Law Mender" (1263–1280) still survive.[50] This is particularly true of landownership, which in Norwegian law was allodial or "udal", rather than feudal: that is, the landowner owned his land absolutely, and did not hold it, as in the feudal system, directly or indirectly of the Crown. Twice in the twentieth century special rights attaining to udal ownership were upheld – in respect of salmon fishing and the foreshore – and distinguished from the position under Scots law proper.[51] A third attempt, which sought to establish special udal rights over buried treasure, failed but raised some fundamental questions concerning the nature of Crown sovereignty in the northern isles – questions later further explored in relation to salmon farming and the sea bed.[52]

---

especially at 150–152; "Canon law as a source [in Stair's *Institutions*]", in D M Walker (ed), *Stair Tercentenary Studies* (SS vol 33, 1981) 112; "Canon law" [in "Sources of law (general and historical)"], *SME*, vol 22 (1987) paras 580–586; "Scottish legal research in the Vatican Archive: a preliminary report" (1988) 2 *Renaissance Studies* 339.

50  The Gulathing Code applied in south-west Norway, around Bergen, and west-over-sea in Iceland, the Faroes, Orkney and Shetland.

51  *Smith v Lerwick Harbour Trustees* (1903) 5 F 680 (foreshore); *Lord Advocate v Balfour* 1907 SC 1360 (salmon-fishings).

52  *Lord Advocate v University of Aberdeen and Budge* 1963 SC 533 and *Shetland Salmon Farmers Association v Crown Estate Commissioners* 1991 SLT 166. See further J Ryder, "Udal law" and Sir T B Smith's "Editorial excursus" thereon in *SME*, vol 24, paras 301–316 and 317–329; and see further Sellar, "Custom" at paras 385–388; and "Custom in Scots law", in J Gilissen (ed), *La Coutume: Custom* (1990) 411 at 417–418 ("In fact, cases based on Udal law raise, not only the question of custom and its reasonableness but also the matter of conflict between two legal orders.")

## D. RENAISSANCE AND REFORMATION

### (1) The foundation of the Court of Session

Scots lawyers have always regarded 1532, the traditional date for the foundation of the Court of Session, as a key date in legal history. In that year Parliament passed the College of Justice Act "Concerning the ordour of Justice and the institutioun of ane college of cunning and wise men for the administracioun of Justice".[53] This central civil court was to have a complement of fifteen judges, "Lords of Council and Session" alias "Senators of the College of Justice": seven lay lawyers and seven ecclesiastical under the presidency of a churchman. Some recent historians have doubted the significance of the events of 1532.[54] They point to over one hundred years of earlier institutional development. In 1426 Parliament legislated for the holding of regular judicial sittings or "sessions" to "examine and finally determine all and sundry complaints causes and querellis that may be determined before the King's Council".[55] These "sessions" appear to have been more spasmodic than regular, but throughout the fifteenth century there were further attempts to improve the quality of central justice through the king's council and the judicial committees of Parliament. By the end of the century in the reign of James IV, a specialist judicial body had begun to emerge within the council, the forerunner of the Lords of Council and Session. Fourteen of the fifteen judges appointed in 1532 had already sat on council sessions in 1531.

However, if the focus shifts from institutional development to jurisdictional competence, the importance of the establishment of the Court of Session as a College of Justice in 1532 becomes clearer. The Act gave the court authority "to sitt and decyde apoun all actions civile",[56] and the new body is soon found determining the most fundamental questions of feudal land law, that is, matters of "fee and heritage". This marked a radical new departure, as jurisdiction over fee and heritage had previously been a

---

53 RPS 1532/6.
54 See the writings of R K Hannay, conveniently gathered in H L MacQueen (ed), *The College of Justice* (SS supp vol 1, 1990), and A A M Duncan, "The central courts before 1532", in *ISLH*, 321.
55 RPS 1426/25.
56 See further A L Murray, "Sinclair's practicks", in A Harding (ed), *Law-Making and Law-Makers in British History* (1980); G Dolezalek, "The Court of Session as a *ius commune* court", in H L MacQueen (ed), *Miscellany IV* (SS vol 49, 2002) 51; J W Cairns, "Revisiting the foundation of the College of Justice", in H L MacQueen (ed), *Miscellany V* (SS vol 52, 2006) 27; A M Godfrey, *Civil Justice in Renaissance Scotland: The Origins of a Central Court* (2009); Simpson and Wilson, *Scottish Legal History* (n 3) ch 6.

jealously guarded privilege of the ordinary feudal courts.[57] Time and again in the fifteenth century the council and the Lords Auditors of Causes and Complaints had declined jurisdiction because it concerned fee and heritage. In 1471, for example, Robert Hamilton, provost of the collegiate church of Bothwell, raised an action before the Auditors touching the payment of mill dues, or "multures", but was fined forty shillings, "for his persute of the said matter quhare it aucht not to be folowit", because it concerned fee and heritage.[58]

Lord Cooper described the central judicial bodies of the late fifteenth century as "Scotland's ersatz substitute for a supreme court".[59] A better comparison can be made with the Chancellor's jurisdiction in England, which supplemented the common law and ordinary justice by providing extra-ordinary judicial remedies. In England, where the central courts of common law and a lay legal profession had been established since the thirteenth century, the supplementary jurisdiction of the Chancellor eventually gave rise to a system of "Equity", distinct from Common law. For hundreds of years, in England, "Equity" in this technical sense ran parallel to Common law, with its own courts, rules and judicial procedures. It was only with the Judicature Acts of 1873 and 1875 that the courts of Equity and of Common law in England finally merged. Even today, English lawyers think in terms of "common law" rules and "equitable" ones. In Scotland, however, in the much-quoted words of the first Lord President Clyde, "In the law of Scotland, law is equity and equity law, and when a Scots lawyer uses the term 'common law', he uses it to distinguish it from Acts of Parliament."[60] That this is so owes much to the establishment of 1532. The new court was much more than the old session writ large, for it combined the extra-ordinary equitable jurisdiction of the council with the ordinary common law jurisdiction over fee and heritage.[61]

---

57 Godfrey, *Civil Justice* (n 56) ch 7, argues that the court had acquired jurisdiction in fee and heritage cases before 1532. See also A M Godfrey, "The College of Justice, Court of Session and Privy Council in sixteenth century Scotland, 1532–1603", in A M Godfrey and C H van Rhee (eds), *Central Courts in Early Modern Europe and the Americas* (2020) 151.
58 T Thomson (ed), *Acts of the Lords Auditors of Causes and Complaints* (1839) at 21.
59 Cooper, *Selected Papers* (n 3) at 227.
60 *Gibson's Trustees* 1933 SC 190 at 198.
61 This idea has its germination in A Harding, "The medieval brieve of protection and the development of the common law", 1966 *JR* 115. Godfrey, *Civil Justice* (n 56) ch 5, sees the Session's jurisdiction as essentially "supervisory" and does not pursue the idea that it combined equity and common law. See further on that theme J D Ford, "Conciliar authority and equitable jurisdiction in early-modern Scotland", in M Godfrey (ed), *Law and Authority in British Legal History, 1200–1900* (2016) 140; and the same author's *Law and Opinion in Scotland during the Seventeenth Century* (2007) ch 6; also A R C Simpson, "Power, reason and equity: two juristic accounts of royal authority in sixteenth-century Scotland", in J O Sunde (ed), *Constitutionalism*

The emergence of a central civil court in Scotland at this period can be viewed as part of a more general European pattern.[62] In Germany, for instance, the *Reichskammergericht* was established in 1495 for the Holy Roman Empire. The slow evolution of a lay legal profession in Scotland in the fifteenth and sixteenth centuries also finds more ready parallels on the Continent than in England. It is possible to point to some laymen in the practice of law in Scotland in the mid-fifteenth century and considerably more by 1500.[63] However, lay lawyers remained overshadowed by churchmen until well into the sixteenth century. The first four Presidents of the Court of Session were all churchmen trained in Canon and Civil law.

## (2) The Reformation

The Scottish Reformation of 1559/60 brought to an end the old division between lay and ecclesiastical jurisdiction. In place of the courts of the Official new "Commissary" courts were set up. Like their predecessors, these Commissary courts dealt with marriage and legitimation, wills, executors and moveable succession. They also had jurisdiction over divorce, now permitted on the grounds of desertion and adultery. Unlike their predecessors, however, and in contrast with the situation in England after the Reformation, these were lay courts, from which appeal ran after 1609 to the Court of Session.[64] The courts of the Reformed Church – Kirk Session, Presbytery, Synod and General Assembly – were restricted increasingly, although not exclusively, to internal ecclesiastical matters.[65]

---

*before 1789: Constitutional Arrangements from the High Middle Ages to the French Revolution* (2014) 128.

62 See Godfrey and Van Rhee (eds), *Central Courts* (n 57); G Rossi (ed), *Authorities in Early Modern Courts* (2021).

63 See MacQueen, *Common Law* (n 23) at 75–84; A R Borthwick and H L MacQueen, "'Rare creatures for their age': Alexander and David Guthrie, graduate lairds and royal servants", in B E Crawford (ed), *Church, Chronicle and Learning in Medieval and Renaissance Scotland: Essays presented to Donald Watt on the occasion of the completion of the publication of Bower's Scotichronicon* (1999) 227; and two articles by A R C Simpson: "Men of law in the Aberdeen Council Register? A preliminary study, circa 1450–1460", 2019 *JR* 136; "Andrew Alansone: man of law in the Aberdeen Council Register, c.1440–c.1475?", in J W Armstrong and E Frankot (eds), *Cultures of Law in Urban Northern Europe: Scotland and its Neighbours c.1350–c.1700* (2020) 247.

64 See further T M Green, *The Spiritual Jurisdiction in Reformation Scotland: A Legal History* (2019); T M Green (ed), *The Consistorial Decisions of the Commissaries of Edinburgh, 1564–1576/7* (SS vol 61, 2014); T Green, "The sources of early Scots consistorial law: reflections on law, authority and jurisdiction during the Scottish Reformation", in Godfrey (ed), *Law and Authority* (n 61) 120; Simpson and Wilson, *Scottish Legal History* (n 3) ch 8.

65 G Donaldson, *Scottish Church History* (1985) at 50–52. For an argument that the Reformation

## (3) Roman law

The scope of the common law, then, increased greatly in the course of the sixteenth century. The establishment of the College of Justice in 1532 nipped in the bud any incipient division between common law and equity, and the extensive legal jurisdiction enjoyed by the church before the Reformation was largely transferred to secular courts. The development of the common law was also strongly affected by Roman law.[66] Much Roman law – more than is generally realised – had already percolated by way of the Canon law. The humanist scholarship of the Renaissance saw a quickening of interest throughout Europe in the original texts of Justinian's *Corpus Iuris Civilis*. As a consequence, in many jurisdictions, Roman law came to exercise a more direct influence over the development of the law. Roman categories and Roman solutions supplemented and even supplanted the customary law. This stage in European legal history is often referred to as the "Reception" of Roman law. English law remained comparatively unaffected by the Reception. Scots law corresponded more to the European norm. The late sixteenth century represents the high-water mark of Roman influence. John Leslie, Lord of Session and Bishop of Ross, wrote in 1578:

> this far to the lawis of the Realme we are astricted, gif ony cummirsum or trubilsum cause fal out, as oft chances, quhilke can nocht be agriet be our cuntrey lawis, incontinent quhatevir is thocht necessar to pacify this controversie, is citet out of the Romane lawis.[67]

led to an infusion of Protestant morality into the criminal law, see C Kennedy, "Criminal law and religion in post-Reformation Scotland" (2012) 16 *Edin LR* 178.
66 Cairns (n 3) 57–74 and passim; Simpson and Wilson, *Scottish Legal History* (n 3) ch 7. See also on this theme many of Professor Cairns' papers, collected as *Law, Lawyers and Humanism: Selected Essays on the History of Scots Law, Volume 1* (2015).
67 J Lesley or Leslie, *De Origine Moribus et rebus gestis Scotiae* (1578) as translated into Scots in 1596 (see E G Cody and W Murison (eds), *The historie of Scotland, written first in Latin by . . . Jhone Leslie* (1888) at 120). Further on the influence of Roman law in the development of Scots law P Stein, "The influence of Roman law on the law of Scotland", 1963 *JR* 205, reprinted in P G Stein, *The Character and Influence of the Roman Civil Law: Historical Essays* (1988) ch 19; the same author's "Roman law in medieval Scotland", *Ius Romanum Medii Aevi*, pars V, 13b (1968) 1, reprinted in Stein, *Character and Influence*, ch 18. Important collections are R Evans-Jones (ed), *The Civil Law Tradition in Scotland* (SS supp vol 2, 1995) and D L Carey Miller and R Zimmermann (eds), *The Civilian Tradition and Scots Law* (1997). For a useful bibliography, see W M Gordon, "Roman law and Scots law – a bibliography", in Evans-Jones (ed), *Civil Law Tradition* 310; also two other contributions, "Roman law as a source [of Stair's *Institutions*]", in *Stair Tercentenary Studies* (n 46) 107 and "Roman law", in *SME*, vol 25, paras 548–556. See also the papers collected under the headings "Roman law and Scots law" and "Roman law influence" in W M Gordon, *Roman Law, Scots Law and Legal History: Selected Essays* (2007). Alan Watson has made telling use of examples drawn from Scots law in his various publications as, for example, *The Making of the Civil Law* (1981). Some of the essays in A D E Lewis and D J Ibbetson

This was undoubtedly an exaggeration. Scots land law remained firmly rooted in Anglo-Norman feudalism, and family law and procedure continued to develop on lines laid down by the Canon law. However, the terminology of Roman law came increasingly to pervade Scots law. For example, the legal rights of children, arising on the death of their parents, earlier known as "bairns' part", were renamed *"legitim"* after the *legitima portio* of Roman law. Some areas of law, such as moveable property and servitudes over land (*anglicé* "easements") took on a decidedly Roman appearance, and writers on Scots law came increasingly to compare their native law with the Roman model.

### (4) Legislation

From the fifteenth century onwards many statutes were passed to enact new law, and not merely to reinforce and explain the old. The nineteenth-century lawyer and historian, Cosmo Innes, wrote of "those brief, terse statutes which shame the legislation of a later wordy age".[68] A surprising number of these acts remained on the statute book until the late twentieth century. Lord Cooper wrote in 1951 of "a long succession of pivotal reforms around which whole chapters of Scots law continued to revolve for centuries and many of which are still in force".[69] Since Cooper wrote many of these ancient statutes have been repealed. The Prescription Acts of 1469, 1474 and 1579 disappeared with the Prescription and Limitation (Scotland) Act of 1973, while the Requirements of Writing (Scotland) Act 1995 repealed the Subscription of Deeds Acts of 1540, 1579 and 1681 as well as the Blank Bonds and Trusts Act 1696.[70] The Marriage and Incest Acts of 1567 were repealed in 1977 and 1986 respectively, 400 years too late.[71] The Bankruptcy Acts of 1621 and

---

(eds), *The Roman Law Tradition* (1994) also consider Scots law and Roman law. Two articles expressing very different points of view as to Scots law and Roman law are A Rodger, "Roman law in practice in Britain" (1993) 12 *Rechtshistorisches Journal* 261, and R Evans-Jones, "Roman law in Britain (sic) Scotland" (1994) 13 *Rechtshistorisches Journal* 494.

68 Innes, *Scotch Legal Antiquities* (n 38) at 159. See further A M Godfrey, "Parliament and the law", in K M Brown and A R MacDonald (eds), *The History of the Scottish Parliament Volume 3: Parliament in Context, 1235–1707* (2010) 157; A R C Simpson, "Legislation and authority in early-modern Scotland", in Godfrey (ed), *Law and Authority* (n 61) 85.

69 Cooper, *Selected Papers* (n 3) at 230.

70 For the Acts mentioned see *RPS* 1469/18, A1474/5/9, 1579/10/36 (prescription); *RPS* 1540/12/92, 1579/10/33, 1681/7/27 (subscription of deeds); *RPS* 1696/9/143 (blank bonds and trusts). On prescription see further A R C Simpson, "Legal learning and the prescription of rights in Scotland", in H Dorndorp, D Ibbetson and E J H Schrage (eds), *Limitation and Prescription: A Comparative Legal History* (2019) 263.

71 By the Marriage (Scotland) Act 1977 and the Incest and Related Offences (Scotland) Act 1986

1696 were repealed, but largely re-enacted, by the Bankruptcy (Scotland) Act of 1985 (now itself replaced by the Bankruptcy (Scotland) Act 2016).[72] The earliest act to remain on the statute book is the Royal Mines Act of 1424, which reserves gold and silver found in the ground to the Crown.[73] Important acts still in force are the Leases Act of 1449/50, which remains the foundation of the law of leases in Scotland, and the Registration Act of 1617 which set up the Register of Sasines to record deeds conveying title to land.[74]

## (5) Legal writing

The late sixteenth and early seventeenth centuries saw the rise of Scottish legal writing.[75] The *Jus Feudale* of Thomas Craig (1538–1608), which expounds the feudal land law of Scotland and compares it with English law, setting both in a broad European context, is the first of a series of works still regarded as authoritative by the Scottish courts today. Craig was a jurist of European stature, a pioneer of the historical and comparative method, whose reputation has been rehabilitated by modern historical scholarship.[76] Another Scottish jurist with a European reputation was William Welwood (d 1622), whose *Sea Law of Scotland* "shortly gathered and plainly dressit for the reddy use of all sea-faring men" appeared in 1590, and his *Abridgement of All Sea Laws* in 1613.[77] Of more purely Scottish interest are the works

respectively. The 1986 Act was repealed by the Criminal Justice and Licensing (Scotland) Act 2010 Sch 7 para 15; the law is now contained in the Criminal Law (Consolidation) (Scotland) Act 1995 ss 1, 2 and 4. For the post-Reformation Marriage and Incest Acts, see *RPS* A1567/12/14 and 15, and see further ch 10 below.

72 For the 1621 and 1696 Acts see *RPS* 1621/6/30, 1696/9/57.
73 *RPS* 1424/15.
74 *RPS* 1450/1/16, 1617/5/30. See also Simpson and Wilson, *Scottish Legal History* (n 3) ch 10.
75 See further Cairns (n 3) at 93–101; Simpson and Wilson, *Scottish Legal History* (n 3) chs 14–16. See also G Dolezalek, *Scotland under Jus Commune* (SS vols 55–57, 2010), an inventory and census of handwritten legal texts 1500–1660 but also including information on legal literature outside that time-range. Professor Dolezalek finds "superabundant evidence that Scotland fully achered to Europe's shared culture of *Jus Commune* from 1500 to 1800" (at 1).
76 See particularly J G A Pocock, *The Ancient Constitution and the Feudal Law* (1957; reissued with a retrospect 1987). See also J W Cairns, "The *breve testatum* and Craig's *Jus Feudale*" (1988) 56 *Tijdschrift voor Rechtsgeschiedenis* 311 (dating the composition of *JF* from the late 1590s to at least as late as 1606); J Finlay, "The early career of Thomas Craig, advocate" (2004) 8 *Edin LR* 298; Ford, *Law and Opinion* (n 61) index sv "Craig, Thomas"; and three contributions by L Dodd, "Thomas Craig's aetiology of law and society: literary dependence and independence in the *Jus Feudale*" (2016) 37 *JLH* 121; the editorial introduction to *Jus Feudale Tribus Libris Comprehensum by Sir Thomas Craig of Riccartoun Book I* (SS vol 64, 2017); and "The *Vita Cragii* of James Baillie", in A M Godfrey (ed), *Miscellany VIII* (SS vol 67, 2020) 265.
77 See J W Cairns, "Academic feud, bloodfeud, and William Welwood: legal education in

of Sir John Skene, Lord Clerk Register (c 1543–1617). He was concerned that the wording and terminology of the older Scottish law was becoming obscure and unintelligible to his contemporaries and was in danger of being displaced by Roman law. Skene's legal glossary, *De Verborum Significatione*, published in 1597, has been described as "a magnificent legal dictionary . . . a goldmine whose riches extend far beyond the strictly legal".[78] Skene's greatest achievement was his edition of the key medieval text *Regiam Majestatem*, together with others of the "auld lawes", published in both Latin and Scots in 1609.

## E. CONSOLIDATION

Throughout Europe from the sixteenth century onwards, as the modern nation state emerged, systematic and analytical treatises consolidating the work of the Reception and expounding the law on a national basis began to appear. Such works were sometimes entitled "Institutes" or "Institutions" after the famous *Institutes* of the Emperor Justinian. An early example is Guy Coquille's *Institution au Droit Français* published in 1607. Later examples are Selchow's *Institutiones Iurisprudentiae Germanicae* (1757), and Asso and Manuel's *Instituciones del Derecho Civil de Castilla* (1771). Scotland fits well into this European pattern, although in modern Scottish legal parlance the term "Institutional" has come to be applied to a small canon of works on Scots law, starting with Craig's *Jus Feudale*, which are regarded as having particular authority. A leading Continental legal historian has suggested that it would be appropriate to use the term in its original and primary meaning and refer to the "Institutional phase" of European legal history.[79]

During the sixteenth and seventeenth centuries the academic writings of Craig and Skene were complemented by more practical manuals on the law, often known simply as "Practicks". John Sinclair (d 1566), Bishop of

---

St Andrews" (1998) 2 *Edin LR* 158, 255 (2 parts); J D Ford, "William Welwod's treatise on maritime law" (2013) 34 *JLH* 171; J D Ford (ed), *Alexander King's Treatise on Maritime Law* (SS vol 65, 2018), especially at lxxxiii–xc, and appendix II.

78 J Wormald, *Court, King and Community: Scotland 1470–1625* (1981) at 181. See further on Skene's career, J W Cairns, T D Fergus and H L MacQueen, "Legal humanism in Renaissance Scotland" (1990) 11 *JLH* 40 at 44–48 (also as "Legal humanism and the history of Scots law: John Skene and Thomas Craig", in J MacQueen (ed), *Humanism in Renaissance Scotland* (1990) 48 at 52–56).

79 K Luig (trans S MacCormack), "The institutions of national law in the seventeenth and eighteenth centuries", 1972 *JR* 193.

Brechin and Lord President of the Court of Session, compiled an early set of Practicks.[80] The best known Practicks are those of Sir James Balfour of Pittendreich (d 1583), who was, like Sinclair, Lord President of the Court of Session, and of Sir Thomas Hope (d 1646), Lord Advocate to Charles I.[81] Balfour's *Practicks*, though hardly systematic, is an invaluable guide to the practice of law in the later sixteenth century. References to the "auld lawes" and to *Regiam Majestatem* rub shoulders with decisions of the Court of Session in titles such as "Marriage", "Tocher", "Beggars", "Bastards" and "Muirburn".[82]

## (1) Stair

At the end of the seventeenth century theory and practice were triumphantly combined in the most influential work ever written on Scots law, *The Institutions of the Law of Scotland*, by James Dalrymple, Viscount of Stair (1619–1695), published in 1681. Stair, like Sinclair and Balfour, was able to draw on his experience as Lord President of the Court of Session. His *Institutions* fit comfortably into the European mould – the systematic exposition of a national legal system – and are universally accepted as the greatest of Scotland's "Institutional" writings. Lord Cooper's celebrated encomium bears repetition:

---

80 A text of Sinclair's practicks is accessible at https://home.uni-leipzig.de/jurarom/scotland/dat/sinclair.html. See further A L Murray, "Sinclair's practicks", in A Harding (ed), *Law-making and Law-makers in British History* (1980) 90; G Dolezalek, "The Court of Session as a ius commune court – witnessed by 'Sinclair's practicks'", in H L MacQueen (ed), *Miscellany IV* (SS vol 49, 2002) 51; A L Murray and G Dolezalek, "Legal argumentation and citation of *jus commune* sources in pleadings in the Court of Session, 1549/1550", in A M Godfrey (ed), *Miscellany VIII* (SS vol 67, 2020) 113; Simpson and Wilson, *Scottish Legal History* (n 3) ch 7.

81 Balfour's *Practicks* circulated extensively in manuscript before the first printed edition of 1754. Balfour's *Practicks* and Hope's *Major Practicks* have both been reprinted by the Stair Society (vols 3, 4, 21 and 22). It is pleasant to record that Lord Hope of Craighead, formerly Lord President of the Court of Session, Lord of Appeal in Ordinary and Deputy President of the UK Supreme Court, is a direct descendant of Sir Thomas, via the 19th-century Lord President Charles Hope of Granton. See further A Hope, "Sir Thomas Hope: Lord Advocate to Charles I", in H L MacQueen (ed), *Miscellany IV* (SS vol 49, 2002) 145.

82 See further two articles by W M Gordon: "The acts of the Scottish lords of council in the late fifteenth and early sixteenth centuries: records and reports", in C Stebbings (ed), *Law Reporting in Britain* (1995) 55; and "Balfour's *Registrum*", in H L MacQueen (ed), *Miscellany IV* (SS vol 49, 2002) 127 (both reprinted in Gordon, *Roman Law* (n 67) chs 20 and 21); and Simpson and Wilson, *Scottish Legal History* (n 3) at 211–213. Note also, for a contemporary of Balfour whose "dictionary of Scotch law" remains unpublished, A R C Simpson, "Counsel and the Crown: history, law and politics in the thought of David Chalmers of Ormond" (2015) 36 *JLH* 3; Simpson and Wilson, *Scottish Legal History* (n 3) 184–187.

The publication of his *Institutions* in 1681 marked the creation of Scots law as we have since known it—an original amalgam of Roman Law, Feudal Law and native customary law, systematised by resort to the law of nature and the Bible, and illuminated by many flashes of ideal metaphysic. To this work and its author every Scots lawyer has since paid a tribute of almost superstitious reverence, and the resort still occasionally made to Stair in the House of Lords and the Privy Council suggests that it is not only in the estimation of his fellow-countrymen that he falls to be ranked amongst the great jurists of all time.[83]

Modern studies of Stair's work, including those by scholars outwith Scotland, have served only to emphasise the magnitude of Stair's achievement.[84]

Stair was the architect of modern Scots law, and in that sense his work marks a new beginning. Yet it was also very much a consolidation of what had gone before. Stair himself would have rejected any suggestion that he had cut loose from the past. Time and again he refers to Craig and cites decisions of the Court of Session to support a proposition. He himself collected and published the decisions of the Court of Session from 1661 to 1681. In the preface to his second edition of 1693 he writes,

> I have been very sparing to express my own opinion in dubious cases of law, not determined by our custom and statutes, but have rather congested what the Lords [of Session] have done . . . But I have used more freedom in opening the fountains of law and justice, and the deductions thence arising, by the law of nature and reason.[85]

The last sentence is significant. Stair believed that the essence of law derived ultimately from equity and morality, rather than from power and authority: "Equity is the body of the law, and the statutes of men are but as the ornaments and vestiture thereof."[86] In keeping with this view, he regarded Roman law, which he cited frequently in his *Institutions*, as a rule or system not binding for its authority, but to be followed rather for its equity.[87] It is interesting to note that Thomas Craig before him, in his *Jus Feudale*, had adopted the same attitude towards Roman law as a source:

> We, in this kingdom, are bound by the laws of the Romans to the extent they agree with the laws of nature and correct reasoning . . . [T]here is scarcely any wider tract of natural equity nor any more fertile field of meticulous judgments

---

83 Cooper, *Scottish Legal Tradition* (n 1) at 9–10.
84 See particularly Ford, *Law and Opinion* (n 61); also *Stair Tercentenary Studies* (n 48); and "Stair Tercentenary Papers", being the second part of the *JR* for 1981.
85 Stair, *Inst*, advertisement prefixed to the second edition, 1693 (1981 edn, at 65).
86 Stair, *Inst*, 1.1.17.
87 See W M Gordon, "Stair's use of Roman law", in Harding (ed), *Law-making* (n 80) at 120–126.

and arguments drawn from the very principles of nature than the books of the jurisconsults . . .[88]

## (2) Mackenzie

Contemporary with Stair was Sir George Mackenzie (1636–1691), King's Advocate, a strong supporter of the royal prerogative, and more inclined than Stair to view law as a command. Mackenzie was a considerable scholar and prolific writer, the author of *Aretina*, which has some claim to be regarded as the first Scottish novel, as well as many works on literature and law. His *Institutions of the Law of Scotland* (1684) is essentially a short primer, which nevertheless provides an instructive counterpoint to Stair's great work. Mackenzie's *Law and Customs of Scotland in Matters Criminal* (1678), deeply imbued with Civilian learning, is a treatise on an altogether larger scale, and marks an important stage in the exposition of Scotland's criminal law.[89]

## (3) The Criminal Procedure Act

One act of the last Scots Parliament, which sat from 1689 until the Union of 1707, deserves special mention: the Criminal Procedure Act of 1701, repealed and effectively re-enacted in 1887 and again in 1975 and 1995.[90] Scots law knows neither Magna Carta nor Habeas Corpus, but the 1701 Act laid down important safeguards against detention without trial. No one can be detained in custody for more than 80 days unless an indictment has been served; or more than 110 days unless trial has commenced. Otherwise the charge is dropped and cannot be brought again. These salutary rules are striking enough in their original context, but still appear remarkable in twenty-first century Europe, where far longer periods of detention without trial are a commonplace, even in England.

---

88 Craig, *JF* 1.2.14 (Dodd translation, at 53).
89 See the edition by O F Robinson (ed), *Mackenzie, Matters Criminal* (SS vol 59, 2012).
90 *RPS* 1701/10/234. See further Criminal Procedure (Scotland) Act 1887 s 43; Criminal Procedure (Scotland) Act 1975 s 101; Criminal Procedure (Scotland) Act 1995 s 65 as amended by the Criminal Procedure (Amendment) (Scotland) Act 2004 s 6 and the Criminal Justice (Scotland) Act 2016 s 79.

## (4) The Union of 1707

In 1603, on the death of Queen Elizabeth, James VI of Scotland succeeded to the English throne. The "Union of the Crowns", however, had little direct effect on the development of Scots law. King James did, indeed, promote a scheme for the harmonisation of Scots and English law, but, in the event, little came of it or of similar proposals later in the seventeenth century.[91] Personal union was followed by political union in 1707. In that year the Parliament of Scotland passed the Act of Union with England, and the English Parliament passed the Act of Union with Scotland. As a consequence, the new United Kingdom of Great Britain came into being on 1st May 1707. The Acts of Union contained important safeguards for Scots law. No alteration was to be made in the laws concerning "private Right" – "except for the evident utility of the subjects within Scotland".[92] The Court of Session and the High Court of Justiciary (which had been established in 1672) were to remain within Scotland in all time coming; and no Scottish cases were to be "cognoscible by the Courts of Chancery, Queens-Bench, Common-Pleas, or any other Court in Westminster-hall".[93] This provision did not prevent appeals being taken from the Court of Session to the House of Lords, nor was it intended to.[94] All

---

[91] See particularly B R Galloway and B P Levack (eds), *The Jacobean Union: Six Tracts of 1604* (SHS, 1985), and B P Levack, *The Formation of the British State: England, Scotland, and the Union 1603–1707* (1987). For earlier discussions of unification of Scots and English law see J D Ford, "Four models of union", 2011 *JR* 45, reprinted with an appendix of documents in H L MacQueen (ed), *Miscellany VII* (SS vol 62, 2015) 179).

[92] Article XVIII. See further J D Ford, "The legal provisions in the Acts of Union", (2007) 66 *Cambridge LJ* 106 at 108–18; and three articles by J W Cairns: "Scottish law, Scottish lawyers, and the status of the Union", in J Robertson (ed), *A Union for Empire: Political Thought and the British Union of 1707* (1995) 243; "Natural law, national laws, parliaments and multiple monarchies: 1707 and beyond", in K Haakonssen and H Hortsbøll (eds), *Northern Antiquities and National Identities: Perceptions of Denmark and the North in the Eighteenth Century* (2008) (both of these reprinted in J W Cairns, *Enlightenment, Legal Education, and Critique: Selected Essays on the History of Scots Law, Volume 2* (2015) chs 5 and 6); and "The origins of the Edinburgh Law School: the Union of 1707 and the Regius Chair", (2007) 11 *Edin LR* 300 at 313–326.

[93] Article XIX.

[94] A J MacLean, "The 1707 Union: Scots law and the House of Lords" (1983) 4 *JLH* 50 (also printed in A Kiralfy and H L MacQueen (eds), *New Perspectives in Scottish Legal History* (1984)); R S Tompson, "James Greenshields and the House of Lords: a reappraisal", in W M Gordon and T D Fergus (eds), *Legal History in the Making: proceedings of the Ninth British legal History Conference, Glasgow* 1989 (1991) 109; J Finlay, "Scots lawyers and House of Lords appeals in eighteenth-century Britain" (2011) 32 *JLH* 249. Important pre-Union background is discussed in J D Ford, "Protestations to Parliament for remeid of law" (2009) 88 *SHR* 57; see also the same author's "Adjudication in the Scottish Parliament, 1532–1707", in Godfrey and Van Rhee (eds), *Central Courts* (n 57) 189.

laws and statutes contrary to, or inconsistent with the terms of the Articles of Union were to be void.⁹⁵

The status of these provisions and their relation to the doctrine of the sovereignty of Parliament has often been debated. According to the English constitutional theorist, Dicey, writing before 1900, "neither the Act of Union with Scotland nor the Dentists Act 1878, has more claim than the other to be considered as supreme law."⁹⁶ However, Professor John Mitchell concluded that, as regards some at least of the provisions of the Act of Union, the element of entrenchment was apparent. He put the question: "Was Parliament born unfree?"⁹⁷ Lord Cooper made a notable contribution to the discussion in the leading case of *MacCormick v Lord Advocate* in 1953, in which he said, "The principle of the unlimited sovereignty of Parliament is a distinctively English principle which has no counterpart in Scottish Constitutional law."⁹⁸ The debate continues.⁹⁹

## (5) The '45

The aftermath of the 1745 Rebellion saw the passing of the Heritable Jurisdictions Act which brought to an end the courts of regality and stripped the baron courts of most of their power. It came into force on 25 March 1748, a date which has been described as one "which should rank with the Union of the Crowns in 1603 and the Union of the Parliaments of 1707 in

---

95 Article XXV. See further on the articles of union Simpson and Wilson, *Scottish Legal History* (n 3) at 374–382.
96 A V Dicey, *The Law of the Constitution*, quoted in J D B Mitchell, *Constitutional Law* (2nd edn, 1968) at 19.
97 Mitchell, *Constitutional Law* (n 96) chs 4 and 5; see also at 98 and 69.
98 *MacCormick v Lord Advocate* 1953 SC 396 at 411.
99 T B Smith, "The Union of 1707 as fundamental law", 1957 *Public Law* 99, reprinted in T B Smith, *Studies Critical and Comparative* (1962) 1–27, and Mitchell's *Constitutional Law* (n 96) are crucial. Further contributions are M Upton, "Marriage vows of the elephant: the constitution of 1707" (1989) 105 *LQR* 79; C R Munro, "The Union of 1707 and the British constitution", in P S Hodge (ed), *Scotland and the Union* (1994); T Harris, "The people, the law, and the constitution in Scotland and England: a comparative approach to the Glorious Revolution" (1999) 38 *Journal of British Studies* 28; J Robertson, "The idea of sovereignty and the Act of Union", in H T Dickinson and M Lynch (eds), *The Challenge to Westminster: Sovereignty, Devolution and Independence* (2000) 33; C Kidd, "Sovereignty and the Scottish constitution before 1707", 2004 *JR* 225; A O'Neill, "The sovereignty of the (Scottish) people: 1689 and all that", 2013 *JR* 446. For consideration of what the relevant principles of Scottish constitutional law might have been, see A McHarg, "The Declaration of Arbroath and Scots law", in K P Müller (ed), *Scotland and Arbroath 1320–2020: 700 Years of Fighting for Freedom, Sovereignty, and Independence* (2020) 423 and R Sutherland, "Aspects of the Scottish constitution prior to 1707", in J P Grant (ed), *Independence and Devolution: The Legal Implications for Scotland* (1976) 15.

the slow destruction of the traditional Scottish polity".[100] In this case, at least, the destruction was all to the good.

## (6) The eighteenth century

The eighteenth century has been described as the classical age of Scots law. There was little statute law reform, but the tradition of institutional writing continued. Andrew M'Douall, Lord Bankton, published his *Institutes* in 1751 in which he expressly compared Scots with English law.[101] *An Institute of the Law of Scotland,* the major work of John Erskine (1695–1768), professor of Scots law at the University of Edinburgh, appeared posthumously in 1773. Erskine's shorter *Principles of the Law of Scotland* (1st edition, 1754) succeeded Sir George Mackenzie's *Institutions* as a student primer, and was not itself displaced until the twentieth century by Gloag and Henderson's *Introduction to the Law of Scotland*.[102] Erskine is cited more frequently in the Court of Session today than Stair, perhaps because he is nearer in time, perhaps because his language is less opaque. At the beginning of the nineteenth century George Joseph Bell (1770–1843), like Erskine, professor of Scots law at the University of Edinburgh, contributed his *Commentaries on the Mercantile Jurisprudence of Scotland* (1804). If Erskine's *Institute* looked backwards as a consolidation or apotheosis of the feudal land law, Bell's *Commentaries,* constructed around the topic of bankruptcy, looked forward to Scotland's industrial and mercantile future. Stair, Erskine and Bell are generally held to be the greatest writers on Scots private law, although this judgement may underestimate Craig and Bankton. At the end of the eighteenth century, the *Commentaries on the Law of Scotland respecting Crimes* (1797) of David Hume (1756–1838), Baron (judge) of the Court of Exchequer, and, like Erskine and Bell, professor of Scots law at Edinburgh University, provided the classic statement of Scottish criminal law.

The eighteenth century marked the highpoint of the Faculty of Advocates. Advocates and judges dominated polite society and made notable contributions to the "Scottish Enlightenment". The achievements of the Enlightenment belong more to the history of ideas than to the history

---

100 B Lenman, *The Jacobite Risings in Britain* (1980) at 278.
101 This is reprinted with an introduction by W M Gordon as vols 41–43 in the Stair Society series. See also A R C Simpson, "Learning, honour and patronage: the career of Andrew McDouall, Lord Bankton 1746–61", in H L MacQueen (ed), *Miscellany VI* (SS vol 54, 2009) 121.
102 Now in its 14th edn (2017).

of Scots law.¹⁰³ However, the legal writing of Henry Home, Lord Kames (1696–1782), particularly his *Historical Law Tracts* (1758) and *Principles of Equity* (1760), had a considerable impact on the domestic Scottish scene, besides being widely read in England, the Continent and America. Kames's *Principles of Equity*, indeed, is still cited occasionally as an authority in the Scottish courts.¹⁰⁴ Some advocates, such as James Boswell and Sir Walter Scott, achieved great fame outwith the law. Others moved south to practise at the English bar, two of them, Alexander Wedderburn (1733–1805) and Henry Brougham (1778–1868) attaining the office of Lord Chancellor. One of the greatest of all English judges, William Murray, Lord Mansfield, Lord Chief Justice of the King's Bench from 1756 to 1788, was also a Scot, although his legal training took place entirely in England.¹⁰⁵

## (7) Codification

Towards the end of the eighteenth century there was a movement on the Continent for the codification of law. A civil code was issued for Bavaria in 1756, and a code for Prussia in 1794, In 1804 Napoleon promulgated his famous *Code Civil*. Scots law, too, was ready for codification; it had been expounded systematically and succinctly by a succession of gifted writers, and the long static years of the eighteenth century, relatively free of law reform, had aided consolidation. Yet Scots law has never been codified. The reason why must be ascribed, at least in part, to Union with England, and to the absence of a competent legislative assembly in Scotland itself.¹⁰⁶ As a consequence, the continuity of Scots law has remained unbroken to an extent surprising to a Continental lawyer.

---

103 The work of Professor John Cairns on this theme has however been fundamental: see a collection of his papers published as *Enlightenment, Legal Education, and Critique* (above n 92). See also J Finlay, *The Community of the College of Justice: Edinburgh and the Court of Session, 1687–1808* (2012) and the same author's *Legal Practice in Eighteenth-Century Scotland* (2015).

104 There have been two modern reprints of Kames' *Principles of Equity*, edited with introductions by D J Carr (2013) and M Lobban (2014). See further A Rahmatian, *Lord Kames: Legal and Social Theorist* (2015).

105 See further J Finlay, "Scots lawyers, England, and the Union of 1707", in H L MacQueen (ed), *Miscellany VII* (SS vol 62, 2015) 243; N S Poser, *Lord Mansfield: Justice in the Age of Reason* (2013).

106 See further J W Cairns, "Ethics and the science of legislation: legislators, philosophers, and courts in eighteenth-century Scotland", in Cairns (n 92) 341; also Cairns (n 3) at 176–177.

## F. THE MODERN LAW

The law of the eighteenth century is now remote from the modern practitioner, and the medieval law an arcane mystery. From the early nineteenth century onwards, however, much remains which is familiar. Hume's *Commentaries* had consolidated the criminal law, and Bell's *Commentaries* the civil. By 1830, after some decades of reform, the Court of Session had assumed its present aspect, both as regards form – an Inner and an Outer House, the former being comprised of two Divisions – and as regards procedure.[107] Nineteenth-century cases are cited regularly in the courts today. It is not, then, entirely surprising that Lord Cooper ended his historical survey about 1820. "That may seem a long time ago", he wrote in 1949, "but the purpose of history is not to chronicle events but to isolate and interpret controlling tendencies; and we are still too near the trees of the nineteenth century to see the wood. In law the last one hundred and twenty years belong to the dynamic present rather than to the historic past."[108]

Nevertheless, Cooper did point to two leading characteristics of the modern period, both of which he disliked. There would probably be general agreement as to the first, the ever increasing volume of statute law and delegated legislation, or, as Cooper put it, "the formidable and still rising torrent of acts, regulations and orders . . . the subject of many an unavailing protest from lawyers and laymen alike".[109] Since the mid nineteenth century, not least in the last 25 years, a steady stream of legislation has reformed many core areas of private law and transformed some almost out of recognition. Areas most affected include land law and the law of succession, and family law in all its aspects. So extensive indeed have been the changes that it would scarcely be possible to write now, as Cooper did, that "as in 1820 the great bulk of the law of Scotland is still common law – improved, simplified and modified in details, but in essence the same."[110] There has been much statutory reform, too, of commercial law.

Not all the changes in private law have been the consequence of legislative reform. The law of obligations – contract, delict (*anglicé* tort) and unjust enrichment – has developed largely through the slow operation of

---

107 See N Phillipson, *The Scottish Whigs and the Reform of the Court of Session 1785–1830* (SS vol 37, 1990); D R Parratt, *The Development and Use of Written Pleadings in Scots Civil Procedure* (SS vol 48, 2006).
108 Cooper (n 1) at 12.
109 Cooper (n 1) at 12.
110 Cooper (n 1) at 13.

the common law, that is, by decisions reached by the courts in particular cases on the basis of past precedent and legal principle. Recognition of the power of the High Court of Justiciary to declare conduct criminal also dates from this period.[111] Important areas of criminal law, such as homicide and theft, have remained dominated by the principles of the common law. One example is the concept of diminished responsibility, developed and refined by the Scottish common law in the nineteenth and twentieth centuries, and only introduced into English criminal law by statute in 1957.[112]

Lord Cooper was particularly disparaging about the content of much modern law, referring to "vast tracts of so-called 'law'", and to "sub-legal matters" containing no more than "a faint tincture of juristic principle".[113] He had in mind areas such as income tax, social security and local government. Here too the torrent has continued unabated since he wrote. Although the insidious growth of delegated legislation remains a cause for concern, in some respects Cooper's comments now appear rather high-minded. The distinction between public and private law no longer seems as clear as once it did; and new classifications of law which combine both public and private, such as "consumer law" and "labour law", have become widely accepted. It would be unrealistic to dismiss these as "sub-legal". One important development in public law has been the growth of the procedure of "judicial review", by which the administrative actings of public bodies have been brought under close scrutiny by the courts.

The second leading characteristic which Lord Cooper discerned in the development of the modern law was the ever-rising influence of English law, not, as he put it, "through the conscious pursuit by Scots lawyers of a desirable foreign contact", which would have been quite acceptable, even beneficial, "but unsought and indirect".[114] He complained of "the haphazard inoculation of one system with ideas taken from another".[115] There were two main channels of this English influence. The first was the process by which, in Cooper's view – and having been Lord Advocate he was in a position to

---

111 See C Kennedy, "Declaring crimes" (2017) 37 *Oxford Journal of Legal Studies* 741.
112 See further C Kennedy, "'Ungovernable feelings and passions': common sense philosophy and mental state defences in nineteenth century Scotland" (2016) 20 *Edin LR* 285. Another problematic area is dealt with in C Kennedy, "Counterfeit currency and the criminal law in commercialising Scotland", in A M Godfrey (ed), *Miscellany VIII* (2020) 285. See more generally L Farmer, *Criminal Law, Tradition and Legal Order: Crime and the Genius of Scots Law 1747 to the Present* (1997), reviewed by W D H Sellar (1998) 42 *American Journal of Legal History* 105).
113 Cooper (n 1) at 12.
114 Cooper (n 1) at 13.
115 Cooper (n 1) at 14.

know – Scottish legislation was all too often initiated. A statute might be drafted in London by English lawyers, thinking in English legal categories, and with the English legal system in mind. Only at the last minute, and with a minimum of alteration, would it be "adapted" to Scottish use. Such haphazard legislation with its roots in another legal system could not be conducive to the smooth running and orderly development of Scots law. The comments of Lord Dunedin in *Governors of George Heriot's Trust* v *Caledonian Railway Company* in 1915 on the Lands Clauses Consolidation (Scotland) Act of 1845 provide one example out of many to illustrate Cooper's complaint:

> The genesis of the 1845 Act is plain enough. It is a copy of the English Act of the same year, the copy being adapted to Scottish needs by a person with a very hazy notion of Scottish real property law. Indications of ignorance crop up all through the statute, in small things as well as great.[116]

The second channel for English influence was to be found in the decisions of the House of Lords. After the Union of 1707 the House of Lords became the supreme court of appeal from Scotland in civil matters. Yet it was not until 1876, with the passing of the Appellate Jurisdiction Act, that there was any provision for the presence there of judges trained in Scots law. Even then they were almost invariably outnumbered in any given appeal by their English-trained counterparts. The results could hardly be beneficial to Scots law as, inadvertently or otherwise, legal concepts appropriate to one system were applied to another through binding decisions at the highest level. A notorious example which illustrates this complaint of Cooper occurs in the speech of Lord Chancellor Cranworth in 1858 in *Bartonshill Coal Company* v *Reid*.[117] This case decided that the "doctrine of common employment", already accepted in English law, was also the law in Scotland. The doctrine prevented a workman, injured in the course of his employment through the negligence of a fellow employee, from suing his employer in delict, on the fiction that by taking employment in the first place he had accepted the risk that a fellow employee might be negligent. The doctrine remained part of both English and Scots law until its abolition by statute in 1947. In *Bartonshill*, Lord Cranworth reviewed the English case law and then continued,

> I consider . . . that in England the doctrine must be regarded as well settled; but if such be the law of England, on what ground can it be argued not to be the law

---

116 1915 SC (HL) 52 at 65.
117 *Bartonshill Coal Company v Reid* (1858) 3 Macq 266.

of Scotland? The law, as established in England, is founded on principles of universal application, not on any peculiarities of English jurisprudence.[118]

Undoubtedly Lord Cooper was right to point to English influence as a major factor in the development of Scots law since the early nineteenth century. Undoubtedly, too, he was right to warn of the perils of uncritical acceptance, and the dangers inherent in a legislative and judicial structure so dominated by a powerful neighbour. His criticism of the legislative procedure in particular has often found an echo since he wrote. In 1974, for example, Professor David Walker wrote of the Consumer Credit Bill (later Act) of that year: "The Bill is just another piece of the extinction of Scots law by draftsmen, officials, Ministers and a Parliament who neither know nor care about Scots law."[119] Lord Cooper, a keen Unionist, did not go on to point the moral that it is difficult to serve a legal system adequately without a distinct legislature; but others found in the quixotic position a strong argument for devolution. Scots law stood almost alone in the world as a legal system without a legislature within the jurisdiction. The danger of being shunted down a branch line was all too clear until the emergence of the devolved Scottish Parliament in 1999.

In some respects, however, it can be argued that Cooper overdrew the picture of the baneful influence of English jurisprudence. Not all English influence came "unsought and indirect".[120] Not all of it has been inimical to the regular development of Scots law. In some areas, such as defamation and trusts, English doctrines have been harmonised with Scots in the best eclectic tradition of the Scottish common law. Sometimes prior English legislation has provided a stalking horse for later Scots reform, as in the case of divorce for irretrievable breakdown. Sometimes, of course, the process has operated in reverse, notoriously so in the case of the community charge or "poll tax" in the late 1980s and early 1990s.

English lawyers, too, tend to be more sensitive now to the existence of a separate system north of the Border. The borrowing of the concept of diminished responsibility into English criminal law this century from Scots has already been noted. More recently, the Crown Prosecution Service has been established in England and Wales partly on the Scottish model. The House

---

118 *Bartonshill*, at 285. See further H L MacQueen and W D H Sellar, "History of negligence in Scots law", in E J H Schrage (ed), *Negligence: The Comparative Legal History of the Law of Torts* (2001) 273 at 300.
119 D M Walker, "Bad dreams realised: the Consumer Credit Bill", 1974 SLT (News) 6 at 8. The article is a remarkable example of sustained invective.
120 Cairns (n 3) at 161–162, 166–167.

of Lords in its judicial capacity, anomalously constituted though it may have been, has been replaced by the UK Supreme Court, which attracts little criticism from Scotland.[121] This may be partly due to the long and distinguished contribution of Lord Reid to British justice as a Scots Lord of Appeal from 1947 to 1971 and successors such as Lord Fraser of Tullybelton, Lord Clyde, Lord Hope of Craighead and Lord Rodger of Earlsferry. One might almost say that the boot was on the other foot with the 1987 appointment for the first time of a practising Scots lawyer, Lord Mackay of Clashfern, as Lord Chancellor of Great Britain. In 2020 the Scottish Justices, Lord Reed and Lord Hodge, became respectively President and Deputy President of the UK Supreme Court.

The decades since Cooper wrote and, especially, the period since the mid-1960s, have been marked by a great transformation in Scots law, greater perhaps than in any period of similar duration since the twelfth and thirteenth centuries. Much of the law with which Cooper was familiar has now been wholly superseded. There have been far reaching reforms in both public and private law. Despite this transformation, to quote for the last time from Lord Cooper, "the anchors of the common law of Scotland have not yet dragged".[122] If anything, Scots law is in better heart, and Scots lawyers more conscious of their proud and independent legal tradition than when Cooper wrote. That this is so is in no small measure due to the inspired leadership of Lord Cooper himself, and of his principal disciple, the late Sir Thomas Smith. Landmarks in the rejuvenation of Scots law and legal scholarship include the founding in 1949 of the Law Society of Scotland, the establishment in 1960 of the Scottish Universities Law Institute with a remit to publish works on Scots law, and the setting up in 1965 of the Scottish Law Commission. A Smith initiative, *The Laws of Scotland: Stair Memorial Encyclopaedia*, the first volume of which appeared in 1987, is the classic statement of the law of Scotland at the close of the twentieth century, continuing into the twenty-first. The law schools of the Scottish Universities have also played their part. The honours degree in law was introduced in the 1960s, and writing on Scots law, much of it centred on the Universities, but also – and this is a sign of vitality – coming from practitioners, is as buoyant now as at any time in its history. The European connection has drawn attention to rather than

---

121 A notable exception to this occurred following the Court's decision in *Cadder v Her Majesty's Advocate* 2011 SC (UKSC) 13. See further H L MacQueen, "Public law, private law, and national identity", in C Mac Amhlaigh, C Michelon and N Walker (eds), *After Public Law* (2013) 168 at 168–171.
122 Cooper (n 1) at 15.

detracted from the separate standing of Scots law and may be expected to survive Brexit in 2021. With its Civilian credentials secure and its Common law credentials acknowledged Scots law remains well placed to play a part, albeit a modest one, in any movement towards overall European harmonisation. The last Lord Chancellor of an independent Scotland, Lord Seafield, is reported to have said when he signed the engrossed copy of the Act of Union in 1707: "Now there is ane end of ane auld sang".[123] So far at least as the law of Scotland is concerned, his words were happily premature.

---

[123] D Szechi (ed), *"Scotland's Ruine": Lockhart of Carnwath's Memoirs of the Union (1714)* (1995) at 204.

# 2 Celtic Law and Scots Law: Survival and Integration*

The O'Donnell Lecture in Edinburgh and the corresponding lectures in Oxford, Dublin and Wales arise from the terms of the will, dated 1934, of the late Charles James O'Donnell who left bequests designed to demonstrate that the extent of Celtic survival in these islands in the face of Anglo-Saxon invasion and cultural influence was much greater than was commonly supposed. O'Donnell was born in the middle of last century. Like his better-known brother Frank Hugh, he was a prominent Irish Home Ruler. He joined the Indian civil service and in India, as in Ireland, he espoused the cause of home rule. Indeed his agitation and pamphleteering for land reform in India led in 1881 to his demotion and eventual departure from the service.[1] I have not attempted to discover what interest, if any, O'Donnell took in the contemporary land agitation in Scotland which was to lead in 1886 to the first Crofters Act, modelled partly on earlier Irish legislation; but I have a suspicion that he might have considered the mere fact that a man named Sellar was to deliver an O'Donnell Lecture to be as much a confirmation of his views on Celtic survival as anything I may actually say. However, I believe I may fairly claim that my theme today – Celtic Law and Scots Law: Survival and Integration – would have commended itself to O'Donnell.

It is a theme I speak on with considerable hesitation as I am only too well aware that the difficult and scattered nature of the surviving evidence, legal, historical and linguistic, calls for a greater combination of talents than I possess. I am also very conscious of how much I owe to other scholars, some of them my recent predecessors as O'Donnell Lecturer here, without whose work today's lecture would hardly have been possible. My debt to Professor Geoffrey Barrow in particular will be clear to all familiar with his writing.

---

\* The O'Donnell Lecture, delivered in the University of Edinburgh on 9 May 1985. Originally published as "Celtic law and Scots law: survival and integration" (1989) 29 *Scottish Studies* 1–27.
1 D E Evans, "Celts and Germans" (1982) 29 *Bulletin of the Board of Celtic Studies* 230; H V Brasted, "Irish home rule politics and India 1878–1886: Frank Hugh O'Donnell and other Irish 'Friends of India'" (University of Edinburgh PhD thesis, 1974).

Many of my comments and conclusions will, inevitably, be tentative, even speculative.

At first blush the survival of Celtic law may seem a distinctly unpromising theme. We do not need to turn to the writings of mischievous English historians – I name no names[2] – for indications that Scots law has no history, or at least no history worth the telling, and that little has survived from a remote past, least of all from the Celtic past. "Before James V instituted the Court of Session in 1532," wrote that fine lawyer and historian, Aeneas Mackay, in 1882, "there was no system of jurisprudence to which the name of Scots law could properly be applied."[3] In 1896 Professor Dove Wilson of Aberdeen noted that "The Celtic Scots were the ancestors in the male line of our kings", and that there had been in Scotland a great mixture of Celtic and Germanic blood, but then continued:

> These things make it almost inexplicable that distinct traces of Celtic law are not to be found. Yet so it is . . . Celtic law seems, indeed, to have disappeared as thoroughly as if it had never existed.[4]

More recently the Regius Professor of Law at Glasgow, David Walker, has sung much the same tune: "Very little is known of legal institutions in Scotland prior to the year AD 1000 and nothing from any earlier period can be shown to have exercised any material or permanent influence on the development of the modern law."[5] More surprisingly, Lord Cooper lent his great authority to the notion that Scots law has no history. "There is a sense," he wrote, "in which it is true to say that Scots law has no history; for the continuity of its growth has been repeatedly interrupted, and its story is a record of false starts and rejected experiments."[6] In *Celtic Law* John Cameron wrote: "It is true to state that, in the history of the law of Scotland, we have little real continuity."[7] Most depressing of all, the great Daniel Binchy once wrote, in the course of a mercilessly critical review of Cameron's book, that "henceforward the student of Celtic institutions will at least know that, apart from some unimportant technical terms, nothing is to be learned from Scottish legal sources . . .".[8]

---

2 Save those of the late Hugh Trevor-Roper (Lord Dacre) and Sir Geoffrey Elton.
3 A J G Mackay, "A sketch of the history of Scots law" (1882) 26 *Journal of Jurisprudence* 113, 225 (2 parts), at 113.
4 J Dove Wilson, "The historical development of Scots law" (1896) 8 *JR* 217 at 221.
5 D M Walker, *The Legal System of Scotland* (5th edn, 1981) at 86. But see D M Walker, *A Legal History of Scotland volume I* (1988) at 27–37.
6 Lord Cooper, *Select Scottish Cases of the Thirteenth Century* (1944) at lxi.
7 J Cameron, *Celtic Law* (1937) at 154.
8 D A Binchy, "Review of John Cameron's *Celtic Law*" (1938) 53 *English Historical Review* 684.

Now if I were not convinced that all these learned gentlemen were quite mistaken, I would not be standing here. So far from the history of Scots law being, in Lord Cooper's words, "a record of false starts and rejected experiments", I believe that the single most striking feature about the history of our legal system is its continuity, a continuity unbroken from a very remote past. The influence of Anglo-Norman law, the Canon law and the Civil law on the later development of Scots law is well known, but Celtic law too is part of the continuing inheritance. It is true, certainly, that the older the influence the more difficult it is to uncover its traces – sometimes one feels more of a legal archaeologist than a legal historian – but I am fortified in my views by an alternative line of authority which has sought to emphasise continuity with the past. This line includes, among lawyers, Sir John Skene in the sixteenth century, Lord Kames in the eighteenth, and George Neilson at the beginning of last century. In the unjustly neglected introduction to the second volume of *Acta Dominorum Concilii* Neilson wrote:

> Scotland was a land of Customary Law, its customs reflecting more or less faithfully the racial movements which had made its history . . . Anglican [sic] and Norman cords intertwined in thirteenth century law with the weakening threads of Celticism.[9]

This statement finds an exact counterpart in Professor Barrow's comment that in Scotland after 1214, "thenceforward, although feudal tenure and custom were irreversibly entrenched within the law of Scotland they would be interwoven with traditional rules and practice to form a distinctively Scottish common law."[10] Historians have probably always been more conscious of continuity than lawyers, and recent historical scholarship, coupled with that of W F Skene and Croft Dickinson in the past, should make it hardly necessary to labour the point.[11] On the legal front, too, there have been reminders of the antiquity of our system, as in the case of *M'Kendrick v Sinclair* (1972) in which a bemused House of Lords found itself having to pronounce on assythment,[12] or in the faintly ludicrous attempt in 1985 to revive trial by combat.[13]

---

9 G Neilson and H M Paton (eds), *The Acts of the Lords of Council in Civil Causes*, vol 2 (1918) at lviii.
10 G W S Barrow, *Kingship and Unity: Scotland 1000–1306* (2nd edn, 2003) at 67.
11 I have particularly in mind the work of Professors Barrow and Duncan, of Dr John Bannerman, of Jenny and Patrick Wormald, and of Professor Derick Thomson.
12 *M'Kendrick v Sinclair* 1972 SC (HL) 25.
13 *The Scotsman* 19, 23 April; *The Glasgow Herald* 27 April; *The Times* 19 April, all 1985. For a comment on this episode see H L MacQueen, "Desuetude, the cessante maxim and trial by combat in Scots law" (1986) 7 *JLH* 90.

One survival which has now been well charted is that of the judge or lawman of pre-feudal times – the *breitheamh* (early Gaelic *brithem*) or brieve, latinised *iudex*.[14] In a sense the history of this office typifies the story of the survival and integration of Celtic law. We can distinguish between a mainstream dimension in which the traces of Celtic law become ever more faint until they are barely recognisable, and a Highlands and Islands dimension in which Celtic law survives longer in a more pristine form, and perhaps even undergoes a revival in the medieval MacDonald Lordship of the Isles. As regards the mainstream we find that the *breitheamh* still retains considerable importance after the introduction of feudalism: he is mentioned in royal ordinances, he appears in the witness list of charters, he assists in perambulations. Barrow has described his continuing presence as "nothing less than the tenacious survival of an ancient judicial caste".[15] Eventually he disappears from witness lists and declines further in status, becoming in the end not *iudex* but *iudicator*, the doomster or dempster of court, responsible for pronouncing sentence of doom; yet still one of the essential "keys of the court" (*claves curiae*) without whose presence the court was not complete.[16] In the High Court of Justiciary the doomster fell further still, for his office was conjoined with that of executioner, and the unfortunate prisoner at the bar had to suffer the spectacle of his executioner entering the court to pronounce sentence of doom. Gradually the doomster disappeared from Scottish courts, although in the case of the High Court not until 1773, late enough for Sir Walter Scott to immortalise the double office of doomster and executioner in *The Heart of Midlothian*.[17] Even after the office of doomster was abolished, some trace of his function remained, for the final words spoken in the High Court after the death sentence was pronounced remained (until the abolition of capital punishment in 1965) "which is pronounced for doom", the judge of the High Court thus being, although I am sure he was unaware of it, in some sense the descendant and representative of the *breitheamh* of Celtic law.

In the Lordship of the Isles, by contrast, the *breitheamh* continued to exercise his original function until the close of the middle ages.[18] "There

---

14 W C Dickinson (ed), *The Sheriff Court Book of Fife, 1515–1522* (SHS, 1928) at lxvi; G W S Barrow, *The Kingdom of the Scots* (2nd edn, 2003) ch 2; A Taylor, *The Shape of the State in Medieval Scotland 1124–1290* (2016) at 121–123, 129–132, 222–224.
15 Barrow, *Kingdom* (n 14) at 57.
16 Balfour, *Practicks*, at 273 (ch viii); Skene, *DVS* sv Curia.
17 Sir W Scott, *The Heart of Midlothian* (first published 1818) ch 23 (above, at 22).
18 D S Thomson, "Gaelic learned orders and literati in medieval Scotland" (1968) 12 *Scottish Studies* 57, at 58–60; J W M Bannerman, "The Lordship of the Isles", in J M Brown (ed), *Scottish*

was a judge in every Isle for the discussion of all controversies," writes "Hugh Macdonald", "who had lands from Macdonald for their trouble, and likewise the eleventh part of every action decided".[19] These judges still bore the title *breitheamh*. Sometimes they witness Lordship charters and documents: *"Donaldus Judex"* in 1447, *"Donald Brehiff"* in 1456 – presumably the same man – and, most significantly, *"Donaldus M'Gillemor iudex insularum"* in 1457; also *"Hullialmus archiudex"* in 1485.[20] From these judges appeal lay to the Council of the Isles with its base at *Eilean na Comhairle* (the Council Isle) on Loch Finlaggan in Islay. These *breitheamhan* ceased to function with the end of the lordship, but some are remembered to this day in Gaelic oral tradition. Even now the Gaelic title for those who adjudicate at the annual national Mod is *breitheamh*.

The long survival of the office of *breitheamh* is not exceptional, and I shall be referring to some comparable cases later. However, the most obvious example of continuity in office – so obvious that it is often passed over in silence – is the monarchy. The Queen's title to rule in Scotland, despite the occasional displacement of a senior line, stems ultimately from her descent from Malcolm Canmore, Kenneth mac Alpin and Fergus Mor mac Erc. The kings of Scots until the time of David II were inaugurated, rather than crowned and anointed, in a ceremony of pre-Christian antiquity which has exact parallels in Ireland and the Isle of Man.[21] In his account of the

---

*Society in the Fifteenth Century* (1977) 209, at 227 (reprinted in J W M Bannerman, *Kinship, Church and Culture: Collected Essays and Studies* (2016) 297 at 315–316); J W M Bannerman, "The Scots language and the kin-based society", in D S Thomson (ed), *Gaelic and Scots in Harmony* (1990) 1 (reprinted Bannerman, *Kinship*, 379); W Matheson, "The Morisons of Ness" (1979) 50 *Transactions of the Gaelic Society of Inverness* 60.

19 J R N Macphail (ed), *Highland Papers I* (SHS, 1914) at 24–25.

20 See J and R W Munro (eds), *Acts of the Lords of the Isles 1336–1493* (SHS, 1986) at xliv, 94, 96, 188, 205, 250 and 257.

21 Among many references to the ceremony of inauguration the following may be noted: for Ireland, D A Binchy, *Celtic and Anglo-Saxon Kingship* (1970) at 11–12; K Nicholls, *Gaelic and Gaelicised Ireland* (1972) at 28–30; D Ó Corráin, *Ireland before the Normans* (1972) at 35–37; F J Byrne, *Irish Kings and High-Kings* (1973) at 15–22; K Simms, *Gaelic Ulster in the Middle Ages: History, Culture and Society* (2020), index sv 'inauguration of Irish kings, sites, ceremonies'. For Scotland, see A A M Duncan, *Scotland: The Making of the Kingdom* (1975) at 115–116, 552–556; Bannerman (n 18) at 224–225 (Bannerman, *Kinship* (n 17) at 313–314); and for the Isle of Man, B Megaw, "Norseman and native in the kingdom of the Isles" (1976) 20 *Scottish Studies* 1 at 24 (revised edition of this paper in British Archaeological Reports, British Series 54(ii), P Davey (ed) *Man and Environment in the Isle of Man* (1978) 265). I am most grateful to Mr Megaw for lending me the typescript of a lecture, "Three Royal Inauguration Rites: Scone, Tullaghoge and Tynwald Hill", delivered by him to the British Association for the Advancement of Science in 1968. A constantly recurring feature in descriptions of inaugurations in Scotland and Ireland is the mention of the white rod of kingship handed to the new ruler in token of his authority (see further ch 4 text accompanying nn 61–65). This makes the more interesting the

coronation of Alexander III in 1249 Fordun narrates that *quidam Scotus montanus* recited the royal genealogy.²² We need not doubt that this was the official historian or *seanchaidh,* without whose presence no inauguration was complete. The Lords of the Isles continued to be inaugurated in the old manner until the fifteenth century, their *seanchaidh* MacMhuirich reciting the catalogue of their ancestors. The late Sir Thomas Innes, Lord Lyon King of Arms, was wont to claim that the origins of his office antedated both heraldry and feudalism, and that he was the *seanchaidh* of the king of Scots as well as an heraldic King of Arms.²³ That he was correct in this claim is, I believe, conclusively shown by a recent study of the Scottish coronation service, in which the Scottish, English and French coronation services are compared.²⁴ In the English service a key role is played by the archbishop of Canterbury, in the French service by the archbishop of Rheims; the corresponding role in the Scottish service is played, not by a bishop or an archbishop, but by the Lyon King of Arms. One of Lyon's functions at the coronation was to recite the royal pedigree through several generations, as his predecessor had done in the time of Alexander III: "The forme of the coronatioun of the Kings of Scotland" prepared for the Scots Privy Council in 1628 refers to Lyon commanding the king to be crowned, and "repeating sax generatiouns of his descent".²⁵

It used to be fashionable, following the researches of Professor Binchy and others into the early Irish law tracts, to emphasise the archaic features of Dark Age Celtic kingship and Gaelic society. The society portrayed in the law tracts was represented as a remarkable fossil survival, little changed since a remote Indo-European past, and the king as a sacral figure, expected to fight and die in battle certainly, but devoid of real authority, his actions circumscribed by the dead weight of tradition, and lacking in legislative and judicial power. This approach emphasised the differences between Celtic society and society elsewhere in early medieval Europe. At its most extreme, as Patrick Wormald noted in his Edinburgh O'Donnell lecture in 1983, it led

---

reference to a white rod in Fordun's account of the deposition of John Balliol in 1296: "regiis exutus ornamentis et virgam albam in manu tenens" (*Chron Fordun,* vol 1 at 327). G G Simpson, "Why was John Balliol called "Toom Tabard"?" (1968) 47 *SHR* 196 overlooks the significance of this reference in a Celtic context.

22 *Chron Fordun,* vol 1 at 294.
23 Sir T Innes of Learney, "Heraldic law", in *SLSL* 379 at 381–382.
24 R J Lyall, "The medieval Scottish coronation service: some seventeenth century evidence" (1977) 28 *Innes Review* 3.
25 *RPC* 2nd series vol 2, at 393–395. On the foregoing see further ch 4 below.

to the portrayal of Dark Age Ireland as a kind of "Tolkienian 'Westernesse'".[26] More recently, however, this approach has been strongly challenged by scholars such as Professors Ó Corráin and Byrne, and by Wormald himself.[27] They place a greater emphasis on similarities between Ireland and mainstream European tradition. They have demonstrated that the Dark Age Irish king was far from powerless or devoid of legislative and judicial authority. Ó Corráin has suggested that the transformation from wider kin-group to narrow lineage, noted on the Continent by Leyser, Duby and others, can be paralleled in Ireland also.[28] He has shown how powerful overkings were able to mediatise lesser dynasties, or competing segments of their own dynasty, and convert their representatives into royal officers and leading churchmen. Such royal officers appear with increasing frequency in the Annals from the tenth century on: the royal governor or viceroy (*airrí*), the steward (*rechtaire*), the head of household (*toísech lochta tighe*), and the commander of cavalry (*toísech marcshlúaighe*).[29] Of particular interest is the judge or chief judge, the *ollamh* or *ard-ollamh breitheamhnais*.[30] It is now recognised that by the end of the first millenium the leading Irish kings not only had judicial powers, but were also able to appoint judicial officers. The European parallels for all this are obvious, and it is clear too that Irish rulers aspired to the European model. The O'Brien kings of Munster, for instance, are complimented in the *Cogadh Gaedhel re Gallaibh* by the description "Fraine na Fotla ... Meic ... Israeil na hErend" (the Franks of Ireland ... the sons of Israel of Ireland).[31] This admiration of the Franks as the chosen people recalls the oft-quoted comment on Malcolm IV and his brother William, kings of Scots: "The modern kings of Scotland count themselves as Frenchmen in race, manners, language and culture."[32] Malcolm and William, indeed, had good reason to be proud of their Frankish connections,

---

26 P Wormald, "Celtic and Anglo-Saxon kingship: some further thoughts", in P E Szarmach (ed), *Sources of Anglo-Saxon Culture* (1986) 151 at 172.
27 D Ó Corráin, "Nationality and kingship in pre-Norman Ireland" in T W Moody (ed), *Nationality and the Pursuit of National Independence* (1978) 1. I also rely here partly on Wormald (n 26), and on lectures given by Professor Byrne in Glasgow in February 1984 on "The Nature of Irish Kingship from the Seventh to the Twelfth Century", and by Professor Ó Corráin in Glasgow at The Barbarians Conference in January 1985 on "Early Historic Ireland".
28 Ó Corráin (n 27) at 33.
29 Ó Corráin (n 27) at 26–29.
30 Ó Corráin (n 27) at 14–15. Note also R R Davies, "The administration of law in medieval Wales: the role of the *ynad cwmwd (judex patrie)*", in T M Charles-Edwards, M E Owen and D B Walters (eds), *Lawyers and Laymen: Studies in the History of Law Presented to Professor Dafydd Jenkins on his seventy-fifth birthday* (1986) 258.
31 Ó Corráin (n 27) at 34.
32 A O Anderson, *Scottish Annals from English Chronicles, A.D. 500—1286* (1908) at 330n.

being inheritors through their mother's mother, Isabelle of Vermandois, of the blood of Charlemagne. On one point both Ó Corráin and Binchy are agreed: by the twelfth century Irish society was already ripe for feudalism. "The type of society that was emerging in Ireland in the eleventh and twelfth centuries", writes Ó Corráin, "was one which was moving rapidly in the direction of feudalism";[33] and Binchy has described the institution of *célsine* (clientship) found in the Irish law tracts as "a forerunner of feudal commendation".[34] Thus, although it is hardly possible to speak of "Irish feudalism" as some have written of "Anglo-Saxon feudalism", the seeds were there.

All this has considerable relevance for Scotland. It helps to explain how the institutions of Anglo-Norman feudalism spread so readily in a Scotland still governed by its native Celtic dynasty and its native Celtic earls. The Scottish inheritance was, of course, more varied than the Irish, and Professor Duncan has warned us that we must not "fill out the exiguous evidence for the dark ages . . . by a wholesale importation of Irish institutions".[35] Pictish, British, Anglo-Saxon and Scandinavian influences are all in evidence, yet there can be little doubt that the prevailing ethos of the kingdom of Alba from the time of Kenneth mac Alpin to that of Malcolm Canmore was Gaelic. There is some evidence to suggest that the earliest borrowings from Anglo-Saxon law were consolidated in this predominantly Gaelic context. The result may have been a further predisposition, greater in Scotland than in Ireland, towards feudalism. Professor Barrow has argued that the Anglo-Saxon terms *scir* (shire, Gaelic *sgìre*) and *thegn* (thane) – sometimes equated with the native Gaelic term *tòiseach* – became deeply embedded in legal administration and the Gaelic language at an early date.[36] Another Anglo-Saxon term which I would be inclined to regard as a significant early borrowing is *(ge)mót* or moot. "Moot" or "mute" is well known in Scots, of course, as are moot-hills, but *mót* was also borrowed early into Scots Gaelic as *mòd*,

---

33 Ó Corráin (n 27) at 32.
34 D A Binchy, *The Linguistic and Historical Value of the Irish Law Tracts* (Rhys Memorial Lecture 1943) reprinted in D Jenkins (ed), *Celtic Law Papers* (1973) 92. Although Professor Binchy more than once declared his intention to write more fully on *célsine*, he does not appear to have done so. See instead K Simms, *From Kings to Warlords* (1987) at 96, 101, 103, 130, 132, 141, 172; F Kelly, *A Guide to Irish Law* (1988) at 29–33.
35 Duncan, *Scotland* (n 21) at 106.
36 Barrow, *Kingdom* (n 14) ch 1. See further now A Grant, "The construction of the early Scottish state", in J R Maddicott and D M Palliser (eds), *The Medieval State: Essays Prsented to James Campbell* (2000) 47; D Broun, "Statehood and lordship in 'Scotland' before the mid-twelfth century" (2015) 66 *Innes Review* 1; Taylor, *State* (n 14) ch 1.

meaning a court or assembly.[37] In Gaelic poetry there is regular reference to the holding of a *mòd* by a chief, while today the Mod *par excellence* (at which, as we have seen, the adjudicators go by the title of *breitheamh*) is held every year. The word seems unknown in Irish Gaelic. I would argue, then, for the early borrowing of a number of key Anglo-Saxon terms. Their ready incorporation surely reflects a strengthening of royal authority. Be that as it may, Scottish society in the eleventh century, like contemporary Irish society, was moving in the direction of feudalism. We need not accept Fordun's account, as it stands, of Malcolm II (1005–34) apportioning the kingdom to his vassals from the moot-hill of Scone,[38] but we may note that even so cautious a historian as Croft Dickinson was prepared to entertain the notion of pre-Norman feudalism in Scotland,[39] while Professor Barrow, in his concluding Rhind lecture this year, used the term "proto-feudalism".[40]

So far as the history of Scots law is concerned we may accept that the introduction of Anglo-Norman feudalism gave rise to a legal Reception, a Reception in every way as significant as the later Reception of the Civil law, but a Reception which did not mark a complete break with the past. Without doubt there were new departures, but as is often the way with legal Receptions, existing institutions might be modified, re-named and adapted without doing too much violence to the native tradition. Sometimes the old institution would continue to exist under a new guise. Sometimes the old name would remain although the institution itself had changed. More often, perhaps, there would be harmonisation leading to further development on a dual foundation. We should expect to find parallel traditions and dual origins. Some sheriffdoms, as Dingwall, Auchterarder, Cromarty, Kinross and Clackmannan, may have taken the place of earlier thanedoms;[41] and many thanes became feudal barons and knights.[42] King David I had a *rannaire* or food-divider[43] and (almost certainly) a *seanchaidh*, as well as a seneschal

---

37 Scandinavian *mót* may also have been an influence, but not, I believe, to the exclusion of Anglo-Saxon *(ge)mót*.
38 *Chron Fordun*, vol 1, at 186.
39 Dickinson, *Fife* (n 14), at 376.
40 Professor Barrow's Rhind Lectures for 1985 were entitled *Patterns of Settlement in Medieval Scotland* but remain unpublished. For different views on the development of "feudalism" in Scotland, see Taylor, *State* (n 14) at 176–184; R D Oram, *David I King of Scots 1124–1153* (2020) chs 9 and 10.
41 Dickinson, *Fife* (n 14), at 378; Duncan, *Scotland* (n 21) at 161–163, 596–597.
42 Skene, *Celtic Scotland* (2nd edn, 3 vols, 1886–1890) vol 3, at 246–283; Dickinson, *Fife* (n 14), at 377; G W S Barrow, *The Anglo-Norman Era in Scottish History* (1980) at 140, 157; Taylor, *State* (n 14) at 227–228.
43 *RRS* vol 1, at 32–33.

and a chancellor. There is the tantalising record of a provincial court of Fife and Fothrif held in 1128 to settle a dispute between the Culdees of Loch Leven and that "furnace and fire of all iniquity" (*fornax et incendium totius iniquitatis*) Sir Robert "the Burgundian".⁴⁴ The account is written by a monastic chronicler whose intoxication with language resembles on one hand the *hisperica famina* of earlier Irish writing and on the other the prose of Anthony Burgess. We read of satraps and satellites and the army of Fife (*cum satrapys et satellitibus et exercitu de Fyf*) and of leaders, commanders and luminaries of the Bishop's host (*primicerios et duces et lumnarcas exercitus Episcopi*) and would dearly like to know what native words, if any, lie behind these terms.⁴⁵ But we read also of three *iudices*, clearly *breitheamhan*, one of whom, Constantine, earl of Fife, is described as *magnus iudex in Scotia*. Is this the *ard-ollamh breitheamhnais* of the king of Scots, the representative of a discarded segment of the ruling dynasty?⁴⁶ And given that Duncan, earl of Fife, later in the century, is the earliest recorded justiciar of Scotia⁴⁷ and the institutional ancestor, therefore, of today's Lord Justice General, should we not trace that office back in part to Celtic roots?

Feudalism was very adaptable. The forms of feudalism could be used to clothe and camouflage and, on occasion, legitimate older practice. The earldom of Fife itself was feudalised under its Celtic earls as early as 1136 and held thereafter in chief of the crown.⁴⁸ Ancient burdens on land such as *cáin* and *conveth*, and obligations to common army service as *fecht* and *slúagad* could readily be incorporated into feudal charters.⁴⁹ Feudal forms too could regulate the position of the learned orders of Gaelic society – doctors, historians, musicians, poets and others – who held their land in

---

44 A C Lawrie (ed), *Early Scottish Charters* (1905) at 66–67. On Sir Robert "the Burgundian" as Sir Robert de Bourgogne (possibly de Bourguignon), see G W S Barrow, "The origins of the family of Lochore" (1998) 77 *SHR* 252.
45 Barrow, *Kingdom* (n 14), at 58, 84; Duncan, *Scotland* (n 21) at 167–168; E J Cowan, "The Scottish chronicle in the Poppleton manuscript" (1981) 32 *Innes Review* 3 at 16–18, and Taylor, *State* (n 14) at 40–42, all refer to this case. There are examples of *satrapas* being used in a Scottish context for mormaor, of *satelles* in a Welsh for serjeant of the peace (*cais*), and of *dux* in an Irish for *toíseach*.
46 Although the exact origins of the earls of Fife are not certain, it seems clear from their arms, privileges and forenames that they represented a branch of the dynasty of Kenneth mac Alpin. See most recently M Hammond, "The development of *mac* surnames in the Gaelic world", in M Hammond (ed), *Personal Names and Naming Practices in Medieval Scotland* (2019) 100 especially at 126–129.
47 Barrow, *Kingdom* (n 14), at 84. Cf Taylor, *State* (n 14) at 214, 222–233.
48 Barrow, *Anglo-Norman Era* (n 42) at 84–90. Again, cf Taylor, *State* (n 14) at 47–52.
49 See below text accompanying nn 119–122; also D Broun, "Re-examining *cáin* in Scotland in the twelfth and thirteenth centuries", in S Duffy (ed), *Princes, Prelates and Poets in Medieval Ireland: Essays in Honour of Katharine Simms* (2013) 46; Taylor, *State* (n 14) ch 2.

return for professional services rendered.[50] As late as 1609 Fergus MacBeth or Beaton was confirmed for life in his hereditary office of principal physician of the Isles and granted the family lands of Ballinaby and others in Islay. The granter was no MacDonald, but James VI himself, acting for his son, Frederick Henry, Prince and Steward of Scotland and Lord of the Isles.[51] Even the position of head of a kindred could be granted in standard form: the collection now known as *Formulary E* contains a style used by the royal chancery about the time of Robert Bruce "*Ad constituendum capitaneos super leges Galwidie*", which begins, "*Sciatis quod constituimus concessimus tali ut sit capitaneus de tota parentela sua vel de parentela tali quatinus de iure et secundum leges et consuetudines Galwydie hactenus usitatas in capitaneis esse debet*".[52] As has been seen, the institution of *célsine* paved the way for feudalism. Might it not also, and with greater force, since it deals with commendation and not with tenure, be viewed as a precursor of that typically Scottish arrangement, the bond of manrent?[53]

I should like to consider now, in rapid succession, various areas of law, public and private, substantive and procedural, seeking out further examples of survival and integration. As already noted, the long survival of the office of *breitheamh* was not exceptional. Parallels can readily be drawn in the case of other offices such as those of *mormaor, maor, tòiseach*, toiseachdeor and *deòradh* (dewar). Time prevents me from lingering on these. The transition from mormaor to earl is well known. In one case at least, that of the earldom of Mar, the present holder of the dignity appears to be the representative and inheritor of a Celtic mormaor, for the countess of Mar descends, like all her predecessors in title, from Morgund, earl of Mar, immediate successor to Ruari, mormaor of Mar in king David I's reign.[54]

---

50 Thomson (n 18); Bannerman (n 18) at 232–239 (Bannerman, *Kinship* (n 18) at 320–328); Bannerman, *The Beatons* (1986).
51 *RMS* vol 7 no 109.
52 *Scottish Formularies*, no E83.
53 Or, if not *célsine*, then its later medieval successor *sláinte* in the sense of buying the protection of a great man (Nicholls, *Ireland* (n 21) at 41). On this tack Dr John Bannerman suggests to me that there may be a connection between the compact or treaty of *cairde*, literally "friendship" (D A Binchy, *Crith Gablach* (1970) at 80; J M W Bannerman, *Studies in the History of Dalriada* (1974) at 165–167 (Bannerman, *Kinship* (n 18) at 165–167)) and the later Scottish bonds of alliance. J Wormald, *Lords and Men in Scotland: Bonds of Manrent 1442–1603* (1985) does not really explore these possibilities, although she notes that "manrent raises questions about the nature of lordship and vassalage, and therefore of Scottish 'feudalism', too insistent to be ignored" (at 33). "Manrent" is itself, of course, a word of Anglo-Saxon origin. See also Skene, *Celtic Scotland* (n 42) vol 3, at 319–321.
54 *Complete Peerage*: sv Mar. The exact relationship between Morgund and his predecessor is not known. See further R D Oram, "Continuity, adaptation and integration: the earls and earldom

The title "mormaor", indeed, in the modern form of *"morair"* is still in use in Gaelic, signifying a lord: thus the countess of Sutherland is *bana-mhorair Chait*, Lord MacDonald is *morair Soléibhte* (of Sleat) and Lord Stockton is *morair Stockton*. Croft Dickinson traced the later history of the *maor* ("mair" in Scots) as an officer of the sheriffdom, often hereditary – that is "of fee".[55] This office was readily equated with that of serjeant. Again, the word is still in use in modern Gaelic, meaning a sheriff-officer or a ground officer. It also figures in one of the less comprehensible titles still borne by the hereditary keeper of Dunstaffnage, that of "marnichty" to the duke of Argyll: this, it seems, stands for the hereditary *maor(s)neachd* or mairship. The term *tòiseach*, too, long survived, both in the original sense of head of a kindred, and also, under the guise of "thane".[56] In the meaning of head of a kindred the *tòiseach clainne* has his counterpart in the *ceann cinéil* of Carrick.[57] The grant by Niall, earl of Carrick, 1250–1256, of the office of *caput progeniei* or *kenkynolle* (that is *cenn cineóil*, later *ceann cinéil*) to his first cousin, Roland of Carrick, is well known, and was the subject of royal confirmation to the Kennedies in later centuries.[58] As already noted, the royal chancery had a set style for appointing the head of a kindred in Galloway, and a number of such confirmations are known. One northern thane yet remains, the thane of Cawdor, holding his lands *in unum et integrum thanagium*, rather than simply *in liberam baroniam*, as many of his fellows came to do.[59] The Cawdor lands in the Black Isle became known as *an Tòiseachd*, the thaneage, or as Ferintosh, "land of the tòiseach",[60] and gave their name to Ferintosh whisky.

The dewar (*deòradh*) likewise, in charge of his sacred relics, is a notable survivor throughout the medieval period and down to the present day. The

of Mar, c.1150–c.1300", in S Boardman and A Ross (eds), *The Exercise of Power in Medieval Scotland c.1200–1500* (2003) 46.
55 Dickinson, *Fife* (n 14), at lxii–lxvi; see also Barrow, *Kingdom* (n 14), at 55–56.
56 Skene, *Celtic Scotland* (n 42) vol 3, at 246–283; K H Jackson, *Gaelic Notes in the Book of Deer* (1972) at 110–114; Barrow, *Kingdom* (n 14), ch 1; A Grant, "Thanes and thanages from the eleventh to the fourteenth century", in A Grant and K J Stringer (eds), *Medieval Scotland: Crown, Lordship and Community – Essays Presented to G W S Barrow* (1993) 39; D Broun, "The property records in the Book of Deer as a source for early Scottish society", in K Forsyth (ed), *Studies on the Book of Deer* (2008) 313; Taylor, *State* (n 14) at 54–69.
57 See Duncan, *Scotland* (n 21) at 108–110, and three articles by H L MacQueen: "The laws of Galloway: a preliminary survey", in R D Oram and G P Stell (eds), *Galloway: Land and Lordship* (1991) 131; "The kin of Kennedy, 'kenkynnol' and the common law", in Grant and Stringer (eds) (n 56) 274; and "The laws of Galloway revisited", in M Ansell, R Black and E J Cowan (eds), *Galloway: Gaelic's Lost Province* (forthcoming).
58 *RMS* vol 1 nos 508 and 509; vol 2 nos 379, 414. I am indebted to Professor William Gillies for the older form *cenn cineóil*. See further MacQueen, "Laws of Galloway revisited" (n 57).
59 *RMS* vol 2 no 1241. The title is now merged in that of Earl Cawdor.
60 W J Watson, *Place-Names of Ross and Cromarty* (1904, reprinted 1976) at 114.

two best-known dewars are the keeper of the *bachull mór* (the *baculus* or pastoral staff) of Saint Moluag, and the keeper of the *coigreach* of Saint Fillan. The first has regained custody of his relic in the island of Lismore, although not without some intervening adventures. The second finally relinquished his relic and all rights and duties attaching to its possession to the Society of Antiquaries of Scotland in 1877, although the title of Dewar of the Coigreach remains, and the holder recently matriculated arms with the Lord Lyon.[61] It is instructive to note that these rights and duties were established by the characteristic Scoto-Norman procedure of the inquest. On 22 April 1428, at the Bridgend of Killin, before John Spens, bailie of the crown lands of Glendochart, an inquest of fifteen found Finlay Dewart to be the keeper of the *coigreach* ("*lator ipsius reliquiae de Coygerach, qui Jore vulgariter dicitur*"). They noted *inter alia* that if any goods or cattle were stolen from an inhabitant of Glendochart who did not care to pursue the thief, he could send for the dewar of the *coigreach* along with four pennies or a pair of shoes and food for one night, and the dewar was bound to pursue the goods wherever they might be found in the kingdom of Scotland. The privileges of the dewar were confirmed by James III in 1487, this confirmation being recorded in the Books of Council and Session as late as 1734 by the then holder of the office.

Another officer whose exact function may still be in doubt but whose late survival is not is the toiseachdeor.[62] The etymology of the word remains obscure, but I take toiseachdeor to be the name of the officer and toiseachdeorachd the name of the office. In Croft Dickinson's interesting but ultimately rather despairing article about this office, he gives many instances of its occurrence both in charter and in statute. I have been able to add some further examples to Dickinson and have little doubt that others could be found. The results are shown on the map.[63] In each case the earliest date

---

61 For these dewars see *inter alia* J Stuart (ed), *Miscellany III* (Spalding Club, 1846) at xxi–xxiv; *Reports of the Royal Commission on Historical Manuscripts* (1870–), 4th Report at 514a; C Innes, *Sketches of Early Scotch History* (1861) at 390–393; A Carmichael, "The barons of Bachuill", (1909) 5 *Celtic Review* 56; N D Campbell (later Duke of Argyll), "Note: the barons of Bachuill" (1910) 6 *Celtic Review* 190; W A Gillies, *In Famed Breadalbane* (1938) at 64–73; W C Dickinson, "The toschederach" (1941) 53 *JR* 85 at 91 and 100–109; I Carmichael, *Lismore in Alba* (1948) at 63–66, 171–81; and Sir I Moncreiffe of that ilk, *The Highland Clans* (2nd edn, 1982) at 117–119, 177.

62 Skene, *Celtic Scotland* (n 42) vol 3, at 278–291, 300–302; Dickinson (n 61).

63 The additions are (a) Asswanly in Strathbogie and (b) the earldom of Carrick, both discussed in the text; (c) MacLachlan's land of Glassary (K A Steer and J W M Bannerman, *Late Medieval Monumental Sculpture in the West Highlands* (1977) at 143); (d) "the *Tosheadorach* of the lands lying west of Lochfyne", apparently including Glenorchy, the two Lochawes, Glenaray,

**Figure 2.1 The toiseachdeor.** From Peter G B McNeill and Hector L MacQueen, *An Atlas of Scottish History to 1707* (Edinburgh: The Scottish Medievalists and Department of Geography, University of Edinburgh, 1996), p 212. Reproduced with permission of the Trustees of the Scottish Medievalists: The Society for Scottish Medieval and Renaissance Studies. Patterns of equivalent names for officers in late medieval Argyll; (1) Bailie: Seneschal, Steward; (2) Toiseachdeor: Coroner; (3) Maor: Officer, Serjeant.

at which a particular toiseachdeor is mentioned is noted. The geographical spread is impressively wide. One of the additions to Dickinson's list supplies the most northerly instance – at Asswanly in Strathbogie – of a toiseachdeor. The source for this is Sir Robert Gordon's *Genealogical History of the Earldom of Sutherland*: "Sir Adam Gordon, slain at Homildoun, had tuo bastard sones, by Elizabeth Crushshanks (daughter of the laird of Assuanly, called Toshdiragh)."[64] A more significant addition is that of a toiseachdeor for the earldom of Carrick. The source here is Sir John Skene (c 1543–1617), who noted in his Latin edition of *Regiam Majestatem* in 1609 that David II *"dedit et concessit Ioanni Wallace suo Armigero, et fideli, officium Serjandiae Comitatus de Carrik, quod officium, Toschadorech dicitur, vulgo ane mair of fee"*.[65] Croft Dickinson noted a toiseachdeor in Nithsdale, but later seemed to cast doubt on this when he wrote that there were no examples of the office to be found in the Lothians and the south west.[66] The Carrick example supports that in Nithsdale, and both are nicely *en route* for the Isle of Man. In view of the absence of the toiseachdeor in Ireland, his presence in the Isle of Man (Manx, *toshiagh jiorrey*), one for each of the six sheadings of the island, raises some interesting questions, both for Man and for Scotland.[67] The Carrick example brings to three – Carrick, Mar and Lennox – the ancient earldoms with which a toiseachdeor is known to have been associated. It is worth reflecting that, despite the obscurity of the office, there are many more examples on the record of the occurrence of the toiseachdeor

---

Glenshira, Ardscotnish, Melfort and Barbreck (Skene, *Celtic Scotland* (n 41) vol 3, at 301); and (e) Knapdale for which see H Campbell, "A MacNeill inventory", in (1920) 36 *The Genealogist* 121. I am indebted to Mr R W Munro for this last reference. Dickinson's "Strathdoune" or "Strathoune" is Strathavon in Banffshire, "Davachindore" and "Fidelmonth" correspond to Auchindoir and Wheedlemont near Rhynie, while "Kerctollony" or "Artholony" appears to be Ardtalnaig on the south side of Loch Tay.

64 Sir R Gordon of Gordonstoun, *A Genealogical History of the Earldom of Sutherland* (1813, written 17th century) at 61.

65 Skene, *RM (Latin)* at 13 (gave and granted to John Wallace his faithful squire the office of sergeant of thee earldom of Carrick, which office is called Toschadorach, vulgarly a mair of fee). This grant does not appear in the *Regesta*, although a charter by David II to John Wallace is known (*RRS* vol 6 at 499 and *RMS* vol 1 no 363 and app 2, no 1650); David II petitioned for a marriage dispensation for Wallace (*RRS* vol 6 at 47). On Skene's career see J W Cairns, T D Fergus and H L MacQueen, "Legal humanism in Renaissance Scotland" (1990) 11 *JLH* 40 at 44–48 (also as "Legal humanism and the history of Scots law: John Skene and Thomas Craig", in J MacQueen (ed), *Humanism in Renaissance Scotland* (1990) 48 at 52–56); and see further two articles by A D M Forte: "'Ane horss turd'? Sir John Skene of Curriehill – a Gaelic-speaking lawyer in the courts of James VI" (2007) 23 *Scottish Gaelic Studies* 21; "'An marcach': a Gaelic sexual metaphor in the legal works of Sir John Skene of Curriehill?" (2011) 28 *Scottish Gaelic Studies* 49.

66 Dickinson (n 61) at 86, 103 and 108.

67 Megaw (n 21) at 24.

under his Gaelic title than there are of the *breitheamh*. In Scotland and the Isle of Man the office of toiseachdeor was regularly equated with that of coroner.[68] In most Scottish examples the native term changes to "coroner" soon after it first appears, and we may take it as certain that behind the "coroner" who appears on the record in some other instances there would have been originally a "toiseachdeor": we may suspect this of the hereditary coroners of Bute and of Arran;[69] and perhaps also of the foresters and coroners of the Garioch in Aberdeenshire, and of the earldom of Strathearn,[70] for the offices of forester and toiseachdeor are also sometimes combined. Noted below the map is a pattern of equivalent names for officers, including the toiseachdeor and the mair, which seems to emerge in late medieval Argyll. How old these equivalents are and how far they represent regular practice throughout Scotland I cannot say, but the subject is worth further investigation.

Turning now to the criminal law, the outstanding example of survival is, of course, the action of assythment, or compensation for wounding or slaughter, revived in the case of *M'Kendrick v Sinclair* (1972),[71] and formally abolished by the Damages (Scotland) Act 1976 as a result. The legal background to the case has been discussed by Robert Black and Christopher Gane, while the wider context of the blood-feud in early modern Scotland has been explored in a seminal article by Jenny Wormald, so little more need be said here.[72] The payment of compensation to pacify the rancour of the kin was not peculiar to Celtic society, and in *M'Kendrick's* case there is mention of Anglo-Saxon *wer* and *wite* as well as Gaelic *crò*. However, one feature which clearly betrays the Gaelic origins of the later Scottish action of assythment is the letter of slains, so essential for remission, granted by the kin of the dead man; for it has recently been shown that, so far from "slains" being a form derived from the English verb "to slay", as one might imagine, it derives from *sláinte*, a technical term of Celtic law.[73] "The basic idea of this Irish word [*sláinte*]," writes Kenneth Nicholls, "is that of 'guarantee'

---

68 Dickinson (n 61); Megaw (n 21) at 24.
69 C Innes and others (eds), *Origines Parochiales Scotiae* (2 vols in 3, Bannatyne Club, 1851–1855, henceforth *OPS*), vol 2(1), at 229, 248.
70 *RMS* vol 2 no 2755 (Garioch); *RMS* vol 2 no 1160 (Strathearn).
71 *M'Kendrick v Sinclair* 1972 SC (HL) 25.
72 R Black, "A historical survey of delictual liability in Scotland for personal injuries and death (part one)" [1975] *Comparative and International Law Journal of Southern Africa*: 46; C H W Gane, "The effect of a pardon in Scots law", 1980 *JR* 18; J Wormald, "Bloodfeud, kindred and government in early modern Scotland" (1980) 87 *Past and Present* 54. And see K M Brown, *The Blood Feud in Scotland, 1573–1625* (1986).
73 Wormald (n 72) at 62.

or 'indemnification'."[74] Indemnification from the further rancour of the kin was the precise function of a letter of slains. The term *cró* for compensation is also of considerable interest. It occurs in the *Leges inter Brettos et Scotos* and in *Regiam Majestatem* and is repeated in the form "croy" in Scots in the legislation of James I in 1432.[75] The late David Greene studied the various meanings of *cró* in Irish and Scots Gaelic and concluded:

> Strange to say, it was in Scotland that it was absorbed into the legal system, maintaining its meaning of the compensation or satisfaction made for slaughter of any man according to his rank ... It is attested [in this meaning] only from Scots; there are no examples of Sc G *cró* in this meaning.[76]

"Croy" then represents a fossil survival in Scots of Celtic law. Stranger still, the word "croo" appears like a *leitmotif* in a historical novel, *The Camerons*, published in 1973 and set in a West Fife mining community last century before the passing of the Workmen's Compensation Acts of 1880 and 1897. The author, Robert Crichton, is American but claims to draw much of his inspiration from his grandmother who came from just such a mining community. In the novel the term "croo" is used of the compensation paid at the discretion of the mine-owner for death or injury in the mines. On the face of it, this argues for the survival of the Gaelic legal term *cró* in the Scots speech of mining communities in Fife until last century, and, if authentic, is truly remarkable.[77]

More generally, one feature which sharply distinguishes the criminal law of Scotland from that of England is the late recognition in Scotland of the public right to prosecute crimes such as theft and homicide regardless. Only at the end of the sixteenth century, and not always even then, can it be said that the Crown's interest in prosecuting for homicide (or "slaughter") took precedence over the wishes of the kin of the victim.[78] Viewed from a wider European standpoint Scotland is by no means unique in this respect, yet the Celtic heritage must be seen as a major factor in the Scottish equation.

In the law of persons one notable survival which I have attempted to chart elsewhere is Celtic secular marriage, which allowed for polygamy,

---

74 Nicholls, *Ireland* (n 21) at 187; Kelly, *Irish Law* (n 34) at 321.
75 *LMS* at 428 ff (*LBS*); *RM* (*APS*) 4.30 (APS vol 1 at 637), *RM* (*Cooper*) 4.24 (at 269); *RPS* 1432/3/6.
76 D Greene, "CRÓ, CRU and similar words" (1983) 15 *Celtica* 1 at 8.
77 I have to thank Dr Athol Murray, Keeper of the Records of Scotland, for drawing my attention to R Crichton, *The Camerons* (1973). Dr Murray suggests that the novel's "Pitmungo" can be loosely equated with Fordel, "Brumbie Hall" with Fordel Castle, "St Andrews" with St David's Harbour, and "Lord Leitch" with the earl of Buckinghamshire.
78 Black (n 72); Wormald (n 72).

concubinage and easy divorce, and is described in the early Irish law tracts.[79] Nicholls has written:

> In no field of life was Ireland's apartness from the mainstream of Christian European society so marked as in that of marriage. Throughout the medieval period, and down to the end of the old order in 1603, what could be called Celtic secular marriage remained the norm in Ireland and Christian matrimony was no more than the rare exception grafted on to this system.[80]

Celtic secular marriage had a long history in Scotland as in Ireland, and did not finally disappear in the Highlands and Islands until the seventeenth century, although its traces are not so easily uncovered in mainstream development.[81] Two late practitioners of such marriage alliances, Ranald MacDonald of Benbecula and Ruairi Macneil of Barra, are still remembered in oral tradition.[82] We have noted that feudal forms were very flexible and could incorporate and express older landholding arrangements without appearing to alter their essentials. The marriage law of the medieval church, too, could camouflage Celtic survival: although Canon law prohibited divorce in the modern sense, there were so many possibilities for the dissolution of marriage on the grounds of consanguinity and affinity that it must often have been easy for practitioners of Celtic secular marriage to present their divorces as dissolutions under the Canon law, the more so as the marriage of near relatives was a commonplace.

Fosterage is an institution given considerable space in the early law tracts, and there is abundant evidence for the continuing existence of fosterage of this type until a very late period in Scotland. Many contracts of fosterage in Scots, and one (dated 1614) in Gaelic, survive.[83] Robert Bruce, it would seem, was fostered.[84] The chiefs of the Campbells continued to be fostered

---

79 See ch 3 below.
80 Nicholls, *Ireland* (n 21) at 73. A Cosgrove, "Marriage in medieval Ireland", in A Cosgrove (ed), *Marriage in Ireland* (1985) 25 suggests that "this sweeping statement needs some qualifications" (at 30). See further Simms, *Gaelic Ulster* (n 21) at 435–441.
81 See also G W S Barrow, "The lost Gaidhealtachd of medieval Scotland", in W Gillies (ed), *Gaelic and Scotland: Alba agus a 'Ghàidhlig* (1989) 67 at 72–73 (reprinted in G W S Barrow, *Scotland and Its Neighbours in the Middle Ages* (1992) 105 at 114–115). This paper was first delivered on the centenary of the chair of Celtic in Edinburgh.
82 See ch 3 text accompanying nn 87–96.
83 For the 1614 contract see Cameron, *Celtic Law* (n 7) at 220–225, 247. Mr William Matheson assures me that the surname of the foster family in this case was Campbell, rather than MacKenzie. See also Innes, *Sketches* (n 61) at 366–372; Skene, *Celtic Scotland* (n 42) vol 3, at 321–323, G Mac Niocaill, *Ireland before the Vikings* (1972) at 58–59; Nicholls, *Ireland* (n 21) at 79; and Barrow, *Anglo-Norman Era* (n 42) at 158.
84 R Nicholson, *Scotland: The Later Middle Ages* (1974) at 73.

until the seventeenth century,[85] and the chiefs of many other clans until the eighteenth. The obligations arising from the tie of fosterage are a frequent theme in Gaelic tradition, both prose and verse. The institution survived long enough to be remarked on by Boswell and Johnson on their famous tour; and I am informed by Mr William Matheson that there died only in the last few years a Mr Olaus Martin whose grandfather, a native of Skye, had been fostered in the ancient manner, and who still kept kindness with his grandfather's foster family. Given the strength of the institution, it is surprising that no trace of it was incorporated into the regular Scots law of persons, although no doubt a claim based on a contract of fosterage would have been legally recognised.

On the borders of marriage law and succession there is another example of dual inheritance in the equation of the Gaelic *tochradh* (Scots "tocher") with the *maritagium* of Feudal law. Some notion of tocher, indeed, still survives: many Scots today would recognise the phrase "a tocherless lass wi' a lang pedigree", although few, I think, could define *maritagium*. One of my favourite examples in this field is the contract of marriage entered into in 1462 between Ewen MacLachlan and Gilchrist Lamont in respect of Gilchrist's sister Marjory. In the event of Ewen refusing to marry Marjory he obliges himself and others as cautioners to pay the following in name of tocher: Celestin Lauchlan [Gillespie MacLachlan], forty cows; Donald the poet, twenty cows; Ewen M'Gillecattan, ten cows; Ewen the clerk, twenty cows; and Duncan Finlae, twenty cows.[86]

In the law of succession proper the institution of tanistry provides examples of integration and survival. Loosely defined, tanistry is the name given to the system whereby succession to office, typically the office of king or chieftain, is open to various members, or to different segments, of a ruling kindred, rather than descending by primogeniture down the one line, as under Feudal law.[87] More strictly, the term "tanist" (*tánaiste, tànaistear, tanister*) – "he who comes second, the awaited or expected one" – describes a successor-designate formally recognised in advance. Such recognition became a common although not invariable practice, and there are accounts from both Ireland and the Isle of Man of the inauguration of a tanist at the

---

85 Innes, *Sketches* (n 61) at 368.
86 Sir N Lamont of Knockdow (ed), *An Inventory of Lamont Papers (1231–1897)* (1914) no 42.
87 There is a wide literature on tanistry, of which the following may be noted: G Mac Niocaill, "The 'heir-designate' in medieval Ireland" (1968) 3 *Irish Jurist* 326; Binchy, *Kingship* (n 21) at 24–30; Nicholls, *Ireland* (n 21) at 25–29; D Ó Corráin, *Ireland before the Normans* (1972) at 37–42 and D Ó Corráin, "Irish regnal succession: a reappraisal" (1972) 2 *Studia Hibernica* 7.

same time as the king.[88] Tanistry in Ireland left its mark on the English Common law, for *Le Case de Tanistry* of 1608,[89] concerning the O'Callaghan succession, is still a leading case on custom as a source of law. In Scotland the system of tanistry operated among the descendants of Kenneth mac Alpin until the death of Malcolm II in 1034, although there is no indisputable evidence for the formal appointment of a *tánaiste*. Later, after the death of his only son Henry in 1152, David I had his eldest grandson Malcolm solemnly paraded around Scotland by the earl of Fife, the hereditary inaugurator of the king of Scots, and recognised as his heir. To some no doubt, perhaps to David himself, Malcolm would be *rex designatus* with clear echoes of the contemporary Capetian monarchy – Malcolm's father Henry had been described as *rex designatus* in a number of charters[90] – but to others among his Celtic subjects, Malcolm would be the nominated *tánaiste*.[91] In the reigns of William I and Alexander II, the Mac William claimants, descending from Duncan II, the eldest son of Malcolm Canmore, surely favoured tanistry. The Mac Williams apart, there was a dearth of males in the royal house for over two centuries, until the accession of Robert II in 1371, which rather precluded the question of tanistry from arising. The only king between 1094 and 1390 who died survived by both a brother and a son was William I, and he took good care that his younger brother David should formally recognise his son Alexander as heir to the throne.[92] There is an echo of tanistry in the arguments for the crown put forward by Bruce the Competitor in the Great Cause in 1291–1292, when he pointed to the alternating succession after Kenneth mac Alpin, and when he claimed that he had been at one stage Alexander II's nominated successor.[93] The mysterious "Appeal of the Seven Earls" which backed Bruce's claim is as likely to refer to the Celtic past as to the imperial German electors, as Barrow points out,[94] although whether it should be viewed as "an example of that semi-antiquarian revival of things

---

88 Megaw (n 21) at 24.
89 *Le Case de Tanistry* 1608 Dav 28.
90 Lawrie (ed), *Charters* (n 45) nos 124, 126, 128.
91 On this I reluctantly dissent from G W S Barrow, *David I of Scotland (1124–1153): The Balance of New and Old* (Stenton Lecture 1984, University of Reading, 1985) at 7–9 (reprinted in Barrow, *Scotland* (n 81) at 50–51). He was unwilling to see the notion of tanistry as part of the background in this instance. See also Duncan, *Scotland* (n 21) at 172–173, and A A M Duncan, *The Kingship of the Scots 842–1292* (2002) at 68–70.
92 K J Stringer, *Earl David of Huntingdon, 1152–1219* (1985) at 42–43.
93 G W S Barrow, *Robert Bruce* (4th edn, 2005) at 56; E L G Stones and G G Simpson, *Edward I and the Throne of Scotland* (2 vols, 1978) vol 1, at 175, 178, 201; vol 2, at 144–145, 170, 185.
94 Barrow, *Bruce* (n 93) at 59–61.

Celtic which was not uncommon in thirteenth century Scotland"[95] is another matter.

In Highland Scotland tanistry had a longer life. Dr John Bannerman has detected tanistry in operation among the MacNeill chieftains of Gigha in the fifteenth and sixteenth centuries, and among the Beaton physicians of Pennycross in Mull a century later.[96] The epithet "tanist" or "tanister" was in use in the Highlands from the fourteenth to the eighteenth centuries. The immediate younger brother of Donald of Isla, Lord of the Isles, John Mor, was remembered as "the Tanist" – *Eoin Mór Tánaiste*.[97] In his case I take the designation to signify, not that John was Donald's nominated successor, but that John, rather than his elder half-brothers Ranald and Godfrey, the sons of Amie MacRuari, would have succeeded to the Lordship, failing Donald and his issue. Later examples seem to equate the *tánaiste* of Celtic law with the *tutor* of Feudal and Roman law, the tutor being the nearest male agnate – again a dual inheritance.

Far from the influence of the Lordship of the Isles, the term "tanistry lands" is used to describe an *appanage* – to use a good feudal term – granted to a younger son. Buchanan of Auchmar, writing in 1723 about his own family, states:

> The Interest of *Auchmar* was for sometime Tanistrie or Appenage-Lands, being always given off to a Second Son of the Family of *Buchanan* for Patrimony, or rather Aliment during Life, and at his Death returning to the Family of *Buchanan*. These Lands were in some Time after disponed irreversibly to the Ancestor of the present Family of *Auchmar*, and his Heirs.[98]

The "irreversible disposition" took place in 1548. Far to the east, in Aberdeenshire, the same arrangement obtained and the same term was apparently in use in the family of Skene. Six small farms in Midmar belonging to the laird of Skene "formed what were called Tanistry lands" and were used in the sixteenth and seventeenth centuries "to make a provision for the younger sons of the family, who occupied them during their lives as kindlie tenants".[99] One of the possessors of these lands was James Skene, the second son of Alexander Skene of Skene, and the father of Sir John Skene

---

95 Barrow, *Bruce* (n 93) at 60.
96 Steer and Bannerman, *Sculpture* (n 63) at 148; Bannerman, *Beatons* (n 50) at 25–40.
97 "The Book of Clanranald", in A Cameron (ed A Macbain and J Kennedy), *Reliquiae Celticae* (2 vols, 1894) at 158, 212.
98 W Buchanan of Auchmar, *Ancient Scottish Surnames* (1732, reprinted 1820) at 42.
99 W F Skene (ed), *Memorials of the Family of Skene of Skene* (Spalding Club, 1887) at 23, 24, 37, 49, 90.

of Curriehill, Lord Clerk Register and legal historian. A similar custom is referred to by John MacPherson writing in 1768:

> In the Highlands and Western Isles the Tierna's [*Tighearna* or chief] next brother claimed a third (Trian Tiernis) part of the estate during life, by virtue of a right founded on an immemorial custom. It is not above two hundred years back since the Tanistry regulation, and the disputes consequent upon it, prevailed in the Highlands. There have been some instances of it much later.[100]

Tanistry, then, was a long-lasting legal concept, capable of being harmonised with others from a quite different background, such as *rex designatus*, tutor, *appanage* and even "kindlie tenants".

There are other aspects of succession which would repay investigation, such as destinations-over in favour of members of a particular patrilineal kindred, as *heredibus suis et suis assignatis cognomen de Cambel* in 1358,[101] or to "Donald MacGilliephadrick, his airs-mail and assignees, of the clan of Clan Chattan allenarly [only]" in 1632;[102] or the use of the regular forms of feudal conveyancing to legitimise the succession of an heir male rather than a female heir general, as in the case of Mary MacLeod of Dunvegan in the sixteenth century;[103] but I should like to move on now to consider courts and their procedure. An outstanding feature of the Scottish legal landscape until the middle of the eighteenth century were the all-pervasive franchise courts – courts of barony and courts of regality – whose jurisdiction covered as large an area of the kingdom as the regular royal courts themselves. One of the most jealously guarded privileges of these courts was the right to repledge to their own jurisdiction inhabitants of the barony or regality accused before other courts, including the sheriff court and the justice court.[104] When repledging took place a cautioner had to be found to ensure that justice would be done. The word used for such a cautioner – and this remained true until the end of repledging itself – was "culrath" or "culrach". The term occurs in both *Regiam Majestatem* and *Quoniam Attachiamenta*, and also ("culrehath") in the *Fragmenta Collecta*.[105] Sir John Skene states

---

100 J Macpherson, *Critical Dissertations on the Origin, Antiquities etc. of the Ancient Caledonians* (1768) at 184. I am grateful to Dr John Bannerman for bringing this passage by MacPherson to my attention.
101 *RRS* vol 6 no 166.
102 *MacGillivray v Souter* (1862) 24 D 759.
103 I F Grant, *The MacLeods: The History of a Clan* (2nd edn, 1981) at 117–126, 273.
104 Dickinson, *Fife* (n 14), at 344.
105 *RM (APS)* 4.23 (*APS* vol 1 at 636; see also *RM (Cooper)* at 289–290); *QA* at 130–131; *APS* vol 1 at 735 (*Fragmenta Collecta*). To judge from the Table of Authorities in *APS* vol 1 at 258–259, this last text appears to have been part of the *Leges Portuum* whence it moved to the *Liber de*

in his *De Verborum Significatione* that "Culrach sumtimes is called a furth comandborgh, bot mair properly it may be called an backborgh, or cationer . . .".[106] There are many examples of the term to be found in court records. Thus in 1518/9 Thomas Forrester "baillie & commissar to the lard of balgony" appeared in the Fife sheriff court to repledge an action there to the laird's baron court: "And the said Thomas Forestar pleige & culrach to the schiref to do Justice in the said actione . . .".[107] In 1539, the abbot of Coupar Angus granted the office of bailliary to James, Lord Ogilvie, with power to repledge *"et Reducendo Cautionem et colerache pro Justicia"*.[108] In 1564 the powers of the bishop of Caithness included *"cautionem lie colerath pro administratione iustitie diebus et locis oportunis prout moris est auferendi et reddendi"*.[109] A late example occurs in 1700, when in a process against "Egiptianis" at Banff there was an unsuccessful attempt to repledge some of the accused to the regality of Grant and to lodge caution of "culriach".[110] One of the accused was James MacPherson (although repledging was not attempted in his case), and the end of that story is well known:

> The reprieve was coming frae the brig o' Banff
> Tae set MacPherson free
> But they pit the clock a quarter afore
> And they hanged him frae the tree.

Although different spellings of the word are legion, there can be no doubt that culrath represents a technical term of Celtic law (*cúlráith*) being composed of the elements *cúl* meaning "back", and *ráth* a "pledge" or "surety", the etymology of the term providing a good explanation of its function in law. *Rath* is a key term in early Irish law and occurs in many situations.[111] It is found in Scotland in at least one other compound word: *fulráith*, used as an equivalent for bloodwite, the element *fuil* meaning "blood": *"bludwytys que Scotice dicitur fuilrath"*.[112] Here, as with "slains" and "croy" in assythment, we find a technical term of Celtic law deeply embedded in a cardinal process

---

*Judicibus*. The text thus does not appear in *LMS*, although see at 55 editorial comments on W J Windram, "What is the *Liber de Judicibus*?" (1984) 5 *JLH* 176.
106 Skene, *DVS*, sv Culrath; and see the articles by Forte cited n 65 above.
107 Dickinson, *Fife* (n 14), at 131.
108 D E Easson (ed), *Charters of the Abbey of Coupar Angus* (2 vols, SHS, 1947) vol 2, at 152 (and reducing caution and culrath for justice).
109 *OPS* (n 69) vol 2(2), at 614n (offering and rendering caution, i.e. culrath, for the administration of justice at the right days and places as is the custom).
110 J Stuart (ed), *Miscellany III* (n 61) at 175–191.
111 Binchy, *Crith Gablach* (n 53) at 102–104; D A Binchy, "Celtic suretyship. a fossilized Indo-European institution?" (1972) 7 *Irish Jurist* 355.
112 J Dennistoun (ed), *Cartularium Comitatus de Levenax* (Maitland Club, 1833) at 45.

of later Scots law. In his short discussion of repledging Croft Dickinson noted that "this extensive right has been traced by Lord Kames back to the time when each tribe or clan claimed to be under the jurisdiction only of its own judges . . . It is more likely, however," he continues, "that it was the outcome of pure feudalism under which justice was bound up with the holding of land".[113] With all respect to Croft Dickinson, I would suggest that Lord Kames was at least half right, and that here again we have a dual inheritance. Another pointer towards the Celtic past is the fact that repledging could on occasion apply to an entire kindred, membership of which was the essential prerequisite. Thus, *"homines de progenie et consanguinitate makcaroun vulgariter nuncupatur Kynmaccaroun"* could be repledged to the regality of the Dunfermline abbey, this privilege being restored by James II in 1459.[114] The "Law of Clan MacDuff", itself an interesting survival, provides a better-known example: this Law granted the privilege of repledging in cases of homicide to those within the ninth degree of kin to the earls of Fife.[115] The privilege was claimed as late as 1458 in the case of *Kininmonth v Spens*, mentioned by both Balfour and Skene.[116]

If there was continuity in procedure, it seems likely that there must have been some continuity in the court structure as well, both franchise and royal. The case of Sir Robert the Burgundian in 1128, already mentioned, in the court of Fife and Fothrif, gives some clues as to the functioning of pre-feudal courts. On this topic Professor Barrow has suggested that behind place-names such as "cuthill", "cuthal" and the like there lies a *comhdháil* or pre-feudal Celtic assembly, a record of which survives in a Mearns charter of around 1317 and an agreement of 1329 under the name of "couthal" or "conthal".[117] Another tack which might be followed here is the investigation of the various saints' fairs which were such a feature of community life in

---

113 Dickinson, *Fife* (n 14), at 34.
114 C Innes (ed), *Registrum de Dunfermelyn* (Bannatyne Club, 1842) at 351–352 (the men of the kindred of Maccaroun vulgarly known as Kynmaccaroun); J M Webster and A A M Duncan (eds), *Regality of Dunfermline Court Book, 1531–1538* (1953) at 11–12.
115 Skene, *DVS*, sv Clan-Makduf.
116 Balfour, *Practicks*, at 511; Skene (n 115). The date "1548" is given by Balfour; but see M Wasser, "Celtic law and printing errors: dating the application of the Law of Clan MacDuff in Balfour's *Practicks*" (1996, unpublished), where it is pointed out that the parties to the case were most probably alive in 1458 rather than 1548. See also A D M Forte, "'A strange archaic provision of mercy': the procedural rules for the *duellum* under the law of *Clann Duib*" (2010) 14 *Edin LR* 418.
117 G W S Barrow, "Popular courts in early medieval Scotland: some suggested place-name evidence" (1981) 21 *Scottish Studies* 1; G W S Barrow, "Popular courts . . . additional note" (1983) 27 *Scottish Studies* 67 (reprinted together in Barrow, *Scotland* (n 81) ch 11).

all parts of Scotland until recently. No doubt some of these fairs have their origin in feudal grants of trading privileges, but others seem older. Most of the saints' names are Celtic, some of them very obscure; and I am reminded that the day of the Tynwald court in the Isle of Man was known in Gaelic as "Latha Féill Eoin" (the day of Saint John's Fair) and in English still as "the Fair Day".[118]

Moving now to land law, we have already met the litany "*cáin* and *conveth, fecht* and *slúagad*" incorporated into many feudal charters. The long survival of the render of *cáin* as "cane fowl", "reek hen" and the like, and of conveth is well known. A nice late example is recorded by Sir William Fraser. He was informed, near Luss, in August 1862, by a man of 88 that Lady Helen, the wife of Sir James Colquhoun, had kept a ring to gauge eggs rendered as "kain fowl" by the tenants: any eggs small enough to pass through were rejected.[119] The survival of *fecht* and *slúagad* – the obligation to expedition and hosting – is less well known, despite the researches of Professors Barrow and Duncan. This pre-feudal obligation to army service was readily incorporated into feudal charters, usually under the name of *servitium Scoticanum* or common army service.[120] Occasionally it appears with the Gaelic terms unaltered, as in the charter granted in 1240 by Ewen MacDougall, lord of Argyll, to the bishop of Argyll of land in Lismore, free of all dues, including "*cáin, conveth, feact, slagad* and *ich*".[121] In the twelfth and early thirteenth centuries the formula *exercitus et expeditio* is found.[122] About 1295 a grant of land in Cowal speaks of the provision of two men *in congregationibus Ergadie* – presumably the *slúagad* or hosting – for the two

---

118 Megaw (n 21) at 24.
119 G Donaldson, *Sir William Fraser* (1985) at 26.
120 J R N Macphail (ed), *Highland Papers II* (SHS, 1916) at 227–245; Barrow, *Kingdom* (n 14), at 161–166; Barrow, *Anglo-Norman Era* (n 42) at 161–162; Duncan, *Scotland* (n 21) at 378–383. Taylor, *State* (n 14) at 184–185 suggests that all survived into charter form because each related to resource extraction, unlike *cro, kelchin, enach* and others, which "regulated the relations between people" and are found only in legal tractates and legislation.
121 See e.g. *RRS* vol 2 no 228; C Innes (ed), *Liber Sancte Thome de Aberbrothoc* (Bannatyne Club, 1848–1856) no 50; A A M Duncan and A L Brown, "Argyll and the Isles in the earlier middle ages" (1956–7) 90 *Proceedings of the Society of Antiquarians of Scotland* 192 at 219. Professor William Gillies suggests to me that *ich* must represent Old Irish *ic(c)* "payment, requital, atonement". Dr Alexis Easson has directed me to a Great Seal confirmation in 1581 of a charter granted the previous year by Neil Campbell, rector of Craignish, to James Campbell of lands in Craignish and Ardscotnish, which contains the following: "cum clausula warrantizationis a solutione de [with clauses of warrandice for the payment of] lie kane, conveiff, garraze, eicht [the same as *ich*?], sornyng . . . et ab omni lie oisting, watching, fecht, flwarize et downaze" (*RMS* vol 5 no 131).
122 Innes (ed), *Liber S. Thome de Aberbrothoc* (n 121) no 50.

pennylands conveyed.[123] Professor Barrow has demonstrated how the older "Scottish service" or "common army service" continued to co-exist after the advent of feudalism beside new-style feudal military service. In a notable passage in his *Anglo-Norman Era* he has suggested how this undoubted survival in Scotland may throw light on one of the more vexed controversies of English medieval history, the question of the survival of the Anglo-Saxon *fyrd* after 1066.[124] The obligation to render common army service long outlasted the Scoto-Norman era. It raised men for Flodden as it had raised them for Bannockburn, and was an important factor, so Sandy Grant has argued, in Scotland's successful struggle against English dominion.[125]

Both the obligation to render common army service and the consequences of trying to escape it are recorded over very many centuries. In 1221 an ordinance of Alexander II dealt with the penalties to be imposed on those absent from the host, particularly in Fife.[126] Nearly 500 years later *Fountainhall's Decisions* carries the report of a prosecution, in 1680, of 35 Fife gentlemen for absence from the king's host.[127] There were Defence of the Realm Acts in 1318, 1456, and 1481.[128] The Act of 1456 ordained that "all maner of man" between the ages of sixteen and sixty "that has landis and gudis be ready horsit and geryt efter the faculty of his landis and gudis for the defence of the Realm". An Act of 1484 laid down that rolls be kept of all "defensible personis" for the defence of the realm and the resisting of the king's enemies;[129] this seems to be the origin of the term "the fencible men". In 1596 the army was called out to the Highlands and Islands, including all freeholders between 16 and 60.[130] In 1685 the estates of Parliament declared the whole nation between 16 and 60 to be in readiness for the king's service, according to their abilities.[131] In 1689 the Estates enacted that heritors and fencible men absent from the host should be prosecuted.[132] In 1704 the Act for the Security of the Kingdom again refers to the obligations

---

123 Lamont (ed), *Inventory* (n 86) no 10.
124 Barrow, *Anglo-Norman Era* (n 42) at 161–168.
125 A Grant, *Independence and Nationhood: Scotland 1306–1469* (1984) at 33–34, 154–156.
126 *LMS* at 608–609. Note that the text is also found as ch 23 in the *Capitula Assisarum et Statutorum Domini David Regis Scocie* (*LMS* at 506–509). See further the editor's introduction at 295, 349–350, and Taylor, *State* (n 14) at 103–111.
127 Sir J Lauder of Fountainhall, *Decisions of the Lords of Council and Session, 1678–1712* (2 vols, 1759–1761), vol 1, at 87–90.
128 *RPS* 1318/29, 1456/4, 1481/4/4–9.
129 *RPS* 1484/2/30.
130 *RPS* A1596/5/3.
131 *RPS* 1685/4/16.
132 *RPS* 1689/6/41.

of the heritors and fencible men.¹³³ It is curious to reflect that the Acts of 1456, 1481, 1484 and 1689 were only finally repealed *ob maiorem cautelam* in 1906 just ten years before the re-introduction of conscription.¹³⁴

Just as we can follow the obligations of *fecht* and *slúagad* forward from Scoto-Norman times, so too can we trace them back to the limit of the historical horizon. John Bannerman has drawn attention to their presence in the *Senchus Fer nAlban* compiled in Dalriada about AD 700;¹³⁵ and was it not precisely *fecht* and *slúagad* that was at issue at the Convention of Druim Cett in Ireland in AD 575 when Saint Columba mediated between Aidan, king of Dalriada, and the Ui Neill overking? The decision of the meeting is recorded in the Preface to the *Amra Choluim Chille* as follows:

> And this is the judgement which he gave; their expedition and their hosting [*a fecht ocus a sloged*] to the men of Ireland always, for the hosting belongs to the territories always, their tax and their tribute [*a cáin ocus a cobach*] belong to the men of Scotland. Or their fleet alone belongs to the men of Scotland; all else however belongs to the men of Ireland.¹³⁶

The obligation to hosting and expedition was not, of course, unique to Celtic society, nor was *fecht* and *slúagad* the only element behind later Scottish army service, but when the history of the army in Scotland comes to be written it will surely take note of this astounding example of continuity and survival from the sixth century to early modern times. It may also point a connection between the naval obligations recorded in the *Senchus*¹³⁷ and the galley service of so many later West Highland charters.

Another field where there may be continuity, although this is more speculative, lies in the higher reaches of constitutional law. Two leading twentieth-century cases, *MacCormick v Lord Advocate* (1953) and *Glasgow Corporation v Central Land Board* (1956), recognised that there may still be differences between Scots and English constitutional law.¹³⁸ That there were once very considerable differences in the matter of the royal prerogative has been pointed out by a number of commentators.¹³⁹ There were, for

---

133 *RPS* 1704/7/68.
134 Statute Law Revision (Scotland) Act 1906.
135 Bannerman, *Studies* (n 53) at 146–148 (Bannerman, *Kinship* (n 18) at 146–148).
136 Bannerman, *Studies* (n 53) at 155, 157–170 (Bannerman, *Kinship* (n 18) at 155, 157–170). There are also accounts of the Convention of Druim Cett in F J Byrne, *Irish Kings and High-Kings* (1973) at 110–111, and M O Anderson, *Kings and Kingship in Early Scotland* (2nd edn, 1980), at 146–148.
137 Bannerman, *Studies* (n 53) at 148–154 (Bannerman, *Kinship* (n 18) at 148–154).
138 *MacCormick v Lord Advocate* 1953 SC 396; *Glasgow Corporation v Central Land Board* 1956 SC (HL) 1.
139 See J R Philip, "The Crown as litigant in Scotland" (1928) 40 *JR* 238; W I R Fraser, *An Outline*

example, different rules on the position of the Crown as litigant and on crown exemption from statute and tax. The English rules consistently favour the Crown. The Scottish rules are more in keeping with the maxim *rex utitur iure communi*.[140] In the interpretation of statute the Crown was particularly favoured in England, and this from an early time: *ea interpretacio sequenda sit que pro rege fecit*.[141] The precise reason for these differences has never been convincingly explained, but it is tempting to associate the less favourable position of the Crown in Scotland with the Scottish libertarian tradition discerned and described by Ronald Cant:[142] that tendency towards libertarianism and against despotism which has surfaced at regular intervals in Scottish history – in the Declaration of Arbroath, in Barbour's *Bruce*, in John Major's *History*, in George Buchanan's *History* and *De Jure Regni*, in the Scottish constitution of 1640, and in the stark declaration in the Claim of Right of 1689 that James VII had forfeited his throne, contrasting with the more polite English fiction that he had merely abdicated:

> Therefor the Estates of the kingdom of Scotland Find and Declare That King James the Seventh ... hath ... Invaded the fundamentall Constitution of the Kingdome and altered it from a legall limited monarchy To ane arbitrary despotick power and hath Exercised the same to the subversione of the protestant religion and the violation of the lawes and liberties of the Kingdome inverting all the Ends of Government whereby he hath forfaulted the right to the Croune and the throne is become vacant.[143]

---

*of Constitutional Law* (2nd edn, 1948) at 146–176; J D B Mitchell, "The royal prerogative in modern Scots law" [1957] *Public Law* 304; and J T Cameron, "Crown exemption from statute and tax in Scotland" (1962) 7 *JR* 191.

140 Thus Baron Sir John Clerk of Penicuik and Mr Baron Scrope, writing in 1726 on the powers of the post-Union Court of Exchequer, note that, as the law concerning private rights in Scotland had to be followed, the lands of Crown debtors in Scotland "cannot be subjected to extents, inquisitions and seizures but must be effected in the same manner as the real estates of debitors are by the laws of Scotland, that is by adjudications, inhibitions, decreets of sale and other diligences; because by the laws of Scotland, *rex utitur jure communi*, and because by the articles of Union the laws of Scotland in relation to private rights are continued" (Sir J Clerk of Penicuik and J Scrope, *Historical View of the Forms and Power of the Court of Exchequer in Scotland* (published 1820) at 138). I owe this reference to A J MacLean, "The 1707 Union: Scots law and the House of Lords" (1973) 4 *JLH* 50 at 56 (also printed in A Kiralfy and H L MacQueen (eds), *New Perspectives in Scottish Legal History* (1984)).

141 E W Ives, *The Common Lawyers of Pre-Reformation England* (1983) at 193.

142 R G Cant, "Kingship in the medieval Scottish realm", and "Scottish libertarianism in theory and practice" (1976) 3 *Proceedings of the Conference on Scottish Studies* 11 and 20; R G Cant, *The Identity of Scotland: An Historical Survey* (St Andrews Day Lecture, University of St Andrews, 1982); and see G W S Barrow, "The idea of freedom in late medieval Scotland" (1979) 30 *Innes Review* 16.

143 *RPS* 1689/3/108.

It is true that behind the Declaration of Arbroath lies the writing of John of Salisbury,[144] and behind Major and Buchanan the Council of Constance,[145] but is it not also legitimate to speculate, as Cant does, that there may also have been an indigenous native inheritance? The very conservatism of Scottish society, indeed, may have helped to preserve an older, less despotic order of things. In his *De Jure Regni*, as also in his *History of Scotland*, George Buchanan claimed that among the ancient Scots the monarchy had been elective within the ruling kindred, and that unsuitable rulers had been deposed or worse.[146] There is some evidence to support this view in the vestigial evidence surviving for early Scottish kingship; rather more in the arrangements of Gaelic society in Ireland. Buchanan also asserted that this position still obtained among the Highland clans in his own day[147] and this appears to have been true, the succession to the chiefship of the MacDonalds of Keppoch and of Clan Ranald being cases in point.[148] It is certainly interesting, and perhaps significant, that Buchanan, himself a Gaelic speaker from the Lennox, drew upon the Celtic past and present. Buchanan, in turn, supplied a justification for the events of 1689.

I should like to conclude on a more personal note by mentioning some further survivals that have come my own way. When I was an apprentice some time ago in a large Edinburgh office I saw the annual account for an estate in Kinross-shire. Many of the incomings were feu duties, and beside the column in which these were entered, a few pounds at a time, there was another column in which sums of one penny, two pennies, three old pennies, were still being religiously entered up every year – they may be still. This column was headed "cane" (I cannot now vouch for the exact spelling) but when I asked, no one could tell me what "cane" was, or what it was doing there: a remarkable example of legal conservatism.[149] Moving from

---

144 See G G Simpson, "The Declaration of Arbroath revitalised" (1977) 56 *SHR* 11.
145 See F Oakley, "On the road from Constance to 1688: the political thought of John Major and George Buchanan" (1962) 1 *Journal of British Studies* 1.
146 See R A Mason and M S Smith (eds), *George Buchanan's Law of Kingship* (2006) at 98–109. See further *inter alios* H R Trevor-Roper, "George Buchanan and the ancient Scottish constitution" (1966) *English Historical Review* supplement 3; R A Mason, "*Rex stoicus*: George Buchanan, James VI and the Scottish polity", in J Dwyer, R A Mason and A Murdoch (eds), *New Perspectives in the Politics and Culture of Early Modern Scotland* (1982) 9.
147 See Bannerman (n 18) at 221, 226 (Bannerman, *Kinship* (n 18) at 309, 314).
148 D Gregory, *History of the Western Highlands and Isles*. Edinburgh (1836, reprinted 1881, 1975) at 108–109, 157–158.
149 Sad to relate, payments in respect of cane, although still within office memory in 1985, had ceased to be entered up. I am grateful to Mr Ivor Guild of Shepherd and Wedderburn, WS, for this information.

the written to the oral, I have heard traditions of *breitheamhan* in Lewis, Skye and Islay. The traditions of the Morrison brieves of Lewis are mostly now in print,[150] but those about Tadhg MacQueen, the Skye brieve, are not, and I hope they may be collected.[151] In Barra I was given the *sloinneadh* or pedigree of a lady whose maiden name was MacNeil.[152] This included an eighteenth-century ancestor whom she named as *Eachann Óg an Tànaistear* (young Hector the tanister), although she was unable to explain this designation. On checking my books I found that this ancestor corresponded with Hector Og MacNeil of Ersary – the designation "tanister" was not mentioned – who took charge of the estate of Barra in 1776 in the absence of his chief.[153] I also checked the oral pedigree with a lady then in her nineties who confirmed that she had heard of this ancestor.[154] "That is a strange nickname," I said innocently. "What does it mean?" "That is not a nickname," I was reproached, "it is a title." This seems, in fact, to be the latest known example in Scotland or in Ireland of the use of the title of tanist.

Nor is the scope of oral tradition confined to the West Highlands and Islands. Croft Dickinson noted that a record of the offices of serjeant and mair is preserved in placenames such as "mairsland", "mairstoun", "le Serjand aker" and "le serjand croft".[155] In the fifteenth century a family named Comrie are recorded as mairs to the earls of Strathearn and were granted a croft referred to as "le Mariscroft", later as "the Serjeant's croft", to the west of the castleton of Fowlis, as part of the perquisites of office.[156] The mairship passed to another family, but the Comries remained, and, remarkably, remain to this day, as tenants in the neighbourhood of Fowlis Wester. I was informed recently by Miss Jean Comrie, who was brought up on the farm of Drummy, by Fowlis Wester, that a field on that farm still goes by the name of "the sergeant". Such continuity in central Perthshire was quite unlooked for.[157]

I fear I have tried your patience with this catalogue. Long though it has been, it could readily have been extended. I have said nothing, for example, about the church, or rights of sanctuary, or land measurement, about calp

---

150 See in particular Matheson (n 18).
151 I have heard traditions of Tadhg MacQueen and his descendants from Dr Sorley Maclean, Mr William Matheson and Dr John MacInnes.
152 The late Mrs Marion Somerville (née MacNeil).
153 R L Macneil of Barra, *The Clan MacNeil* (1923) at 93.
154 The late Miss Rachael MacLeod, formerly schoolteacher in Barra, who lived to see her century.
155 Dickinson (n 61) at 96n.
156 *RMS* vol 2 nos 1248 and 2296; A Porteous, *History of Crieff* (1912) at 46–48.
157 I am indebted to Miss Comrie for her assistance.

or colpindach. I have left unexplored the possibility that behind the very frequent resort to arbitration in Scottish legal history, or the device of the wadset, there may lie elements of procedures under Celtic law. I have not even mentioned the famous Gaelic charter of 1408 or the recently discovered Gaelic lease of around 1600.[158] I have concentrated almost entirely on the Gael north of Forth and Clyde, to the exclusion of Picts and Britons, and the Gael of the south west. I hope, however, that I have said enough to demonstrate that the story of Celtic law in Scotland did not come to an abrupt end with the advent of feudalism. On the contrary, many institutions of Celtic law survived for centuries, to an extent perhaps not previously realised, and traces are to be found to the present day. Such survivals are to be seen not as isolated curiosities, of antiquarian interest only, but as part of the very fabric of a legal system one of the outstanding features of which has been continuity with the past.

---

158 R Black, "A Gaelic contract of lease", in W D H Sellar (ed), *Miscellany II* (SS vol 35, 1984) 132.

# 3 Marriage, Divorce and Concubinage in Gaelic Scotland*

According to *A Description of the Western Isles of Scotland,* written about 1695, by Martin Martin,

> It was an ancient custom in the islands that a man should take a maid to his wife, and keep her the space of a year without marrying her; and if she pleased him all the while, he married her at the end of the year, and legitimised these children; but if he did not love her, he returned her to her parents, and her portion (i.e. her tocher) also; and if there happened to be any children, they were kept by the father: but this unreasonable custom was long ago brought into disuse.[1]

Many later writers on the history and customs of the Highlands and Islands before the breakdown of the old Gaelic social order in the sixteenth and seventeenth centuries have commented on what they take to have been peculiar customs of marriage and concubinage. Prominent among them are these two great pioneers of the history of Celtic Scotland, Donald Gregory and W F Skene.

Gregory was puzzled by the status of two half-brothers of John, Lord of the Isles (d 1503), Celestine (or Gillespic) MacDonald of Lochalsh, and Hugh (or Uisdean) MacDonald of Sleat. He notes the application of the terms *frater naturalis* and *frater carnalis* to them in contemporary documents; yet he writes:

> The history of Celestine and Hugh and their descendants sufficiently shows that they were considered legitimate, and that, consequently, the words *"naturalis"* and *"carnalis"*, taken by themselves, and without the adjunct *"bastardus"*, do not necessarily imply bastardy. It is probable that they were used to designate the issue of those handfast or left-handed marriages, which appear to have been so common in the Highlands and Isles. Both *naturalis* and *carnalis* are occasionally applied to individuals known to be legitimate in the strictest sense of the word.[2]

---

* Address given to the Gaelic Society of Inverness, 1 December 1978. Originally published as "Marriage, Divorce and Concubinage in Gaelic Scotland" (1981) 51 *Transactions of the Gaelic Society of Inverness* 464–493.
1 Martin Martin, *Description of the Western Isles of Scotland*, ed D J MacLeod (1934) at 175.
2 D Gregory, *History of the Western Highlands and Isles* (1836) at 41 n l.; for the use of *"naturalis"* and *"carnalis"* see J C Barry (ed), *William Hay's Lectures on Marriage* (SS vol 24, 1967) at 234–235.

Later, commenting on the so-called "Statutes of Iona", imposed in 1609 as part of the Crown's drive to tame the West Highland chiefs, Gregory says of Article One, which set out that "mariageis contractit for certane yeiris" should be "simpliciter dischairgit and the committaris thairof haldin, repute and punist as fornicatouris", that this is "a proof that the ancient practice of handfasting still prevailed to a certain extent."[3]

Skene, like Gregory, was puzzled by the high incidence of apparently irregular succession in the Highlands, and also suggested that the answer might lie in the

> probable supposition that the Highland law of marriage was originally very different from the feudal, and that a person who was feudally a bastard might in their view be considered legitimate, and therefore entitled to be supported in accordance with their strict ideas of hereditary right and their habitual tenacity of whatever belonged to their ancient usages.[4]

In elaborating on this Skene, like Gregory, made use of the term "handfasting". In a passage which is reminiscent of Martin, he speaks of

> a singular custom regarding marriage retained to a very late period among the Highlanders, which would seem to infer that their original law of marriage was different from that of the feudal. This custom was termed handfasting, and consisted in a species of contract between two chiefs, by which it was agreed that the heir of the one should live with the daughter of the other as her husband for twelve months and a day. If in that time the lady became a mother, or proved to be with child, the marriage became good in law, . . . but should there not have occurred any appearance of issue, the contract was considered at an end, and each party was at liberty to marry or handfast with any other.[5]

The case for the existence of an ancient custom of trial marriage or handfasting for a year and a day was reviewed in 1958 by A E Anton.[6] Anton pointed out that the notion that such a custom once existed in Scotland – in the Borders, where it was claimed by no less than Sir Walter Scott, as well as in the Highlands – has had a wide currency, and appears not only in works on Highland history and law, but also in such seminal studies on anthropology and jurisprudence as Westermarck's *History of Human Marriage,* Jolowicz's *Historical Introduction to Roman Law,* and Vinogradoff's *Historical Jurisprudence.* However, Anton believed that accounts of the custom betray a fundamental ignorance of medieval Canon law. He was able to show that

---

3 Gregory, *Western Highlands* (n 2) at 331; the Statutes of Iona are included in G Donaldson, *Scottish Historical Documents* (1970) at 171 (from *Reg, Privy Council*, ix, 26–30).
4 W F Skene (ed A. MacBain), *The Highlanders of Scotland* (1836, new edn 1902) at 108.
5 Skene, *Highlanders* (n 4) at 108.
6 A E Anton, "'Handfasting' in Scotland" (1958) 37 *SHR* 89.

those who have used the term "handfasting" have not appreciated the meaning of that term in medieval parlance, nor its relationship to the law of the Church. There had been confusion between an engagement to marry, or betrothal, and marriage itself. "The ceremony of joining hands," he writes, "became so closely associated with betrothals in medieval times that in Scotland, and apparently in the North of England, the ordinary term for a betrothal was a handfasting."[7] When betrothal was followed by intercourse on the faith of the promise to marry, then a valid although irregular marriage resulted (*sponsalia per verba de futuro subsequente copula*). Despite Skene's view to the contrary, the presence of a priest was not required to make a marriage good in law: although disapproving, the church recognised as valid not only marriage *per verba de futuro* as above, but also marriage *per verba de praesenti* contracted without ecclesiastical ceremony. On all these points Anton is convincing.[8] The appropriation of the term "handfasting" by Gregory and Skene to describe Highland marriage customs was inept and has given rise to much confusion.

However, it is more difficult to agree with Anton when he concludes, paraphrasing a remark by Cosmo Innes, that "there is no proof, or approach to proof, that handfasting in Skene's sense or any other peculiar customs of marriage were recognised in medieval Scotland after the introduction of Christianity had given one rule of marriage to the whole Christian world."[9] Cosmo Innes too was misled by the use of the term "handfasting" which he knew to be inappropriate. His views on Celtic law, however, do not bear examination and do this great legal historian no credit. "I have said," wrote Innes "that the law of marriage was viewed as one of the peculiarities of the Celtic race, but there is nothing more likely to mislead us in a subject necessarily of much obscurity than to found upon the loose practice of a half savage people, a theory of a definite system of law."[10] How much weight should be attached to this remark can be judged by his later comment on the *Leges inter Brettos et Scotos,*

> I have not troubled you with the ancient Scotch terms applicable to these laws of compensation. Some of them are more or less intelligible to the Celtic scholar;

---

7 Anton (n 6) at 91.
8 See also Archbishop J Scanlan, "Husband and wife: pre-Reformation Canon law", in *ISLH* 69; Barry (ed), *Hay's Lectures* (n 2). These two types of irregular marriage continued in later Scots law and were only brought to an end by the Marriage (Scotland) Act 1939. See further chs 9 and 10 below.
9 Anton (n 6) at 102.
10 C Innes, *Scotland in the Middle Ages* (1860) at 178.

but I cannot venture to speak of etymologies from that language, of which I am entirely ignorant.[11]

Contrary to the views of both Anton and Innes, there is in fact a great deal of evidence which indicates that "peculiar customs of marriage" were recognised in Gaelic Scotland long after "the introduction of Christianity had given one rule of marriage to the whole Christian world". The clue lies in Ireland and in Irish law and custom.

John of Fordun's account of Macbeth tells the story, later popularised by Holinshed and Shakespeare, of how Malcolm Canmore tests the loyalty of Macduff by pretending himself to be unsuited to wear the crown: "Malcolm adduces various instances of kings having lost their kingdoms through sensuality." The examples given by Fordun include Tarquinius, who "lewdly violated Lucretia", Sardanapalis, King of Assyria, "a man more dissolute than a woman", Chilperic of France, Edwy of England and Culen of Scotland. The crowning example – an anachronistic one, alas not referred to in Shakespeare – is Roderic of Ireland:

> The kingdom of Hibernia, likewise, came to an end with the lustful king Roderic (begotten, forsooth, of the stock of our own race), who would have six wives at once, not like a Christian king, and would not send them away, in spite of the loss of his kingdom — though he had often been warned by the whole Church, both archbishops and bishops, and chidden with fearful threats, by all the inhabitants, to Ruairi (Rory) O'Connor (d 1198), High King of Ireland both chiefs and private persons.[12]

The reference is clearly at the time of the Anglo-Norman invasion. Fordun's reference to Ruairi is remarkably close to the entry *sub anno* 1233 in the contemporary Annals of Connacht. After recording a battle in which two sons and two grandsons of Ruairi were killed, the Annal continues:

> Here ends the rule of the children of Ruairi O Conchobair, King of Ireland. For the Pope offered him the title to [the kingship of] Ireland for himself and his seed for ever, and likewise six wives, if he would renounce the sin of adultery henceforth; and since he would not accept these terms God took the rule and sovranty from his seed for ever, in punishment for his sin.[13]

These comments on Ruairi O'Connor, taken from medieval Scottish and Irish sources, illustrate dramatically the fact, now universally accepted by

---

11 Innes, *Scotland* (n 10) at 181.
12 *Chron Fordun*, vol 1, at 198–199 (trans vol 2, at 185–186).
13 A M Freeman (ed), *The Annals of Connacht* (henceforth *AC*) (2 vols, 1944 and 1970), sv AD 1233. Fordun's account is remarkably close to that in *AC*; it would be interesting to know where he got his information.

Irish scholars, that the ancient Irish law of marriage allowed for polygamy, concubinage and divorce, and that customs reflecting this law continued to flourish for over a thousand years after the introduction of Christianity.

Sir Henry Maine noted in his *Early Institutions* that there was "nothing like an intimate interpenetration of ancient Irish law by Christian principle" and commented that "the tract on 'Social Connections' appears to assume that the temporary cohabitation of the sexes is part of the accustomed order of society".[14] More recently many scholars have emphasised the peculiarities of Irish marriage customs. Gearoid MacNiocaill states that royal fertility was expected and admired and that this "was rarely attainable without a plurality of wives." He quotes from the canons of the Dark Age Church: "the greater the dignity a king has received, the greater should be the fear he has; for many women debase his soul; and his spirit, divided by a multitude of spouses, slips deeply into sin."[15] One of these early canons is entitled *De concubinis non habendis cum legitima uxore*.[16] However, native jurists, anticipating the Mormons by a thousand years, were able to point to the example of the Old Testament patriarchs: "God's chosen people lived in a plurality of unions, so that it is not easier to condemn it than to praise it."[17] Donncha Ó Corráin states that "Irish dynasties, as the laws and other sources conclusively prove, were polygamous from the earliest period until the collapse of the Gaelic System."[18] This view is echoed by Kenneth Nicholls.

> In no field of life was Ireland's apartness from the mainstream of Christian European society so marked as in that of marriage. Throughout the medieval period, and down to the end of the old order in 1603, what could be called Celtic secular marriage remained the norm in Ireland, and Christian matrimony was no more than the rare exception grafted on to this system.[19]

Celtic secular marriage was no mere survival of inarticulate folk custom. Its origins are to be found in the highly organised legal order of early Ireland and in the Irish law tracts. These tracts represent the committing to paper by a professional learned class of oral legal tradition preserved by the joint

14 Sir H Maine, *Early History of Institutions* (7th edn, 1897) at 58, 59.
15 G Mac Niocaill, *Ireland before the Vikings* (1972) at 58.
16 H Wassersohleben, *Die Irische Kanonensammlung* (1885) at 190.
17 As quoted by Mac Niocaill, *Ireland* (n 15) at 58.
18 D Ó Corràin, *Ireland before the Normans* (1972) at 38. See further D Ó Corràin, "Marriage in early Ireland", in A Cosgrove (ed), *Marriage in Ireland* (1985) 5.
19 K Nicholls, *Gaelic and Gaelicised Ireland in the Middle Ages* (1972) at 73. A Cosgrove, "Marriage in medieval Ireland", in A Cosgrove (ed) (n 18) 25 suggests that "this sweeping statement needs some qualifications" (at 30). See further K Simms, *Gaelic Ulster in the Middle Ages* (2020) at 435–441. Note also Wales: R R Davies, "The status of women and the practice of marriage in late medieval Wales", in D Jenkins (ed), *The Welsh Law of Women* (1980) 93.

memory of the ancients, the transmission from one ear to another, the chanting of the poets, to quote the *Senchus Mór*, the best known of these compilations, or, to use Professor Binchy's memorable phrase, "oral tradition congealed in ink". Already in writing in the seventh century, the texts attained canonical form by the end of the eighth century and reflect the customs of an archaic society whose roots lay deep in the Indo-European past.[20]

The law tracts recognise many types of sexual union, some lasting, some temporary and some merely transient. The legal consequences of these unions as regards status, contract, and property law are regulated in considerable and complicated detail. As well as a first or chief wife, known as a *cétmuinter*, it was recognised that a man could have a second wife. The usual purpose of such a second marriage was to produce sons. The violation of a secondary wife rated only half the sum in compensation to the husband as the violation of a chief wife. The technical name given to this secondary wife, at least in the later texts, is *adaltrach*, literally "adulteress", a term which clearly reflects the Church's disapproval of such unions. Various types of concubine inferior to an *adaltrach* were also recognised. The children of most of these unions would be regarded as legitimate for the purpose of succession.

Divorce was a recognised institution and available to both parties on a number of grounds. For example, a woman might divorce her husband if he slandered her or ill-treated her physically. She could divorce him if he took an *adaltrach*, if he became insane, or if he was sexually unsatisfactory – impotent, sterile or a homosexual. A man might divorce his wife if she was sterile, if she dishonoured him, for adultery, for "general mischief in the house,"[21] or if she procured an abortion. An *adaltrach* who did not bear a male child within a year could be summarily dismissed. Here, perhaps, we may recognise the ultimate source of Martin and Skene's trial marriage for a year, or for a year and a day. Divorce by mutual consent was also possible. All this, of course, was clean contrary to the teaching of the Church, as was the Irish predilection for marrying their close kin.[22]

---

20  There is a large literature on the Irish law tracts especially in relation to the legal status of women. Key studies are R. Thurneysen and others, *Studies in Early Irish Law* (1936); D A Binchy, "The linguistic and historical value of the Irish law tracts" (1943) 29 *Proceedings of the British Academy* 195, reprinted in D Jenkins (ed), *Celtic Law Papers* (1973) 71; and D A Binchy, "Irish history and Irish law: I and II" (1975 and 1976) 15 and 16 *Studia Hibernica* 7 and 7. For the original texts themselves see D A Binchy (ed), *Corpus Iuris Hibernici* (7 vols, 1978).
21  Translation from A Gwynn, "The first synod of Cashel" (1946) 67 *Irish Ecclesiastical Record* 109.
22  For the Irish law on the legal status of women see, in addition to works already quoted, Gwynn

It is difficult to be certain how far legal theory reflected actual practice, and this is a difficulty which increases as the centuries pass. However, it is not difficult to discern the influence of Celtic secular marriage in the career of the notorious and much married Gormlaith described in that great work of literature *Njal's Saga*, as well as in more sober historical sources. Wife of Olaf Cuaran, King of Dublin, mother of his son Sitric Silkenbeard, discarded wife of Brian Boru, sometime wife of King Máel Sechnaill II, prospective spouse of Sigurd of Orkney,

> She was endowed with great beauty and all those attributes which were outside her own control, but it is said that in all the characteristics for which she herself was responsible, she was utterly wicked. She had been married to a king called Brian, but now they were divorced.[23]

From the eleventh century onwards more evidence becomes available from external sources on the Irish law of marriage. It is not flattering. Pope Gregory VII writes to Lanfranc, Archbishop of Canterbury, to say that he has heard that the Irish – *quod de Scotis audivimus* – not only desert their wives but also sell them.[24] Lanfranc himself writes in 1074 to the king of Munster, Turlough O'Brien, complaining that

> in your kingdom every man abandons his lawfully wedded wife at his own will, without the occasion of any canonical cause; and with a boldness that must be punished, takes to himself some other wife . . . according to a law of marriage that is rather a law of fornication.[25]

Lanfranc's successor, St Anselm, writes two letters to the king of Munster, Muirchertach O'Brien. In the first he says:

> It is reported among us that marriages are dissolved in your kingdom without any reason; and that kinsfolk are not ashamed to have intercourse, either under the name of marriage or under some other name, publicly and without rebuke, against all the prohibitions of the Canon Law.

---

(n 21); K Hughes, *The Church in Early Irish Society* (1966); A Gwynn, *The Twelfth-Century Reform* (1968); K Simms, "The legal position of Irishwomen in the later middle ages", 1975 *Irish Jurist* 96; D Ó Corráin, "Women in early Irish society" and K Simms, "Women in Norman Ireland", both in M MacCurtain and D O Corráin (eds), *Women in Irish Society* (1978).

23  M Magnusson and H Pálsson (trans), *Njal's Saga* (Penguin Classics, 1960) at 342.
24  A W Hadden and W Stubbs, *Councils and Ecclesiastical Documents relating to Great Britain and Ireland* (3 vols, 1869–1878), vol 2, at 160; J Robertson, *Concilia Scotiae* (2 vols, Bannatyne Club, 1866), vol 1, at xxiv (n), takes this to refer to Scotland rather than Ireland, but this is not at all likely.
25  C R Elrington (ed), *The Whole Works of James Ussher* (1847–1864) at 492–494 (Gwynn's translation).

In the second he writes: "It is said that men exchange their wives with the wives of others as freely and as publicly as a man might exchange his horse ....".[26]

In 1101 a synod held at Cashel forbade a man from marrying his stepmother or his step-grandmother, his stepdaughter, his wife's sister or his brother's wife – a far cry indeed from the seven forbidden degrees of kinship of the contemporary Canon law, and good evidence that such unions were in fact taking place.[27] Despite several further reforming synods the old marriage customs continued, and the desirability of ecclesiastical reform bulks large in Pope Adrian IV's famous grant of the Lordship of Ireland to Henry II in 1155. On the political level, indeed, the abduction by Dermot MacMurrough, king of Leinster, of Devorgilla, the wife of Tighearnan O'Rourke, in 1152 was an important factor in precipitating the Anglo-Norman invasion of Ireland. The great Turlough O'Connor (d 1156), king of Connacht, had seventeen sons by four wives, and, as already seen, later generations ascribed to the polygamous habits of his son the high-king Ruairi the downfall of his dynasty as kings of Ireland.[28] In 1172 Pope Alexander III wrote to Henry II, now overlord of much of Ireland in fact as well as name, complaining that the Irish married their stepmothers, and their brother's wives while the brother was still alive, and "that a man might live in concubinage with two sisters; and that many of them, putting away the mother, will marry the daughter".[29] Katherine Simms comments:

> Anyone reading the letter written by Pope Alexander III to King Henry II in 1172 might be forgiven for thinking that a prime object of the Norman invasion of Ireland had been the reform of the Irish customs with regard to marriage and concubinage.[30]

Simms has made a detailed study of the position of women in medieval Ireland, relying not only on Gaelic material but also on the original registers of the archbishops of Armagh. Her conclusion is that although Irish law in the middle ages differed in many ways from the ancient law tracts, the law on marriage remained remarkably constant.[31] Kenneth Nicholls

---

26 Elrington (ed), *Ussher* (n 25) at 490–491, 521 (Gwynn's translation).
27 Gwynn (n 21); Hughes, *Church* (n 22) at 263 ff. There are orthographical ambiguities in the text, and it is just possible, although not likely, that the prohibition is on marrying one's own daughter, or sister.
28 For Turlough's wives see O Corráin (n 22) at 7.
29 M P Sheehy (ed), *Pontificia Hibernica* (1962), vol 1, at 21.
30 Simms, "Legal position" (n 21) at 97.
31 Simms, "Women" (n 21) at 14.

takes the same view in his pioneering study of Gaelic Ireland in the middle ages.[32] Thus we should not be too surprised to read that in 1243 Tadg O'Connor, on being released from captivity by O'Reilly, led a company of men to MacDermot's house and abducted MacDermot's wife, who was his own mother, and gave her to O'Reilly as ransom for himself; nor that in 1365 MacMahon was forced by Somhairle MacDonald to divorce his wife and marry Somhairle's daughter.[33] In 1339, Turlough O'Connor, king of Connacht, "took a new wife, and put away [i.e. divorced] the old one". According to Nicholls the new wife was his aunt![34] Cablaigh Mor O'Connor died in 1395, "to wit, a propertied woman of great substance was she, that lived with noble men, namely Niall O'Donnell, king of Tirconell, and Aedh O'Rourke, king of Brefne, and Cathal, royal heir of Connacht and other men that are not reckoned here." From the fact that three of her husbands were deadly enemies she was named *Port-na-dtri-namhad* – "the meeting place of the three enemies".[35] The second earl of Clanrickard (d 1582) was said to have been six times married, with five wives living at the same time, four of them having been "put away" by him.[36] At the end of the sixteenth century it was still possible to comment on Irish marriage customs in these terms:

> In old time they much abused the honourable state of marriage, either in contracts unlawful, meeting the degrees of prohibition, or in divorsements at pleasure, or in retaining concubines or harlots for wives; yea even at this daie, where the clergie is faint, they can be content to marrie for a year and a daie of probation; and at the years end, or anie time after, to returne hir home with hir marriage goods, or as much in valure, upon light quarels, if the gentlewoman's friends be unable to revenge the injurie. In like maner maie she forsake hir husband.[37]

However, although Celtic secular marriage and marriage under the Canon law were poles apart in legal theory, the contrast in practice, at least as regards divorce, as Simms points out, was not as great as might have been expected. Under the Canon law marriage was for life and divorce was not permitted, but the increasing ease with which annulments were granted in

---

32 Nicholls, *Gaelic and Gaelicised Ireland* (n 19) at 73–77.
33 *AC* (n 13) AD 1243; W M Hennessy and B MacCarthy (eds), *Annals of Ulster* (1887–1901, henceforth *AU*), AD 1365. For commentary on the 1365 annal, see Simms, "Legal position" (n 21) at 110.
34 *AC* (n 13) AD 1339; Nicholls, *Gaelic and Gaelicised Ireland* (n 19) at 75; Simms, "Legal position" (n 21) at 98.
35 *AU* (n 33) AD 1395; Nicholls, *Gaelic and Gaelicised Ireland* (n 19) at 73.
36 Nicholls, *Gaelic and Gaelicised Ireland* (n 19) at 74.
37 R. Stanihurst, "A Treatise conteining a plaine and perfect description of Ireland", in *Holinshed's Chronicles* (1586), vol 2, at 45 – see Simms, "Legal position" (n 21) at 103. Once again a period of a year and day is referred to; cf text accompanying nn 5, 20–21 above.

the later middle ages, especially on the grounds of consanguinity and affinity, made a mockery of the permanence of marriage. Not only in Gaelic society did men and women have a succession of spouses. Again, Irish lords were as likely – perhaps more likely – to marry their close kin as their counterparts in Western Europe.[38] Increasingly they found it politic to present their divorces as annulments under the Canon law, and to seek for their marriages, if all went well, the blessing of a dispensation from the prohibited degrees. It might be difficult to deduce from the consistorial records of the church alone that Celtic secular marriage continued to flourish. However, it is possible to detect differences, as Simms has done, between petitions on the Irish side and petitions on the Anglo-Irish side. Typically, on the Anglo-Irish side a wife will petition because she wants to be separated from her husband; on the Irish side, by contrast, the petition is more likely to come from a wife who claims she has been dismissed "without reasonable cause".[39]

Celtic secular marriage then survived in Gaelic Ireland until the end of the old order. As a legal institution its origin is to be seen in the ancient Irish laws. As a social institution it continued to reflect the aspirations of an archaic kin-based society.[40] Given the tenacity of the institution in Ireland one would expect to find Celtic secular marriage also in Scotland, a country united by a dynasty of Gaelic-speaking kings of Irish origin. In the Highlands and islands of Scotland, as in Ireland, an archaic kin-based Gaelic society survived the middle ages. MacDonald in Islay had as much in common with O'Neill in Tyrone and O'Donnell in Donegal as he had with any lowland Scottish magnate. The history of Celtic law in Scotland remains to be written, but the parallels in law and society between Gaelic Scotland and Gaelic Ireland are unmistakable: parallels true of the mainstream of Scottish development until at least the twelfth century, and remaining true of the western Highlands and islands for a further five hundred years.[41] There are parallels in the nature of kingship, especially as regards the ceremony of inauguration, in the law of succession to the throne, in burdens in land such as *cain*, in the professional learned orders, such as doctors, poets and judges. Parallels too in the church, as one would expect in the adopted country of St Columba:

---

38 For example, the AD 1339 entry in *AC* (n 13) and the decisions of the Synod of Cashel of 1101, text accompanying nn 23–26. See also Nicholls, *Gaelic and Gaelicised Ireland* (n 19) at 75–76. It has not been possible to explore in any depth this aspect of matrimonial custom in this paper.
39 Simms, "Women" (n 21) at 15, 16.
40 This paper concentrates on Celtic secular marriage as a legal institution; a great deal of groundwork remains to be done on the social and anthropological side.
41 See further ch 2 above.

in ecclesiastical organisation and office-bearers; as regards relics and their custodians; and in reform movements such as the Culdees. It is true that the surviving Scottish record, especially from the Gaelic side, is sparser than the Irish, but enough has survived to indicate that Celtic secular marriage had a long history in Gaelic Scotland as in Ireland.

Little evidence has survived before the reign of Malcolm Canmore (1058–1093). His queen, St Margaret, according to her biographer Turgot, held at least one council in which she attempted some reform in the Celtic Church, one malpractice specifically mentioned being the fact that marriage was permitted with a stepmother and a deceased brother's wife. Some years later, 1112 –1114, Pope Paschal II sent two letters to Scotland, one of them to Turgot, now bishop of St Andrews, condemning abuses in the Church. Once again, uncanonical customs concerning marriage are hinted at, although this time obliquely: *"Coniugia inter vos pudicitia serventur"* (let marriage serve modesty among you), writes Paschal.[42] The parallels with contemporary Irish reform, as at the synod of Cashel in 1101, are too close to be accidental. Later in the twelfth century the biographer of Ailred of Rievaulx refers thus to the marital habits of the Galwegians:

> *Ibi castitas tociens patitur naufragium, quociens libido voluerit, nec est inter castam et scortum ulla distancia nisi quod castiores inibi mulieres per menses viros alternent et vir pro una bucula vendat uxorem.*[43]

So far the record evidence. There is, however, an intriguing tradition recorded by the fifteenth-century historian Andrew of Wyntoun about the birth of Malcolm Canmore himself. According to Wyntoun, Malcolm's father King Duncan "gat two sownnys off lauchfull bed," one of them being the later king Donald Ban. One day, however, when out hunting, Duncan chanced to come by the mill of Forteviot, where he met and fell in love with the miller's daughter. The story unfolds:

> This milnare had a dowchtyr fayre,
> That to the Kyng had offt repayre . . .
> (He) tuk, and chesyd that woman

---

42 D Bethell, "Two letters of Pope Paschal II to Scotland" (1970) 49 *SHR* 33; R Somerville (ed), *Scotia Pontificia: Papal Letters to Scotland before the Pontificate of Innocent III* (1982) nos 1 and 2. A A M Duncan, *Scotland: The Making of the Kingdom* (1975) at 123, 129, is perhaps too sceptical about the existence of Queen Margaret's council, given the constant repetition of complaints about similar abuses in Ireland.

43 F M Powicke (ed), *Vita Ailredi Walteri Danielis* (1950) at 45 (chastity suffers shipwreck as many times as lust desires, nor is there any difference between a chaste woman and a whore except that the more chaste will change their husbands by the month and a man will sell his wife for a heifer – *my translation*).

To be fra thine hys luwyd lemman.
That ilke nycht, that the Kyng
Tuk wyth the mylnare hys gesnyng,
in to bede wyth hyr he lay,
And gat on hyr a sowne or day,
That wes Malcolme, off Scotland
Thare-efftyre crownyd Kyng regnand.[44]

The fact that Wyntoun tells such a story of an ancestor of the reigning line suggests that it had achieved a very wide currency. Wyntoun was clearly fascinated by the genealogical implications, and devotes several lines to demonstrating that many kings, an Emperor, and even a Pope descended from the miller of Forteviot's daughter.[45] It is worth remembering too that Donald Ban's heir-at-law, John Comyn, was a claimant for the throne of Scotland during the Great Cause of 1291, although the exact grounds of his claim are unknown.[46] According to Fordun, both Malcolm Canmore and Donald Ban were sons of Duncan's union with a cousin of Earl Siward of Northumbria, but this evidence, like that of Wyntoun, is late, and it must remain at least a possibility that Malcolm Canmore was the son of a union with a concubine or an *adaltrach*.[47]

The status, legitimate or otherwise, of Malcolm Canmore's eldest son Duncan, king in 1094, has been much debated by historians. Duncan was not the son of St Margaret, but of Malcolm's earlier wife Ingibjorg. In his 1094 charter to Durham he describes himself as king *constans hereditarie*, yet in the next century William of Malmesbury calls him *nothus*, a bastard.[48] Historians have speculated that Duncan may have been technically illegitimate under the Canon law, and have constructed none too convincing tables of consanguinity and affinity to back up this thesis. Again, there has been some dispute as to the identity of Duncan's mother, Ingibjorg. According to *Orkneying Saga* Ingibjorg was the wife of Thorfinn the Mighty, jarl of Orkney — and mother of his sons, Paul and Erlend – before she married Malcolm Canmore. However, Thorfinn is thought to have died around 1065, and as there are chronological difficulties in supposing that Ingibjorg

---

44 D Laing (ed), *Orygynale Cronykil of Scotland by Androw of Wyntoun* (3 vols, 1872), vol 2, at 120 (lines 1625–1642).
45 Laing (ed), *Wyntoun* (n 44) at 121–122 (lines 1663–1696).
46 E L G Stones and G G Simpson, *Edward I and the Throne of Scotland* (2 vols, 1978), vol 1, at 15; vol 2, at 138.
47 *Chron Fordun*, vol 1, at 187; vol 2, at 179.
48 A C Lawrie (ed), *Early Scottish Charters prior to 1153* (1905), no XII; A A M Duncan, "The earliest Scottish charters" (1958) 37 *SHR* at 127–8.

married Malcolm after that date, a second Ingibjorg, daughter of the first and wife of Malcolm, has been postulated. However, the difficulties as to Duncan's status and parentage disappear if one supposes that Ingibjorg was the divorced wife rather than the widow of Thorfinn when she married Malcolm. Thorfinn, let us suppose, had put her away, and so in the eyes of the Church, but not, one imagines, of Ingibjorg or Malcolm, her second marriage was bigamous and her son Duncan an adulterine bastard.[49]

After the accession to the throne of the sons of Margaret, and the increasing influence of the Canon and the Feudal law, one would expect the practice of Celtic secular marriage to disappear rapidly from the mainstream of Scottish political life. Nevertheless it may be that the continuation of just such a practice was an element in the disputes, a present barely understood, about succession to several earldoms, such as Mar, Menteith and Atholl, in the twelfth and thirteenth centuries. Historians have recognised that different customs of succession may underly these disputes but have so far tended to consider the question of status, legitimate or otherwise, solely within the context of Canon law. The practice of Celtic secular marriage may have its bearing too on the matrimonial alliances of William, the son of Duncan II, and on the claims to the crown put forward by his descendants, the MacWilliams.[50]

If the influence of Celtic law declined in lowland Scotland from the twelfth century onwards, it survived in more pristine form, and perhaps even underwent a revival, in the Highlands and islands.[51] The main focal point of Gaelic Scotland in the later middle ages was the Lordship of the Isles. In the Lordship, stationed on various islands, were judges who still bore the Celtic title of *breitheamh*: the best known of these judges or "brieves" are the Morrisons of Ness in Lewis. From these judges appeal ran to the Council of the Isles with its headquarters at *Eilean na Comhairle* at Loch Finlaggan in Islay. In 1485 *Hullialmus archiiudex* witnesses an island charter.[52] Both Gaelic and official Scots sources indicate that laws other than those of the

---

49 J Anderson (ed), *Orkneyinga Saga* (1873), ch 23 (at 45–46 and note); A O Anderson (ed), *Early Sources of Scottish History, 500 to 1286* (2 vols, 1922), vol 2, at 4, 25–26. There is also a discussion in Duncan (n 48) at 128. In the Scandinavian world as in the Celtic, pre-Christian marriage customs long continued. In the twelfth century Harald Maddadson, Iarl of Orkney, repudiated his wife. Mr Hermann Pálsson has kindly pointed out to me that concubinage remained commonplace in twelfth-century Iceland.
50 For the general background see Duncan, *Scotland* (n 42). Professor G W S Barrow discusses the MacWilliam claims in *RRS*, vol 2, at 11–13.
51 See n 40 above.
52 J and R W Munro (eds), *Acts of the Lords of the Isles 1336–1493* (SHS, 1986) no 119 (at 188).

kingdom of Scotland were applied. Dean Monro, writing in 1549, speaks of "the Laws made be Renald McSomharkle callit in his time King of the Occident Iles" (this is the MacDonald ancestor Ranald, son of Somerled).[53] In 1504 the Scots Parliament enacted: "Item that all our soverane lordis liegis beand under his obesance and in speciale all the Ilis be Reulit be our soverane lordis aune lawis and the commoune lawis of the Realme and be nain other lawis."[54]

Political and personal alliances between West Highland magnates and native Irish lords were frequent. In the thirteenth century the MacSweens of Knapdale formed marriage alliances with the O'Connor kings of Connacht and the O'Donnell rulers of Tyrconell. In 1259 the daughter of Dugald MacRuairi, king of Innse Gall and a descendant of Somerled, married Aedh O'Connor, king of Connacht, and brought her husband a dowry of one hundred and sixty galloglasses. In 1290 Aedh O'Donnell deposed his brother as leader of the O'Donnells with the aid of his mother's kin, the Clan Donald. The marriage of Angus Og MacDonald of Islay with Aine, daughter of Cumuighe O'Cathan, is well known. Aine's second husband was an O'Neill chieftain. Many later MacDonalds, especially of the family of Dunivaig and the Glens, married Irish wives.[55]

Given this background, there is, as one would expect, considerable evidence for the continuing existence of Celtic secular marriage in the later middle ages in the Highlands and Islands. Unfortunately the evidence is rarely direct or unambiguous, and is difficult to interpret. The official records of the Lordship are lost. No trace of the laws of Ranald, son of Somerled, survives. No judgement of an island *breitheamh* exists in original form. Much of the evidence which does survive from the Gaelic side about the history of families and their marriage alliances, and about the state of society in general, was not written down until the seventeenth century or later, long after the end of the Lordship, and "the daunting of the Isles". These accounts are an invaluable record of tradition, but are often confused, garbled and biased.

The Vatican archives do, indeed, contain a wealth of contemporary material on medieval Scotland, including the Highlands, much of which concerns annulments, legitimacy and dispensations from the prohibited degrees. The study of this material has barely begun, but it may not disclose as much

---

53 R W Munro (ed), *Monro's Western Isles of Scotland* (1961) at 57.
54 *RPS*, A1504/3/124.
55 W D H Sellar, "Family origins in Cowal and Knapdale" (1971) 15 *Scottish Studies* at 30–31; *AC* (n 13) AD 1259, 1290; *AU* (n 33) AD 1290.

about Highland marital habits as we might expect.[56] The official record tells us how the relationships which it records were presented in Rome; it does not necessarily tell us how they were viewed within Gaelic society. The Irish experience indicates that it was not difficult to present relationships resulting from Celtic secular marriage in Canon law guise, and that it was often politic to do so.[57] An official dispensation to marry, long after the event, the official legitimation of a son and heir, may often have been considered politic and desirable, but they do not indicate that within the context of Gaelic society, the marriage was not already considered valid or the son legitimate. In the same manner feudal forms were used to clothe Celtic customs regarding succession, as in the case of the heiress Christiana MacRuairi, bypassed in Robert Bruce's time in favour of the male line, or in the case of Mary MacLeod, the sixteenth-century heiress of Dunvegan, similarly excluded from the succession.[58]

The evidence then is difficult to interpret. However, it is impossible to review the history of the West Highlands in the later middle ages, or to read through the later traditional accounts of the Highland clans, without reaching the conclusion that Skene and Gregory were right in detecting the existence of peculiar customs of marriage. Almost regardless of which family is studied, there are examples of disputed legitimacy and marriage, of succession disputes with uncle ranged against nephew, and brother against half-brother, of tales of repudiated and abandoned wives, and of uncanonical unions. Between 1550 and 1650 there were three particularly fratricidal succession disputes, among the MacLeods of Lewis, the Macneils of Barra and the MacLeods of Assynt.[59] It is impossible to regard these examples as springing simply from unusual political unrest or from technical breaches of the Canon law so common throughout Europe. They are different in kind and intensity, and their explanation is to be found in the continuance of customs of Celtic secular marriage.

---

56 The Department of Scottish History at Glasgow University now holds a great deal of Scottish material from the Vatican Archives on microfilm, the result of many years of systematic investigation. Indices and calendars are being gradually compiled, and some of the material is published in the series *Calendar of Scottish Supplications to Rome* (1934–2021, continuing). See also J J Robertson, "Scottish legal research in the Vatican Archive: a preliminary report" (1988) 2 *Renaissance Studies* 339 at 345.

57 Simms, "Women" (n 21).

58 G W S Barrow, *Robert Bruce and the Community of the Realm of Scotland* (4th edn, 2005), at 377–378; R C MacLeod, *The MacLeods of Dunvegan* (1927) at 91–93; I F Grant, *The MacLeods* (1959) at 116–126.

59 The disputes in relation to Lewis and Barra are discussed in text accompanying nn 84–85 and 87–96 below.

As noted above, Gregory regards Gillespic MacDonald of Lochalsh (d 1473) and Hugh MacDonald of Sleat (d 1498) as providing examples of peculiar Highland marriage custom. Gillespic and Hugh were sons of Alexander, Lord of the Isles, and half-brothers – perhaps elder half-brothers – of John, Lord of the Isles. Neither contemporaries nor tradition ever claimed that they were the sons of a regular canonical union. Gillespic, described as a "base son" in the traditional Sleat history, was the son of a daughter of MacDuffie (MacPhee), while Hugh's mother was a daughter of Gillepatrick O'Beolan of Carloway.[60] The Sleat history itself describes Hugh's mother as a concubine, and says that "MacDonald could not be induced to part with her, on occasion of her great beauty".[61] Neither MacDuffie nor O'Beolan, it may be noted in passing, were men of humble birth: both belonged to the aristocracy. Some further information on the chequered matrimonial career of Alexander, Lord of the Isles, has survived. In 1446 he was admonished by Pope Eugenius IV for putting away his lawful wife, Elizabeth, perhaps the mother of John – *ipsam Elizabeth a se de facto repulit* – and for impudently adhering to yet another woman named Christiana MacLaide *quem in concubinam tenere non trepidat* – whom he did not fear to keep in concubinage.[62] One is reminded here of Simms' finding that consistorial petitions from women in Irish Gaelic society typically allege dismissal by their husbands without reasonable cause.[63] In addition, the Vatican records give the name of Alexander's wife in 1433 as *Jacobella*, and Papal letters of legitimation were granted in 1445 in favour of three sons of Alexander – Hugh, Alexander and Donald – by an unnamed mother.[64]

Nor were the matrimonial affairs of Gillespic and Hugh themselves free from complication. According to the Sleat history Giliespic "got [his son] Alexander by his father's brother's daughter, and finding no clergyman to marry them, he cohabited with her all his lifetime against the consent

---

60 "History of the Macdonalds," attributed to Hugh MacDonald, a Skye *seanchaidh* (hereafter cited as *History*), in J R N Macphail (ed), *Highland Papers I* (SHS, 1914; hereafter cited as *Highland Papers I*) at 34–5, 47, 53–4; *The "Black Book" of Clanranald* (hereafter cited as *Clanranald*); A Cameron, *Reliquiae Celticae II*, ed A Macbain and J Kennedy (1894) at 211, 213. *History* mistakenly fathers Gillespie on John, Lord of the Isles.
61 *History* (n 60) at 35.
62 *Highland Papers I* (n 60) at 93–95. There is doubt whether Elizabeth was a Seton or a Haliburton.
63 See text accompanying n 39 above.
64 Vatican Archive, Register of Supplications, 289 fo 253 v (I am grateful to Mr and Mrs R W Munro for drawing my attention to this reference); *Highland Papers I* (n 60) at 92–93. As Sheriff Macphail observes, this legitimation is in very ample terms, allowing not only succession *ab intestato* but also a right to the father's armorial bearings.

of all his friends."[65] Nevertheless this son Alexander, the product of two uncanonical alliances in two generations, appears as the acknowledged heir of his uncle, John, Lord of the Isles.[66] The fate of Alexander of Lochalsh's two daughters and ultimate heiresses, according to the Sleat account, is not without interest. Alexander MacDonald of Glengarry "married first a brother's daughter of his grandfather . . . and having turned her off, he married the second daughter;" again, "having dismissed his lawful wife . . . he ravished Alexander MacGillespig's daughter merely to advance his fortune . . . but could not get himself married to her while his former wife lived." The elder daughter of Alexander of Lochalsh was married to Dugald, son of the deposed chief of Clanranald, but "Glengarry and others by threats compelled him again to dismiss his wife," who later married Dingwall of Kildun.[67]

Hugh MacDonald of Sleat died leaving six sons, each by a different mother: Donald Gallich by Elizabeth Gunn ("Austine [Hugh] having halted at Caithness he got a son by the Crowner of Caithness' daughter"); John by MacIan of Ardnamurchan's daughter; Donald Harrich by MacLeod of Harris' daughter; Gillespic by MacLeod of Lewis' daughter; Angus Collach by MacLean of Coll's daughter; and Angus Dubh by the daughter of the vicar of South Uist.[68] Again the mothers are of noble birth, but it is straining credulity too far to believe that Hugh was canonically married to each of them in turn. A charter under the great seal survives confirming a grant by John, Lord of the Isles, in favour of Hugh and the mother of son number two, with the unusual destination-over – believed by Sheriff MacPhail to be unique – to their heirs male *legitime sive illegittime procreatis seu procreandis*.[69] One can guess why this proviso was necessary! Son number two did indeed succeed his father, but the later house of Sleat descend from son number one, Donald Gallich. Donald Gallich, incidentally, would appear to have married the mother of his son and heir, Donald Gruamach, when her former husband, Torquil MacLeod of Lewis was still alive, while of Donald Gruamach the Sleat history records:

---

65 *History* (n 60) at 54, 64. Donald Gregory, however, makes the mother of Alexander of Lochalsh "Fynvola", daughter of Lachlan Bronnach MacLean (Gregory, *Western Highlands* (n 2) at 60).
66 Gregory, *Western Highlands* (n 2) at 55–57; J W M Bannerman, "The Lordship of the Isles", app II in K A Steer and J W M Bannerman (eds), *Late Medieval Monumental Sculpture in the West Highlands* (1977) at 207.
67 *History* (n 60) at 54, 55, 64, 65.
68 *History* (n 60) at 62–63; *Clanranald* (n 60) at 213.
69 *Highland Papers I* (n 60) at 96–99; *RMS*, vol 2, no 2286.

He afterwards had Gilespig Cierich by a daughter of Torkill MacLeod his married wife being then alive for she slipt away from her own child without the least offence being given her.[70]

Although the Sleat history calls Angus Og the legitimate son of John, Lord of the Isles, by the earl of Angus' daughter, he is usually accounted illegitimate. He was certainly not the son of John's only known wife, Elizabeth Livingston. Yet two Crown charters in 1476 and 1478 explicitly recognised Angus as heir to his father's lands should John have no legitimate issue in the male line.[71] The status of Angus' son Donald Dubh is notoriously also a matter of dispute: his mother was a daughter of the first earl of Argyll, but his legitimacy was always, it seems, denied by the Crown, and always asserted by the islanders.[72]

Other branches of the house of the Isles also had their share of uncanonical associations. It is generally accepted that the great Clanranald chief John Móideartach, who succeeded his father Alexander in 1530, was illegitimate. The Sleat history describes him as being of natural birth but "without doubt . . . a man truly worthy of the preferment."[73] He was legitimised by Crown grant in 1532.[74] The Black Book of Clanranald simply gives his mother's name as Dearbhfail (Dorothy), without any indication of her paternity. She may have been a commoner. The mothers of two other families of John's father Alexander are named as the daughter of Tormod (Norman) son of Gillepatrick O'Beolan, and the daughter of MacIntosh.[75] The "Black Book" credits many other Clanranald chiefs and notables with a number of partners, the most striking example being that of Ranald of Benbecula which will be considered later. The MacDonalds of Keppoch descend from Angus son of Alexander Carrach. The Sleat account regards them as being of legitimate descent, but the "Black Book" says that Angus' mother was a daughter of MacDuffie but was not married to his father.[76] After John Mor MacDonald of Dunivaig was hanged on the one gallows in 1499 with his son John Cathanach and two of

---

70 *History* (n 60) at 67, 72. Torquil MacLeod was also married to Catriona, daughter of Colin, Earl of Argyll (Steer and Bannerman (eds), *Sculpture* (n 66) at 114, citing *The Book of the Dean of Lismore* and *RMS* (n 69) vol 2, no 2424). Donald Gruamach's "married wife" was Catriona, daughter of Alexander of Clanranald, and formerly the wife of John "Brayach" MacIan of Ardnamurchan *(History* (n 60) at 72; *Clanranald* (n 60) at 213).
71 *History* (n 60) at 47; *RMS*, vol 2, nos 1246 1410.
72 *History* (n 60) at 50; *Clanranald* (n 60) at 163.
73 *History* (n 60) at 65.
74 *RSS*, vol 2, no 1117.
75 *Clanranald* (n 60) at 171.
76 *History* (n 60) at 26–27; *Clanranald* (n 60) at 213.

his grandsons, the representation of the family devolved on John Cathanach's son Alexander, ancestor of the later MacDonalds of Islay and of Antrim. Of Alexander's birth the Sleat history says that he was "begotten by the Savages daughter in the County of Downe in Ireland and spouse of Achilles Bay MacCartin, they being both at the time his [John Cathanach's] prisoners".[77] One is reminded of the association between Shane O'Neill and Catherine MacLean, widow of the fourth earl of Argyll and wife of Calvagh O'Donnell: this association, which produced several sons, began when Catherine and her husband Calvagh were Shane's prisoners.[78]

The history and traditions of other families disclose similar irregularities. The legitimacy of several sixteenth-century chiefs of MacKay was very much in question, as Ian Grimble has shown, and for two of them at least, John (d 1529) and his brother Donald (d 1550), formal letters of legitimation were sought from the Crown.[79] Sir Robert Gordon (no lover of the MacKays) writes:

> Y-Roy Macky had, by a woman of the West Yles, four bastard sones and two daughters: Neill, John, Donald and Angus ... his sone John Macky succeeded ... whereupon Neill Naverigh, the brother of Y-Roy ... maid clame ... alleging his nephues to be bastards.[80]

Kenneth MacKenzie of Kintail (d 1492) is said to have repudiated his first wife, Margaret, daughter of John, Lord of the Isles, and taken a second one. The legitimacy of John of Killin, born of this second alliance and ancestor of the later chiefs of Kintail, was hotly disputed by his uncle, Hector Roy MacKenzie of Gairloch. According to tradition MacKenzie returned his wife, who was blind in one eye, to her kinsmen mounted on a one-eyed horse and accompanied by a one-eyed servant and a one-eyed dog.[81] Not surprisingly a battle resulted. The repudiation by Alexander (Alastair Crotach) MacLeod of Harris of his MacDonald wife led, according to the Sleat history, to his imprisonment and broken back.[82] Lachlan Cattanach

---

77 History (n 60) at 61. G Hill, The MacDonnells of Antrim (1873, reprinted 1976) at 375 reads MacFirbis as stating that Alexander's mother was Sile (Julia), daughter of MacIntosh. This is incorrect: MacFirbis too makes Alexander's mother the daughter of Savage.
78 G A Hayes-McCoy, Scots Mercenary Forces in Ireland (1565–1603) (1937) at 149–152.
79 I Grimble, Chief of Mackay (1965), especially ch 2; RSS, vol 1, no 2286.
80 Sir R Gordon, Earldom of Sutherland (1813), 304–205. Sir Robert (at 306) calls Donald's son Aodh (d 1572) likewise a bastard.
81 See A MacKenzie, History of the MacKenzies (1894).
82 History (n 60) at 68. According to MacLeod tradition, however, Alexander became a humpback as the result of a sword-wound received in battle: MacLeod, MacLeods (n 58) at 70; Grant, MacLeods (n 58) at 53.

MacLean of Duart (d 1523), another chief for whom letters of legitimation were sought and obtained from the Crown, attempted a more final repudiation of his wife Elizabeth Campbell, when he exposed her on a tidal rock, still known as Lady's Rock, between Lismore and Mull. The lady was saved and Lachlan was killed in revenge.[83]

Just as Irish tradition ascribed the end of the kingdom of Ireland to the polygamous habits of Ruairi O'Connor, so too, and with considerably more justification, did later Highland tradition ascribe the end of the MacLeods of Lewis to the polygamous habits of their sixteenth-century chief, Ruairi. The story has been often told and needs no lengthy repetition.[84] Ruairi repudiated his first wife, Janet MacKenzie, and disowned her son Torquil Conanach, claiming that he was the result of an adulterous liaison with the Morrison brieve of Lewis. It would appear that Janet later married MacLeod of Raasay. Ruairi recognised the son of his second marriage, another Torquil, as his heir, but he predeceased his father. By a third marriage Ruairi had two more sons, Torquil Dubh and Tormod, whom he wished to succeed him. Torquil Conanach, however, with the aid of his mother's kin, the MacKenzies, maintained that he was the true heir. Five further bastard sons of Ruairi took one side or the other in the ensuing dispute. Brother eliminated brother, and uncle nephew. The power of the MacLeods was destroyed and the way open for the "Fife Adventurers" and the MacKenzie takeover of Lewis.

One account indicates that the old marriage customs lingered in Lewis into the seventeenth century. In 1610, according to *The Genealogy of the MacRas*, Kenneth MacKenzie, Lord Kintail, brought the Reverend Farquhar MacRae to Lewis,

> where he preached the Gospel to the inhabitants, who were great strangers to it for many years before, as is evident from his having to baptize all under forty years of age, which he did, and married a vast number who lived there together, as man and wife, thereby to legitimate their children, and to abolish the barbarous custom that prevailed, of putting away their wives upon the least discord.[85]

When all these examples – and there are others which have not been referred to – are set against the Irish background, one cannot doubt that Celtic secular marriage survived late in Gaelic Scotland as in Gaelic Ireland. Admittedly, many of the traditional accounts, such as the Sleat history and

---

83 Gregory, *Western Highlands* (n 2) at 127–128; *RSS*, vol 1, no 68 (letter of legitimation, 3 Oct 1496).
84 See Grant, *MacLeods* (n 58) at 127–130, 188–207.
85 *Highland Papers I* (n 60) at 226. I am grateful to Dr John Bannerman for this reference.

the Book of Clanranald, are strongly biased in favour of the family for whom they were written and seek to discredit rival branches. The Sleat history is not slow to stigmatise most rival branches of the Clan Donald as being of uncanonical descent. However, neither the Sleat nor the Clanranald accounts try very hard to conceal the irregular descent of their own branch. The Sleat historian rather lamely defends the legitimacy of Hugh MacDonald (Uisdean, Austin), the founder of the house of Sleat. Other MacDonald families, he says, deny the pre-eminence to Sleat "pretending that he [Hugh] was of natural descent whereas almost all of themselves have doubled or tripled that kind of generation, before or after the birth of Austin". "Besides," he continues disingenuously, "every person must grant that by the law of nature of two brothers illegitimately begotten the eldest should have pre-eminence over the younger."[86] Again, it might be argued that some of the feuding between uncle and nephew, and between brother and brother, may reflect a survival of succession by tanistry. If this is so it merely strengthens the argument for the late survival of Celtic law.

Two final and conclusive examples of the survival of Celtic secular marriage may be given: the alliances of Ruairi Macneil of Barra (Ruairi an Tartair) and of Ranald MacDonald of Benbecula (Raonull Mor). Both these men lived in the Outer Hebrides, well out of reach of central authority. Both lived into the seventeenth century. An account of Barra, thought to be contemporary and to date to around 1630 has been preserved in *MacFarlane's Geographical Collections*:

> The Inhabitants thereoff are verie antient Inhabitants and the Superior or Laird of Barray is called Rorie McNeill, he is sex or sevin score of years as himself did say. This ancient man in tyme of his youth being a valiant and stout man of warr ... This McNeill had severall Noblemens daughters and had sundrie bairns, and at last everie one of them thinking and esteeming himself to be worthie of the Countrie after the fathers deceass being on lyff as yet. the saids sons having sundrie mothers, at last everie one of them did kill others except one that is alyff and another drowned in the sea.[87]

Some memory of the marital exploits of Ruairi MacNeil has survived in oral tradition to the present day. Mrs Marion Somerville (née MacNeil), Ardveenish, Barra, tells me she heard that the "Weaver's Castle" on the Stack Islands between Eriskay and Barra was built by Ruairi for one of his

---

86 *History* (n 60) at 64; text accompanying nn 57–58 above.
87 W MacFarlane, *Geographical Collections* (SHS, 1906–1908), vol 2, at 179–180. For a review of the evidence for Ruairi's wives and sons and the succession dispute in Barra see J L Campbell, "The MacNeils of Barra and the Irish Francisans" (1954) 5 *Innes Review* 33.

ladyloves, the stones being carried up in panniers on the back of a white mare.[88]

Of Ranald Mor of Benbecula, who died in 1636, the Book of Clanranald records:

> Ranald, son of Allan, a good man according to the times in which he lived; he was hospitable and generous, thrifty and friendly. He took unto him as his first wife the daughter of Ranald, son of James, i.e., Tanist of South Oirear, and she bore him a good son, Angus Mor, son of Ranald. He put her away, and she was afterwards married to Coll Mac Gillespie. She was the mother of the Clann Coll, namely, Gillespie, Ranald and Alaster, and a good family of daughters, who were married to good gentlemen. Ranald, son of Allan, after having put away the daughter of Ranald, took Fionnsgoth Burke, a lady of the Burkes of the Province of Connaught, in the County of Mayo, and she bore three sons for him, namely Alexander, Rory, and Farquhar. He put away Fionnsgoth, and married Margaret, the daughter of Norman Macleod of Harris, the wife whom Norman Og Macleod of Lewis had.[89] She bore a family to the son of Allan, namely, Allan Og, son of Ranald. That good wife died from him. After her he took Mary, the daughter of Gillespie of Medhe Connaill[90] and she bore a son to him, namely, Donald Gorm, son of Ranald, and he put her away. After all these he married Margaret, the daughter of Angus, son of James, and her issue were made heirs of Benbecula and of Ardnish. She bore him a good family, namely Ranald Og, the heir, and John Og, Angus, Ranald, and Rory.[91]

This account thus credits Ranald with ten sons by five wives, three of whom he put away. One is reminded of the six wives of the second earl of Clanrickard.[92] For once, however, there is official confirmation of Ranald's matrimonial activities and a cross-reference on Gaelic tradition. On 5 October 1633, criminal letters were raised by Archibald, Lord Lorne, heritable justiciar of Argyll and the Isles, against "Rannald Mcallen VcEan alias Mcrannald of Castle Vorreiff", i.e. Ranald son of Allan son of John alias MacRanald of Castle Borve – Ranald MacDonald of Benbecula. The letters charge Ranald with murder and polygamy. After accusing him of poaching deer in Rhum and slaying the minister of Barra, they continue:

> Item having shakkin aff all feare of god and obedience to His Majesties Lawes he in 1603 with out any Lawful devorcement putt away [blank] nyn Rannald Vcdonald his first mareit wyiff and mareit umquhile Margaret nccleoyd sister to

---

88 For alternative stories on the building of "Weaver's Castle" see J L Campbell (ed), *Tales of Barra told by the Coddy* (1961) at 81–91.
89 The translation is at fault here: the Gaelic reads Torquil Og, rather than Tormod (Norman).
90 This should be "MacDonald".
91 *Clanranald* (n 60) at 173–175. Dr Alasdair Maclean further informs me (letter to the author dated 16 February 1977) that "the Clanranald oral traditions have a strong thread of incest" – brother and sister, and even father and daughter. See also n 38.
92 See text accompanying n 36 above.

> umquhile sir Rorie Mccleoyd of Dounvegoune. Efter quhais deceis he mareit Marie Ncconnell sister to Sir Donald McDonald of Sleatt and keepit house with her Ten yeires and thaireftir in ane most godles and Lawles manner without any Decreit of Devorcement patt the said Marie away and mareit Margaret Nc-Connell Sister[93] to Angus McConnell of Dounnavaig with quhome he keipes present companie and societie and sua at this present hour he hes thrie mareit wyiffes alive.[94]

One could hardly wish for better contemporary confirmation of the traditional Clanranald account, even if one wife has got lost in the passing. The succession to Benbecula passed to Ranald Og, the son of the fifth marriage; he was the ancestor of the later chiefs of Clanranald, and also, of the famous Flora MacDonald.

Memory of the marital exploits of Ranald of Benbecula has also survived in oral tradition to the present. Dr Alasdair Maclean, of Daliburgh, South Uist, after referring to the historical evidence about Ranald, and the fact that he was a patron of the Franciscan mission, tells me:

> Curiously enough the local tradition looks at it all in a very different light. Ranald forced the priest at gunpoint to marry him – the priest being unwilling as his "legal" wife was still alive. Having married them under threat the priest then wished them *Moran sliochd air bheagan toinisg* (much progeny of little sense). And so it was. Ragnal Mor na Corpaich (Mac-Eachen) had the job of feeding them all from wooden coggies on the floor.[95]

Ranald is also remembered in oral tradition as a persecutor of nuns. He is said to have evicted nuns from Benbecula as a result of which a curse was pronounced that no man born in Benbecula should ever be a priest.[96]

In conclusion, Skene and Gregory were correct in drawing attention to peculiar Highland marriage customs, although their misappropriation of the word "handfasting" to describe these customs was unfortunate and has confused the issue. In Scotland, as in Ireland, customs of marriage based ultimately on ancient Irish law, continued until the seventeenth century. It is convenient to refer to these customs, adopting recent Irish usage, as "Celtic secular marriage". Referring back to the beginning of this paper, these were indeed the customs to which Martin Martin refers, albeit in garbled fashion, and which were struck at by Article One of the Statutes of Iona, when it forbade "mariageis contractit for certane yeiris".

---

93 This is a misreading for "dochter".
94 J R N Macphail (ed), *Highland Papers IV* (SHS, 1934) at 225–227; and see R Black, "Colla Ciotach" (1972–4) 48 *Transactions of the Gaelic Society of Inverness* 215.
95 Letter to the author dated 16 February 1977.
96 This story appeared in *The Sunday Post* ("The curse of Benbecula", 26 September 1976).

# 4 The Lyon and the *Seanchaidh**

This paper is concerned to review the proposition that the office of Lord Lyon King of Arms to an extent subsumed the office of *seanchaidh* (sennachie) which existed under the Gaelic-speaking kings of Scots, before the advent of feudalism and the birth of heraldry. It perhaps may even be seen as a seamless continuation of one office into the other.

Sir Thomas Innes of Learney (Lord Lyon 1945–1969) propounded this thesis in print on many occasions. There is an early version of it in the first Stair Society publication of 1936, written when Innes was Albany Herald.[1] He referred to the Court of the Lord Lyon as "the most ancient judicature in Scotland" which preserved "many of the surviving elements of what appear to be the ceremonial and social code of the Celto-Pictish kingdom".[2] He continued:

> Lyon Court is in origin that of the High Sennachie of Scotland, on whom rested the duty of preserving the genealogy of the Royal line, and under the system of "tanistry", of certifying at coronations the eligibility of the candidate for inauguration as *ArdRigh Alban* (High King of Albany). That the duties were originally of a priestly nature appears from the whole ceremonial proceeding on Lyon's command. . . . In Scotland no chivalric official required to be created, for the High Sennachie, supreme judge in genealogies and family representation, remained with the glamour of a long and ancient past behind him.[3]

Sir Thomas returned to this theme many times, including in his *Scots Heraldry*,[4] and in the later editions of Frank Adam's *Clans, Septs and*

---

* This paper was first delivered to the Heraldry Society of Scotland as the St Andrew Lecture on 4 December 2011. It was left unfinished when David Sellar died, and it was put into publishable shape by Alex Maxwell Findlater. This involved reordering small bits, some rewriting and expansion, and creating the footnotes. It is hoped that David's characteristic style is not disguised, or even debased, by this. The first publication was as "The Lyon and the Seanchaidh" (2021) 44 *The Double Tressure* 19–36. Alex Maxwell Findlater is grateful to David Sellar's wife Susan and their sons for permission for the paper to be published, and to both Elizabeth Roads, Snawdoun Herald and Professor Gillian Black for their help, and particularly to Professor Hector MacQueen for help, encouragement and attention.
1 T Innes, "Heraldic law", in *SLSL* 379.
2 Innes (n 1) at 381.
3 Innes (n 1) at 381–382, 383.
4 Sir T Innes of Learney, *Scots Heraldry* (1st edn, 1934) at 7–8; (2nd edn,1956) at 9–10; (3rd edn, edited (very lightly) by his son, Sir M Innes of Edingight, 1978) at 5.

*Regiments of the Scottish Highlands*,[5] which he edited. Not everyone has been convinced, however. Many historians have been sceptical, and some have been downright dismissive. Others simply ignore the hypothesis. It is worth noting, however, that so careful a historian as Croft Dickinson wrote,

> It is difficult to say when Lyon gained his court and jurisdiction in matters relating to [arms], together with the verification and registration of genealogies (birth brieves). It may be that, to an original genealogical jurisdiction, a jurisdiction in points of heraldry was later added in feudal times.[6]

There are two particularly interesting references in Sir Thomas's chapter in the first volume of the Stair Society: the first, a reference to a Report written in 1628 by Lyon Sir Jerome Lindsay of Annatland in response to a request from King Charles I, transmitted by the Scottish Privy Council, for information about the Scottish Coronation service;[7] and the second, the statement in a footnote that, "The earliest reference to a Scottish 'King of Arms' as such is in 1278", citing Joseph Edmondson's *Complete Body of Heraldry* published in two large folio volumes in London in 1780.[8] I shall come back to these two references later.

What is the basis of the proposition that Lyon is in some sense the successor of the *seanchaidh* of the early kings of Scots? The most important source is a description of the inauguration of the boy king Alexander III at Scone in 1249 given in Book XLVIII of the *Gesta Annalia* or "Annals", often attached in manuscripts to the main text of *Johannis de Fordun Chronica Gentis Scotorum*, or John of Fordun's History.[9] Fordun was at work on his History in the third quarter of the fourteenth century.

Book XLVIII describes how Malcolm, earl of Fife, Malise, earl of Strathearn, and other nobles led Alexander to the cross by the graveyard at the east end of the Church of Scone. The account continues (in translation):

> There they set him on the royal throne, which was decked with silken cloths inwoven with gold; and the Bishop of St Andrews, assisted by the rest, consecrated him king as was meet. So the king sat down upon the royal throne – that

---

5 F Adam, *Clans Septs and Regiments of The Scottish Highlands*, edited by Innes for the 3rd and 4th editions of 1965 and 1970 respectively. See also n 26 below.
6 W C Dickinson, "Courts of special jurisdiction", in *ISLH* 396 at 397.
7 Innes (n 1) at 382 (citing *Register of the Privy Council*, second series (8 vols, 1899–1908) vol 2, at 393ff).
8 Innes (n 1) at 383, n 5 (and further below text accompanying n 59).
9 *Chron Fordun*, vol 1, at 254–383 (in Latin); vol 2, at 249–372 (in English translation by F J H Skene). This is the only full printed text of *Gesta Annalia*. Note however the edition of the genealogy of Alexander III in D Broun, *The Irish Identity of the Kingdom of the Scots* (1999) at 183–187.

is, the stone – while the earls and other nobles, on bended knee, strewed their garments under his feet, before the stone. But, lo! When all was over, a highland Scot (*quidam Scotus montanus*) suddenly fell on his knees before the throne, and, bowing his head, hailed the king in his mother tongue, saying these words in Scottish (Gaelic) 'Benach de Re Albanne [Blessings of God King of Albany] Alexander, MacAlexander, MacVleyham, MacHenri, MacDavid' and, reciting it thus, he read off, even unto the end, the pedigree of the kings of Scots. [*The text then gives the full pedigree, only in Latin.*][10]

The next source is the account of the same event given by Walter Bower in his *Scotichronicon*, written between 1440 and 1447. The *Scotichronicon* has been edited to the highest academic standards in nine volumes (1989–98) by a team of scholars under the guiding hand of the late Professor Donald Watt. The account of the inauguration there is heavily based on *Gesta Annalia*, although somewhat elaborated and embroidered. This is what Bower says about the Highland Scot, again in translation:

> ... there suddenly appeared a venerable, grey-haired figure, an elderly Scot (*quidam Scotus venerabilis*). Though a wild highlander (*silvester et montanus*), he was honourably attired after his own fashion, clad in a scarlet robe. Bending his knee, in a scrupulously correct manner and inclining his head, he greeted the king in his mother tongue, saying courteously: "God bless the king of Albany, Alexander mac Alexander, mac William, mac Henry, mac David." And so reciting the genealogy of the kings of Scots he kept on to the end ... .[11]

This genealogy conforms to the style and form of medieval Irish manuscript genealogies, the form of which changed little over many centuries, with this being a particularly fine example.[12] For a comparison, the famous MS 1467,[13] named after its date of 1467, so some 200 years later than the inauguration of Alexander III, is in an almost identical format. The recto is

---

10  *Chron Fordun*, vol 1, at 294 (*Gesta Annalia* Latin); vol 4, at 290 (English translation).
11  S Taylor and D E R Watt with B Scott (eds), Scotichronicon by Walter Bower volume 5 (1990) at 292–295. [Editorial comment: The whole phrase is "*et quidam Scotus venerabilis caniciei senex quamvis silvester et montanus honeste tamen pro modulo suo indutus et pallio scarletico coopertus morose satis genuflectens materna lingua regem inclinato capite salutavit huiusmodi verbis satis curialiter dicens: Benach de re Albane . . .*" The translation in the Watt edition breaks up the description at the word '*senex*' (old man), while in the original all that follows is in apposition to '*senex*'. The *seanchaidh* has high status clothing; the illustration below shows that he wore a sword and elegant shoes. Alex Maxwell Findlater's translation would be: "and a notable venerable Scot, an old man with white hair, if you like a countryman from the highlands, nobly attired for his part in the ceremony, covered in a scarlet cloak (*pallium*), bending his knee with appropriate care, hailed the king in his mother tongue with his head bowed, saying with words in a manner appropriate and courtly: 'May God bless you, king of Albany . . .'". This significantly improves the apparent standing of the *seanchaidh*.]
12  Broun, *Irish Identity* (n 10) at 189, argues that "the royal genealogy would, in particular, have proclaimed the Scottish king's descent from the kings of Ireland in the deep past."
13  NLS, Adv MS 72.1.1.

displayed in an appreciation of W F Skene by the author to mark the 110th anniversary of Skene's death.[14] As an example, the MacLean pedigree, as given in MS1467, is shown below:[15]

| *Original* | *Translation* |
|---|---|
| [do] genilach cl[oinn]i gil[l]eai[n] .i. | Of the genealogy of the MacLeans i.e. |
| laclai[n] mac eoin mhic kll[e]c[olaim] | Lachlan son of John son of Gille Colaim, |
| mhic maeil is[o]g mhic g[ill]e[ain] | son of Mael Íoság son of Gilleain, |
| mhic mhic raith mhic suthain | son of Mac Raith son of Suthain, |
| mhic neill mhic con duiligh .i. | son of Niall son of Cú Duiligh i.e. |
| ab lesa mor sanabi | abbot of Lismore, formerly abbot of Iona, |
| mhic raing r[uaidh?] mhic s | son of [red-haired?] Francis son of |
| an dubg[aill] a lis | old Dugald from Lismore, |
| mhic fh[erchair] abhr[adruaidh] | son of Fearchar of the red eyebrows, |
| mhic feradhaigh, mhic [Fergus] | son of Fearadhach son of [Fergus], |
| mhic nechtain mhic colm[ain] | son of Neachtán son of Colmán, |
| mhic leat ain.i. | son of Leathan i.e. |
| mhic morgainn mhic dom[hnaill] | son of Morgann son of Donald, |
| mhic cathmhael mhic ruaid[hri] | son of Cathmhael son of Ruairi, |
| mhic [ ]rullaigh mhic cgac | son of Fergus the Proud, son of Eochaidh. |

There is a famous, contemporary, illustration of the event at Scone in one of the manuscripts of Bower (Corpus Christi College, Cambridge, MS 171 fo 206).

It is now generally accepted that the scene shown on the medieval seal of the abbey of Scone (Court of the Lord Lyon, cast) is also a pictorial representation of the inauguration of Alexander III: the boy king flanked by the earls of Fife and Strathearn, on the left an ecclesiastic with a reliquary or perhaps a gospel book, and on the right the *seanchaidh* reading the genealogy from a roll of parchment.

There was, for a while, a lively debate about the date of the Scone seal which focussed to some extent on the heraldry of the three shields depicted at its foot. Professor Duncan argued in the 1970s that the shields were those of, in the middle, the king of Scots, to the dexter the earl of Fife and to the sinister the earl of Strathearn.[16] Professor Barrow, however, was not convinced. In 1997 he suggested that the seal might depict, not the inaugura-

---

14 W D H Sellar, "William Forbes Skene (1809–92): historian of Celtic Scotland" (2001) 131 *Proceedings of the Society of Antiquaries of Scotland* 3, at 10.
15 R Black, "1467 MS: The MacLeans" (2013) 22 (series 3) *West Highland Notes & Queries* 3, at 5–6.
16 A A M Duncan, *Scotland: The Making of the Kingdom* (1975) at 554–556.

tion of Alexander III in 1249, but rather that of John Balliol in 1292.[17] The main reason for suggesting the later date was that he took the paly shield to dexter to be that of the earl of Athol rather than the earl of Fife. In ripostes published in 2002 and 2003 Professor Duncan countered Barrow's arguments and reiterated his earlier view that the paly shield was that of the earl of Fife.[18]

Neither Barrow nor Duncan seem to have been aware of a seminal article, *Double Coats at the Dawn of Scottish Heraldry* by Sir Iain Moncreiffe of that Ilk, given as the St Andrew Lecture of the Heraldry Society of Scotland in 1977.[19] Charles, Prince of Schwarzenberg, a distinguished Continental heraldist, had drawn Sir Iain's attention to the existence at the dawn of heraldry:

> of a number of cases of two separate coats of arms being borne simultaneously by the same noble. Where they appear, the one has a device such as an eagle or a lion, the other is a geometrical pattern or "ordinary"; and usually the tinctures are the same in each.[20]

Sir Iain set out to investigate the position in Scotland and found much evidence to support the theory. In particular, he suggested that the early earls of Fife had used two coats: "the one a lion Gules, the other paly of six, presumably of the same colours." "Both coats", he continued, "appear on their seals in the thirteenth century."[21] The Fife paly coat, Moncreiffe believed, was "differenced" later by changing the colours from Or and Gules to Or and Sable for their cadets, the earls of Atholl.[22]

Bruce McAndrew, who was, of course, aware of Sir Iain's article, has since demonstrated the use of a paly coat Or and Gules, by the thirteenth-century earls of Fife.[23] As a complementary survival, the first evidence for use of a lion rampant by an earl of Atholl was by John, earl of Atholl (d 1307), where

---

17 G W S Barrow, "Observations on the coronation stone of Scotland" (1997) 76 *SHR* 115.
18 A A M Duncan, *The Kingship of the Scots 842–1292* (2002), ch 7 ("*Creacio regis*: making a king"), esp at 136ff; A A M Duncan, "Before the coronation: making a king at Scone in the 13th century", in R Welander, D J Breeze and T O Clancy (eds), *The Stone of Destiny: Artefact and Icon* (2003) 139.
19 Sir I Moncreiffe of that Ilk, "Double coats at the dawn of Scottish heraldry", first published in *The Armorial*, and later published in (1977/78) 1 *Journal of the Heraldry Society of Scotland* (normally known as the Jubilee Edition of *The Double Tressure*) 57. The article is also published in a posthumous collection of Sir Iain's papers: H Montgomery-Massingberd (ed), *Lord of the Dance: A Moncreiffe Miscellany* (1986) 160, and this is the version cited below.
20 Moncreiffe of that Ilk (n 19) at 160.
21 Moncreiffe of that Ilk (n 19) at 162.
22 Moncreiffe of that Ilk (n 19) at 162.
23 B McAndrew, *Scotland's Historic Heraldry* (2006) at 38–39.

**Figure 4.1** Inauguration of Alexander III, from Bower's Scotichronicon, courtesy of the Master and Fellows of Corpus Christi College, Cambridge

**Figure 4.2** Seal of Scone Abbey around 1250, showing the inauguration of Alexander III, courtesy of Lord Lyon King of Arms/Crown Copyright: RCAHMS

both above and below the shield there is a lion passant guardant.[24] Barrow's argument for a date after 1292 then falls; and it seems likely that the Scone seal does indeed represent the inauguration of Alexander III, being created not long after the event.

Having considered the debate on the arms depicted on the Scone Abbey seal, we can be sure that the king is flanked by two earls, Fife and Strathearn, as depicted by their arms in the base of the seal. On either side of the enthroned boy king are two clerics, the bishop of St Andrews and the abbot of Scone, flanked by the two earls; behind are two figures, the bishop of Dunkeld with a portable house-shrine, and the other the *seanchaidh* holding the roll from which he reads the pedigree of the king. By the *seanchaidh* we

---

24 W R MacDonald, *Scottish Armorial Seals* (1904) seal no 2729; see also J H Stevenson and M Wood, *Scottish Heraldic Seals* (3 vols, 1940), vol 3, at 625.

see another figure, identified by the late John Bannerman as the harpist.[25] That the *seanchaidh* is shown on the seal tells for the importance of his role in the inauguration, while the fact that this is the last appearance of the *seanchaidh* known to us argues strongly for the dating of the seal to be close to the 1249 inauguration. It is thus a third, near-contemporaneous source for what happened at the inauguration.

With the accounts of the inauguration of Alexander III in both the *Gesta Annalia* and Bower's *Scotichronicon* we should compare the description of the inauguration of the MacDonald Lords of the Isles ascribed to "Hugh [or Uisdean] MacDonald" writing towards the end of the seventeenth century, some 200 years after the fall of the Lordship:

> The Ceremony of proclaiming the Lord of the Isles. At this the Bishop of the Isles and seven priests were sometimes present; but a bishop was always present, with the chieftains of all the principal families, and a *Ruler of the Isles*. There was a square stone, seven or eight feet long, and the tract of a man's foot cut thereon, upon which he stood, denoting that he should walk in the footsteps of his predecessors, and that he was installed by right in his possessions. He was clothed in a white habit, to shew his innocence and integrity of heart, that he would be a light to his people, and maintain the true religion. *The white apparel did afterwards belong to the poet by right. Then he was to receive a white rod in his hand, intimating that he had power to rule* . . .[26]

Note particularly these last two sentences in italics. The poet was MacVurich, also genealogist and historian – *seanchaidh* if you like – to the Lord of the Isles. Lachlan MacVurich, styled *archipoeta*, was a witness as *Lacclanno Mac Muredhzaich archipoeta* to an island charter in 1485.[27] Martin Martin's well-known *Description of the Western Isles of Scotland*,[28] written even later, preserves some memory of the same event when he writes, in the chapter on custom, of, "the orator [*who*] pronounc'd a Rhetorical Panegyrick, setting forth the ancient Pedigree, Valour, and Liberality of the Family," and in the note on Finlaggan, the seat of the Lords of the Isles, of "the orator [*who*] rehears'd a catalogue of his Ancestors, etc,".

"Hugh MacDonald's" description of the inauguration of the Lords of the Isles has had a very wide circulation. It was printed as Appendix IX in the

---

25 J Bannerman, "The king's poet and the inauguration of Alexander III" (1989) 68 *SHR* 120 at 134 (also in J W M Bannerman, *Kinship, Church and Culture: Collected Essays and Studies* (2016) section 2 ch 4, at 266).
26 F Adam, *Clans, Septs and Regiments of the Scottish Highlands* (1908) appendix IX. The appendix remains in the later editions of the book edited by Sir T Innes.
27 J and R W Munro (eds), *Acts of the Lords of the Isles 1336–1493* (SHS, 1986) at 188.
28 Martin Martin, *Description of the Western Islands of Scotland* (1703, 2nd edn 1716, reproduced in facsimile 1970) at 102, 241.

very first 1908 edition of Frank Adam's popular and influential *Clans, Septs and Regiments of the Scottish Highlands*. Elizabeth FitzPatrick, an Irish student of royal inaugurations in Scotland and Ireland, has referred to it as "the fullest surviving account of a Scottish ceremony (of inauguration)", and draws parallels between it and inauguration ceremonies in Gaelic Ireland.[29] The role of the *seanchaidh* is also referred to memorably in the *History of the Campbells of Craignish*, written about 1720, where we read that,

> It is well known to any who have the least smattering of the old Scottish affairs that every considerable family in the Highland had their Bards and Shenachies . . . their work was to hand down to posterity the valorous actions, Conquests, batles, skirmishes, marriages and relations of the predicessors by repeating and singing the same at births, baptisms, marriages, feasts and funeralls, so that no people, since the Curse of the Almighty dissipated the Jews, took such care to keep their Tribes, Cadets and branches so well and so distinctly separate.[30]

Sir Thomas Innes was, of course, also familiar with, and much influenced by William Forbes Skene's great late nineteenth-century work, *Celtic Scotland*. There is surprisingly little about the inauguration of Alexander III in Skene's book, and what there is, to my mind, reads rather oddly:

> The boy king then received the homage of the feudal baronage of the kingdom, and a strange ceremony followed, probably now for the first time, and intended to mark the cordial acceptance of the king by the entire Gaelic population of Scotland as the heir and inheritor of a long line of traditionary monarchs. A Highland sennachy advanced, and, kneeling before the fatal stone, hailed him as the "Ri Alban", and repeated his pedigree according to Highland tradition through a long line of Gaelic kings, partly real and partly mythic, till he reached Gaithal Glas, the "eponymus" of the race.[31]

However, in 1869 Skene had discussed the inauguration at greater length in his earlier publication on the Stone of Scone where he set out parallel texts from Fordun and Bower. Skene did not realise that the *Gesta Annalia* were not intrinsic to Fordun, as will be discussed further below. The first thing that caught my eye there was Skene's translation of the key phrase *quidam Scotus montanus* ("a certain Highland Scot") as "a certain Scotch mountaineer". But on reflection, this just shows how words can change their meaning. Skene continued:

---

29 E FitzPatrick, *Royal Inauguration in Gaelic Ireland c1100–1600* (2004), at 7. [Editorial comment: See also K Simms, *Gaelic Ulster in the Middle Ages: History, Culture and Society* (2020), index sv "inauguration of Irish kings, sites, ceremonies".]
30 H Campbell (ed), "The manuscript history of Craignish by Alexander Campbell", in *Miscellany IV* (SHS, 1926) 175 at 190.
31 W F Skene, *Celtic Scotland*, 3 vols (2nd edn, 1886), vol 1, at 490.

Fordun's description is so graphic we can almost depict the scene. A Scottish July day; the cross in the cimiterium; before it the fatal stone, covered with gold-embroidered clothes; upon it the boy king; at his side the two Bishops and the Abbot of Scone; before him the barons of Scotland kneeling before the ancient symbol of Scottish sovereignty; the eager Highland *Sennachy* pressing forward to utter his barbarous Celtic gutturals . . .[32]

Having considered the sources, I should like now to review Sir Thomas' hypothesis in the light of scholarship over the last forty years or so. An important point is that there has been a significant re-dating of the passage in *Gesta Annalia* formerly attributed to Fordun. Until recently it was thought that the *Gesta Annalia* were written in or after 1371 by Fordun himself, that is, over 120 years after Alexander's inauguration. More recently Professor Dauvit Broun has shown that the *Gesta Annalia* was a separate document from Fordun's history, in fact two documents. The first is the original up to February 1285, finished before April 1285 (GA I), with the second being a continuation from October 1285 to 1363 (GA II).[33] Thus the section of the *Gesta Annalia* which describes the inauguration of Alexander III, which is part of GA I, is not contemporary with Fordun, but must have been written no later than Easter 1285, that is, less than forty years after the events which it describes. It is thus also closely contemporaneous with the depiction of the inauguration on the Scone seal discussed earlier.

One of the results of the great renaissance in Scottish historical writing pioneered by Professors Barrow and Duncan has been the realisation that, contrary to the earlier prevailing view that nothing of any significance survived from the earlier Celtic kingdom into feudal Scotland and beyond, it is now clear that a great deal did survive. So much so, that Professor Dauvit Broun has written a book on *The Irish Identity of the Kingdom of the Scots* in the twelfth and thirteenth centuries.[34] At the same time there has also been a renaissance in Irish historical writing, especially about the history of Gaelic Ireland, which has made it easier to recognise and point to parallels between Gaelic Scotland and Gaelic Ireland. A seminal work here has been Kenneth Nicholls' *Gaelic and Gaelicised Ireland in the Middle Ages*.[35]

Among those who have drawn attention to survivals from the Gaelic past well into feudal times and beyond are Professor Derick Thomson on the

---

32 W F Skene, *The Coronation Stone* (1869) at 9 (finishing with an astonishing sentiment from the author of *Celtic Scotland*).
33 D Broun, *Scottish Independence and the Idea of Britain, from the Picts to Alexander III* (2007) at 175; and see further on the *Gesta Annalia* at 216–229.
34 Above, n 9.
35 K Nicholls, *Gaelic and Gaelicised Ireland in the Middle Ages* (1973).

hereditary learned orders of Gaelic society,[36] drawing on Irish parallels; and John Bannerman on the dynasty of Beaton[37] (alias MacBeth) physicians as well as (as we have already seen) on the king's poet. Professor Geoffrey Barrow charted the survival of the judge in Gaelic society – known as *breitheamh* in Gaelic, *brieve* or *brehon* in English, and *iudex* in Latin – and his integration into the new feudal framework in Scotland.[38]

It is also now recognised that some legal terms of art from Celtic law survived in Scots law right through the feudal period and beyond. One example is the term *culrath* ("back security") which described a caution or cautioner and was used in the cardinal procedure of repledging a suspect from one court to another as late as the eighteenth century.[39] An even more remarkable example of survival comes from the action of assythment, or compensation for slaughter, with its accompanying letter of *slains*, another technical term from Celtic law, by which the kin of the dead man accepted compensation from the kin of the slayer and remitted their rancour against him. The action of assythment was originally used to help settle a blood feud; it survived in Scots law, astonishingly, until the 1970s when it was abolished after a belated attempt at revival which reached the House of Lords.[40] The etymology of the word *slains* as in letters of slains, surprisingly, has nothing at all do with the English words "slay" or "slain", but is cognate with one of the few Gaelic words which everyone knows: *slan* or *slainte*, signifying a salutation of health. Monarchy, the mainstay of Gaelic society, of course, has continued, merging into the pan-European concept.[41]

I turn now to the article by John Bannerman to which reference has already been made in connection with the king's harpist.[42] In that article Bannerman mainly considers the evidence for the existence of the office of king's poet (in Gaelic *OllamhRi*) in Scotland in the twelfth and thirteenth centuries. The word *ollamh* in both Scotland and Ireland denoted a leading member of the professional classes, a doctor, for example, or a lawyer, or a historian, or a poet, such as "a learned doctor"; "a Doctor of the Church". Bannerman writes that

---

36  D S Thomson, "Gaelic learned orders and literati in medieval Scotland" (1968) 12 *Scottish Studies* 57.
37  J Bannerman, *The Beatons: A Medical Kindred in the Classical Gaelic Tradition* (1986).
38  G W S Barrow, *The Kingdom of the Scots* (2nd edn, 2003) ch 2.
39  See ch 2 text accompanying nn 105–111.
40  *M'Kendrick v Sinclair* 1972 SC (HL) 25; see ch 2 above, text accompanying nn 73–74. Assythment was abolished by s 8 of the Damages (Scotland) Act 1976.
41  Chapter 2 above, text accompanying n 21.
42  Bannerman (n 25).

One of the duties of the *ollamh*, as will become clear, was to maintain his master's pedigree and produce it when required, and the poet to the king of Scots comes most clearly into view at the inauguration of Alexander III at Scone on 13th July 1249.[43]

In Bannerman's view then, the *"seanchaidh"* who appeared at Alexander's inauguration was, in fact, the king's poet – the *ollamh*, or *ard-ollamh* (arch-poet), of the king of Scots. He argues against the use of the word *seanchaidh*, on the grounds that that word has now been degraded to a story-teller, but also quotes an *Ollamh* from 1464–66 who describes himself as *seanchaidh*, arguing that it was *qua seanchaidh* that he performed the inauguration.[44] We might see *ollamh* as a status, while the *seanchaidh* performed a role.

Bannerman argues, I believe correctly, that the phrase *"quidam Scotus montanus"* identifies the *seanchaidh* as a Gaelic speaker, and that the sword shown in the Corpus Christi illustration confirms him as a man of rank. He also comments that "the impression of rusticity . . . was further compounded by the habit of later commentators on Fordun . . . of referring to him as a *seanchaidh*".[45] Bannerman regards this, though, as "a legitimate label" especially in connection with genealogy.[46] He compares the role of the poet in 1249 with that of the poet in Ireland where, for example, the poet Ó Maol-Chonaire officiated at the inauguration of O'Connor kings. An Irish scholar, Professor Donnchadh Ó Corráin, has written that, "the royal and dynastic genealogy was the equivalent of a charter of right and was the proof of the king's title to rule."[47] Bannerman says: "only the poet is mentioned in connection with the ceremony itself."[48] He also quotes the account of the inauguration of the Lord of the Isles by "Hugh MacDonald":

> the white apparel did afterwards belong to the poet by right. Then he was to receive a white rod in his hand, intimating that he had power to rule . . . Then he received his forefather's sword.[49]

Bannerman also suggests that the rod of office was in 1249 represented by the sceptre, and that the sceptre was given to the king by the poet:

> Significantly, in a passing reference to the inauguration of Donald as lord of the Isles c. 1387, the only aspect mentioned by the seventeenth century MacMhuirich

---

43 Bannerman (n 25) at 120 (Bannerman, *Kinship* (n 25) at 252).
44 Bannerman (n 25) at 123 (Bannerman, *Kinship* (n 25) at 255).
45 Bannerman (n 25) at 122 (Bannerman, *Kinship* (n 25) at 254).
46 Bannerman (n 25) at 122 (Bannerman, *Kinship* (n 25) at 254).
47 D Ó Corráin, *Ireland before the Normans* (1972), 36.
48 Bannerman (n 25) at 123 (Bannerman, *Kinship* (n 25) at 255).
49 Bannerman (n 25) at 131 (Bannerman, *Kinship* (n 25) at 264).

poets and authors of the Red and Black Books of Clan Ranald was the presentation to Donald of *slat an tigernais*, "the staff of lordship".⁵⁰

In the main text of his article Bannerman makes no mention of the Lyon King of Arms: at one point he writes that, "the office [of poet] had almost certainly ceased to exist by the fifteenth century";⁵¹ and later that, "as far as royal inaugurations in particular are concerned, 1249 may have seen the last occasion of that kind on which [the poet's] presence was required . . ."⁵² However, in a footnote to that last quotation, Bannerman writes, it would seem as an afterthought,

> Except in so far as the Lyon King of Arms seems to have taken over his duty of reciting the royal pedigree at later coronations . . . However, the preservation of the format of the coronation ceremony seems also to have fallen to the Lyon King. Was this once a function of the king's poet? The existence of the Ó Conchobhair inauguration tract already quoted might suggest so.⁵³

Some ten years earlier Roderick Lyall compared the report compiled by Lyon Sir Jerome Lindsay of Annatland in 1628, at the request of King Charles I, on the form or *ordo* of the ancient Scottish coronation service ["*the Forme*"], with the account of the coronation of Robert II in 1371 compiled by Sir Jerome's successor as Lyon, the well-known Sir James Balfour of Denmilne.⁵⁴ There is no doubt that the two accounts are related, but there is considerable doubt as to the accuracy of Balfour's account of the coronation of Robert II. In fact, Balfour has a bad name among historians. The record scholar Maitland Thomson summed up the general opinion when he wrote that Balfour was "one of our most industrious antiquarians, but alas! also one of the least trustworthy."⁵⁵ Sir Jerome's account has, I believe, suffered unfairly, by association with Balfour. Lyall compared Lindsay's *Forme* or *ordo* with late medieval accounts of the coronation service in England and in France. He considered that the Scottish service was firmly within the western European tradition, although with some notable variations. One was the more secular nature of the Scottish ceremony, indicated by the prominence given to the Lyon King of Arms. Another variation was the

---

50 Bannerman (n 25) at 133 (Bannerman, *Kinship* (n 25) at 266).
51 Bannerman (n 25) at 122 (Bannerman, *Kinship* (n 25) at 254).
52 Bannerman (n 25) at 137 (Bannerman, *Kinship* (n 25) at 270).
53 Bannerman (n 25) at 137 n 6 (Bannerman, *Kinship* (n 25) at 270 n 103).
54 R J Lyall, "The medieval Scottish coronation service: some seventeenth-century evidence" (1977) 28 *Innes Review* 3. The report by Lindsay of Annatland is the first of the references by Sir T Innes of Learney mentioned above, note 7. The other main source used by Lyall is Sir James Balfour of Denmilne, *Ancient Heraldic and Antiquarian Tracts* (1837) at 36ff.
55 J M Thomson, *The Public Records of Scotland* (1922) at 139.

introduction of the recitation by the Lyon King of Arms of "sax generations of the king's descent". This, of course, brings to mind the ceremony in 1249, and also Martin Martin's account of the "orator" reciting a catalogue of the royal ancestors.[56] Lyall's article has been largely ignored by historians, but it seems to me that Sir Jerome's account merits further research.

In his 2009 St Andrew Lecture to the Heraldry Society of Scotland, Adrian Ailes pointed to some early references to the office of Lyon King of Arms which he had found in the English records.[57] Previously it had been thought that the first reference to the office was in the reign of Robert II, and that the first named Lyon on record was Henry Grieve in 1399. Ailes had found another reference to Henry "Greve", as King of Heralds of the Scots, in 1401, and a reference to the puzzling name "Average, Rex Heraldus de Scotia" in 1367, that is, in David II's reign. But he had also found much earlier references to a James or Jack Caupeny or Capigny. Ailes first finds him in 1290 as King Caupeny of Scotland when "he came" to King Edward I; also at the marriage of Edward I's daughter the same year, perhaps on the same occasion. In 1306 Caupeny was paid by the English Exchequer as *rex heraldorum*, and in the following year as *"Rex Haraldorum de Scocia"*. Ailes speculated that he might previously have been a herald to Alexander III and John Balliol.[58]

Now we come back to the second reference given by Sir Thomas Innes, quoting Edmondson's *Complete Body of Heraldry* of 1780.[59] I consulted Edmondson and was astounded to find that the 1278 entry, again from the English household accounts, was an even earlier reference to Caupeny as *regi Caupeny de Scotia*, in the company of four other Kings of Heralds, one of whom was from France.[60] Now we see that Caupeny is on record

56 See above, text accompanying n 28.
57 A Ailes, "Scots heralds and heraldry in The National Archives (UK)" (2010) 33 *The Double Tressure* 2, at 8–11.
58 Ailes (n 57) at 10–11.
59 J Edmondson, *Complete Body of Heraldry* (1780), vol 1, at 92b. The full quotation is:

Comp hospitii 6 Ewd I in the Tower records
– Hertolino regi heraudorum,
– regi Grey Hunel qui est rex Heraldorum in partibus Franciae
– regi Caupeny de Scotia
– duobus regibus heraldorum, [whose names were presumably forgotten]

60 [Editorial comment: After some discussion with Ronald Black and William Gillies, for which many thanks, it is clear that Caupeny is most unlikely to be derived from a Gaelic word. However, Coupigny is the name of two places, one in the Pas de Calais, the other in the Calvados. It is conceivable that this king of arms was from one of these or descended from a family originating there.]

from 1278 to 1306, so for almost 30 years. Moreover, the gap of about 120 years once thought to exist between King Alexander's inauguration in 1249 and the account once attributed to Fordun has shrunk to less than 30 years. It is worth noting further that in 1278 Alexander III was still on the throne. The last reference to a *seanchaidh* or *ollamh* in relation to the king of Scots in Scottish records seems to be the 1249 ceremony of inauguration of Alexander III. Hard on the heels of this comes the "king of heralds", the first known record being of Caupeny, King [of Heralds] of Scotland, in 1278.

Finally, one aspect of the ceremony of inauguration has attracted little attention, in Scotland at least: the white rod. The significance of the white rod does not seem to have been realised by Scottish historians. Remember the quotation from "Hugh MacDonald":

> The white apparel did afterwards belong to the poet by right. Then he was to receive a white rod in his hand, intimating that he had power to rule . . .[61]

Then there is the account of the deposition of John Balliol when he was compelled to surrender the kingdom of Scotland to Edward I in 1296 in a humiliating ceremony which earned Balliol the name of *Toom Tabard*. Ailes wrote that when in 1296 Edward I stripped Balliol of arms, "It is quite probable that he now stripped the Scots king of his own herald", noting that this "deserves more research".[62] The *Gesta Annalia* narrate that in 1296,

> King John, stripped of his kingly ornaments, and holding a white rod (*virga alba*) in his hand, surrendered up with staff and baton, and resigned into the hands of the King of England, all right which he himself had, or might have, to the kingdom of Scotland.[63]

This white rod is well known in Ireland where it was recognised as the "rod of kingship" or the "rod of lordship" – the *slat an tighernais*. This corresponds to the proposal of Bannerman already mentioned, that the rod is the sceptre.[64] It is surely also the origin of the White Rod in the medieval Scottish Parliament, the symbol of the right to exercise power; however, the White Rod was latterly carried by the Usher of Parliament, so was by then much modified from its early significance.[65]

I shall sum up briefly, by suggesting that research over the last forty years or so has greatly strengthened the case for seeing in Lyon King of Arms a

---

61 Text accompanying n 49 above.
62 Ailes (n 57) at 11.
63 *Chron Fordun*, vol 1, at 327 (Latin); vol 2, at 320 (English translation).
64 See above text accompanying n 50.
65 *SME*, vol 7 (1995) "The Crown", para 829.

successor to the *seanchaidh* of the early kings of Scots or, as we should now say, the *OllamhRi* or king's poet. In 1936 Sir Thomas Innes was a lone, and possibly disregarded, forerunner of much modern scholarship, with more evidence still to be uncovered. Research since 1970, especially the work of John Bannerman, demonstrates that there was real substance in the small material with which Innes had to work. The paper which he wrote in 1936 seems to have been worked in at the very end of the first Stair Society volume as an after-thought, and almost appears wishful thinking; but now the weight of evidence and our greater understanding of the Gaelic world, particularly informed by work from Ireland, has brought us to a closer understanding of the ancient culture of ritual and ceremony in thirteenth-century Scotland.[66]

---

66 See further D Sellar, "Sueno's stone and its interpreters", in W D H Sellar (ed), *Moray: Province and People* (Scottish Society for Northern Studies, 1993) 97 at 106–110, for the suggestion that the panel at the base of the Stone's western face has many similarities to the Scone seal (above, text accompanying nn 16–25) and may represent the inauguration ceremony of Kenneth mac Alpin as king of Scots after the final defeat and overthrow of the Pictish monarchy.

# 5 Birlaw Courts and Birleymen*

"Birlaw courts and birleymen" may seem an obscure title, but the birlaw was a well-known and widespread institution in Scotland for many hundreds of years.[1] It was once known in England also, although apparently not in Ireland.[2] My interest in birlaw courts was first aroused by a short appendix entitled "The Burlaw Men" in Croft Dickinson's classic 1937 study of barony courts in Scotland, *The Court Book of the Barony of Carnwath*.[3] That appendix still remains the essential starting point for anyone interested in the history of the birlaw in Scotland. In fact, apart from the occasional references, little has been written since about this long-standing institution, and the birlaw court and its history remains largely unknown even to Scottish legal historians and record scholars. This is partly no doubt because birlaw courts in Scotland have left little by way of written record of their proceedings, subject to one or two exceptions to be noted later.[4]

---

* Originally published as "Birlaw Courts and Birleymen", in P Brand, K Costello and W N Osborough (eds), *Adventures of the Law: Proceedings of the Sixteenth British Legal History Conference, Dublin, 2003* (2005) 70–87; revised version in H L MacQueen (ed), *Miscellany VII* (SS, 2015) 163–177. In writing this paper, I have acquired debts over the years to audiences in Edinburgh, Durham, Dublin and Oslo, and also to the many friends who have generously supplied me with information and references to the birlaw and to birleymen in Scotland. I trust that it does not seem invidious to single out by name Dr Athol Murray, former Keeper of the Records of Scotland, and Dr Alan Borthwick of the NRS. I am also grateful to the staff of the NRS for general assistance at a time before the existence of a computer index. My thanks too to Stefan Brink and Doreen Waugh for advice on questions of etymology. Finally I should like to record my gratitude to the Senter for Grunnforskning in Oslo for supporting the Landscape Law and Justice programme in 2002–3, and to Michael Jones of the University of Trondheim for inviting me to participate in it.
1 The variant spellings of "birlaw" and "birleymen" are legion (below, text accompanying n 16), with no agreed modern form. I have chosen to use "birlaw" and "birleymen", rather than Dickinson's "burlaw" and "burlaw men", as a matter of convenience. I also sometimes refer to "the birlaw", rather than "the birlaw court", for the reasons given below, 130.
2 I am most grateful to Fergus Kelly and Kenneth Nichols for advising me that they are not aware of references to birlaw courts or birleymen in Irish sources.
3 W C Dickinson (ed), *The Court Book of the Barony of Carnwath 1523–1542* (SHS, 1937), appendix A, "The burlaw men", at cxiii–cxvi.
4 Below, 129–133. For the position in England see below, 134–138. Since this paper was first published "birlaw" has been discussed in a wider context by A Grant, "Franchises north of the border: baronies and regalities in medieval Scotland" in M Prestwich (ed), *Liberties and Identities in Medieval Britain and Ireland* (2008) 155 at 179; and R Houston, "Custom in context: medieval and early modern Scotland and England" (2011) no 211 *Past and Present* 35 at

Dickinson notes the presence of birley men (*Birlawmen*; *berla men*; *barle men*) in the Carnwath record, all at Whitsun courts. These courts were particularly concerned with economic matters and the keeping of "good neighbourhood". The birleymen helped to enforce the "styles and statutes" of the courts and might act on occasion as arbiters in matters concerning neighbourhood. Dickinson pointed to references to the birlaw in the medieval treatise *Regiam Majestatem*, and in Sir John Skene's *De Verborum Significatione* of 1597. He gave several examples of birlaws and birleymen on the record from 1479 onwards. He noted that in the barony of Forbes in the seventeenth century birleymen were appointed for each parish, and in the burgh of Peebles for each "quarter" of the town. The system, he believed, "was an ideal one for preserving the peace of the community and for ensuring that each tenant paid a proper regard to the welfare of his neighbours."[5] He refers to the nine birleymen [Bourlawmen] appointed to the barony of Stitchill in 1655, "to desyde all matters questionable and debaitable among neybors . . .", and to the "birly men" of the barony of Forbes in 1668, concerned with the "keiping of guid nightbourheid".[6] Birleymen might be concerned with, for example, the maintenance of hedges and ditches to prevent animals from straying into the corn, disputes as to pasturage, questions as to boundaries, and the assessment of compensation.

Dickinson believed that birlaw courts had at first been independent of the barony court but were later subsumed into it. "Undoubtedly," he wrote, "burlaw courts were at first held by the tenants themselves, but before long we find the baron and his baillie choosing the birlaw men, whilst in the barony of Skene, in 1615, the burlaw court ("barla court") was presided over by the laird and the baillie."[7] He cited the record of the barony court of Stitchill as evidence that baron courts might uphold the decrees of the birlaymen, or of the birlaw court, and interpone authority to them: all tenants were to "obey the Sentences and Decreits to be pronounced be the Bourlawmen in tym cumeing and that non oppose them neither be word nor deid nor scold,

---

49, 73. On custom more generally see Sellar, "Custom"; A Perreau-Saussine (ed), *The Nature of Customary Law: Legal, Historical and Philosophical Perspectives* (2008); and D J Bederman, *Custom as a Source of Law* (2010).

5 Dickinson, *Carnwath* (n 3) at cxv.

6 Dickinson, *Carnwath* (n 3) at cxiv–cxv, citing C B Gunn (ed), *Records of the Baron Court of Stitchill* (1905) at 2, and J M Thomson (ed), "The Forbes baron court book, 1659–1678", in *Miscellany III* (SHS, 1919) 205 at 275. The editor of *Stitchill* notes that the term "stent maisters" is used elsewhere rather than birleymen.

7 Dickinson, *Carnwath* (n 3) at cxv–cxvi, n 8; "Extracts from the court books of the baronies of Skene, Leys and Whitehaugh, 1613–1687", in J Stuart (ed), *Miscellany V* (Spalding Club, Aberdeen, 1852) 215 at 218.

raille, nor outcry against ther proceedings in tym cumeing utherwyas nor be order of Law and justice under the paine of five punds and personall punishment at the Lairdis pleasure . . ."⁸ The etymology of "birlaw" suggested by Dickinson was particularly intriguing. Following the *Oxford New English Dictionary*, he wrote that "the word is probably derived from the Old Norse *býjar-lög*, that is, "law community" or "law district", and so came to mean the local law governing small townships or villages."⁹ Dickinson, however, did not suggest how the name or the institution came to Scotland.

Professor Archie Duncan, in a passage which clearly draws on Dickinson, wrote that our knowledge of the village community in medieval Scotland is "shadowy". He notes the role of the "burlaw men" in the keeping of good neighbourhood in the later medieval period, then adds these challenging comments:

> The antiquity of this institution is uncertain but the derivation of its name from Old Norse suggests that it developed between the ninth century and the twelfth. We must be chary of assuming that it arose among the peasantry rather than by the landlord's command, but nonetheless it is the nearest we shall get to a 'popular' institution in Scottish society.¹⁰

This article explores the history of the birlaw and birleymen in Scotland further, and seeks to answer a number of questions. What type of business was transacted in birlaw courts? How long did birlaw courts and birleymen continue to function? When did birlaw courts first appear in Scotland? Finally, if the etymology of "birlaw" is indeed Scandinavian, how and when did that Scandinavian influence arise?

As Dickinson noted, the first known reference to birlaw appears in the treatise *Regiam Majestatem*, now generally believed to have been compiled in the first half of the fourteenth century. The chapter *De effusione sanguinis* ("On the shedding of blood") sets out a tariff calculated in cows for the shedding of blood, according to the rank of the victim: nine cows for the shedding of blood from the head of an earl, six for the son of an earl, or for a thane, and so on down the scale:

> *Item sanguis de capite unius comitis aut filii Regis sunt novem vaccae. Item sanguis filii comitis aut unius thani sunt sex vaccae. Item de sanguine filii thani tres vaccae. Item de sanguine nepotis thani duae vaccae et duae partes unius vaccae. Item de sanguine unius rustici una vacca.*

---

8 Dickinson, *Carnwath* (n 3) at cxiv–cxvi; Gunn (n 6) at 24.
9 Dickinson, *Carnwath* (n 3) at cxiii, citing *Oxford New Law Dictionary*, sv *Burlaw*. Dictionaries generally are an invaluable source of reference on this subject: see, for example, below, 134–135.
10 A A M Duncan, *Scotland: The Making of the Kingdom* (1975) at 349–350.

The chapter then deals with blood drawn below the breath (*subtus anhelitum*), the rights of unmarried women, and a blow not causing the shedding of blood, before concluding with the sentence:

> *Cetera omnia et singular quae currunt in curiis dominorum secundum auxilium et favorem terminantur, exceptis legibus de Burlawis quae per consensum vicinorum erunt.*[11]

This may be translated as follows: "All other matters brought before lords' courts are determined in accordance with the strength and favour enjoyed by the parties excepting the laws of Burlaw which are determined by the consent of neighbours."[12]

In his English edition of *Regiam Majestatem*, published in 1609, Sir John Skene translates the same sentence as follows: "All other sundrie things, quhilk occurres in Barone courts, are determined at the discretion and will of the Lord of the court. Except Birlaw courts, the quhilkis are rewled be consent of neighbours." In his Latin edition, published in the same year, Skene glosses the sentence thus:

> Apud Germanos Baur rusticum significat & Lauch vel law <u>lex dicitur</u>, hinc Burlaw, rusticorum leges, de re rustica latae. Nos hodie Birlaw courtis, & Birlawmen, dicimus.

The chapter on the shedding of blood is one of four chapters not originally part of *Regiam Majestatem*, as noted by both Lord Cooper and Sir John Skene. These chapters constitute a tract long referred to, on grounds which are not quite clear, as *Leges inter Brettos et Scotos*, "the Laws of the Bretts and the Scots", and of which French and Scots versions also survive. It is older, perhaps much older, that the main body of *Regiam Majestatem*, although the passage on the birlaw appears to be an addition to the original core text.[13] However, even if this passage was added to the original provi-

---

11 *RM (Cooper)*, 4.39; *RM (APS)*, 4.58 (*APS*, vol 1, at 641), where the relevant clause reads *exceptis burlawis que per consensum vicinorum concurrunt*. See now *LMS* at 438–439, giving the reading *exceptis de byrlawis que per consensum uicinorum currunt*.
12 I am grateful to Paul Brand for advice on this translation which differs from that of Lord Cooper. The *LMS* translation (at 439) is "Each and all the above which run in lords' courts are determined by aid and favour, saving birlaws which proceed by the consent of neighbours."
13 The final sentence, including the reference to the birlaw, does not appear in the version of the *Leges* given in *APS*, vol 1 at 665 or in *LMS* at 430–431 from the late 13th-century Berne MS. Note, however, the editor's comment in *LMS* at 431 n 6, citing this article and adding: "There is no firm evidence, in my view, that the '*LBS*' section was not part of *Regiam*, as *Regiam* itself was unfinished, with 'book IV', in particular, showing such a range of subject matter that it is difficult to determine what would – and what would not – have been used by the original compiler. It is, however, probable that this last sentence (beginning 'Cetera omnia . . .') was added on to the

sions on the shedding of blood, it seems reasonable to conclude that the birlaw was already old and well established by the early fourteenth century.

Sir John Skene's *De Verborum Significatione* of 1597 contains this entry:

**BURLAW**, *Byrlaw*. Laws of *Burlaw* are maid, and determined be consent of nichtbors, elected and chosen be common consent, in the courtes, called the *Byrlaw* courts. In the quhilk, cognition is taken of complaints betuixt nichtbour & nichtbour ... The quhilk men sa chosen, as judges and arbitrators to the effect foresaid, are commonly called *byrlaw* men. It is an dutch word [that is, German], for *baur* or *baursman* in dutch, is *rusticus*, an husbandman. And sa *byrlaw* burlaw or baurlaw, *leges rusticorum*: Lawes maid be husbandmen, concerning nichtbour-heid to be keeped amangs themselues.

This entry tallies with Skene's gloss on the sentence in the *Regiam*. It is valuable also as giving Skene's own contemporary comment on birleymen and birlaw courts. Again there is an emphasis on neighbours, neighbourhood and common consent. Skene's etymology, echoed in his comments on *Regiam Majestatem*, is plausible enough, though not correct. His three variant spellings could be multiplied many times over.[14]

It is indicative of the poverty of the Scottish record, as compared with the English, that the first known reference to birlaw courts in practice occurs 150 years after *Regiam Majestatem*: the Coupar-Angus example of 1479 cited by Dickinson. The rental book of the Abbey of Coupar-Angus requires that a leaseholder "sal kepe gud nychtburhede ... And owkly [weekly] he and his nychtburis sal halde a byrlay courte amang thame self, for commown profit of the town [that is, of the farmtown or "township"] and correccioun of al fautis."[15] Again the emphasis is on neighbours, neighbourhood and the common weal. A few years later, from 1488–1492 inclusive, "birlawmen" are among the burgh officials appointed at the Michaelmas head court of the burgh of Dunfermline.[16] Later courts there refer to "the haill comonis", *communitatem dicti burgi*, and "the nychtbouris". Even for the sixteenth century few references survive. In addition to the examples from *Carnwath*, the Forbes rental of 1532 shows joint tenants being bound to keep good neighbourhood "at the sight of umpires called 'birleymen', chosen by

---

LBS-chapter." With respect, the last of these editorial sentences is in fact the argument of this chapter at this point.

14 Variants include birlaw, birlawe, burlaw, byrlaw, bourlaw, boorlaw, bierlaw, byerlaw, berlaw, baurlaw, birley, birla, barla and birlie; also birlaw-man, byrlaw man, birley men, berla men, barle men and barleymen! See also *OED* under "birlaw", "birlie", "bourlaw", "burley" and "byrlaw".

15 C Rogers (ed), *Rental Book of Cupar-Angus* (2 vols, 1879–80) vol 1, at 230 (see Dickinson, *Carnwath* (n 3) at cxiv).

16 E Beveridge (ed), *Burgh Records of Dunfermline* (1917) at xvii, 4, 16, 22, 30, 39.

themselves".[17] Sir James Balfour in his *Practicks*, referring to a case decided in 1552, notes of "landis lyand togidder in rin-rig" that "everie ane of thame may be compellit at the instance of ane uther, to concur in keeping of gude nichtbourheid ane with the uther, in tilling, labouring, sawing, scheiring, pastouring, and dykeing, and in all uther thingis pertening to gude and thriftie nichtbourheid".[18]

After 1600, however, references become more frequent, both in the surviving record and in non-legal sources. This is so throughout Scotland, Highland and Lowland, although Lowland examples predominate. Some further examples may be added to those given by Dickinson. In 1660 the bailie of the regality of Melrose upheld a decision of the "birlawmen" of Darnick: "The bailie absolves the Defenders, and interpones his decreit to the said condescendence and stent agreed on in the said birlaw court."[19] Dr Athol Murray has drawn my attention to a declaration made by the birlawmen of the barony of Fintry in 1685 and by those of the barony of Buchanan in 1719.[20] In Kintyre in 1672, four named "birlawmen" were appointed for each of nine parishes by "Acts of Bailyierie . . . made and sett doun be ane Noble Earle Archibald [9th] Earle of Argyll".[21] These birleymen were drawn from the local gentry, including, for example, the laird of Ralstoun, the laird of Sanda and Lachlan MacNeill of Tirfergus. The 1672 Acts followed earlier "Acts of Neighbourhood" for Kintyre, promulgated by the ninth earl's father, the marquis of Argyll, in 1653 "for better settling the condition of the countrey; and for keeping good neighbourhood . . ."[22] In Erskine's *Institute* (1773) there is a reference to the role of Birleymen in valuing or appraising the value of a debtor's goods in the execution of poinding [impounding].[23] The *Balgair Court Minutes* – the court of a landowner in Stirlingshire, but apparently not a baron court – record the laird presenting two "Birlawmen" to his court in 1709, birleymen conducting a perambulation and division of lands in 1713, and one James Whyte being fined fifty pounds Scots in 1726 by Balgair's

---

17 The reference and quotation are from C Innes, *Scotch Legal Antiquities* (1872) at 254.
18 Balfour, *Practicks*, vol 2, at 536–537. I owe this reference to R A Dodgshon, "Farming in Roxburghshire and Berwickshire on the eve of Improvement" (1975) 54 *SHR* 140 at 151.
19 C S Romanes (ed), *Records of the Regality Court of Melrose, 1547–1706* (3 vols, 1914–17) vol 1, at 311. There are further references to birlaw courts held in the Borders in the 18th century in Dodgshon (n 18).
20 NRS GD220/6/693/25 and 220/6/1790/7.
21 A I B Stewart, "Regulation of agriculture in seventeenth century Kintyre", in W M Gordon (ed), *Miscellany III* (SS, 1992) at 220–221.
22 Stewart (n 21) at 216–217.
23 Erskine, *Inst*, 3.6.23. I am indebted to Professor Bill McBryde for this reference.

bailie "for refusing to be a birlaman".[24] In the island of Islay, references to "two sworn birleymen" for the assessment of damage done to grass or corn became standard in leases granted by Campbell of Shawfield from 1724 onwards.[25] However, I have not found any references to birlaw courts or birleymen in the Outer Hebrides, Orkney and Shetland, all areas of intensive Scandinavian settlement, despite the suggested Scandinavian etymology.[26]

The great nineteenth-century record scholar and legal historian, Cosmo Innes, wrote of the birleymen in his *Scotch Legal Antiquities* in 1872:

> Let me say something of this rural officer chosen by the people. I think he is not yet extinct in some northern districts – not forgotten anywhere in Scotland. The birleymen were the arbiters – the referees in rural differences – between tenants of the same estate.

He added that, "In the old time, to dispute the award of the birleymen left a stain on a man's character".[27] Innes believed that the institution had spread north from England. Elsewhere, when discussing "constant quarrels" about the souming of cattle and sheep in the forfeited estate of Robertson of Struan in 1755, which had been referred by the baron-bailie to the birleymen of the district to resolve, Innes commented, "You see how far the Saxon institution had penetrated into the Highlands."[28]

Most references to the birlaw and the birleymen are of a secondary nature, actual records of Scottish birlaw courts and their proceedings being extremely rare. One record, however, which does survive is "The Boorlaw Book of Yester and Gifford" in East Lothian, written in the later eighteenth century.[29] This sets out 40 acts of the birlaw in the form of "Act anent . . ." The last act is dated the 19th of July 1780, and the 38th the 24th of June 1761. The first 37 acts are written in the same hand as the last three, which are preceded by the note, "The above 37 Acts has been time Immemorial the Boor law or commonly pronounced the Birla of Yester". The first two acts read as follows:

---

24 J Dunlop (ed), *Court Minutes of Balgair 1706–1736* (1957), at 8, 10–11, and 24 (see also at 26, 27, 28 and 30). I am most grateful to Dr Athol Murray for these references.
25 F Ramsay (ed), *The Day Book of Daniel Campbell of Shawfield 1767 with relevant papers concerning the Estate of Islay* (1991) at 6 (1724), 73 (1748), 71 (1752) and 223 (1777).
26 An explanation for this is suggested below, 139–140.
27 Innes, *Scotch Legal Antiquities* (n 17) at 254.
28 Innes, *Scotch Legal Antiquities* (n 17) at 268. "Souming" refers to the number of beasts which a tenant was allowed to put on the common grazings.
29 NRS, Records of the Feuars of Gifford, GD/1/16/2. See further Marquis of Tweeddale, "The boorlaw book of Yester and Gifford" (1958) 7 *Transactions of the East Lothian Antiquarian and Field Naturalists Society* 9; and J H Simpson, *The Feuars of Gifford, 1750–1980* (1986) ch 1 ("The eighteenth century").

1. Act anent over Soumes. If any person dwelling in the neighbourhood holding sumes above their stent [allowed number] being warned by the Birlamen to remove them of the ground, for ilk twenty four hours they shall keep them after the command of the Birlamen they shall pay Twenty shillings scots.
2. Act anent Night Lairs. Whosoever shall have a beast lying out of the house betwixt the 3rd of may & the corns being all shorn & led home to the barn yard, for ilk night lair shall pay to the birla twelve shillings scots and they shall pay to the complainer what damage corn is comprised to.

Several acts are concerned with the digging and use of turf and peat. For example, the seventh act reads: "Act anent Casting [digging] of Elding. Whosoever shall cast Peits, truffs, diviots or faill upon their Neighbours ground, they shall pay to the Birla Twenty Shillings for breaking the ground . . ."[30] Other acts seek to uphold the authority of the birleymen and the birlaw court:

11. Act anent abusing of the Birlawmen. Whosoever shall revile scold or abuse the Birlemen . . . with base or unbecoming words or speeches they shall for each fault of that nature pay to the Birlaw Twenty shillings scots.
17. Act anent Absenting from the Birla. Whosoever absents himself from the Birla being in health and at home and sends others in his stead for ilk absence they shall pay to the Birla half a merk.

Other matters covered by the acts include the tethering of horses, "wanton Staigs [young horses] in the harigg", wrongous complaints about neighbours, and "Blowen Pease in the Harvest time".

The vocabulary used might repay further study. Much of it is now impenetrable without the aid of a good Scots dictionary, and it would be interesting to know how common it was in the eighteenth century. The use of the phrase "the Birla" – "commonly called the Birla of Yester" – rather than "the Birlaw court" at the beginning of the record and in several of the acts is also a point of interest.[31] This birlaw, which had earlier been closely associated with the barony of Yester, merged into, or was assimilated by, a body known as "the Feuars of Gifford", which emerged in the mid-eighteenth century and survives to the present as a trust with charitable status. The last entry in the Boorlaw Book, dated 22 August 1793, concerns a general meeting of the Feuars of Gifford.

New birlaw courts were still being set up as late as the eighteenth century. In 1715 farmers in and around Edinburgh and Leith petitioned Leith Town

---

30 "Fuel, feal and divot" is one of the rural servitudes recognised by Scots law: the right to cut peat for fuel and turf for walling.
31 See above, 129.

Council to have "Burlay Baillies [that is, birleymen] chosen and elected" to make the necessary "acts and statutes".[32] The petition was granted and the Council appointed "the said byrlaw Court to commence from Lammas next". The court was to be maintained by the members, rather than at public expense. From 1724 there is a record of the proceedings of this birlaw court – perhaps the only reasonably full record of the proceedings of a Scottish birlaw court to have survived.[33] The emphasis is again very much on neighbours, neighbourhood and common consent. An Entry for 20 July 1724 notes that:

> The persons hereto subscryving being admitted and entered Members of the Burlaw Court of Leith Doe hereby bind and oblidge themselves to stand to abyde and fulfil all the Acts and statutes of the said Burlaw Court Made and to be Made for the better regulation of the neighbourheid and Members of the said Court, and oblidgs them to obey the sentences of the said Burlaw Court in all tyme coming.[34]

The court met weekly or fortnightly from Spring until Autumn. At first it met in the open air at the "Ducatt yeard" (Dovecote yard) by Leith Links, but soon the birlaw bailies petitioned the bailies of South Leith to be allowed to sit inside a house when the weather was "foull, stormy or rigidly cold"![35] The birlaw's activities were not confined to Leith, but ranged widely over farmland around Edinburgh, including Broughton, Canonmills and Inverleith.

This birlaw too had its own acts and statutes, some in language almost as impenetrable as that of the Boorlaw of Yester, as for example, in an act of 28 September 1719 which concerned the liability of persons setting out "Scabbed or Colded horses on the Grass Stanks or Seughs of the Ground".[36] The index to the acts discloses much about animals, as one would expect – cows, "duks", dogs, fouls, geese, hens, horses, sheep and

---

32 D Robertson, "The burlaw court of Leith" (1927) 15 *Book of the Old Edinburgh Club* 115 at 116–117, citing the minutes of Edinburgh City Council. This informative article was known also to Dickinson. Robertson notes (at 170) that the court's jurisdiction extended as far as Curriemuirend to the west of Edinburgh. There stands in the modern suburb of Currie a small stone roadside cross known as The Corslet Cross, relocated there around 1970 from its original position a mile to the north at Riccarton South Strip. The plaque upon its plinth narrates that the cross was the meeting-place of the "byrlae" or birlaw court for the district of nearby Corslet. See further S Harris, *The Place Names of Edinburgh* (1996) sv "Corslet", "The Corslet Cross".
33 Edinburgh Council Archives [ECA], SL 86/11/1–3 (Leith Burlaw Court, 3 vols). These three Sederunt Books cover the period 1724–1750. The first volume also contains (loose at end) an "Alphabeticall Indix of the Boorlaw Court Acts" by subject matter for the period 1715 to 1729.
34 ECA, SL 86/11/1–3, vol 1, loose paper; see Robertson (n 32) at 171.
35 ECA, SL 86/11/1 (n 34), petition at the end of vol 1; Robertson (n 32) at 172.
36 ECA, SL 86/11/1 (n 34), "Alphabeticall Indix": "Colded"; and see Robertson (n 32) at 181.

swine. One intriguing entry indexed under "Bullets" refers to a complaint by Thomas Sheills, tenant at Broughton, that "Severall people when playing att the Bullets on [Broughton loan] Upon pretence of Seeking for their Bullets, Trade doun and Spoil his growing Corn". The birlaw ordained that any person so transgressing should pay a fine of one pound scots and empowered Thomas Sheills "to Seize the bullets of the transgressors And to Detain them till the said One Pund be paid".[37] The reference is evidently to the game of bullets, once widely popular, which involved pitching a rounded stone (the "bullet") from point to point in as few chucks or throws as possible.[38] The Leith birlaw court ceased to function about the middle of the eighteenth century.

As Cosmo Innes suggests, the birleyman remained a familiar figure in rural Scotland until well into the nineteenth century. Already in 1602 John Colville, attempting to reconvert his countrymen to Roman Catholicism, wrote of the Ecumenical Councils of the Church "as far in maiestie and authoritie exceeding your Synods as a gret parlament doth exceed a poor birla court".[39] Sir Walter Scott wrote in *Waverley* of "Jamie Howie, wha's no fit to be a birlieman, let be a bailie".[40] In 1866 it was noted that "Birley Court, in the tradition of the Borders, [was] a name for any particularly stormy meeting."[41] The birleyman, or burlaw-bailie, even has his place in verse, although the words are not flattering and the verse is not good. Allan Ramsay's "The Lure: A Tale" contains this stanza:

> This Falconer has tane his Way
> O'er *Calder*-moor; and gawn the Moss up,
> He there forgather'd with a Gossip:
> And wha was't, trow ye, but the Deel [the devil],
> That had disguis'd himsell sae weel
> In humane shape, sae snug and wylie;
> *Jude* took him for a Burlie-baillie:[42]

---

37 ECA, SL 86/11/1–3 (n 34), vol 1, 27 May 1728.
38 The game of "lang bullet" also figures in *Mathiesone v Anderson*, a case of accidental slaughter in 1640, in which stones had been rolled down the "bank or bra[e] of the castell of Edinburgh" with fatal consequences (*Justiciary Cases* II at 395).
39 J Colville, *The Paranaese or admonition of Io. Colville . . . unto his cuntrey men* (1602) epistle, at 23. Colville also wrote that the General Assembly of the Church of Scotland in relation to Ecumenical Councils was "in proportion as a flee is to ane Elephant"! See also *Dictionary of the Older Scottish Tongue* [*DOST*], "Birlaw". An electronic version of both *DOST* and the *Scottish National Dictionary* [*SND*] is available online: www.dsl.ac.uk.
40 Sir W Scott, *Waverley* (first published 1814) ch 42.
41 (1866) Proceedings of the Berwickshire Naturalists Club at 261.
42 A Ramsay, *Poems II* (1728) at 238. Allan Ramsay the poet (1686–1758) was the father of Allan Ramsay the painter (1713–1784).

Birlaws and birleymen gradually disappeared in the course of the nineteenth century, although some were remembered well into the twentieth. For example, it was said in Banffshire in 1928 that, "I min' fin the vailyations for an oot-gyaan [out-going] tenant wis deen [was done] by the birley man".[43] One late example is to be found at St Boswells, near Melrose, where an annual birlaw court was held by the proprietors of the undivided common green. The court's function was restricted to letting the green, dividing the income, and appointing "Birleymen". The existing record begins in 1823 – surprisingly late. The last description of the meeting as a "Birly Court" is in 1840; but the meeting continued to be held for many more years, appointing named birleymen until 1873. The record of lettings continues in scrappy fashion until 1969.[44] There is a marvellous description of the St Boswells Fair in *Change at St Boswells* by Lieutenant-Colonel Frederick G Peake (Peake Pasha):

> Until about 1840 the opening of the Fair was an occasion for ceremony. In the early morning of 18th July the Burleyman, David Stoddart of Ancrum, known as Black Davie, arrived in St Boswells wearing buckled shoes, gorgeous knee breeks, green coat with brass buttons, and a tall hat. After showing himself in all his glory to the assembled crowds he went to the east end of the village. Then, carrying the drum and escorted by two halberdiers and the legal representative of the Duke of Buccleuch, he slowly marched to the Smithy. At the stroke of 8 a.m., he smote the drum and in a loud voice declared the St. Boswells Fair open. Having marched round the Fair, drum beating, and with his escort, this was known as Crying the Fair . . .[45]

One set of birleymen survives to the present day in the Border town of Selkirk where they remain an integral part of the annual and highly symbolic "Selkirk Common Riding", the riding of the marches of the burgh. "Burleymen" are now appointed by a trust set up in 1975 after the old town council disappeared in local government reorganisation. An attractive leaflet on the history of the Common Riding provides yet another misleading etymology of "birleymen": that they are so called because their function was to carry out the burgh law.[46]

How did this legal institution come to Scotland? As already noted, Cosmo Innes believed that it had come from England, describing it as "the Saxon

---

43 *SND* (n 39) sv "Birlie".
44 NRS, GD1/1152/1.
45 Lieut-Colonel Frederick G Peake (Peake Pasha), *Change at St Boswells* (1961) at 89. I owe this reference to Sue Sellar. For Peake Pasha (1886–1970) see http://en.wikipedia.org/wiki/Frederick_Peake.
46 *Selkirk Common Riding History – Alive in the present*, published by Selkirk Chronicles (no date).

institution".⁴⁷ A check through the *Oxford English Dictionary* reveals that the birlaw was indeed once common in England.⁴⁸ The main entry (under "byrlaw", of which "birlaw" is said to be an obsolete form) describes "byrlaw" as

> The local custom or "law" of a township, manor or rural district, whereby disputes as to boundaries, trespass of cattle, etc., were settled without going into the law courts; a law or custom established in such a district by common consent of all who held land therein, and having binding force within its limits.

These definitions, it will be seen, fit well into the Scottish birlaw also. The earliest form of the word given, "Birelag", comes from the record of Furness Abbey in Lancashire in 1257; and the second, "Birlawe", from Devon in 1292. The suggested etymology is given as "apparently" ON [Old Norse] from a hypothetical "*býjar-log*, f. *býjar* gen. case of *bý-r* (=<u>BY</u> n.)", a dialect variant of *baer*, a village, town or farm, plus "*log* (pl. of *lag*) law, 'law community, communion, also a law district'", with a note cautioning that the existence of *býjar-*, *baejar-log* in Old Norse has scarcely been proved.

A separate entry under "by-law" describes "by-law" as

> apparently the same as BYRLAW; occurring in the thirteenth century. As the name of a custom (in Kent) according to which disputes were settled outside the law courts, on the testimony of neighbours, by official or specially deputed arbitrators.

The earliest forms given here are "bilage" in 1283 and again in 1303, both from Kent. The suggested etymology notes that the word appears to be a doublet of byrlaw in sense, the difference in form being perhaps explicable by "the derivation of *bylaw* from the stem instead of the genitive case of ON *bý-r*, Sw. and Da. *by*, dwelling-place, farm, village, township, town". However, it is also noted, with a view to the earliest examples of the word, that "the difficulty of assigning a Scandinavian etymology to the local name of a Kentish custom is obvious, but cf quot 1292 under BYRLAW from an assize held in Devonshire . . .". The more recent Danish and Swedish forms *bylag* and *byalag*, both describing a village community, are also noted.⁴⁹

This short excursion has been necessary to show that although the ultimate Scandinavian etymology of the word birlaw is not in doubt, some details remain unclear, not least the exact relationship between "birlaw" and

---

47 Above, 129.
48 I have used *OED Online* (https://www.oed.com/) which for "byrlaw" etc is based on the 1989 edition updated.
49 Below, 140.

"by-law". *OED* also notes, under "byrlaw", here following place-name scholars, that the Yorkshire place-names Brampton Bierlow, Eccleshall Bierlow and Brightside Bierlow, appear to incorporate the word "birlaw".[50]

There can be little doubt that the name "birlaw", and probably the institution also, came to Scotland from England. Given the Scandinavian derivation of the word the most likely area of origin within Britain is the Danelaw. Although surprisingly little has been written about the birlaw in studies of the medieval village community or in general works on English legal history, there is ample evidence for the functioning of birlaw courts throughout England from the late thirteenth century onwards.[51] Particularly relevant here is an article published in 1965 by Warren O Ault on open-field husbandry, the village community and agrarian by-laws in medieval England.[52] Ault noted that Vinogradoff had pointed to the existence of village by-laws already in the fifteenth century, and had suspected that there must be some from an earlier date.[53] Through the study of the rolls of manorial courts, courts baron and courts leet, Ault was able to point to the existence of such village by-laws already in the late thirteenth and fourteenth centuries. These regulated a wide variety of matters, including conservation of grain, gleaning and reaping, protection of sheaves against theft, peas and beans, stubble, right of fallow, tethering of animals, pasturing of sheep, control of pigs, fencing of fields, ploughs and ploughing, rights to hay, boundaries, access and rights of way.[54]

The regulations are typically described as "statutes", "ordinances" and "customs". Examples given by Ault include the phrases *statutum ville* (1290, Newington, Oxon), *statute et ordinanciones autumpnales* (1290, Great Hornwood, Bucks), *sicut statutum fuit per le byrlawe* (1317, Abbot's Ripon, Hunts), *birlawe* (1322, Burwell, Cambs), *ordinacio bilegis* (1325, Littleport Manor, Cambs) and *consuetudines vocate belawes* (1379, Heyford, Oxon).[55] There is regular emphasis on common consent and assent. Ault discusses the various phrases used by way of description and notes as the "simplest of all, most frequent, and least informing" *ordinatum est ex commune assensu*, a

---

50 See, for example, A Goodall, *Place-Names of South-West Yorkshire* (1914), "Bierlaw"; and A Mawer (ed), *The Chief Elements used in English Place-Names* (1924), "byarlog".
51 A notable exception is Angus Winchester whose work on birlaw courts is noticed below, 137–138.
52 W O Ault, "Open-field husbandry and the village community: a study of agrarian by-laws in medieval England", in (1965) 55 (ns) *Transactions of the American Philosophical Society*, part 7, 5. I am most grateful to Paul Brand for alerting me to this article some years ago. See also W O Ault, *Open-Field Farming in Medieval England: A Study of Village By-Laws* (1972).
53 Ault (n 52) at 12.
54 Ault (n 52) at 12–40.
55 Ault (n 52) at 40–41. Ault gives "le bye-law" for the 1317 entry in the main text, but "le byrlawe" in the documentary appendix (at 59, no 34).

phrase which occurs more than fifty times in the rolls of Durham's halmotes.[56] More informative are phrases such as *per communitatem tocius villate* (1324, Newington, Oxon), *ex commune assensu tocius villate* (c1425, Wimeswold, Leics) and *ex commune tocius vicinorum* (1383, Durham Halmote).[57] Ault notes and disagrees with Maitland's comment on the community of the vill being "generally a body of men whom the lawyers call serfs" and shows that, on the contrary, they were usually freemen.[58] He emphasises that "when it comes to the statutes of autumn the assent of the whole community – lord, freemen and villains – was essential."[59] Ault calls those responsible for the observance of the laws, termed in the record *custodes, conservatores* and *prepositi*, "wardens" or "overseers". He describes them as being usually "among the more substantial and responsible members of the farming community", and notes that they were elected: "In general, then, it may be said that the wardens of the by-laws were elected by the same authority that enacted the by-laws."[60]

The courts were free-standing inasmuch as they were not an integral part of the feudal structure:

> The wardens of the village by-laws ... performed no services for the lord as such. They were not subject to inquest in his court as to the discharge of their duties. They were not officers of the manor but of the community that chose them and they served without pay.[61]

If vill and manor co-incided, then the manor court might act as a forum. However, Ault notes that evidence of non-manorial meetings is plentiful in the sixteenth century, adding that, "For evidence of such non-manorial meetings we have to rely on inference in the earlier centuries, but it is clear and inescapable."[62] Ault does not mention Scotland, nor does he speak of "birlaw courts" or "birleymen". Yet it is clear that he is describing the same institution, and we may suspect that in some instances at least the vernacular word which lies behind *custodes* and *conservatores* and the like is not "warden" but "birleyman". Ault's descriptions of the "wardens" as being "among the more substantial and responsible members of the farming community" tallies with the later Scottish evidence.

---

56 Ault (n 52) at 41.
57 Ault (n 52) at 41.
58 Pollock & Maitland, vol 1, at 624.
59 Ault (n 52) at 43.
60 Ault (n 52) at 44, 46.
61 Ault (n 52) at 49.
62 Ault (n 52) at 54.

The institution of the birlaw seems to have disappeared, or to have been subsumed into other bodies, rather earlier in England than in Scotland. Birlaw courts and birleymen perhaps survived longest in north-west England, where their survival is attested to by dialect dictionaries. Angus Winchester has described rural life in northern England and the Scottish Borders between 1400 and 1700.[63] His work is based on a detailed study of manorial courts, occasionally including birlaw courts, in the northern counties of England (Cumberland, Westmorland, Northumberland, County Durham, and the North and West Ridings of Yorkshire) in the sixteenth and seventeenth centuries. He provides the best account to date of the functioning of the birlaw in England.

In a chapter entitled, "Law, Custom and Good Neighbourhood", Winchester notes the antiquity of manor courts. He speculates that they "represent the incorporation into the manorial system of the village folk-meeting, assumed to be an ancient institution common to much of rural Europe".[64] He notes Ault's work and the emphasis placed in the records which Ault studied on agreement "by the community of the vill", and "by agreement of all the neighbours". "Byrlaw courts," writes Winchester, "sometimes described in Latin as *plebiscitum*, were known over much of northern England and in Scotland."[65] He is aware of Dickinson's appendix and the suggested Scandinavian derivation. Two documents in Winchester's own appendix set out articles laid down by sixteenth-century birlaw courts in Yorkshire and Lancashire.[66] These documents, he believes,

> bring us as close as it is possible to come to decision-making in the hill farming hamlets. Both are brief statements of local byelaws, apparently drawn up by hamlet communities and enrolled in the record of the manor court of which the hamlet in question was a member.[67]

These by-laws are reminiscent of the acts of the birlaws of Yester and of Leith already noticed. Thus the first of the by-laws from Halton Gill in Yorkshire in 1579 reads: "Imprimis that no habitator ther shall kepe any riggold tuppes to com emonges ther ewes in ryding tyme, peyn [under pain

---

63 A Winchester, *The Harvest of the Hills: Rural Life in Northern England and the Scottish Borders, 1400–1700* (2000). I am grateful to Andrew Humphries, a fellow participant in a "Commons Old and New" workshop in Oslo, for alerting me to Angus Winchester's work.
64 Winchester, *Harvest of the Hills* (n 63) at 42.
65 Winchester, *Harvest of the Hills* (n 63) at 34, 42. For the use of *plebiscitum* see also Ault (n 52) at 41 (*plebiscitum* [1433], *plebeicitum et bilages villate* [1494]), and 43 (*plebiscitum*).
66 Winchester, *Harvest of the Hills* (n 63) at 172–175 (documents 5 and 6).
67 Winchester, *Harvest of the Hills* (n 63) at 172.

of fine of] iiis.iiiid."; and the fifth that "every inhabitant shall kepe ther stint both winter & somer in field and pasture in peyn of iiis.iiiid."

The other regulations, from Outhwaite in Lancashire in 1580, are headed, "A byarley and orders maide by the tenants of Hulthwatt as is hereunder sett downe in articles the xiith daie of October by the consentes of all the said tenants". Winchester emphasises the role of customary law, the regulation of rights in commons and the preservation of "good neighbourhood" in the work of the birlaw and manorial courts.[68] Spellings of birlaw range from "byrlaw" and "byarley" to *"curia sive birelagium"* (in Millom, South Cumbria), "court barron or byerlaye", "bierlays", "birelag", "bierlow", "byerlay" and "barley jury".[69] Birleymen, "burlawmen" or "barleymen" appointed by manorial courts are also in evidence.

Detailed consideration of the reasons for the decline and disappearance of the birlaw is beyond the scope of this article. Writing on the Leith birlaw court in 1927, David Robertson singled out the Heritable Jurisdictions Act 1746 as an agent of change, and pointed also to new agricultural methods of draining, dyking and especially enclosure as bringing to an end the usefulness of the court.[70] In fact, the agents of change were well under way by the mid-eighteenth century, and earlier legislation, such as the Winter Herding Act 1686, the Division of Commonties Act 1695 and the Runrig Act of the same year had already made an impact. Angus Winchester also considers the reasons for the decline of manorial courts, including birlaw courts, in northern England. He regards the centuries covered by his book as "the heyday of manorial regulation of common land", partly brought about by the increasing enclosure of pasture in the sixteenth and seventeenth centuries.[71] He sees the forces of agricultural change gaining momentum in the eighteenth century as part of a long transition towards individual as against communal ownership, involving "an assault on the ideals of "ancient custom" and good neighbourhood" which underpinned the workings of the manorial courts".[72] The decline of the birlaw, then, is intimately connected with "the tragedy of the commons", the gradual disappearance of commons or commonties before a more aggressive private ownership.

---

68 See especially Winchester, *Harvest of the Hills* (n 63) at 45–48.
69 Winchester, *Harvest of the Hills* (n 63) at 174, 43, 44 and 48.
70 Robertson (n 32) at 169–170 and 204–205.
71 Winchester, *Harvest of the Hills* (n 63), ch 7 ("Manor courts in a changing world, 1400–1700"), and at 148.
72 Winchester, *Harvest of the Hills* (n 63) at 148.

What more can be said of this legal institution? And what of the apparent Scandinavian provenance? I was fortunate enough to be in Oslo for much of the academic year 2002–3 and was able to discuss the birlaw with Scandinavian scholars. There seems no doubt that the Scandinavian etymology is correct. Indeed it was pointed out to me that to talk of birlaw *courts* is otiose as the notion of a court or assembly is implicit in the second element of the word "birlaw". One thinks here of the "Boor Law or commonly pronounced the Birla of Yester", and of the payment of fines "to the birla".[73] It also seemed agreed that the etymology of the word is likely to be Old Eastern Scandinavian rather than Old Western Scandinavian. This supports the conclusion already reached that the institution is likely to have spread to Scotland from the south, from England, the Danelaw being the obvious source, rather than from Norwegian settlements in the north and west. Either route is, in principle, quite credible: another Scandinavian institution, the "ting", is commemorated in several Scottish place-names, particularly in Orkney and Shetland; while the ceremony of "fencing the court", once a regular feature of Scottish court procedure, is found also in Scandinavia and the Isle of Man, but apparently nowhere else.[74]

It seems probable then that the institution spread north to Scotland from the Danelaw at some time well before the fourteenth century.[75] It is suggested that the birlaw is equally likely to have spread south to other parts of England at an early date, some considerable time before the name was first

---

[73] Above at 129–130. A further possible instance is the text of *Regiam Majestatem* in *APS* and *LMS*, which give *exceptis burlawis* rather than *exceptis legibus de Burlawis* (above, 126).

[74] For the "ting" see *inter alia*, *SND* (n 34); G Fellows-Jensen, "Tingwall, Dingwall and Thingwall", in *Twenty-eight Papers Presented to Hans Bekker-Beilsen on the Occasion of his Sixtieth Birthday* (1993) 53; S Brink, "Law and legal customs in Viking Age Scandinavia", in J Jesch (ed), *The Scandinavians from the Vendel Period to the Tenth Century: An Ethnographic Perspective* (2002) 87; A Sanmark, *Viking Law and Order: Places and Rituals of Assembly in the Medieval North* (2017). "Fencing the court" marked the official constitution of the court, latterly by a mere form of words, but originally, no doubt, by some kind of physical barrier: see W C Dickinson (ed), *The Sheriff Court Book of Fife 1515–1522* (SHS, 1928), appendix A ("The procedure of the court") at 309; W C Dickinson, "Some Scandinavian influences in Scottish legal procedure?" (1960) 15 *Arv* 155; Balfour, *Practicks*, vol 1, at 273, "Of courtis" ch viii; and *DOST* (n 34) sv "Fens, Fence". The procedure of "fencing the court" does not appear to be recorded in Anglo-Saxon law, although the possibility cannot be entirely ruled out. I am also grateful to the late Patrick Wormald for assistance on this point.

[75] Barbara Crawford makes the same suggestion in "Scandinavian influence II: historical background", a paper given at a conference of the Tayside and Fife Archaeological Committee (TAFAC) in Perth in 2002 on the topic of Scottish urban origins. This can be accessed at www.tafac.freeuk.com/perthcon/scandinavian2.htm, at 4. I am grateful to Dr Crawford for drawing this paper to my attention.

recorded in the thirteenth century, and that the hesitation of the compilers of *OED* regarding the etymology of the word "by-law" is unjustified.[76]

The case for origin in the Danelaw is further strengthened by the fact that the birlaw, or an institution very similar, can be found in both Denmark and Sweden, in early modern times at least, and quite possibly earlier, under the name of *bylag* and *byalag*, whereas there seems to be no corresponding nomenclature in Norway. Village communities have been studied extensively in Scandinavia over recent years, following similar studies in Germany and England. Professor Michael Jones of the University of Trondheim has studied institutions for local self-government at what he terms "the lowest regional level", that is, the "village", "farm community" or "neighbourhood unit". Building on the work of Danish legal historian Poul Meyer and others, he has compared such institutions in Ostrobothnia, Sweden, Denmark and Norway.[77] He notes, in particular, the existence of village by-laws termed *byordning* and village leaders termed *byaman* in Ostrobothnia, and the institution of the *byalag* in Sweden. The *byalag* still functions in the south of Sweden in Skane or Scania (formerly an integral part of Denmark) where membership of the body can be considered a mark of esteem.[78] Given the astonishing longevity of the birlaw in Scotland, and to an extent in England also, it would not be surprising if the *byalag* in Denmark and Sweden had an equally long history.

My initial assumption had been that this adventure of the law had travelled from Scandinavia, probably Denmark, to the Danelaw, and from there to Scotland. However, Professor Stefan Brink of the University of Uppsala, who has made a study of early Scandinavian institutions, while accepting the link between the birlaw and the Danelaw, questioned whether this adventure of the law had begun life in Scandinavia. Rather, he suggested, the borrowing might have taken place in the other direction, from the Danelaw to Scandinavia. Whichever is correct, the reign of Cnut, king of both Denmark

---

76 Above, 134.
77 See M Jones, "Law and landscape – some historical-geographical studies from Northern Europe", in T Peil and M Jones (eds), *Landscape, Law and Justice: Proceedings of a Conference Organised by the Centre for Advanced Study at the Norwegian Academy of Science and Letters, Oslo 15–19 June 2003* (2005) 95 at 96–98. See also his unpublished paper (presented at the seminar "Custom, Law and Landscape", Landscape, Law & Justice research group, Centre for Advanced Study at the Norwegian Academy of Science and Letters, Oslo, 11 November 2002), "The role of neighbourhood and village institutions for the regulation of land and the shaping of landscape in Norden: a historical overview", and his articles, "The 'two landscapes' of north Norway and the 'cultural landscape' of the south", in M Jones and K Olwig (eds), *Nordic Landscapes: Region and Belonging on the Northern Edge of Europe* (2008); and "Landscape, law and justice - concepts and issues" (2006) 60 Norsk Geografisk Tidsskrift 1.
78 I am grateful to Dr Wilhelm Ostberg of the National Museum in Stockholm for this information.

and England (1016–35), would seem as likely a period as any.[79] The suggestion that the birlaw was forged in England raises further intriguing questions which cannot be followed in detail here. Could the institution have evolved on an Anglo-Saxon base, but with an added Scandinavian dimension and a Scandinavian name? The "Wantage Code" of Ethelred II (978–1016) and the laws of the West Saxon king Ine (688–726) may be relevant here. It is entirely possible that in Scotland too, the birlaw may also have drawn on an existing native institution such as the *comhdhail*. The late Professor Geoffrey Barrow suggested, in particular, that the reference to "Couthal" [for *comhdhail*] in an Arbroath agreement of 1329 "is used in such a casual manner as to suggest that in Angus at least it was a well-known term applied to a species of birlie or burlaw court, so humble indeed that Abbot Geoffrey speaks somewhat contemptuously of its dealing with the '*innumerosis actibus inter semetipsos tantummodo contingentibus*'".[80]

The story of the birlaw in Scotland provides a remarkable example of survival. Always a low-key institution, but one with extra-ordinary staying power, the birlaw continued to function, little altered in its essentials and seldom keeping a formal record, for upwards of half a millennium. At its heart, even after the institution had been subsumed into other bodies, notably the courts of feudal lords, lay the consent and active participation of the community concerned. The birlaw and the birleymen must have impinged on the daily lives of those living on the land in a way that better recorded superior courts never did. It seems clear that the institution, in the form in which we know it, came to Scotland from the Danelaw before legal records began, perhaps in the tenth or early eleventh century. Whether it originated in the Danelaw, or came from Scandinavia, it may already have had hundreds of years of history behind it. Warren Ault writes of the open-field system so closely associated with the birlaw that, "Some scholars are able to discern elements of it in what Tacitus wrote about the Germanic tribes . . ." In addition to Tacitus' *Germania*, Ault also points to the laws of King Ine; while Angus Winchester, as noted above, writes of "the village folk-meeting, assumed to be an ancient institution common to much of rural Europe".[81]

---

79 Crawford (n 75) at 3 suggests that the institution might have travelled north with Malcolm Canmore in 1054.
80 G W S Barrow, "Popular courts in early medieval Scotland: some suggested place-name evidence" (1981) 21 *Scottish Studies* 1 (quotation at 3); G W S Barrow, "Popular courts . . . additional note" (1983) 27 *Scottish Studies* 67 (reprinted together in G W S Barrow, *Scotland and its Neighbours* (1992), ch 11 (quotation at 220)).
81 Ault, *Open-Field Farming* (n 52) at 16; and above, 137.

# 6 English Law as a Source of Stair's *Institutions**

One of the main objects which Lord Bankton had in mind in writing his *Institute of the Laws of Scotland* (1751), as he makes clear in his preface, was to compare the law of Scotland with that of England. In this he distinguished his work from Stair's *Institutions*, saying "The Lord Stair had no occasion to observe any thing of this kind, nor was it of great use in his time."[1] More recent writers have assigned a minimal role to English influence in Stair's *Institutions*, or have denied that there is any English influence to be found there at all. Lord Cooper, writing in 1946, while admitting that "there are a number of passages in his *Institutions* which disclose an acquaintance with, and even an appreciation for, points of English doctrine", goes on to say that "it would be impossible even to suggest that this typically Scottish treatise owed anything specific to English influence or transmitted that influence to the law of Scotland".[2] In 1979, a leading English legal historian stated that there is in Stair's *Institutions* "no hint of English influence whatever".[3] It will be argued in this essay that, contrary to the general view, the influence of English law on both the theory and the substance of Scots law, as exemplified and expounded in Stair's *Institutions*, is by no means negligible. Even in the seventeenth century, and, indeed, for some hundreds of years previously, Scots law was, in the words of Hélène David, "à cheval entre droits romano-germaniques et droits de la common law".[4]

In one sense, however, and the point is an important one, the author of the *Institutions* would not have admitted that English law or any other system of law had influenced his work. Stair's purpose, as he repeatedly informs us, was to expound the law of Scotland as it existed in his time. He did not con-

---

* Originally published as "English Law as a Source", in D M Walker (ed), *Stair Tercentenary Studies* (SS vol 33, 1981) 140–150.
1 Bankton, *Inst*, preface, p. ix.
2 Lord Cooper of Culross, *Selected Papers 1922–1954* (1957) at 115.
3 J H Baker, *An Introduction to English Legal History* (2nd edn, 1979) at 32. The statement continues to appear in the 5th edn (2019) of Baker's book (at 41).
4 H David, *Introduction à l'Étude du Droit Ecossais* (1972) at 298 ("it rode between Romano-germanic and Common laws").

ceive himself to be free to alter or amend that law. Where there were conflicting views or lines of decisions it was his avowed policy to make this clear, and on many undecided matters of substantive law he refrained from giving his own opinion, preferring to leave the question open. The rules of other systems of law, Feudal, Civil and Canon, and the customs of neighbouring nations might be of historical and comparative value, illuminating the origin and development of Scots law, but Stair would have rejected the suggestion that he had imported any such rules, at his own hand, into the body of Scots law. Re-casting and systematising the law was, however, another matter:

> I have been very sparing to express my own opinion in dubious cases of law, not determined by our customs or statutes, but have rather congested what the Lords have done . . . But I have used more freedom, in opening the fountains of law and justice, and the deductions thence arising, by the law and light of nature and of reason.[5]

By systematising an area of law in a particular manner Stair sometimes did in fact determine its future course: thus his arrangement of Restitution (1.7) and Recompence (1.8) set the law of unjust enrichment along Civilian lines to this day.

With that proviso, however, it is worth noting that English law is referred to more frequently in the *Institutions* than the municipal law of any other jurisdiction contemporary with Stair. There are about fifty separate references to English law and English practice. The only other jurisdiction given anything like similar prominence is France. Germany and the Netherlands come a poor third, and of other countries there is barely a mention. A number of the references to English law concern points of terminology, for Stair, like a true philosopher, was always interested in the definition and meaning of words. Thus "the English by *reversion* do not understand a right of redemption, but a right of survivancy or succession; . . . and that which we call a wadset, they call a *Mortgage*".[6] Sometimes Scottish usage is approved, sometimes English: "These we call decernitures or decreets; the English call them judgments, or decrees, which do more properly signify a resolution upon choice in any free thing, than the determining the rights of parties";[7] Scots law talks of ward-holdings "when the fee is holden for military service, or, as the English better express it, by knight service . . .";[8] the

---

5 Stair, *Inst*, Advertisement to the Second Edition (1981 edn at 65). See also text accompanying n 41 below.
6 Stair, *Inst*, 2.10.3.
7 Stair, *Inst*, 4.46.2.
8 Stair, *Inst*, 2.4.33.

Scots talk of *horning* but "The English do more properly call this execution *outlawry* . . .".[9] Other references allude to the English distinction between Equity and Common Law,[10] compare proof before answer with English procedure,[11] and inform us that the English have two sorts of lawburrows – binding over to keep the peace, and binding over to good behaviour.[12] A well known passage refers to the English practice of seeking damages for patrimonial loss in defamation actions: "Such actions upon injurious words, as they may relate to damage in means, are frequent and curious among the English".[13] However, the bulk of the references to English law concern matters of property and succession, and in this, as we shall see, Stair largely follows Thomas Craig.

Where did Stair learn his English law? The first manuscripts of the *Institutions* are thought to date from as early as 1662. Probably then Stair's acquaintance with English law is referable in great part to the period of the Protectorate, at the end of which he sat in tandem with English lawyers as Judge Dalrymple, Commissioner for the Administration of Justice, appointed by Cromwell. Lord Cooper indeed suspected that the period of the Protectorate might have left a lasting impact on the development of Scots law and on the shape of the *Institutions*, but on investigation he concluded, no doubt correctly, that this was not so, and that "so far as direct and tangible consequences to the law of Scotland are concerned, the years between 1650 and 1661 were years which the locusts had eaten".[14] Stair himself was later at some pains to play down and excuse the part he had played during the Protectorate. Stair's references to English law do not, in fact, suggest any deep study of that system, and he never cites authors or cases. Rather he shows the casual acquaintance which one would expect of a practical lawyer and man of affairs. In this Stair differs from his great predecessor Thomas Craig whose *Jus Feudale* and *De Unione Regnorum Britanniae* betray a considerable and detailed knowledge of English law,

---

9 Stair, *Inst*, 3.3.1.
10 Stair, *Inst*, 2.10.3; 4.3.1.
11 Stair, *Inst*, 4.39.4 and 5.
12 Stair, *Inst*, 4.48.14.
13 Stair, *Inst*, 1.9.4.
14 Cooper (n 2) at 115. It is conceivable, however, that some of the procedural reforms made by Stair when Lord President may owe something to his experience under the Protectorate. This has never been investigated, and might, in any case, be difficult to prove. Further on the Interregnum court see J D Ford, *Law and Opinion in Scotland during the Seventeenth Century* (2007) ch 2.

and who mentions various English authorities by name, including Bracton, Littleton, Dyer and Plowden. Craig is a prime source for Stair.[15]

The subject of Craig's *Jus Feudale* is, of course, the feudal land law, not only of Scotland, but also of Europe more generally, expecially England and France. Craig perceived the parallels between the land law of the countries of western Europe and was concerned to demonstrate and explain them by the historical and comparative method. Professor Pocock in his *The Ancient Constitution and the Feudal Law* has reminded us of the magnitude of Craig's intellectual achievement and his place in European historiography:

> Craig had been able to construct an impressively broad historical synthesis, explaining the general history of European law since the barbarian invasions and fitting both Scotland and England into their place in this pattern. If we are to think of him as a product of what is called the Reception in Scotland, it is plain that in him at least reception of civil law principles produced no contempt for or desire to displace native customs; rather a new understanding and respect, produced by his new found ability to see them in their historical context as part of the universal law of the western world.[16]

Craig's historical perspective, as Pocock makes clear, was in sharp contrast to the blinkered and unhistorical approach of contemporary English Common lawyers, such as Sir Edward Coke, thirled to the myth of the Ancient Constitution, unchanged since time immemorial.

Craig was particularly interested in exploring the similarities between Scots law and English law and in emphasising the suitability of the two systems for harmonisation. He was the main Scottish legal apologist for James VI and his cherished scheme to unite his two British kingdoms in an incorporating union.[17] The Epistle Dedicatory to *Jus Feudale* refers to this scheme:

> In order that this union or conjunction should be strong and perfect in all ways, you established a convention of legal experts (*jurisconsultorum*) from each kingdom some time ago and they consulted with one another regarding the laws of either nation in order to discover the similarities and differences and whether it could be arranged that the same laws and the same customs would be observed in each kingdom (*si fieri possit, ut in utroque eaedem leges iidemque mores observentur.*)

---

15 Craig, *JF*; Craig, *De Unione*. I have followed Terry's translation of *De Unione:* but have not always adhered to Lord President Clyde's rather free translation of *Jus Feudale*, to which that of Dodd is preferable. Latin quotations from *JF* are also from the Dodd edition where published, otherwise the Baillie edition of 1732. I am grateful to Dr John Durkan for pointing out to me that there appears to be no contemporary evidence for the title "Sir" generally accorded to Craig.
16 J G A Pocock, *The Ancient Constitution and the Feudal Law* (1957), at 88.
17 On the various schemes for union see B P Levack, "The proposed union of English law and Scots law in the seventeenth century", 1975 *JR* 97.

Some thought that "each nation had completely different institutes and customs which were not only incompatible with each other but were diametrically opposed," Craig continues, but after some research, "I discovered the same foundations for each system of law presently observed both in England and Scotland. Having compared them, I ascertained that there was clearly the greatest affinity between them in the arguing and deciding of cases".[18] This conclusion he supported in detail with a wealth of learning (and not a little special pleading) in chapter VI of his *De Unione*.[19] Craig was not the first to point to the parallels between Scots and English law: in 1560 the Scots commissioners to England, seeking to promote a marriage between Queen Elizabeth and James Lord Hamilton, wished to emphasise how much the two countries had in common:

> ... we present no straunger, but in a maner your owne countrey man, seeing the Ile is a common countrey to us both, one that speaketh your owne language, one of the same religion ... Neither yet neade youe to feare any alteracion in the lawes, seeing the lawes of Scotland wer taken out of England and therfore booth ther realmes are ruled by one fashion.[20]

Nor was Craig the last to underline the similarities between Scots and English law with a view to harmonisation: Lord Kames wrote in his *Statute Law of Scotland* (1757): "One must be ignorant of the history of our law, who does not know, that the laws of Scotland and England were originally the same, almost in every particular";[21] and elsewhere he spoke of the need for "a regular institute of the common law of this island, deducing historically the changes which that law hath undergone in the two nations".[22] However, although Craig was well aware of the similarities between Scots and English law, both historical and contemporary, and wished to further the schemes of his royal master, King James, he remained a patriotic Scot, proud of his country's traditions, unwilling to see Scotland lose face. If there were to be a legal union then there should be a genuine harmonisation of laws. Scots law had as much to offer as English law could give in return. After mentioning his conclusion that there was a fundamental identity in the principles of Scots and English law, Craig continued:

18 Craig, *JF*, Epistle Dedicatory, at lxxii (Dodd translation at lxxiii).
19 Craig, *De Unione* (n 15) at 68 ff (Latin) and 297 ff (translation). The title of this chapter is "Whether for the perfecting of the proposed union the laws of the two countries should be identical. With some remarks on the existing English and Scottish systems".
20 A H Williamson, *Scottish National Consciousness in the Age of James VI* (1979) at 14, citing PRO (TNA): SP52/5/49 and 50.
21 H Home, Lord Kames, *Statute Law of Scotland* (1757) at 429.
22 Kames, *Historical Law Tracts* (1758), preface, at xiv.

We are all aware that different forms of action and forensic procedure are observed in our country and theirs, but I would say, with all respect to our neighbours, that our forms of action and judicial proceedings are preferable over the forms of all the other nations I have ever seen – and I do not think I am making this declaration rashly.[23]

As a result Craig found himself in a dilemma in tracing the history of Scots feudal law. Many Scots and English feudal customs were so similar that one could not doubt their common origin. But was one to admit that such customs had come direct to Scotland from the "auld enemy"? Surely it was better to suppose that they had come directly and independently from Normandy to Scotland, preferably at a time prior to the arrival of these customs in England. And if *Regiam Majestatem* was in large measure a copy of a late twelfth-century English lawbook, *Glanvill*, as Craig knew it to be, then surely it could not be part of the law of Scotland. And so the Epistle Dedicatory to *Jus Feudale* explains how the "feudal system of law", expounded first in Lombardy, reached Scotland direct from France and only later reached England;[24] while *Regiam Majestatem* is described in *Jus Feudale* as "a blot on the jurisprudence of our country . . . the work of some obscure plagiarist . . ." and no part of Scots law.[25] Craig, however, can hardly have believed all this. The truth was that the "feudal system of law" in Scotland had largely been borrowed from England, although no doubt adapted to meet native needs, and that *Regiam Majestatem* was an important, although not necessarily authoritative, repository of Scottish customary law. Craig was too good a scholar not to realise this, and on occasion he shows it. Thus, in his *De Unione* he admits the possibility that England was the immediate source: "Whether our feudal system came to us from England, as on many grounds is possible, or whether we adopted it from the French Consuetudinary law, or from some other source, I cannot positively state". While in his discussion of procedure by brieve in *Jus Feudale* the truth slips out: "It is more probable that this procedure was imported into Scotland from England, than that we derived it from the Feudal Law" (*scil*, of the Continent).[26] As regards *Regiam Majestatem* it has been demonstrated that despite Craig's castigation of that work as a source he himself

---

23 Craig, *JF*, Epistle Dedicatory, at lxxii (Dodd translation at lxxiii).
24 Craig, *JF*, Epistle Dedicatory, at lxxii (Dodd translation, at lxxiii).
25 Craig, *JF*, 1.8.11.
26 Craig, *De Unione* (n 15), at 311; Craig, *JF*, 2.17.25 (Clyde translation). Craig also admits entails to be a direct borrowing from Engand: Craig, *JF*, 2.16.1.

relies on it many times in *Jus Feudale*.[27] The main source of influence then on that native customary law of Scotland for which, as Pocock says, Craig had found a new understanding and respect, was English law, and Craig can hardly have failed to realise this.

What place does Stair give to customary law in his *Institutions*? Stair makes a clear distinction between ancient custom, existing from time immemorial, and more recent custom. It will be argued that in both these categories the influence of English law is apparent.[28]

For Stair the three formal sources of Scots law are ancient custom, statute, and recent custom or practice. This division appears throughout the *Institutions*, for example, in the reference in the Dedication to "our statutes, our ancient customs, and the more recent decisions of our Supreme Courts",[29] but it is set out and explained as follows:

> Next unto equity, nations were ruled by consuetude, which declareth equity and constituteth expediency . . . So that every nation, under the name of law, understand their ancient and uncontroverted customs, time out of mind, or their first and fundamental laws. . . . In like manner, we are ruled in the first place by our ancient and immemorial customs, which may be called our common law.[30]

Stair then contrasts the "common law" of Scotland with the other senses in which the term "common law" is used: the common law of nations, and the *jus commune* of the Civilian tradition. He continues:

> By this law, is our primogeniture, and all degrees of succession, our legitim portion of children, communion of goods between man and wife, and the division thereof at their death, the succession of the nearest agnates, the terces of relicts, the liferent of husbands by the courtesy, the exclusion of deeds on deathbed; which are anterior to any statute, and not comprehended in any, as being more solemn and sure than those are.[31]

All Stair's examples of ancient custom are taken from the law of property and succession, the very area covered by Craig's treatise, and in which, although discerning many similarities with the law of England, Craig was reluctant to admit direct English influence. Can it be that Stair's ancient

---

27 See *RM (Cooper)*, introduction, at 6. The credit for identifying the references to *Regiam Majestatem* in Craig's work does not belong, however, to Lord Clyde, as Cooper suggests: they are already to be found in the 3rd edition of 1732, edited by James Baillie.
28 For an appraisal of the role of custom from a quite different standpoint see J T Cameron, "Custom as a source of law in Scotland" (1964) 27 *MLR* 306.
29 Stair, *Inst*, Dedication, at 59. See further on Stair's preference for customary law, Ford, *Law and Opinion* (n 14) at 407–417, 534–539.
30 Stair, *Inst*, 1.1.16.
31 Stair, *Inst*, 1.1.16.

custom, the common law of Scotland, was originally derived in the main from England? Certainly, this seems to be the case. The origin of all the customs mentioned by Stair, including even deathbed which later took on a distinctive Scottish appearance, is to be found in the Anglo-Norman law. All are to be found in *Regiam Majestatem*, and in that part of the *Regiam* which owes most to *Glanvill*.[32] Some indeed, such as legitim and *jus relictae*, have remained virtually unchanged from *Glanvill*'s day until our own. Some, such as courtesy, were peculiar to England, Scotland and Normandy. Craig was well aware of this, even if many English writers in his day (and one might add our own) were not; "The English call this right the courtesy of England as if it was a peculiarly English institution; but this is a mistake, for both in Scotland and among the Normans the right of courtesy finds observance."[33]

Did Stair realise that his examples of ancient custom were of English origin? It is difficult to believe that he did not. At best he may have shut his eyes to what he did not care to see. Stair knew his Craig, and frequently refers to him. The treatment of the law of property and succession in the *Institutions*, a substantial proportion of the whole, owes much to Craig, including the references to English and French law. Stair also knew his *Regiam Majestatem*, but, like Craig, affected to believe that it was not part of Scots law: "Craig doth very well observe . . . that those books called *Regiam Majestatem* are no part of our law, but were compiled for the customs of England";[34] and

> though the book called *Regiam Majestatem* treat thereof [of deathbed], yet does not introduce it, and it hath been compiled by some stranger, who hath not fully known our law, but by mistake hath resolved most cases by the customs of other nations, especially of England.[35]

Stair's contemporary, Sir George Mackenzie, held a different opinion. In his *Institutions*, published only three years after the first edition of Stair's *Institutions*, Mackenzie lists *Regiam Majestatem* among the sources of Scots law, referring to "the Books of Regiam Majestatem, which are generally looked upon as a Part of our Law".[36]

We can only speculate as to why Stair was so reluctant to acknowledge the influence of England on Scottish customary law. Stair was heavily involved in politics and had many enemies. He may have been sensitive to the charge

---

32 *RM (Cooper)*, 2.16, 18, 37, 58 and especially 25–34; relying on *Glanvill*, Books VI and VII.
33 Craig, *JF*, 2.22.40 (Clyde translation). Unfortunately Craig goes on to deduce courtesy from a rescript of the Emperor Constantine!
34 Stair, *Inst*, 1.1.16.
35 Stair, *Inst*, 3.4.27.
36 Mackenzie, *Inst*, 1.1.

of being an angliciser, especially in view of his past as a judge in the "English time".[37] Like Craig, Stair was involved as a commissioner in Union negotiations with the English. Like Craig, Stair was convinced of the intrinsic merit of Scots law:

> The law of Scotland in its nearness to equity, plainness and facility in its customs, tenors and forms, and in its celerity and dispatch in the administration and execution of justice, may well be paralleled with the best law in Christendom.[38]

When talk of union and the assimilation of laws was in the air, Stair may not have wished to give too many hostages to fortune.

The ancient custom of Stair's *Institutions* then, the common law of Scotland, that part of Scots law most comparable to the *droit coutumier* of the Continent, had been largely borrowed from English law. There is also a case for seeing English influence in the prominence given by Stair to recent custom as a source of law. By recent custom Stair meant above all the decisions of the Court of Session, and to these he gave great weight. He wrote in the Dedication to the first edition,

> I have, as distinctly and clearly as I could, by this Essay, given a view of law and of our customs, and the decisions of the Session, since the institution of the College of Justice, as they have been remarked and reported by the most eminent judges and pleaders from time to time.[39]

And in the Advertisement to the second edition he wrote:

> The former edition was collected by me in many years, and designed chiefly for my particular use, that I might know the decisions and acts of Session, since the first institution of it, and that I might the more clear and determine my judgment in the matter of justice. And to that end I made indexes of all the decisions, which had been observed by men of the greatest reputation, and did cite the same . . . I have been very sparing to express my own opinion in dubious cases of law, not determined by our customs and statutes, but have rather congested what the Lords have done, than what my opinion would have been in cases when they were free . . . I have omitted no material decision of the Lords that I found, especially where they were contrary, and seemed to be inconsistent, that judges might not be overruled by adducing some decisions, where others about the same time were opposite.[40]

He writes again in the same vein at the beginning of Book IV in the second edition, saying that in this Book, as it deals with process, he is going to

---

37 Stair's own phrase: *Decisions* vol 1 (below, n 52) at 328 (*Kilbocho v Kilbocho* (1665) Mor 3058).
38 Stair, *Inst*, 1.1.16.
39 Stair, *Inst*, Dedication, at 62–63.
40 Stair, *Inst*, Advertisement, at 64, 65.

give his own opinion and cite few decisions, in contrast to the rest of the *Institutions*.

In the body of the work there is ample evidence that Stair carried out his declared policy. Commenting on the casualty of relief he notes,

> there is scarce a controversy or decision observed about it by any since the institution of the College of Justice, so that we must rest in the common custom used betwixt superior and vassal, the nature of this casualty, and the opinions of some few of our lawyers who have written upon it.[41]

Discussing the Bankruptcy Act 1621 he says

> This excellent statute hath been cleared by limitations and extensions, in multitudes of decisions occurring since, relating to defrauding of creditors: which being of the greatest importance for public good and security, we shall distinctly, and in order, hold forth the several cases that have been decided in this matter.[42]

Another significant passage, which is worth quoting in full, occurs at the beginning of Stair's treatment of feudal rights, where he explains his attitude towards Craig's *Jus Feudale*:

> Our learned countryman, Craig of Rickertoun, hath largely and learnedly handled the feudal rights and customs of this and other nations, in his book *De Feudis;* and therefore we shall only follow closely what, since his time, by statute or custom hath been cleared or altered in our feudal rights, which is very much; for he having written in the year 1600, there are since many statutes and variety of cases, which did occur, and were determined by the Lords, and have been *de recenti* observed, as they were done by the most eminent of the Lords and lawyers, as by Haddingtoun, who was President of the Session, and by President Spotiswood, and by Dury, who continued in the Session from the year 1621 until his death in the year 1642. And though these decisions have been intermitted, since that time, till Charles II's return, the loss is not great, these times being troublesome, and great alterations of the Lords;[43] but the decisions of the Lords have been constantly observed since that King's return, by which most of the feudal questions are determined; and those things which Craig could but conjecture from the nature of the feudal rights, the customs of neighbouring nations, and the opinion of feudists, are now commonly known, and come to a fixed custom; neither doth he observe any decisions particularly further than his own time, in which our feudal customs could be but little determined, seeing the Lords of Session were mutable and ambulatory, till the year 1540, in which King James V did perfect the establishment of the Session in a College of Justice, who, at first, could not be so knowing and fixed in their forms and customs; and therefore, it cannot be thought strange, if the feudal customs, as they are now settled, do much differ from what Craig did observe.[44]

---

41 Stair, *Inst*, 2.4.27.
42 Stair, *Inst*, 1.9.15.
43 The "years which the locusts had eaten", above text accompanying n 14.
44 Stair, *Inst*, 2.3.3.

There are many examples of Stair preferring decisions of the Session to Craig's opinion: "Though Craig insinuateth, that . . . yet posterior decisions have, upon good grounds, cleared, that . . .";[45] "It is also related by Craig that . . . These are most part overruled by custom . . .";[46] "Craig in the forementioned place relates the opinion of the Feudists, whereunto he agrees, . . . but the contrary was found in the case of the *La. Carnegie contra Lo. Cranburn*".[47] Frequently too Stair prefers Scots custom to a known Roman law or Canon law solution.[48]

In all, despite his declared aversion to "the nauseating burden of citations",[49] Stair cites more than 2,000 decisions of the Court of Session in his *Institutions* – too many for Lord Kames who wrote, rather unfairly, that "Lord Stair, our capital writer on law, was an eminent philosopher; but as he was not educated to the profession of law, his Institutes [sic] consist chiefly of decisions of the court of Session; which with him are all of equal authority, though not always concordant".[50] Stair also, like several of his predecessors as Lord President, collected the decisions of the Court of Session.[51] Unlike them, he published them. His *Decisions*, published in 1683, and covering the years 1661–81, was the first published collection of decisions in Scotland, and his Epistle Dedicatory thereto sets out once again his views on the importance of case law.[52] Stair clearly thought of his *Institutions* and *Decisions* as being complementary. They are mentioned together in Charles II's Gift and Privilege for Printing, dated 11 April 1681,[53] and the *Decisions* are referred to at least once explicitly in the *Institutions*: "As to the meaning and interpretation of special clauses, they are congested in the Indexes of the Decisions of the Lords observed by me".[54]

---

45 Stair, *Inst*, 2.4.22.
46 Stair, *Inst*, 2.7.23.
47 Stair, *Inst*, 2.11.22, citing *Lady Carnegie v Lord Cranburn* (1663) Mor 10375.
48 The passing of risk on sale (Stair, *Inst*, 1.14.7) provides a controversial example of Stair arguing from a negative as to Scots custom and rejecting the settled Roman rule that *periculum rei venditae nodum traditae est emptoris*. Stair's view has the support of Hope, Balfour and *Regiam Majestatem*. Sir George Mackenzie accepted the Roman rule, and by the nineteenth century it was possible to assert that *periculum est emptoris* was the common law of Scotland.
49 Stair, *Inst*, Dedication, at 60.
50 Kames, *Elucidations respecting the Common and Statute Law of Scotland* (1777), preface.
51 See Stair, *Inst*, 2.3.3; above, text accompanying n 40; also *An Apology for Sir James Dalrymple of Stair, President of the Session, by Himself* (1690) at xxii (". . . and I did seldom eat or drink, and scarcely ever slept, before I perused the informations that passed every sederunt-day, and set down the decisions of the Lords . . ."). The *Apology* was reprinted by the Bannatyne Club in 1825 and again in J S More's edition of Stair's *Institutions* (1832).
52 J Dalrymple, *Decisions of the Court of Session* (2 vols, 1683, 1687).
53 Printed in Stair's *Decisions* (n 52) after the Epistle Dedicatory.
54 Stair, *Inst*, 4.42.22.

It is no accident that two Continental scholars, writing recently on Scottish legal history, have singled out Stair's citation of cases as an outstanding feature of his work. "The text of Stair's exposition is based mainly on the decisions of the Court of Session . . .," writes Luig in his survey of the 'Institutes of National Law', "unlike the contemporary continental lawyers, in particular those in Germany, Stair regarded the development of the law by the judges as more important than academic legal science".[55] In like manner Hélène David refutes the notion that Stair cites comparatively little authority:

> On a parfois reproché à Stair de n'avoir pas assez tenu compte des decisions de la Cour de Session . . . Ce reproche me paraît mal fondé . . . Si nous ouvrons les *Institutions*, nous voyons au contraire que la jurisprudence y tient une grande place: on compte en effet dans les quatre livres des *Institutions* environ 2315 décisions citées, . . . Ces nombres paraissent, pour l'époque, considérables.[56]

In the prominence which he gives to decisions, Stair is in no way exceptional among Scottish legal writers, either contemporary or subsequent. Even Sir George Mackenzie, for whom statutes were "the chief Pillars of our law,"[57] could emphasise on occasion the importance of decided cases. In the high-flown oration which he delivered at the opening of the Advocates Library in 1689 he said,

> Superest tantum ut gratias, quas possumus maximas, agamus Senatui nostro illustrissimo, sub cujus auspiciis nostra crevit Bibliotheca, et cujus Decisiones (veras illas et immortales Judicum imagines) in hoc Parnasso, Musarumque sinu, honore merito concelebrabimus.[58]

The citation of decisions is in fact, such a commonplace of Scots law and legal writing that the manifold citation of cases in Stair's *Institutions* does

---

55 K Luig, "The institutes of national law in the seventeenth and eighteenth centuries", 1972 *JR* 193 at 221 and 222.
56 David (n 4), at 333 (Stair has sometimes been reproached for not having taken sufficient account of the decisions of the Court of Session . . . This reproach seems to me to be ill-founded . . . If we open up the *Institutions*, we see on the contrary that case law plays a large role: we find indeed in the four books of the *Institutions* about 2315 cited decisions . . . These numbers seem, for the time, considerable.)
57 The *Works of that eminent and learned lawyer, Sir George Mackenzie of Rosehaugh, Advocate to Charles II and James VII. With many learned treatises of his, never before printed* (2 vols, 1716), vol 1, *Treatises (Observations on the Acts of Parliament)* at 166.
58 Mackenzie, *Oratio inauguralis in aperienda Jurisconsultorum Biblioteca* (1689), at 30; reprinted with introduction by J W Cairns and A M Cain (1989) with this translation of the quoted passage by J H Loudon at 76: "There remains only the duty of rendering the warmest possible thanks to our illustrious Senators under whose protection our library has grown, and whose Decisions (which faithfully reveal to posterity the characters of judges) we shall in this Parnassus, this bosom of the Muses, crown with the honour which they so well deserve."

not strike the Scots lawyer as being in any way remarkable. Yet Luig has noted that it sets Stair apart from contemporary continental writing. What is the explanation? It is true, as Luig remarks, that comparatively little Scots customary law had been written down – although Sir John Skene's collection *Regiam Majestatem Scotiae Veteres Leges et Constitutiones* (1609), to give it its full title, is an important contribution. Luig also points to a lack of active legislation; yet for Mackenzie statutes were "the chief Pillars of our law", and the Scots statutes from 1424 to 1633, albeit liable to desuetude, take up over five hundred folio pages in the "Glendook" folio edition of 1681. Although collections of "Practicks" were not unknown on the Continent, surely the main explanation for the frequent citation of cases in Stair's *Institutions* and other Scottish legal works lies in the geographical proximity and influence of England, the case-law system *par excellence*. Stair was not the only President of a supreme court who wrote an institutional work and published a collection of decisions in the seventeenth century. Sir Edward Coke, Lord Chief Justice of the Common Pleas and later of the King's Bench, edited eleven volumes of law reports between 1600 and 1616, and after his dismissal from the Bench in 1616 he set to writing his *Institutes of the Laws of England*.[59] Coke's rambling style could hardly be more different from Stair's systematic approach, nor Coke's blinkered insularity from Stair's wider vision, yet the comparison is surely apt. "Common law comes from the court, Continental law from the study", write Zweigert and Kötz in their *Introduction to Comparative Law*, "the great jurists of England were judges, on the continent professors".[60]

It is suggested then that the English influence on Scots law in Stair's day, the law set out and expounded in the *Institutions*, is by no means negligible. The very common law of Scotland, those ancient and immemorial customs referred to by Stair, was in great part derived from the Anglo-Norman law. Indeed, it is clear that the legal and administrative reforms of the Norman and early Plantagenet Kings of England, at the infancy of the Common law, had a lasting influence in Scotland second only to their influence in England. The influence of English law can also be seen in Stair's treatment of recent custom, the decisions of the courts, as a source of law: throughout the *Institutions* great reliance is placed on the decisions of judges, and behind these statute takes a poor second place. In addition, although Stair does

---

59 Baker (5th edn) (n 3) at 194, 200.
60 K Zweigert and H Kötz (trans T Weir), *An Introduction to Comparative Law* (3rd edn, 1998) at 69.

not make many comparisons with contemporary systems of law, he takes more examples from England than from any other jurisdiction. This essay has necessarily been condensed, and many areas of comparison between the English and Scottish legal systems, especially in procedure and judicial administration, have not been touched upon. It cannot be denied that the Scottish legal system has strong Civilian affinities, and that these affinities were more pronounced in Stair's day than they are in our own. Yet it is also true that Scots law in the seventeenth century owed much to the Common law. In some measure Scots law has always been a "mixed" system.

# 7 The Resilience of the Scottish Common Law*

One of the outstanding features of the history of Scots law has been the continuity of legal development; a continuity which stretches back, without serious interruption or political dislocation, to a very remote past, to a time indeed before our earliest legal records begin.[1] One of the guiding threads which, in my view, helps to explain this continuity of development – perhaps the most important guiding thread – is the concept of a Scottish "common law". This paper considers the rise of the common law of Scotland and its relations with the Feudal law, the Canon law and the Civil law.[2] It seeks to demonstrate the resilience and adaptability of the common law in the face of the incoming tide of the Civil law and, in particular as regards the "Reception" of Roman law; and to suggest some reasons to this resilience.[3]

## A. THE EMERGENCE OF A SCOTTISH COMMON LAW

The idea of a specifically Scottish common law is first articulated about the middle of the thirteenth century. The emergence of such a concept at such a time can be explained by the combination of two crucial factors. The first was the extension of the terms "Scots" (*Scoti* or *Scotti*) and "Scottish" to cover all the peoples within the territory of the king of Scots; and of the term "Scotland" or *Scotia* to describe that territory. These terms as applied to land and people alike originally had a purely Irish frame of reference, but by the beginning of the eleventh century had become as apt to attach to the

---

* Originally published as "The resilience of the Scottish common law", in D L Carey Miller and R Zimmermann (eds), *The Civilian Tradition and Scots Law: Aberdeen Quincentenary Essays* (1997) 149–164.
1 As argued in ch 1 above. For a contrary view, see Lord President Cooper in his original *Scottish Legal Tradition* (1949); reprinted in 1991 as above. See also Sellar, "Common law".
2 For the rise of the Scottish common law, see Sellar (n 1), and Sellar, "Custom"; and H L MacQueen, *Common Law and Feudal Society in Medieval Scotland* (1993, reprinted 2016). Note the controversial reassessment in D Carpenter, "Scottish royal government in the thirteenth century from an English perspective", in M Hammond (ed), *New Perspectives on Medieval Scotland 1093–1286* (2013) 117.
3 See ch 1 nn 66 and 67 for references to writings on Roman law and Scots law.

longstanding colony of the Gaels in Britain as to the Gaels of Ireland.[4] At the end of that century, in 1094, in the earliest surviving Scottish charter, the style used by King Duncan II, son of Malcolm Canmore, is *rex Scottae*.[5] The regular style of his brother Edgar (and of his successors for centuries to come) was *rex Scottorum*.[6] At first, however, the Scots were only one of several people addressed by the kings of Scots in their charters, and not usually the people addressed first at that. Thus, a typical charter of King David I (1124–53), or of his grandson Malcolm IV (1153–64) would address the king's subjects *Franci, Angli,* and *Scotti* alike. Sometimes the address might include other peoples also: *Walenses* in the territory of the old kingdom of Strathclyde; and *Galwalenses* (Galwegians) in the far south-west. The pecking order is reasonably clear: French first, English second, and Scots a poorish third. In the south-east of the kingdom, indeed, the Scots might not be mentioned at all.[7] Thus when King William I (1165–1214) granted a toft of land in Berwick to the abbey of Kelso, the address is restricted to *Franci* and *Angli*.[8] The term *Scotia* had at first a similarly restricted meaning. In King David's time it denoted the country north of the Forth and Clyde. Earlier still it may have excluded land north of the Spey. By the middle of the thirteenth century however, this terminology was rapidly changing. The farsighted policy of King David and his royal successors was succeeding in melding the various peoples in their kingdom into a single nation, the nation of the Scots: and the growing perception was that of one people, the Scots, under one king, within the kingdom of Scotia.

The second factor which helps to explain the emergence of the concept of a Scottish common law at this time requires little further elaboration: the rise of the English common law. There can be no doubt that the terminology of a "common law" as it came to be used in Scotland (*communis lex* or *jus commune* in Latin; *la commune lei* in French) was borrowed direct from England.[9] To these two factors a third should be added, a corollary of the first: the fact that the kings of Scots, like the kings of England, had

---

4 On this see D Broun, "The origin of Scottish identity", in C Bjørn, A Grant and K J Stringer (eds), *Nations, Nationalism and Patriotism in the European Past* (1994) 35; see also E J Cowan, "Myth and identity in early medieval Scotland" (1984) 63 *SHR* 111.
5 A C Lawrie, *Earliest Scottish Charters* (1905), no XII. The authenticity of this charter has been disputed on a number of occasions, but now appears to be generally accepted.
6 Lawrie, *Charters* (n 5) nos XVIII–XXII.
7 G W S Barrow, *RRS*, vol 1, at 73 ff, and *passim*; and G W S Barrow, "Witnesses and the attestation of formal documents in Scotland, 12th–13th centuries" (1995) 16 *JLH* 1 at 6.
8 C Innes (ed), *Liber Sancte Marie de Calchou (Cartulary of Kelso Abbey)* (Bannatyne Club, 1846); vol 1, no 32.
9 See below text accompanying nn 11–16.

been remarkably successful in bringing their various subjects under a single body of law common to all the kingdom, declared in the king's courts. In this Scotland and England were unlike, for example, France and Germany, where there was one king, but not for many centuries a single body of law.

## B. THE SYMBOLISM OF THE CROWN

The concept of the common law of Scotland has had a continuous history from the thirteenth century until the present day. I have tried to chart its progress elsewhere, and Hector MacQueen has studied the early centuries of the common law in his *Common Law and Feudal Society in Medieval Scotland*.[10] The earliest reference to the Scots common law so for observed occurs in 1264, in a royal brieve (*jus commune*).[11] In the course of the judicial competition for the Crown of Scotland in 1291–2, known as "The Great Cause", there are frequent references to "*la commune lei e les usages de Escoce e du reaume de Engleterre*", or similar, and at least one reference to "*la commune lei expresse de Escoce*".[12] There are references also, incidentally, to that other long-lived *jus commune*, which denoted a blending of the Civil and Canon learned law: the "Paris lawyers" consulted by Edward I in the form of a *quaestio* for their opinion on the Scottish succession, refer to *leges communes scilicet imperiales*, and to *leges communes imperiales tam juri canonico quam Civili*.[13] In Robert the Bruce's legislation of 1318, passed after his victory at Bannockburn, the phrase *communis lex et communis iusticia* describes the law of the realm.[14] In 1399, as is well known, the Scots Parliament was concerned about "the mysgouvernance of the Reaulme and the defaut of the kepyng of the common law".[15] Later the Scots Parliament passed Acts in 1426 and 1504 which stress that the laws in use in the realm of Scotland should be the king's own statutes and the common law of the realm, and no "particular" laws, nor the laws of other countries or realms.[16]

---

10 For the main sources drawn on here, see above n 2. See further A Taylor, *The Shape of the State in Medieval Scotland, 1124–1290* (2016) chs 3–5.
11 Innes, *Liber* (n 8), vol 1, no 309.
12 E L G Stones and G G Simpson, *Edward I and the Throne of Scotland* (1978), vol 2, at 336 and 326.
13 Stones and Simpson, *Edward I* (n 12) vol 2, at 359 and 363 (the common imperial laws both Canon and Civil). See also G J Hand, "The opinions of Paris lawyers upon the Scottish succession c1292" (1970) 5 *Irish Jurist* 141.
14 *RPS* 1318/4.
15 *RPS* 1399/1/2.
16 *RPS* 1426/6; *RPS* A1504/3/124.

What other laws are struck at by these ordinances of 1426 and 1504? Without doubt, any laws in particular parts of the kingdom, such as the Western Isles, which might be in conflict with the king's common law, for these are mentioned specifically. But laws external to the kingdom are intended also. For, and this is highly relevant to the story of Scots law in its relations with the Civil law, the kings of Scots were determined to be masters in their own house, or as it was sometimes expressed emperors in their own kingdom. It is well known that the French attitude towards the authority of Roman law as a source was partly conditioned by the determination of the kings of France to demonstrate their independence of the Holy Roman Emperor: and that what was true of Philip the Fair of France was true also of Edward I of England. In Scotland too, it can be argued, that the desire of the Scottish kings to be seen to be independent of the Empire, coupled with the existence of a Scottish common law, prevented an uncritical adoption of Roman law in the late medieval period, when it had, in Maitland's famous phrase, "gone half-way to meet the medieval facts".[17]

In the first half of the fifteenth century a cohort of Scotsmen can be found studying the law, Canon and Civil, at the University of Leuven (Louvain).[18] One of them was William Elphinstone senior, father of the William Elphinstone the Quincentenary of whose foundation of Aberdeen we celebrate. In fact, William Elphinstone senior's lecture notes are the earliest to survive from the University of Leuven.[19] Many of these law students rose later to prominent positions in Scotland, none more so than Archibald Whitelaw, royal secretary from 1462 to 1493, first to King James III, and then to his son James IV. Yet it was in the reign of James III (1460–88) in particular, that the fact that the Scottish kingdom was an empire in itself came to be emphasised.

In 1469 the Scots Parliament enacted in striking language that notaries licensed by imperial authority would no longer be recognised in Scotland unless licensed by the king of Scots:

> Item It ls thocht expedient that sen Oure Soverane lord hes ful Jurisdictioune & fre Impire within his Realme that his hienes may mak notaris & tabellionis quhais Instruments sal have ful faith in all contractis Civile within the Realme And in

---

17 Pollock & Maitland, vol 1, at 223: "Roman law must come sooner or later; the later it comes the stronger it will be for it will have gone half way to meet the medieval facts."
18 R J Lyall, "Scottish students and masters at the universities of Cologne and Louvain in the fifteenth century" (1985) 36 *Innes Review* 55.
19 L Macfarlane, *William Elphinstone and the Kingdom of Scotland 1431–1514: The Struggle for Order* (2nd edn, 1995) at 18.

tyme cumyn that na notaris maid nor to be maid be the Imperouris Autorite have faith in contractis Civile within the Realme les than he be examinyt be the ordinare & approvit be the kings hienes.[20]

James III also used the symbolism of empire in his coinage. The groats and half-groats of James's last issue of c1484–88 display one of the most striking portraits in the whole range of the Scottish coinage. The king is shown three-quarter face – a fine Renaissance portrait, and one of the few successful three-quarter portraits in numismatic history – and wearing, in token of the independent status of his kingdom, a closed or "imperial" crown.[21] A few years later, in the reign of James IV, the same symbolism was used in the building of the new University of Aberdeen: for the tower of Bishop Elphinstone's foundation of King's College was surmounted by an imperial crown. As David McRoberts has suggested, "[i]f, as seems probable, the imperial crown over King's College was gilded, then Bishop Elphinstone's assertion of the independent sovereignty of King James IV would have looked even more spectacular than it does at the present day."[22] It is this crown in stone, renewed in 1633, which the University has taken as the symbol of its Quincentenary. A few hundred yards away the same symbolism recurs in the heraldic ceiling of St Machar's Cathedral, which dates from early in the reign of James V, for there again the king of Scots is given an imperial crown.[23]

## C. SCOTTISH COMMON LAW AND ENGLISH COMMON LAW

The common law of Scotland which emerged in the thirteenth century was not only named in imitation of the English common law, then in its own early

---

20 *RPS* 1469/20.
21 I H Stewart, *The Scottish Coinage* (2nd edn, 1967) at 67. The groat is displayed in N Macdougall, *James III: A Political Study* (2nd edn, 2009) plate 1. D McRoberts, *The Heraldic Ceiling of St Machar's Cathedral Aberdeen* (Friends of St Machar's Cathedral Occasional Papers no 2, 1981) at 12 discusses the use of the closed or imperial crown by James III and James IV, noting its adoption by Charles VIII of France in 1495, and Henry VII of England in 1485. Macfarlane, *Elphinstone* (n 19) at 330 also discusses the matter, and notes that Hector Boece specifically describes the crown on King's College as imperial, rather than royal. See also two contributions by W Ferguson: "Imperial crowns: a neglected facet of the background to the Treaty of Union of 1707" (1974) 53 *SHR* 22, and "James Anderson's *Historical Essay[,shewing that the Crown and kingdom of Scotland, is imperial and independent]*", in W M Gordon (ed), *Miscellany III* (SS vol 39, 1992) 1; and R A Mason, *Kingship and the Commonweal: Political Thought in Renaissance and Reformation Scotland* (1998) at 128–137. I am most grateful to Dr Ferguson for discussing the symbolism of the imperial crown with me. See also below n 53.
22 McRoberts, *Heraldic Ceiling* (n 21) at 12.
23 McRoberts, *Heraldic Ceiling* (n 21) at 12.

years, but derived much of its content from that source also. As Lord Cooper wrote, "[f]or roughly 200 years after the accession of David I the legal statesmen of Scotland were actively engaged in the construction of a legal system founded upon Anglo-Norman law".[24] I differ from Lord Cooper, however, in his belief that this period was marked by "a false start and a rejected experiment". On the contrary, I see the period as crucial in the formation of a specifically Scottish common law.[25] It is true, of course, that after the thirteenth century, and especially after the Wars of Independence, English law ceased to exercise such a direct influence on the development of Scots law: although its influence in the later Middle Ages was never entirely negligible. But the foundations had been solidly laid. At the very core of the later common law of Scotland lies what Lord Cooper called the "Scoto-Norman" law, based to a considerable extent on the Anglo-Norman law of England. I do not think that it is misleading to talk of a "Reception" of the Anglo-Norman law, so complete was its influence on substantive law, legal administration and procedure. Indeed, this earlier Reception had a sharper chronological focus, and was in many ways more dramatic and transparent, than the later Reception of Roman law.

The Anglo-Norman law which came from England was, of course, a variant of the Feudal law of western Europe, which found its most influential expression in the *Libri Feudorum*, "The Books of the Feus", of the Lombard jurist Obertus de Orto, compiled in the mid-twelfth century. The Feudal law was in a very real sense the common law of post-Carolingian Europe, and the *Libri Feudorum*, which incorporated the Constitutions of several of Charlemagne's imperial successors, were often regarded as an appendix to the Civil law of the Emperor Justinian himself.[26] The English common law in its infancy, it should not be forgotten, was very much in tune with contemporary European legal culture. It was its precocious development which set it apart. As Michael Clanchy has written:

> The distinctive style of English common law derived from many sources and traditions Anglo-Saxon, Norman, ecclesiastical, Roman and scholastic. The system took the form it did because it developed in the period of the twelfth-century Renaissance and it retained that form for centuries thereafter because bureaucracy perpetuated it. Hence later lawyers praised as peculiarly English something

---

24 Lord President Cooper, "From David I to Bruce, 1124–1329: the Scoto-Norman law", in *ISLH* 3 at 3.
25 Sellar (n 1).
26 For the *Libri Feudorum* see, for example, O F Robinson, T D Fergus and W M Gordon, *European Legal History* (3rd edn, 2000) at 37–38; S Reynolds, *Fiefs and Vassals: The Medieval Evidence Reinterpreted* (1994) at 215–230 and appendix.

that was really peculiarly 12th century and cosmopolitan . . . Its distinctive form was therefore a product of England's close contacts with the continent at the time and not in opposition to them.[27]

As will be noted below, one early Scottish jurist at least, Thomas Craig, was well aware of the historical background to the English common law.

The strength and lasting effect of the influence of the Anglo-Norman law on the common law of Scotland can nowhere be better observed than in Stair's treatment of custom as a source of Scots law in his *Institutions of the Law of Scotland*.[28] For Stair custom is the best and purest source of law, superior to statute. In an elegant and memorable passage he concludes:

> Yea and the nations are more happy whose laws have entered by long custom wrong out from their debates upon particular cases, until it come to a consistence of a fixed and known custom. For thereby the conveniences and inconveniences thereof through a tract of time are experimentally seen; so that which is found in some cases convenient, if in other cases afterwards it be found inconvenient, it proves abortive in the womb of time before it attain the maturity of law.[29]

Stair distinguishes between "our ancient and immemorial customs, which may be called our common law", and recent custom, by which he meant the gathering body of judicial decisions emanating from the Session. The ancient customs to which Stair referred were so well established that they needed no proof. Stair instances "our primogeniture, and all degrees of succession, our legitim portion of their death, the succession of the nearest agnates, the terces of relicts, the liferent of husbands by the courtesy, which are anterior to any statute, and not comprehended in any, as being more solemn and sure that they are".[30] Each of these customs particularly mentioned by Stair can be found in *Regiam Majestatem*, which draws on these matters virtually word for word from *Glanvill's De Legibus et Consuetudinibus Angliae*.[31] And so we are faced with the apparent paradox that the core of our common law, as understood by our greatest legal writer, is to be found in the leading text on Anglo-Norman law.

Several of the imports from the Anglo-Norman law were long to outlast Stair's time. The law of deathbed, for example, survived, much embroidered, until 1871.[32] The law of conquest – the law which governed succession to

---

27  M T Clanchy, *England and its Rulers 1066–1272* (3rd edn, 2006) at 135.
28  See ch 6 text accompanying nn 28–56.
29  Stair, *Inst*, 1.1.15.
30  Stair, *Inst*, 1.1.16.
31  See ch 6 text accompanying nn 29–33.
32  The law of deathbed was abolished by the Law of Deathbed Abolition (Scotland) Act 1871.

acquired as opposed to inherited land – survived until 1874, some 600 years after it had ceased to apply in England.[33] The division between heritable and moveable succession continued until 1964; and the six rules identified by Maitland as most characteristic of succession to land in England at the close of the reign of Henry III in 1272, remained true of heritable succession in Scotland until 1964 also.[34] The legal right of courtesy, with its peculiar rules which puzzled English lawyers already in Edward I's reign, and also that of terce, again survived until 1964: while the legal rights of *jus relictae* and *legitim* in favour of widows and children which, despite their Romanistic names, came to Scots law from the Anglo-Norman law by way of *Glanvill* and *Regiam Majestatem*, are with us still.[35]

All these examples concern "succession to defuncts", considered by Stair to be "the most important title in law".[36] But survivals from the Reception of Anglo-Norman law can be found elsewhere: for example, in the office of sheriff and that of justiciar, later Lord Justice General.[37] In criminal matters, our solemn procedure of trial by jury following on indictment can also be traced back to the Anglo-Norman law.[38]

## D. SCOTTISH COMMON LAW AND CELTIC CUSTOMARY LAW

However, if the Feudal law in Anglo-Norman guise was at the heart of the common law of Scotland, that law did not entirely supersede the older customary law, much of it Celtic in origin, but containing also elements of Anglo-Saxon and Scandinavian (or Anglo-Danish) law. This customary law too, often remodelled or reinterpreted, had its influence on the later common law of Scotland. This is in no way surprising. All over Europe, Feudal law merged with customary law; and in Scotland, unlike England, there had been no Norman Conquest to mark a break with the past. Indeeed, there can be few if any parts of Europe where there has been such longstanding political continuity as in Scotland. In Scotland north of Forth and Clyde, there has been no clean break with the past for over a thousand years – since the time of Kenneth the son of Alpin (843–858) – and arguably for longer still.

---

33 The special rules relating to conquest were abolished by the Conveyancing (Scotland) Act 1874 s 37.
34 Pollock & Maitland, vol 2 at 260; Sellar (n 1) at 89. See Succession (Scotland) Act 1964.
35 On courtesy see ch 14 and Sellar (n 1) at 90.
36 Stair, *Inst*, 3.4.
37 See Barrow, "Justiciar".
38 Sellar (n 1) at 88 ff.

The influence of Celtic law, in particular, can be found in the mainstream of later Scots common law.[39] This influence is not always easy to recognise or trace, but three instances of the tenacious survival of a technical term of Celtic law down to modern times may be noticed in passing. The term "culrath", meaning literally a back security, is found in regular use in connection with the procedure of repledging an accused from one jurisdiction to another, until repledging itself came to an end in the mid-18th century. "Letters of Slains", from *"slán"* meaning "indemnity", indicating full and formal remission of rancour by the kin of the victim, were in constant use in connection with actions for assythment until the same century.[40] A style of these letters is given as an appendix to Lord Kames' *Historical Law Tracts*.[41] The phrase last surfaced judicially (although its Celtic origins were not recognised) in the early 1970s, when the action of assythment was reviewed, albeit without success, in the case of *M'Kendrick v Sinclair*.[42] The third term is *"cáin"*, a payment made to a lord in token of his authority, comfortably traceable in a legal context until the nineteenth century, and last noticed occurring in accounts drawn up annually in an Edinburgh legal office in the 1960s.[43]

### E. THE INFLUENCE OF CANON LAW AND CIVIL LAW

If the thirteenth century marked the emergence of the Scottish common law, it also marked an important stage in the consolidation of the medieval Canon law, with the promulgation in 1234 of the Decretals, compiled for Pope Gregory IX through the genius of St Raymond of Peñafort; and the appearance later in the century of the standard manual on Romano-canonical procedure, the *Speculum Judiciale* of William Durantis. Together with the Civil law, Canon law became the *jus commune* of western Christendom: the learned law, known and influential everywhere. Where did the emerging common law of Scotland stand in relation to the *jus commune*?

Unlike Civil law, the Canon law, as Walter Ullmann always emphasised, was a living law, the living law of western Christendom.[44] The Church had its own courts and its own procedures, governed by Canon law. In Scotland,

---

39 For a discussion and examples see ch 2 above.
40 See ch 2 above text accompanying nn 73–74.
41 Henry Home, Lord Kames, *Historical Law Tracts* (1st edn, 1758) appendix.
42 *M'Kendrick v Sinclair* 1972 SC (HL) 25.
43 See ch 2 text accompanying n 149.
44 See, for example W Ullmann, *Law and Politics in the Middle Ages* (1975) chs 4 ("The Canon law") and 5 ("The scholarship of Canon law").

as elsewhere, these courts of the Church existed side by side with the lay courts, and were possessed of a wide jurisdiction, which included the constitution and dissolution of marriage, contracts entered into under oath, and, at least in Scotland and England, executry matters and moveable succession.[45] This jurisdiction continued, exclusive to the Church and no part of the common law of Scotland, until the Scottish Reformation in 1559–1560. After the Reformation, however, jurisdiction in these matters, still heavily influenced by the Canon law, became the concern of the secular courts, and merged gradually into the common law, the Court of Session being described by Act of Parliament in 1609 as "his majesteis great consistorie".[46]

However, the Canon law had influenced the development of the common law of Scotland long before this merger of jurisdictions. For example, as is well known, the Canon law doctrine of legitimation *per subsequens matrimonium* was accepted early into the Scots common law, and applied to succession to heritage, in marked contrast to the position in England.[47] Another clear borrowing is the rule enshrined in the Terce Act of 1504, by which a widow claiming her terce (that is, her right to a liferent over one third of her deceased husband's heritable estate) was allowed, if her marital status was challenged, to point to the fact that she and her alleged husband had been generally held and reputed spouses ("that the woman ask and this terce beand repute & haldin as his lauchfull wife in his life tyme") as *prima facie* evidence of her status, pending determination of the question, if required, in the Church courts.[48] In later centuries, as memory of the Canon law background grew dim, the Act of 1503 (actually 1504) was mistakenly believed to have introduced the doctrine of marriage by cohabitation with habit and repute into Scots law.[49] Other significant pre-Reformation imports from the Canon law, or rather from the *jus commune* for these drew partly on the Civil law as well – were rules on arbitration which appear already in *Regiam Majestatem*; and the Romano-canonical procedure increasingly in used in the central judicial bodies in the fifteenth century, and adopted by the Session from 1532, and the sheriff courts from 1540.[50]

---

45 G Donaldson, "The church courts", in *ISLH* 363.
46 *RPS* 1609/4/20.
47 A E Anton, "Parent and child", in *ISLH* 116, at 117; above, ch 1 n 41.
48 *RPS* 1504/3/42.
49 See ch 9 below.
50 On arbitration, see *RM (Cooper)* 2.1.10 (*RM (APS)* 2.1–7); A M Godfrey, *Civil Justice in Renaissance Scotland* (2009), 361–393. For Romano-canonical influence in *Regiam Majestatem* generally, and the debt to the Canonist Goffredus de Trano (d 1245), see P G Stein, "The sources of the Romano-canonical part of *Regiam Majestatem*" (1969) 48 *SHR* 107.

There were imports from the Civil law also. These have been considered by others, as also the question as to whether and at what time such imports into Scots law should be regarded as constituting a Reception.[51] The point to emphasise here is that the common law of Scotland, as it developed from the thirteenth century onwards, remained open to the influence of the learned laws, both Canon and Civil, in a way not equally true of the common law of England. One channel of this influence, undoubtedly, was provided by those who sat in a judicial capacity. Many of those who served on the central judicial bodies before 1532 were churchmen with a formal training in Canon law, and who had cut their teeth as Bishop's Official. The prime example is, of course, William Elphinstone, whose service to the Crown as a lord of council and lord auditor of causes and complaint between 1478 and 1514 was second to none. He studied Canon law at Paris, and also Civil law at Orleans, and was from 1471 to 1478 Official of Glasgow, and from 1478 to 1483 Official of Lothian.[52] After 1532, half the judges on the newly constituted Session, now established as the College of Justice, as also the Lord President of the Court, were by statute churchmen.

## F. SIR JOHN SKENE'S VIEWS ON THE SCOTTISH COMMON LAW

I should like to conclude by examining what two of the principal writers on Scots law at the turn of the sixteenth and seventeenth centuries, Sir John Skene and Thomas Craig, had to say about the relationship between the common law of Scotland and the other laws we have had under consideration – the Canon law, the Civil law, the Feudal law and Anglo-Norman law. How did they perceive the historical relationship between these laws? How did they rate them as formal sources of law? And how far were they conscious of Scots law as a system in itself?

As a young man Skene, as he informs us himself in the elegant dedication to James VI in his Latin edition of *Regiam Majestatem* published in 1609, had spent seven years abroad, and had studied Civil law at the university of Wittenberg.[53] Skene makes a clear distinction between Scots law (*jurispru-*

---

51 See generally, the references above (n 3).
52 For Elphinstone's judicial career see Macfarlane, *Elphinstone* (n 19) passim; also A L Brown, "The Scottish "establishment" in the later 15th century", 1978 *JR* 89.
53 An engraving of an imperial crown figures prominently in Skene, *RM (Latin)*, appearing, for example, on the title page and at the beginning of the dedication to the King. For Skene's career and writings see J W Cairns, T D Fergus and H L MacQueen, "Legal humanism in Renaissance

*dentia Scotica*) and Civil law (*jus Civilis Romanorum*). He was interested, he says, in exploring the similarities and differences between these laws – *quae varia est, et multiplex* – and in combining the foreign and the municipal (*peregrina cum domesticis*).⁵⁴ In an oft-quoted passage Skene complains that all too often aspiring Scots jurists had studied the Civil law, but neglected their own Scots law, because, in Peter Stein's translation, "[they] found the old Scottish laws obscure and their language distasteful (*stylo horrido et aspero scriptas*)."⁵⁵

The dedication flatters King James in fulsome terms, paying tribute to the singular erudition of this pupil of George Buchanan. Skene notes that James had long wished to see the laws of his ancestors (*tuorumque majoram leges*) clarified and expounded for the greater utility of his subjects in the kingdom of Scotland. Skene adds that these laws of the king's ancestors agreed for the most part with the laws of the kingdom of England, to which James had just succeeded. Skene's edition includes not only the text of *Regiam Majestatem*, but other legal texts also, such as *Quoniam Attachiamenta*, and statutes ascribed to various Scottish kings before the reign of James I (1406–37); collected, as he says, from the public records and from old books and manuscripts. In the same year Skene also published a separate Scots edition of the same texts, "translated out of the Latine into the Scottish language, to the *use and knowledge of all the subjects within this Realme*".⁵⁶ Of Skene's commitment to Scots law as a separate and independent system there can be no doubt.

In the preface to his Latin edition of *Regiam Majestatem*, Skene explains he had tried to establish the best text from the many variant readings in the manuscript sources by making comparisons with relevant passages from the Civil law, the Canon law, the Norman law (*jus Nortmannicus*) – for this is how Skene refers to the Feudal law – and from English law (*jus Anglicus*). He notes that Civil law, Canon law, Norman law and English law were the sources from which nearly all the older Scots law had been drawn, or with which it agreed. He adds that the debt to English law (*leges Regni Angliae*)

---

Scotland" (1990) 11 *JLH* 40 at 44–48 (also as "Legal humanism and the history of Scots law: John Skene and Thomas Craig", in J MacQueen (ed), *Humanism in Renaissance Scotland* (1990) 48).

54 "*Jurisprudentiam Scoticam perscrutari ejusque coginitionem, cum juris Civilis Romanorum scientia conferre, et utriusque communionem et differentem (quae varia est, et multiplex) annotare, et ad meam utilitatum, peregrine cum domesticis conjungere decrevi.*"

55 P G Stein, "The influence of Roman law on the law of Scotland", 1963 *JR* 205 at 217, reprinted in P G Stein, *The Character and Influence of the Roman Civil Law: Historical Essays* (1988) 319 at 331.

56 Skene, *RM (Scots)* (his italics).

was such that anyone able to understand English law would understand a great part of Scots law also.⁵⁷ Skene, therefore, while recognising Civil law, Canon law and Feudal law as historical sources of this Scottish common law, particularly stresses the value of this study of English law, which he expressly distinguishes from Norman or Feudal law, as an aid to understanding the older Scottish laws.

## G. THOMAS CRAIG AND HIS VIEWS ON THE SCOTTISH COMMON LAW

### (1) Scottish common law and English common law

In his insistence that there was substantial common ground between Scots law and English law, Skene was at one with his contemporary Thomas Craig.⁵⁸ In both his celebrated *Jus Feudale* and the less well known *De Unione Regnorum Britanniae* Craig made much of points of comparison between Scots and English law.⁵⁹ In *Jus Feudale* he wrote of his discovery of "the same foundations for each system of law presently observed both in England and in Scotland", and of "the greatest affinity between them in the arguing and deciding of cases".⁶⁰ In the *De Unione* he asserted "that at the present day there are no two nations whose laws and institutes more closely correspond than England and Scotland".⁶¹ In *Jus Feudale* Craig cites up to eighteen "axioms" as he terms them, or adages, taken from English law which "to a large extent are also followed by ourselves [i.e., *Scots law*]".⁶² Most of these examples are taken from land law or succession: thus, "the

---

57 '*Fontes ipsos unde singulae fere leges desumtae sunt, aut cum quibus consentiunt, annotavi, ex Jure Civili, Canonico, Nortmannico. Et ex legibus Regni Angliae, cum quibus nostrae magna ex parte concordant, adeo ut qui has intellexerit, illas quoque magna ex parti intellegere possit.*" Note, however, that despite his recognition of the debt owed by the Scottish common law to English law, Skene continued to maintain that *Glanvill* was copied from *RM* rather than the other way round; on which see H L MacQueen, "*Glanvill* resarcinate: Sir John Skene and *Regiam Majestatem*", in A A MacDonald, M Lynch and I B Cowan (eds), *The Renaissance in Scotland Studies in Literary, Religious, Historical and Cultural History Offered to John Durkan* (1994) 385.
58 Sellar (n 1): and see Cairns/Fergus/MacQueen (n 53) especially at 48–60.
59 See ch 6 above, text accompanying nn 15–27.
60 Craig, *JF*, Epistle Dedicatory at lxxiii (Dodd translation).
61 Craig, *De Unione* at 304. Craig continues: "On fundamental principles of jurisprudence they agree perfectly, though in procedure they differ, a fact which by no means obscures the general resemblance between their systems of law. Though I am not deeply versed in English law . . . I should say, from such study as I have given to the subject, that there is not that diversity between the two systems of law as is popularly supposed to exist."
62 Craig, *JF*, 1.7.13–14.

firstborn son succeeds to the whole inheritance whereas daughters succeed *per capita*"; "Movable goods pertain not to the heirs but to the executors appointed in the deceased's last will"; and, "the rights of guardianship and the marriage of heirs, and also of relief (as they are called), belong to the lord". In the *De Unione* Craig ranges through English law, public and private, in order to demonstrate the similarities between Scots and English law.[63] Again he concentrates on land law and succession, but he also points, for example, to the use of the jury in criminal proceedings in both countries, and towards a similarity of approach towards sources of law.

Some of Craig's examples, there can be little doubt, are somewhat strained. His views are those of an apologist for closer union between the kingdoms of Scotland and England, and, therefore, to an extent, partisan. Such views were not universally held by his contemporaries, as Craig freely acknowledges. There were jurists, he notes, who held that England followed her own municipal law while Scots law was founded on Civil law.[64] However, Craig's reflections on the similarities between Scots and English law need to be set in a wider context. It was the breadth of Craig's vision and the depth of his historical understanding that enabled him to make comparisons where others saw none.

## (2) Feudal law and Civil law

If Craig thought that there was a fundamental identity between Scots law and English law, it was partly because he saw both systems within the wider context of the Feudal law and the Civil law. Craig reckoned the Feudal law to be part of the native law, the *jus proprium*, of Scotland, broadly defined: *hoc jus proprium huius regni dici potest (si latius juris proprii nomen extendamus)* –"we may call this the *jus proprium* of this kingdom, if we take a broad view of the definition of *jus proprium*." "For feudalism", continued Craig, "is the source and origin from which most of the law in daily use in our courts, and all our legal usages and practice are derived."[65] English law too owed much to the Feudal law, even if English lawyers were reluctant to acknowledge this fact. One reason, says Craig, why he gave so many exam-

---

63 Craig, *De Unione* at 305–327.
64 Craig, *De Unione* at 326. *Plus ça change, plus c'est la même chose!*
65 Craig, *JF*, 1.8.16. The translation of this passage is my own. Dodd (n 59) reads (at 179): "this [feudal law] can be said to be the proper law of this kingdom (if we take the term *jus proprium* broadly), because all the law which we employ today in court and all usage and practice flows from its spring and fonts."

ples of similarities between the "axioms" of English law and Scots law, was to "shew that the law of England owes much to the Feudal law, little as the debt may be openly acknowledged in a system which rather professes to be independent of all others".[66] In the *De Unione* he writes to the same effect: "Our English neighbours are therefore far out in their reckoning in their belief that their legal system is indigenous and unlike those of other countries".[67]

If English law, like Scots, was grounded in the Feudal law, it also, in Craig's estimation, owed much to the Civil law. Craig's views on this subject are worth quoting at some length. In the *De Unione* he writes:

> The Civil law, so the English imagine, has but little vogue among them. Indeed though you will find in every branch of study very learned men in England, there are very few who have made the study of Civil law their main pursuit. They are content to merely salute it from the threshold, and in its room to give consideration to the institutes and customs of their native law. It has indeed been held by some jurists that England follows her own municipal law, whereas Scotland's system is rooted in Civil law. But in fact the Civil law has never been so exiled from English practice as to prevent its principles and decisions from flashing light on every point and illuminating every controversy. But this illumination they prefer to ascribe to their own jurists rather than to the ancient jurisconsults. And yet, however little Civil law may be professed among them, it none the less shines so clearly amid all their legal controversies that any one skilled in it will very readily discover that all of them are easily capable of solution by the Civil law and the responses of the jurisconsults or rescripts of the Caesars, as is frequently noticeable in the cases reported by Plowden and Dyer.[68]

It is against the wider background, therefore, of a common European legal tradition, that Craig's comparison of Scots law with English law must be understood.

### (3) The hierarchy of sources

Craig also considered the ranking of the formal sources of Scots law, the earliest of our Institutional writers to do so.[69] His treatment of these sources is consistent with his understanding as to the historical origins of the law. When controversy arises, says Craig, the first question to ask is whether the matter is covered by the *jus scriptum* of Scotland – effectively the Acts of

---

66 Craig, *De Unione* at 311.
67 Craig, *De Unione* at 311.
68 Craig, *De Unione* at 326 ff. There is a passage in Craig, *JF* (1.7.22) to the same effect. See also Gordon (n 51). For a telling re-assessment of the debt of English common law to the *jus commune*, which supports Craig's view, see D J Seipp, "The reception of Canon law and Civil law in the common law courts before 1600" (1993) 13 *Oxford JLS* 388.
69 Craig, *JF*, 1.8.9.

the Scots Parliament. Failing this, the next source is Scottish customary law, a settled course of judicial decisions or practice: *judicatarum consuetudo observatur, quam nos "praxin" vocamus*. If neither the written nor the customary law of Scotland can provide the answer, the next place of resort is the written Feudal law: *post consuetudinem tertium locum juri Feudali scripto tribuemus*. This is to be preferred to the Civil or Canon law. Failing Feudal law, says Craig, we must have recourse to the Civil law, but he adds that the Civil law must give way to Canon law where they differ. This is in keeping with his account of the Canon law earlier in *Jus Feudale*, where he says that even although Scotland has "shaken off the papal yoke, the Canon law's great authority still survives in our country, to the extent that where it deviates from the Civil law" – and Craig says that this is often the case, and that much has been written about the differences – "the Canon law is preferred by us" (*jus Canonicum praeferamus*).[70] The Civil law, therefore, as an independent system of law, rates surprisingly low in Craig's hierarchy of sources.

The same approach towards sources of law is to be discerned in Craig's *De Unione*. At the close of his discussion on Scots and English law, Craig considers how they might best be harmonised. "Should the attempt be made," he says, "it would be necessary to revert to the sources of feudal law, that is . . . to the Norman law (*Jus Normannicum*), in whose idiom the laws of England were and still are written." If that did not provide an answer, it would then be necessary to go back beyond the Norman law, "to the feudal law (*Jus Feudale*) from which that of Normandy was derived". If common ground could not be found even there, then, says Craig, it would be necessary to have recourse to the Civil law, "whose principles are so equitable and of such widespread acceptance that it deservedly merits the appellation, common law (*Jus commune*)".[71] This view of the relationship between Civil law and Scots law, namely that the Civil was followed for its equity rather than any inherent authority, appears also in *Jus Feudale*, where Craig states that in Scotland Roman law is accepted in so far as it accords with nature and right reason (*quatenus legibus naturae et rectae rationi congruunt*).[72] Craig's

---

70 Craig, *JF*, 1.3.24; note also 1.8.17 ("*in eis jus pontificium a nostris praefertur*" – in these differences the papal law is preferred by us).
71 For all these quotations see Craig, *De Unione*, at 327–328.
72 Craig, *JF*, 1.2.14. Craig does note in the same title: "So it is that we follow the decisions and rules of the Civil law, especially in the management of moveables . . . [W]e closely follow the Civil law in paction, transactions, restitution, arbitrations or (as we say nowadays) arbitraments, servitudes, contracts both *bonae fidei* and *stricti iuris*, and both nominate and innominate, evictions, pledges, tutory, legacies, actions, exceptions, obligations and finally in punishing delicts. In fact, I would say that the Civil law is so diffused through all of our affairs and around all our concerns

assessment in turn is in full agreement with Stair's later and better known statement that Roman law was not acknowledged in Scotland as a law binding for its authority, but was followed rather for its equity.[73]

At the heart of Craig's ever widening circles of generality lies the native law of Scotland, and to this, despite his arguments in favour of harmonisation, he, like Skene, was strongly attached: "We are all aware that different forms of action and forensic procedure are observed in our country [*Scotland*] and theirs [*England*]," he wrote in the "Epistle Dedicatory" to his *Jus Feudale*, "but I would say, with all respect to our neighbours, that our forms of action and judicial proceeding are preferable over the forms of all the other nations I have ever seen – and I do not think I am making this declaration rashly."[74] Again this puts us in mind of Stair who wrote that, "[t]he law of Scotland in its nearness to equity, plainness and facility in its customs, tenors, and forms, and in its celerity and dispatch in the administration and execution of justice, may be well paralleled with the best law in Christendom."[75]

Lord President Dundas' remark, made towards the end of the eighteenth century, has often been quoted: "I respect the Civil law; but I will not haul it in to destroy our own institutions."[76] Whatever view one takes of the Reception of Roman law in Scotland, can one doubt that the same sentiment could have been expressed by Stair at the end of the seventeenth century or Thomas Craig at the end of the sixteenth? This is not, of course, to deny the importance of the Civilian tradition in the shaping of Scots law. On the contrary: in some areas of Scots law, for example, unjustified enrichment, an appreciation of the Civilian background is the beginning of understanding. But the story of the Reception of Roman law in Scotland is a complex one which can only be properly understood against the background of a strong and resilient native tradition.

---

that practically no inquiry and no sort of case occurs in which its singular force and function are not manifestly apparent. Whenever something difficult arises in court or judgments, the solution is to be sought therein" (Dodd trans at 55). See further two articles by J W Cairns: "The Civil law tradition in Scottish legal thought", in D L Carey Miller and R Zimmermann (eds), *The Civilian Tradition and Scots Law* (1997) 191; "*Ius Civile* in Scotland, c 1600" (2004) 2 *Roman Legal Tradition* 136 (the latter reprinted in J W Cairns, *Law, Lawyers and Humanism: Selected Essays on the History of Scots Law*, Vol 1 (2015) ch 3).

73 Stair, *Inst*, 1.1.12. Neither Craig nor Stair quote the well-known tag *non rationae imperii sed imperio rationis*, but such was undoubtedly their view.
74 Craig, *JF*, Epistle Dedicatory, at lxxiii (Dodd trans).
75 Stair, *Inst*, 1.1.16.
76 Hailes, *Decisions*, vol 2, at 987.

# 8 Scots Law: Mixed from the Very Beginning? A Tale of Two Receptions*

The 1990s witnessed a welcome, albeit sometimes impassioned, debate about the nature of Scots law and its relationship, past, present and prospective, with the English Common Law on the one hand, and the Civil Law tradition on the other. The debate was to an extent ideological and touched on the most appropriate way of teaching Scots law in our universities, as well as looking forward to the possible emergence of a new European *jus commune*. Even the sober discipline of legal history did not escape a touch of the ideological brush. Some of us who have written on the history of Scots law were labelled "revisionists" – "arraigned as revisionists" might not be putting it too strongly. As one of these revisionists, perhaps the revisionist-in-chief, I am grateful for the opportunity to reconsider my position and express my views.[1]

The title of this paper refers back to a passage, in an article on the history of unjust enrichment, written jointly by Hector MacQueen and myself, which attracted particular criticism:

> Large and unjustified claims have sometimes been made as to the extent to which Scots law is based on Roman law. In fact, from the time of its emergence in the Middle Ages, the common law of Scotland has been open to influence from both the common law and the Civilian tradition. It has been a "mixed" system from the very beginning.[2]

---

* The Stair Society Annual Lecture, delivered 7 November 1997. Originally published as "Scots law: mixed from the very beginning? A tale of two receptions" (2000) 4 *Edin LR* 3–18.
1 Various prior contributions to the debate are noticed below: they include N R Whitty, "The Civilian tradition and debates on Scots law", 1996 *Tydskrif vir die Suid-Afrikaanse Reg* 227 and 442; H L MacQueen, "Mixture or muddle? Teaching and research in Scottish legal history" (1997) 5 *Zeitschrift für Europäisches Privatrecht* 369; R Evans-Jones, "Civil law in the Scottish legal tradition", in R Evans-Jones (ed), *The Civil Law Tradition in Scotland* (SS supp vol 2, 1995); and R Evans-Jones, "Receptions of law, mixed legal systems and the genius of Scots private law" (1998) 114 *LQR* 228, published after this paper was delivered.
2 H L MacQueen and W D H Sellar, "Unjust enrichment in Scots law", in E J H Schrage (ed), *Unjust Enrichment; The Comparative History of the Law of Restitution* (1995) at 289; the pas-

This passage was singled out for criticism by Niall Whitty in the course of a far-ranging paper on Scots law and the Civilian tradition.[3] In a section headed "The revision of the legal-nationalist interpretation of Scottish legal history", Whitty accepts that the "revisionists", to adopt for a moment his terminology, have made some important original contributions, but continues "Some (not all) of their writings however have unduly downgraded the role of the *ius commune* and exaggerated that of English law in the historical development of Scots law, as in the following misleading passage . . .".[4] Then follows the passage quoted above, which is glossed by Whitty as follows:

> Yet it has not been established that any contemporary English source at all was cited to the Court of Session between its establishment as a College of Justice in 1532 and Stair's *Institutions* (1681 and 1693). Virtually all the 50 or so references to English law in Stair are by way of comparison not by way of authority. It is misleading to say that Scots law was "open to" English Common Law influence between 1500 and 1700 if that influence never, or scarcely ever, arrived in that period. For one might as well say that in that sense it was also open to *Chinese* influence. Moreover, the above passage gives the concept of "a mixed system" a sense different from its usual meaning in comparative law of a civilian system overlaid by the common law.[5]

My co-author and fellow revisionist, Hector MacQueen, in a powerful rejoinder entitled "Mixture or Muddle? Teaching and Research in Scottish Legal History", has adhered to the original passage complained of, defending the use of the phrase "large and unjustified claims", as also the adjective "mixed" as applied to Scots law.[6] He declares himself to be "an unashamed revisionist", but denies downplaying the role of the *jus commune*.[7] I am not so sure that I welcome the description of "revisionist", conscious as I am of the ideological baggage which it carries. On the other hand, I notice that Peter Birks, writing recently on Scots law and the Civilian tradition, has described Stair as a "revisionist", clearly intending this as a compliment to him, as compared to his more conservative contemporary Sir George Mackenzie.[8] In that sense, at least, I am happy to be called a revisionist.

---

sage goes on, however, to identify unjustified enrichment as an area which shows little trace of English influence during the formative period of its development.
3 Whitty (n 1).
4 Whitty (n 1) at 230–233 (especially at 232).
5 Whitty (n 1) at 232 (emphasis supplied).
6 MacQueen (n 1) at 376. MacQueen's article and this article are to an extent complementary.
7 "As an unashamed revisionist, I must nevertheless deny conscious downplaying of the role of the *ius commune* in Scottish legal history. Until recently, it was the non-Civilian elements in Scots law which were downplayed, ignored, misrepresented or misunderstood" (MacQueen (n 1) at 379).
8 "Stair, by contrast, was a revisionist, forceful and independent in his attempt to modify and

It is perhaps misleading to say that it all began in the Edinburgh University Staff Club, but that is as good a place to start as any. One evening, in the late 1970s, in the Staff Club of the University of Edinburgh, at the bar of that great but sadly now defunct institution, the late John Mitchell asked me if I were to sum up the history of Scots law in a word, what that word would be.[9] After some anxious reflection, I replied "Continuity". Not exactly the light on the road to Damascus. More the sort of thing one thinks better of the next morning. However, in this case, even in the cold light of day, the idea seemed worth pursuing. I had been teaching Scottish legal history for some years, and had naturally relied much on and had, indeed, been inspired by the work of Lord Cooper. The view propagated by Lord Cooper, as is well known, was that the history of Scots law was a story of false starts and rejected experiments. On one occasion he even went so far as to suggest that, in a sense, Scots law has no history.[10] For Cooper the false start and rejected experiment *par excellence* was what he termed the "Scoto-Norman" period of Scottish legal history.[11] This period, beginning with the reign of King David I in 1124, was characterised by borrowing from the Anglo-Norman law, but came to a sudden end, according to Cooper, at the time of the Wars of Independence, to be succeeded by a "Dark Age". It is not entirely clear exactly when Lord Cooper's "Dark Age" came to an end, but after the Dark Age came Stair.

Cooper's view was challenged almost immediately by Hector McKechnie who made some rather caustic comments about belief in a Dark Age.[12] Cooper's scheme was further undermined by contributions from, among others, Geoffrey Barrow, writing about the office of Justiciar, James J Robertson and Alan Harding.[13] Thus there was room for doubt. About the time of the Staff Club conversation, I had been asked to write on English

---

improve the overview inherited from the past" (P Birks, "The foundation of legal rationality in Scots law", in Evans-Jones (ed), *Civil Law Tradition* (n 1) at 93–94).

9 J D B Mitchell, Professor of Constitutional Law, 1954–67, first Salvesen Professor of European Institutions, 1969–80. For a perceptive assessment of Mitchell's contribution, see M Loughlin, "Sitting on a fence at Carter Bar: in praise of J D B Mitchell", 1991 *JR* 135.
10 T M Cooper, *Select Scottish Cases of the Thirteenth Century* (1944) at lxi.
11 See, for example, T M Cooper, "From David I to Bruce, 1124–1329; the Scoto-Norman law", *ISLH* 3.
12 H McKechnie, "Judicial Process upon Brieves, 1219–1532" (David Murray Lecture, Glasgow University, 1956) at 19: "While there are dark patches I think the description 'The Dark Age' is unfortunate. It is only dark to those who have not searched for the light that is hidden under the bushels in our charter rooms."
13 Barrow, "Justiciar"; J J Robertson, "The development of the law", in J M Brown (ed), *Scottish Society in the Fifteenth Century* (1977) 136; A Harding, "The medieval brieve of protection and the development of the common law", 1966 *JR* 115.

influence in Stair for the *Stair Tercentenary Essays* later published by the Stair Society.[14] A thankless task, you might think. And so indeed I thought. However, as I started to read through Stair I was struck by what he said about custom as a source of law. Stair, alone among our institutional writers, is passionate about the virtues of custom as a source of law compared to statute, and his praise of custom gives rise to some purple passages in the *Institutions*. "Every nation," says Stair, "under the name of law, understand their ancient and uncontroverted customs time out of mind, as their first and fundamental laws." "The English," he notes, "by their common law, in opposition to statute and recent customs, mean their ancient and unquestionable customs." "In the like manner," he continues, "*we* are ruled in the first place by *our* ancient and immemorial customs, which may be called *our* common law."[15] The examples of ancient custom which Stair then gives can all, in fact, be traced back to *Regiam Majestatem*, and beyond that to *Glanvill*, the key text at the very beginning of the English Common law.[16] Here indeed was food for thought when set against Lord Cooper's alleged false start and rejected experiment.

I came, therefore, to believe that Cooper's characterisation of the history of Scots law as a series of false starts and rejected experiments was deeply flawed. It wholly obscured the remarkable and continuous history of the Scottish common law from its origins over 700 years ago in the thirteenth century until the present day. The model for the emerging Scottish common law was undoubtedly the Common Law of England, to such a degree that it is legitimate, I believe, to speak of a Reception. This early Reception of the English Common Law, so integral to the emergence of Scots law as a separate system, was sharply focused, both as regards time and substantive legal content, to the extent that by the end of the thirteenth century both could be subsumed, with some colour of truth, under the description *lex anglicana*.[17] However, the common law of Scotland and the Common law of England were never the same, and came increasingly to diverge, a process already well under way before the end of the thirteenth century and the Wars of

---

14 See now ch 6 above.
15 Stair, *Inst*, 1.1.16 (emphasis supplied).
16 Examples of "ancient custom" given by Stair include primogeniture and heritable succession generally, legitim, terce and courtesy. For a more detailed discussion see ch 6 above. For custom as a source of Scots law, see also J T Cameron, "Custom as a source of law in Scotland" (1964) 97 *MLR* 306; and Sellar, "Custom". It is doubtful how far Stair was aware of the link between *RM* and *Glanvill*: see H L MacQueen, "*Regiam Majestatem*, Scots law and national identity" (1995) 74 *SHR* 1.
17 G W S Barrow, *The Anglo-Norman Era in Scottish History* (1980) at 119.

Independence.[18] There was no false start and rejected experiment. There was no Dark Age.[19]

I have put forward these views on many occasions now, drawing attention to the continuous history and remarkable resilience of the Scottish common law.[20] Others have written in the same vein, notably Hector MacQueen in his *Common Law and Feudal Society in Medieval Scotland*.[21] It would not be appropriate to rehearse these arguments again in any detail today. I would like, however, in view of the challenge thrown out in the critical passage already quoted, to focus for a time on the years between 1500 and 1700, and explain what I had in mind when we wrote that Scots law was always open to English influence, even during this period. Substitute, if you wish, as the story progresses, for the words "England" and "English" the words "China" and "Chinese", and see if that works as well. I would suggest that there are at least three ways in which substantial English influence can be measured, and shall deal with each in turn. The first lies in the continuing legacy of the Scoto-Norman law; the second in further occasional direct borrowing from England (although I certainly would not wish to contend that such borrowings amount to a further Reception); and the third in the views of contemporary writers, particularly towards the close of the sixteenth century, on the relationship between Scots and English law.

First, the continuing legacy of the Scoto-Norman law. This is, of course, necessarily restricted to those areas which formed part of the common law of Scotland in the thirteenth century, notably land law and heritable succession, but in those areas the continuing influence is clear enough. Witness, for example, Stair's discussion of "ancient custom" referred to above, the first of which was "primogeniture, and all degrees of succession", custom so integral to the law and so well accepted as to need no proof. That Stair regarded these as important parts of the law is evident from his statement, at the beginning of his discussion of succession, that "succession to defuncts is the most important title in law".[22] The rules of intestate heritable succession,

---

18 See Sellar, "Common law"; H L MacQueen, "Scots law under Alexander III", in N H Reid (ed), *Scotland in the Reign of Alexander III, 1249–1286* (1990) 74; and H L MacQueen, *Common Law and Feudal Society in Medieval Scotland* (1993, repr 2016). See too the controversial reassessment by D Carpenter, "Scottish royal government in the thirteenth century from an English perspective", in M Hammond (ed), *New Perspectives on Medieval Scotland 1093–1286* (2013) 117.
19 Although one might conceivably speak of arrested development.
20 For example, in chs 1, 6 and 7 above; also Sellar (n 18).
21 MacQueen, *Common Law* (n 18); also MacQueen (n 1) and MacQueen (n 16).
22 Stair, *Inst*, 3.4.

indeed, received from Anglo-Norman law, remained little altered until 1964, so much so that the principal rules of succession to land in England towards the end of the thirteenth century are virtually indistinguishable from the principal rules of succession to heritage in Scotland before 1964.[23] The "legal rights" of *jus relictae* and legitim (formerly known as "bairns' part"), also borrowed early from England, are with us still, and still confined to moveables.

Secondly, there was further occasional borrowing from England, which shows that a close eye was being kept on developments south of the Border. In 1572 the English Parliament enacted that vagabonds above the age of fourteen years were to be "adjudged to be grievously whipped, and burned through the Gristle of the right Ear with a hot Iron of the Compass of an Inch, unless some credible Person will take him into Service for a Year".[24] Three years later the Scots Parliament enacted that strong and idle beggars between the ages of fourteen and seventy "be adiugeit to be scurgeit and burnt throw the girssill of the richt eare with ane het Irne of the compasse of ane inche about" unless they were taken into service for a year.[25] A modern Secretary of State for Scotland shadowing English Home Office legislation could hardly do better.[26]

A second example is more mainstream, namely the claim of Thomas Craig, who was in a position to know, that the inspiration behind the celebrated series of statutes which culminated in the setting up of the Sasine Register in 1617 lay in the legislation of Henry VIII.[27] In his *Jus Feudale* Craig writes of the beginning of registration of sasine (*anglicé* seisin) in Scotland:

> There is, however, one point of English law which is particularly worthy of notice, because it removes opportunities for a great many frauds and tricks and has spread its example to our country in the last five or six years. Specifically. It was enacted by a general statute of Henry VIII that no contract or feudal grant (other than burgage) had validity in England unless, within a six-month period, it had been introduced and registered in the public records among the books of Westminster or in the books of the county in which the alienated estate is located

---

23 On this see also Sellar (n 18) at 89. See Succession (Scotland) Act 1964.
24 14 Eliz c 5.
25 *RPS* A1575/3/5.
26 Or now, perhaps, First or Justice Minister. These two examples are both given in Sellar (n 18) at 92.
27 Craig, *JF*, 2.7.23. The text here from nn 27–30 is drawn from Sellar, "Common law" at 92. Further, on the development of the Register of Sasines and its significance, see A R C Simpson, "Earth and stone: history, law and land through the lens of sasine", in M M Combe, J Glass and A Tindley (eds), *Land Reform in Scotland: History, Law and Policy* (2020), ch 6.

and in the presence of the justices of the peace or of one justice of the peace along with the relevant clerk.[28]

Craig's "five or six years" must refer back to the Act of 1599 which set up the "Secretary's Register", the precursor of the 1617 Act still in force.[29] Later Craig comments that the design of "Queen Mary's Act" for the registration of sasines – that is, the Sasines Act of 1555 – "closely resembled the well-known statute of Henry VIII", the reference being apparently to the English Statute of Enrolments of 1535.[30] It is more than a little intriguing to find the inspiration for the Register of Sasines, the keystone of Scottish conveyancing for centuries, in a statute of Henry VIII.

Another statute of Henry VIII also appears to have had a far-reaching effect in Scotland: the Marriage Act of 1540, passed to allow Henry to marry Katharine Howard as his fifth wife. Katharine was a first cousin of Anne Boleyn, Henry's second wife, and stood, therefore, within the prohibited degrees of relationship as then laid down by Canon law.[31] Henry's Marriage Act restricted the prohibited degrees to those mentioned in Leviticus, thereby allowing first cousins to marry.[32] Twenty-seven years later, after the Scottish Reformation, a similar Marriage Act was passed, allowing first cousins to marry in Scotland also.[33] The Incest Act 1567, passed on the same day, and clearly intended as the criminal counterpart of the Marriage Act, referred in terms to Leviticus, chapter 18.[34] First cousins have married freely in both Scotland and England since these respective Marriage Acts. In a European context this is exceptional. Although the Reformers everywhere reduced the prohibited degrees, it remained for a long time distinctly unusual, even in the Protestant lands, to permit marriage between such close kin as first cousins. It is difficult to resist the conclusion that the Scottish legislation in this field was influenced by the English.[35]

---

28 Craig, *JF*, 1.11.30 (Dodd trans at 303).
29 *RPS* 1599/7/6; see also *RPS* 1600/11/49 (the Sasines Act 1600); *RPS* 1617/5/30; and J M Thomson, *The Public Records of Scotland* (1922) at 106–107. Lord Clyde and Dr Dodd are mistaken in identifying the Act referred to by Craig with one passed in 1584.
30 Craig, *JF*, 2.7.23; *RPS* A1555/6/22; Statute of Enrolments 1535, 27 Hen VIII, c 16.
31 Henry and Katharine were in the second degree of affinity, well within the four degrees prohibited by Canon law.
32 32 Hen VIII c 38: ". . . and that no Reservation or Prohibition, God's law except, shall trouble or impeach any Marriage without the Levitical Degrees".
33 Marriage Act 1567, *RPS* A1567/12/15.
34 *RPS* A1567/12/14.
35 The Marriage and the Incest Acts of 1567 were repealed belatedly in 1977 and 1986 (by the Marriage (Scotland) Act and the Incest and Related Offences (Scotland) Act respectively). It should be stressed that English law did not make incest a statutory offence until 1908. For a

In the field of public law also there is further evidence that Scottish legislators were influenced by English practice. Thus an Act of 1428 regulating the Scots Parliament looked to English parliamentary practice, in setting out that the commissioners from the sheriffdoms should choose "a wise and ane expert man callit *the common spekar* of the parliament the quhilk sal propone all and sindry nedis and causis pertening to the commonis in the parliament or generall consal . . ."; and the 1587 Barons in Parliament Act gave the franchise to "sic as hes fourty schilling land in fre haldin of the king" in clear imitation of the English forty shilling freeholder.[36] Another example of English influence is the patent of the Winton peerage, conferred on Robert, Lord Seton in 1600, which employed the phraseology of English law.[37] Another and very different example of similarity between Scots and English public law was set out by Brian Levack in his 1996 Stair Society Lecture, in which he suggested that the law relating to judicial torture in Scotland, contrary to what is usually assumed, had more in common with English law and procedure than with the Romano-Canonical procedure of the Continent.[38]

Another example of English influence is provided by the use of the phrase "feoffees in trust" in connection with that quintessentially Scottish institution, George Heriot's Hospital or Trust. George Heriot – "jingling Geordie" – jeweller to King James VI, died in 1624 in the parish of Saint Martins-in-the-Fields in London, his will being proved in the Prerogative Court of Canterbury. The bulk of Heriot's fortune was assigned to the Town of Edinburgh to set up a hospital. The Governors of the Hospital were to be the Provost, Magistrates, Minister and Councillors of Edinburgh, named and appointed in the will as "feoffeis of trust".[39] These Governors,

---

full discussion of the history of the Acts of 1567, and their relationship with each other and the Canon law, see ch 10 text accompanying nn 74–105 below.

36 RPS 1428/3/3 (emphasis supplied); RPS 1587/7/143. A "common speaker" was never, in fact, appointed for the Scottish Parliament, so far as is known: while the qualification of a "forty shilling freeholder" covered a very different social grouping in Scotland than in England. Nevertheless the English influence is clear. These points were emphasised by Julian Goodare in a subsequently published paper to the British Legal History Conference in Edinburgh in July 1999: "The admission of lairds to the Scottish Parliament" (2001) 116 *English Historical Review* 1106. I am most grateful to Dr Goodare for discussing them with me.

37 G Seton, *Memoir of Alexander Seton, Earl of Dunfermline* (1882) at 45–46; and see "Historical notes on titles of nobility in Scotland" (1881) 25 *Journal of Jurisprudence* 561 at 568 (no author given).

38 B P Levack, "Judicial torture in the age of Mackenzie", in H L MacQueen (ed), *Miscellany IV* (SS vol 49, 2002) 185.

39 W Steven, *Memoir of George Heriot* (1845) appendix VI at 44. This example is also noted and discussed by G L Gretton, "Scotland: the evolution of the trust in a semi-Civilian system", in

in accepting the first statutes of the new institution in 1627 describe themselves as "Feoffis in trust guydaris and Guvernouris of the Hospitall to be foundit within this brugh to be called George Heriot his Hospitall . . .".[40] The Governors again describe themselves as "feoffis in trust of the hospitall" in an agreement reached "with the fermers of the lands of Brughtoun [Broughton] pertaining to the guid towne" (of Edinburgh) that same year.[41]

My third example of English influence in the period in question is to be found in the views of contemporary writers. Thomas Craig's views on the close relationship between Scots law and English law in his time are now well known, and cannot be lightly disregarded. In his treatise *De Unione Regnorum Britanniae*, for example, he said: "I assert that at the present day [c 1605] there are no nations whose laws and institutions more closely correspond than England and Scotland."[42] Craig backed up his views with many examples. It is also clear from his discussion of sources of law that he had in mind not only the historical debt owed by the Scots common law to the Anglo-Norman law, but also more recent contact between the two systems.[43] The same is true of Craig's contemporary, Sir John Skene, who wrote of the debt owed by Scots law not only to Feudal or Norman law (*jus Nortmannicum*), but also to the laws of the kingdom of England (*leges Regni Angliae* and *jus Anglicum*).[44] Another witness is the Reverend Robert Pont (father of the map-maker Timothy), an almost exact contemporary of Bishop John Leslie, whose views on the authority of Roman law are so often quoted, and like Leslie a Lord of Session.[45] In his dialogue on a prospective union between Scots and English law, written in 1604, Pont has one character (*Hospes*) say, "But, say they, their will be a mutation of the lawes . . .", to which *Polyhistor* replies, "This is not to be feared, for the lawes of England and Scotland are almost the same in substance; and if any small differences

---

R Helmholz and R Zimmermann (eds), *Itinera Fiduciae: Trust and Treuhand in Historical Perspective* (1998) at 519. Gretton considers the phrase to be "truly striking", especially given the use of Scottish legal terminology elsewhere in the deed.

40 Steven, *Memoir* (n 39) appendix VII at 83.
41 Steven, *Memoir* (n 39) at 51 n.
42 Craig, *De Unione*, at 304. Compare the very similar statements made by Craig, *JF*, Epistle Dedicatory (accessible in the first volume of Dodds' ongoing edition (SS vol 64, 2017) at lxviii–lxxix).
43 For a more detailed account of Craig's views on the relationship between Scots and English law, see Sellar (n 18) and ch 7 above, text accompanying nn 58–68; and also J W Cairns, "The Civil law tradition in Scottish legal thought", in D L Carey Miller and R Zimmermann (eds), *The Civilian Tradition and Scots Law* (1997) 191, especially at 191–195 and 200–203.
44 Sir J Skene, *Regiam Majestatem Scotiae Veters Leges et Constitutiones* (1609), preface. For a more detailed account see ch 7 at text accompanying nn 53–57.
45 For Leslie's views see n 60 below.

arise, a parliament of each kingdome being summoned, they wil be by sage counsel easily reconcyled."⁴⁶ An earlier example of the same sentiment can be found in 1560, when commissioners for the earl of Arran, who was seeking the hand of Elizabeth of England in marriage, played down worries about legal change, saying: "Neither yet neade youe to feare any alteracioun in the lawes, seing the lawes of Scotland wer taken out of England and therfor booth ther realmes are ruled by one fashion."⁴⁷ At the end of the sixteenth century, therefore, although there may have been some special pleading, there was a lively awareness in Scotland of the close links between Scots and English law.

I would like to turn now, in a rather more tentative manner, to the Reception of Roman law in Scotland. Until quite recently, despite many *ex cathedra* statements, surprisingly little had been written by way of general survey on the relationship between Scots and Roman law. There was Peter Stein's pioneering article, "The Influence of Roman Law on Scots Law", first published in 1963 and revised in 1988, but little else.⁴⁸ Now, however, the situation has changed utterly. There has been a flurry of combative articles, followed by two splendid collections of essays: *The Civil Law Tradition in Scotland*, edited by Robin Evans-Jones, and, more recently, *The Civilian Tradition and Scots Law*, essays celebrating the quincentenary of the University of Aberdeen, edited by David Carey Miller and Reinhard Zimmermann.⁴⁹ One of the most interesting things about these essays is the extent to which, although approaching the matter from diverse angles, different authors tell substantially the same story. Certainly I have learnt much from them.

One caveat, made forcefully by a number of contributors in the two collections, is the need to distinguish clearly, when considering Roman law as a source, as has not always been done, between the law of Justinian and the later Civilian tradition of the Middle Ages and beyond. Another point which emerges from recent writing is the extent to which borrowings from Roman law, once adopted into Scots law, take on – to use the phrase applied by Geoffrey Barrow to earlier importations from English law – "the protective

---

46 R Pont, "Of the Union of Britayne", in B R Galloway and B P Levack (eds), *The Jacobean Union: Six Tracts of 1604* (SHS, 1985) at 24. Others, it may be noted, such as J Russell (*Jacobean Union* at 88), were strongly against this proposition.

47 Quoted in A H Williamson, *Scottish National Consciousness in the Age of James VI* (1979) at 14.

48 P Stein, "The influence of Roman law on the law of Scotland", 1963 *JR* 205, reprinted in P G Stein, *The Character and Influence of the Roman Civil Law: Historical Essays* (1988) 319.

49 Evans-Jones (ed), *Civil Law Tradition* (n 1) and Carey Miller and Zimmermann (eds), *Civilian Tradition* (n 43). See also further literature references gathered in ch1 at nn 66 and 67.

colouring of a thoroughly native species".⁵⁰ Here one might instance *donatio mortis causa*, or the *conditio si testator* and the *conditio si institutus*, investigated some years ago by Bill Gordon,⁵¹ or the *condictio causa data causa non secuta*, excoriated recently in its modern Scottish guise by Robin Evans-Jones.⁵² To these caveats a third and very important further one needs to be entered, not least because it is so often overlooked: a recognition of the contribution of Canon law, both on its own account, and as part of the *jus commune*. Some of the most ardent Romanists, it seems to me, consistently underestimate the importance of the Canon law.

One way to study the Reception of Roman law in Scotland is to approach the matter chronologically, and to collect examples of the influence of Roman law on Scots law century by century. Bill Gordon's essay in *The Civil Law Tradition in Scotland* does just this, charting importations from Roman law from the thirteenth century until the present day.⁵³ The obvious question which arises from such an approach is: when did the Reception take place? But here we run into difficulties, for very different dates have been suggested for the Reception of Roman law in Scotland. Some point to the long eighteenth century, extending from the publication of Stair's *Institutions* in 1681 until the Napoleonic wars; others choose the seventeenth century; others again plump for the sixteenth.⁵⁴ That fine historian of our medieval

50 Barrow, *Kingdom* (n 13) at 98.
51 W M Gordon, "Roman and Scots law – the conditiones si sine liberis decesserit", 1969 *JR* 108 (reprinted in W M Gordon, *Roman Law, Scots Law and Legal History: Selected Essays* (2007) 87). See also A R Barr, "The conditio si institutus sine liberis decesserit in Scots and South African law", in K G C Reid, M J de Waal and R Zimmermann (eds), *Exploring the Law of Succession: Studies National, Historical and Comparative* (2007) 177; R R M Paisley "The Roman and Civilian origins of the conditio si testator sine liberis decesserit" (2015) 19 *Edin LR* 1. The *conditio si testator sine liberis decesserit* was abolished and replaced by the Succession (Scotland) Act 2016 ss 6 and 29. Donation *mortis causa* was likewise abolished by the Succession (Scotland) Act 2016 s 25(1). The classic exposition of donation *mortis causa* in modern Scots law was given by Lord President Inglis in *Morris v Riddick* (1867) 5 M 1036 (quoted below, at 274). See further W M Gordon, "Donation", *SME* Reissue (2011), paras 7, 30 and 46; and ch 12 text accompanying nn 46 and 47 below.
52 R Evans-Jones, "Unjust enrichment, contract and the third Reception of Roman law in Scotland" (1993) 109 *LQR* 663; see also G MacCormack, "The condictio causa data causa non secuta", in Evans-Jones (ed), *Civil Law Tradition* (n 1) 253; and A Rodger, "The use of the Civil law in Scottish courts", in Carey Miller and Zimmermann (eds), *Civilian Tradition* (n 43) 198 at 227–228.
53 W M Gordon, "Roman law in Scotland", in Evans-Jones (ed), *Civil Law Tradition* (n 1) 13.
54 It is only possible to record a few opinions here. Sir T B Smith, in *A Short Commentary on the Law of Scotland* (1962) at 23, suggests that "the full influence of Roman law was subsequent to the publication of Stair's *Institutions* in 1681". Elsewhere, however (*Short Commentary* at 29), Smith refers to the establishment of the Court of Session as a College of Justice in 1532 "as the watershed between the pre-Roman and the Roman phase of Scottish legal history", a view shared by Stein (n 48) at 215, 249. D M Walker, on the other hand, writes that before 1600, "the

law, George Neilson, even suggested that the Reception may have come, by way of France, in the fourteenth and fifteenth centuries.[55] It may then be that the question – when did the Reception take place? – is not well framed, as it pre-supposes that the Reception can be pinned down to a fixed point in time, or at least to a relatively limited period. In truth, it seems that the Reception of Roman law in Scotland was a very gradual process, although none the less real for that.

Another way of approaching the study of the Reception is to look at the various divisions of Scots law in turn – family law, obligations, property and so on – seeking out Roman influence. This is the approach favoured by Peter Stein in his seminal article already mentioned.[56] The question which arises naturally from this approach is: in what areas of our law did Roman law exert the greatest influence? Here again, however, we encounter problems. One objection is that in looking at the law in this way, area by area, we lose our sense of chronological perspective. Another more serious objection becomes apparent if we turn the exercise inside out, as it were, and, taking each of the various divisions of the law in turn, we ask what were the most important external influences – custom, Feudal law, Civil Law, Canon law and the like – on their overall development. If we do this, we may find that our perception of the contribution of Roman law in any given area alters somewhat. Thus we may find – for the sake of argument – that although the law of servitudes wears a Roman mask, the crucial influence on our land law has been Feudal law in its Anglo-Norman guise; that although the Roman division into pupils and minors, tutors and curators, was part of our law for many hundreds of years, until superseded a few years ago, the crucial influence on our law of persons has been the Canon law; that our law of succession was long divided into heritable and moveable, but that in neither branch were the rules of Roman law generally adopted; and so on. The original question – in what areas of our law did Roman law exercise the greatest influence? – may not have been wrongly framed, but the answer does not tell us as much as we might at first imagine. Even in an area where it is clear that Roman law was a major influence, namely the law of moveable

---

influence of the Civil law had indeed been small, even negligible" (*A Legal History of Scotland*, vol 3, *The Sixteenth Century* (1995) at 827). Birks (n 8) at 93 points to the seventeenth century.
55 G Neilson and H M Paton (eds), *The Acts of the Lords of Council in Civil Causes*, vol 2 (1918) at lxxvi.
56 Stein (n 48). Another example of the same type of approach is D L Carey Miller, "A Scottish celebration of the European tradition", in Carey Miller and Zimmermann (eds), *Civilian Tradition* (n 49) 19.

property, it has been shown that Scots law departed substantially from the original Roman rules.[57]

Another question we might ask admits of a more satisfactory answer: what authority has been accorded to Roman law as a source of law in Scotland? *En passant*, we may note that Alan Watson has suggested that the answer to the question as to whether any given system may be called "Civilian" is linked to this question of authority. Thus a "Civilian" system is one "in which parts or the whole of Justinian's *Corpus Iuris Civilis* have been in the past or are at present treated as the law of the land, or, at least, are of direct and highly persuasive force; or else it derives from some such system."[58] The answer to the question is more satisfactory because it is clear and consistent. From the time of Craig and Skene, the first of our jurists to weigh Roman law as a source deliberately against other sources of law, the answer has been that Roman law has been accepted not by reason of any innate authority, but because of the good sense and equity of its solutions. Thomas Craig's opinion that Roman law was received in so far as it was in harmony with the laws of nature and right reason is entirely in line with Stair's better-known statement that Roman law is not acknowledged as a law binding for its authority, but as a rule – that is, as a system – followed for its equity.[59] Therefore, says Stair, in a surprisingly understated phrase, "It shall not be amiss here to say something of it." There is, of course, Bishop Leslie's well-known statement about Roman law, already referred to: ". . . this far to the lawis of the Realme we ar astricted, gif ony cummirsum or trubilsum caus fal out, as oft chances, quhilke can nocht be agreit be our cuntrey lawis, incontinent whatever is thocht necessar [*statim quicquid . . . necessariam censetur*] to pacifie this controversie, is citet out of the Romane lawis."[60] Whatever this means, and it may be no more than an emphatic statement of the common European position that the *jus commune* should be regarded as a subsidiary source of

---

57 See Carey Miller (n 56) at 35; and, by the same author, "Systems of property: Grotius and Stair", in D L Carey Miller and D W Meyers (eds), *Comparative and Historical Essays in Scots Law: A Tribute to Professor Sir Thomas Smith QC* (1992) 13; "Stair's property: a Romanist system", 1995 *JR* 70; and "Derivative acquisition of moveables", in Evans-Jones (ed), *Civil Law Tradition* (n 1) 128.
58 A Watson, *The Making of the Civil Law* (1981) at 4.
59 Craig, *JF*, 1.2.14 (Dodd edn (n 42), 52–55); Stair, *Inst*, 1.1.12. See W M Gordon, "Stair's use of Roman law", in A Harding (ed), *Law-Making and Law-Makers in British History* (1980) 120, and "Roman law as a source", in Walker (ed), *Stair Tercentenary Essays* (n 14) 107; also Cairns (n 43), especially at 200–206.
60 J Lesley or Leslie, *De Origine Moribus et rebus gestis Scotiae* (1578) as translated into Scots in 1596 (see E G Cody and W Murison (eds), *The historie of Scotland, written first in Latin by . . . Jhone Leslie* (1888) at 120); above, n 45. See also ch 1 text accompanying n 67.

law, Leslie's opinion cannot stand against the carefully considered views of later jurists. The immediately succeeding passage in Leslie's *History* is not so often cited: it extols and sets forth in detail king "Kennedie his lawis, baith haly and ancient, set furth afor sevin hundir and fiftie yeirs", comparing them to the Twelve Tables![61] An earlier expression of the general point about the importance of Roman law as a subsidiary source of law occurs in Regent Morton's speech to Parliament at Stirling in 1571, when he referred to the Civil law as "the common lawe and the lawe receaved in Scotland in all decisions wher ther is no expresse municipall lawe wrytten".[62]

It would seem then that we cannot say that Roman law was ever in itself authoritative in Scotland. We cannot point to any narrow band of time and say that this was the period of the Reception of Roman law. We cannot assert that Roman law has been the major influence in shaping most of the areas of our substantive law – certainly not if we leave the Canon law out of account. This Reception then, the Reception of Roman law, was not like the earlier Reception of English law. It was not specific as regards time or substantive legal content. Its character was entirely different. This Reception lay not so much in the adoption of one piece of Roman law or another, at any particular time; it lay in the gradual acceptance of a vision of law as a dynamic whole, as an intellectually coherent entity, as set out first by Gaius and Justinian and refined by the jurists of the medieval *jus commune*.[63] It lay in the recognition of the law as a system, and an understanding of the relationship of the parts of that system to the whole; in the acceptance also of legal categories and terms of art such as "obligations". It is striking how often this theme surfaces in the two books of essays on the Civilian tradition already mentioned.[64] Nowhere is it put forward more elegantly and convincingly than by Peter Birks in his two contributions, entitled "The Foundation of Legal Rationality in Scotland", and "More Logic and Less Experience:

---

61 MacQueen (n 1) at 381 draws attention to the fact that the immediately *preceding* passage in Leslie gives an account of the principal written laws of Scotland, including the burgh laws, *Regiam Majestatem* and the Acts of Parliament.
62 Quoted in Williamson, *Scottish National Consciousness* (n 47) at 184. The speech is thought to have been written for Morton by George Buchanan. For an earlier example still, in 1548, see A L Murray, "Sinclair's Practicks", in Harding (ed), *Law-Making* (n 59) 90 at 101. See also J W Cairns, "*Ius Civile* in Scotland, c 1600" (2004) 2 *Roman Legal Tradition* 136 (reprinted in J W Cairns, *Law, Lawyers and Humanism: Selected Essays on the History of Scots Law, Vol 1* (2015) ch 3).
63 Including also Canon lawyers.
64 Above, nn 1 and 43. Compare also Watson, *Making* (n 48), chs 2 ("The block effect of Roman law") and 3 ("The formal rationality of Civil Law").

The Difference between Scots Law and English Law".[65] In the first of these pieces occurs this memorable quotation:

> The one invaluable inheritance which Scots law took from the Roman past was its gift for systematic overview and the aspiration to principled rationality which went with it, making precedent the handmaid to reason rather than, as some would say of English law, reason the slave of precedent.[66]

And so the Reception of Roman law affected not only the vocabulary but also the very grammar of Scots law. Of no area of the modern law is this more obviously true than unjustified enrichment. Despite 300 years of absence from the common Civilian table, Scots lawyers, with their talk of the *condictiones*, *quantum lucratus* and *negotiorum gestio*, still speak recognisably the same language as lawyers from the Continent, albeit perhaps a rather archaic variant. By contrast, English lawyers speak what sometimes appears to be a different language entirely.[67]

Peter Birks described the tradition of principled rationality inherited by Scots law from Roman law as stretching "back to the middle of the seventeenth century".[68] I would suggest that the tradition goes back at least a century earlier.[69] The second half of the sixteenth century was a time of particular intellectual ferment when at least four separate factors can be identified as being at work. In the first place, there was English law: comparisons with English law, as has been seen, were well remembered and actively pursued in this period. Then there was the Civil law: the importance and value of Roman law were regularly emphasised, and not just by Bishop Leslie. Thus the commission given in 1567 to "sufficient personis to mak ane body of the civile and Municipale lawis devidid in heidis conforme to the fassone of the law Romane" may be seen as an early nod in the direction of principled rationality.[70]

A third factor was the Canon law. It is only possible to note briefly the importance of this influence here. The Canon law had already made a

---

65 Birks (n 8); and P Birks, "More logic and less experience: the difference between Scots law and English law", in Carey Miller and Zimmermann (eds), *Civilian Tradition* (n 43) 167.
66 Birks (n 8) at 97.
67 See further MacQueen and Sellar (n 2).
68 Birks (n 8) at 93.
69 Compare MacQueen (n 1) at 380: "A key period of development is obviously the sixteenth century . . ."; and P G Stein, "Roman law in medieval Scotland", *Ius Romanum Medii Aevi,* pars V, 13b (1968) at 49, reprinted in Stein, *Character and Influence* (n 48) ch 18 at 315: "Consequently, as their predecessors had done haphazardly and intermittently, the sixteenth century Scots lawyers turned systematically and regularly to Roman law."
70 *RPS* 1567/12/54.

significant impact on Scots law before the Reformation in 1560. It had also, of course, melded to a considerable extent with Roman law in the medieval *jus commune*. After the Reformation, the old Canon law jurisdiction over obligations, marriage and testaments came gradually to be integrated into the common law of Scotland. Questions must inevitably have arisen on occasion as to whether to follow the Canon or the Civil law. When they did, we have it on the authority of Thomas Craig that it was usually the Canon law which was followed.[71] The fourth factor was, of course, the common law of Scotland itself. A continuing attachment to, and a determination to retain, the common law of Scotland is very evident. In 1584, for example, Parliament enacted, in words copied from an earlier statute of 1504, and reminiscent of a statute of 1426 earlier still, that "All his hienes leigeis (being under his obeissance) man be rewllit be his awin lawis and the commoun lawis of this realme and be nane uther lawis".[72]

I conclude with some thoughts on Stair and the Civil law, and a brief personal coda. It is arguable that Stair, so far from opening the gates to further Civilian influence, actually began to close them. Stair, of course, wrote his *Institutions* in English rather than in Latin, thereby rendering his work less accessible to the wider scholarly community of his time. In addition, his revisionist genius was such as to re-order the law on occasion into categories of his own, rejecting the Roman classification. This is famously true of Stair's classification of obligations into obligations conventional and obligations obediential.[73] Within obediential obligations, when Stair considers delinquence, or delict, rather than insist on the terminology of Roman law, he elects to follow delinquences "as they are known by the terms in *our law*".[74] And in the area now known as unjust or unjustified enrichment, Stair's treatment marks a radical new exposition of the Civilian tradition,

---

71 Craig, *JF*, 1.3.24 (Dodd edn (n 42) at 82–85). Examples would appear to be later Scots law on *pacta nuda*, promise and *jus quaesitum tertio*. This theme is explored further in ch 15 ("Promise") below; see also H L MacQueen and W D H Sellar, "Scots law: *ius quaesitum tertio*, promise and irrevocability", in E J H Schrage (ed), *Ius Quaesitum Tertio* (2008), 357.
72 *RPS* 1584/5/10; the 1504 Act is to be found at *RPS* A1504/3/124; and the 1426 Act at *RPS* 1426/6. See also ch 7 above and MacQueen (n 16).
73 Stair, *Inst*, 1.3.2: "Obligations by the Romans are distinguished in four kinds: in obligations ex contractu, vel quasi ex contractu, ex maleficio, vel quasi ex maleficio. Which distinction insinuates no reason of the cause or rise of these distinct obligations, as is requisite in a good distinct division: and, therefore, they may be more appropriately divided, according to the principle or original from whence they flow, as in obligations obediential, and by engagement, or natural and conventional."
74 Stair, *Inst*, 1.9.4 (emphasis supplied).

200 years or so ahead of its time.[75] Thus we are left with the paradox that although Stair himself was deeply imbued with the Civil law, and did more than any other writer to ensure that Scots law was ordered and structured in the best tradition of the Reception, the force of his genius was such as to open a gap between Scots law and the mainstream Civilian tradition.

I end, as I began, on a personal note. It has sometimes been suggested that the Civilian tradition in Scots law has been played down and devalued in recent years, and that the teachers of private law at our universities have relied uncritically on English law, neglecting the institutional writers and the roots of our own law.[76] I cannot speak for others – although Hector MacQueen has spoken for himself[77] – but I, for one, plead not guilty. In my teaching of private law and legal history over the years I have regularly referred to Stair's *Institutions* and sought to place Scots law in the wider context of the *jus commune* and the European legal tradition, although I have certainly also drawn comparisons with English law when these seemed relevant. In 1987 Hector MacQueen, John Cairns and I introduced a course entitled "Scots Law and the Western Legal Tradition" into the curriculum of the Faculty of Law at Edinburgh.[78] In 1991, I and others were instrumental in establishing a Centre for Legal History within the Faculty. The second head of the proposals promoting the Centre read: "The object of the Centre shall be to encourage and foster the study of legal history in general, with particular attention being paid to Scots law and to Roman law and the Civilian tradition."[79] And I have frequently urged the Faculty to refill the Chair of Civil Law, left vacant by the departure of Peter Birks in 1987, although without success. I therefore deny the charges in so far as laid against me.[80]

As to the future, I do not share the gloomy prognostications of some, but remain an optimist. A Parliament for Scotland has been established. Writing

---

75 As argued in MacQueen and Sellar (n 2); and W D H Sellar, "Unjust enrichment", *SME*, vol 15 (1995), paras 10–86.
76 For some particularly sweeping statements see Evans-Jones (n 1a); and Evans-Jones (n 1b), for example at 246. And see W A Wilson, "The importance of analysis", in Carey Miller and Meyers (eds), *Comparative and Historical Essays* (n 54) 162 at 171.
77 MacQueen (n 1), especially at 382–384.
78 And see MacQueen (n 1) at 383. The course was effectively discontinued in 1995, but immediately reincarnated as an Honours course in European Legal History and a Masters course in European Legal Tradition.
79 The Centre continues within the present Edinburgh Law School, under the direction of Professor John Cairns.
80 The Chair lay vacant until 2012 when it was filled by Professor John Cairns, previously Professor of Legal History.

on Scots law has never been in such a healthy state. Writing on Scottish legal history, in particular, has shown that it is capable of generating light as well as heat. Stair's *Institutions* are known outwith Scotland as never before. We are far better placed now than formerly to appreciate the history of our legal system and the nature of our heritage.[81] Scots lawyers are now routinely involved in international comparative enterprises. There is certainly room for improvement, but I would suggest that the future looks bright.[82]

---

81 As recognised by Lord President Hope in *Morgan Guaranty Trust Co of New York v Lothian Regional Council* 1995 SC 151 at 157: "I believe that we are better placed now than our predecessors were at two critical stages in our history, at the start of the nineteenth century, and when *Glasgow Corporation v Lord Advocate* was being debated 36 years ago, to reach an informed decision as to whether the error of law rule really is part of Scots law."
82 For a very different view of some of the matters covered in this paper, and one from which this author cordially differs, see Evans-Jones (n 1b).

# 9 Marriage by Cohabitation with Habit and Repute: Review And Requiem?*

The doctrine of marriage by cohabitation with habit and repute (MCHR) has long been established in Scots law but has not always been well understood. There has been disagreement about the origins of the doctrine, let it be traced to an Act of the Scots Parliament passed in 1503, or to the medieval Canon law. There has been controversy too about the role of the doctrine in modern Scots law: is it merely a method of proof, or is it, as has been argued from time to time, and with some force by Eric Clive in particular,[1] in some sense also part of the constitution of marriage?

This article seeks, first, to explain the background to the Act of 1503 (actually 1504) and to demonstrate the relationship of that Act to the medieval Canon law; and secondly, "were it decent to criticise upon our favourite author",[2] to argue that MCHR was always no more than a method of proof. The scope for irregular or common law marriage in Scots law before the statutory abolition of MCHR in 2006 will also be touched on.

### A. THE ACT OF 1503

A well-known passage in Erskine's *Institutes*, worth citing in full, traces the origins of MCHR to the law of nature, and to a Scots statute of 1503:

---

* Originally published as "Marriage by cohabitation with habit and repute: review and requiem?", in D L Carey Miller and D W Meyers (eds), *Comparative and Historical Essays in Scots Law: A Tribute to Professor Sir Thomas Smith QC* (1992) 117–136.
1 E M Clive, *The Law of Husband and Wife in Scotland* (2nd edn, 1982) at 59–76; and see below text accompanying nn 66–75. The 3rd edn of *Husband and Wife* was published more or less contemporaneously with the original version of this article; in the 4th edn (1997) at paras 05.019–05.060, however, Professor Clive cited this paper about the Canon law origins of MCHR while continuing to disagree with the argument that CHR was never more than a method of proving matrimonial consent.
2 Lord Kames on Thomas Craig: *Statute Law of Scotland* (1737) at 434.

Marriage may also be entered into where the consent is not express, but is discovered *rebus ipsis et factis*. In this way it is presumed or inferred from cohabitation, or the parties living together at bed and board, joined with their being habite, or held and reputed, man and wife. Cohabitation therefore does not itself establish this presumption; for a man and woman may thus cohabit to gratify their unlawful desires, without any intention of being bound in marriage. This legal presumption is grounded not only on the nature of things, but on statute 1503, c 77, which provides that a woman, who has been reputed the wife of a man till his death, shall be entitled to and enjoy the terce as his widow, till it be proved that she was not his lawful wife. Hence it may be observed, that the presumption of habite and repute is not so strong an evidence of marriage as to exclude a contrary proof; it only throws the burden of it on him who denies the marriage.[3]

Erskine's exposition of the doctrine of MCHR is accurate and helpful, as is his explanation of the purport of the Act of 1503. The Act, "Anent the exceptioun proponit aganis wedowis persewand and followand their brevis of terce", was designed to help a widow, pursuing her terce in her deceased husband's heritable estate, to counter the allegation that she had not been a lawful wife. As long as she could show that the marriage had not been questioned in her husband's lifetime, and that she had been "repute and haldin as his lauchfull wife", she was to be served to her terce, unless and until "it be clearly decernit and sentence gevin that scho [she] was not his lauchfull wife".[4]

Erskine's suggestion that the doctrine finds its origin in the Act of 1503 has been widely followed, but it is quite mistaken. It was given further credence by Lord Fraser in his treatise on *Husband and Wife*. It has long been recognised, however, that Fraser's work, learned though it is, is vitiated by his insistence that in the Middle Ages both England and Scotland had a national ecclesiastical law of their own, influenced by, but not identical with that of the church of Rome. This belief caused Fraser to misdirect himself comprehensively on the origins of MCHR in Scotland, and the background to the Act of 1503. He wrote:

> This rule of evidence rests in Scotland upon the authority of a statute passed in the year 1503, in the reign of James IV. It was the rule of the Roman law, but in the year 1503 the Roman law had no footing in Scotland ... But this rule was also that of the Canon law; and if the Canon law had been the law of Scotland (a matter that has been already considered), the Act of Parliament of 1503 would have been unnecessary. Nothing can be more distinct than the rule as stated in the decretals, promulgated in 1234, that cohabitation and habit and repute proved marriage; and if this decretal had been considered binding in Scotland,

---

3 Erskine, *Inst*, 1.6. 6.
4 *RPS*, 1504/3/42.

the hardships which the statute of 1503 was intended to remove, would never have been heard of.[5]

The assertion that the doctrine has its origin in the Act of 1503 has often been repeated this century. It is to be found, for example, in all the editions of Walton, *Husband and Wife;* in Sheriff Ireland's treatment of husband and wife in the Stair Society's *Introduction to Scottish Legal History*, in Sir Thomas Smith's *Short Commentary;* and in Professor David Walker's *Principles*.[6] Only in the first edition of Wilson and Clive, *Husband and Wife*, tentatively, and more firmly in Clive's second edition, has it been conceded that the probable origin of the doctrine lies in the medieval Canon law.[7]

The fact is that an Act passed by the Scots Parliament in 1503 (actually in 1504) did not and could not make any alteration to the law of marriage.[8] Questions involving the status of marriage lay outwith the jurisdiction of Parliament and the king's courts. Such matters fell within the province of the ecclesiastical courts, which looked to the Canon law and to Rome. Lord Fraser was quite mistaken on this point, as already noted. Further evidence as to the operation of the Canon law in Scotland in the decades preceding the Reformation, should such be required, can be found in William Hay's *Lectures on Marriage*, delivered in the 1530s at the University of Aberdeen, and in Simon Ollivant's *Court of the Official in Pre-Reformation Scotland*, both published by the Stair Society.[9] The king's courts could, however, deal with questions of heritage, including succession to land. This provides the context for the statute of 1504.

The doctrine of legitimation *per subsequens matrimonium*, whereby a child born to parents unmarried, but free to marry, was held to be legitimated by the subsequent marriage of its parents, provides a parallel. This too was a rule of the medieval Canon law. In Scotland, the rule was adopted

---

5 P Fraser, *Treatise on Husband and Wife* (2nd edn, 1876) vol 1, at 393–394. The decretal is considered below at text accompanying n 27.
6 F P Walton, *A Handbook of Husband and Wife* (1893) at 20; 2nd edn by J L Wark (1922) at 26; 3rd edn by W E R Hendry and A M Johnston (1951) at 34; R D Ireland, "Husband and wife: (a) Post-Reformation Canon law of marriage of the Commissaries' courts and (b) modern common and statute law", in *ISLH* 89; T B Smith, *A Short Commentary on the Law of Scotland* (1962) at 313; D M Walker, *Principles of Scottish Private Law* (4th edn, 1988) vol 1, at 240.
7 E M Clive and J G Wilson, *The Law of Husband and Wife in Scotland* (1974) at 116–117; Clive, *Husband and Wife* (n 1) at 59–60; and see further n 1 above.
8 For the Act passed on 15 March 1504, see *RPS* 1504/3/42. Under the Julian calendar which prevailed in Scotland until 1600, a year began on 25 March rather than 1 January; hence, for contemporaries, the Act anent terce was passed in 1503.
9 J C Barry (ed), *William Hay's Lectures on Marriage* (SS vol 24, 1967); S Ollivant, *The Court of the Official in Pre-Reformation Scotland* (SS vol 34, 1982).

early by the king's courts and applied to succession to heritage.[10] In England, however, it is notorious that the rule was rejected. When the suggestion was put to the Barons of England assembled at Merton in 1236 that they should adopt the rule and apply it to succession to land, they replied memorably *"noiumus leges Angliae mutare"*; and so it remained until 1926.[11]

The statute of 1504, then, was directed at the royal courts. It concerned fee and heritage and not status. It introduced to the king's courts – or conceivably confirmed there – the rule, already well established in the ecclesiastical courts, that cohabitation with habit and repute raised a presumption of marriage. The same presumption was to apply in the case of a widow pursuing her terce in the king's courts. The object of the Act may have been to prevent defenders playing off one jurisdiction against the other.

Although Thomas Craig does not refer specifically to the Act of 1504 in his *Jus Feudale*, he notices its effect in his treatment of procedure on a brieve of terce.[12] A widow claiming her terce, Craig notes, should obtain a brieve from Chancery directed to a sheriff and inquest, or jury, of fifteen. One question which the inquest must determine is whether the petitioner was the lawful wife of the deceased. There will rarely be a challenge on this point except by the heir. Should objection be taken, Craig comments that the law is more favourably disposed towards the widow claiming her terce than towards the prospective heir whose legitimacy has been impugned. In the latter case, procedure by brieve and inquest is suspended pending determination of the question of legitimacy *in curia christianitatis*. In the case of the widow, procedure on the brieve of terce can continue; restricted, however, to the determination of a single issue – whether the petitioner was habit and repute spouse at the date of the deceased's death (*si conjunx habita et reputata tempore mortis fuerit*). Should it be later determined *in foro Ecclesiastico* that there was no marriage, the findings of the inquest will be null and void. Craig's discussion neatly illustrates the effect of the 1504 Act, and the relationship between secular and ecclesiastical jurisdictions.

It is interesting to note that, as in the case of legitimation *per subsequens matrimonium*, English law was different. The English equivalent of terce was dower, but a claim for dower depended on whether the widow had been endowed by her husband at the church door. Proof of marriage by habit and repute would not suffice. Scots law may once have been the same, for

---

10 See S Marshall, *Illegitimacy in Medieval Scotland 1100–1500* (2021), 26–27, 34–41, 110–116.
11 See J H Baker, *An Introduction to English Legal History* (5th edn, 2019) at 528–529.
12 Craig, *JF*, 2.22.31–32. The Latin text, where quoted, is from the 1655 edition.

*Regiam Majestatem* follows the English rule as set out in *Glanvill*.[13] If that be so, the 1504 Act may mark the relaxation of an older stricter rule.

Elsewhere in *Jus Feudale* Craig notes that although the authority of the Pope was rejected at the Reformation, the Canon law remained authoritative: "to the extent that where it deviates from the Civil law (as it often does, with many books having been written about the differences between the Civil and Canon law)" says Craig, "we prefer the Canon law." This was particularly true of the constitution and dissolution of marriage (*de matrimonio, vel contrahendo vel dissolvendo*).[14] Craig's evidence is particularly valuable, as he practised and wrote in the years immediately following the Reformation.

Some changes, of course, were made to the law at the Reformation. For example, divorce was allowed on the grounds of adultery and desertion; and the prohibited degrees of matrimony were relaxed to allow first cousins to marry.[15] In general, however, the Canon law remained an authoritative source for Scots marriage law, liable to alteration only through the slow evolution of the common law. Much of the jurisdiction of the old ecclesiastical courts passed after the Reformation to the commissary courts. At first there was a measure of continuity in the personnel of these courts, but gradually the commissary courts became secularised.[16] In 1609, the year after Craig's death, appeal was allowed from their decisions to the Court of Session. It is to the commissary courts that Craig refers in the phrases *in curia christianitatis* and *in foro Ecclesiastico* noted above.

## B. THE CANON LAW

According to the Canonists, the essence of the contract of marriage lay in the consent of the parties.[17] At first Canon law looked also for some evidence

---

13 *RM (Cooper)*, 2.16; *RM (APS)* 2.13. For English law see the discussion of dower in Pollock & Maitland, vol 2, at 420–8, especially at 425.
14 Craig, *JF*, 1.3.24 (Dodd trans at 83).
15 Ireland (n 6) at 93–97.
16 See generally T M Green, *The Spiritual Jurisdiction in Reformation Scotland: A Legal History* (2019).
17 The literature on the Canon law of marriage is immense. I have found the following particularly useful: A Esmein, *Le Mariage en Droit Canonique*, 2nd edn by R Genestal (1929); R H Helmholz, *Marriage Litigation in Medieval England* (1974); J A Brundage, *Law, Sex, and Christian Society in Medieval Europe* (1987); and C Brooke, *The Medieval Idea of Marriage* (1989). See also Pollock & Maitland, vol 2, ch VII; and Archbishop J Scanlan, "Pre-Reformation Canon law of marriage of the officials' courts", and R D Ireland, "Husband and wife: (a) Post-Reformation Canon law of marriage of the Commissaries' courts and (b) modern common and statute law", both in *ISLH* 69, 82; O F Robinson, "Canon law and marriage", 1984 *JR* 22.

of consummation, but the position eventually adopted by the developed Canon law of the later Middle Ages, albeit with some hesitation and qualification, was that consent alone was sufficient to constitute a valid marriage.[18] Consent would normally be expressed by words spoken by the parties in the present tense (*per verba de praesenti*). The exchange of such words was in itself sufficient to constitute a valid marriage, even although the formalities which the Church required for regular marriage had not been complied with. A marriage might be clandestine or irregular, but none the less a valid marriage for that.

Ideally the consent should be expressed in words, but tacit consent was also recognised as being sufficient in some circumstances to infer marriage. William Hay, relying here on the Decretals of Gregory IX,[19] noted that a deaf mute could lawfully contract marriage with another deaf mute. Even among those able to speak, Hay continued, matrimonial consent was not restricted to words. It could be expressed in writing or even by signs:

> A timid maiden's silence is sometimes considered sufficient for marriage, without any sign at all (*sine quibuscunque signis*), if she quietly allows all the usual formalities of a wedding to take place in her regard, without making any protest, tor she is presumed to consent, and her silence is taken as a sufficient sign.[20]

The Church also taught that intercourse following on a promise or engagement to marry constituted a valid though irregular marriage. This was the doctrine of *sponsalia per verba de futuro subsequente copula*. The theory was that present consent to marriage could be inferred from the intercourse between the parties.

The surviving record of the ecclesiastical courts in Scotland before the Reformation illustrates clearly the operation of irregular marriage *per verba de praesenti* and *per verba de futuro subsequente copula*. Cosmo Innes brought together cases on marriage from the records of the Officials of St Andrews and Lothian in his *Liber Officialis Sancti Andree*.[21] In *Turnbull v Forrest* it was held that a previous irregular marriage *per verba de futuro carnali copula subsecuta* took precedence over and annulled a later regular marriage *in facie ecclesie solemnizatum per verba de praesenti carnali copula subsecuta*.[22] In *Blak v Robertsone* the pursuer was released from an

---

18 The pontificate of Alexander III (1159–1181) marks the watershed. See, for example, Brundage, *Law, Sex* (n 17) at 331–337.
19 *Hay's Lectures* (n 9) at 176–178, citing X *(Decretals)* 4.1.23.
20 *Hay's Lectures* (n 9) at 179.
21 C Innes (ed), *Liber Officialis Sancte Andree* (Abbotsford Club, 1845).
22 *Liber Officialis* (n 21) at 19.

engagement to marry (*sponsalia per verba de futuro*) which had not been followed by intercourse, on account of a subsequent engagement which had been so followed, and which therefore constituted a valid marriage.[23] In *Johnesoune v Eldare* a regular marriage in *facie ecclesie* between David Johnesoune and Margaret Eldare was held invalid because of earlier *sponsalia* between David and Margaret Abernethy *tam per verba de futuro quam de praesenti . . . carnali copula subsecuta,* the actual words spoken being "I promytt to you Begis Abirnethy that I sall marry you and that I sail nevere haiff ane uther wiff and therto I giff you my fayth".[24] The report continued that David and Margaret Abernethy then cohabited at bed and board (*cohabitaverunt in una domo in mensa tabula et lecto*) and were habit and repute man and wife (*tanquam coniuges fuerunt habiti tenti et reputati*).[25] Here in the language of the medieval Canon law we find the origin of the phrase "cohabitation with habit and repute", or, for that matter, the "repute and haldin" of the Act of 1504. In passing it may be noted that "habiti" or "habite" has sometimes been misunderstood and taken to refer to the passage of time rather than to be a rendering in Scots of the Latin *habiti* or "held".[26]

The teaching of the Canon law on the weight to be attached to cohabitation with habit and repute as a proof of marriage stemmed from a ruling given by Pope Alexander III (1159–81) to the Archbishop of Genoa. This decretal was incorporated in the Decretals of Gregory IX (1234),[27] and gave rise to much later commentary. A man and a woman had cohabited for ten years. The woman denied that they were married. She claimed that witnesses to the *sponsalia* were not available: that a document which named the parties as man and wife was suspect; and that a number of witnesses could testify that the man had firmly denied the fact of marriage. The Archbishop asked for guidance. The Pope replied that when doubts of this kind arose particular attention should be paid to general repute in the neighbourhood (*fama viciniae*). Diligent inquiry should be made whether the couple were

---

23 *Liber Officialis* (n 21) at 14.
24 *Liber Officialis* (n 21) at 21.
25 This last case was known to James Fergusson who printed it in the Appendix to his *Consistorial Law* (1829) at 60–61 with the comment: "This decision proves further that habit and repute was another mode of constituting marriage under the canon law of Scotland." This comment is, at best, ambiguous and misleading as will be seen.
26 E.g. by Sheriff Wilson (n 7) at 120, following Lord Cranworth in *Campbell v Campbell* (1867) 5 M (HL) 115 at 135, and by Temporary Judge R G MacEwan QC in *Kamperman v MacIver*, 20 March 1992, 1992 GWD 15–893.
27 X.2.23 *De Praesumptionibus*, c 11. This is the decretal referred to by Lord Fraser, text accompanying n 5 above.

regarded in the neighbourhood as living together at bed and board as man and wife, or in concubinage. If the former, then the woman should be persuaded to show proper conjugal affection.

The decretal was not free from ambiguity, but from it evolved the later Canon law doctrine that evidence of cohabitation with the necessary repute might be enough, in the absence of further proof, to infer that matrimonial consent had been exchanged. The evidence lay in possession of the state of marriage. There were three elements relevant to this proof: *nominatio*, *tractatus* and *fama*. Little stress was put on the first of these, *nominatio*, for the Canonists recognised that assumption of the name of husband and wife could arise from all sorts of ulterior motives, and was far from conclusive. The conjunction of the other two elements, however – cohabitation over a period of time, and the all-important public repute or *fama* – did raise a presumption of marriage. Initially there was some hesitation about the doctrine. The Church had expended much energy over the centuries in combatting concubinage, both lay and clerical, and enjoining Christian matrimony. It did not wish to appear to be re-admitting concubinage by the back door. However, by the time of the great Canonist, Panormitanus (Niccolo de Tudeschis, 1386–1445, Archbishop of Palermo), author of a famous commentary on the Decretals, the doctrine was generally accepted.[28] It was always merely a presumption, a method of proof; the constitution of marriage was another matter.

## C. SCOTS LAW

As already noted, Canon law remained an authoritative source of Scots law after the Reformation. To Thomas Craig's testimony on this point we can add that of Stair, one hundred years later:

> And so deep hath this canon law been rooted, that, even where the Pope's authority is rejected, yet consideration must be had to these laws, not only as to these by which church benefices have been erected and ordered, but as likewise containing many equitable and profitable laws, which because of their weighty matter, and their being once received, may more fitly be retained then rejected.[29]

The rules of Canon law gradually merged with, and became part of, the common law of Scotland. This was particularly true of the constitution of

---

28 Panormitanus, *Commentaria* ad X.2.23.11. See Esmein, *Le Mariage* (n 17), vol 1, at 222–225; Helmholz, *Marriage Litigation* (n 17), at 46–47 and 195–196; and Brundage, *Law, Sex* (n 17), at 444–447 and 514–517.
29 Stair, *Inst*, 1.1.14.

marriage.³⁰ Over the centuries, certainly, there might be changes. Thus the impediment of affinity, relevant to the prohibited degrees, which under the Canon law had arisen from previous intercourse, came to be founded rather on previous matrimony; this being finally established by the case of *Hamilton v Wylie* (1827).³¹ Again, the rule that a previous adulterous relationship with the prospective spouse might raise an impediment to marriage, while still apparently insisted on in *Irvine v Ker* in 1695,³² no longer presented a barrier by the mid-nineteenth century. Much, however, remained unaltered. Irregular marriage *per verba de praesenti* continued to be recognised and was re-affirmed in pristine canonical form in *Walker v M'Adam* (1813).³³ Irregular marriage *per verba de futuro subsequente copula* also continued to be recognised, the classic doctrine of the Canon law being affirmed in *Pennycook v Grinton* (1752)³⁴ and again in *Mackie v Mackie* (1917),³⁵ after some intermittent uncertainty caused largely by the inaccuracies of Lord Kames in the eighteenth century and Lord Fraser in the nineteenth.

One thing above all remained constant: the emphasis placed on consent as the cardinal factor in the constitution of marriage. Stair writes, "Though the commixtion of bodies seem necessary for the constitution of affinity arising from marriage, yet the opinion of the canon law is true, *consensus, non coitus, facit matrimonium*".³⁶ In his discussion of irregular marriage he notes that:

> the matter itself consists not in the promise, but in the present consent, whereby they accept each other as husband and wife: whether that be by words expressly; or tacitly by marital cohabition or acknowledgment; or by natural commixtion, where there hath been a promise or espousals preceding, for therein is presumed a conjugal consent *de praesenti*.³⁷

---

30 See further T M Green (ed), *The Consistorial Decisions of the Commissaries of Edinburgh, 1564 to 1576/7* (SS vol 61, 2014), introduction, at xlvi–lv, especially at xlix–l; T Green, "The sources of early Scots consistorial law: reflections on law, authority and jurisdiction during the Scottish Reformation", in M Godfrey (ed), *Law and Authority in British Legal History, 1200–1900* (2016) 120.
31 *Hamilton v Wylie* (1827) 5 S 716.
32 *Irvine v Ker* (1695) in F P Walton (ed), *Lord Hermand's Consistorial Decisions 1684–1777* (SS vol 6, 1940) 91; and see Ireland (n 6) at 93–94.
33 *Walker v M'Adam* (1813) 5 Pat 675. For a failed attempt at abolition by statute see B Dempsey, "The Marriage (Scotland) Bill 1755", in H L MacQueen (ed), *Miscellany VI* (SS vol 54, 2009) 75.
34 *Pennycook v Grinton* (1752) Mor 12677.
35 *Mackie v Mackie* 1917 SC 276.
36 Stair, *Inst*, 1.4.6.
37 Stair, *Inst*, 1.4.6.

Stair also notes that "public solemnity" – that is, regular marriage – "is a matter of order, justly introduced by positive law for the certainty of so important a contract, but not essential to marriage."[38]

Later in the *Institutions*, under the title of "Probation Extraordinary", Stair considers proof of marriage by CHR:

> Cohabitation, and behaving as man and wife for a considerable time, presumeth marriage, though there be neither contract, promise, nor *sponsalia* preceding, nor evidence of copulation by children . . . These are presumptions so strong, that the confession or oath of either, or both parties, will not elide the same, though they should acknowledge that they neither promised marriage *de futuro*, nor contracted the same *de praesenti*; yea, though they should acknowledge that they so cohabited to cover their fornication, that they might be free to marry others when they pleased: for all these and such things would be presumed as collusion, to dissolve the marriage upon dissonance of humors, or other designs . . .[39]

There is nothing here that a Canon lawyer would disagree with; indeed, the example is reminiscent of Alexander III's original decretal. Neither is Stair suggesting, as has sometimes been claimed,[40] that the presumption is virtually irrebuttable.

Erskine, too, emphasises that consent is both necessary and sufficient: "Marriage is truly a contract, and so requires the consent of parties . . . And it is constituted by consent alone . . .".[41] He notes that a promise or engagement to marry is "quite distinct from the marriage itself, which requires present consent",[42] and that "the consent essential to marriage is either express or tacit".[43] The passage in which Erskine discusses MCHR, "where the consent is not express, but is discovered *rebus ipsis et factis*", has already been noticed.[44] Erskine's *rebus ipsis et factis* equates with the Canonists' "possession of the state of marriage".

Baron David Hume introduces the discussion of the constitution of marriage in his *Lectures* by noting that:

> the doctrine of the Law of Scotland may be delivered in few words, being very simple and compendious. It is founded on that of the Canon law, which is the basis of the matrimonial law of Europe . . . Thus, the general precept of our practice as of the old Canon law, is that marriage is a civil contract, and is established

---

38 Stair, *Inst*, 1.4.6.
39 Stair, *Inst*, 4.45.19.
40 E.g. by Ireland (n 6) at 89.
41 Erskine, *Inst*, 1.6.2.
42 Erskine, *Inst*, 1.6.3.
43 Erskine, *Inst*, 1.6.5.
44 See above text accompanying n 3.

by the interposition of consent, *which is the one thing sufficient and indispensible to its completion.*[45]

Like Stair, Hume emphasises that "mere form or solemnity is in nowise essential to a marriage by our law".[46] Hume later discusses what he terms "the form and mode" of interposing matrimonial consent.[47] MCHR is introduced with the words, "Indeed, from what has already been said of the spirit of the Law of Scotland, it will be evident to you that there must be still further modes of substantiating the intervention of the matrimonial consent."[36] Consent in this case, he notes, is tacit, *rebus ipsis et factis*, "inferred from a continued trial of consistent conduct".[48]

In his notes to Hume's *Lectures* the editor, Dr Campbell Paton, drew attention to a passage in More's *Lectures* in which More comments that what writers call the constitution of marriage is really proof of exchange of consent.[49] The point is a valuable one, even if not unique to More.[50] To describe *sponsalia per verba de praesenti* and *sponsalia per verba de futuro subsequente copula* as methods of contracting marriage is unlikely to cause misunderstanding, but when the same terminology is applied to marriage by cohabitation with habit and repute, confusion is bound to arise. The fact that the cohabitation and repute is merely a mode of inferring consent may be lost sight of, and the period of cohabitation itself be viewed as being in some sense integral to the constitution of marriage. This indeed was the argument advanced by Eric Clive.[51]

Although the terminology used may occasionally have been rather loose, much later commentators on the marriage law of Scotland were agreed that cohabitation with habit and repute (CHR) was merely a method of proof. For example, F P Walton, the acknowledged authority on the law of husband and wife at the end of the nineteenth century, wrote of MCHR, echoing the comments of More:

> This is not, properly speaking, a separate mode of marriage, but it is convenient to treat of it by itself. It is more correct to describe it as another way in which it may be proved that two persons had interchanged matrimonial consent. As I

---

45 Hume, *Lectures* vol 1, at 21–22 (emphasis supplied).
46 Hume, *Lectures* vol 1, at 40.
47 Hume, *Lectures* vol 1, at 33.
48 Hume, *Lectures* vol 1, at 55.
49 Hume, *Lectures* vol 1, at 33 n 2.
50 See also, for example, Sheriff Wilson (n 7) at 108: "all marriages require consent *de praesenti* and what are usually called the three forms of irregular marriage were often regarded as strictly three methods of proving that consent had been exchanged."
51 See below text accompanying nn 66–74.

have explained already, all that is necessary to prove a marriage in Scotland is to show that two people, who are free to marry each other, have agreed then and there to do so.[52]

The main support for the argument that MCHR is something more than a method of proof is to be found in one of the opinions delivered in the Court of Session in the case of *Campbell v Campbell* ("The Breadalbane Peerage Case") in 1866: the joint opinion of Lord Justice-Clerk Inglis, Lord Neaves and Lord Mure.[53] On fuller inspection this support proves to be distinctly unreliable. Their Lordships put forward the view (now also advanced by Dr Clive) that Scots law recognises two distinct types of cohabitation with habit and repute. The first is a "presumption, not peculiar to the law of Scotland, that the parties have been married at some time or another, and in some way or another according to law"; the second is "peculiar to the law of Scotland, as they [cohabitation and repute] are a recognised mode of contracting marriage". "The history and probable origin of this doctrine in the law of Scotland", they continue, "throws some light on the subject". They note that the principle of CHR is "indeed a very natural one" (an echo here of Erskine) which has been recognised in several systems. They then refer to the operation of *usus* in Roman law and to the practice of "Teutonic nations" quoting an "old Jutish law" – *Concubinam quamdiu habere licet* – for which no reference is given. This is the extent of the reference to history and origins! There is no mention of the Canon law.

It is difficult to know what to make of this extraordinary excursus. Certainly the ignorance displayed as to origins tends to shake one's faith in the exposition of the current law. Roman law did indeed have a doctrine of *usus*, built on by the medieval Civilians; but it was partly the Roman lawyers' readiness, following Modestinus in Digest 23.2.1 to allow that long cohabitation might itself constitute marriage, that made the Canon lawyers at the first reluctant to allow cohabitation even as a mode of proof.[54] In 1867 the House of Lords was polite but firm about the theory that Scots law recognised two types of cohabitation with habit and repute, and that consent alone might not be sufficient to constitute marriage. In a passage worth quoting at length, which was clearly aimed at the joint opinion, Lord Westbury took some pains to counter any suggestion that CHR might in some sense constitute marriage:

---

52 F P Walton, *Scotch Marriages, Regular and Irregular* (1891) at 131.
53 *Campbell v Campbell* (1866) 4 M 867 at 924–926.
54 See Helmholz (n 17) at 46–47 and 195–196; Brundage (n 17) at 444–447 and 514–517.

It is not pretended by any of the learned Judges that marriage is constituted by CHR, but they, one and all, I think, treat the evidence upon that subject as evidence to prove that which alone constitutes marriage, namely, the consent of the parties. Some exception may possibly be taken to some few words occurring in one of the judgments in which CHR is spoken of as a mode of contracting marriage. It is quite plain what is meant by the learned judges; but perhaps it may not be strictly correct to say that it is a mode of contracting marriage. It is, rather (as I have already stated) a mode of making manifest to the world that tacit consent, which from the conduct of the parties the law will infer to have been already interchanged between them.[55]

Lord Cranworth observed: "I cannot, however, think it correct to say that habit and repute, in any case, make the marriage."[56] Lord Colonsay, who had advised on the case earlier in the Court of Session as Lord President, saw no reason to alter his previous opinion to the effect that CHR was merely a mode of indicating consent to matrimony: "Marriage is constituted by consent, and there may be various *indicia* or proofs of consent; the question always is, whether there are such proofs."[57]

### D. THE 1939 ACT

As long as marriage by declaration *per verba de praesenti* and *pe verba de futuro subsequente copula* continued to be recognised, the exact definition and scope of the doctrine of MCHR was a matter of more academic than practical interest, as one method of proof tended to shade into another. In 1939, however, Section 5 of the Marriage (Scotland) Act enacted that, "No irregular marriage by declaration *de praesenti* or by promise *subsequente copula* contracted after the commencement of this Act shall be valid."[58]

The Departmental Committee on the Law of Marriage, chaired by Lord Morison, whose Report had preceded the legislation, had recommended the abolition of these two forms of irregular marriage. The Committee had also recommended the abolition of MCHR, under the impression that this too was a method of constituting marriage, but this recommendation was successfully resisted in Parliament. What effect then did the Act have on MCHR? A number of interpretations were possible.

---

55 *Campbell v Campbell* (1867) 5 M (HL) 115 at 140.
56 *Campbell* (1867) (n 55) at 135.
57 *Campbell* (1866) (n 53) at 946.
58 On the background to the 1939 Act see B Dempsey, "Making the Gretna blacksmith redundant: who worried, who spoke, who was heard on the abolition of irregular marriage in Scotland" (2009) 30 *JLH* 23.

On one interpretation there had been only two forms of irregular marriage recognised by Scots law: marriage *per verba de praesenti* and marriage by promise *subsequente copula*. The abolition of marriage "by declaration *de praesenti*" might be thought to embrace all forms of *de praesenti* matrimony. The effect of the Act, therefore, was to abolish all forms of irregular marriage in Scots law, notwithstanding the clear intention of Parliament, as evidenced by Hansard, to the contrary. This appears to have been the view taken by A E Anton, who noted, *en passant*, in 1958 that the Act abolished irregular marriages in Scots law.[59] It was not, however, the view taken by the courts who, without troubling to discuss the matter, continued to recognise irregular marriages based on CHR.[60]

On another view, CHR was indeed in some sense a method of constituting marriage in Scots law. It thus remained unaffected by the 1939 Act. At least some of the opinions expressed by Sir Thomas Smith in his earlier writings can be construed in that light, as D I C Ashton-Cross noted:

> The doctrine of "habit and repute" [*Sir Thomas had written*], is not limited to the aspect of presumption of evidence that a man and woman who have cohabited must at some time have been married . . . In Scotland cohabitation with habit and repute may actually result in marriage and the court may pronounce a decree of declaration of marriage, though it cannot single out with certainty any particular date on which mutual consent to marriage was exchanged.[61]

Ashton-Cross argued strongly for the contrary view that CHR was not in any sense a method of constituting marriage, but merely a method of proving or inferring the exchange of tacit consent. The Departmental Committee had been mistaken on this point. He then reviewed various decisions and writings of authority, some of them already referred to in this article. He noted the dictum of Lord Moncreiff in *Lapsley v Grierson*: "The proper doctrine is, that the consent, by which marriage is constituted in the law of Scotland, may be proved by such cohabitation and repute".[62] He summed up his views on the effect of the Act in this delphic sentence: "If, then, 'habit and repute' was before the Act a mode of marriage it still is; if it was not, it still is not." He concluded: "The authority to the effect that it was never a mode seems to me overwhelming."[63]

---

59 A E Anton and Ph Francescakis, "Modern Scots 'runaway marriages'", 1958 *JR* 253 at 255.
60 See below section E.
61 D I C Ashton-Cross "Cohabitation with habit and repute", 1961 *JR* 21 at 22–24, quoting T B Smith, *The United Kingdom, The Development of its Laws and Constitutions: Scotland* (1955) at 791.
62 *Lapsley v Grierson* (1848) 8 D 34 at 81.
63 Ashton-Cross (n 61) at 23.

Sir Thomas took heed of Ashton-Cross's criticisms. In his *Short Commentary* he referred to Ashton-Cross and noted:

> It would seem that the view which regards habit and repute as being a method of constituting marriage is erroneous. Habit and repute is a method of proving consent and this may not have been realised by the legislature in 1939.[64]

This is in line with the third edition of Walton on *Husband and Wife*, published in 1951, which states that irregular marriage constituted "by the interchange of consent to be inferred from proof of cohabitation and habit and repte" had not been affected by the 1939 Act.[65]

The same view, broadly speaking, was taken by Sheriff Wilson, who wrote the text of the relevant chapter of Clive and Wilson on *Husband and Wife*, published in 1974.[66] There are clear indications of disagreement, however, in some of Clive's footnotes.[67] Clive's second edition, published in 1982, made a radical shift of opinion, which was reflected also in the Scottish Law Commission discussion paper (March 1990) entitled "Family Law: Pre-consolidation reforms".[68] Clive effectively revived the view expressed by Lord Justice-Clerk Inglis, Lord Neaves and Lord Mure in *Campbell v Campbell*, although in more sophisticated form. He argued that Scots law recognises two types of CHR: one is purely evidential, the other helps to constitute a type of irregular marriage. He wrote:

> If there were nothing more to cohabitation with habit and repute than the rule of evidence noted above then irregular marriages by cohabitation by habit and repute would have been abolished incidentally by the Marriage (Scotland) Act 1939 as a necessary consequence of the abolition of marriages by declaration *de praesenti* and promise *subsequente copula*.[69]

In a key passage, Clive continues:

> Irregular marriages by cohabitation by habit and repute survive. The explanation is that the Scottish courts departed from, or developed, the canon law and recognised that tacit consent inferred from, *and combined with*, the requisite cohabitation by habit and repute was sufficient to constitute marriage. In other words, cohabitation by habit and repute ceased to be merely evidence from which an express exchange of consent could be inferred and became, in addition, a recognised way of exchanging tacit consent. It became as meaningful to talk of

---

64 Smith, *Short Commentary* (n 6) at 314.
65 Walton, *Handbook* (n 6) at 24.
66 Clive and Wilson, *Husband and Wife* (n 7) at 107–122, especially at 121–122.
67 See, for example, Clive and Wilson, *Husband and Wife* (n 7) at 117 n 38, the argument in which is replicated in Clive, *Husband and Wife* (n 1).
68 Scottish Law Commission Discussion Paper No 85 (March 1990), paras 2.1–2.19.
69 Clive, *Husband and Wife* (n 1) at 60.

marriage by cohabitation by habit and repute as to talk of marriage by declaration *de praesenti*.[70]

With the greatest respect, this argument does not appear to be well founded. There can be no doubt that the doctrine of MCHR was inherited from the Canon law; and also, that the Canon law was subject to change after the Reformation both by statute and at common law. There was, however, no statutory alteration of MCHR, and there is little to support the view that the courts developed the common law in the manner stated by Clive. On the contrary, as argued in this chapter, the weight of the evidence is overwhelming that there was little change, if any, in the understanding and exposition of the doctrine of MCHR between Panormitanus in the fifteenth century and Walton in the twentieth. It does not, incidentally, appear to be the case that the Canon law required evidence of *express* consent to marriage, as Clive suggests. The terms of Alexander III's original decretal and of *William Hay's Lectures on Marriage*, already referred to, are enough to negate that proposition. In any event, the joint opinion of the Lord Justice-Clerk, Lord Neaves and Mure in *Campbell* is a poor support on which to rest any exposition of the modern law. Their Lordships were clearly mistaken in their history and were corrected in their exposition of the law by the House of Lords. Further, it does not necessarily follow that if CHR were merely a rule of evidence the 1939 Act would have had the incidental effect of abolishing MCHR. We may agree with Clive when he writes that, "Cohabitation and repute do not in themselves constitute a marriage", and that "Outward actings do not make a marriage in Scots law".[71] But surely he is mistaken when he continues:

> Mere consent does not in itself constitute a marriage either. Marriage requires both a mental element (mutual consent to marry) and an outward or factual element (nowadays either a regular marriage ceremony or cohabitation by habit and repute). Both are necessary. Neither is sufficient.[72]

The belief that consent in itself is insufficient is re-iterated more starkly when Clive counters Ashton-Cross's argument that CHR is merely a method of proof, with the comment that this "seems to proceed on the fallacious assumption that consent is sufficient as well as necessary for the constitution of marriage".[73]

---

70 Clive, *Husband and Wife* (n 1) at 60–61 (emphasis supplied).
71 Clive, *Husband and Wife* (n 1) at 62.
72 Clive, *Husband and Wife* (n 1) at 62 n 1.
73 Clive, *Husband and Wife* (n 1) at 62 n 1.

On the contrary, the clear teaching of the law from the twelfth century to the twentieth is that the consent of the parties is enough by itself to constitute marriage, that it is both necessary and sufficient, always so long as there exists proof adequate to demonstrate the exchange of that consent. That is the fundamental proposition. It may, of course, be enacted that certain formalities must be complied with in order to constitute a valid marriage, but this has not happened in Scotland, or particular modes of marriage or, more properly, modes of indicating exchange of the necessary matrimonial consent may be declared invalid by statute. This is what happened in 1939 in regard to marriage by declaration *de praesenti* and promise *subsequente copula*. Subject to this exception, however, the basic proposition still holds. The burden of proof on those seeking to show the displacement or qualification of such a cardinal point of doctrine is very heavy. It has not been discharged.

As Clive recognises, some practical consequences flow from the theory that CHR is more than just a method of proof. The most obvious is that the cohabitation must have taken place "for a considerable time".[74] Consonant with this, Clive writes that:

> It is, however, totally illogical to back-date marriages by CHR to a date when there has been neither cohabitation nor repute. It is submitted that the only original date for such a marriage is the date by which there has been sufficient relevant cohabitation . . . and reputation to satisfy the law's requirements.[75]

## E. CASE LAW SINCE 1939

It is time now to consider the case law since the 1939 Act. It does not support the propositions put forward by Eric Clive, but rather bears out the traditional view that CHR is no more than a method of proof. *Nicol v Bell*[76] concerned a period of cohabitation which began many years before the Act came into force and continued until 1950. The pursuer sought declarator that she had been lawfully married to the defender by cohabitation from 1929 to 1950 and the habit and repute arising therefrom. She had come to live with the defender, a married man, in 1929. His sister was then still living in the house. During the course of 1929, the sister left, the defender's marriage was dissolved by divorce (on 8 June), and the pursuer became pregnant by the defender. A child, James, was born on 2 June 1930, and registered

---

74 Clive, *Husband and Wife* (n 1) at 62–64.
75 Clive, *Husband and Wife* (n 1) at 73.
76 *Nicol v Bell* 1954 SLT 314.

under the defender's surname. The Lord Ordinary granted the declarator sought, and this was confirmed on appeal by the Second Division.

In the Division Lord Justice-Clerk Thomson noted that cohabitation might begin in a number of different situations and "that it may not always be possible for the Court . . . to single out with any certainty any incident or even point of time in the association of the partners from which the married state should run."[77] In this case, however, he thought that there were points of time that could be looked at:

> The Lord Ordinary chose the point preceding James's birth. I am quite satisfied with that but I should have thought an equally good case could be made out for the date when the sister left and the whole household was rearranged.[78]

The Lord Justice-Clerk, then, was prepared to allow that the marriage had taken place a good deal less than a year after the defender became free to contract.

Lord Patrick emphasised the role of consent. He did not agree with the Lord Ordinary that tacit consent could be inferred from actings immediately before James's birth, but he thought that "the tacit consent to marriage may be held to have existed from the same year as the Lord Ordinary has affirmed, namely 1930."[79] Lord Mackintosh noted that:

> It is well settled law that cohabitation and the habit and repute arising therefrom do not in themselves constitute marriage but if the proof of these be sufficient they give rise to the presumption that *at some possibly unascertained date* the parties tacitly interchanged consent to be husband and wife and so contracted a marriage.[80]

He approved Lord Glenlee's "classic statement of the law of marriage by cohabitation and repute" in *Elder v M'Lean*, including the words, "Marriage is founded on consent, *and there may be single facts so strong as to supersede everything else.*"[81]

The interlocutor in *Nicol v Bell* held that marriage had been established "by cohabitation from 1930 until 1950 and the habit and repute arising there from". Ashton-Cross criticised the form of this interlocutor as not distinguishing properly between constitution and proof. "If the inference was of consent," he wrote, "the wording of the interlocutor is unfortunate."[82] It

---

77 *Nicol v Bell* (n 76) at 319.
78 *Nicol v Bell* (n 76) at 321.
79 *Nicol v Bell* (n 76) at 325–6.
80 *Nicol v Bell* (n 76) at 326 (emphasis supplied).
81 *Elder v M'Lean* (1829) 8 S 56 at 62 (Lord Mackintosh's emphasis).
82 Ashton-Cross (n 61) at 26.

is clear from the passages quoted above, from the emphasis on points of time and on single facts so strong as to supersede everything else, that the inference was indeed of consent, and that the Lord Ordinary and two of the Division were quite prepared to infer that consent from actions within a year or so of the parties being free to marry. There was no consideration of the effect, if any, of the 1939 Act, but in the circumstances of the case, this is not surprising.

The lack of such consideration in *AB v CD*[83] is altogether more remarkable, as this is the first reported case involving a period of cohabitation which began after the Act came into force. In *AB* the pursuer sought declarator of nullity of marriage on the ground that she was under age at the time of the marriage ceremony. The Age of Marriage Act 1929 had raised the age of consent to marriage to sixteen. In *AB*, the marriage ceremony took place on 27 July 1942, although the pursuer did not become sixteen until 12 August. The defender raised a cross-action for declarator of marriage on the ground that he and the pursuer had cohabited as married persons with habit and repute until 1948. Five children had been born of the marriage. The Lord Ordinary, Lord Guthrie, granted declarator of marriage. He noted that:

> Under the old common law, whereby a pupil was incapable of entering marriage "if the married pair shall continue alter puberty, such acquiescence makes the marriage valid" – Erskine's Institute, I, vi, 2. In my opinion, the same result flows from continued cohabitation as man and wife after time has removed the impediment to marriage imposed by the Act of Marriage, 1929.[84]

Lord Guthrie did not refer to Lord Justice-Clerk Thomson's remarks on the relevance of points, as opposed to tracts, of time in particular cases, but it is clear that he considered 12 August 1942, when the pursuer attained the age of 16, to be the relevant point in time.

In *Low v Gorman*[85] the cohabitation of the parties began in adultery in 1961, when they set up house together after a sham wedding reception. The parties became free to marry only on the divorce of the defender on 26 February 1966. The defender left the pursuer on 27 December that same year. The pursuer failed in her petition for declarator of MCHR. The Lord Ordinary, Lord Robertson, accepted that the parties would have married in 1961 had they been free to do so; but he did not assent to the proposition that the parties should therefore be regarded as married whenever the

---

83 *AB v CD* 1957 SC 415 (also reported as *Woodward v Woodward* 1958 SLT 213).
84 *AB v CD* (n 83) at 427.
85 *Low v Gorman* 1970 SLT 356.

impediment was removed. In this case there were three difficulties. The most important of these was the fact that "the parties became estranged at the beginning of 1966 and relations between them steadily deteriorated."[86] There was also a difficulty as regards repute, in that a number of relatives were well aware that the parties had not been married. The third difficulty was time, given that the tract of time available was only ten months. On this last point Lord Robertson relied on the somewhat uncertain authority of the Second Division case of *Wallace v Fife Coal Company*,[87] in which Lord Ardwall appeared to set an absolute minimum in excess of the ten and a half months there available.[88]

In *Mackenzie v Scott*,[89] the Lord Ordinary, Lord Ross, refused to grant the declarator of marriage sought, being unable to find that there ever was tacit consent. Lord Ross referred with approval to the dicta on consent by Lord Cranworth and Lord Westbury in *Campbell v Campbell* noted above.[90] This case furnishes a modern example of the uncertain value of evidence regarding what the Canonists termed *nominatio*, for there was evidence here of the exchange of birthday cards addressed to "My Dear Wife" and "Dearest Husband".

In *Shaw v Henderson*[91] the question of time was very much at issue. The pursuer began to cohabit with James Henderson about June 1977, both being at that time married to others. They did not become free to marry until Henderson was divorced on March 1978. Henderson was killed in a road accident on 31 January 1979. The period available, therefore, was less than eleven months. Was this sufficient to establish the necessary cohabitation with habit and repute? The Lord Ordinary, Lord Stott, held that it was. He observed: "Counsel for the defender submitted, in my opinion correctly, that marriage is constituted not by cohabitation and repute but by the consent of the parties to be inferred therefrom."[92] He had little difficulty in distinguishing *Low v Gorman* because of the deteriorating relationship between the parties evident in that case; and he was unimpressed by the authority of *Wallace v Fife Coal Company* cited by Lord Robertson in *Low*. He pointed out that Lord Ardwall, who had appeared to set a tract of time

---

86 *Low v Gorman* (n 85) at 361.
87 *Wallace v Fife Coal Company* 1909 SC 682.
88 Discussed further below, this page.
89 *Mackenzie v Scott* 1980 SLT (Notes) 9.
90 See above text accompanying nn 55–56.
91 *Shaw v Henderson* 1982 SLT 211.
92 *Shaw v Henderson* (n 91) at 212.

longer than the ten and a half months available in *Wallace*, had not been supported by the other two judges in the Division: the Lord Justice-Clerk had made it clear he was deciding the case on its particular facts. Lord Stott said:

> That in my respectful opinion is the correct approach. What I have to do is to bear in mind the comparatively short period of cohabitation and determine whether on the evidence in relation to that period an inference of consent to marriage ought to be drawn.[93]

In the past few years there has been a positive flurry of further decisions. In *Hill v Hill* Lord Davidson refused the declarator of marriage sought. He did, however, note with approval Lord Glenlee's statement in *Elder v Maclean*, already referred to, that "Marriage is founded on consent, and there may be single facts so strong as to supersede everything else."[94] In *Davies v Sutherland's Executrix* Lord Mayfield refused declarator of marriage. In so doing, he observed:

> It is of course well recognised that marriage is not constituted by cohabitation with habit and repute but cohabitation with habit and repute is the evidence from which the court may infer the consent of the parties which alone can constitute marriage.[95]

The circumstances in *Mullen v Mullen*[96] were unusual. The couple in question had been divorced in March 1974 but had resumed cohabitation in October the same year. About six months later the wife's initial doubts as to the wisdom of renewing the relationship had been overcome, and she suggested they should go through a civil marriage ceremony. The husband declined on religious grounds as he did not accept that the first marriage had ever been dissolved. They remained together, universally accepted as husband and wife, until the death of the husband in 1989. Lord Murray held that the divorce between the parties was no bar to their subsequently establishing a marriage by CHR, and granted declarator of marriage as from 4 April 1975, six months after the resumption of cohabitation.

In *Donnelly v Donnelly's Executor*,[97] the pursuer and John Donnelly began to cohabit as husband and wife in or about 1979, both being free to marry. They remained together until Donnelly's death in 1987, but never went through a formal ceremony of marriage. Lord Mayfield did not find it

---

93 *Shaw v Henderson* (n 91) at 212.
94 *Hill v Hill*, 15 July 1986 (unreported); *Elder v M'Lean* (above n 81).
95 *Davis v Sutherland's Executrix*, 20 December 1989, 1990 GWD 8–433.
96 *Mullen v Mullen* 1991 SLT 205.
97 *Donnelly v Donnelly's Executor* 1992 SLT 13.

difficult to infer tacit consent on the evidence and granted declarator that the pursuer and Donnelly had been lawfully married by cohabitation and repute on 1 January 1980; that is, very shortly after they began to cohabit.

In *Kamperman v MacIver* R G McEwan, sitting as a temporary Judge, held that a period of six months and two weeks cohabitation was too short, and could never be categorised as "considerable". He believed that Lord Stott in *Shaw v Henderson* had misconstrued the decision in *Wallace v Fife Coal Company*. But that approach was overturned by the Second Division.[98]

The decisions of the Social Security Commissioners (determining status for social security purposes only) are in line with those of the Court of Session. The Commissioner (J G Mitchell QC) in *R(G) 4/84* quoted with approval the definition of marriage by cohabitation with habit and repute adopted by a Tribunal of Commissioners in *R(G) 2/82*, including the words "Cohabitation with habit and repute does not in itself constitute marriage. It raises a presumption that there has been tacit consent to marriage but such a presumption can be rebutted or displaced." In *R(G) 5/83*, a claim for widow's allowance, despite accepting that cohabitation should be "for a considerable period", a Tribunal of Commissioners found MCHR established although the period available was only three and a half months (13 May to 31 August 1982) – far shorter than in *Shaw v Henderson*. The sufficiency of the period was to be judged in the light of the circumstances of the case. Here the couple began to cohabit in 1970 when neither was free to marry. In 1972 the man placed a ring on the claimant's left hand in a church. In 1977 the claimant was divorced. In 1980, in the knowledge that he was seriously ill, the man raised divorce proceedings against his wife, to pave the way for a formal marriage ceremony with the claimant. Divorce was granted on 13 May 1982, but illness delayed the preparations for a formal marriage and the man died on 31 August 1982.

The burden of the case law is clear. In the first place the courts have treated the 1939 Act as irrelevant to the operation of the doctrine of MCHR. This has been entirely a matter of practice, as there seem to be no judicial dicta on the point. Any argument that the effect of the Act had been to abolish all forms of irregular marriage in Scots law has simply been passed over in silence. This is quite remarkable, and not entirely to the credit of the judiciary.

Secondly, it is clear that the view that CHR is something more than a method of proof has not won judicial acceptance. The courts have continued

---

98 *Kamperman v MacIver* 1994 SC 230.

to emphasise the all-important role of consent, and to regard CHR merely as a method of inferring that consent. As already noted, it is integral to Clive's view that CHR in part constitutes as well as proves the marriage that cohabitation should have taken place over a tract of time – "for a considerable time".[99] Yet in *Nicol v Bell* Lord Justice-Clerk Thomson emphasised that in some cases events occurring at particular points in time could be crucial in inferring consent; and Lord Glenlee's dictum in *Elder v M'Lean* that there may be "single facts so strong as to supersede everything else" has been cited with approval more than once. In *Nicol v Bell* the Lord Ordinary and two of the Division were prepared to infer consent within a year, perhaps well within a year, of the start of the relationship. In *AB v CD* Lord Guthrie chose the earliest available point in time, namely the date when the pursuer acquired the necessary capacity to marry. In *Shaw v Henderson* Lord Stott went out of his way to emphasise that the time factor was purely evidentiary, and that there could be no question of fixing an absolute minimum period; in the circumstances he held just under eleven months to be sufficient. The same approach was taken by the Social Security Commissioners in *R(G) 5/83*, where three and a half months were found to be sufficient. In *Mullen v Mullen*, as in *AB v CD*, the Lord Ordinary chose the earliest available point in time, six months after the resumption of cohabitation, when the pursuer became reconciled to living again as a married woman. In *Donnelly v Donnelly's Executor*, also, an early date was selected at which to infer consent.

## F. CONCLUSION

The essential element in the constitution of marriage is consent. Requirements of capacity and form always excepted, consent is both necessary and sufficient. On this point the common law of Scotland remains in agreement with the medieval Canon law. The doctrine of CHR was inherited from the Canon law as a mode of inferring consent, as a method of proof and no more; and so it remains. Declaration *per verba de praesenti* and promise *subsequente copula* were likewise modes of inferring consent, inherited from the Canon law. They ceased to be recognised as a result of the 1939 Act. The crucial role of consent in marriage, however, remained unaffected by the Act. It could not have been altered by statute save by the most explicit and unambiguous language. Nor could it have been altered by

---

99 Clive, *Husband and Wife* (n 1) at 62–64; above text accompanying n 74.

a side-wind in the Court of Session. Certainly it is paradoxical that marriage by expressly declared consent should have been abolished, yet marriage by tacit consent retained. This does, however, appear to represent the present position in Scots law.

One further point may be made. Although the term "MCHR" is commonly and conveniently used to describe such irregular marriage as is still recognised as valid in Scots law, it is not exact, and that for two reasons. In the first place, *pace* Clive, there are not two separate doctrines of cohabitation with habit and repute, the one relevant to regular marriage, and the other to irregular. There is only one doctrine of CHR, relevant to regular and irregular marriage alike; although short of a general conflagration at the Register House, it is difficult to imagine the circumstances in which such evidence might be necessary to prove the existence of regular marriage in a purely Scottish context.

Secondly, there may be other facts and circumstances apart from CHR, from which the courts may infer the tacit consent which constitutes marriage. *AB v CD* seems such a case; declarator was granted from the day on which the pursuer attained the age of sixteen. As Lord Guthrie noted, this was consonant with "the old common law" as expounded by Erskine;[100] it was also in line with the Canon law. *Mullen v Mullen* was not dissimilar: here the Lord Ordinary was prepared to backdate the declarator to the date at which the wife ceased to have reservations about once more cohabiting as a spouse. A further, hypothetical example may be posited. Suppose a wife disappears and is declared dead under the Presumption of Death (Scotland) Act 1977. The effect of that declarator will be to dissolve the marriage beyond recall. Shortly after pronouncement of the declarator the wife returns and immediately resumes cohabitation with her former husband without going through a second ceremony of marriage. Is it not likely that declarator of marriage would be granted as from the date of the resumption of cohabitation? The true position under Scots common law then appears to be that declarator of marriage will be granted if there exist facts and circumstances from which consent to marriage can lawfully be inferred; such facts and circumstances will usually, but need not necessarily, include cohabitation with habit and repute.

Given the scope of this paper it has not proved possible to draw comparisons with the role of cohabitation with repute in English law, contemporary or historical; nor to consider the role played by cohabitation with

---

100 *AB v CD* (above n 83) at 427.

repute in the irregular or common law marriages which still exist, or are being reinvented, in a number of jurisdictions in the United States. Neither has the question posed by the Scottish Law Commission, "Should marriage by cohabitation with habit and repute be retained or abolished?" been addressed. At the very least, however, that question needs reformulation. Anomalous it may be, but irregular marriage does not yet appear to have outlived its usefulness in Scots law.[101]

---

101 See further on Scots irregular marriage law E Gordon, "Irregular Marriage: Myth and Reality", (2013) 47 *Journal of Social History* 507; R Probert, M Harding and B Dempsey, "A Uniform Law of Marriage? The 1868 Royal Commission Reconsidered", (2018) 30 *Child & Family Law Quarterly* 217. MCHR was abolished by the Family Law (Scotland) Act 2006 s 3, following a recommendation in the Scottish Law Commission's Report on Family Law (Scot Law Com No 135, 1992). For its development in the period between the original publication of this chapter and its abolition see E Sutherland, *Child and Family Law* (3rd edn, 2022) vol 2, ch 2 ("Intimate Adult Relationships in Scotland: Definition and Formation").

# 10 Marriage, Divorce and the Forbidden Degrees: Canon Law and Scots Law[*]

The last few years have seen some notable studies in the history of marriage and divorce, and in the related topic of women's rights. Both English law and Irish law have come in for their fair share of attention.[1] Rather less, however, has been written about Scots law.[2] Another topic which has engaged the attention of legal historians of late is the fate of Canon law in the Protestant

---

[*] Discourse delivered to the Irish Legal History Society at the Faculty of Law, Roebuck Castle, University College Dublin, on 9 October 1992. Originally published as "Marriage, divorce and the forbidden degrees: Canon law and Scots law", in W N Osborough (ed), *Explorations in Law and History: Irish Legal History Society Discourses, 1988–1994* (1995) 59–82.

1 For example, L Stone, *The Family, Sex and Marriage in England, 1500–1800* (1977) and *Road to Divorce* (1990); R B Outhwaite (ed), *Marriage and Society: Studies in the Social History of Marriage* (1981); R Phillips, *Putting Asunder: A History of Divorce in Western Society* (1988); M MacCurtain and D Ó Corráin (eds), *Women in Irish Society: The Historical Dimension* (1978); A Cosgrove (ed), *Marriage in Ireland* (1985).

2 Contributions on the subject include T C Smout, "Scottish marriage, regular and irregular, 1500–1940", in Outhwaite (ed) (n 1); K M Boyd, *Scottish Church Attitudes to Sex, Marriage and the Family, 1850–1914* (1980); R Mitchison and L Leneman, *Sexuality and Social Control: Scotland 1660–1780* (1989), especially chs 3 and 4 on regular and irregular marriage; A D M Forte, "Some aspects of the law of marriage in Scotland: 1500–1700", in E Craik (ed), *Marriage and Property* (1984) 104; T M Green (ed), *The Consistorial Decisions of the Commissaries of Edinburgh, 1564–1576/7* (SS vol 61, 2014); and R H Helmholz, "The medieval Canon law in Scotland: marriage and divorce", in A M Godfrey (ed), *Miscellany VIII* (2020) 95. In two articles J W Cairns shows how the distinctive Scots law of marriage and divorce informed Sir Walter Scott's novels *The Bride of Lammermoor* (first published 1819) and *Saint Ronan's Well* (first published 1823 with a title page dated 1824): "A note on *The Bride of Lammermoor*: why Scott did not mention the Dalrymple legend until 1830" (1993) 20 *Scottish Literary Journal* 19; and "The noose hidden under flowers: marriage and law in *Saint Ronan's Well*" (1995) 16 *JLH* 234 (both reprinted in J W Cairns, *Enlightenment, Legal Education, and Critique: Selected Essays on the History of Scots Law, Volume 2* (2015) chs 14 and 15). See also nn 5 and 33 below. One of the main theses put forward by Mitchison and Leneman is that church and state operated a different law of marriage in Scotland in the centuries following the Reformation. I should state at the outset that I am not at all convinced of this, although there may be some questions of definition involved. However, this paper is not the place to investigate the matter further. The leading modern legal work is E M Clive, *The Law of Husband and Wife in Scotland* (3rd edn, 1992). [A 4th edn appeared in 1997.]

lands.³ Again, comparatively little has been written about Scotland, although here there is an interesting story to tell, as Canon law remained an important influence on Scots law after the Reformation.⁴ In this short paper I hope to combine these themes, and consider the impact of the Canon law on the later Scots law of marriage and divorce. I shall also consider one of the blackest chapters in Scottish legal history, the story of the law on the prohibited degrees of matrimony and incest, in which the continuing influence of the medieval Canon law is all too apparent.

## A. CONSTITUTION OF MARRIAGE

In earlier centuries, before the Canon law established a common rule, the marriage law of Gaelic Scotland was similar to that of Gaelic Ireland. Both recognised "Celtic secular marriage", set out in the early Irish law tracts, which permitted divorce, concubinage and even polygamy.⁵ A late practitioner in Scotland of this type of matrimony was Ranald MacDonald of Benbecula (d 1636), lineal ancestor of the later chiefs of Clan Ranald and of Flora MacDonald. *The Book of Clanranald* credits him with five wives, three of whom he "put away", that is, divorced. The official record, in the shape of criminal letters raised against him in 1633, accuses him of polygamy and other crimes, including murder. Flora MacDonald and the later chiefs descend from Ranald's fifth wife.⁶

The interest of the story of marriage and divorce after the Reformation, however, lies in contrast, rather than comparison. The law in Scotland developed very differently from that in England or in Ireland. This paper focuses mainly on Scotland, with occasional reference to England and Ireland. It does not consider the property consequences of marriage.

In 1560 the Parliament of Scotland repudiated the authority of the Pope, enacting "that the bishope of Rome haif na Jurisdiction nor autoritie within this realme in tymes cuming".⁷ At the same time the extensive jurisdiction

---

3 R H Helmholz (ed), *Canon Law in the Protestant Lands* (1992), being volume 11 of the Gerda Henkel Stiftung series of Comparative Studies in Continental and Anglo-American Legal History.
4 See J J Robertson, "Canon law" [in "Sources of Law (General and Historical)"], *SME*, vol 22 (1987) paras 580–586.
5 See ch 3 above. For Ireland, see F Kelly, *A Guide to Early Irish Law* (1988) and the works cited in n 1 above. For the description "Celtic secular marriage", see K Nicholls, *Gaelic and Gaelicised Ireland in the Middle Ages* (1972) at 73.
6 Chapter 3 text accompanying nn 87–96; see also R Black "Colla Ciotach", in (1972–74) 48 *Transactions of the Gaelic Society of Inverness* 215.
7 *RPS* A1560/8/4.

of the old church courts in matters such as marriage, testate succession and contract came to an end. After some years of confusion new "commissary courts" were established in 1563–64 to exercise this jurisdiction: a chief commissary court in Edinburgh, and inferior commissary courts elsewhere.[8] Questions of marriage and divorce lay within the exclusive jurisdiction of the chief commissary court. The commissary courts were distinct from the court of the new reformed church. Although at first they were in some sense spiritual courts, they gradually became secularised. From the beginning, the Court of Session, Scotland's supreme secular civil court, exercised a supervisory or appellate jurisdiction, being described by Act of Parliament in 1609 as the King's "great consistory".[9]

Despite these changes, however, the Canon law remained an important source of law in Scotland. Thomas Craig, the author of *Jus Feudale*, whose working life spanned the half century after the Reformation, is quite explicit about this.[10] So, too, is James Dalrymple, Viscount Stair, whose great work, *The Institutions of the law of Scotland*, first appeared in 1681:

> So deep hath this Canon law been rooted, that, even where the Pope's authority is rejected, yet consideration must be had to these laws, as . . . containing many equitable and profitable laws, which because of their weighty matter, and their being once received, may more fitly be retained than rejected.[11]

In no area was the continuing influence of the Canon law more evident than in the constitution of marriage.[12] Before the Reformation the church had encouraged people to marry in a regular fashion, exchanging matrimonial consent *in facie ecclesie* in the presence of a priest and witnesses, after due proclamation of banns. But it had also recognised as valid marriages contracted in irregular fashion by a simple exchange of present consent between the parties, that is *per verba de praesenti*; or by a promise to marry, followed by intercourse on the faith of that promise, that promise, that is, *per verba de futuro subsequente copula*. Present consent to marriage was inferred from the act of intercourse. For such irregular marriages to be valid neither the proclamation of banns, nor the presence of a priest was necessary. The Roman church phased out such irregular marriages by

---

8 For the years of confusion see T M Green, *The Spiritual Jurisdiction in Reformation Scotland: A Legal History* (2019); also D B Smith, "The spiritual jurisdiction 1560–4" (1993) 25 *Records of the Scottish Church History Society* 1.
9 *RPS* 1609/4/20.
10 Craig, *JF*, 1.3.24.
11 Stair, *Inst*, 1.1.14.
12 For writings on the law of marriage see ch 9 n 17.

the bull *Tametsi* promulgated at the Council of Trent in 1563. The law of England continued to recognise them until Lord Hardwicke's Marriage Act of 1753 – an Act which did not apply in Ireland.[13] In Scotland, where the Reformation took place three years before the Trent decree, marriages *per verba de praesenti* and *per verba de futuro* continued to be valid until 1940.[14]

Despite their long existence in Scots law, irregular marriages were often subject to criticism. As early as 1562, in the period between the repudiation of the pope and the establishment of the commissary courts, the kirk session of Aberdeen fulminated against such marriages in terms which clearly questioned their validity:

> Item, Becaus syndrie and many within this town ar handfast, as thai call it, and maid promeis of mariage a lang space bygane, sum sevin year, sum sex yeir, sum langer, sum schorter, and as yit will noch mary and compleit that honourable band, nother for fear of God nor luff of thair party, bot lyis and continewis in manifest fornicatioun and huirdom. Heirfor, it is statut and ordanit, that all sic personis as hes promeist mariage faythfully to compleit the samen. . .[15]

In the seventeenth century a number of Acts laid down penalties for those contracting irregular marriages.[16] In the eighteenth century it was anticipated that irregular marriage would be abolished in Scotland in the wake of Lord Hardwicke's Act in England. A bill for that purpose was actually read in Parliament in 1755, but nothing further came of it.[17] The judge and antiquarian Lord Hailes (d 1792) reflected gloomily,

> All the European nations, Scotland excepted, have departed from the more ancient common law [that is, the *jus commune*], and have required the interposition either of Church or of State to validate a marriage. Thus what was the law of all Europe, while Europe was barbarous, is now the law of Scotland only, when Europe has become civilised.[18]

---

13 An Act for the Better Preventing of Clandestine Marriages 1753, 26 Geo II, c 33.
14 See below, text accompanying nn 32–34. This paper does not explore the history of regular marriage in Scotland after the Reformation.
15 J Stuart (ed), *Selection from the Records of the Kirk Session, Presbytery and Synod of Aberdeen, 1562–1681* (Spalding Club, Aberdeen, 1846) at 11.
16 For example, the Acts of 1661 (*RPS* 1661/1/302) and 1698 (*RPS* 1698/7/113); and see Mitchison & Leneman, *Sexuality* (n 2) at 103. These Acts were only finally repealed *ob maiorem cautelam* by the Statute Law Revision (Scotland) Act 1964.
17 Report of the Royal Commission on the Laws of Marriage [4059] HC 1867–68, xxxii, appendix, at 77; and see Smout (n 2) at 208 and B Dempsey, "The Marriage (Scotland) Bill 1755", in H L MacQueen (ed), *Miscellany VI* (SS vol 54, 2009) 75.
18 Lord Hailes in *Scruton v Gray* (1772) Hailes' Decisions 499, quoted in the 1868 Report (n 17), appendix, at 83.

Lord Hardwicke's Act, as we have noted, did not apply in Ireland, but in 1844 it was held as the result of a tie in the House of Lords in the controversial Irish case of *R v Millis* that the presence of a clergyman of the established church (in Ireland, the Church of Ireland), or of a person authorised by statute to celebrate marriage, was essential to constitute a valid marriage, even an irregular one *per verba de praesenti*.[19] In Scotland, however, the common law on irregular marriage continued unchanged. In 1844, the year of the decision in *Millis*, there occurred the following exchange before a House of Lords select committee on divorce. The Scottish Lord Advocate, Duncan M'Neill, later to be Lord President of the Court of Session and to sit in the House of Lords as Lord Colonsay, was giving evidence:

> QUESTION: Is a marriage [in Scotland] irregular which is performed by any other than a clergyman?
> LORD ADVOCATE: It is.
> QUESTION: And equally valid with one performed by a clergyman?
> LORD ADVOCATE: Quite so.
> QUESTION: Is it sufficient to constitute a marriage in Scotland that the two parties, being of the proper age, the man fourteen, the woman twelve, should say to each other, "I take you for my husband?"
> LORD ADVOCATE: That constitutes a valid marriage, if there is no fraud.
> QUESTION: That is to say if there is real consent.
> LORD ADVOCATE: Quite so, present consent.
> QUESTION: Would this marriage be enough to carry the estates and honours?
> ANSWER: It would.
> QUESTION: Suppose a young nobleman of fourteen is trepanned into a marriage by a woman of bad character of thirty or thirty-five, and he says, in such a way that it can be proved, "I take you for my wife," and she says, "I take you for my husband," at this moment would that be a valid marriage, and carry a Dukedom and large estates to the issues?
> LORD ADVOCATE: It would do so, if it was a deliberate interchange of present consent for the purpose of constituting the relation of husband and wife.
> QUESTION: Does it require any domicile in Scotland for one minute more than the time the marriage is performing to make it a valid marriage?
> ANSWER: No.
> QUESTION: Suppose an English Duke of the age of fourteen years, and a women of bad character of the age of thirty-five, go to Gretna Green, and before a witness say that they take one another for husband and wife; Would that, by the law of Scotland, be a perfectly valid marriage?
> ANSWER: A valid marriage, if deliberately done before witnesses, and proved.
> QUESTION: No consent of parents or guardians is required?

---

19 *R v Millis* (1844) 10 Cl & Fin 534. The marriage regarded as invalid in this prosecution for bigamy had been entered into by two Protestants, one of them Presbyterian, and celebrated by a Presbyterian minister. The decision is now generally regarded as "a misreading of history": see J H Baker, *Introduction to English Legal History* (5th edn, 2019) at 522.

LORD ADVOCATE: No.
QUESTION: Nor any domicile?
LORD ADVOCATE: No.[20]

The scenario of the innocent young English nobleman seduced by a scheming Scotswoman of uncertain age and virtue was clearly one which caused considerable concern south of the Border. When the former Lord Chancellor, Lord Brougham, himself educated at Edinburgh University and admitted to both the Scots and English bars, gave evidence to a select committee on marriage in 1849, he said this about the attitude of the aristocracy towards the suggestion that their sons should go to Edinburgh University: "'Edinburgh,' was always the answer—'the very last place in world we should think of sending our son to: he would be married in twenty four hours; there is no saying what would happen.'"[21] It was Lord Brougham who was later responsible for the Marriage (Scotland) Act of 1856 which provided that no irregular marriage should be valid unless one of the parties usually resided in Scotland, or had lived there for the twenty-one days preceding the marriage.[22]

The exchange with Lord Advocate M'Neill illustrates two further points in which the Scots law of marriage continued to follow Canon law. The age of capacity remained 14 for males and 12 for females. The law did not alter until 1929, when the age was raised to 16 for both sexes, where it still remains.[23] This in itself is not surprising. In other jurisdictions also the Canonical ages were not altered until this century. What is surprising is the other survival, especially when considered along with the early age of capacity to marry: in Scots law it remained the case, as under the pre-Reformation Canon law, that there was no requirement of parental consent to marriage. Indeed, this is still the law. This contrasts strongly with the trend elsewhere in Europe, both Catholic and Protestant, from the sixteenth century onwards.[24] In Scotland, although there were occasional rumblings about reforming the law, as in 1581 when an article anent marriages without

---

20 19 March 1844, First Report of the Commissioner appointed to enquire into the Law of Divorce, [1604] HC 1852–53, xl, 66 [hereafter 1853 Report]; a version of this exchange appears in *Yelverton v Yelverton* (1864) 4 MacQueen 743.
21 Report of the Select Committee on Marriage (Scotland), HC 1849, xii, at 13, quoted in Smout (n 2) at 207.
22 Marriage (Scotland) Act 1856.
23 Age of Marriage Act 1929, repealed and replaced by the Marriage (Scotland) Act 1977 ss 1 and 5(4). For those born after the commencement of the Age of Legal Capacity (Scotland) Act 1991, the age of 16 is attained on the first moment of the sixteenth birthday.
24 For example, see Helmholz, *Canon Law* (n 3) at 138, 161, 175, 189.

consent of parents was remitted to a committee of parliament, in the event nothing was done.[25]

Over the centuries, as memories of the Canon law grew fainter, doubts began to arise on the finer points of *de praesenti* and *de futuro* marriage. As regards the former, was a mere exchange of consents enough, or did consent have to be followed by a period of cohabitation, however short? As regards *de futuro* marriage, did intercourse following on a promise of marriage actually constitute marriage in itself (or, more properly, prove that marriage had been irrevocably constituted), or did it merely create an indissoluble pre-contract? These and other questions, reminiscent of debates which had taken place during the formative period of the Canon law 500 years or more previously, were canvassed by writers and gave rise to considerable litigation.[26] In the event the rules of the developed Canon law were re-established in pristine form. Three cases are worth noting.

*Walker v M'Adam*, decided by the House of Lords in 1813, concerned the effect of an exchange of *de praesenti* consents, with no subsequent cohabitation.[27] The facts are memorable. An Ayrshire laird, whose name might well adorn the novels of Sir Walter Scott, Quintin M'Adam of Craigengillan, took into his house Elizabeth Walker, the sister of a neighbouring farmer, intending to live with her but with no immediate intention of marriage. Quintin and Elizabeth lived together for five years and three children were born. One day in March 1805, M'Adam wrote to his lawyer saying that he wanted to marry the mother of his children and asking him to come and draw up a marriage contract. The following morning, before posting the letter, M'Adam called three of his servants into his dining-room, took Elizabeth by the hand, and said: "I take you three to witness that this is my lawful married wife, and the children by her are my lawful children."[28] Elizabeth said nothing, but curtsied assent. Later M'Adam told his factor of the marriage. On the afternoon of the same day, before his lawyer had a chance to arrive, M'Adam shot himself. The question as to whether mere consent without any subsequent cohabitation was sufficient to constitute marriage could hardly have been raised more sharply. The House of Lords declared in favour of marriage *per*

---

25 See Smout (n 2) at 213–215; RPS 1581/10/28; also 1698/7/46.
26 Many of the difficulties arose from the writings of two distinguished Scottish judicial authors: Henry Home, Lord Kames, in the eighteenth century, and Patrick Fraser, Lord Fraser, in the nineteenth (see n 31 below).
27 *Walker v M'Adam* (1813) 5 Paton 675.
28 Scots law, unlike English, recognised legitimation *per subsequens matrimonium*: ch 9 above, text accompanying nn 9–10.

*verba de praesenti*. (Unsurprisingly the mental state of M'Adam was raised in the litigation, but it was not proved that he was insane.)

The cases of *Pennycook v Grinton* in 1752, and *Mackie v Mackie* in 1917 concerned the doctrine of *de futuro* marriage.[29] In *Pennycook* it was held that a promise of marriage followed by intercourse constituted a valid marriage, and a subsequent regular marriage between the man and another woman was set aside as invalid. This decision is entirely in line with medieval authority.[30] In *Pennycook* the matter was taken somewhat further, for at the same time as the lady successfully petitioned for declarator of marriage, she also obtained a divorce on the grounds of her newly declared husband's adultery, namely his subsequent supposed marriage!

Following *Pennycook* further doubts arose as to the nature of *de futuro* marriage, caused largely by the writings of the Court of Session judge, Lord Fraser, author of the standard Victorian work on husband and wife in Scots law.[31] Fraser put forward the proposition that a promise of marriage, followed by intercourse, merely set up an indissoluble pre-contract, and did not of itself constitute marriage. One consequence of this view, if correct, was that if one of the parties to the alleged pre-contract died before further solemnisation there could be no marriage. The facts of *Mackie* raised this case exactly: there had been promise with intercourse following, but death had intervened without further solemnisation. It was held, in line with *Pennycook*, that intercourse on the faith of the promise of itself constituted marriage, and that an action for declarator could competently be brought after the death of one of the parties.

Both marriage by declaration *de praesenti* and *per verba de futuro* were abolished by the Marriage (Scotland) Act 1939, section 5 of which reads:

> No irregular marriage by declaration *de presenti* or by promise *subsequente copula* contracted after the commencement of this Act shall be valid.[32]

One might have thought that the wording of the 1939 Act was sufficient to end irregular marriage in Scotland, but it was apparently not so intended, and has certainly not so proved. Scots law still recognises irregular marriage by cohabitation with habit and repute. There has been a great deal of

---

29 *Pennycook v Grinton* (1752) Mor 12677; *Mackie v Mackie* 1917 SC 276.
30 See *X (Decretals)* iv.1, ch 30.
31 P Fraser, *Treatise on Husband and Wife* (2nd edn, 2 vols, 1876), especially vol 1, at 322–358.
32 Marriage (Scotland) Act 1939. On the background to the 1939 Act see B Dempsey, "Making the Gretna blacksmith redundant: who worried, who spoke, who was heard on the abolition of irregular marriage in Scotland", (2009) 30 *JLH* 23.

confusion, which unfortunately still subsists, as to the origin and nature of this type of marriage. In fact, like most of the rules of Scots common law regarding the constitution of marriage, it can be traced back to the medieval Canon law.[33] In the eyes of the Canonists, cohabitation over a period of time with sufficient reputation of marriage was a competent way of establishing that consent which was both necessary and sufficient to establish marriage. After the Reformation this rule continued to be applied in Scottish courts, although by the eighteenth century its origin came to be ascribed mistakenly to an act of the Scots Parliament passed in 1504. In the nineteenth and twentieth centuries controversy arose as to whether the cohabitation with habit and repute should be viewed as in some sense contributing towards the actual constitution of marriage, or whether it remained merely a method of proof. This debate continues. I favour the latter view, and the courts have, on the whole, continued to regard cohabitation with habit and repute as a method of proof, but the former view has been strongly put forward by the leading writer on modern Scots family law, Eric Clive.[34]

Be that as it may, the Scottish courts have continued to recognise as valid irregular marriages established by cohabitation with habit and repute. Surprisingly, they have never considered the argument that the 1939 Act might be interpreted as sweeping away such marriages, albeit inadvertently. It is a curious anomaly of modern Scots law that although an explicit declaration of consent cannot constitute an irregular marriage, an inference of tacit consent raised by cohabitation with habit and repute still appear regularly in the law reports.[35] However, the Scottish Law Commission have recommended the abolition of marriage by cohabitation with habit and repute, although there seems to be no public pressure to do so.[36]

*En passant*, the celebrated case of *Yelverton v Yelverton* illustrates the various methods of proving the existence of an irregular marriage in Scots common law. The parties to the case were Miss Theresa Longworth, an Englishwoman, and the Honourable Charles Yelverton, the heir to an Irish peerage. The case was litigated in England, Ireland and Scotland. In the Scottish proceedings, Miss Longworth sought declarator of marriage on four grounds: (a) *per verba de praesenti*; (b) *per verba de futuro subsequente*

---

33 See ch 9.
34 Clive, *Husband and Wife* (n 2) at 48–67 (see 4th edn (1997) at 51–65).
35 For example, *Mullen v Mullen* 1991 SLT 205; *Donnelly v Donnelly's Executor* 1992 SLT 13.
36 Scottish Law Commission, Family Law: Pre-Consolidation Reforms (Discussion Paper No 85, March 1990); Report on Family Law (Scot Law Com No 135, 1992). MCHR was abolished by the Family Law (Scotland) Act 2006 s 3.

*copula*; (c) by cohabitation with habit and repute; and (d) on account of a marriage ceremony conducted in Ireland in a Roman Catholic chapel by a Catholic priest.[37] She failed on all four counts. The fourth count fell foul of the Irish Act of 1745[38] which invalidated a marriage contracted according to the forms of the Roman Catholic church between a Catholic (which Miss Longworth was) and any party professing to be a Protestant during the previous twelve months. Major Yelverton had been born and brought up a Protestant. At the ceremony in question he had very prudently described himself as "a Protestant Catholic".[39]

The Marriage (Scotland) Act 1939 also broke new ground in providing for the first time for the civil celebration of regular marriage.[40] Scots law was late in introducing this measure, the corresponding provision for England and for Ireland having been passed over one hundred years previously. In many jurisdictions, a civil ceremony once introduced becomes the only type of marriage recognised as valid by the state. Neither in England nor in Scotland is this the case, both civil and religious ceremonies being recognised as equally valid.

It is notorious that after Lord Hardwicke's Act of 1753 put an end to irregular marriage in England, a lively trade in marriage for a predominantly English clientèle grew up in a number of places in Scotland, particularly near the Border; notorious too that some of the beneficiaries of this trade were successors of Hardwicke as Lord Chancellor. Lack of a Scottish domicile, as already noted from Lord Advocate M'Neill's evidence, and in the case of *Yelverton*, did not affect the validity of an irregular marriage in Scots law.[41] Gretna, near Carlisle, is the best-known spot where such marriages took place, with so-called "priests" officiating over what was in law only an irregular marriage *per verba de praesenti*. But marriages were also contracted at Lamberton Toll, near Berwick; at Coldstream; at Annan; and indeed in Glasgow and Edinburgh.[42] Of Hardwicke's successors as chancellor, John Scott, Lord Eldon, had married at Blackshiels, near Coldstream in 1772; Henry, Lord Brougham, at Coldstream in 1819; and Thomas, Lord Erskine, after travelling disguised in woman's clothes with his mistress, married her at

---

37 *Yelverton v Yelverton* (1864) 4 MacQueen 745. The original grounds maintained before the Lord Ordinary are given at 779. See also (1864) 2 M (HL) 49 and (1862) 1 M 161.
38 Act 19 Geo II, c 13, s 1.
39 See *Yelverton* at 769, 862, 894.
40 Section 1.
41 Above, nn 20 and 37–39.
42 "Claverhouse" (Meliora Smith), *Irregular Border Marriages* (1934) provides a very readable account.

Gretna in 1818. Other beneficiaries of Scotland's marriage laws were Percy Bysshe Shelley, married in Edinburgh in 1811, and John Peel, the huntsman, married at Gretna in 1797.[43]

Less well known is a marriage with an Irish connection which took place at Gretna in 1836. The Gretna register discloses that on 7 May 1836 Carlo Ferdinando Borbone (or Bourbon), prince of Capua, contracted marriage with Penelope Caroline Smythe, of Ballynatray, Co Waterford, daughter of the late Guy Smythe.[44] The prince was the immediate younger brother of Ferdinand II, king of Naples and the Two Sicilies (known also as "Bomba"). The Gretna declaration was apparently the fourth marriage ceremony entered into between the couple, who were trying to circumvent a decree of Bomba to the effect that no marriage of a prince of the blood was to be valid without the consent of the reigning sovereign. Carlo Ferdinando and Penelope were married first at a royal villa in Lucca, secondly in Madrid, and thirdly in Rome by a cardinal. After the ceremony at Gretna they sought licence to marry in the Church of England, but a *caveat* was lodged on behalf of Bomba. Ignoring this, they married again for the fifth time at the church of St George, Hanover Square, London.[45] The marriage does not appear to have been recorded by the *Almanach de Gotha* while Bomba lived, but the 1861 *Gotha* notes against Prince Carlo Ferdinando, "marié en 1830, morganatiquement à Miss Penelope Smith". The 1862 edition improves on this, giving "marié 5 April 1836 à Penelope-Caroline, née 19 juill. 1815, fille de Grice [sic] Smyth de Ballynatray, (comté de Waterford)", and recording two children of the marriage: a daughter, and Prince Francisco-Ferdinando-Carlo, count of Mascali.[46]

Another marriage of Irish interest took place at Gretna in November 1834 between John P Lahy, also known as "Rambling Jack", and Dorcas Stratford ("Lady Dusty"), the sister of his former wife. This marriage is said to have been declared valid by the Dublin chancery court in 1910.[47]

---

43 See the entries for Eldon, Brougham, Erskine, Shelley and Peel in the *Oxford Dictionary of National Biography* (2004).
44 "Claverhouse", *Irregular Border Marriages* (n 42) at 109 gives 7 May 1846 as the date; but this must be a mistake for 7 May 1836, as given in E W J M'Connell (ed) *Marriages at Gretna Hall, 1829—Ap. 30 1855* (Scottish Record Society, 1949).
45 This follows the account given in "Claverhouse" (n 42) at 109–111.
46 Almanach de Gotha for 1861, (Deux-Siciles) at 18; for 1862, (Deux-Siciles) at 83.
47 "Claverhouse", *Irregular Border Marriages* (n 42) at 107. I have been unable to confirm this statement. The marriage took place before Lord Lyndhurst's Act of 1835 (which did not apply in Scotland) declared null and void, and not merely voidable, marriages contracted within the forbidden degrees.

## B. DISSOLUTION OF MARRIAGE

Moving now from the constitution of marriage to its dissolution, the pre-Tridentine Canon law allowed for the annulment of marriage on various grounds, such as defect of consent, lack of capacity and, above all, pre-marital relationships – the forbidden degrees of matrimony. It also permitted judicial separation on the grounds of adultery and cruelty. Cruelty, however, had to be such as to endanger life and limb; there had to be *saevitia*, with connotations of ferocity and savagery as much as cruelty. For both these actions the Canon law, confusingly to our eyes, used the term *divortium* or "divorce". Nullity was described as divorce *a vinculo*, and separation as divorce *a mensa et thoro*, that is, from bed and board. Of divorce in the commonly accepted modern sense of the dissolution of a valid marriage, there was none.

The history of separation in Scots law after the Reformation can be swiftly told: little changed for 400 years. The expression "divorce *a mensa et thoro*" continued in use until this century. Adultery and cruelty remained the sole grounds for separation until 1903 when habitual drunkenness was added.[48] Even after cruelty was introduced as a ground for divorce proper in 1938, and interpreted increasingly widely, the necessity for *saevitia* in actions for separation continued to be emphasised. As late as 1962 it was held in the case of *Jack v Jack*[49] that although unreasonable conduct falling short of *saevitia* might be sufficient reason for non-adherence in an action of divorce for desertion, it was not enough to found an action for separation; changes in the law were for the legislature and not the court. Only with the passing of the Divorce (Scotland) Act of 1976 and the assimilation of the grounds for separation with those for divorce was there a clear break with the past.

If the law on the formation of marriage and on separation continued to owe much to the Canon law, the case was quite different with divorce. Scotland admitted divorce immediately after the Reformation. Two grounds were recognised, adultery and desertion, these remaining the sole grounds of divorce until this century. Actions for divorce were raised before the head commissary court at Edinburgh, it being a matter of indifference to the law whether the pursuer was male or female. These changes in the law were in keeping with Protestant theology, both Lutheran and Calvinist, although

---

48 Licensing (Scotland) Act 1903.
49 *Jack v Jack* 1962 SC 24.

divorce for desertion was more readily allowed by the former than by the latter.[50]

Divorce for adultery was introduced by judicial decision rather than by legislation, the kirk sessions of the reformed church at first competing with the commissary courts for jurisdiction. Smith notes that the kirk session of St Andrews granted eleven divorces on the ground of adultery between February 1560 and August 1563.[51] Although the Catholic church had not permitted the dissolution of a valid marriage, later Scottish divorce practice did inherit a number of doctrines from the Canon law, including the oath of calumny and the defences of recrimination, condonation and *lenocinium* (connivance). The oath of calumny survived, somewhat altered, until 1976.[52] Recrimination disappeared in the eighteenth century, but the defences of condonation and *lenocinium* still survive, despite numerous statutory changes in divorce law in the last century. It is curious to find the post-Reformation Spanish Canonist Sánchez (1550–1610) being cited with approval as an authority on *lenocinium* in 1908 by Lord President Dunedin in the case of *Thomson v Thomson*, and in 1952 by Lord President Cooper in *Riddell v Riddell*, Lord Dunedin referring to Sánchez as "one who, though not a jurist, is considered an authority on this matter".[53]

The Reformers founded divorce for adultery on scriptural authority. The Old Testament had prescribed the death penalty for adultery. Even if the death penalty was not insisted on it could be argued that the guilty party should be treated as civilly dead so far as re-marriage by the innocent spouse was concerned. Sometimes, however, the death penalty was exacted. In Scotland "notour", that is, notorious adultery, was made a capital offence in 1563, and although there were few executions, the statute was not a dead letter.[54]

---

50 Phillips, *Putting Asunder* (n 1) at 40–94; for Scotland, see C J Guthrie, "The history of divorce in Scotland" (1911) 8 *SHR* 39; D Baird Smith, "The Reformers and divorce: a study on consistorial jurisdiction" (1912) 9 *SHR* 10; Ireland (n 12) at 82; Forte (n 2) at 112–114; Smith (n 8); T M Green (ed), *The Consistorial Decisions of the Commissaries of Edinburgh, 1564 to 1576/7* (SS vol 61, 2014), introduction, at lv–lxiv.
51 Smith (n 8); and see D Hay Fleming (ed), *Register of the Kirk Session of St Andrews, 1559–1600* (2 vols, SHS, 1889, 1890).
52 It was finally abolished by s 9 of the Divorce (Scotland) Act 1976.
53 *Thomson v Thomson* 1908 SC 179 at 185; *Riddell v Riddell* 1952 SC 475 at 482–83; see also *Annan v Annan* 1948 SC 532, a case on condonation which refers to Sánchez, Carpzovius and Voet. I am not entirely in agreement with Lord Sorn's view (*Annan* at 537) of the continuing influence of the Canon law on Scots law after the Reformation as being the result of "essentially a process of adoption".
54 *RPS* A1563/6/10.

There were objections, both moral and logical, to the re-marriage of the guilty spouse, especially with a paramour. In 1598 it was noted that marriage was "ane blessing of God . . . quhilk aught not to be grantit and given to adulteriris,—for the honorabil band of marriage ought not to be ane cloke to sic unlawful and dishonest copulation".[55] In 1600 an act was passed annulling any marriage between the guilty party and a paramour named in the decree of divorce.[56] But practice went further: at the end of the seventeenth century a regular marriage between Dr Christopher Irvine (or Irving) and his former mistress, was treated as invalid, even although there had been no preceding action for divorce. The petitioner was the son of the original marriage, also Dr Christopher Irvine, of Castle Irving in Ireland.[57] By the nineteenth century, however, matters had changed. A leading case on irregular marriage, *Campbell v Campbell* ("the Breadalbane peerage case"), which went to the House of Lords, concerned the elopement of Eliza Ludlow, a doctor's wife from Chipping Sodbury, with Lieutenant James Campbell in 1781.[58] James and Eliza went through a ceremony of marriage, and held themselves out as husband and wife, while Doctor Ludlow was still alive. After Ludlow's death they continued to live together as husband and wife. Could they be regarded as having contracted an irregular marriage after Dr Ludlow's death? The case revolved around the evidence necessary to establish marriage *per verba de praesenti* and the role of cohabitation with habit and repute; but it was not suggested that the adulterous liaison in itself barred the subsequent marriage of the parties. The 1600 Act remained on the statute book until 1964.[59] Long before then, however, it had become standard practice to avoid naming the paramour in the decree of divorce.[60]

Divorce for desertion was regulated by statute in 1573, the act apparently being passed to allow Archibald, earl of Argyll, to divorce his wife, Lady Jane Stewart, a bastard daughter of King James V, and then re-marry.[61]

---

55 Ireland (n 12) at 94, and J Riddell, *Inquiry into the Law and Practice of Scottish Peerages* (1842), vol 1, at 392, citing *Whytlaw v Ker* (1598).
56 *RPS* 1600/11/42.
57 *Irvine v Ker* (1695), in F P Walton (ed), *Lord Hermand's Consistorial Decisions, 1684–1777* (SS vol 6, 1940), at 91; see also F J Grant (ed), *The Commissariot of Edinburgh: Consistorial Processes and Decreets, 1658–1800* (Scottish Record Society, 1909) no 66. Compare the situation described in J Witte jr, "The plight of Canon law in the early Dutch Republic", in Helmholz (ed) *Canon Law* (n 3) 135 at 155.
58 *Campbell v Campbell* (1867) 5 M 115.
59 It was repealed by the Statute Law Revision (Scotland) Act 1964.
60 Smith, *Short Commentary*, at 316.
61 *RPS* 1573/4/2; Riddell, *Scottish Peerages* (n 55), vol 1, at 547; D Baird Smith "A note on divorce for desertion" (1939) 51 *JR* 254; J E A Dawson, "The noble and the bastard: the earl of Argyll and

The statute narrated that divorce for desertion had been available since the Reformation, but it is not clear that this is so. The period required for desertion was four years, reduced to three in 1938. The procedure, at first cumbersome, was simplified in the nineteenth century. Not until 1938 were the grounds for divorce altered, the Divorce (Scotland) Act of that year adding cruelty together with incurable insanity, sodomy and bestiality as grounds.[62]

So far as I am aware, no one has yet searched through the commissary court records, still extant in manuscript in abundance, to determine the incidence of divorce at any particular time, or in any particular part of the country, to record the sorts and condition of men and women who raised the actions; to distinguish between male and female pursuers; or to calculate the cost of litigation.[63] Information on all these points would be of considerable interest. However, I know of nothing to suggest that there was a bias in favour of men, or that the rules effectively excluded all but the very rich. Quite the contrary. Lord Hermand's collection of consistorial decisions covering the years 1684–1777 reveals many female pursuers; and also pursuers of humble social standing, such as Robert Wood, baker in Glasgow, who sued for divorce for desertion in 1756.[64] The Edinburgh commissariat register confirms this impression: thus, in 1729, Marion Stuart, spouse to Alexander Herbertson, wright and looking-glass maker in Glasgow, sued for divorce; and in 1788 Archibald Muir, residing in Glasgow, "sometime one of the drivers of the Newcastle waggon, now riding clerk and book-keeper for said wagon", raised an action against his wife.[65]

Lord Advocate Duncan M'Neill gave evidence to the 1844 select committee on the frequency of female pursuers in divorce actions as follows:

> QUESTION: Has any inconvenience been found to result from giving the wife an equal remedy with the husband in obtaining a Divorce a *vinculo*?
> ANSWER: I am not aware of any inconvenience.
> QUESTION: Can you state what proportion of instances are of Divorces a *vinculo* at the suit of the wife?

---

the law of divorce in Reformation Scotland", in J Goodare and A A MacDonald (eds), *Sixteenth-Century Scotland: Essays in Honour of Michael Lynch* (2008) 147.

62 I have not taken the story of divorce beyond this Act.
63 See F P Walton, "The courts of the Officials and the commissary courts", in *Sources and Literature of Scots Law* (SS vol 1) at 133; also J Fergusson, *Consistorial Law in Scotland, with reports of cases (1696–1826)* (1829); Walton (ed) *Hermand* (n 57); and Mitchison & Leneman, *Sexuality* (n 2). See now L Leneman, *Alienated Affections: The Scottish Experience of Divorce and Separation, 1684–1830* (1998).
64 Walton (ed) *Hermand* (n 57) at 71.
65 Grant (ed), *Commissariot of Edinburgh* (n 57) nos 262, 910.

ANSWER: No, I cannot state the proportion.
QUESTION: Are they frequent?
ANSWER: I would say they are about as numerous as the others. I am merely guessing. Those that have been most litigated on the merits have been at the instance of the husband.[66]

When asked about the expense of an unopposed action for divorce, he replied, "That is more in the department of a solicitor than in mine; but, perhaps forty or fifty pounds."[67]

A paper taken from the *Law Magazine* of May 1843, attached to the 1853 *Report*, also covers these questions. It states that the average cost of a divorce in Scotland was thirty pounds, or, if the action was unopposed, fifteen. It also notes that in the period from November 1836 to November 1841 ninety-five divorces *a vinculo* were granted, and that "the parties litigant were almost all of the humbler classes, including four servants, four labourers, three bakers, three tailors, two soldiers, one sailor, a butcher, a shoemaker, a carpenter, a weaver, a blacksmith, an exciseman, a rope-maker, a hairdresser, a quill-seller, a plasterer, a carver, a tobacconist, and a last-maker,—as well as every variety of small tradesmen and petty shopkeepers."[68]

The history of divorce in Scotland, then, presents a stark contrast to the story in England, Wales and Ireland. In Scotland divorce was open to all immediately after the Reformation on the grounds of adultery and desertion; the law showed no preference to either sex; and actions were determined in courts which became secular in all but name. In England, as is well known, the picture is very different.[69] Shortly after the Reformation the Church of England sets its face against divorce, although the church courts continued to grant separation *a mensa et thoro*. In 1670 Lord de Roos, separated from his wife on the ground of her adultery, persuaded Parliament to pass an Act allowing him to marry again. Thereafter, until 1857 in England, and for longer in Ireland, the only possibility of divorce and remarriage was by private Act of Parliament, and the only ground adultery.[70] By its nature, this procedure was restricted to the very rich, and until 1801 to men. Between 1670 and 1857 there were 300 private Acts passed,

---

66 19 Mar 1844, 1853 Report (n 20) at 65.
67 19 Mar 1844, 1853 Report (n 20) at 65.
68 1853 Report (n 20) at 73.
69 See, for example, Stone, *Road to Divorce* (n 1); Phillips, *Putting Asunder* (n 1) at 227–241. For a time Scotland functioned as a divorce haven: Stone, *Road to Divorce* (n 1) at 357–359; Phillips, *Putting Asunder* (n 1) at 238–240.
70 The Matrimonial Causes Act 1857 ended the divorce jurisdiction of the church courts in England, and re-marriage by private Act of Parliament.

only four of them in favour of women. In Ireland there were ten private Acts passed before 1800.[71] A female plaintiff, unlike her male counterpart, had to prove not only adultery, but also some further ground such as cruelty or desertion. Even after 1857 the law continued to discriminate against women and in favour of the rich. Only in 1923 were the sexes placed on an equal footing in English law.[72] Adultery remained the sole ground of divorce until "A P Herbert's Act" of 1937.[73] Anyone tempted to draw far-reaching conclusions about the nature of law and society, or male attitudes towards women, from this lamentable story should first take into account the very different course of divorce law north of the Border.

## C. PROHIBITED DEGREES AND INCEST

My third topic, which I have already characterised as one of the blackest chapters in the history of Scots law, is the law of incest and the prohibited degrees of matrimony. If the continuing influence of the Canon law in the areas already discussed may be considered neutral, or even benefical, in this area it was wholly malign. The extensive prohibitions placed on marriage by the developed Canon law on the grounds of pre-existing relationship between the parties are well known.[74] Even after a relaxation of the rules in 1215, marriage to any blood relative up to and including the fourth degree of Canonical computation was still not permitted: that is to say, marriage between parties who shared a common great-great-grandparent, or any close ancestor, was forbidden. This was the impediment of consanguinity. Nor was it permitted, to marry anyone related in the fourth degree to a previous spouse. This was the impediment of affinity. But affinity went further: the impediment arose, not merely from a previous marital relationship, but also from extra-marital intercourse. Thus a man might not marry the second cousin once removed of a woman he had slept with twenty years before. To do so was to commit incest in the eyes of the church. There were further impediments still based on prior spiritual relationship (*cognatio spiritualis*), or on pre-contract. It was possible, however to obtain a dispensation to marry within the forbidden degrees, and in the century or two before the Reformation this became increasingly frequent.

71  Stone, *Road to Divorce* (n 1) at 359.
72  Matrimonial Causes Act 1923.
73  Matrimonial Causes Act 1937.
74  See, for example, Pollock & Maitland, vol 2, at 387–388; Scanlan (n 12) 69; and J Goody, *The Development of the Family and Marriage in Europe* (1983).

The reason behind these extensive prohibitions has been much debated, but nobody has yet produced a wholly convincing explanation.[75] You will recall Maitland's view, memorable, if more than a little unfair: "Reckless of mundane consequences, the church, while she treated marriage as a formless contract, multiplied impediments which made the formation of a valid marriage a matter of chance . . ."; and again: "Behind these intricate rules there is no deep policy, there is no strong religious feeling; they are the idle ingenuities of men who are amusing themselves by inventing a game of skill which is to be played with neatly drawn tables of affinity and doggerel hexameters."[76]

The Scottish Reformers, like Henry VIII, and many of their continental counterparts, reduced the prohibited degrees.[77] In England, Henry's Marriage Act of 1540 allowed first cousins to marry.[78] In Scotland the matter was regulated by the Marriage Act of 1567, which set out that "secundis in degreis of consanguinitie and affinine and all degreis outwith the samin contenit in the word of the eternal God and that are not repugnant to the said word mycht and may lauchfullie marie".[79] This permitted first cousins to marry, and they have married freely in Scotland ever since. However, the Scots Parliament had passed another Act on the same day, the Incest Act 1567, which declared incest, which before the Reformation had been purely an ecclesiastical offence, to be a crime, and a crime punishable by death.[80] In fact, incest appears to have been treated as a crime at common law immediately after the Reformation, there being a prosecution for adultery and incest in 1565.[81] This was entirely unlike developments in England, where incest was not made criminal until 1908;[82] but quite in keeping with other Acts passed by the Scots Reformers – like that on "notour" adultery already noted – which sought to equate sin and crime, and were not sparing in their use of the death penalty.[83]

---

75 For a review and an innovative theory, see Goody, *Family and Marriage* (n 74). For a review and critique of Goody see the issue of *Continuity and Change* for December 1991. See also S Wolfram, *In-laws and Out-laws: Kinship and Marriage in England* (1987).
76 Pollock & Maitland, vol 2, at 389.
77 *Cognatio spiritualis* appears to have disappeared in Scotland with the Reformation. For similar developments elsewhere in reformed Europe, see Goody, *Family and Marriage* (n 74) at 194–204.
78 Marriage Act 1540: 32 Hen VIII c 38.
79 *RPS* A1567/12/15.
80 *RPS* A1567/12/14.
81 See the prosecution of Master John Craig for adultery and incest in 1565: R Pitcairn, *Criminal Trials in Scotland* (2 vols, 1833) vol 1, at 459°.
82 Punishment of Incest Act 1908.
83 See J Irvine Smith, "Criminal law", in *ISLH* 280 at 283. There were similar developments in the

The Incest Act, like Henry VIII's statute of 1540, referred to Leviticus, chapter 18. It ordained that

> quhatsumever persoun or personis committeris of the said abhominabill cryme of incest that is to say quhatsumever person or personis thay be that abusis thair body with sic personis in degre as Goddis word hes expreslie forbiddin in ony tyme cuming as is contenit in the xviii Cheptour of Leviticus salbe puneist to the deith.

It was not clear, however, how the statute was to be interpreted. Was Leviticus to be strictly construed, or merely used as a guideline? For example, did the prohibition on intercourse between aunt and nephew also include uncle and niece? Should prohibitions affecting the direct line of ascent or descent be extended *ad infinitum*?[84] And what was the relationship between the Incest Act and the Marriage Act? Were they to be regarded as independent of each other, or were they to be construed together? To the eternal disgrace of Scots law, although the Acts remained on the statute book for over 400 years, these questions were never satisfactorily answered.[85] In the seventeenth century the forfeit for faulty interpretation was death.

Doubts about the proper interpretation of the Acts began immediately. In 1569 the Regent Moray put this hypothetical question to the General Assembly of the Church of Scotland (not, be it noted, to the Court of Session): did a man who slept with a woman who had been his mother's brother's paramour commit incest? The question was carefully framed. The answer was that he did. The editor of the Stair Society's *Justiciary Cases*, Sheriff Irvine Smith, who recounts the question, adds the comment that the General Assembly "so set on its way a principle in which hardly any limits were set to the crime of incest."[86] With respect, although it is true that prosecutions for incest over the next century do indeed comprise a horrifying and bloody catalogue, it is possible to discern an underlying principle.

Evidence of the reformed church's wide interpretation of the sin of incest and its determination to root it out are to be found in records of visitations,

---

Dutch Republic: Witte (n 57) at 157–158 observes that there "the church's jurisdiction over sin coincided closely with the state's jurisdiction over crime".

84 For differing views on the interpretation of Leviticus, see Goody, *Family and Marriage* (n 74) at 168ff, 176ff.

85 The Marriage Act 1567 was repealed by the Marriage (Scotland) Act 1977. For the repeal and replacement of the Incest Act 1567 see ch 1 above (text accompanying n 71). For further comments see W D H Sellar, "Forbidden degrees of matrimony: the Marriage (Scotland) Bill and the law of incest", 1977 *SLT (News)* 1, and "Leviticus xviii, the forbidden degrees and the law of incest in Scotland" (1978) 1 *Jewish Law Annual* 229.

86 Justiciary Cases II at xliv.

for example, in Dunblane in the year 1586 to 1589, and in kirk session and synod records.[87] But it is the justiciary records which reveal the full horror of the transmutation of sin into crime. The examples which follow concentrate on cases which might not at first sight appear to involve incest at all. They all concern affinity. In 1626 Alexander Gourlay was accused of incest in that he had slept with his wife's aunt, her mother's sister. The death penalty was demanded by the prosecution. Happily Gourlay was acquitted, it seems on technical grounds.[88] In 1628 George Sinclair was accused and convicted of incest in respect of intercourse with two sisters. He was not married to either woman. He was sentenced to be drowned.[89] Similar cases occurred in 1669 and 1673, as discussed below. In 1629 John Weir of Clenachdike was accused and convicted of incest for marrying (in England) the widow of his great uncle (the "relict of umquhile Mr James Weir guidsiris brother to the said Jon Weir"). He was sentenced to have his head "strucken from his bodie" at the market cross of Edinburgh, although the sentence was later commuted to banishment.[90] In 1646 there occurred what the institutional writer Hume refers to as a "still more shameful and scandalous case": Jean Knox was accused and convicted of incest in that being pregnant to one man she married his brother five months later. She was sentenced to be hanged on a gibbet on the castle hill of Edinburgh.[91]

Two further examples may be given. In 1669 Callum Oig MacGregor was accused of incest, as George Sinclair had been in 1628, in respect of intercourse with two sisters. He was found guilty of incest and sentenced to be hanged, but as the other crimes of which he was accused included sorning and oppression, hamesucken and blackmail, incest may not have been the determining factor![92] In 1673 John M'Kennan and Mary N'Thomas were accused of incest before the Argyll justiciary court on the grounds that Mary had previously had carnal relations with John's uncle. Mary was found guilty and sentenced "to be taken to the gallows of Rothesay and there hanged to the death". John apparently escaped conviction on the ground of

87 J Kirk (ed), *Visitation of the Diocese of Dunblane and other churches, 1586–1589* (Scottish Record Society, 1984); J Kirk (ed), *Records of the Synod of Lothian and Tweeddale, 1589–1596, 1640–1649* (SS vol 30, 1977); for kirk session records, see nn 15 and 51 above; also Mitchison & Leneman, *Sexuality* (n 2), and, for example, J Kirk (ed), *Stirling Presbytery Records, 1581–1587* (SHS, 1981).
88 *Justiciary Cases* I at 48.
89 *Justiciary Cases* I at 95.
90 *Justiciary Cases* I at 121.
91 *Justiciary Cases* III at 690. For Hume's comment, see Hume, *Commentaries*, vol 2, at 298. Hume also discusses some of the other cases noted here.
92 *Justiciary Records* I at 315–319.

his ignorance of the earlier relationship. The editor of the volume recording this case finds the conviction "difficult to follow", and wonders whether Mary and John's uncle might have been regarded as being married by habit and repute.[93]

In fact, the logic behind this terrible line of prosecutions, and the General Assembly's answer to the Regent Moray in 1569, is clear. The Reformers interpreted Leviticus chapter 18 in the light of the pre-Reformation Canon law, except inasmuch as it had been altered to allow first cousins to marry. In every one of the cases just cited marriage between the parties would have been forbidden by the Canon law on the ground of incest. The express prohibition in Leviticus on marriage between aunt and nephew was given a parallel interpretation to include uncle and niece also; this being in keeping with the interpretation of Reformers elsewhere, including England, although different from that applied in Jewish law.[94] The prohibition on marriage with the sibling of a parent was understood to include siblings of all ancestors, however remote. Such relationships were treated as if in the first degree. This had been the teaching of the Canon law. In pre-Reformation Scotland, Father William Hay expounded it in his lectures on marriage at Aberdeen university, citing Petrus de Palude (d 1342) as authority.[95] In post-Reformation Scotland the same doctrine is to be found in Stair's *Institutions*.[96] In addition the Canon law definition of affinity as arising from intercourse rather than marriage was maintained. All this is quite in keeping with Goody's observation that Calvinist doctrine generally regarded the prohibitions in Leviticus chapter 18 as merely illustrative, and treated affinity as arising from intercourse rather than marriage.[97]

There was one attempt to provide a complete statutory guide to the law of incest. The "Act for punishing the horrible crime of Incest with death", passed on 9 July 1649, disapproved a strictly literal interpretation of Leviticus, "considering also that there be many other degrees of Incest both in affinity and consanguinity, no less heinous and punishable than these expressed in the letter of that Text, because they be either nearer or fully as

---

93 J Cameron (ed), *Justiciary Records of Argyll and the Isles, 1664–1705, volume 1* (SS vol 12, 1949) at 21.
94 See Goody, *Family and Marriage* (n 74) at 176.
95 J C Barry (ed), *William Hay's Lectures on Marriage* (SS vol 24, 1967) at 198–205.
96 Stair, *Inst*, 1.4.4. Lord President Normand's comments on this passage in the leading case of *Philp's Trustees v Beaton* 1938 SC 733 at 746 are wide of the mark, as is much else said in that case about the history of the law.
97 Goody, *Family and Marriage* (n 74) at 176; see also the discussion on Calvin and Leviticus in Boyd, *Scottish Church Attitudes* (n 2) at 258–261.

near . . .".⁹⁸ It declared and ordained that those sinning in such degrees were equally worthy of death, and published a table – the first and last to appear in Scotland before 1976 – setting out the prohibited degrees for clarification.⁹⁹ The table takes into account the Marriage Act of 1567, but otherwise follows the pre-Reformation law. A footnote, added by way of further explanation, is quite explicit as to siblings of those in the direct line, and on the definition of affinity:

> No person may marry or lie with those that are in the direct line ascending or descending; or with a brother or sister of one in the direct line; or with relicts of those in the direct line; though never so far asunder in degree: Because all these are Parents and children, or in the place of parents and children one to another. Consanguinity and affinity impeding matrimony is contracted between them that are of kindred on the one side, as well as by them that are of kindred by both sides; and by unlawful company of men and women, as well as by Marriage.

Some have treated the Act as breaking new ground,¹⁰⁰ but it is apparent that it was intended to clarify the law and expound existing practice. Act and table were repealed by the general Act Rescissory at the Restoration. This, however, did not affect the interpretation of the Acts of 1567, as is illustrated by some of the cases already considered. In 1690 a further Act was passed setting out that a man might not marry "any of his wife's kindred nearer in blood than he may of his own".¹⁰¹ This again may be regarded as declaratory of the existing law.

Although the death penalty for incest was not abolished until 1887, as the eighteenth century progressed there were fewer prosecutions, and the more technical offences based on affinity were not pressed to the limit of the law.¹⁰² By 1827 the definition of affinity had altered: it was now regarded as arising from marriage alone and not from intercourse. In *Hamilton v Wylie* it was held to be irrelevant as a defence to an action for declarator of marriage that the wife had previously slept with the husband's brother.¹⁰³ Changed days indeed since the case of Jean Knox in 1646! In the twentieth century, in Scotland as in England, enabling Acts were passed to allow marriage with a deceased wife's sister, a deceased husband's brother and a deceased spouse's niece or nephew. In 1961 marriage was permitted to a *former* spouse's

---

98 RPS 1649/5/219.
99 For English tables setting out the prohibited degrees, see Goody, *Family and Marriage* (n 74) at 179–180.
100 Hume, *Commentaries*, vol 2, at 291–292, 299–300; *Justiciary Cases* II at xlv.
101 RPS 1690/4/33, ch 24(4). The Act ratified the 1647 Confession of Faith.
102 The death penalty was abolished by the Criminal Procedure (Scotland) Act 1887 s 56.
103 *Hamilton v Wylie* (1827) 5 S 716; compare *Wing v Taylor* (1861) 2 Sw & Tr 278 in England.

relatives in these categories.[104] In 1977 the Marriage Act 1567 was finally repealed, and in 1986 the Incest Act.[105] Their continuing presence on the statute book had long been a standing disgrace to Scottish jurisprudence.

The Scottish Reformers' predilection for incorporating moral offences into the criminal code had turned the Canon law into an engine of death, the more so as in the new law, unlike the old, there was no provision for dispensation. Maitland's comment on "the idle ingenuities of men who are amusing themselves by inventing a game of skill which is to be played with neatly drawn tables of affinity and doggerel hexameters" takes on a new and terrible meaning in the light of Scottish practice in the seventeenth century. Here, indeed, Canon law proved to be a *damnosa haereditas*.

---

104 The first Act in this sequence was the Deceased Wife's Sister's Marriage Act of 1907. For attitudes in Scotland, see Boyd, *Scottish Church Attitudes* (n 2) at 255–297.
105 Above, n 85.

# 11 Forethocht Felony, Malice Aforethought and the Classification of Homicide*

*Lord Morton of Shuna*: There seems to be a reluctance on the part of English legal minds to engage in a moral judgement so to speak, and bring in wickedness and evil intent. Does that in your view represent an essential element in the crime of murder?
*Lord Emslie (Lord Justice General)*: I think it does certainly in murder. We have not for centuries, found it difficult to invite juries to make what people call a moral judgement.[1]

The mental element in the crime of murder, and the meaning to be attached to the term "malice aforethought", is a topical issue in modern English law. A succession of controversial cases, notably *DPP v Smith*,[2] *R v Hyam*,[3] *R v Moloney*[4] and *R v Hancock and Shankland*[5] have given rise to prolonged debate on the proper definition of murder. In 1988 Lord Goff set out an eloquent plea for law reform in an article entitled "The Mental Element in the Crime of Murder" in the *Law Quarterly Review* in which he considered Scots as well as English law.[6] This prompted the appointment of a House of Lords Select Committee which heard evidence from both jurisdictions before reporting in 1989.

A parallel debate regarding the medieval English law of homicide, which might equally be entitled "The Mental Element in the Crime of Murder",

---

* Originally published as "Forethocht felony, malice aforethought and the classification of homicide", in W M Gordon and T D Fergus (eds), *Legal History in the Making: Proceedings of the Ninth British Legal History Conference, Glasgow 1989* (1991) 43–59. There has been added to this version part of "Was it murder? John Comyn of Badenoch and William, earl of Douglas", in C J Kay and M A Mackay (eds), *Perspectives on the Older Scottish Tongue* (2005).
1 Report of the House of Lords Select Committee on Murder and Life Imprisonment (1989), vol 3, 470.
2 [1961] AC 290.
3 [1975] AC 55.
4 [1985] AC 905.
5 [1986] AC 455.
6 (1988) 104 *LQR* 30; and see also Glanville Williams, "The mens rea of murder: leave it alone" (1989) 105 *LQR* 387.

has also taken place since the 1960s, leading contributors being J M Kaye in the *Law Quarterly Review* for 1967,[7] and Thomas Green in the *Michigan Law Review* for 1975–76.[8] This debate has revolved around the exact meaning to be attached to the words "malice prepense", or "malice aforethought" in the leading statute of 1390 and the century following. In simple terms the question has been in what circumstances, if any, did "malice aforethought" carry its obvious and literal meaning of premeditation, and when did it merely signal a deliberate and intentional killing – one committed, it may be, on the spur of the moment without premeditation. The answer to this question affects an understanding of the later development of the law of homicide in England, and in particular the rise of the distinction between murder and manslaughter, and the relationship between both these terms and the concept of "chance medley".

It would be both impertinent and unwise for a Scots lawyer to intervene in the English debate, medieval or modern. So far as the modern law is concerned the Scottish witnesses who gave evidence to the Select Committee declared, virtually without exception, that they were satisfied with the existing position under Scottish common law, and were against the drafting of a new statutory definition of the crime of murder for Scotland. Sheriff Gordon indeed, the author of the leading modern work on Scots criminal law, professed himself puzzled at the need to consider the Scottish definition of murder at all. It was "almost impossible for a Scottish judge to go astray when directing a jury on the mens rea of murder".[9] All he had to do was to quote the classic definition of murder in Macdonald's *Criminal Law*: "Murder is constituted by any wilful act causing the destruction of life, whether intended to kill, or displaying such wicked recklessness as to imply a disposition depraved enough to be regardless of the consequences."[10] The Select Committee recommended a new statutory definition of the crime of murder for England but, noting the strength of the Scottish evidence in favour of the existing common law, concluded that however desirable uniformity of definition might be in theory they "could not justify the imposition on Scotland of changes which would

---

7 J M Kaye, "The early history of murder and manslaughter" (1967) 83 *LQR* 365 and 569 (2 parts).
8 T A Green, "The jury and the English law of homicide" (1975–76) 74 *Mich LR* 414. A revised version appears in T A Green, *Verdict According to Conscience* (1985, 1988), ch 3 ("Judge, jury, and the evolution of the criminal law in medieval England").
9 Select Committee Report (n 1), vol 3, at 553.
10 J H A Macdonald, *A Practical Treatise on the Criminal Law of Scotland* (5th edn, 1948) at 89. Macdonald, who subsequently became Lord Justice-Clerk, was 30 years old when he first framed this definition in 1866.

be so unwelcome".[11] They also noted that statutory definition of "the elusive concept of 'wicked recklessness' would be very difficult", and considered that "that very flexibility of 'wicked recklessness' which is seen as its virtue in Scotland precludes the use of precise and definite language which is normally and rightly expected in a statute defining a criminal offence."[12]

This essay considers the historical development of the classification of homicide in Scotland, with particular reference to the use of the term "forethocht felony", the native Scottish equivalent of the English lawyer's "malice aforethought". As the Scottish evidence has occasionally been brought into play in the medieval English debate, I hope that this study will provide further ammunition for English legal historians. I believe, too, that the study of the historical development of the law of homicide in these islands and, in particular, the changing meanings attached to the term "murder" prompts reflection on the modem debate as to how far it is desirable or even possible to frame a watertight statutory definition of the crime. Many Scots lawyers will be surprised, incidentally, to learn that the notion of malice aforethought or "forethocht felony" was part and parcel of their law for over 500 years, as it plays no part in Scots law today.

To return briefly to the history of homicide in England, Maitland believed that *"malice prepense"* in the statute of 1390 did indeed signify premeditation, and that this constituted the essential ingredient in the crime of murder. During the fifteenth century, he argued, premeditated killing or murder could be contrasted with killing in the heat of the moment, deliberately perhaps, but without premeditation. Maitland, like Stephen before him, argued for a continuous development in the law from the statute of 1390, through the fifteenth century, to the distinction made in the sixteenth century between murder and manslaughter. He used Scottish evidence from the fourteenth and fifteenth centuries as a link in the chain of his argument. He also pointed back to the English case of *John de Warenne v Alan de la Zouche* in 1270, in which actings *ex praecogitata malitia* were contrasted with those *ex motu iracundiae* in apparent anticipation of the later distinction between malice aforethought and chance medley or *chaudemellee*.[13]

Maitland's view was generally accepted until the publication in 1967 of Kaye's articles. Kaye set out to prove that *malice prepense* in the statute of 1390 denoted a killing done "wickedly" or "wilfully" or "without lawful

---

11 Select Committee Report (n 1), vol 1, at para 42.
12 Select Committee Report (n 1), vol 1, at para 43.
13 F W Maitland, "The early history of malice aforethought" [1883], in H A L Fisher (ed), *Collected Papers* (3 vols, 1911) vol 1, 304. See also Pollock & Maitland, vol 2, at 468–469 and 485–488.

excuse", but not necessarily with premeditation. He saw no line of continuous development between the statute of 1390 and the emergence of the distinction between murder and manslaughter in the sixteenth century. In Kaye's view the courts redefined murder and manslaughter in the middle of the sixteenth century "making the distinction between them depend on the presence or absence of premeditation: thus manslaughter, or chance medley, came to mean a deliberate killing 'upon a sudden occasion'". Manslaughter or chance medley, argued Kaye, had previously described not a deliberate, but "an accidental killing which took place in the course or furtherance of an act of violence not directed at the person slain or any member of his company".[14] He also argued that "chance medley" was distinct, not only etymologically but also conceptually, from *"chaudemellee"* – actings in hot blood.[15] Kaye was unimpressed by the relevance of the Scottish evidence, and regarded *De Warenne v De la Zouche* as an isolated case from which no safe conclusion could be drawn.[16]

Kaye's view became the new orthodoxy. Reservations have been expressed, however, by both Thomas Green and John Baker. Green writes that "the weight of the evidence suggests that by 1390 *malitia precogitata* had come at least temporarily and in one significant context – that of homicide – to have the meaning of true malice aforethought."[17] He notes that in a charge to a grand jury in 1403 homicide "of those who lie in wait *par malice devant pourpense*" was distinguished from homicide *chaude melle*.[18] Green further points out that the term "chance medley" (*chance melle*) appears as early as 1388, and believes that in the late fourteenth and early fifteenth centuries "the two terms *chaude melle* (literally 'hot medley') and *chance melle* (literally 'chance medley') appear to have been interchangeable."[19] However, he believes that the distinction drawn by the statute of 1390 was relatively short-lived. Baker comments that "the notion of malice aforethought was not much discussed [in the fifteenth century], and it is uncertain whether it denoted actual premeditation." "At least by the end of the fifteenth century," he writes, "lawyers recognised a second kind of felonious homicide which they called chance-medley."[20]

14 Kaye (n 7) at 369–370.
15 Kaye (n 7) at 376.
16 Kaye (n 7) at 374–375.
17 Green (n 8) at 463 and n 182.
18 Green (n 8) at 467 and n 200.
19 Green (n 8) at 467 and n 200.
20 J H Baker, *Reports of Sir John Spelman*, 2 vols (Selden Society vol 94, 1978), introduction, at 304. See also J H Baker, *An Introduction to English Legal History*, 5th edn (2019) at 570–572.

Compared with the richness of the English record, the sources for the history of homicide in Scotland in the middle ages are sparse indeed. The most we can hope to discern is the bare outline of the law as set forth in treatises, formularies and statute. We have no record of coroners' indictments, no trial rolls to guide us. The detailed research into the workings of the jury which has proved so fruitful in England, and the distinction which it has been possible to draw even in medieval times between societal and purely legal concepts of crime, including murder, are quite impossible to parallel in Scotland. Thomas Green has exposed the workings of the "nullifying" jury in medieval English practice, reaching its own decisions in spite of, rather than in accordance with strict law.[21] We may suspect – in view of Green's work, we must suspect – that the nullifying jury was at work in Scotland, as in England, but we cannot demonstrate the proposition. More surprising perhaps, at least to an English legal historian, than the poverty of the Scottish record, for that is well known, is the lack of comment on what little does exist. Apart from some able studies on assythment (that is, compensation payable to the kin for mutilation or slaughter), and the blood feud so closely associated with it, little has been written about the development of the law of homicide in Scotland to set against the veritable torrent of research and writing recently in England.[22] This essay should, therefore, be regarded as tentative.

The prominence of assythment and the blood feud in the Scottish record points to a significant difference between the operation of the law of homicide in Scotland and in England in the later middle ages. Although much in the early Scots law of homicide was clearly borrowed from Anglo-Norman England, including trial by jury and the process of indictment, in Scotland the Crown's right to prosecute for homicide was circumscribed for centuries by the right of the kin of the victim to seek vengeance or, alternatively, to accept assythment. Even after the Crown's right to proceed, regardless of the wishes of the kin, was clearly recognised towards the end of the sixteenth century, the right to assythment – known also, significantly, as "kinboot" – remained in cases where the death penalty had not been exacted; and a full pardon, or remission, from the Crown remained conditional on satisfying

---

21 Green, *Verdict According to Conscience* (n 8), especially ch 2 ("Societal concepts of criminal liability and jury nullification of the law in the thirteenth and fourteenth centuries").
22 See particularly J Wormald, "Bloodfeud, kindred and government in early modern Scotland" (1980) 87 *Past and Present* 54; and also R Black, "Historical survey of delictual liability in Scotland for personal injuries and death – part i, early history", (1975) 8 *Comparative and International LJ of Southern Africa* 46; C H W Gane, "The effect of a pardon in Scots law", 1980 *JR* 18; and K M Brown, *Bloodfeud in Scotland, 1573–1625* (1986).

the just demands of the kin of the deceased for compensation.[23] Examples of assythment occur with some regularity until the middle of the eighteenth century, and it was only in 1976, after a belated attempt at revival in the case of *M'Kendrick v Sinclair*,[24] which was argued up to the House of Lords, that the action of assythment was finally abolished in Scots law.[25] The operation of the law of homicide in Scotland, therefore, involved a delicate counterpoint between public and private right long after private considerations ceased to play any part in English law.

As is well known, the word "murder" is cognate with Germanic *"mord"* and Scandinavian *"morð"* signifying a secret killing; and there can be little doubt that "murder" was first used in Scotland as in England in this sense. In Celtic law too, to judge from the Irish evidence, a secret killing was regarded as a particularly heinous form of homicide.[26] This early meaning of "murder" is to be understood against the background of the blood feud and private vengeance. It antedates public justice. All killing potentially gave rise to a blood feud or claim for compensation. A secret killing was particularly reprehensible because – among other reasons – the kin of the murdered man would not know against whom to seek redress. This early definition of murder as a secret killing long survived the growth of the king's peace and the recognition of "pleas of the Crown" in both Scotland and England.

The term *murdrum* first appears on record in Scotland in the reign of William I (1165–1214) when it appears as one of the pleas of the Crown, excepted from the grant of Annandale to Robert de Brus: *"Exceptis regalibus que ad regalitatem meam spectant Scilicet . . . Causa de murdra"*.[27] At this time it presumably bore its original meaning of a secret killing. In a text dated 1244, the *Statuta Regis Alexandri* distinguishes *murthra* (and robbery – *roboria*) from other homicides and thefts (*furta*): the former pertain to the Crown and entail forfeiture of all the perpetrator's chattels, while in the latter the perpetrator's lord takes the chattels.[28] The earliest known classification of homicide in Scots law occurs in the treatise known as *Regiam Majestatem*, once thought to date from the first half of the thir-

---

23 See, in addition to the authorities cited in n 22, J Irvine Smith and I Macdonald, "Criminal law", in *ISLH* 280; and *Justiciary Cases* II, introduction.
24 1972 SC (HL) 25.
25 Damages (Scotland) Act 1976 s 6.
26 F Kelly, *Guide to Early Irish Law* (1988) at 128.
27 RRS vol 2 at 179.
28 LMS at 576–581. See further A R C Simpson, "Procedures for dealing with robbery in Scotland before 1400", in idem, S C Styles, E West and A L M Wilson (eds), *Continuity, Change and Pragmatism in the Law: Essays in Memory of Professor Angelo Forte* (2016) 95.

teenth century, but now dated later, probably to the years shortly after 1318. This section of *Regiam* is lifted almost verbatim from *Glanvill's De Legibus*, compiled over a century previously, and reflects the ancient use of the term "murder" to denote a secret killing:

> *Duo autem genera sunt homicidii: unum quod dicitur murdrum quod nullo vidente vel sciente clam perpetratur . . . secundum genus homicidii est illud quod dicitur simplex homicidium.*[29]

"Murder", therefore, is contrasted in the *Regiam* with "simple" homicide.

The next evidence for the classification of homicide in Scotland comes from two well-known statutes of 1369/70 and 1371/72. The 1370 statute of David II enacted that the king should not grant a remission for homicide until an inquest had determined whether the killing had been committed *per murthyr vel per praecogitatam malitiam*.[30] The statute of Robert II, two years later – perhaps rather statutes, as there are a number of separate provisions – follows the same classification, and enacts that when homicide has been committed an inquest or assize should determine whether the killing was committed *ex certo et deliberato proposito vel per forthouchfelony sive murthir vel ex calore iracundiae viz chaudemellee*.[31] The 1372 statute also uses the shorter formulation of *per forthouchfelony vel per murthir* in contrast to *per chaudemellee*: if the assize finds forethocht felony or murder then sentence is to be carried out without delay; if, on the other hand, it finds *chaudmellee* the accused is to have the exceptions and defences already permitted by law and custom – "*habebit dilaciones et defensiones legitimas et debitas per leges Regni et consuetudines hactenus approbatas.*" The statute continues that in the case of a killer seeking sanctuary an assize should determine whether the deed was *per murthir sive per forthouchfelony* or whether it was *per chaudemelle*. Only in the latter case should benefit of sanctuary be allowed.

Two near contemporary formularies, the Bute manuscript and Formulary E, show that these statutes were no dead letter. Each contains a style directing the holding of an inquest to determine whether someone had killed another by forethocht felony or not. The texts are nearly identical and mirror the words of the statute of 1372:

---

29 *RM (Cooper)*, 4.5; *RM (APS)*, 4.4 (at 663). And see *Glanvill*, 14.3.
30 *RPS* 1370/2/36. Note the slightly different version of this statute in *RPS* 1370/2/12. On sanctuary and the forethocht felony/*chaudmellee* distinction, see further H L MacQueen, "Girth: society and the law of sanctuary in Scotland", in J W Cairns and O F Robinson (eds), *Critical Studies in Ancient Law, Comparative Law & Legal History* (2001) 333 at 344–345.
31 *RPS* 1372/3/9. See also *RPS* 1372/3/7.

Inquisitio si talis interfecit talem per forthought felony vel non. Jacobus dei gracia vicecomiti et balliuis suis salutem. Mandamus etc. quatinus per probos et fideles homines patrie per quos rei veritas melius sciri poterit, magno sacramento interveniente, diligentem et fidelem inquisicionem fieri faciatis si talis lator presencium talem *ex iracundie inconsulto calore nec per murthir nec per forthocht felony interfecit. Et si et in quantum ei alias dederit occasionem et causam sue mortis ex predicto inconsulto iracundie calore vel aliter.* Et que et quales circumstantie intervenerunt in morte et causa mortis dicti talis. Et quid per dictam inquisicionem diligenter et fideliter factam esse inveneritis sub sigillo vestro vicecomitis et sub sigillis eorum qui dicte inquisicioni intererunt faciende ad capellam nostram mittatis et hoc breve.[32]

The wording of the rubric, incidentally, clearly incorporating the category of "murder" within forethocht felony, shows that the *vel* and *sive* occurring in David II's statute between *murthyr* and *praecogitatam malitiam*, and in Robert II's statute between *ex certo et deliberato proposito, forthouchfelony* and *murthir*, are conjunctive.

At least two fifteenth-century Scottish statutes also mention forethocht felony and contrast it with actions on a "suddante" or *chaudemellee*. The first, an Act of James I in 1426, is concerned not so much with homicide specifically but more generally with breaches of the king's peace.[33] Should anyone complain that the king's peace has been broken upon him, it runs, the appropriate officer of the law is to summon both parties and inquire diligently and without favour whether the deed was done upon forethocht felony or "throw suddande chaudemellay". "Ande gif it be fundyn forthocht

---

32 Inquest [to determine] whether one killed another through forethocht felony or not.

James by the grace of God to his sheriff and bailies greeting. We command etc. that you cause a diligent and faithful inquest to be held, under application of the great oath, by good and faithful men of the country by whom the truth of the matter can be better known to determine whether the bearer of these presents [i.e. the petitioner] killed another *in anger in the heat of the moment and not through murder or forethocht felony; and whether and in what respect he [the deceased] gave him occasion and cause for his death arising out of anger in the heat of the moment foresaid or otherwise;* and what were the general circumstances of the death and the cause of the death of the said R. And send whatever you find transacted diligently and faithfully by the said inquest along with this brieve to our chapel under your own seal as sheriff and under the seals of those who served on the said inquest.

The text is taken from *Scottish Formularies* at 55 (E14). The emphasis is mine. Formulary E is Edinburgh University Library MS Borland no 207. Professor Duncan describes this manuscript "as derived from an earlier collection of state documents of period c1280–1329" (*Scottish Formularies* at xv) and states that it "can confidently be dated 1424–82" (*Scottish Formularies* at 39). Compare the Bute MS text, which runs in the name of King Robert (*Scottish Formularies* at 149–150 (B68)). In the text given above and in translating I have utilised Bute's *"et si et in quantum ipse ei alias dederit"*, which is clearly preferable to the *"et si et in quantum R ei dedirit"* of Formulary E). Duncan dates Bute to c1424 (*Scottish Formularies* at 117–118).

33 *RPS* 1426/10.

felony," the statute continues, "the party salbe chalangyt incontinent of the kingis pece breking be the officiaris of the lawe the quhilkis sall ger the party hurte be fullely assythit [compensated] efter the quantite of the skaithe [harm] that he has sustenyt." Thereafter the malefactor is to be in the king's mercy as regards life and limb. If, on the other hand, "the trespass be done of suddande chauldemelly the party scathit sall folowe [pursue the action] and the party trespassande sall defende eftir the coursis of the auld lawis of the realme". This last sentence is in line with the provision in the 1372 statute that if the inquest finds *chaudemellee* the defender is to have the exceptions and defences allowed by law and custom.

The second statute dates from 1469 in James III's reign.[34] The preamble complains of "gret slachteris quhilkis has bene Richt commone ymang the kingis liegiis now and of late baith of forethocht felony and of suddante". Many of those who have committed slaughter hope to be granted sanctuary, but the law does not permit those who have committed "forthocht felony *tanquam Incediator viarum et per Industriam*" to enjoy sanctuary. An assise is therefore to determine whether there has been forethocht felony or not and only if it finds "suddante" is sanctuary to be granted. As Lord Cooper pointed out, the statute's *tanquam Incediator viarum et per Industriam* follows the Vulgate's rendering of Exodus 21.14, which speaks of a manslayer coming *tanquam insidiator et per industrium*.[35] This passage would have been familiar to all Canon lawyers as it heads the treatment of homicide in *Decretals* V, xii. According to the rubric there, the incorrigible manslayer (*homicida incorrigibilis*) is to be handed over to the secular arm to be put to death – *ut moriatur* – Exodus xxi, 14 being cited as authority for this proposition.

It is clear then that from the last third of the fourteenth century at latest a new classification of homicide was beginning to replace the division between murder and simple homicide found in *Regiam Majestatem*. Or rather, the new classification came to exist alongside the old; it did not entirely supersede it. The term "murder" began to extend its ambit and move from its older and more restricted meaning of a secret killing to cover all killing done with forethocht felony. Killing by forethocht felony was contrasted with killing in the heat of the moment, *chaudemellee*, killing which – or so it would appear – was not premeditated. This second type of killing, although clearly culpable, was not viewed with such outright disfavour as murder:

---

34 *RPS* 1469/25.
35 *RM (Cooper)* at 255; see also Maitland (n 13) at 326–327.

unlike murderers, killers by *chaudemellee* were not excluded from benefit of sanctuary, nor necessarily from a royal pardon. This new classification has moved away from the world of the blood feud towards a public criminal law. The king's peace extends over all the land. All killing becomes technically criminal. The mental element in homicide – never entirely disregarded – becomes more important. Which killers are to be allowed to claim sanctuary? To whom shall the king extend his pardon? Cases of pure misadventure and self-defence certainly, but what else besides?

There is a further example of the use of the term "forethocht felony" in fifteenth-century Scots which is very instructive. It occurs in Sir Gilbert of the Hay's translation into Scots (around 1456) of Honoré Bonet's *Arbre des Batailles*.[36] Bonet lived between around 1340 and 1410 and his *Arbre des Batailles* is a celebrated early work on what would now be termed public international law.[37] In his third chapter Bonet discusses the morality of a challenge to combat as a means of settling a dispute. He aims to show that such a challenge is expressly forbidden by all laws, God's and man's. First, he says, it is against the law of nature. Here he is in Hay's rather free translation:

> Bot before or I schaw thir casis [some exceptional cases], I will first prove opynly that gage of bataille be all lawis is forbedyn expressly, bathe in Goddis law and mannis law, in commoun lawe and canoune lawe, and als, be gude resoun naturale, quhilk is callit lawe of nature, and als, be the law civile to geve gage of bataill or to tak. And for sik querele, to fecht is a thing condampnyt bathe and reprovit be all lawis. *And first and formast, I preve it be resoun naturale. For gage of bataill cummys ay [comes always] of forethocht felouny. Bot naturaly all maner of creature naturale has a passioun of nature that is callit the first movement; that is, quhen a man or beste is sudaynly sterte, thair naturale inclinacioun gevis thame of thair complexioun to a brethe, and a sudayn hete of ire of vengeance quhilk efterwart stanchis efter that hete. Bot bataill taking cumis of lang forset and forethocht purpos of malice that is nocht naturale to man.*[38]

---

36 J H Stevenson (ed), *Gilbert of the Haye's Prose Manuscript*, i, *The Buke of the Law of Armys* (Scottish Text Society, vol 44, 1901).
37 The standard modern French edition is Ernest Nys (ed), *L' Arbre des Batailles* (1883), and the standard modern English translation G W Coopland (ed), *The Tree of Battles of Honoré Bonet* (1949).
38 Stevenson (n 36), at 256 (emphasis supplied). See further below, text accompanying nn 89–90. Note too Hay's listing in this passage of various types of law: *Goddis law, mannis law, common lawe, canoune lawe, the lawe of nature* and *the law civile*. Compare Coopland's translation of Bonet's original, following the original text more closely:

> But before I name them I wish to show plainly how, according to divine law (*droit divin*), the law of nations (*droit des gens*), the law of decretals (*droit des decrets*), and civil law (*droit civil*), to give wager of battle and to receive it for the purpose of combat is a thing reproved, and is condemned by reason (Coopland (n 37), 4.111; original French from the Nys edition 1883).

This is a most valuable passage, for not only does it duplicate the terms of art used in the law, but it gives an insight into the mentality, the way of thinking, which distinguished between slaughter "on a suddanty", or *chaudemellee*, and forethocht felony. Hay writes of "forethocht felony", of "lang forset and forethocht purpos of malice", of "a sudayn hete of ire of vengeance", and of being "sudaynly stert". But the greater value of the passage lies in its disclosure of the way of thinking which lay behind these legal distinctions. The division into slaughter by forethought felony and slaughter chaude-melle reflects a very real difference in the way men thought about these two types of killing. Killing by forethought felony was unnatural, against the law of nature. Killing chaude-melle, on the other hand, although clearly sinful, was the result of natural passion. The first deserved the description of "murder", a term, then as now, reserved for the type of killing deemed most reprehensible by society. The second did not. One might compare the distinction in Scots law today between murder and culpable homicide, or murder and manslaughter in England. If, therefore, we describe killing in hot blood as "murder" at this period, we are not only guilty of an anachronism, but are also in some danger of misunderstanding and misjudging the reaction of contemporaries.[39]

At this point it is worth noting in parenthesis that Lord Cooper, in the notes to his edition of *Regiam Majestatem*, interpreted the development of the law of homicide in Scotland rather differently.[40] Partly, it would seem, through misdating the style which appears in the Bute formulary, Cooper placed the first appearance of the distinction between murder and forethocht felony, on the one hand, and homicide *ex iracundiae inconsulto calore* on the other, in the thirteenth century – a hundred years or more too early. He then continued:

> It is likely enough that these humane distinctions tended to become blunted and obscured during the Wars [of Independence with England], and it may be on this account that the matter had to be taken up afresh under French influence two generations later.

He then pointed to the French *Ordonnance* of 1356 which classified the more serious forms of homicide as those *perpetrés de mauvaiz agait, par mauvaise volonté et par deliberacion*,[41] and suggested that David II brought back from France the ideas which prompted the Scottish legislation of 1370

---

39 This paragraph is drawn from Sellar, "Was it murder?" (n °) at 135.
40 *RM (Cooper)* at 255.
41 *Ordonnances des Rois de France* (1723–1849), vol 3, 129.

and 1372. Even if one lays aside the misdating of the Bute style, this scenario is quite speculative and would need considerable further supporting evidence to be rendered credible. In fact, it is the close correspondence between Scots and English law which is really remarkable.[42] The parallels with France are best understood in the context of a wider European background.

The distinction drawn in the law of homicide between forethocht felony and *chaudemellee* had a very long run in Scots law, and was only finally laid to rest by Baron Hume's great work on the criminal law at the end of the eighteenth century. It can be traced in legal writings and, from the late fifteenth century onwards, in actual cases. Pitcairn's *Criminal Trials* provides a useful guide to the terms of art used in practice in prosecutions for homicide from the end of the fifteenth century, as evidenced by the following examples:[43]

- 1493 "art and part of the forethought felony done . . . by way of Murder" *(William Tayt)* (vol 1, part 1, at 17°);
- 1497 "art and part of the Murther and Slaughter of . . ." *(Patrik McKowloche)* (vol 1, part 1, at 99°);
- 1509 "Convicted of art and part of the cruel Slaughter . . . committed upon forethought felony" *(Alexander Lecprevik)* (vol 1, part 1, at 62°);
- 1512 "art and pairt of the Slauchtir and Murthure" *(William Douglas of Drumlanrig)* (vol 1, part 1, at 79°);
- 1530 Accused of "Cruel Slaughter . . . acquitted of forethought felony . . . Wherefore they were restored to the sanctuary of Torphichen" *(Robert Manderstoune)* (vol 1, part 1, at 151°).

By the middle of the sixteenth century the indictments become more formulaic, usually combining the elements of old feud, provision, set purpose and forethocht felony:

- 1539 "indict and accusit for art and pairt of the felloune and cruell Slauchter . . . apoun auld feid and forthocht felony . . . comitit the said Slauchtir upon provisioune and foirthocht fellony" *(James Reid)* (vol 1, part 1, at 220°);
- 1562 Convicted of "the crewell and unmercyfull Slaughter . . . upone ald ffeid, sett purpois, provisione and foirthoicht fellonye" *(William Fergusone)* (vol 1, part 1, at 425°);
- 1581 Accused of *slaughter* "upoune sett purpois, provision, auld feid and foirthocht fellonie"; defence claims that it was "done on suddantie . . . and denyis foirthocht fellonie" *(William Bikartoune)* (vol 1, part 2, at 98–99).

---

42 For a reassessment which builds on the work of several scholars see Sellar, "Common law"; also chs 7 and 8 above.
43 R Pitcairn, *Criminal Trials in Scotland from 1488 to 1624* (3 vols, Bannatyne and Maitland Clubs, 1833). The following section is derived from Sellar, "Was it murder?" (n °), at 134–135.

Sir James Balfour, writing towards the end of the sixteenth century, notes (here following *Regiam Majestatem*):

> Thai ar twa kindis of man-slauchter, the ane is callit murther, and the uther callit simple slauchter. Murther is done privatlie, na man seand nor kanawand the samin bot allanerlie [only] the slayer and his complices, swa that the cry of the people followis not suddenlie thairupon, as is usit in the law of slauchter.

But he also writes that "na slaughter done be chance or chaud-melle, sould be callit murther; for all murther is committit be foirthocht felonie."[44]

In his *De Verborum Significatione*, published in 1597, Sir John Skene notes under "FORTHOCHT":

> FORTHOCHT felony, praecogitata malitia, quhilk is don and committed wittinglie and willinglie, after deliberation and set purpose, and is different from chaudemelle;

and under "CHAUD-MELLE":

> In Latin Rixa, an hoat suddaine tuilzie or debaite, quhilk is opponed as contrar to forthoucht fellonie, vide Melletum;

and under "MELLETUM ":

> Ane French word *Melle*, dissension, strife, debate ... And in the actes of Parliament, and practique of this realme, *Chaud-mella* is ane faulte or trespasse, quhilk is committed be ane hoate suddaintie, and nocht of set purpose or *praecogitata malitia*.

Skene also printed an interesting but almost entirely neglected tract *Of Crimes and Judges in Criminall Causes* along with his English translation of *Regiam Majestatem* in 1609. Here we find 'Of Slaughter – Manslauchter, committed voluntarlie be forethought-felonie or casualy be chaudemelle, generally is punished be death . . .".[45] The juxtaposition of "voluntary" and "casual" in this passage is of particular interest. It points forward, as will be seen, to the Act of 1649 and to Hume, but also back to the Civilians and the Canon law.

*Irvings v Bell* in 1646 illustrates the use of the various terms in practice.[46] The case concerned the scope of a royal remission from "suddane slaughter and killing". There was much discussion of *Regiam Majestatem* and the old statutes on homicide; and the contrast was made between "*murthour quod*

---

44 Balfour, *Practicks*, vol 2, at 512.
45 Sir J Skene, *Of Crime, and Judges in Criminall Causes conform to the Lawes of this Realme* (1609) 2.6.1.
46 *Justiciary Cases* III at 583–588.

*factum fuit per precogitatam malitiam*" and "*naikit slauchter be chaudmella per rixam vel per infortuniam*".[47] The term "naikit slauchter" is, of course, an echo of the *Regiam's* "*simplex homicidium*". The two classifications – the older distinction between murder and simple homicide, and the later contrast between forethocht felony and *chaudemellee* – seemed to co-exist side by side reasonably well in practice, the term "murder" being increasingly equated with forethocht felony, although its original meaning of a secret killing was long remembered. It would have been quite logical had Scots law developed a further classification in the sixteenth century, based on provocation, corresponding to the division between "murder" and "manslaughter" in contemporary England, but this did not happen. Instead, all was thrown into confusion by a further statute, passed initially in 1649, and re-enacted in 1661.[48]

The main purpose of this statute was to detail the types of homicide which should not carry the death penalty. It introduced to the statute book the term "casual homicide", already encountered in the tract printed by Skene in 1609:

> *Act anent severall Degrees of Casuall homicide*
> The Estats of parliament etc for removeall of all questiounes and doubts that may arise heereafter in Criminall persuits for slaughter Statuts and ordaines that the cases of homicide after following viz Casuall homicide Homicide in laufull defence and Homicide committed upon theives and robbers breaking hous in the night or incase of masterfull Depredatioun or in the persute of Denounced or Declared rebellis for Criminall causes or of such who assist and Defend the rebellis by armes and by force opposes the persute and apprehending of thame whilk shall happin to fall out in tyme comeing nor any of thame shall not be punished by death And that notwithstanding of any Lawis or acts of parliament or any practik made heretofore or observed in punishing of slaughter Bot that the Manslayer in any of the cases aforesaid shall be assoilzied [absolved] from any Criminall persute pursued against him for his lyfe for the said slaughter before any Judge Criminall within this kingdome . . .

Unfortunately, the statute omitted to define what was meant by "casual homicide". Standing the previous legislation, which still remained in force, save where specifically altered by the statute, a number of different interpretations were clearly possible. A killing *chaudemellee* might be said to be a killing by chance, *casu*, in so far as there had been no premeditation or forethocht felony. Was such a killing, therefore, "casual homicide"? If so,

---

47 *Justiciary Cases* III at 585–586.
48 *RPS* 1649/1/118: an Act of Charles II, passed on 13 February 1649; re-enacted in 1661 after the Restoration (*RPS* 1661/1/265).

*chaudemellee* would not carry the death penalty. Alternatively, did casual homicide refer only to killing by chance in the quite different sense of mere accident, or pure misadventure? If so killing *chaudemellee* was a capital offence. And what about a death caused by culpable negligence? These and other points of interpretation were raised in case after case, and the relevant passages in *Regiam Majestatem* and the fourteenth-century statutes trotted out again and again.

In *Dalmahoy or Ralstoun v Mason*, for example, in 1674 the deceased, Ralstoun, had apparently been drunk and had provoked and assaulted the pannel [accused], Mason.[49] Mason retaliated and beat Ralstoun who fell and cut open his head on the edge of a bunker or chest. Ralstoun, who in addition to being drunk was said to have been aged and infirm and recently recovered from sickness, took no proper care of the wound but stayed "in frosty weather for three hours after". He died some time later from "defluxion and swelling" rather than directly from the wound. A number of possible defences were clearly available to the pannel on the facts, but the case reveals considerable uncertainty about terminology. The pannel denied "precogitate malice" and forethocht felony. If the wound was his fault he pleaded either casual homicide or self-defence. The widow insisted on "simple slauchter" and said that casual homicide was only relevant where the effect was not and could not have been foreseen. The Lord Advocate, acting with the widow and children of the deceased, argued that the defence of casual homicide did not apply in that *culpa casui precedens* the pannel *causam rixae dedit* to the defunct, and after giving him the wound pursued him further.[50] The pannel then denied *culpa precedens* and maintained that the killing was "clearly casual being neither intended not expected to be repute deliberate and resolved".[51] The court found the libel [indictment] relevant only to *poenam extraordinanam* – that is, they excluded the death penalty – and remitted the case and defences to an assize. The assize found self-defence "all in one voice except one"[!].[52]

In the course of time the balance tilted towards interpreting casual homicide to exclude *chaudemellee*. Thus Sir George Mackenzie in his *Matters Criminal*, published in 1678, defines casual homicide in these terms: "*Homicidium casuale* is when a Man is killed casually, without either the Fault or Design of the Killer", and "Casual Slaughter, or Homicide, then, is

---

49 *Justiciary Records* II at 278–294.
50 *Justiciary Records* II at 292.
51 *Justiciary Records* II at 293.
52 *Justiciary Records* II at 294.

which is occasioned by Mistake and just Ignorance."[53] He notes, however, that "Slaughter and Murder did of old differ": murder, properly so called, was committed upon forethocht felony, in contrast with "*Chaudmella*, or Slaughter committed upon Suddenty". "All casual Slaughter," he writes, "was of old comprehended under the Word *Chaudmella*."[54] Mackenzie then discusses the wording of the 1649 Act and points out that the definition of casual homicide there is ambiguous and inadequate in that its relationship to *chaudmellee*, and generally to "*homicidium culposum*", is not clear. However, he writes that William Douglas's case determined "that in our Law, though Murder was not at first designed, yet if it was designed the Time the Stroke was given, the Killer is guilty of Murder: That Premeditation is requisite to make Murder capital, being only such as *antecedit actum, licet non congressum*."[55] In other words, killing *chaudemellee* should not fall under the protection of the Act.

Mackenzie contrasts "murder" and "slaughter", but it is clear that the unqualified term "slauchter", or "manslauchter", was used in a general way – as for example by Balfour and Skene in the passages quoted above – to cover the entire field of homicide. Lord Kames, too, uses "manslaughter" in a general sense in 1757 in his *Statute Law of Scotland* where he writes of "murder, which is manslaughter upon forethought felony".[56] In English law, of course, the term "manslaughter" came to be used in the sixteenth century in a narrower sense and was distinguished from "murder"; yet it is interesting to note Baker's comment, "It might have been more logical if the English word had been retained for the genus, and 'murder' and 'chance-medley' used for the species."[57]

*Chaudemellee* was referred to in 1752 in one of the most notorious murder trials in eighteenth-century Scotland: the "Appin murder", immortalised by Robert Louis Stevenson in *Kidnapped*, in which James Stewart of the Glens was charged with the murder of "the Red Fox", Colin Campbell of Glenure. In the course of the trial, Stewart's counsel, Thomas Millar, said:

> And, first, it will be observed, that the murder is not said to have been committed from sudden passion, or *chaudmelle*, as the law expresses it, but to have been premeditated and resolved upon for some days before it was committed. Now,

---

53 Mackenzie, *Matters Criminal*, 1.11.6 ((Robinson edn at 92).
54 Mackenzie, *Matters Criminal*, 1.11.11 ((Robinson edn at 96).
55 Mackenzie, *Matters Criminal*, 1.11.12 (Robinson edn at 97).
56 H Home, Lord Kames, *Statute Law of Scotland* (1757) at 204.
57 Baker, *Spelman's Reports* (n 20) at 305.

to render malice of so high a nature probable, some very strong ground or cause ought to have been assigned for it.[58]

He went on to refer to *Regiam Majestatem* and the various statutes.

The old classification was finally consigned to well-deserved oblivion by Baron David Hume in his magisterial *Commentaries on Crime* (1797). Hume distinguished four categories of homicide "though perhaps not fully distinguished in our practice by appropriated names": aggravated murder, murder, culpable homicide, and homicide "free of all blame", this last comprising casual homicide and justifiable homicide.[59] With the exception of the first, these categories are, broadly speaking, still in use today. Hume noted that "casual homicide" had sometimes been taken to include *chaudemellee* in the past, but considered that it was more appropriate to restrict the term to "pure misadventure without any act of the killer's will".[60] Of murder he said, "The characteristic of this sort of homicide is that it is done wilfully and out of malice aforethought".[61] Note that in Hume the polite English "malice aforethought" has taken over from the native forethocht felony. After Hume the familiar question arose again as to whether "malice aforethought" necessarily involved premeditation, or whether it merely signified a deliberate and wilful killing. The point was finally settled in favour of the latter in the case of *Charles MacDonald* in1867.[62] After that the term "malice aforethought" was otiose and gradually passed out of Scots law after a life of 500 years or more.

The Scottish evidence may be sparse but it seems clear enough. It points to the consistent and uninterrupted use of the term "malice aforethought" to describe a premeditated, rather than a merely deliberate homicide, from at least the later fourteenth until the eighteenth century. The actual legal term of art changes from the Latin *praecogitata malitia* of the statute of 1370, through the Scots "forethocht felony", to the more familiar "malice aforethought". Maitland thought the Scottish evidence was relevant to an understanding of the development of the English law of homicide. Kaye was not convinced. He wrote that the evidence of the statutes of David II and Robert II should not be pushed too far in view of the generally accepted belief that Scots law at this period owed more to France and the Civil law

---

58 (1752) *Scots Magazine* at 231.
59 Hume, *Commentaries*, vol 1, at 282.
60 Hume, *Commentaries*, vol 1, at 369–376, discusses the 1649 Act and *chaudemellee*. The quotation is at 283.
61 Hume, *Commentaries*, vol 1, at 390.
62 (1867) 5 Irv 525.

than to England.⁶³ Here Kaye relies too much on Lord Cooper's distinctly speculative account of the development of homicide noted above. There is, *per contra*, good reason to believe that the impact of the Anglo-Norman law on most areas of Scots law, including the criminal law, was a lasting one – or, at any rate that it lasted until long after the Wars of Independence put an end to amicable relations between Scotland and England. For my part, I am at least as impressed by the English as by the French connection, and, like Maitland, would be inclined to view the English case of *De Warenne v De la Zouche* in 1270, dismissed by Kaye, with its reference to *praecogitata malitia*, as part of the jigsaw.⁶⁴

Kaye points to the dearth of early recorded cases in Scotland. From the standpoint of the richer English record this is undoubtedly true; yet the burden of the Scottish evidence is clear. Kaye also believed there to be a danger of making a false analogy in the later middle ages between the "chaudemellee" of Scots law and the English "chance medley".⁶⁵ Since Kaye wrote, however, as already noted. Green has pointed to the use of "chance melle" in England as early as 1388, and suggested that the terms chaudemelle and *chance melle* (or medley) were at that stage interchangeable.⁶⁶ It is curious, certainly, that *chaudmellee* should appear on the Scottish record in 1372, sixteen years before the first recorded English use of *chance melle*. I doubt, however, if Kaye is right to suggest that the term "chance medley" would have been "meaningless" to the judges of Edward III.⁶⁷

The correspondence between Scots law, where the distinction between forethocht felony and *chaudemellee* appears already in 1370, and English law can hardly be accidental; and the borrowing is more likely to have been from English law to Scots rather than vice versa.⁶⁸ The meaning to be attached to "malice aforethought" or "malice prepense" in the English law of homicide in the late fourteenth and fifteenth centuries should surely be re-examined, the more so given the light which Bonet's *Arbre des Batailles* throws on contemporary patterns of thought about homicide.

63 Kaye (n 7) at 376.
64 In fact, the wording of the French *Ordonnance* of 1356 (*perpetrés de mauvaiz agait, par mauvaise volonté et par deliberacion*) seems closer to the 1390 statute's *par agait, assaut ou malice prepense* than to any Scottish parallel.
65 Kaye (n 7) at 376. It is perhaps worth noting that Sir James Balfour in Scotland equated chance medley and *chaudemellee* (above at n 40) just as did Sir Edward Coke in England.
66 Above, at nn 17–19.
67 Kaye (n 7) at 583.
68 A closer examination of the various terms of art used in England and Scotland in connection with homicide than has been possible in this paper might help to settle the issue.

Be that as it may, the divergence between the later Scots and English law of homicide is instructive. The widening of the meaning of "murder" to extend from a secret killing to all cases of forethocht felony or malice aforethought was related in both jurisdictions to a strengthening of public justice and an increasing emphasis on the mental element in the crime of murder. In the sixteenth century the English courts advanced a stage further by developing the defence of provocation and distinguishing between "murder" and "manslaughter". The Scottish courts did not follow suit; nor indeed did Scots law develop the exception of "benefit of clergy" to temper the strict severity of the law and further develop the classification of homicide, as happened in England. The Scottish debate on the place of the doctrines of provocation and self-defence and their relationship to the mental element in homicide did not gather momentum until the later seventeenth century. By then the Act of 1649 and increasing Civilian influence determined that Scots law would follow a different course from England.

The term "casual homicide", already present in Skene's tract of 1609, and sanctioned by the statute of 1649, has been in regular use in Scots law ever since. Sir George Mackenzie, and later Hume, devote some space to its proper definition. Hume divided homicide into murder, culpable homicide casual homicide and justifiable homicide. Gerald Gordon classifies homicide in modern Scots law as criminal or non-criminal: criminal homicide comprises "murder" and "culpable homicide", the latter being either "voluntary" or "involuntary"; non-criminal homicide is either "casual" or "justifiable".[69] What is the source of these terms of art: "casual" and "voluntary", "culpable" and "justifiable"? The answer again will surprise modern Scots lawyers. These terms all derive, at one remove or another, from the medieval canon law; more particularly from Book V, chapter xii of the Decretals, compiled by St Raymond of Peñafort for Pope Gregory IX and promulgated in 1234. This chapter has already been mentioned as the likely source of the quotation from Exodus xxi in the Scots Act of 1469.[70] It is entitled *De Homicidio Voluntario vel Casuali* and is full of decisions on the nature of "casual homicide" and the role played by fault or *culpa*. Earlier still the canonist Bernard of Pavia (d 1213) had already divided homicide into four Categories – *iustitia, necessitate, casu et voluntate* – discussing each at some length.[71] The

---

69 G H Gordon, *Criminal Law of Scotland*, 2nd edn (1978) at para 23–09. In the current (4th) edition of 2017 by J Chalmers and F Leverick, see para 30.09.
70 Above, at n 35.
71 For Bernard of Pavia, see F W Maitland (ed), *Bracton and Azo* (Selden Society vol 8, 1894), appendix ii.

same St Raymond who compiled the *Decretals* also compiled the *Summa de Casibus Poenitentiae*, which has been identified as a key source for Bracton's treatment of homicide in thirteenth-century English law.[72] And so the wheel turns full circle.[73]

With all this in mind, it is worth revisiting two of the most famous killings in later medieval Scotland, almost invariably referred to by historians as "murder", to see how they are described by contemporaries:[74] the killing of John Comyn of Badenoch by Robert Bruce and others in the Church of the Greyfriars in Dumfries in February 1305–6; and the killing of William 8th earl of Douglas by James II and others in Stirling Castle in February 1451–2. Did these killings amount to murder in the eyes of contemporaries? The context of both these killings is well known and is taken for granted here.

Was Bruce's killing of Comyn premeditated? Early Scottish sources suggest that it was not. English sources, however, such as the chronicle of Walter of Guisborough and Sir Thomas Gray's *Scalacronica*, antagonistic towards Bruce, suggest that it was. The very earliest accounts are both English. The first, a newsletter written within weeks of the killing, gives a detailed account of Bruce's recent movements, but has only a glancing and neutral reference to the killing of John Comyn (*la mort le dit monsire Johan*).[75] However in the "confession" of Bishop Lamberton recorded only a few months later in August 1306, Robert de Cottingham, an English royal clerk, uses the term *murdrum* to describe the killing of Comyn (*tam de murdro et interfectione quondam domini Johannis Comyn*), and refers to the "premeditated iniquity" (*excogitate nequicia*) of Robert Bruce.[76] The considered view of modern historians appears to be that Bruce's killing of Comyn was not premeditated. This was the view taken by Geoffrey Barrow in his biography of Bruce:

> It is contrary to everything we know about Bruce's character that he should have called Comyn to the Greyfriars' church with the secret intention of killing him. ... [T]he murder [*sic*] itself was surely an act of un-premeditated violence.[77]

---

72 F Schulz, "Bracton and Raymond of Peñafort" (1945) 61 *LQR* 286.
73 The main channel of influence so far as later Scots law was concerned was undoubtedly Civilian. Mackenzie, *Matters Criminal*, 1.11.1 (Robinson edn at 88), for example, notes that the Civilians divide homicide into four categories; homicide committed casually; in defence; culpably; and "wilfully" [i.e. "voluntarily"]. English law was heavily influenced at the outset by the Canon law. The topic is a large one and is clearly worth further study.
74 From this point to the text immediately after n 89 below the text is that of Sellar, "Was it murder?" (n °) at 135–138, updated to take account of more recent writings.
75 E L G Stones, *Anglo-Scottish Relations 1174–1328: Some Selected Documents* (Oxford, 1965, repr 1970), no 34 (at 266–267).
76 Stones, *Anglo-Scottish Relations* (n 75) no 35 (at 274–275).
77 G W S Barrow, *Robert Bruce and the Community of the Realm of Scotland* (4th edn, 2005) at

The historian of the Comyns, Alan Young, is of the same mind: "It is unlikely that the murder was premeditated."[78] Archie Duncan too believed that there was no premeditation: "It is surely clear that the murder was unpremeditated, but there must be a suspicion that Comyn, who had shown himself a violent man, was provocative."[79] Edward I"s biographer Michael Prestwich agrees: "Comyn"s death was not premeditated, but was the result of a quarrel over Bruce's plans."[80] Historians, I think, have sometimes found it difficult to explain why Bishop Wishart of Glasgow and Bishop Lamberton of St Andrews, among others, continued to give Bruce their full support apparently undeterred by the murder of Comyn, Wishart absolving Bruce from his sin shortly after the event, and Lamberton saying pontifical high mass at Bruce's inauguration as king later in 1306. The answer is clear. They did not see Bruce's deed as murder. It is worth recalling at this point that the medieval Church was capable of a far more advanced analysis of homicide than the rough distinction between forethought felony and *chaude-melle* under review.[81]

The only detailed contemporary account of the killing of William, earl of Douglas, by King James II in February 1452, despite the king's special assurance and respite, is given in the Auchinleck Chronicle's distinctly breathless prose:

> That samyn zer Erll William of Douglas wes slane in the castell of striuling be king James the second that had the fyre mark in his face . . . and this samyn Monday [Douglas] passit to the castell and spak with the king that tuke richt wele with him be apperans and callit him on the morne to the dynere and to the supper and he come and dynit and sowpit and thai said thair was a band betuix the said erll of Douglas and the erll of Ross and the erll of Crawford and efter supper at sevyne houris the king then beand in the Inner chalmer and the said erll he chargit him to breke the forsaid band he said he mycht nocht nor wald nocht/ Than the king said fals tratour sen yow wil nocht I sall/ and stert sodanely till him with ane knyf and straik him at the colere and down in the body and thai sayd that Patrick Gray straik him nixt the king with ane pollax on the hed and strak out his braines and syne the gentills that war with the king gaf thaim Ilkane a straik or twa with knyffis . . .[82]

---

189–191. Cf M Penman, *Robert the Bruce King of the Scots* (2014) at 86–91; A Grant, "Murder will out: kingship, kinship and killing in medieval Scotland", in S Boardman and J Goodare (eds), *Kings, Lords and Men in Scotland and Britain, 1300–1625: Essays in Honour of Jenny Wormald* (2014) 193 at 220.

78 A Young, *Robert the Bruce's Rivals: The Comyns, 1212–1314* (1997) at 198.
79 A A M Duncan, *John Barbour: The Bruce* (1997) at 80n.
80 M Prestwich, *Edward I*, 2nd edn (1997) at 505.
81 Above, text accompanying notes 69–73.
82 The Auchinleck Chronicle is transcribed from the Asloan MS (NLS MS Acc. 4233) in C McGladdery, *James II* (2nd edn, 2015), appendix (quoted passage at 265).

Was this killing done with forethocht felony? Most modern historians, although referring to the deed as "murder", have concluded that it was not. In the first edition of her biography of James II, Christine McGladdery wrote of "the hot-blooded stabbing of the earl by the king", and concluded that "the murder of Douglas is unlikely to have been premeditated".[83] Annie Dunlop took the view in her biography of Bishop Kennedy that "No doubt James was carried away by a sudden outburst of unbridled fury".[84] McGladdery seems however to lean the other way on this question in her second edition, partly because the king stabbed the earl more than once.[85] In fact, the language of the Auchinleck Chronicle is that of suddenty or chaud-melle. The chronicler is clear that the slaughter of Douglas was not premeditated, using the words "the king ... stert sodanely till him with ane knyf". This statement should be compared with the passage from Sir Gilbert Hay already given, written less than five years after the killing of Douglas, which contrasts killing by forethocht felony with killing "quhen a man or beste is sudaynly sterte" and experiences "a sudayn hete of ire of vengeance".

Douglas's killing, therefore, was not murder. It was right, however, that the king should make amends, so far as possible, to the kindred of the man he had slain. He should not profit from his misdeed. This is why, I would suggest, King James entered into a bond of manrent with William Douglas's brother and successor, James 9th earl of Douglas, in January 1453, and personally petitioned the Pope to grant the necessary dispensation to allow the new earl to marry William's widow, the heiress Margaret of Galloway, and thereby acquire control over her lands.[86] This behaviour has surprised historians. Ranald Nicholson comments, "Even more astonishingly James bound himself to aid the earl to consolidate his territorial power by furthering a marriage betwixt Earl James and the latter's sister-in-law";[87] while in her first edition McGladdery followed Dunlop in considering that James's promotion of the marriage is proof of his impotence and the insecurity of his position.[88] On the contrary, the king's promotion of the marriage should be

---

83  C McGladdery, *James II* (1st edn, 1990) at 69.
84  A I Dunlop, *The Life and Times of James Kennedy Bishop of St Andrews* (1950) at 133.
85  McGladdery, *James II* (n 82) at 116–117. She also appears persuaded by Grant's counter (above n 74) to the argument presented in the original version of this paper. Cf A R Borthwick and H L MacQueen, *Law, Lordship and Tenure: The Fall of the Black Douglases*, ch 3 (forthcoming).
86  R Nicholson, *Scotland: The Later Middle Ages* (1974) at 365; McGladdery, *James II* (n 79) at 140.
87  Nicholson, *Scotland* (n 86) at 365.
88  McGladdery, *James II* (n 83) at 83; Dunlop, *Bishop Kennedy* (n 84) at 43. McGladdery, *James II* (n 82) at 140–141, again takes a different view, this time following M Brown's analysis in "The

seen above all as a fitting act of expiation, a just and necessary assythment for the slaughter of Earl William in hot blood, done to prevent further feud.[89]

What of the terms of art used in the passage from Hay which conform so closely to those used in Scots law? What terms do they translate or mirror in the original French of Honoré Bonet, composed some seventy years before? Might the original and the translation, taken together, throw some light on the comparative legal history of homicide? The answer to these questions came as a surprise. There is no parallel passage in Honoré Bonet.[90] The entire passage given in italics earlier in this paper is an interpolation. Why?

One can only speculate. Hay's patron, as he tells us, was that great survivor of Scottish fifteenth-century politics, William Sinclair, earl of Orkney (later earl of Caithness) and lord of Roslin. The interpolated passage which echoes so closely the slaughter of the earl of Douglas by the king, must, at the very least, have stirred memories of that death in Hay's patron. Is there any reason to suppose that William Sinclair, earl of Orkney, had a particular interest in the fate of the Douglases? Every reason, it transpires. His relationship to the Douglas kin could not have been closer: his mother was a Black Douglas; his first wife was a Black Douglas; and his sister was married to a Black Douglas. Through his first wife, Elizabeth, the earl of Orkney was the uncle of William 6th earl of Douglas and of David his brother, who were both executed judicially after "the Black Dinner" at Edinburgh Castle in 1440. He was uncle also, through his sister Beatrice, of William 8th earl of Douglas, killed by King James at Stirling.[91] The earl of Orkney was also, like most of the higher nobility, a close cousin of the king, being a great grandson of Robert II. He is likely to have reflected more than most on the events of that February day in 1452 when the king "stert sodaynly" towards the earl of Douglas with a knife. Is it not likely that William earl of Orkney may have had a hand in this interpolation?

Although I have argued that the expression "forethocht felony", or "malice aforethought", has quite definite overtones of premeditation in the medieval law, the final word must be one of caution. It would be a mistake to attach

---

Lanark Bond", in Boardman and Goodare (eds), *Kings, Lords and Men* (n 76) at 227. Once more, cf Borthwick and MacQueen, *Law, Lordship and Tenure* (n 82), ch 3.

89 It does not appear that this precedent for marrying a brother's widow was cited in the case of Henry VIII and Catherine of Aragon.
90 There is no parallel in Nys's standard edition (n 37), nor, I suspect, in any manuscript of the original. I am assured by Sally Mapstone, who has made a close study of Hay's work, that this is far from the only occasion on which Hay departs from Bonet's original text.
91 For these relationships, which are uncontroverted, see M Brown, *The Black Douglases* (1998) at 98, 228 (genealogical tables).

too strict or precise a meaning to the various terms discussed: terms such as "casual", "deliberate" and "malice aforethought". These terms all have several shades of meaning, some of which overlap. Which precise nuance is to be attached will depend on circumstance, and the circumstances of homicide are infinitely varied. The perception of what constitutes the most heinous form of homicide, to which the name "murder" can properly be applied, varies from generation to generation. If a study of the historical background suggests anything, it is that there is little merit in attempting too precise a definition of murder, particularly where a jury is concerned. Gerald Gordon has noted for modern Scots law that there is "no academically satisfactory definition of murder", "nothing to delimit murder clearly from culpable homicide".[92] The same, apparently, might be said of modern English law. There the *mens rea* of murder is "malice aforethought"; this, of course, being now a technical term which need no longer infer either real malice or premeditation. Murder is an unlawful killing with malice aforethought. Manslaughter is an unlawful killing without malice aforethought.[93] There is no reason to believe that medieval definitions were any more clear cut than that. It is as well that the jury should have considerable scope. The rise in convictions for murder as against culpable homicide or manslaughter after the abolition of capital punishment in 1965 tells its own story.

---

92 Gordon, *Criminal Law* (n 69) para 23–19. In the 4th edition (above n 69), see para 30.21. On 27 May 2021 the Scottish Law Commission published its Discussion Paper No 172 on the Mental Element in Homicide, looking to reform the law as it stands following the cases of *Petto v HM Advocate* 2012 JC 105 and *Drury v HM Advocate* 2001 SLT 1013.
93 See, for example, J C Smith, B Hogan and D Ormerod, *Criminal Law*, 15th edn (2020) at 512–514.

# 12 Juridical Acts Made in Contemplation of Death*

When Scotland joined with England in 1707 to form the United Kingdom of Great Britain the independent status of Scots law was preserved, and Scots law remains today distinct from English law, a separate system in international law. This *rapport* considers the topic of *l'acte à cause de mort* (juridical acts made in contemplation of death) in the law of Scotland over a period of four hundred years: from the Scottish Reformation in 1559–1560 until the coming into force of the Succession (Scotland) Act in September 1964.

## A. INTRODUCTORY – MEDIEVAL SCOTS LAW

Scots law has a long continuous history which extends back to a remote past. Part of the original inheritance was Celtic and part Germanic. However, the main influences in the forging of a distinctively Scottish system of law in the Middle Ages and beyond were the Feudal law (or feudal custom) in its Anglo-Norman guise, and the Canon law. The medieval law on succession was largely determined, as regards land or "heritage", by feudal custom, interpreted by the king's court and amended by the Scottish Parliament, and, as regards moveable property, by the Canon law. Although Anglo-Norman influence was particularly marked in questions of heritage, it was not entirely absent in the law of moveables. In Scotland, as in England, the term "common law" came to be applied to the emerging national law.[1]

There was no clear break with the Celtic past, and survivals from Celtic law are to be found into the later Middle Ages and beyond. Two relevant to the theme of *l'acte à cause de mort* may be briefly mentioned. Niall, earl of the then Gaelic-speaking area of Carrick in south-west Scotland, died in 1256, leaving no sons. His lands and his comital title passed through his daughter Marjory to his grandson Robert Bruce, later king of Scots

---

* Originally published as "Juridical acts made in contemplation of death in the law of Scotland", in *Actes à Cause de Mort; Acts of Last Will* (Jean Bodin Society, 1993) 159–170.
1 See, for example, Sellar, "Common law".

(1306–29). However, Gaelic society was strongly agnatic, and before he died Niall made a grant of the office of *caput progeniei* or "*kenkynolle*" (Gaelic *cenn cineoil*), that is, head of his kin, to his first cousin, Roland of Carrick. This grant received royal confirmation on several occasions in the fourteenth and fifteenth centuries.[2] Thus it seems that the chief of a kindred had the right, no doubt with due consents, to nominate his successor. Even today, the Lyon Court, which has jurisdiction in matters of heraldry and genealogy in Scotland, accepts – although perhaps controversially – that the chief of a name is entitled to nominate his successor.[3]

Another survival was the taking of "calp". In the Highlands and Islands of Scotland it was the custom when a man died to tender his best animal – ox, or horse, or cow – to the chief of his name in token of lordship. This exaction was known as calp (from the Gaelic word *colpthach* – a young heifer).[4] It was possible to indicate a change of allegiance by contracting *inter vivos* to whom calp should be paid on death. This could be done both by individuals and by heads of families contracting on behalf of their surname. Various sixteenth-century contracts of this description survive, as for example that entered into in 1591 between Alexander MacGregor of Glenstrae and Aulay MacAulay of Ardincaple by which the latter promised that on his death a calp would be payable to the former ("I, the said Awlay, grantis me to gyff to the said Alexander ane calpe at the deceiss of me") as a sign and token that the MacAulays were believed to descend from a cadet branch of MacGregor's house.[5] The custom of taking calp was abolished by Act of the Scots Parliament in 1617.[6]

With the advent of feudalism from the beginning of the twelfth century, the transmission of land or heritage was increasingly controlled by feudal custom approved and sanctioned by the king's court. The common form of feudal grant was to the grantee, his heirs and assignees (*heredibus et assignatis*), and, in the standard case, land would descend on death according to

---

2 *RMS* vol 1, nos 508, 509; vol 2, nos 379, 414. See further three articles by H L MacQueen, "The laws of Galloway: a preliminary survey", in R D Oram and G P Stell (eds), *Galloway: Land and Lordship* (1991) 131; "The kin of Kennedy, 'kenkynnol' and the common law", in A Grant and K J Stringer (eds), *Medieval Scotland: Crown, Lordship and Community – Essays Presented to G W S Barrow* (1993) 274; and "The laws of Galloway revisited", in M Ansell, R Black and E J Cowan (eds), *Galloway: Gaelic's Lost Province* (forthcoming).
3 *Maclean of Ardgour v Maclean* 1941 SC 613, explained in *Captain Alwyne Farquharson of Invercauld* 1950 SLT (Lyon Ct) 13. See further *SME* Courts and Competency Reissue (2016) para 277.
4 Skene, *DVS*, sv "Cavpes".
5 W Fraser, *Chiefs of Colquhoun* (1869) vol 2, 112–113.
6 *RPS* 1617/5/35.

the rules of intestate succession. By the end of the thirteenth century these rules were well understood and were comparable to those which obtained under contemporary English law: within any given degree males were preferred to females; among males the eldest succeeded to the whole inheritance as "heir-at-law"; if the succession opened to females they partitioned the inheritance equally between them as "heirs-portioners"; and at all levels of succession the right of representation to both male and female heirs was recognised. Certain "legal rights" were exigible from heritage, again comparable to English law: the widow had right to her "terce" (*anglicé* "dower") – the liferent of a third part of her deceased husband's heritage; and the widower had right to "courtesy" (*curialitas Scotie*) – the liferent of the whole of his deceased wife's heritage. Courtesy, however, was only exigible where a child had been born of the marriage, alive and heard to cry.[7]

At first it may have been possible to alter the succession to heritage by will, but, if so, this soon ceased to be the case. Even alienation of land *inter vivos* was subject to strict controls. One device which became increasingly popular in the later Middle Ages was the entail, or, in Scots dialect, "tailzie" – from the French *tailler*, to cut; signifying that the succession had been cut off from its natural course and diverted into other channels. This was effected by documents drawn up *inter vivos*, and normally required the consent of the feudal superior. A favourite form of entail was one which limited the succession to heirs-male, excluding female heirs and their descendants from the succession. Such a scheme accorded well with the strongly agnatic bias of Gaelic society. An interesting variant was the entail in favour of a particular "name", an early example of which is the grant of land in 1358 by King David II to Gillespic Campbell *tenendas et habendas eidem Gillaspic heredibus suis et suis assignatis cognomen de Cambell habentibus*.[8] Another regular form of entail was one by which succession was limited to the heirs of the grantee's own body – *heredibus suis de corpore suo legitime procreandis*.[9]

Another scheme which might be said to have been entered into in contemplation of death was one whereby a landowner passed on the title to his lands to another, typically his eldest son, by process of resignation and

---

7 *ISLH*, chs 9 and 16; on courtesy see also ch 14 below.
8 *RRS* vol 6, no 166.
9 For entails in Scots law generally see *ISLH* at 177ff; C D'O Farran, *The Principles of Scots and English Land Law* (1958) Part II; C F Kolbert and N A M Mackay, *History of Scots and English Land Law* (1977), chs 17, 20 and 21; and W M Gordon, *Scottish Land Law* (1989) ch 18. Farran, Kolbert & Mackay, and also A W B Simpson, "Entails and perpetuities", 1979 *JR* 1, compare Scots and English law. The rise of the Scottish tailzie is considered by A A M Duncan in his introduction to *RRS* vol 5 at 62–69.

regrant, while reserving to himself a liferent and many of the rights of ownership. In technical parlance he divested himself of the fee (*feodum*) while retaining the franktenement (*liberum tenementum*). Such devices are first found in the fourteenth century and became increasingly popular. By this means the succession to the lands was secured.[10]

In the developed medieval law, alteration to the succession to land or heritage was effected not by *mortis causa* deed, but by arrangements entered into *inter vivos*. Many such arrangements, however, may reasonably be described as having being made in contemplation of death. The successor to heritage was regarded as the "heir" par excellence, the term applied by the later Scots law to the successor to heritage on intestacy being "heir-at-law".

The position as regards succession to moveables was quite different. From the late twelfth century moveable succession in Scotland, as in many other European countries, lay within the province of the Church and was governed by ecclesiastical law. Moveables could be left by will or testament, and intestacy was strongly discouraged. The faithful were particularly encouraged to make gifts for pious uses. The administration of the moveable estate lay in the hands of the "executor" – the "executor-nominate" in the case of testacy, and the "executor-dative" where the deceased died intestate. The executor was entitled to a share of the estate and was responsible to the Church courts for its administration.[11]

Certain "legal rights" were exigible from the moveable estate. As was the case with heritage, these were comparable to similar rights allowed under medieval English law. The Scottish text *Regiam Majestatem* (c 1318) mirrored the earlier English *Glanvill* in this regard: where the deceased died survived by a widow and children, the widow was entitled to a third part of the moveable estate as her *jus relictae*, and the children were likewise entitled to a third part divided equally between them as "bairns' part" (later termed *legitim*); if there were no children the widow took a half; similarly if there was no surviving spouse the children took a half. These "legal rights" could not be defeated by testament.[12]

---

10  T M Cooper, "Freehold in Scots law" (1945) 57 *JR* 1; W C Dickinson, "Freehold in Scots law" (1945) 57 *JR* 135.
11  A E Anton, "Medieval Scots executors and the courts spiritual" (1955) 67 *JR* 129.
12  *ISLH* at 113, 212; Sellar, "Common law" at 91.

## B. THE LAW OF SCOTLAND: 1559–1964

### (1) Historical summary[13]

Shortly after the Scottish Reformation in 1559–60 the Church courts lost their jurisdiction over moveable succession to newly established "commissary courts". The principal commissary court of Edinburgh was established in 1564, and, although at first there was some continuity of personnel with the pre-Reformation courts, the new courts where soon staffed by laymen rather than by churchmen. Appeal ran from the commissary courts to the Court of Session.[14] This was in contrast to the situation in England where ecclesiastical courts continued to exercise extensive jurisdiction until 1857, although after the Reformation these were courts of the Church of England rather than of the Church of Rome.

Nevertheless, the old distinction between heritable and moveable succession, between the "heir" par excellence and the "executor", continued little changed for many hundreds of years. Even after commissary jurisdiction merged in the course of the nineteenth century with that of the sheriff court and Court of Session the distinction continued. Over the centuries a number of Acts, first of the Scots and later of the United Kingdom Parliament, made changes in the law, and removed some anomalies and anachronisms. An important change took place in 1868, when it at last became competent for a landowner to settle the succession to his heritage by testamentary or *mortis causa* deeds or writings.[15] Until then a testamentary bequest of heritage had continued to be invalid, although various devices had developed to circumvent this prohibition.[16] However, it was not until the passing of the Succession (Scotland) Act in 1964 that the law was radically reformed. The 1964 Act abolished the centuries-old distinction between heritable and moveable succession, between heir and executor, and introduced a unitary law of succession, closely modelled on the former rules of moveable succession. Since 1964 the executor has been responsible for the ingathering and administration of the whole estate of the deceased, both heritable and moveable.

---

13 See also Appendix – Select Table of Events.
14 See ch 1 text accompanying nn 64 and 65.
15 Titles to Land Consolidation (Scotland) Act 1868 s 20.
16 See text accompanying n 42 below.

## (2) The reasons behind juridical acts made in contemplation of death

The reasons for taking legal action to control the destination of property after death in Scots law appear to have been familiar and conventional: the repayment of debts and obligations, recompense for services rendered, legacies to friends and relatives, gifts to charities, donations for religious purposes and the like (although in Presbyterian Scotland this last was not of such importance as in Catholic countries). Sometimes a testator sought to preserve his name or that of his family by founding a school or an institution to be named after him, or by directing the erection of an elaborate funerary monument.

A celebrated example of this last purpose is provided by the last will of John Stuart M'Caig, who died in 1902. M'Caig directed the erection on the Stuart M'Caig Tower – a circular construction which he himself had built in a prominent position overlooking the town of Oban in Argyll – of

> . . . large Figures of all my five brothers and of myself namely Duncan Dugald Donald Peter and of my father Malcolm and of my mother Margret and of my sisters Jean Catherine Margaret and Ann and that these Statues be modelled after photographs. And where these may not be available that the Statues may have a family likeness to my own photograph . . .

The testator's brother Peter had died in infancy. He further directed that artistic towers should be built at prominent points on his lands. The Court of Session struck down both bequests on the grounds that they were neither charitable, nor educational, and conferred no beneficial interest on anyone.[17] Remarkably, M'Caig's sister Catherine, who died in 1913, left a bequest in very similar terms directing the erection of bronze statues of her parents and their nine children within the Stuart M'Caig Tower. This too was struck down.[18] Despite the failure of these bequests the M'Caigs were successful in preserving their name for posterity: the Stuart M'Caig Tower still dominates Oban and is universally known as M'Caig's Folly!

In earlier centuries, the preservation of the family name was an overriding consideration. The practice of limiting the succession to heritage to those bearing a particular surname by means of an entail or special destina-

---

17 *M'Caig v University of Glasgow* 1907 SC 231. See also for similarly unenforceable bequests *Aitken's Trustees v Aitken* 1927 SC 374 (erection of massive bronze equestrian statue in Musselburgh in memory of testator and ancestors); *Lindsay's Executor v Forsyth* 1940 SC 568 (weekly supply of fresh flowers at testator's grave).

18 *M'Caig's Trs v Lismore United Free Kirk Session* 1915 SC 426.

tion has already been noted. One destination of lands, drawn up originally in 1632, when the clan system was still in full vigour, gave rise to later trouble. The destination was in favour of "Donald MacGilliephadrick, his airs-mail and assignees, of the clan of Clan Chattan allenarly [only]". Over 200 years later questions arose as to the succession, and the Court of Session decided after protracted litigation that the destination was too vague, and that the law knew not the Clan Chattan. "A description sufficient for being hanged or shot," remarked Lord Deas, referring to former penal statutes, "is not necessarily a sufficient description for being served heir of destination to an estate."[19]

Concern to preserve the name, however, was not confined to the clannish Highlands. The leading institutional writer on Scots law, Lord Stair, wrote in 1681 that "The expediency of tailzies is the same with primogeniture, to preserve the memory and dignity of families."[20] More recently, when comparing the Scottish entail with the English strict settlement, Professor Brian Simpson was struck by the predominance of considerations of family and name in the Scottish institution.[21] In 1685 the means of setting up a strict and binding entail were laid down by statute in the Entail Act, and it was only by stages and over centuries that it became possible to "loosen the fetters of the entail". The further creation of new entails was finally prohibited by the Entail (Scotland) Act of 1914, but there must still be a number of entails in force.[22] Another device used to perpetuate the family name, and one which still remains competent, was to attach a "name and arms clause" to the inheritance of property: the insertion of such a clause made succession conditional on the assumption of the name and coat of arms of the family in question.[23] As noted above, the Lyon Court still recognises the right of the chief of a name to nominate a successor.[24]

---

19 *MacGillivary v Souter* (1862) 24 D 759 at 772–773.
20 Stair, *Inst*, 3.4.33 (at 679).
21 Simpson (n 9) at 10–20.
22 For authorities see n 9.
23 eg *Munro-Lucas-Tooth* 1965 SLT (Lyon Court) 2.
24 See above n 3.

## (3) Scope of, and limitations on, juridical acts made in contemplation of death

### (a) Incorporeal property rights

Scots law recognises both corporeal and incorporeal property rights. Incorporeal heritable rights include the right to a title (such as "earl" or "duke") and to a coat of arms. Such rights descended according to the rules of intestate heritable succession; indeed, they still do, forming an exception to the scheme of unitary succession laid down by the Succession (Scotland) Act 1964.[25] In this connection the device of including a "name and arms clause" in a deed, and the possibility of naming a successor as head of a "name" or family, have already been mentioned.[26] Incorporeal moveable rights include the right to intellectual property. However, the vast majority of juridical acts made in contemplation of death in the period under review concerned corporeal property.

### (b) Corporeal heritable rights

In the period up to 1964 land in Scotland was held in feudal form either immediately or mediately of the Crown.[27] The effective owner of the land (the tenant at the bottom of the feudal chain) was termed the "vassal"; those above him were termed "superiors", including "mid-superiors" and "over-superiors". The vassal had the right of *dominium utile* over the land, while the right of the superior was termed *dominium directum*. Both *dominium utile* and *dominium directum* could be the object of dispositions of land made with a view to altering the succession on death. In the case of the *dominium utile* it was not unusual to grant a life interest ("liferent", cf usufruct) over the *dominium utile* to one party and a right of property ("fee") to another. The liferenter enjoyed the property while he or she lived but could not alienate any part of it or alter the succession. By the nineteenth century it was common to set up a trust and appoint trustees to hold property on behalf of both liferenter and fiar. Leasehold rights (or "tacks" of land) having some years still to run could also be the object of juridical acts.

---

25 1964 Act s 37(1); also Law Reform (Parent and Child) (Scotland) Act 1986 s 9(1)(c); *Baronetcy of Pringle of Stichill* 2016 SC (PC) 1 (discussed by C Agnew and G Black, "The significance of status and genetics in succession to titles, honours, dignities and coats of arms: making the case for reform" (2018) 77 *Cambridge LJ* 321).

26 See above sections A (text accompanying nn 2–10) and B(2).

27 This continued to be the position until the Abolition of Feudal Tenure etc (Scotland) Act 2000 came into force on 28 November 2004.

## (c) Corporeal moveable rights

In the case of moveables a last will would normally contemplate the transmission of a full right of property, although there might, of course, be conditions attached to acceptance.[28] Scots law recognised the doctrine of *legatum rei alienae*: if a testator bequeathed something knowing that it was not his, it was not to be presumed that he did not intend to give, and so the executor was required to purchase the object in question or, if this proved impossible, to pay its value to the beneficiary; if, on the other hand, the testator believed mistakenly that the object was his, the legacy failed.[29]

## (d) Limitations on testing on heritage

As already noted, by the common law of Scotland it was not competent to settle the succession to land by testamentary or *mortis causa* deeds or writings; and this remained the rule until altered by statute in 1868.[30] However, it gradually became possible to circumvent this prohibition by means of various forms or devices which enabled the owner of land, in practice, to determine the succession at his death.[31] Entails and special destinations also, in effect, circumvented the prohibition. Another type of limitation which affected the transmission of heritable property arose from the law of "deathbed", discussed below.[32]

## (e) Limitations arising from legal rights

The "legal rights" existing at common law in medieval times exigible from both movables and heritage in favour of a surviving spouse and children have already been noted: the widower's "courtesy" and the widow's "terce" from the heritable estate; and the widow's *jus relictae* and the surviving children's *legitim* or "bairns' part" from the moveable estate.[33] These rights continued to be recognised throughout the period under review and constituted limitations on the power of disposal. One peculiarity was that, until 1855, a widow was only entitled to her *jus relictae* if the marriage had lasted for at least a year and a day, or a living child had been born. The legal rights recognised at common law were added to by the Married Women's Property (Scotland)

---

28  See further below section B(4)(d).
29  Erskine, *Inst*, 3.9.10; *Meeres* v *Dowell's Executor* 1923 SLT 184.
30  Above, n 15.
31  Below, section B(4)(c).
32  See section B(5) below.
33  See text accompanying nn 7 and 12 above.

Act 1881, which allowed the widower to claim *jus relicti* out of the moveable estate, corresponding to the widow's *jus relictae*.[34] The same Act extended the children's right to *legitim*, previously restricted to the father's estate, to the mother's estate also (although representation in *legitim*, allowing grandchildren to represent a predeceasing parent, was not permitted until 1964).[35] These legal rights could not be defeated by will. Thus, the testator had power of disposal over that portion of his movable property only which remained after legal rights had been claimed. This remaining portion was known, therefore, as the "dead's part". The legal rights of terce and courtesy in heritage were abolished in 1964 by the Succession (Scotland) Act, but the rights of *jus relicti*, *jus relictae* and *legitim* in moveables remain.

### (f) Limitations on accumulations of income and successive liferents

Unlike English law, Scots law has never operated a general rule against the settlement of land in perpetuity, although the legislation permitting a breach of entail and, eventually, prohibiting the creation of new entails goes some way towards achieving this end. However, the Accumulations Act of 1800 (otherwise known as "the Thellusson Act"), which imposed restrictions on the accumulation of income, applied equally in England and Scotland. The Act introduced four periods beyond which accumulation was prohibited: (1) the life of the grantor of the deed; (2) a term of twenty-one years from the death of the grantor; (3) the duration of the minority or minorities of any person or persons living or *in utero* at the death of the grantor; and (4) the duration of the minority or minorities of any person or persons who, under the terms of the deed directing accumulation would for the time being, if of full age, be entitled to the rents or income directed to be accumulated. Periods (2), (3) and (4) constituted limitations on disposal made in contemplation of death. These prohibitions give rise to much confusion and generated much litigation.[36] Accumulations struck down as illegal fell into intestacy.

Similar restrictions on the constitution of liferents were introduced by statute in the nineteenth century. It became competent to constitute a liferent interest over either heritable or moveable property in favour only of a person in life at the date of the deed constituting or reserving the liferent.[37]

---

34 Married Women's Property (Scotland) Act 1881 s 6.
35 1881 Act s 7.
36 See R Burgess, *Perpetuities in Scots Law* (SS vol 31, 1979). Reform is proposed by the Scottish Law Commission in *Report on Trust Law* (Scot Law Com No 239, 2014) ch 18.
37 Entail Amendment Act 1848 s 48; Entail Amendment (Scotland) Act 1868 s 17, repealed and re-enacted by the Trusts (Scotland) Act 1921 s 9.

*(g) Negative limitations*

The concept of civil death may be regarded as a negative limitation. After the Reformation there is little evidence in Scots law for the operation of civil death as a consequence of entering a monastery or religious order. Civil death was, however, recognised in other situations. Banishment for life gave rise to civil death.[38] So did a sentence of outlawry, that is, condemnation as a rebel. Remarkably, the status of outlawry continued to be recognised by Scots law until 1949 – although largely as an anachronistic legal technicality – when it was abolished by the Criminal Justice Act of that year.[39] Latterly, outlawry was the consequence of a sentence of "fugitation" pronounced by the High Court of Justiciary against an accused for failing to obey a citation to appear. Formerly outlawry might also arise as a consequence of debt. Originally an outlaw might be killed with impunity as *caput lupinum* (wolf's head), but an Act of 1612 forbade this when an action for debt lay behind the outlawry.[40] The effect of civil death was discussed in the case of *Macrae* in 1836 when it was decided that an outlaw retained the power to dispose of his property in so far as this was not to the prejudice of those with an interest in forfeiture arising as a consequence of outlawry.[41]

## (4) Form and character of juridical acts made in contemplation of death

*(a) Unilateral, bilateral and multilateral*

Juridical acts determining the succession to both heritable and moveable property were overwhelmingly unilateral. However, bilateral acts were competent, and mutual wills by husband and wife were not uncommon. Notoriously, these gave rise to difficulties of interpretation, particularly on the matter of revocability, given that the law recognised as binding an agreement not to alter the terms of a *mortis causa* disposition of property.[42] *Mutatis mutandis*, the same was true of bilateral acts concerning the disposition of heritage. Marriage contracts entered into before or after matrimony

---

38 *Farquhar* (1753) Mor 4669.
39 Criminal Justice (Scotland) Act 1949 s 15(2).
40 *RPS* 1612/10/10.
41 *Macrae* (1836) 15 S 54. The topic of outlawry and its consequences is a complex one and little discussed in Scots law. See J Chisholm (ed), *Green's Encylopaedia of the Laws of Scotland* (1897) sv "Death", "Denunciation", "Fugitation", "Horning" and "Outlawry".
42 See for example *Duthie v Keir's Executor* 1930 SC 645; *Saxby v Saxby's Executors* 1952 SC 352.

were once very common, and frequently contained provisions made in contemplation of death.

Acts of Parliament determining the succession to the throne, although hardly comparable to the standard unilateral act, might be counted multilateral acts made in contemplation of death. The Scots Parliament settled the succession to the throne on a number of occasions by entail or "tailzie": for example, in 1284, 1318 and 1373.[43] The English Act of Settlement of 1701 settling the crown on the Electress Sophia of Hanover and her Protestant heirs was adopted by Article II of the Act of Union with England in 1707.

Further examples of multilateral acts made in order to regulate the succession to office can be found in the practice whereby the gentleman of a particular "name" or clan might enter into a formal agreement as to the chiefship of the clan. Thus a Bond of Union recognising a chief was agreed between the various branches of the Clan Chattan in 1609;[44] and the leading men of the surname of MacGregor met to acknowledge a chief in 1714 and again in 1774.[45]

*(b) Written or oral?*

In general any juridical act intended to alter the succession to property after death had to be expressed in writing. *Donationes mortis causa,* however constituted a partial exception to this general rule. The doctrine was recognised on the analogy of the Civil law. The institutional writer Bankton wrote that donations *mortis causa* "savour much indeed of legacies".[46] For such donations to be effective, however, in the later law at least, writing was not essential. Lord President Inglis defined *donatio mortis causa* in Scots law as

> a conveyance of an immoveable or incorporeal right, or a transference of moveables or money by delivery, so that the property is immediately transferred to the grantee, upon the condition that he shall hold for the grantor so long as he lives, subject to his power of revocation, and, failing such revocation, then for the grantee on the death of the grantor.[47]

Another exception to the requirement of writing was the recognition as valid of oral or "nuncupative" legacies up to the value of £100 Scots (£8.33

---

43 *APS* vol 1 at 424; *RPS* 1318/30, 1373/3.
44 C Fraser-Mackintosh, *Minor Septs of Clan Chattan* (1898) at 188–191; and see above text accompanying n 19.
45 W R Kermack, *The Clan MacGregor* (1963) 28–31.
46 Bankton, *Inst*, 1.9.16. Donation *mortis causa* was abolished by the Succession (Scotland) Act 2016 s 25(1).
47 *Morris v Riddick* (1867) 5 M 1036 at 1041.

sterling).⁴⁸ A further exception lay in the device of the "trust". Trusts were normally constituted in writing, but not invariably so; although by the Blank Bonds and Trusts Act 1696 proof of trust was restricted to the writ, or to the judicial oath, of the alleged trustee.⁴⁹

Documents conveying heritage were subject to requirements of form prescribed by a series of statutes from 1540. The deed needed to be subscribed at the end by the grantor before two witnesses. Where the deed had a number of pages "bookwise", that is, in modern form as opposed to a continuing roll, each separate page required to be subscribed by the grantor. Wills and testaments were subject to these requirements of form, and had, therefore, to be subscribed and attested. There was, however, an important exception in favour of holograph writing, which was admitted as valid so long as subscribed. This privilege was further extended to deeds or wills to which the grantor or testator appended the words "adopted as holograph" in his own handwriting above his signature. Latterly it was even accepted that a typewritten testamentary writing might count as holograph so long as it was typed by the grantor, that being his customary method of writing, and contained a clause *in gremio* that it had been typed by him.⁵⁰ Holograph wills gave rise to much litigation. Where a testator was blind or unable to write the law made special provision for "notarial" execution. A will could be executed notarially by a notary public – latterly by any qualified solicitor – by a justice of the peace, or by a parish minister (that is, a minister of the Church of Scotland) acting within his parish.

Finally, the general rule was that no particular words of style need be used to make a testamentary bequest effective provided the intention was clear. A partial exception to this was the rule which developed late, and was only abolished in 1874, that it was necessary to use the word "dispone" to render a disposition of heritage effective.⁵¹

*(c) Revocable or irrevocable?*

Wills were, in principle, revocable and ambulatory. It was possible, however, to enter into a binding contract not to alter a testamentary provision.

---

48 E.g. *Kelly v Kelly* (1861) 23 D 703. The rule was abolished by the Requirements of Writing (Scotland) Act 1995.
49 *RPS* 1696/9/143. This too was abolished by the 1995 Act.
50 *M'Beath's Trs v M'Beath* 1935 SC 471; *Chisholm v Chisholm* 1949 SC 434.
51 Conveyancing (Scotland) Act 1874 s 27; and see *ISLH* at 215–216 and the case of *Kirkpatrick v Kirkpatrick's Trustees* (1874) 1 R (HL) 37.

This gave rise to problems in relation to mutual wills, as already noted.[52] Normally revocation was a matter for the testator. Exceptionally, the courts might hold a last will to have been revoked by the subsequent birth of a child to the testator, through the operation of the Roman law *conditio si testator sine liberis decesserit*, a version of which was received in Scotland.[53]

The prohibition on *mortis causa* dispositions or settlements of heritage before 1868 has already been noted.[54] It was, however, possible to convey heritage, effectively in anticipation of death, by *de praesenti* deed. Such deeds would not become effective until delivery, at which point they became irrevocable. Later it became permissible to include within the deed a clause allowing revocation notwithstanding delivery. Eventually even the requirement of delivery was dropped. It thus became possible in practice, although not – until 1868 – in theory, to make a *mortis causa* disposition of heritage which was both revocable and ambulatory. It became commonplace to execute a "Trust Disposition and Settlement" to settle the succession to heritage and circumvent the archaic prohibition on *mortis causa* deeds.[55] The trust disposition and settlement remains in regular use in modern Scots law, but few contemporary conveyancers, I suspect, are aware of its origin.

### (d) Gratuitous or conditional?

Conditions might be attached to gifts. Such conditions generated a large volume of case law distinguishing between various types of conditions and declaring some void for reasons including uncertainty and public policy, the case of *M'Caig's Trustees* discussed above being a leading example.[56] If the condition failed it was treated as *pro non scripto*, and the legacy or bequest took effect unconditionally.

---

52 See section B(4)(a) above.
53 See further ch 13 below. The *conditio si testator sine liberis decesserit* was abolished and replaced by the Succession (Scotland) Act 2016 ss 6 and 29.
54 See section B(3)(d) above.
55 See the article on Succession in Chisholm (ed), *Green's Encyclopaedia* (n 40); and *ISLH* at 213–214.
56 See section B(2) above.

## (5) Juridical acts in contemplation of death: by whom competent?

"The power of testing is competent to all persons who have the use of reason," wrote Lord Stair in *his Institutions* (1681), "but not to pupils, idiots, furious persons in their furiosity: neither to bastards not having lawful issue."[57] With the exception of the last category, this remained broadly true until the passage of the Age of Legal Capacity (Scotland) Act 1991. Pupils – females under the age of 12 and males under the age of 14 – did not have the capacity to make a will. Minors – females aged 12 to 21 and males aged 14 to 21 in the period under review – did have the necessary capacity.[58] Incapacity arising from insanity is regarded as a question of degree and circumstances; it is accepted that even the insane may have lucid intervals in which they have the capacity to test.[59] The same reasoning applies to senility or other weakness of mind (but see the discussion of "deathbed" below). The disabilities affecting the illegitimate have gradually been relaxed. In this context the important change came with the Bastards (Scotland) Act 1836, which gave illegitimate persons full power to test.[60]

There formerly existed a complicated law of "deathbed" which affected dispositions of heritage. "Dispositions, obligations, or contracts of any heritable right, on death bed," wrote Stair, "are null and reducible, in so far as may prejudge the heir."[61] It was crucial that a deed conveying heritage should have been executed *in legitimam potestatem* or, as it was put *"in liege poustie"*: that is, when the grantor was fully *compos mentis*. Otherwise the deed could be reduced on the ground of deathbed (*ex capite lecti*). By an Act of 1696 there was a presumption that a grant was not *in liege poustie* if it had been executed within 60 days of death; but the presumption could be elided if the deceased had been to kirk (church) or market – both being public places – during this period.[62] There were many hard cases where dying men struggled vainly to give the appearance of health and vitality on the threshold of the grave. The law of deathbed was finally abolished in 1871.

---

57 Stair, *Inst*, 3.8.37.
58 The Age of Majority (Scotland) Act 1969 reduced the age of majority from 21 to 18; but see now Age of Legal Capacity (Scotland) Act 1991 making it 16.
59 *Nisbet's Trustees v Nisbet* (1871) 9 M 937.
60 The status of bastardy was abolished by the Law Reform (Parent and Child) (Scotland) Act 1986.
61 Stair, *Inst*, 3.4.26.
62 *RPS* 1696/9/56.

## APPENDIX

### Select table of events

| | |
|---|---|
| 1559–60 | The Scottish Reformation. |
| 1564 | Commissary court of Edinburgh established. |
| 1681 | Stair's *Institutions of the Law of Scotland*. |
| 1685 | Entail Act: establishment of the strict entail. |
| 1770 | "Montgomery Act": loosens some of the "fetters" of the entail. |
| 1823 | Abolition of inferior commissary courts. |
| 1836 | End of Edinburgh commissary court. |
| 1836 | Bastards (Scotland) Act: bastards given full power to test. |
| 1848 | "Rutherfurd Act": introduction of procedure for disentail. |
| 1855 | Moveable Succession (Scotland) Act: affects "legal rights". |
| 1868 | Titles to Land Consolidation (S) Act: power to test on heritage. |
| 1871 | Law of Deathbed Abolition (Scotland) Act. |
| 1874 | Conveyancing (Scotland) Act: use of the word "dispone" no longer necessary in dispositions of heritage. |
| 1881 | Married Women's Property (Scotland) Act: widower's right to *jus relicti* introduced; children given right to *legitim* in mother's estate. |
| 1914 | Entail (Scotland) Act: further creation of strict entails prohibited. |
| 1964 | Succession (Scotland) Act: assimilation of heritable and moveable succession; "legal rights" of terce and courtesy abolished; representation in *legitim* allowed. |
| 2016 | Succession (Scotland) Act: donation *mortis causa* abolished; *conditio si testator sine liberis decesserit* abolished and replaced. |

# 13 Succession Law*

## A. INTRODUCTION

This chapter aims to provide a historical context for the present law by setting out the main outlines of the law of succession in Scotland before the ground-breaking changes brought about in 1964 by the Succession (Scotland) Act. Before 1964 much of the law of succession was old, almost immemorially old, and in dire need of reform. This was particularly true of the law of intestate succession.[1] The template for the pre-1964 law had been laid down in the Middle Ages, by the fourteenth century at latest. The roots of that earlier succession law lay in the Feudal law, largely mediated through England, in the case of succession to land; and in customary law and the practice of the Church, again strongly influenced by England, in the case of moveables.[2] Roman law was not a major source, although it was certainly not without influence.[3] The terminology of Roman law, in particular, came to be increasingly widely used from the sixteenth century onwards. Some traces of Celtic law did survive into the later Scots common law, including the law of succession, but these are not considered further in this paper.[4]

The history of the Scots law of succession, then, is one of quite remarkable legal conservatism, rooted in a remote past. Crucially, for over 600 years before the reforms of 1964, there was not one law of succession in Scotland but two, depending on whether the property in question was heritable or moveable. In this respect Scots law was completely unlike Roman law which had as its "foundation-stone" the principle of universal succession.[5] In maintaining a division of this type into the twentieth century

---

* Originally published as ""Succession law in Scotland – a historical perspective", in K G C Reid, M J de Waal and R Zimmermann (eds), *Exploring the Law of Succession: Studies National, Historical and Comparative* (2007) 49–66.
1 For the background to the Act, see M C Meston, *The Succession (Scotland) Act*, 1st edn (1964); for the modern law of succession see *SME* vol 25 (1989) "Wills and Succession" (co-ordinator M C Meston); D R Macdonald, *Introduction to the Scots Law of Succession*, 3rd edn (2001); *Gloag and Henderson The Law of Scotland*, 14th edn (2017) Part IIIB.
2 Scots law prefers the spelling "moveable" to "movable".
3 In this chapter the term "Roman law" is used broadly to embrace the Civilian legal tradition.
4 See chs 1 and 12 (text accompanying nn 2–6).
5 B Nicholas, *An Introduction to Roman Law* (1962) at 235.

Scots law lagged far behind most other Western systems, with the conspicuous exception of English law which retained just such a division until the Administration of Estates Act 1925.[6]

Stair considers succession in Book III of his *Institutions*, when, following what Archie Campbell has called its "master-plan", he moves from the constitution and nature of rights to their conveyance or translation from one person to another.[7] "Succession to defuncts," writes Stair, "is the most important title in our law."[8] An earlier passage in Book I of the *Institutions* is also highly relevant to the history of succession. There Stair considers custom or consuetude as a source of Scots law. He distinguishes between recent custom, declared by the Court of Session, and what he terms, "our ancient and immemorial customs, which may be called our common law."[9] These ancient customs include, "our primogeniture, and all degrees of succession, our legitim portion of children, communion of goods between husband and wife, and the division thereof at their death, the succession of the nearest agnates, the terces of relicts, the liferent of husbands by the courtesy, [and] the exclusion of deeds on deathbed." Stair describes these customs as being "anterior to any statute, and not comprehended in any, as being more solemn and sure than those are." The striking thing about these examples is that they all concern the law of succession. In addition, they are all to be found in *Regiam Majestatem*, the most important treatise in early Scots law, which probably dates from the first half of the fourteenth century.[10] Even more striking, these passages in *Regiam* are all derived from *Glanvill*'s great treatise on the laws and customs of England, composed about 1200.[11]

## B. SUCCESSION TO HERITAGE

As already noted, for over 600 years until 1964, Scots law had not one law of succession, but two. As Stair puts it: "The channel of succession is with us divided into two currents."[12] Property in Scotland divides into "heritage" and "moveables", corresponding broadly to the division between "realty"

---

6 For the history of English law, see generally J H Baker, *An Introduction to English Legal History*, 5th ed (2019) chs 15, 16 and 22 (at 405–406, 411–412).
7 A H Campbell, *The Structure of Stair's Institutions* (David Murray Lecture, University of Glasgow, 1954) at 11.
8 Stair, *Inst*, 3.4.
9 Stair, *Inst*, 1.1.16 (at 87); and see Sellar, "Custom"; also ch 6 above.
10 *RM (Cooper)* 2.16, 18, 25–34, 37 and 58; *RM (APS)* 2.13, 15, 22–28, 30 and 53.
11 *Glanvill*, 6 and 7.1.3–5 and 18.
12 Stair, *Inst*, 3.4pr.

and "personalty" in English law. There was one set of rules for succession to heritage, effectively all land; quite another set for moveables. Succession to heritage – the word is significant – concerned the heir ("the successor in immoveables doth only retain the name of heir, and, therefore, immoveables are called heritable rights"[13]); succession to moveables was the province of the executor.

One crucial rule affecting succession to land was that it was not permitted to leave heritage by will. Once again this rule can be traced back to *Regiam Majestatem* and to *Glanvill*. *Regiam* states, *"de hereditate vero in ultima voluntate nihil potest disponere, ut predictum est"*,[14] copying *Glanvill*'s *"de hereditate vero nihil in ultima voluntate disponere potest sicut predictum est."*[15] Elsewhere *Regiam Majestatem* copies *Glanvill*'s statement that only God can make an heir, not man (*". . . solus Deus heredem facere potest, non homo"*) virtually word for word (*". . . solus Deus heredem facere potest, et non homo."*)[16] It remained strict law in Scotland until 1868 that heritage could not be left by will, although over the centuries various devices came to be used to circumvent the prohibition. It is only possible to refer to these briefly here. They might involve the device of surrender and re-grant, that is, surrender of the lands by the vassal into the hands of his feudal superior for a new grant in different form, perhaps reserving the liferent to the original vassal and the fee to his heir; or the use of destinations controlling the succession of the lands in future through a series of heirs, such as heirs male of the original grantee, or heirs bearing his surname. An early example of such a grant is that by King Robert I to Sir Robert Keith the marischal, *"tenendas et habendas . . . predicto Roberto . . . et heredibus masculis . . . legitime procreandis cognomen de Keth et arma gerentibus"*.[17] Destinations to a succession of heirs eventually evolved into the law of entails, or "tailzies" as it was expressed in Scots, which became a specialised branch of the law on its own.[18] A later device was the trust disposition and settlement, notionally

---

13  Stair, *Inst*, 3.4.23.
14  *RM (Cooper)* 2.37; *RM (APS)* 2.30 (nothing can be left from heritage in a last will, as has already been said).
15  *Glanvill*, 7.5.
16  *Glanvill*, 7.1; *RM (Cooper)* 2.20.4; *RM (APS)* 2.17.
17  See *RRS* vol 5 no 261 (and note editorial comments at 67) (to have and to hold to the said Robert and his heirs male lawfully begotten of the surname of Keith and bearing the arms).
18  G L Gretton, "Scotland: the evolution of the trust in a semi-Civilian system", in R Helmholz and R Zimmermann (eds), *Itinera Fiduciae: Trust and Treuhand in Historical Perspective* (1998) 507 at 517 suggests that the *fideicommissum* was arguably a major source of the Scottish tailzie. I would suggest, however, that the institution, like much else in early Scottish land law, came from the English Common law; see A A M Duncan's introduction to *RRS* vol 5 at 60–69.

entered into *inter vivos*, but in fact latterly *mortis causa* and revocable. So successful was this last device that the trust disposition and settlement, or "TD & S", remains a favoured way of making a will.

A significant restriction on the transmission of heritage *inter vivos* was the law of deathbed, the root of which, like the prohibition on testing on heritage, is to be found in *Regiam Majestatem* and *Glanvill*.[19] The object of this law was to prevent a disposal of heritage to the detriment of the legal heir by a grantor who was approaching death and no longer in full possession of his faculties. For an *inter vivos* grant to be valid the grantor had to be *in legitimam potestatem*, or, as it was regularly expressed, *in liege poustie*; "by which", writes Erskine, "is understood a state of health."[20] Otherwise the grant could be reduced *ex capite lecti* - on the ground of deathbed. There was a presumption at common law that a grant had been made *in liege poustie* if the grantor had been seen, after making the grant, going to or coming from kirk (church) or market unaided, both being public places. An Act of 1696 c 4 declared that it was sufficient to repel the objection of deathbed that the grantor had lived for sixty days after executing the deed, even if he had not been to kirk or market during that time. However, a shorter period might suffice if the deceased had been to kirk or market within the sixty days.[21] The law of deathbed was no antiquarian curiosity, but an active area of law well into the nineteenth century, and gave rise to much heart-rending litigation. It was only in 1871 with the Law of Deathbed Abolition (Scotland) Act that it was finally abolished.

First and foremost, the rules governing the law of intestate succession to heritage favoured the eldest son.[22] Males were preferred to females in every degree; and among males in the same degree, the eldest inherited. He was termed the "heir at law" – the heir par excellence. Stair believed that the purpose of this rule of primogeniture was to protect the honour and dignity of families.[23] In Roman law, by contrast, throughout its history, primogeniture had no place. When the succession did open to females, they shared the inheritance equally. A Biblical precedent sometimes cited for this rule, not

---

19 *RM (Cooper)* 2.18.7; *RM (APS)* 2.15; *Glanvill* 7.1 (at 70 and n).
20 Erskine, *Inst* 3.8.95. In the phrase *in liege poustie* we may perhaps discern an echo of 13th-century Scots pronunciation of French.
21 *RPS* 1696/9/56.
22 For the old rules of intestate succession, see, for example, Smith, *Short Commentary*, ch 14; Gloag and Henderson's Introduction to the Law of Scotland (6th edn, 1956); *ISLH*, chs 9 (G C H Paton, "Husband and wife: property rights and relationships") and 16 (J Irvine Smith, "Succession"); and *Green's Encyclopaedia of Scots Law*, 1st ed (1896).
23 Stair, *Inst*, 3.4.33 (at 679).

only in Scotland, but elsewhere, was the Old Testament case of the daughters of Zelophehad in the book of Numbers.[24] According to Lord Macmillan, Sir Frederick Pollock described this case as "the earliest recorded decision which is still of authority."[25] It is referred to by Stair, and was cited in the "Great Cause" for the Crown of Scotland.[26] In Scots law such female co-heirs were termed "heirs portioners". The rules of intestate succession to heritage allowed for representation at every stage: thus the claim of a granddaughter, the daughter of a predeceasing elder son, trumped that of a younger son. Succession, it was said, should descend whenever it could: and so on the death of the middle of three brothers, it was the younger brother, rather than the elder, who inherited. In this scheme of succession a surviving spouse was not a potential heir. Rather, succession was entirely parentelic, the potential heirs in each parentela being exhausted before the succession opened to an earlier parentela. However, only agnatic parentelas counted, that is, the paternal kin, no matter by which route the heritage had in fact descended. This inequitable rule was firmly fixed by 1600, although there are indications that Scots law, like English law, had earlier followed the rule *paterna paternis materna maternis*: namely, that heritage which had descended from the paternal side should go to paternal relatives; while heritage which had descended from the mother's side should go to the maternal kin.[27]

All these rules were true of succession to land in England also. "At the end of Henry III's reign [in 1272]," wrote Maitland, "our common law of inheritance was rapidly assuming its final form."[28] Maitland discerned the following six rules:

> (1) A living descendant excludes his or her own descendants. (2) A dead descendant is represented by his or her own descendants. (3) Males exclude females of equal degree. (4) Among males of equal degree only the eldest inherits. (5) Females of equal degree inherit together as co-heiresses. (6) The rule that a dead descendant is represented by his or her descendants overrides the preference for the male sex, so that a grand-daughter by a dead eldest son will exclude a younger son.

In the Great Cause for the Crown of Scotland at the end of the thirteenth century there was still room for doubt on the question of representation; but

---

24  Numbers 27.7.
25  H P Macmillan, *Law and Other Things* (1938) at 61.
26  Stair, *Inst*, 3.4.9–10; E L G Stones and G G Simpson (eds), *Edward I and the Throne of Scotland 1290–1296* (1978) vol 2 at 365 (the opinions of the consulted foreign lawyers).
27  Pollock & Maitland, vol 2, at 299–300; for earlier Scots law see *RM (Cooper)* 2.25; *RM (APS)* 2.22; and *Alexander* (1696) Mor 14873.
28  Pollock & Maitland, vol 2, at 260.

by the middle of the following century all the rules listed by Maitland were true of Scots law also. They remained true of Scots law until 1964.

There might be some slight variation in these rules in the case of land which had been acquired rather than inherited, that is, by "singular" rather than by "universal" succession. Such acquisitions were known as "conquest". The stock example of succession to conquest involved three brothers, the middle of whom predeceased the others leaving conquest. In this case it was the elder and not the younger brother who inherited. The notion of conquest was also known in English law at an early date, but soon disappeared. The legal historian Theodore Plucknett noted a case in England where the rules of conquest were invoked "as late as 1203".[29] By contrast, the rules regarding conquest remained part of Scots law until 1874 and were still being litigated over as late as 1917.[30]

These rules were odd enough, but until 1874 there was a further hurdle to surmount.[31] It was essential that the ancestor or relative from whom the claim was derived should have taken sasine of the heritage in question, that is, that he should have been "infeft" (enfeoffed) or clothed with the fief.[32] This was expressed by the maxim *"nulla sasina nulla terra"*,[33] as opposed to the contrary maxim, generally expressed in French, *"le mort saisit le vif"*.[34] Thus if a deceased father had not taken sasine it was necessary to derive the succession to the land from the last person who had done so, perhaps an uncle, a grandfather, or an even more remote relative. In cases where the land had descended through the female line, the vagaries of sasine could result in great unfairness.[35]

Although a surviving spouse was not an heir, both widow and widower had rights in the deceased spouse's heritable estate, known respectively as "terce" and "courtesy". These rights, together with rights of spouses and children against the deceased's moveable estate discussed below, have simply been known as "legal rights" in Scots law. They may be regarded as examples of "forced heirship", although that term has rarely been used in Scots law.[36]

---

29 T F T Plucknett, *A Concise History of the Common Law* (5th edn, 1956) at 527 n 1.
30 Conveyancing (Scotland) Act 1874 s 37; *Walker v Walkers Trs* 1917 SC 46.
31 Conveyancing (Scotland) Act 1874 s 9.
32 For sasine and infeftment in Scots law, see J M Halliday, "The tragedy of sasine", 1965 *JR* 105; also G L Gretton, "Sasine and infeftment", in *SME* vol 18 (1993) paras 87–93.
33 (no sasine, no land).
34 (the deceased gives sasine to the living).
35 See *Anstruther v Anstruther* (1836) 14 S 272, considered below, text accompanying nn 46–48.
36 J P Dawson, *Gifts and Promises: Continental and American Law Compared* (1980) is an extended study of "forced heirship", but does not consider Scots law. M C Meston, "Succession – rights or discretion?", 1987 *JR* 1 at 7 writes of "Forced-Share Systems".

The widow's terce was a right to the liferent of a third part of her deceased husband's heritage, a right corresponding to the "dower" once recognised by English law.[37] Until 1924 there was the further requirement that in order for the widow to succeed to her terce – to be "kenned" to her terce, as it was expressed – the husband should have been infeft. Terce was abolished by the Succession (Scotland) Act 1964, although as this was not retrospective, it is conceivable that some widows are still enjoying their terce.[38] In England dower was abolished in 1925.

The widower's courtesy was a right not to the liferent of a third but to the liferent of the whole of his wife's heritable estate. In the case of courtesy, however, there was no requirement to show prior infeftment. There was, however, one further necessary qualification: in order to enjoy courtesy there had to have been a child born of the marriage live and heard to cry. Further survival of the child was not necessary, although in later Scots law, at least, there was the additional requirement that the child, had it survived, should have been its mother's heir. These extraordinary rules find parallels in both English and Norman law which also knew the institution of courtesy. Just why the child should have been born live and heard to cry was already a matter for learned debate among English lawyers in the thirteenth century.[39] In Scotland there was a *cause célèbre* in 1368 involving courtesy, the issue being whether a child had been born live and heard to cry, in which two noble claimants resorted to trial by battle in front of King David II.[40] Sir John Skene waxes eloquent on courtesy in his great dictionary of the older Scots legal tongue, *De Verborum Significatione* (1597):

> CURIALITAS, curialitie, curtesie, from the French Curtoise civilitie, gentelnesse, humanitie, for the law of curtesie, is an gentill and favorable ordinance or constitution, granted and observed in this Realme, and nocht universallie keiped, or used in uther cuntries, And therefore it is called *Curialitas Scotiae*, the curtesie of *Scotland*. And in the laws of *England lex Anglie*, or the curtesie of *England*, within the quhilk [which] twa realmes and nane uther this law is in use. That is quhen onie man maries lauchfullie ane wife, and receivis lande and heritage with her: And it happen that he beget with her ane bairne, quha [who] being borne, is heard cryand betwixt foure walles of ane house . . .

Skene was clearly fascinated by the requirement that the child be born live and heard to cry:

---

37 Baker, *English Legal History* (n 6) at 289–290.
38 Succession (Scotland) Act 1964, s 10.
39 Pollock & Maitland, vol 2, at 418.
40 See ch 14 below.

> The curtesie hes nocht place quhen na bairne is borne in lauchfull mariage, for it is necessar that ane bairne be borne mail or femaill, quick and liveand: And for probation theirof, he mon [must] be heard cryand, for the curtesie hes place *in puero clamante*, (or as it is written in sum buikes) *brayand*, squeiland [squealing], or loudly cryand . . .

In England curtesy, the "curtesy of England" (*curialitas Anglie*), was abolished in 1925.[41] In Scotland, incredibly, courtesy survived, cry and all, until 1964.[42]

The old law of heritable succession was antiquated and irrational, an extraordinary legal fossil. It was quite impossible to justify. In *Clinton v Trefusis*[43] Lord Kinloch said of the law on courtesy:

> This is a right of a very peculiar character . . . It is governed by rules, of which several rest on little better footing than that it has been so fixed. To apply general principles of equity, or the inferences of analogy, to any deliberation of this right, is wholly alien to its legal character.[44]

In *Cuninghame v Cuninghame*[45] it was pleaded that:

> There were several specialties in the law of Scotland which differed from the law of most other nations: the division of succession into heritage and conquest was one of these peculiar rules, founded, however, upon no principle that could be discovered, other than the arbitrary will of the law itself.

It was well recognised that the law was inequitable. In the Full Court case of *Antruther v Anstruther*,[46] which concerned the technicalities of collation *inter heredes* (discussed further below), the consulted judges (Lord President Hope and five others) looked first to the history of that doctrine before expounding its "fundamental rules". They then embarked on a lengthy excursus on the unfairness of the law of heritable succession. "In truth," they said, "the common law of feudal succession uniformly resists the intervention of equity to temper or modify its rules." They gave a number of examples. Suppose a brother dies survived by a sister-german (full sister) and a brother consanguinean (half-brother on the father's side). If the deceased was infeft, his sister takes the property to the exclusion of the half blood; but, if he died uninfeft, the whole estate passes to the half-brother.

---

41 Baker, *English Legal History* (n 6) at 290–291. Baker notes, however, that it survived in equity until 1997.
42 Succession (Scotland) Act 1964 s 10.
43 *Clinton v Trefusis* (1869) 8 M 370.
44 At 373.
45 *Cuninghame v Cuninghame* (1770) Mor 14875.
46 *Anstruther v Anstruther* (1836) 14 S 272.

Or, suppose one of several heirs-portioners dies leaving a child. If the child is uninfeft, her mother's portion will be shared among her aunts. However, if the child has been infeft, then that child's brothers or sisters consanguinean, if any, may inherit, whom failing the child's father. "What is it," lament the judges, "that sends the succession into channels so widely different, in these instances, contrary to every feeling of equity, and every principle of natural justice? Nothing but the mere ceremony of passing an infeftment."[47] Another scholarly opinion was delivered in the same case by Lord Medwyn who also looked to the historical background of the doctrine of collation. He believed, probably correctly, that collation had been introduced by the church courts "from considerations of equity . . . For the churchmen, in their judicial capacity, were the great masters of equity in those times."[48]

## C. SUCCESSION TO MOVEABLES

The rules of moveable succession, it was generally agreed, left more room for the intervention of equity. Stair writes that, "The law and customs of Scotland have reduced the matter of testaments, and succession in moveables, much nearer to natural equity, and made it shorter and plainer than the Roman law."[49] Two hundred years later Maitland noted that,

> the Scottish law of intestate succession to movables has been marvellously unlike that settled by Nov. 118. It has been at once agnatic (refusing to trace through a female ancestor) and parentelic.[50]

As in the case of heritage, then, intestate succession to moveables was parentelic, and narrowly confined to the paternal kin, with limited exceptions in favour of the mother and brothers and sisters uterine being introduced in 1855.[51] Again, in principle, the surviving spouse was not a potential heir. Beyond that the rules were different.[52] Succession went to the "next of kin". There was no rule of primogeniture and no preference for males: everyone in the same degree of relationship to the deceased shared equally. However, the heir at law, if also one of the next of kin, was required to "collate" – that is, to share his inheritance – if he wished to participate in the

---

47 At 287.
48 At 299ff.
49 Stair, *Inst* 3.8.28.
50 Pollock & Maitland, vol 2, 361 n 3.
51 Intestate Moveable Succession (Scotland) Act 1855 s 5; see also Intestate Moveable Succession (Scotland) Act 1919.
52 For the older rules see n 22.

moveable succession. This was known as collation *inter heredes* (collation between the heirs), so called to distinguish it from collation *inter liberos* (among the children) which might arise in connection with the legal right of *legitim*.[53] Unlike the case with heritage, there was no right of representation in intestate moveable succession at common law: the surviving relatives in the nearest degree alone inherited. Thus a surviving child would exclude the children of deceased siblings, and uncles or aunts would exclude cousins. This situation was partially remedied by legislation in 1855, and a measure of representation allowed in the case of descendants and brothers and sisters of the deceased.[54] But the statute was poorly drafted and much litigation ensued.[55] Heirs to moveables under the 1855 statute were known as "heirs *in mobilibus*" as distinct from "next of kin". Until 1823 there was the further requirement that confirmation must have been granted, before the moveable estate could pass to the next of kin.

In moveable succession, whether testate or intestate, the law required the appointment or "confirmation" of an executor to ingather, administer and distribute the estate. In the middle ages, in Scotland as also in England, confirmation of executors was a matter for the Church and its courts. At a Provincial Council at Perth in 1420 it was noted that beyond memory of man "bishops and those holding the jurisdiction of an ordinary have been wont to confirm the testaments and codicils of those who die testate in their respective sees and to appoint executors to those who die intestate."[56] In his seminal article A E Anton notes that the similarities between the Scottish system and the English are "too marked to be accidental".[57] After the Reformation this jurisdiction passed in Scotland to newly erected "commissary" courts which were subject to the Court of Session. Anton comments that:

> A crisis came in 1560 when the jurisdiction of the spiritual courts was abolished. Reforming zeal might well have led to a clean break with the past, but the "natural equity" and practical convenience of the old system ensured its retention, under secular auspices indeed, but substantially unchanged.[58]

Anton also considers that the position of the executor was too well entrenched by this time to be challenged by "a different and more subtle threat – the ubiquitous Roman law":

---

53 For *legitim* see below, text accompanying nn 60–66.
54 Intestate Moveable Succession (Scotland) Act 1855 s 1.
55 For example, *Colville's JF v Nicoll* 1914 SC 62 and *Adam's Executrix v Maxwell* 1921 SC 418.
56 A E Anton, "Medieval Scots executors and the courts spiritual" (1955) 67 *JR* 129 at 131.
57 Anton (n 56) at 153.
58 Anton (n 56) at 153.

The question was rather which characteristics of the Roman law should be applied to the Scottish executor... Certain characteristics of the Roman heir were applied to the Scottish executor, and the only result was that the latter emerged stronger than ever before and better equipped to meet the needs of the world today.[59]

In the nineteenth century commissary jurisdiction was transferred to the sheriff courts and the Court of Session, where it remains. The executor continued to ingather the moveable estate until 1964, after which he (or she) became responsible for the entire estate.

Scots law recognises "legal rights" in moveable succession also.[60] These rights are a restriction on the power of testation, as they apply in testate and intestate moveable succession alike. Originally legal rights in moveables were for the benefit of the widow and children of the deceased. If the deceased died leaving both a widow and children, the widow and the children collectively were entitled to one third each of the free moveable estate. If there was no widow, the children were entitled to a half; while if there was a widow but no surviving children, the widow took a half. There was no representation. These provisions are among the most ancient in Scots common law. They are to be found in *Regiam Majestatem*, in a passage which comes virtually word for word from *Glanvill*:

> ... omnes res ejus mobiles in tres partes dividentur aequales, quarum una debetur heredi, secunda uxori; tercia vero reservatur testatori, de qua tercia parte liberam habebit disponendi facultatem. Verum si sine uxore decesserit, medietas sibi reservetur.[61]

> ... omnes res eius mobiles in tres partes dividentur equales, quarum una debetur heredi, secunda uxori; tercia vero ipsi reservatur, de qua tercia liberam habebit disponendi facultatem. Verum si sine uxore decesserit, medietas ipsi reservatur.[62]

It will be noted that Cooper's and Hall's respective translations[63] differ from each other rather more than the original Latin. Neither explains, as Maitland does, and as practice confirms, that the word "heir" in both *Glanvill* and *Regiam* was construed as meaning children collectively, although Cooper

---

59 Anton (n 56) at 154.
60 For a historical survey see J C Gardner, *Origin and Nature of the Legal Rights of Spouse and Children in the Scottish Law of Succession* (1928) (from articles in the *JR* in 1927 and 1928).
61 [("... all his moveables fall to be divided into three equal parts, of which one goes to his heir, one to his wife and one is reserved to be disponed of by the testator as he pleases. But if at the time of his death he has no wife, one half is reserved to the testator."] *RM (Cooper)* 2.37; *RM (APS)* 2.30. The translation is Lord Cooper's.
62 ["... all his chattels will be divided into three equal parts of which one is due to the heir, and the second to his wife; the third is reserved to himself, and he shall have free power of disposition over this third; but if he dies without leaving a wife, one half is reserved to him."] *Glanvill* 7.5; the translation is Hall's.
63 Given in the footnotes above.

does notice Sir John Skene's translation as "bairns" in his vernacular version of the *Regiam* in 1609.[64] These rules disappeared by slow stages from English law, surviving longest in the northern ecclesiastical province of York (until 1692), and in the custom of London (until 1724), but they remain good law in Scotland today. Maitland writes, "Had our temporal lawyers of the thirteenth century cared more than they did about the law of chattels, wife's part, bairn's part and dead's part might at this day be known south of the Tweed."[65] Unlike terce, legal rights in moveables vest by mere survivance. In modern Scots law the widow's part is known as *jus relictae* and the children's part as *"legitim"*, formerly as "bairns part". Until 1964 *legitim* was exigible from a father's estate only. Until 1855 *jus relictae* was only due if the marriage had lasted for a year and a day or if a child had been born. The rules appear to be of ancient customary origin, pre-dating the Norman Conquest in England, and to owe nothing to Roman law, despite the description *"legitim"*. In Scotland a widower was given a commensurate right by statute in 1881, termed *jus relicti*.[66] Legal rights in moveables were preserved by the 1964 Act, but only then was the principle of representation extended to *legitim*.

It will be apparent, then, that the scope for testation during most of the period under consideration was distinctly limited. In strict legal theory heritage could not be transmitted by will until 1868, while the legal rights of terce and courtesy burdened the succession with liferents. In moveable succession, if the testator was survived by a wife and children, the "dead's part" – the name given to the portion over which the testator has power of disposal – was limited to one-third of the moveable estate. For much of the period a good part even of that third went to the Church, or to the executors *ex officio*. It is not surprising, therefore, that much of what would now be regarded as lying at the heart of the law of succession, including the law relating to legacies, is dealt with briefly by the older writers. Stair's treatment of heritable succession in Walker's 1981 edition of the *Institutions* extends from pages 653 to 737; and his treatment of moveable succession from pages 737 to 770, of which legacies take only pages 752 to 755.[67] Even in Baron Hume's *Lectures*, written at the start of the nineteenth century, the treatment of legacies is far shorter than that of settlements and tailzies; shorter even than the treatment of deathbed.[68]

---

64 Pollock & Maitland, vol 2, at 350.
65 Pollock & Maitland, vol 2, at 355–356.
66 Married Women's Property (Scotland) Act 1881 s 6.
67 Stair, *Inst*, 3.4–7 (heritable); 3.8 (moveable).
68 In Hume, *Lectures*, vol 5, the law of legacies takes up 16 pages as against 27 for deathbed and

Before the Reformation, as already mentioned, testate succession was pre-eminently a matter for the Church, with jurisdiction after the Reformation moving seamlessly to the commissary courts. Wills were revocable and ambulatory as indeed they still remain. They also nominated executors. Hume writes: "The main substance of a testament – its distinctive and peculiar character – consists in the matter of a nomination of executors."[69] All too little is known about the details of legal doctrine in Scotland regarding moveable succession in medieval times. Unlike the position as regards status – marriage, separation and legitimacy – there was no great body of Canon law for the churchmen to turn to. Those presiding in the church courts, and in the later commissary courts, would have been familiar with the *jus commune* and would certainly have regarded that as a potential source. But they would also have looked to Scottish custom and to natural equity, as Stair suggests.[70]

Anton's seminal article must now be read in the light of Reinhard Zimmermann's "*Heres Fiduciarius*? Rise and Fall of the Testamentary Executor", based on the most recent European writing and research.[71] The last section in this article is headed "English Common Law".[72] We may amend Zimmermann's statement that, "The only European country, therefore, where a congenial environment has been retained for the executor is England", to include Scotland also. That done, however, we may adopt many of his conclusions as being true of Scots law also. In Scotland, as in England, the executor "has changed remarkably little over the centuries", always allowing for the extension of his role in 1964 to cover the entire succession. In Scotland, as in England, the executor came to be equated with the heir of Roman law in the sense that he could be described as *eadem persona cum defuncto*. In Scotland, as in England, the executor has come to be regarded as a trustee.[73] We can probably also say, as Zimmermann does of England, that in this area of law, at least, Scotland "formed part of the world of a medieval common law that antedates the intellectual recovery of the Digest".[74]

---

nearly 90 for settlements and tailzies.
69 Hume, *Lectures*, vol 5 at 195.
70 Stair, *Inst*, 3.8.28 (quoted above).
71 R Zimmermann, "*Heres fiduciarius*? Rise and fall of the testamentary executor", in Helmholz and Zimmermann (eds), *Itinera Fiduciae* (n 18) 267.
72 Zimmermann (n 71) at 301–4.
73 For this proposition, once controversial, see Gretton (n 18), 514–516.
74 Zimmermann (n 71) at 301; and see M Lupoi, *The Origins of the European Legal Order* (2000).

## D. THE SUCCESSION (SCOTLAND) ACT 1964

The importance of the 1964 Succession (Scotland) Act can hardly be overestimated. Most of the principal changes introduced by the Act have already been mentioned, but it may be useful to summarise them here. A single system of intestate succession replaced the two-fold system which had existed for centuries. The executor became responsible for the administration of the entire estate, not merely the moveable. The old rules of heritable succession were entirely discarded, as were the legal rights of terce and courtesy. Legal rights in moveables, however, remained, although they were not extended to cover the whole estate, an omission which has led to criticism.[75] Representation was introduced in *legitim*. Further rights, known as "prior rights", were introduced in favour of a surviving spouse. These rights are extensive and may account for much or all of the deceased's estate.[76] Unlike legal rights, however, prior rights arise only on intestacy. The new statutory rules which determine succession to the estate after prior rights and legal rights have been taken into consideration are similar to the old rules regarding moveable succession, inasmuch as there is no primogeniture and no preference for males. However, they are different in that there is representation throughout; also when the succession opens to ancestral lines, all parentelas are now included on an equal basis, paternal and maternal alike. The 1964 Act also placed the half-blood on the mother's side on an equal footing with those on the father's side. A further important change was the recognition of a surviving spouse as a potential heir, postponed to descendants, siblings and parents, but prior to uncles, aunts and grandparents.

---

75 See Meston (n 1) at 35; also Intestate Succession and Legal Rights (Scot Law Com Memo No 69, 1986), and Report on Succession (Scot Law Com No 124, 1996) 3.15–16. The Scottish Law Commission produced a further Report on Succession (Scot Law Com No 215, 2008) which like its predecessor is unlikely to be implemented in full (although see the Succession (Scotland) Act 2016). See further a series of articles by D Reid: "From the cradle to the grave: politics, families and inheritance" (2008) 12 *Edin LR* 391; "Reform of the law of succession: inheritance rights of children" (2010) 14 *Edin LR* 318; "Why is it so difficult to reform the law of intestate succession?" (2020) 24 *Edin LR* 111. See also two papers by K G C Reid, "Mixing without matching: fractions, slabs, and the succession rights of the surviving spouse and children" (2020) 24 *Edin LR* 118; "Legal rights in Scotland", in K G C Reid, M J de Waal and R Zimmermann (eds), *Comparative Succession Law volume 3: Mandatory Family Protection* (2020) ch 14.

76 Prior rights had precursors in the Intestate Husband's Estate (Scotland) Acts 1911 to 1959.

## E. ADOPTED AND ILLEGITIMATE CHILDREN

The 1964 Act also admitted adopted children for the first time into the scheme of intestate succession. Adoption was introduced by statute in 1930, but adopted children had to wait until the 1964 Act to obtain a right to succeed to the estates of their adoptive parents.[77] The 1964 Act, however, made no provision for illegitimate children: so far as intestate succession was concerned the illegitimate child had no claim. This situation had long been substantially ameliorated by the early adoption into Scots law of the Canon law rule of legitimation by subsequent marriage. Unlike the English Common law which notoriously set its face against this doctrine for hundreds of years, the Scottish common law recognised legitimation by subsequent marriage as early as the thirteenth or fourteenth century. In the nineteenth century the place of the doctrine in Scots law was examined with exuberant learning in the Full Court case of *Kerr v Martin* in 1840, a case remarkable for its abundant citation of authority, Roman, Canon and Scots.[78] The end result was perhaps not the best advertisement for such impressive consultation: the Court divided seven to six, with the Lord President and the Lord Justice-Clerk in the minority! Finally, in 1968, Scots law was amended to allow illegitimate children the same rights of succession in the estates of their parents as legitimate children.[79]

## F. ENGLISH LAW; SCOTS LAW; ROMAN LAW

There can be no doubt that the most important influence on the Scots law of succession to heritage during its formative years, amounting to a reception, was the English Common law. However, by the thirteenth century the Scottish common law was already charting its own independent course: some borrowings, once received, took on a life of their own; others, and this is conspicuously true of intestate succession to heritage, seem to have entered a virtual time warp. The influence of Roman law in this area of succession was distinctly limited. For example, there are few references to Roman law in the first 200 pages of Baron Hume's treatment of succession. It is only when he comes to discuss confirmation, *donatio mortis causa* and legacies that Civilian references become more frequent, including nods in the direction

---

[77] Adoption of Children (Scotland) Act 1930; Succession (Scotland) Act 1964 s 23.
[78] *Kerr v Martin* (1840) 2 D 752; also S Marshall, *Illegitimacy in Medieval Scotland, 1100–1500* (2021), at 26–41, 110–116.
[79] Law Reform (Miscellaneous Provisions) (Scotland) Act 1968 s 2.

of Voet and Vinnius.[80] There is an obvious contrast here with Dutch and South African law, as is at once apparent from a glance at Lee's edition of Grotius' *Inleiding*.[81] Thus Lee comments on Grotius 2.27 "Of the degrees of relationship" that, "This chapter is pure Roman law".[82] South African law is, in fact, entirely innocent of feudalism and feudal land rights (rather quaintly termed "feuds" by Lee).[83] Even in the land law of the Province of Holland in Grotius' time, Feudal law played a relatively minor role.

In medieval Scotland moveable succession lay within the province of the Church and its courts, although inspiration came from a blending of customary law and Christian practice, rather than from the Canon law as such. Here again England provides the closest parallel, but in the practice of the English Church and its courts rather than the English Common law. After the Scottish Reformation in 1560 jurisdiction passed to the commissary courts, and the law of moveable succession joined the mainstream of the Scottish common law.

It is difficult to assess the influence of Roman law on the Scots law of succession: it was not negligible, but it certainly did not amount to a reception.[84] It is necessary to distinguish between at least three channels of Roman influence. First, as mediated through and altered by the Canon law, as in the case of legitimation by subsequent marriage. Second, through the *jus commune*: Scotland continued to participate in the *jus commune* throughout the Middle Ages and beyond to a far greater extent than England. And third, through the influence of Justinian's Digest more directly, as studied, for example, by Scots lawyers at the Dutch universities. It is also necessary to distinguish between the terminology and the substance of Roman law.

It was entirely natural that Scots lawyers educated on the Continent should use the terminology of Roman law, but this can be misleading.[85] Sometimes native institutions, such as the legal rights in moveables, were dressed up in Roman garb: thus bairns' part became "*legitim*", in imitation of the *legitima portio* of Roman law, and the widow's right became known as *jus relictae*, with the corresponding right of *jus relicti* being added later by legislation. Sometimes the search for a Roman origin became faintly

---

80 Hume, *Lectures*, vol 5 at 201–234.
81 *Jurisprudence of Holland by Hugo Grotius*, trans R W Lee, with commentary (2 vols, 1926–1936).
82 *Jurisprudence of Holland* (n 81) vol 2, at 178.
83 E.g. *Jurisprudence of Holland* (n 81) vol 1, at 264: "*Hoe leen bekomen werd*", translated (vol 2, at 265) as "How feuds are acquired".
84 There is a burgeoning literature on the influence of Roman law on Scots law, for which see ch 1 (text accompanying nn 66 and 67) and ch 8 above.
85 See D L Carey Miller, "Stair's property: a Romanist system?", 1995 *JR* 70.

ridiculous, as when the legal right of courtesy was traced back to a rescript of the Emperor Constantine.[86] The origins of the trust in Scots law are still far from clear, but most are agreed that they owe little to the contracts of mandate and deposit, despite suggestions to that effect by Institutional writers.[87] The trust has also been compared to the Roman *fideicommissum*, but so too have other institutions.[88] Thus Stair writes: "If there be a nomination of executors, with a material legacy to another, it is fideicommissary succession, to be restored to the universal legatar."[89] Hume, however, although noting Stair's usage, avoids it himself, preferring to refer to the executor as the dominus of the estate or as a trustee.[90] The terminology of fideicommissary succession could also be applied to the heir of entail and, more credibly, to the *conditio si testator*. The executor was regularly described as *eadem persona cum defuncto*, but so too, on occasion, was the heir at law. The situation which gave rise to the *conditio si institutus* in Roman law was bound to arise naturally in most jurisdictions, making it difficult to determine how far the *conditio si institutus* of modern Scots law derived from Roman law and how far it is of native origin.[91] The idea of donation *mortis causa* may have come from Roman law but the institution has been tailored to meet Scottish needs.[92]

As late as 1942, in the case of *Stuart v Stuart*, the question was raised whether the Roman *testamentum militare* was part of the common law of Scotland.[93] The court found it unnecessary to decide the point but showed no great enthusiasm for the proposition. Two years later, in a case involving death in a common calamity, Lord Cooper rejected the suggestion that the rules of Roman law should have any place:

> If the question whether survivance in a common calamity should be determined by evidence or arbitrary presumption had arisen for decision in the later

---

86 See *Hodge v Fraser* (1740) Mor 3119; also Gardner (n 60) at 56 and Stair, *Inst*, 2.6.19.
87 For the origins of the trust, see Gretton (n 18); also R Burgess, "Thoughts on the origins of the trust in Scots law", 1974 *JR* 196. Gretton's views on the mandate and deposit suggestion can be found in his article (n 18) at 506–507.
88 Gretton (n 18) at 490–491; and see *Duke and Duchess of Buccleugh v Marquess of Tweeddale* (1677) Mor 2369. See also G L Gretton, "Fideicommissary substitutions: Scots law in historical and comparative perspective", in K G C Reid, M J de Waal and R Zimmermann (eds), *Exploring the Law of Succession: Studies National, Historical and Comparative* (2007) 156.
89 Stair, *Inst*, 3.8.30.
90 Hume, *Lectures*, vol 5, at 203, 208.
91 See the writings cited at ch 8 n 51. The *conditio si testator sine liberis decesserit* was abolished and replaced by the Succession (Scotland) Act 2016 ss 6 and 29.
92 Donation *mortis causa* was likewise abolished by the Succession (Scotland) Act 2016 s 25(1). See further ch 8 n 51.
93 *Stuart v Stuart* 1942 SC 510.

seventeenth century, Scotland might conceivably have adopted, as being in accordance with equity and expediency, the Roman solution or some modification of it. But Scotland did not do so; and I have the greatest difficulty in entertaining the suggestion that, in relation to a problem which must have arisen on many past occasions, we should now for the first time adopt from Rome or from any other source an entirely new solution; for such a step would in the circumstances partake of judicial legislation.[94]

The words "in accordance with equity and expediency", as Lord Cooper makes clear, are a direct reference to Stair's *Institutions*, where after considering the relationship of the Civil, Canon and Feudal laws to the law of Scotland, Stair writes: "But none of these have with us the authority of law; and therefore are only received according to equity and expediency, *secundum bonum et aequum*."[95]

---

94 *Drummond's JF v HM Advocate* 1944 SC 298 at 301. The rules regarding death in a common calamity in Scots law were altered first by the Succession (Scotland) Act 1964 s 31 and then by the Succession (Scotland) Act 2016 s 9.
95 Stair, *Inst* 1.1.16.

# 14 Courtesy, Battle, and the Brieve of Right, 1368*

Chapter 63 of George Neilson's *Trial by Combat* is headed "Three Half-told Stories, 1362–85". In it Neilson notes that English records give details of preparations being made in 1367 and 1368 for a judicial duel to be fought in Scotland "according to the law of Scotland, for certain causes" – *juxta legem Scotiae ex certis causis* – between James Douglas and Thomas Erskine. Both Douglas and Erskine petitioned Edward III for permission to buy the necessary arms and armour in London. These included a pair of plates, a haubergeon, gauntlets, a helmet, bracers and leg armour, long arms and coverings for two horses, two daggers and the head of a lance for Douglas, and plates, bascinet, bracers, cuisses, greaves, a chaffrein for a horse, a dagger, a long sword, a short sword and a pair of iron gauntlets for Erskine. But there, for Neilson, the story ended:

> As is too often the case in the history of Scotland the intimations of the English records serve only to tantalise. One hears of duels which are to be, but lacks the satisfaction of knowing the event. The story ends with the beginning.[1]

For once Neilson was mistaken. Tucked obscurely away in a Latin footnote to W F Skene's edition of John of Fordun and largely unnoticed save by peerage writers and family historians, there is a near contemporary account of the duel between Erskine and Douglas, fought before King David II himself.[2] We know both the event and the "certain causes" from which

---

* Originally published as "Courtesy, battle and the brieve of right, 1368: a story continued", in W D H Sellar (ed), *Miscellany II* (SS vol 35, 1984) 1–12.
1 G Neilson, *Trial by Combat* (1890) at 216–217; D. Macpherson and others (eds), *Rotuli Scotiae* (2 vols, 1814–19), vol 2, at 915b–917b.
2 *Chron Fordun* vol 1, at 370n. The text in the note is derived from two MSS of *Fordun*: the British Library's Cotton MS Vitellius E. XI Cottonian and the Trinity College Dublin MS 498. Professor Dauvit Broun advises that it probably represents a post-1389 addition to a work mostly completed by 1363. See further his article, "Understanding John of Fordun's *Chronica Gentis Scotorum* as a medieval 'national history'", forthcoming in a festschrift in honour of Roger Mason (ed S Reid). I am most grateful to Dr Alexander Grant for first bringing the note to my attention. It is noticed in J B Paul (ed), *The Scots Peerage* (9 vols, 1904–1914), vol 5, at 597; vol 6 at 345; and in W Fraser, *The Douglas Book* (4 vols, 1885), vol 1, at 253. See also M Penman, *David II, 1329–71* (2004) at 374–376.

the duel arose. As the story is a dramatic one and the causes of considerable interest, we may regret the lack of an account from Neilson's sparkling pen.

In 1353 Sir William Douglas of Liddesdale, a man who had notoriously lived by the sword, was assassinated in Ettrick Forest by his namesake William, lord (and later first earl) of Douglas. He left considerable estates, mainly in the south of Scotland. Some of these were inherited by his only child and heir, Mary; while others went to his nephew and heir-male, James Douglas (later Sir James Douglas of Dalkeith), one of the protagonists in the duel in 1368. James Douglas had already been granted the barony of Aberdour (Fife) by his uncle and on his death he also acquired the baronies of Dalkeith (Midlothian) and Kilbucho and Newlands (Peeblesshire) by virtue of a tailzie executed by Sir William in 1351.

Mary Douglas succeeded to the unentailed lands, which included the baronies of Calderclere (Midlothian), Linton-Rothrik (West Linton, Peeblesshire), Roberton (Lanarkshire), Buittle (Galloway), and half of Preston (Galloway).[3] Mary was married first to Reginald Mure (or More), son of William Mure of Abercorn, but this marriage was annulled, and she then married Thomas Erskine, the other protagonist in the duel. In or about 1367 she died in childbirth and her child died with her, leaving James Douglas as her nearest heir (Figure 14.1). James Douglas claimed the inheritance – he was served heir to Mary in the baronies of Buittle, Preston and other lands, by brieve of succession (otherwise inquest) at Dumfries on 30 June 1367[4] – but Thomas Erskine claimed that he was entitled to a liferent of his wife's not inconsiderable heritage by right of courtesy.

*Fordun* narrates the death of Sir William Douglas of Liddesdale and then provides this vivid account of the duel:

> Hic reliquit post se unicam filiam nomine Mariam heredem, quae nupsit Reginaldo Mure filio et heredi domini Willelmi Mure, sed postea per quasdem causas exquisitas divortiata fuit ab eodem et postea nupsit Thomae de Irskyn filio et heredi domini Roberti de Irskyn quae, impregnata per eundem, in partu periclitata mortua est. Terras vero domini Willelmi de Dowglas idem dixit sibi deberi pro tempore vitae suae ex curialitate Scociae, eo quod, ut dixit, de dicta maritagia genuit prolem vivam, sed Jacobus de Dowglas filius domini Johannis de Dowglas fratris praefati domini Willelmi, se opposuit dixens dictas terras

---

3 See *Scots Peerage*, vol 6, sv "Morton", and C Innes (ed), *Registrum Honoris de Morton* (2 vols, Bannatyne Club, 1853, henceforth *Morton Registrum*). The career and landed interests of Sir James Douglas are considered in A Grant, "The higher nobility in Scotland and their estates, c1371–1424" (Oxford DPhil thesis, 1975) at 240ff. Dr Grant points out that Mary Douglas was a more substantial heiress than *Scots Peerage* suggests.
4 *Morton Registrum* (n 3) vol 2, no 83.

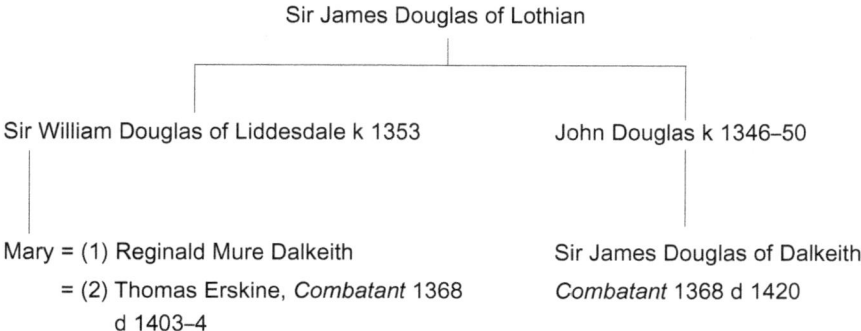

**Figure 14.1 Courtesy 1368**

*sibi debere, jure hereditario, eo quod, ut dixit, dicta proles non fuit viva nata. Super quo debato acceperunt duellum apud Edinburgh coram rege David, et in introitu parcae idem Thomas est effectus miles per patrem suum, et Jacobus per dominum Archibaldum Dowglas est miles effectus; qui simul pugnantes autoritate regia sunt divisi et extra parcam ducti. Sed quia post longos tractatus hinc inde habitos concordare non potuerunt, iterum dominus rex adjudicavit eosdem infra parcam convenire complecturi finaliter. Sed, ipsis ibidem introductis, rex cum magna diligentia tractavit inter eos, et data quadam summa pecuniae dicto Thomae per dictum Jacobum quam ante in prioribus tractatibus optulerat, et alia summa per ipsum regem ex sua magnificentia propter concordiam et dilectionem utriusque personae, idem Thomas cessit esse et, ipsis simul eductis de parca, terrae universae ipsius domini Willelmi penes dictum Jacobum jure hereditario remanserunt.*[5]

He left behind him a single daughter called Mary who married Reginald Mure, the son and heir of William Mure. But afterwards she was divorced from him on certain intricate grounds and she married Thomas Erskine, the son and heir of the lord Robert Erskine. She conceived a child by him but died in childbirth. Now he [Thomas Erskine] said that the lands of the lord William Douglas ought to be his for his lifetime by the courtesy of Scotland, because, he said, he had fathered a live child by the said marriage, but James Douglas, the son of the lord John Douglas, brother of the aforesaid William, opposed him saying that the said lands ought to be his by hereditary right, because, he said, the said child was not born alive. They agreed to a duel at Edinburgh on this debate in the presence of King David to settle the question, and at the entrance to the park the said Thomas was made a knight by his father, and James was made a knight by the lord Archibald Douglas; they then fought but were separated by royal command and led outside the park. But after long further negotiations they were unable to agree and again the lord king adjudged that they should meet in the park to settle the matter finally. But, after they had been led in there, the king mediated very carefully between them, and after the said Thomas had been given a certain sum of money which had already been offered by the said James in previous negotiations, and

---

5 *Chron Fordun* (n 2), vol 1 at 370n.

a further sum by the king himself out of his own magnificence for the sake of concord and because of his affection for both parties, Thomas yielded his claim. Both parties were led simultaneously from the park and the whole lands of that lord William remained with the said James by hereditary right.[6]

The detail and precision of the account is remarkable and must surely be taken from a legal document drawn up to record the event: the knighting of the participants by Sir Robert Erskine, Thomas's father, and by Sir Archibald Douglas; the two stages of the combat; the intervention and anxiety of the king; the final settlement by which neither party lost face; and the simultaneous departure from the lists – *simul eductis de parca* – all are carefully narrated. The relationship of the parties and the nature of their claim is clearly set out. Erskine claimed by the courtesy of Scotland – *ex curialitate Scociae* – while Douglas claimed by hereditary right – *jure hereditario*. The point at issue between them was not one of law – for the law seems to have been clear enough – but one of fact: had the child born to Mary Douglas been born live or stillborn? If live, then Erskine was entitled to his courtesy. If stillborn, then Douglas took his heritage un-trammelled by a liferent. To determine this fact they were prepared to duel, if need be to the death. We are also told that it was Erskine who relinquished his claim – *idem Thomas cessit esse* – which suggests that the issue on which battle was joined had been raised by him. We may be sure, incidentally, that the date of the duel was 1368: at the beginning of that year Erskine was still buying arms and armour, as has been seen, while by December 1368 James Douglas is being styled *"miles"*.[7]

The king's anxiety to achieve a settlement is understandable. Both combatants were closely connected to leading members of the royal circle. To judge from the frequency of their appearance as witnesses to David II's acts, Sir Robert Erskine and Sir Archibald Douglas, who knighted the combatants, were second to none in importance in the counsels of the king.[8] Sir Robert was chamberlain of Scotland and had been justiciar both north of Forth and of Lothian. At the time of David II's death in 1371 Sir Robert controlled Stirling castle, while his son Sir Thomas, the combatant, controlled Edinburgh.[9] Sir Robert was a trusted servant of Robert II, both

---

6 The translation is my own.
7 *RRS*, vol 6, nos 413 and 417.
8 *RRS*, vol 6, *passim*; B Webster, "David II and the government of fourteenth century Scotland" (1966) 16 *Transactions of the Royal Historical Society* 127; Penman, *David II* (n 2), index sv "Douglas, Archibald, 'the Grim', lord of Galloway (d 1400)" and "Erskine, Robert (d 1385)".
9 R Nicholson, *Scotland: The Later Middle Ages* (1974) at 150, 169–170, 185; Penman, *David II* (n 2) at 243–244. Nicholson's account of Erskine's part in the accession of Robert II is not

when steward and when king, as well as of David II. Sir Archibald Douglas, nicknamed "the Grim", was the illegitimate son of the celebrated Sir James. He controlled the rich inheritance of Bothwell and Petty, by virtue of his marriage in 1362 to Joanna Moray. In 1369 David II granted him all royal lands in Galloway between the Cree and the Nith in free barony. Later he became lord of Galloway and earl of Douglas. His daughter Marjorie married Robert III's eldest son, David, duke of Rothesay, and his son Archibald, earl of Douglas, married King Robert's eldest daughter.[10] David II had everything to gain from a reconciliation of the parties.

The dispute between Erskine and Douglas is one of the earliest recorded Scottish cases on the right of courtesy (*anglicé* curtesy), and the point at issue illustrates one of the peculiarities of that law. A widower could not enjoy the courtesy of a liferent of his wife's heritage unless a child had been born of the marriage and that child had been heard to cry. This requirement is as old as the law of courtesy itself.[11] It is to be found in *Glanvill*, it is found in the *Leges Quatuor Burgorum*, it is found in *Regiam Majestatem*.[12] Sir John Skene, in his *De Verborum Significatione*, waxes positively lyrical about it:

> Curialitas, curialitie, curtesie, from the French *Curtoise* civilitie, gentelnesse, humanitie, for the law of curtesie, is an gentill and favorable ordinance or constitution, granted and observed in this Realme, and nocht universallie keiped, or used in uther cuntries, And therefore it is called *Curialitas Scotiae*, the curtesie of *Scotland*. And in the laws of *England lex Anglie*, or the curtesie of *England*, within the quhilk twa realmes and none uther this law is in use. That is quhen onie man maries lauchfullie ane wife, and receivis lande and heritage with her: And it happen that he beget with her ane bairne, quha being borne, is heard cryand betwixt foure walles of ane house: and thereafter his wife deceasis before him, he sail bruik and possesse, all the landes quhilks perteined to her, in-during his lifetime, albeit the bairne live or decease ... The curtesie hes nocht place quhen na bairne is borne in lauchfull mariage, for it is necessar that ane bairne be

---

accepted by A Grant, *Independence and Nationhood: Scotland 1306–1469* (1984) at 177–179, see also Penman, *David II* at 413–414. Sir Robert first appears as justiciar north of Forth in 1358/9 (*RMS*, vol 2, no 3717): see further H L MacQueen, "Tame magnates? The justiciars of later medieval Scotland", in S Boardman and J Goodare (eds), *Kings, Lords and Men in Scotland and Britain, 1300–1625: Essays in Honour of Jenny Wormald* (2014) 93 at 100.

10 See references above at n 8; also *RRS*, vol 6, no 451, and see M Brown, *The Black Douglases* (1998) ch 3.
11 The further requirement in the later Scottish law of courtesy that the child, had he or she survived, should have been the mother's heir, in the sense of heir-at-law, may not have been part of the medieval law.
12 *Glanvill*, 7.18; *Leges Quatuor Burgorum*, ch 41 (*APS*, vol 1, at 340); *RM* (*APS*) 2.53; *RM* (*Cooper*) 2.58. Curtesy is discussed in Pollock & Maitland, vol 2, at 414–420. There is no adequate treatment of the history of courtesy in Scotland, but see P Fraser, *Husband and Wife* (2nd edn, 1878) at 1118 and J C Gardner, *The Origin and Nature of the Legal Rights of Spouses and Children* (1928).

borne maill or femaill, quick and liveand: And for probation theirof, he mon be heard cryand, for the curtesie hes place *in puero clamante,* (or as it is written in sum buikes) *brayand,* squeiland, or loudlie cryand. For in French *brayer,* in the latin *vagire,* is to crie or greite with ane loud voice. Quhilk word in our language is alswa attributed to Horse, Hartes, and uther beastes.[13]

Already in the thirteenth century, as Maitland pointed out, English lawyers were at a loss to account for some of the peculiarities of the law of curtesy, including the requirement that the child be heard to cry. Yet these peculiarities remained part of the Scottish law of courtesy until the end, and in the fourteenth century men were prepared to resort to battle to satisfy them.

The judicial duel in England could be either civil or criminal, and in *Trial by Combat* Neilson demonstrated that this was true of Scotland as well.[14] "The proof for the judicial duel in a plea of land in Scotland", he writes, "is very indefinite, yet there is such a body of floating provisions on the subject that in spite of the poverty of testimony it is reasonable to believe that it had at least some short existence there."[15] The criminal duel was appropriate in the appeal of felony where the appealer appealed the accused of felonious crime and offered proof by his body. The classic situation where the civil duel was competent in England was in procedure on the writ of right, the writ which raised the question of the best and most ancient right to land, rather than more recent possession or seisin. In the writ of right, but not in the "possessory" writs of novel disseisin and mort d'ancestor, the "tenant" (defendant) could choose whether to let the question be decided by an inquest or assize, or whether to defend and prove his right by battle. In the civil duel, but not in the criminal, the parties would be represented by champions (*campiones*), the "demandant" (plaintiff) necessarily so, the tenant at his option. Much has been done to elucidate the history of the brieves (or writs) of right, of novel dissasine and of mortancestry in medieval Scotland.[16] As their name indicates these brieves were modelled on the English writs, although they were by no means exact copies, and once established had a

---

13 Skene, *DVS,* sv "Curialitas".
14 Neilson's *Trial by Combat* (n 1) remains a classic for both Scotland and England. For England, see also M J Russell, "Trial by battle and the writ of right", and "Trial by battle and the appeals of felony", together at (1980) 1 *JLH* 111–164; M T Clanchy, "Highway robbery and trial by battle in the Hampshire eyre of 1249", in R F Hunnisett and J B Post (eds), *Medieval Legal Records* (1978) 26; and J H Baker, *Introduction to English Legal History* (5th edn, 2019) at 66, 80–81, 252, 543–547.
15 Neilson, *Trial by Combat* (n 1) at 87.
16 See H L MacQueen, *Common Law and Feudal Society in Medieval Scotland* (1993, reprinted 2016) chs 4–7. A Taylor, *The Shape of the State in Medieval Scotland, 1124–1290* (2016) ch 5 reconsiders the origins of the brieves in the twelfth and thirteenth centuries.

different history. As in England, the brieve of right appears to have raised deeper and more ancient questions of right than mere recent possession, and as in England, battle was at one time presumably competent on this brieve. The brieve of right was the ultimate touchstone of right to heritage and recognised as such by the poet William Dunbar in his description of hell in *Fasternis Evin in Hell* (written around 1507):

> Na menstrallis playit to thame but dowt,
> For glemen thair wer haldin owt,
> Be day and eik by nicht –
> Except a menstrall that slew a man;
> Swa till his heretage he wan
> and entirt be breif of richt.[17]

As more rational methods of proof were adopted the original duel of law went out of favour, especially in civil matters. After 1300 there appears to be no record of a duel of law actually fought over heritage in either Scotland or England. However, as the duel of law declined it was to some extent replaced, at least in courtly society, by the duel of chivalry. In some respects the duel of chivalry was a continuation of the duel of law, but there were important differences. The duel of chivalry was confined to the knightly classes. The parties fought in person and not through champions. They fought on horseback, fully armoured and bearing weapons of their choice, unlike the combatants in the original duel of law whose dress and whose weapons, prescribed by law, were archaic and repulsive: the combatants in the duel of law fought on foot, shaven-headed and bare-legged in sheepskin coats, and attacked each other with batons tipped with horn which resembled small pick-axes. The duel of chivalry took place before the Constable or the Marshal and not in the ordinary courts. Typically the duel of chivalry arose from an accusation of treason or other serious crime – indeed Neilson habitually refers to it as "the treason-duel of chivalry". But it was also appropriate, to judge from English evidence, to decide the right to armorial bearings, which are a type of heritage, and we need not doubt that it would have seemed appropriate, at least in the fourteenth century, to deal with questions of disputed right such as might arise on the brieve of right.

Neilson argues for, and indeed proved, the existence of a court of chivalry in later medieval Scotland. He pointed to two fifteenth-century manuscripts which regulated procedure in that court: "The Manner of Batale" and

---

17 J Kinsley (ed), *The Poems of William Dunbar* (1979) at 153 lines 103–108 (and for the date see at 335–336).

"The Order of Combats".[18] He also noted, as a further distinguishing mark between the original duel of law and the law of chivalry, that the duel of law could not be stopped by the judge, "for, so to speak, the battle itself was the real judge";[19] whereas the duel of chivalry could be stopped, and frequently was. "As in England", he says, "the duels were rarely fought except in the royal presence, and as in England, they were often stopped in mid-fight by the king. He did this in virtue of a royal *nobile officium* peculiar to chivalry. In both countries he was the head of this battle court."[20] The Scottish court of chivalry may not have been fully choate in 1368, but we may recognise in the combat between Erskine and Douglas a classic example of the duel of chivalry, fought between knights on horseback and in armour, and determining a question of heritage.

It seems more than likely that the duel of chivalry between Erskine and Douglas arose out of some process at common law. The English records speak of a judicial duel to be fought "according to the laws of Scotland, for certain causes"; and Fordun's account mentions several legal words and phrases – *"ex curialitate Scociae"*, *"jure hereditario"*, *"super quo debato acceperunt duellum"*, and *"rex adjudicavit"*.[21] However, we can only speculate as to the exact nature of that process. In England, there was a writ of right of dower (terce) and on this battle was competent.[22] But the widow's right of dower differed in many important respects from the widower's right of curtesy and it appears that there was never a separate writ of curtesy in England.[23] In his great treatise, however, *Bracton* does indicate several methods by which the issue in curtesy of whether a child had been born

---

18 Neilson, *Trial by Combat* (n 1) chs 66 (headed "The Maner of Batale") and 74 ("The Order of Combats"). See also R K Hannay, "Observations on the officers of the Scots Parliament" (1932) 44 JR 125; K Stevenson, *Chivalry and Knighthood in Scotland 1424–1513* (2006) at 64–67; and (on David II's enthusiasm for chivalry) M Penman, "David II (1329–1371)", in M Brown and R Tanner (eds), *Scottish Kingship, 1306–1542: Essays in Honour of Norman Macdougall* (2008) 49 at 64.

19 Neilson, *Trial by Combat* (n 1) at 189.

20 Neilson, *Trial by Combat* (n 1) at 273; the best-known instance of royal intervention is the treason-duel between Hereford and Norfolk in 1398 stopped by Richard II. K Nicholls, "Anglo-French Ireland and after" (1982) 1 *Peritia* 377, suggests that the judicial duel was often used as a device to enforce arbitration rather than as an end in itself.

21 Above, text accompanying n 5.

22 *Glanvill*, 6.11; cf *RM (APS)*, 2.13; *RM (Cooper)*, 2.16.

23 S F C Milsom, "Inheritance by women in the twelfth and early thirteenth centuries", in M S Arnold and others (eds), *On the Laws and Customs of England: Essays in Honour of Samuel E Thorne* (1981) 60, especially at 83: "There was no action by which the husband could claim curtesy, and he never had to sue for it. He had had the land ever since the marriage." This essay is reprinted in S F C Milsom, *Studies in the History of the Common Law* (1985) ch 12 (quotation at 254).

live and heard to cry – or worse, whether a monster and not a child had been born (an eventuality which seems to have caused *Bracton* particular concern) – could be raised.[24] The widower would normally be in possession of the lands on his wife's death. He might then be dispossessed by the heir. In that case the widower would take out a writ of novel disseisin, to which the heir, after the necessary general denial, would admit the disseisin but put forward the "exception" that the widower was not entitled to curtesy because no child had been born live of the marriage. In later English parlance he would "confess and avoid".[25] Thus the birth of a live child would be put in issue. Alternatively the heir might take out a writ of mort d'ancestor (or of cosinage) alleging that the widower stood between him and the land to which he was entitled by ancestral descent. In this case it would be the widower who would "except" and place the birth of the child in issue. Neither of these possibilities would involve battle at common law. But there was a third possibility: instead of a writ of mort d'ancestor the heir might have to proceed, or choose to proceed, by writ of right, claiming that the widower stood between him and the land to which he was entitled by hereditary right. Again the widower would "except" and place the birth of the child in issue. In this third scenario battle would be competent.

The evidence for medieval Scottish pleading is distinctly scrappy and has seldom been studied, but it is clear from legislation, surviving treatises and the early records of Council and Session that the system of pleading by exception existed in Scotland also.[26] It seems probable that in Scotland too the issue of childbirth in courtesy could have been raised in any of the three ways described by Bracton – by brieve of novel dissasine by the widower,

---

24 *Bracton*, fols. 168 (vol 3 at 34), 169b–170 (vol 3 at 38), 216 (vol 3 at 151), 271 (vol 3 at 293), 278 (vol 3 at 311), 438–438b (vol 4 at 362–363); Milsom (n 23) at 83–89 (reprint at 254–260).
25 On exceptions in England, see Pollock & Maitland, vol 2, at 611–620; S F C Milsom, *The Legal Framework of English Feudalism* (1976) at 13–17.
26 On exceptions in Scotland, see *inter alia* P J Hamilton-Grierson in his edition of Habakkuk Bisset's *Rolment of Courtis* (3 vols, Scottish Text Society, 1920–1926), vol 3, at 69; Bisset himself in the text "Anent the ordoure of proponyng of exceptionis" (*Rolment of Courtis*, vol 1, at 172; Balfour, *Practicks*, vol 2, at 343 ("Anent exceptiounis and essonzies"); *RM (APS)* 1.10.11 or *RM (Cooper)* 1.11.12; T D Fergus (ed), *Quoniam Attachiamenta* (SS vol 44 (1996) chs 22, 37 (at 218–219); *APS*, vol 1, at 742 c 7 (probably from the *Liber de Judicibus*); RPS 1426/13, 1427/7/6 and 7, 1430/5, 1471/8/26, A1504/3/140, A1557/12/5; *John son of Walter v Thomas Scot* 1368 (*RPS*, 1368/6/2); T Thomson (ed), *Acts of the Lords Auditors of Causes and Complaints* (1839), index, sv "Exceptions"; T Thomson (ed), *Acts of the Lords of Council in Civil Causes* (1839), index, sv "Dilatory Exceptions". See further H L MacQueen, "Pleadable brieves, pleading and the development of Scots law" (1986) 4 *Law & History Review* 403, and MacQueen, *Common Law* (n 16) at 77, 123. For a discussion of procedure in the church courts see S Ollivant, *The Court of the Official in Pre-Reformation Scotland* (SS vol 34, 1982) 108.

or by brieve of mortancestry or brieve of right by the heir, followed by the necessary exception. In Scotland, however, the scope of the brieve of mortancestry, albeit extended by Robert Bruce's legislation of 1318 to include grandparents as well as parents, brothers and sisters, uncles and aunts,[27] does not appear to have been extended further, as in England, by writs of cosinage, and so it is the more likely that the heir in Scotland would have to rely on the brieve of right. Thus James Douglas would not have been able to use mortancestry to succeed to lands of which his cousin Mary had been in sasine: he would have had to resort to the brieve of right.[28] If then a process at common law lies behind the duel of chivalry between Douglas and Erskine, we may speculate that Douglas, having been served heir by inquest to some of Mary's lands in June 1367,[29] found Erskine unwilling to relinquish possession, and was forced to proceed by brieve of right in the sheriff court. Erskine made the general denial and then pleaded by way of exception that he was entitled to a liferent by the courtesy of Scotland because a child had been born live of the marriage. On this exception issue was joined, and the duel of law competent at common law on the brieve of right was transmuted into a duel of chivalry before the king. The issue was Erskine's: "He who excepts must, like a plaintiff, offer to prove his case," says Maitland:[30] and thus it was Erskine who eventually yielded his claim, as Fordun informs us. This explanation, however, it should be stressed again, is speculative and likely to remain so.

Sir Thomas Erskine and Sir James Douglas both enjoyed long and distinguished careers after 1368. Both were to demonstrate again their appreciation of the finer points of law. After Mary Douglas's death Sir Thomas married as his second wife Janet Keith, great grand-daughter of Gratney, earl of Mar, and, in the eyes of Sir Thomas, the heiress-presumptive to that earldom. In order to safeguard the rights of his wife and of their heirs, Sir Thomas appeared in full Parliament in March 1390/1 before King Robert III and made a protest in the vernacular, using these or similar words – "*dixit in vulgari prout sequitur vel saltem in verbis consimilibus*":

> My lorde the kyng it is done me til understand that thare is a certane contract made bytwene schir Malcolme of dromonde and schir John of Swynton apon the landis of the Erledome of Marr and the Lordship of Garvyauch of the qwhilkes

---

27 *RPS* 1318/25.
28 The reference in *Morton Registrum* (n 3), vol 2, no 107 to a brieve of mortancestry in connection with a dispute between Sir James Douglas and William Cresswell over the barony of Roberton (which was part of Mary Douglas's inheritance) presumably relates to Cresswell's ancestral claim.
29 Above, text accompanying n 4.
30 Pollock & Maitland, vol 2, at 616; Maitland cites *Bracton* and the *Digest* of Justinian.

Erldome and Lordship Issabell the said schir Malcolms wyf is verray and lauchfull ayre And failliand of the ayrez of hir body the half of the forneymt erldome and lordship perteignys to my wyfe of Richt of heritage Tharefore I require you for goddis sake as my lorde and my kyng as lauchful actornay to my said wyfe that in case gif ony sic contract be made in preiudice of my saide wyfe of that at aucht of Richt and of lauch perteigne til hir in fee and heritage failliand of the saide Issabell as is before saide that yhe grant na confirmacion thare apon in hurtyng of the commone lauch of the kynryk and of my wyvis Richt swa that sic contract gif ony be make na preiudice no hurtyng to my fornemyt wife of that at scho aucht to succede to as lauchful ayre To the qwhilk our lorde the kyng answerit saiand that he had weel herd and undirstand his request and said that hym thocht his request was resonable And said als that it suld nocht be his wil in that case no in nane other oucht to do or to conferme that suld ryn ony man in preiudice of their heritage attour the commone lauch and namely in oucht at rynyt the said schir Thomas or his wyfe in sic manner Apon the qwilk our lorde the kynges grant the said schir Thomas and als apone his said Request Requerit me notare before said to make hym ane Instrument.[31]

Interestingly, this notarial instrument appears to be our first record of the vernacular in use in the Scots Parliament. The parliamentary record itself does not change from Latin to Scots until 1399. Erskine was right to suspect double dealing regarding the earldom of Mar, for it is notorious that his descendants were excluded from that earldom, despite frequent protests, for over one hundred years until they were finally granted the title (which still remains in the family) in the sixteenth century. Sir Thomas Erskine died in 1403 or 1404.[32]

Sir James Douglas of Dalkeith enjoyed the favour of successive kings and became one of the most powerful magnates in Scotland.[33] Many surviving documents attest to his close attention to legal matters. There is, for example, in the recently published *Regesta* of David II a brieve of mortancestry taken out by Douglas in 1368, not long after the duel of chivalry, to gain sasine of the lands of the barony of Kilbucho and Newlands, entailed on him by his uncle in 1351.[34] But the best evidence for his legal activity lies in the chartulary of the Douglases of Dalkeith, a treasure of evidence for the medievalist and legal historian, and one of the very few lay chartularies to have survived from medieval Scotland. The bulk of this was published last century

---

31 *RPS* 1391/5. For details of the Erskine claim see S I Boardman, "Erskine family (*per* c1350-c1450)", *Oxford Dictionary of National Biography* (2004) accessible at https://doi-org.ezproxy.is.ed.ac.uk/10.1093/ref:odnb/54181.
32 See Boardman (n 31).
33 On the career of Sir James Douglas of Dalkeith see in addition to Grant, "Higher nobility" (n 3) at 240ff, Innes, *Morton Registrum* (n 3), preface; MacQueen, *Common Law* (n 16) at 260–262; and Brown, *Black Douglases* (n 10), index sv "Douglas, James (I), Lord of Dalkeith (d 1420)".
34 *RRS*, vol 6, no 417; above, text accompanying n 3 for the entail of Kilbucho.

as *Registrum Honoris de Morton*. Perhaps the most interesting documents in the chartulary are two wills drawn up for Sir James in 1390 and 1392, the earliest known Scottish wills extant. In them Sir James makes special mention of his books: books of romances, books of grammar and dialectic, but also books of law, both civil law and Scottish statutes – *libros meos . . . civiles et statuta Regni Scocie*.[35] A direction later in the will to return books which had been borrowed to their owners confirms the impression of a literate, articulate layman. There may have been several such in late fourteenth-century Scotland, but Sir James is one of the few for whom we have clear evidence. Also specified in the will are various items of armour, some of which, one imagines, may date from the combat in 1368! Sir James married first the sister of the earl of March, Agnes Dunbar, whom David II may have wished to make his queen.[36] He married secondly Giles (Egidia), half-sister of Robert II. His eldest son married Elizabeth, daughter of Robert III. Sir James died in 1420, more than fifty years after the combat with Erskine, "a man of enormous territories and great real wealth".[37]

Before concluding, it is worth noting another tantalising reference, in no way less dramatic, to the law of courtesy in medieval Scotland. As the aged Walter Stewart, earl of Atholl, lay in prison on the afternoon of 26 May 1437, awaiting execution later that day for his part in the murder of his nephew King James I, he was visited by Sir Thomas Maule of Panmure, accompanied by various gentlemen and a notary. There, after making his last confession, Walter Stewart swore a solemn declaration that after his wife's death he had possessed the lands of Brechin Barclay by the courtesy of Scotland – *possidebit simpliciter ex curialitate regni Scotie*. Some of these lands he had resigned into the king's hands, but others in Fife he had not. This declaration was recorded for Sir Thomas Maule in a notarial instrument.[38] Atholl's wife had been Margaret Barclay, lady of Brechin, and heir to her father, Sir David Barclay. Maule's interest in the matter is not stated in the instrument, but it appears from a document drawn up in Scots eleven days later on 6 June 1437 – "the soothfast witnesing" of Thomas Bisset of Balwillo.[39] In it Bisset carefully traces the relationship between the countess of Atholl and Sir Thomas Maule:

---

35 *Morton Registrum* (n 3), vol 2, nos 193 and 196.
36 Nicholson, *Scotland* (n 9) at 182–183; Penman, *David II* (n 2) at 412, 415: in 1371, before she married Sir James Douglas, Agnes Dunbar was granted 1000 merks a year from the customs of Aberdeen and Haddington by David II.
37 Innes, *Morton Registrum* (n 3), preface at xv.
38 J Stuart (ed), *Registrum de Panmure* (2 vols, 1874, henceforth *Panmure Registrum*), vol 2, at 228.
39 *Panmure Registrum* (n 38) vol 2, at 230.

suth fastli I make knawin that dam Jehan Barclay the wif umquhil of scher David Flemying was ful systir til the last scher David Barclay umquhile lord of brechyn and at the Said scher David [Barclay] had na brothir that mycht succed til his heritage bot alanerlie a douchtir the quhilk was merit with Walter Stewart Knicht erl of Athol sumtym. Heir atour, suthfastli I mak knawin that the said dam Jehan Barclay the wyf umquhil of the said scher David Flemyng had twa douchters an callit Jonet an uthir Marioun and Jonet bair Alexander of Seytoun, and Marioun Thomas de Maule the quhilk decisit at the Harlaw. Alsua suthfastli I make knawyn that in my yuthed I was servant on to my lord scher Thomas of Erskyn [the duellist of 1368] and of continual houshald and oftymes I herd my lord beforsaid and my lade Dam Jehan his wif that was modir to David Steuart's modir, suthfastli say that failyeand of David Steuart and of his modir that Seytonis and Maulis war verra ayris to the Barclayis landis . . . .[40]

Figure 14.2 overleaf sets out some of the complicated relationships involved. The point is, however, that failing issue of Margaret Barclay and Walter Stewart – and Walter died predeceased by all his descendants, his grandson Sir Robert Stewart having been executed some days before him – Sir Alexander Seton and Sir Thomas Maule were the nearest heirs to the Barclay inheritance, through heirs portioners.[41] It would be pleasant to record that Sir Thomas Maule did actually succeed to some of the Barclay lands, but the evidence is otherwise.

The duel between Erskine and Douglas in 1368 and the last declaration of Walter, earl of Atholl, provide two of the best and most dramatic instances of the operation of the law of courtesy in medieval Scotland before the records of the central judicial bodies and of the Court of Session provide a clearer picture. The duel in 1368 may strike us as an extraordinary combination of a bizarre rule of evidence and an archaic method of proof, but before we rush to condemn our fourteenth-century ancestors we would do well to reflect that the requirement that a child be born of the marriage live and heard to cry remained part of the law until the abolition of courtesy in 1964, and that it is at least arguable, following dicta in *M'Kendrick v Sinclair*,[42] that trial by battle is still competent in Scotland.

---

40 I have followed the text in *Panmure Registrum* but, with the aid of the facsimile included there, corrected some small mistakes.
41 Thus both Seton, who appears to have been the father of the first earl of Huntly, and Maule were heirs to the Barclay inheritance, and not Maule alone, as is often stated.
42 1972 SC (HL) 25; the argument would assume that the Appeal of Murder Act 1819 (59 Geo III c 46), which abolished trial by battle in England after the celebrated case of *Ashford v Thornton* (1818) 1 B & Ald 405, does not apply in Scotland, and follows Lord Reid's view that "Loss of a common law remedy by desuetude would, I think, be a novelty in our law, and I see no advantage in introducing such a principle. No one knows what may happen in the future" (1972 SC (HL) at 54).

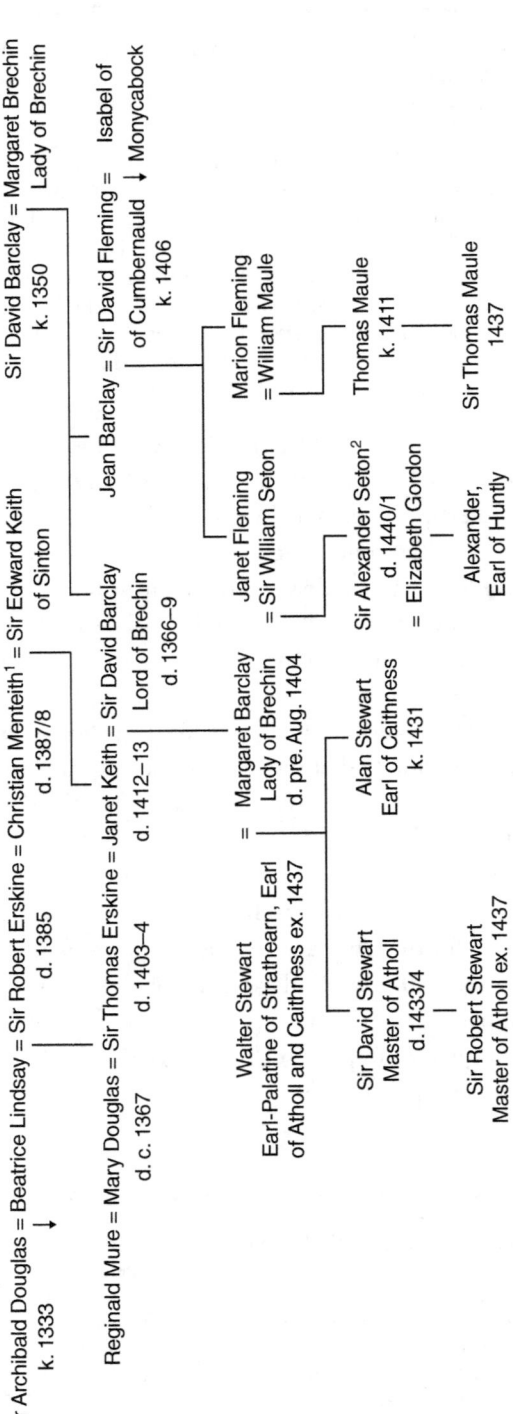

**Figure 14.2** Courtesy 1437

[1] Christian Menteith was both stepmother and mother-in-law to Sir Thomas Erskine. It was through her that the Erskines claimed the Earldom of Mar.
[2] Sir Alexander Seton's elder brother Sir John Seton was probably the son of an earlier marriage.

# 15 Promise*

## A. INTRODUCTION

For several hundred years Scots law has held to the proposition that a promise, seriously intended, is legally binding without the need for acceptance. Stair set out the position clearly in his *Institutions*, and although later writers lacked his clarity of vision and capacity for analysis, the law remained essentially unchanged until the Requirements of Writing (Scotland) Act 1995.[1] In the mid-twentieth century the writings of Sir Thomas Smith gave rise to a renewed interest in the doctrine of promise which was reflected in a number of academic articles and two Scottish Law Commission Memoranda.[2] In two valuable contributions, Bill McBryde has placed the modern law in its historical and comparative setting, and Robert Black has expounded it in the *Stair Memorial Encyclopaedia*.[3] Reinhard Zimmermann and Phillip Hellwege have also commented on the Scots law of promise from a continental perspective.[4] It is hoped, however, that there may still be room for further comment.

---

* Originally published as "Promise", in K G C Reid and R Zimmermann (eds), *A History of Private Law in Scotland* (2000), vol 2, 220–251.
1 It is difficult not to sympathise with J J Gow's comment that "Omne verbum in ore fideli cadit in debitum was the undoubted battle-cry of Stair but his successors unto this present day have lacked his genius and his ardour" (*The Mercantile and Industrial Law of Scotland* (1964) at 1). See below section J.
2 These are discussed below section F, and text accompanying nn 128–50.
3 W W McBryde, "Promises in Scots law" (1993) 42 ICLQ 48 (see also W W McBryde, *The Law of Contract in Scotland* (3rd edn, 2007) ch 2); R Black, "Unilateral promises", in SME, vol 15 (1996) paras 611–618. See also since the first publication of this chapter H L MacQueen and J Thomson, *Contract Law in Scotland* (5th edn, 2020) paras 3.20–3.28; M Hogg, *Obligations* (2nd edn, 2006) ch 2; M Hogg, *Promises and Contract Law: Comparative Perspectives* (2011); and three articles by H L MacQueen: "Unilateral promises: Scots law compared with PECL and the DCFR" (2016) 24 *European Review of Private Law* 529; "Unilateral promises", in A Albanese and A Nicolussi (eds), *Le Parole del Diritto: Scritti in Onore di Carlo Castronovo* (2019) 1893; "My word is my bond: unilateral promises again", 2019 *SLT (News)* 103.
4 R Zimmermann and P Hellwege, "Belohnungsversprechen: 'pollicitatio', 'promise' oder 'offer'?: Schottisches Recht vor dem Hintergrund der europaischen Entwicklungen" (1998) 39 *Zeitschrift für Rechtsvergleichung* 133. For Italian perspectives, see P de Gioia-Carabellese, "The concepts of the Scottish (and Italian) unilateral promise" [2011] *European Business Law Review* 381 and L Vagni, *La Promessa en Scozia* (2008).

This chapter seeks, in particular, to consider Stair's treatment of promise against the background of the Canon law and the *jus commune*, and actual Scottish practice. It investigates, however tentatively, the state of Scots law in the years between the Scottish Reformation in 1559/60 and the appearance of Stair's *Institutions* in 1681; and it explores the influence of the pre-Reformation Canon law on the later Scottish law of obligations. Inevitably, it also addresses some at least of the questions of terminology which so bedevil this entire area of law, notably the much debated question as to what significance, if any, should be attached to Stair's use of the word "pollicitation".[5] Throughout the article the general term used to indicate a promise, seriously intended, and binding in law without the necessity of acceptance, is simply "promise", this being in line with well-established Scottish usage. The term "pollicitation" (or *pollicitatio*) has been rejected as inappropriate for the purpose, and the inclusion of the adjective "unilateral" before "promise" deemed unnecessary.[6]

## B. STAIR'S *INSTITUTIONS*

As is well known, Stair held that promise, seriously intended, was legally binding without the need of acceptance. Promise, for Stair, fell into the category of 'conventional obligations", which "do arise from our will and consent".[7] "We must distinguish", wrote Stair, in a famous passage, "betwixt promise, pollicitation or offer, paction and contract".[8] Sometimes the act of will was "absolute and pure, and sometimes conditional". If conditional, the condition might relate either to the performance of the obligation, or to its very constitution. In the latter case, fulfilment of the condition was necessary to bring the obligation into existence. Thus, in the case of an ordinary contract, "when any offer or tender is made, there is implied a condition, that before it become obligatory, the party to whom it is offered must accept ... So then, an offer accepted is a contract, because it is the deed of two,

---

5 See below section F.
6 This chapter should be read alongside those of G Lubbe, "Formation of contract", and H L MacQueen, "Third party rights in contract: *jus quaesitum tertio*", in K Reid and R Zimmermann (eds), *A History of Private Law in Scotland volume II: Obligations* (2000), at 1 and 220 respectively. See further H L MacQueen and W D H Sellar, "Scots law: *ius quaesitum tertio*, promise and irrevocability", in E J H Schrage (ed), *Ius quaesitum tertio* (2008) 357.
7 Stair, *Inst*, 1.10.1. The term "voluntary obligations" is perhaps to be preferred to "conventional obligations", given that the latter might be thought to refer to contractual obligations alone.
8 Stair, *Inst*, 1.10.3.

the offerer and accepter."[9] By contrast, says Stair, "a promise is that which is simple and pure, and hath not implied as a condition, the acceptance of another".[10] Stair noted that Hugo Grotius (1583–1645) had taken a contrary view, holding that acceptance was necessary to constitute every conventional obligation, and that, accordingly, even a promise required to be accepted for it to become binding in law:

> In this Grotius differeth de iure belli, lib.2.cap. 11.§ holding, "that acceptance is necessary to every conventional obligation in equity, without consideration of positive law;" and to prevent that obvious objection, that promises are made to absents, infants, idiots, or persons not yet born, who cannot accept, and therefore such obligations should ever be revocable, till their acceptance, which in some of them can never be; he answereth, that the civil law only withholdeth, that such offers cannot be revoked, until these be in such capacity as to accept or refuse.[11]

Stair's scheme is crystal clear: he distinguishes between "promise", pure and simple, requiring no acceptance to become binding, on the one hand; and "contract", which becomes binding as the result of "acceptance" following on an "offer", on the other.[12] "Promises now," says Stair, speaking of the practice of Scots law in his own time, "are commonly held obligatory, the canon law having taken off the exception of the civil law, *de nudo pacto*."[13] He continues:

> It is true if he in whose favour they [promises] are made, accept not, they become void, not by the negative non-acceptance, but by the contrary rejection. For as the will of the promiser constitutes a right in another, so the other's will, by renouncing and rejecting that right, voids it, and makes it return.

It is important to note that Stair implies that this doctrine of promise does not rest simply on abstract legal theory, but corresponds to actual Scottish practice, "the canon law having taken off the exception of the civil law". It is also worth noting that although Stair generally uses the term "promise" to refer to promise binding without acceptance, that is, to "simple" or "pure" or "naked" or "perfect" promise, he does occasionally use the term in a wider sense to include also offer: thus, "If the promise be pendent upon acceptation, and no more than an offer . . ."; or, ". . . for promises, when they are

---

9 Stair, *Inst*, 1.10.3.
10 Stair, *Inst*, 1.10.4.
11 Stair, *Inst*, 1.10.4.
12 It will be noted that this very clear analysis of "contract" as being based on "offer" followed by "acceptance" pre-dates by almost 150 years the adoption of such an analysis in English law (for which see M Lobban, "Contract", in W Cornish and others (eds), *The Oxford History of the Laws of England Volume XII: 1820–1914: Private Law* (2010) 295 at 329 ff).
13 Stair, *Inst*, 1.10.4.

parts of bargains about moveables, are probable by witnesses"; and in his discussion of *jus quaesitum tertio*.[14] The context, however, is usually such as to avoid any ambiguity.

There was, however, an important obstacle in the way of an unfettered doctrine of promise in Scots law. Although no particular formalities were required to constitute the obligation, a promise, if challenged, could only be proven by writ or oath (*vel scripto vel iuramento*): that is, by writing under the hand of, or the oath in court of, the party denying.[15] This is so, says Stair, even when the promise is for under £100 Scots (that is, £8.33 sterling), the significance of this remark being that in many cases where Scots law restricted proof, an exception was made if the sum was for less than £100 Scots. The rule restricting proof did not apply, however, where the promise was part of a larger bargain concerning moveables.[16] The rule as to proof by writ or oath had been established long before Stair's time,[17] and its basis was challenged as early as 1580: in *Auchinleck v Gordon*, a case involving a promise to pay a sum of money, it was held that proof could not be by witnesses, *sed vel per scriptum vel per juramentum partis*.[18] The report of the case includes the comment *licet jus commune et sana ratio contrarium tradere videantur*,[19] although it is not clear whether this represents the view of the reporter or of court.

Again and again this harsh rule was confirmed by the Court of Session. Four centuries were to pass before the law was to change, and then in favour of a stricter, rather than a more liberal requirement.[20] It is convenient to note this later history here. In *Deuchar v Brown*, cited by Stair, and decided when he was Lord President, a gratuitous promise, even for a sum under £100 Scots, being "without cause onerous, or commerce", and "not being in the way of a bargain", was held to be not provable by witnesses.[21] The case was clearly intended to set a precedent, the report reading, "The Lords, having considered this case as of general consequence, and to be a

---

14 Stair, *Inst*, 1.10.6; 1.10.4: for *jus quaesitum tertio*, see below text accompanying n 28.
15 For a discussion of the former law on proof by writ or oath, see particularly A G Walker and N M L Walker, *The Law of Evidence in Scotland* (1st edn, 1964); also Scottish Law Commission Memorandum No 39 on Constitution and Proof of Voluntary Obligations: Formalities of Constitution and Restrictions on Proof (1977) and No 66 on Constitution and Proof of Voluntary Obligations and the Authentication of Writings (1985).
16 Stair, *Inst*, 1.10.4; 4.43.4.
17 Balfour cites a case in 1565 (*Practicks* at 366).
18 *Auchinleck v Gordon* (1580) Mor 12382.
19 "Although both the *jus commune* and common sense would seem to suggest the contrary."
20 See below section J.
21 *Deuchar v Brown* (1672) Mor 12386.

practick for the future, did sustain the defence." In *Fotheringham* in 1708 it was noted that, "there was scarce any case where there was a more uniform track of decisions than here that promises are never allowed to be proved by witnesses".[22] Later in the eighteenth century, the rule was again confirmed in the leading case of *Millar v Tremamondo*.[23] Tremamondo had made various promises "in the view of" Millar marrying his daughter. He claimed, however, that he was not bound, "the promises alleged being merely verbal and gratuitous", and therefore not provable by witnesses. The pursuer agreed that "mere gratuitous promise could not regularly be proved by parole-evidence", but pleaded an exception when the promise was made *intuitu matrimonii*, this being, he argued, part of a larger transaction and "highly onerous". The court, however, after a lively debate recorded in some detail in Lord Hailes's Reports, upheld the general rule and, by a majority of seven to six, refused to make an exception in the case of prospective marriage. Hailes makes it clear that the marriage did indeed take place, and notes that: "Millar did not reclaim. He told his counsel that he would not give the Court any farther trouble; and, at the same time, declared that he would not put his father-in-law upon oath lest he should perjure himself!"

*Millar v Tremamondo* remained a leading authority until the law was changed by the Requirements of Writing (Scotland) Act 1995, being followed in *Edmonston* in 1861, *Hawick v Huggan* in 1902 and, definitively, in the First Division case of *Smith v Oliver* in 1911.[24] In *Hawick v Huggan* Lord Kyllachy, and in *Smith v Oliver* Lord President Dunedin, restated the basic rule that gratuitous promise, although in principle just as binding in Scots law as an onerous obligation, could only be proved by writ or oath; there was no scope, it was said, *Millar v Tremamondo* being taken as authority for the proposition, for the doctrine of *rei interventus* as regards proof of promise.

Stair explains the rule regarding writ or oath, rather disingenuously, by comparing it to the position in Roman law regarding naked pactions and *stipulatio*:

> the reason . . . is the same that the Roman law gave no action upon naked pactions, to prevent the mistakes of parties and witnesses in communings, that they should use a set form of words in stipulations so now, when writ is so ordinary,

---

22 *Fotheringham of Pourie v Heir of Hunter of Burnside* (1708) Mor 12414.
23 *Millar v Tremamondo* (1771) Mor 12395, Hailes' Decisions 409.
24 *Edmonston v Edmonston* (1861) 23 D 995; *Hawick Heritable Investment Bank v Huggan* (1902) 5 F 75; *Smith v Oliver* 1911 SC 103.

we allow no processes for promises, as a penalty against those who observe not so easy a method.²⁵

Disingenuously, given that the requirement in Roman law concerning *stipulatio* affected constitution rather than proof, whereas in Scots law, to use Stair's own famous phrase, "every paction produceth action".²⁶ In this matter of proof, it is clear that Stair was again setting forth an existing rule of Scots law.²⁷

Stair also addresses the question of third party rights, or *jus quaesitum tertio*, in the same chapter. As this is covered elsewhere, it is only necessary to refer to it briefly here.²⁸ Stair's discussion of *jus quaesitum tertio* flows directly from his treatment of promise,²⁹ writing

> It is likewise the opinion of Molina [Luis de Molina, 1535–1600], cap 263, and it quadrates to our customs, that when parties contract, if there be any article in favours of a third party, at any time, *est jus quaesitum tertio*, which cannot be recalled by both the contractors, but he [the third party] may compel either of them to exhibit the contract, and thereupon the obliged may be compelled to perform. So a promise, though gratuitous, made in favour of a third party, that party, albeit not present nor accepting, was found to have right thereby.³⁰

Stair cites the case *Achinmoutie v Hay*, decided in 1609, in support of this proposition.³¹ However, the situation is different if the so-called promise in favour of a third party is no more than an offer, binding only on acceptance:

---

25 Stair, *Inst*, 1.10.4.
26 Stair, *Inst*, 1.10.7.
27 For a modern tirade against the rule regarding proof by writ or oath, see J J Gow, "The constitution and proof of voluntary obligations", 1961 *JR* 1 (on which see the contribution of Lubbe (n 6), especially section V). See further below text accompanying nn 135–140, and below section J. It is, of course, the case that Scots law from an early date required that certain obligations (*obligationes literis*), mainly concerning the transfer of heritage, should be *constituted* in writing.
28 See MacQueen and Sellar (n 6).
29 As is recognised, for example, by Sir Thomas Smith and Alan Rodger. See the discussion of the term "pollicitation", below section F.
30 Stair, *Inst*, 1.10, 5. As Rodger pointed out (in "Molina, Stair and the *jus quaesitum tertio*", 1969 *JR* 34, 128, 2 parts) the reference to Molina was properly to Disp 263, rather than to Disp 265, as given in earlier editions of Stair. T Richter, "Molina, Grotius, Stair and the *jus quaesitum tertio*", 2001 *JR* 219, suggests that Stair's reference to Molina may well have been a "blind citation", copied from Grotius and not actually used by Stair himself. See further MacQueen and Sellar (n 6), at 359–360.
31 *Auchmoutie v Hay* (1609) Mor 12126. Rodger (n 30) discusses this case *sub nomine Auchmoutie v Laird of Mainehay* at 139 sqq., and prints the report of the case as given in the manuscript of Haddington's Decisions in the Advocates' Collection in the National Library of Scotland as Appendix A. He notes with regret that the report lacks detail, but believes that it shows that "for some reason or other a *tertius* could sue on a promise which had not been accepted" (at 140). In fact, Haddington's manuscript appears to be the basis for Morison's report. For the case of *Wood v Moncur* in 1591, see below text accompanying n 48.

> If the promise be pendent upon acceptation, and no more than an offer it is imperfect and ambulatory, and in the power of the offerer, till acceptance; ... and so if a promise be made by one to another in favours of a third, importing the acceptance of that third, it is pendent and revocable by these contractors, till the third accept.[32]

As already noted, Stair regards the proposition that a promise seriously intended is binding without acceptance as a consequence of the Canon law taking off the exception of Roman law *de nudo pacto*. His famous formulation that "every paction produceth action" is likewise explicitly founded on Canon law:

> We shall not insist in these [formalities of Roman law], because the common custom of nations hath resiled therefrom, following rather the canon law, by which every paction produceth action, et omne verbum de ore fideli cadit in debitum, C.1 & 3 de pactis. And so observeth Guidelinus, de jure Nov.l.3.cap 5. ult. and Corvinus, de pactis. We have a special statute of session, November 27, 1592, acknowledging all pactions and promises as effectual: and so it has been ever since decided, January 14, 1631, Sharp contra Sharp.[33]

The *jus commune*, then, according to Stair, had followed the Canon law in this matter, rather than the Roman rule, and this has been reflected in Scottish practice. Thus a bare contract, based on offer and acceptance, required no counter-prestation or consideration in response to the offer to be binding in law.[34] Stair, incidentally, does not distinguish between the terms "paction" and "contract":

> Pactions, contracts, covenants, and agreements, are synonymous terms both in themselves, and according to the recent customs of this and other nations; so that it will be unnecessary to trace the many subtilties and differences amongst pactions and contracts in the Roman law.[35]

---

32 Stair, *Inst*, 1.10.6. For the story of *jus quaesitum tertio* in later Scots law, see now, in particular, MacQueen (n 6).

33 Stair, *Inst*, 1.10.7. For the alleged Act of Sederunt, see below text accompanying nn 50–53. The report of *Sharp v Sharp* (1631) Mor 4299, 15562 does not mention the Act of Sederunt, but does indicate that the strict rules of Civil law were not being followed (see also Lubbe (n 6), text accompanying n 107).

34 Thus every edition of Gloag and Henderson's *Introduction to the Law of Scotland* contains the sentence, "Differing in this respect from the law of England, Scots law holds that consent will infer an obligation although there may be no consideration." See now the 14th edn (2017) at para 5.01. As with promise, however, there may be complications regarding proof if the contract is gratuitous. For the formation of contract in Scots law generally, see Lubbe (n 6).

35 Stair, *Inst*, 1.10.10. For a discussion of the different meanings sometimes ascribed to words such as "contract", "pact", and "convention" see, for example, R Zimmermann, *The Law of Obligations: Roman Foundations of the Civilian Tradition* (1990) ch 18.

## C. THE *JUS COMMUNE*

Stair's treatment of promise needs to be considered in the context of the wider European intellectual tradition. Stair refers to "the common custom of nations", that is, the *jus commune*, and more specifically to the opinions of Petrus Gudelinus (1550–1619), Grotius, Molina, and others. This is no mere window-dressing. Rather it indicates that Stair was fully aware of the ongoing debate within the *jus commune* as to the place of promise and *nudum pactum*. The Church had taught that promises seriously intended should be kept, whether standing on their own, or as part of what would now be classified as a contract: *pacta quantumcunque nuda servanda sunt*;[36] this being in clear contrast to the Civil law rule: *ex nudo pacto non oritur actio*. At first the keeping of promises was regarded as primarily a moral obligation, which should not necessarily be given legal effect; but in the later middle ages it came to be accepted by Canon lawyers that such promises should also be legally binding, and various devices, such as the *denunciatio evangelica* and appeal to the *officium judicis*, were used to allow to give legal force to such obligations in the Church courts. As Helmholz notes, "[t]he ethical principle led even to enforcement of unilateral promises".[37] In addition, the Church claimed jurisdiction over obligations supported by an oath, on the basis that the invocation of the name of the deity gave them a *locus* in the matter. The net result was that over much of western Europe, including both Scotland and England, towards the end of the middle ages, the courts of the Church acquired a large and significant jurisdiction in the field of obligations.[38]

This rapid expansion of ecclesiastical jurisdiction at the expense of the secular courts soon came to be resented. In particular, the *nexus* resulting from the use of an oath came to be regarded as little more than a fiction which allowed the Church courts to claim jurisdiction over matters more properly of secular concern. As Helmholz notes, "the reality, in England at least, had gone far beyond the point where it could be argued that there was anything

---

36 *Decretals*, lib I, tit XXXV, ch I.
37 R H Helmholz, "Contracts and the Canon law", in J Barton (ed), *Towards a General Law of Contract* (1990) 49 at 50.
38 For an overview of the Canon law in this area, see Helmholz (n 37). On oaths in particular, see R H Helmholz, *The Spirit of Classical Canon Law* (1996), 145–173. Earlier studies of the development of the Canon law as regards the *denunciatio evangelica* and the appeal to the *officium judicis* include F Spies, *De l'observation des simple conventions en droit canonique* (1928), and J Rousseau, *Le Fondement de l'obligation contractuelle dans le droit classique de l'Église* (1933). See further below section E.

remotely spiritual about the jurisdiction."[39] In England the high point of ecclesiastical jurisdiction in these matters was reached in the last decade of the fifteenth century. Thereafter it rapidly declined, the fourteenth-century statute of *Praemunire* providing the means to cut it down. Helmholz notes that by the 1520s, that is, before the English Reformation, the Church's jurisdiction in contract was "virtually moribund".[40]

Debate, however, continued within the *jus commune* as to the enforceability of promises and *pacta nuda* in *secular* courts. Increasingly exceptions came to be made to the Civilian rule *ex nudo pacto;* earlier distinctions made between "pact" and "contract" began to break down; and more and more agreements came to be regarded or classified as *pacta vestita*, agreements clothed by *causa* and thus actionable, rather than *pacta nuda*. Although the French Humanists were reluctant to abandon the Civilian rule altogether, it gradually came to be accepted, in theory as well as practice, that agreements entered into by mutual consent should be legally enforceable, even if they involved no counter-prestation or *quid pro quo*. This acceptance of the principle *pacta sunt servanda* has sometimes been traced to the writings of Matthaeus Wesenbecius (1531–1586). Certainly it was to become the common currency of the Spanish scholastics and the later natural law school, including Grotius. By the end of the seventeenth century the principle had won general acceptance.[41] The Civilian Franciscus Connanus (1508–51) was unusual in that he did not recognise that gratuitous agreements gave rise even to a moral obligation. Stair goes out of his way to disagree with him:

> But let us inquire whether promises, or naked pactions, are morally obligatory by the law of Nature. Few do contravert it, yet Connanus, lib.1.cap. 6, lib.5.cap. 9 holdeth, that promises, or naked pactions, where there is no equivalent cause onerous intervening, do morally produce no obligation or action, though in congruity and decency it be fit to perform . . .; against which there is not only the

---

39 Helmholz (n 37) at 57.
40 Helmholz (n 37) at 59. Helmholz also cites the example of Barcelona, and does not doubt that the reaction against the Church's claimed jurisdiction was general.
41 This short account of a lengthy and complicated process is necessarily much simplified. It does not, for example, cover differing definitions of *causa* and "consideration". For further details, see Barton, "Introduction", and R Feenstra, "Pact and contract in the Low Countries from the 16th to the 18th century", in Barton, *General Law of Contract* (n 37) 197; also K-P Nanz, *Die Entstehung des allgemeinen Vertragsbegriffs im 16. bis 18. Jahrhundert* (1985) – I have found W M Gordon's review of Nanz in (1987) 8 *JLH* 373 particularly helpful; J Gordley, *The Philosophical Origins of Modern Contract Doctrine* (1991), especially 67–77; Zimmermann, *Obligations* (n 35), chs 16–18; and W Decock, *Theologians and Contract Law: The Moral Transformation of the Ius Commune (ca.1500–1650)* (2013). See further Lubbe (n 6), section IV. Although Stair, *Inst*, 1.10, does not cite Wesenbecius, he does refer to him later in connection with "earnest" in sale (*Inst*, 1.14.3).

testimony of the canon law, which insinuates an anterior reason to its own position; but also the civil law . . .; but especially this is confirmed by the law of God . . .[42]

Naked pactions, then, resulting from a bare agreement between the parties, came to be regarded as enforceable by most writers within the *jus commune* by the end of the seventeenth century. But what about a promise, pure and simple? Although most writers, differing from Connanus, took the view that promises were morally binding, few if any, with the exception of Stair, and perhaps Molina, were prepared to argue that they should be legally enforceable. Grotius was quite explicit that a promise (*promissio*), although intending to confer a legal right on another, was binding only on acceptance. Stair, as noted, indicated his specific disagreement with this view. Grotius also made a subtle distinction between *promissio* and *pollicitatio*; the latter falling short of a resolution to confer a legal right. Few followed him in this, although Samuel Pufendorf (1632–1694) who held, like Grotius, that a bare promise was not enforceable without acceptance, refers to *pollicitatio* as *imperfecta promissio*.[43]

A further question concerned the nature of a right conferred by agreement between two parties on an absent third party (*jus quaesitum tertio*). Although Grotius did not favour the rule *alteri stipulatio nemo potest*, he insisted that there must be acceptance by the third party. This was to have an adverse effect on Roman-Dutch law and on later Dutch and South African law down to the present day.[44] Stair, as already noted, took the view that no acceptance was necessary. In this instance he was not alone, as Molina certainly, and perhaps also Simon à Groenewegen van der Made (1613–1652), were of the same opinion.[45]

## D. THE COMMON LAW OF SCOTLAND

Stair, then, was well informed about the ongoing debate within the *jus commune* as to the potentially binding nature of naked pactions and promises. He was, however, as has been noted, also concerned with the practice of

---

42 Stair, *Inst*, 1.10.10.
43 I have found G MacCormack, "A note on Stair's use of the term pollicitatio", 1976 *JR* 121, helpful on this.
44 See Zimmermann (n 35), 42–45.
45 For Groenewegen, see B Beinart and M L Hewett (eds), *Simon à Groenewegen van der Made, Tractatus de Legibus Abrogatis* (1975), vol 2, ad D 50, 12 *De Pollicitationibus*, and (1984), vol 3, ad C. 2, 3, 13 *in bonae fidei*.

Scots law in his own day and makes frequent reference to it. Thus, in discussing promise, he says, "[p]romises now are commonly held obligatory"; in discussing *jus quaesitum tertio*, he inserts the phrase, "and it quadrates to our customs"; and in the same title he talks of, "the recent customs of this and other nations".[46] Stair also cites Scottish cases, decided by the Session, such as *Auchmoutie* and *Sharp*, to back his propositions.[47] To the cases cited by Stair others can be added, such as *Wood v Moncur* in 1591 where a promise made by contract in favour of a third party was upheld; *Kintore v Sinclair* in 1623 where a bare promise, although *nudum pactum*, was sustained; and *Laird of Clackmannan v Sir William Nisbet* in 1624 where the defenders argued that a promise was not obligatory, but the court held it to be a "perfect stipulation".[48] To these can be added *Deuchar v Brown*, cited by Stair in connection with the restriction on proof.[49] Further, in his discussion of promise Stair claimed that there was an Act of Sederunt in point, "We have a special statute of session, November 27, 1592, acknowledging all pactions and promises as effectual: and so," he continues, "it hath been ever since decided."[50]

This Act of Sederunt of 1592, if accurately reported, is clearly important as regards actual Scottish practice. Subsequent commentators, however, have concluded that Stair's reference cannot be taken at face value. They have consulted the printed Acts of Sederunt, identified an Act of 27 November 1592, but found that it deals with other matters. Thus Erskine notes:

> The effect given in our law to verbal obligations is by Stair ascribed to an act of sederunt, 27 Nov. 1592, which, as he recites it, declares all pactions and promises to be effectual: but that act says no more than that all irritant clauses in contracts, infeftments, bonds and other writings, shall be judged precisely according to the words and meaning of such clauses, without the least mention of pactions or promises.[51]

More recently, Lord Mackenzie Stuart has described the reference as, "but an incidental misdirection in Stair's otherwise remarkable incorporation of

---

46 Stair, *Inst*, 1.10.4; 1.10.5; 1.10.10. For Stair on the authority of custom "which may be called our common law", see ch 6 of the present work; also Sellar, "Custom", at paras 364–369.
47 For *Sharp* and *Auchmoutie*, see above text accompanying nn 31 and 33.
48 *Wood v Moncur* (1591) Mor 7719; *Kintore v Sinclair* (1623) Mor 9425; *Laird of Clackmannan v Sir William Nisbet* (1624) reported in R Spotiswoode, *Practicks of the Law of Scotland* (1706) at 248. For the last of these, see A J Mackenzie Stuart, "Contract and quasi-contract", in *ISLH* 241 at 252.
49 *Deuchar v Brown* (1672) Mor 12386 (and see above text accompanying n 21).
50 Stair, *Inst*, 1.10.7.
51 Erskine, *Inst*, 3.2.1.

native threads into what is largely a foreign pattern".[52] That Stair should have made a mistake on such a matter would indeed be surprising. There is, however, further evidence which confirms Stair's account. At the end of the discussion of pactions (*De Pactis*) in Hope's *Major Practicks*, there occurs this sentence: "C 775 makes mentione of ane statut insert in the sederunt books (27 Nov. 1592) beiring that the conventions of parties should be fulfilled albeit not aggreable to the comone law."[53] C 775 is believed to be a manuscript written by Sir Thomas Hope (d 1643), Lord Kerse, son of the author of the *Practicks*, who died within the lifetime of his father. The reference is clearly to the same Act of Sederunt as that mentioned by Stair. The form of wording used by Hope, differing from that in the *Institutions*, admits both Hope and Stair as independent witnesses, and shows that the Act (or conceivably, it may be, its interpretation) is not a figment of Stair's imagination. No other Act of that date appears in the printed editions of the Acts of Sederunt, and none can be found in the manuscript books, but the presumption must surely be either that another Act did once exist, or that the known Act was generally interpreted along the lines suggested by Stair and by Hope's *Practicks*. Either way, we have important evidence as to the practice of Scots law in the century before Stair.

## E. CANON LAW AND SCOTTISH PRACTICE

Evidence from other sources tends to confirm the importance of the Act of Sederunt (or its interpretation) and to suggest a credible context for it. In Scotland, in the century or so preceding the Reformation the influence of Canon law and of Canon lawyers was particularly strong.[54] As elsewhere in western Europe, the courts of the Church came to exercise a large jurisdiction over contract. Gordon Donaldson has calculated from the surviving record of the Court of the Official Principal of Saint Andrews in the sixteenth century that, excluding appeals, some 24 to 27 per cent of the judgments given related to "the rendering of money or goods by one party to another or for the fulfilment of contracts".[55] This last category, he noted, arose partly from obligations fortified by an oath, partly as a result of agreement between the parties that the Church courts should have jurisdiction,

---

52 Mackenzie Stuart (n 48) at 253–254.
53 Hope, *Practicks*, 2.2.5. The phrase "comone law" in this passage would seem to refer to the common law of Scotland.
54 For the influence of the Canon law in Scotland, see ch 1 text accompanying nn 35–49.
55 G Donaldson, "The church courts", in *ISLH* 356 at 366.

and partly from contracts "actit" or recorded in the books of the Officials. Simon Ollivant's more recent study of the Court of the Official in Scotland has confirmed the importance of this jurisdiction.[56]

As already noted, in many countries, including England, there was a reaction against the extensive jurisdiction claimed by the Church courts, even before the Reformation. In Scotland, however, any reaction was muted. It may be that the strong clerical component built into the Court of Session when it was established in 1532 as a College of Justice militated against such a challenge to ecclesiastical authority: of the fifteen ordinary members of the court, eight, including the President, were to be churchmen. Thus in 1542, in the case of *Barclay v Blackhall*, the Session confirmed that

> a contract or obligation made of any civil and profane matter, such as an assedation of lands, is understood not to be profane or civil, if the same be confirmed by the oath or *fide media* of the contrahentis, or any of them; and therefore the party, albeit he be a temporal man may be called and pursued for fulfilling the same before the Spiritual Judge.[57]

In fact, ecclesiastical jurisdiction over obligations continued unaltered in Scotland until the Reformation in 1559–60. Even after the Reformation, although the authority of the Pope was rejected, the Canon law continued to be regarded as an important source of law, save inasmuch as it conflicted with the Reformation settlement. Both Craig and Stair are quite explicit about this.[58] Much Canon law, both substantive and adjective, had already been incorporated into the common law of Scotland before the Reformation, and many distinguished Canon lawyers had presided over secular courts.[59] After the Reformation there was a further significant fusion of Canon law and Scottish common law. New "commissary" courts were established, under a head commissary court based in Edinburgh, to exercise much of the jurisdiction formerly possessed by the former courts of the Official (and their commissaries) in matters not strictly ecclesiastical. Thus the new commissary courts acquired jurisdiction over marriage and legitimacy, over testaments and moveable succession, and also, to a considerable extent, over contract and voluntary obligations. Although the new courts looked to the Court of Session, rather than to the Church, and soon became quite secularised, there was at first considerable continuity between the personnel of

---

56 Ollivant, *Official* (n 54) at 85–93, 177, and also at 65–66.
57 Balfour, *Practicks*, 29; jurisdiction did not extend, however, to contracts "concerning redemptioun of landis or heritage"; and see Mackenzie Stuart (n 48) at 250.
58 Craig, *JF*, 1.3.24; Stair, *Inst*, 1.1.14; and see, for example, ch 9 above.
59 The most notable, though far from the only example, being William Elphinstone.

the old Church courts and the new commissary courts. Archibald Menzies, for example, served uninterrupted as commissary of Dumfries from about 1543 until 1579, and Archibald Beaton, official general of Glasgow at the Reformation, was still in office as a commissary in 1581.[60] The most striking example of continuity, however, was provided by the appointment of Sir James Balfour of Pittendreich, the last Official of Lothian, as the first chief commissary of Edinburgh. Balfour was later to become Lord President of the Court of Session, and is the author of Balfour's *Practicks*.[61]

In his *Practicks*, Balfour gives a copy of the original instructions given to the commissaries of Edinburgh in March 1564.[62] Article 1 directs that all proceedings should be conducted in Scots: "In the first, that the summoundis, haill processes and sentences, be in the vulgar tongue." Article 13 allows for the registration of "contractis, obligatiounis, actis, and uther writtis", subscribed by the parties, in the books of the court. Article 14, crucially, concerns jurisdiction in contract:

> XIV. That the Commissaris sail be Judges to all contractis registrat in their bukis, quhairunto thair authoritie is interponit, and the partie submittand him to thair jurisdictioun, et hoc cumulative, sed non privative: And siclike, to all uther contractis not beand registrat in uther judges ordinaris bukis; for the fulfilling quhairof the parties is ellis sworn, or sail happen thairefter to be sworn, et hoc cumulative, et non privative.[63]

Article 15 provides that in other actions "quhairin the aith [oath] is not interponit, and persewit as maid *fide media*, and quhilkis the persewar will refer to the defendar's aith," where the sum in dispute does not exceed £40, "the saidis Commissaris to be Judges, *et hoc cumulative sed non privative*". They are to have jurisdiction also in other small actions "quhidder thay be *fide media* or not, of widowis, pupillis, and siclike puir and miserabill persounis, not exceeding the sowme of xx. lib. quhilkis wer wont to be decidit in the consistorie of befoir, *et hoc cumulative,* as said is."

Given the widespread resentment throughout Europe, already noted, against the expansive jurisdiction of the Church courts in the field of obligations, it is distinctly surprising that in Scotland this jurisdiction should have carried over, it would seem entire, from the pre-Reformation church courts

---

60 Donaldson (n 55) at 369.
61 For Balfour's remarkable career, see P G B McNeill's introduction to Balfour's *Practicks* (SS vol 21, 1962).
62 Balfour, *Practicks*, at 655 sqq.
63 These grounds of jurisdiction, it will be observed, compare closely with those instanced by Donaldson (n 55), above text accompanying nn 55 and 56.

to the post-Reformation commissary courts, albeit with cumulative rather than privative effect. Nevertheless, the commissary jurisdiction was confirmed in 1592 when the original instructions of 1564 were ratified by Act of the Scottish Parliament: "Decerning and declaring the said iurisdictioun to be als ample of the same force and auctoritie with the iurisdictioun of the saidis officiallis to quhome thai succeedit."[64] As it was possible to appeal the decisions of the commissaries to the Court of Session (described in 1609 as the King's "great consistorie"),[65] questions are bound have arisen as to what was, or should be, the stance of the common law of Scotland on the matter of promises and "naked pactions": should it follow the Canon law rule *pacta sunt servanda* or the Civil law maxim *ex nudo pacto non oritur actio*? This provides the perfect context for the Act of Sederunt of 1592. In Hope's words, "the conventions of parties should be fulfilled albeit not agreeable to the comone law": that is, *pacta sunt servanda*. The Canon law rather than the Civil law was to be followed, although apparently not previously agreeable to the common law of Scotland.[66] This decision may have been made the easier by the fact that *Regiam Majestatem*, which was still cited in court, however one might view its authority, had borrowed from the distinguished thirteenth-century Canonist Goffredus de Trano in its section on pacts, and this had been repeated by both Balfour and Hope.[67]

The commissary courts lost or gave up most of their jurisdiction over voluntary obligations in the course of the seventeenth century. Crucially in 1639 it was said that *interpositio fidei* should not confer jurisdiction on the commissaries in actions not merely consistorial.[68] Stair merely describes the commissaries as "proper judges in the confirmation of testaments, and in the matter of divorce", although they did still retain some jurisdiction into the following century over civil matters not exceeding £40 Scots in value.[69] But the die was cast: the common law of Scotland had adopted the Canon law

---

64 RATIFICATIOUN of the Commissariot of Edinburgh (*RPS* 1592/4/86).
65 *RPS* 1609/4/20.
66 The context here suggests that by "comone law" is to be understood not the *jus commune* but the common law of Scotland.
67 *RM (Cooper)*, 1.28–31, especially ch 28 (*De pacto et pollicitatione*); *RM (APS)* 1.29–32; and see P Stein, "The source of the Romano-canonical part of the *Regiam Majestatem*" (1969) 48 *SHR* 107. Balfour, *Practicks*, at 188–189 repeats the passage in *Regiam* in the vernacular; see also Hope, *Practicks*, 1.98, and 2.89. Goffredus himself, Canonist though he was, based his account partly on Azo and the *Digest*.
68 *RPS* C1639/8/33 (27 Sept 1639).
69 Stair, *Inst*, 4.1.58. More research into the topic of commissary jurisdiction in the 17th century is clearly desirable. See, however, D Stevenson, "The commissary court of Aberdeen in 1650", in W D H Sellar (ed), *Miscellany II* (SS vol 35, 1984) 144.

rule. The adoption, however, does not seem to have been quite as sudden or complete as Stair's comment on the Act of Sederunt of 1592 suggests: "... and so, it hath been ever since decided".[70] Arguments based on the Civil law continued for some time, as in *Kintore* in 1623 where Haddington argued unsuccessfully that a promise "was *nudum pactum,* having no preceding cause, and that promises of that kind are not obligatory"; *Laird of Clackmannan* in 1624, on which Mackenzie Stuart has commented that "Spotiswoode's humanistic mind is outraged by the Lords finding the promise to be a 'perfect stipulation'"; or *Sharp* in 1631, where arguments based on "the treatises of the lawyers and doctors" were considered not to be relevant.[71]

In an article written in 1955 Helmut Coing looked at the procedures by which the later Canon law sought to give legal force to natural obligations regarded earlier as morally binding only: in particular, the *denunciatio evangelica* and the appeal to the *officium judicis.*[72] Bartolus, he noted, derived *obligatio naturalis*, so far as the procedure of the *denunciatio evangelica* was concerned, from either consent or unjust enrichment. Natural obligations based on consent included *pacta nuda*, promises made under oath, and promises in favour of a third person. From unjust enrichment came the principle *nam hoc natura aequum est, neminem cum alterius detrimento fieri locupletiorem.*[73] Coing sought to explore how far these procedures of Canon law might have influenced the early development of equity in England. He concluded that although some influence was probable, it was necessarily limited because of the nature of the relationship in England between equity and common law.

More recently Richard Helmholz has sought to assess what influence, if any, the Canon law exercised over the development of the English law of contracts, given that the jurisdiction of the Church in England had become "virtually moribund" in the 1520s.[74] He puts forward two possible areas where there may have been influence. The first is in connection with jurisdiction over contracts exercised by the Court of Chancery in the fifteenth century. Helmholz agrees with Coing that "influence of this kind is indeed

---

70 Above text accompanying nn 33 and 50–53.
71 For these cases, and also *Deuchar v Brown*, see above text to nn 21 and 48; and Mackenzie Stuart (n 48), at 252.
72 H Coing, "English equity and the *denunciatio evangelica* of the Canon law" (1955) 71 *LQR* 223. The procedures are discussed by Spies and Rousseau (both n 38).
73 Coing (n 72), at 234.
74 Helmholz (n 37), at 59–65, and above text accompanying n 40.

highly probable." The second is in connection with the action of assumpsit in the courts of common law in the sixteenth century. He believes that the evidence is suggestive, although admitting that the evidence is not direct, and that "the inherent probability of such a connection is less than that there was influence of the canon law in Chancery". He continues:

> It appears less plausible that the common lawyers would have been subject to any influence from the canon law than would the medieval chancellors. Common lawyers were not trained in the canon law; the chancellors or their clerks often were. Common law procedure was not modelled on Romano-canonical rules. The two systems were quite different in many ways, and there has long and properly been resistance to any attempt to suggest something like a "Reception" in England.[75]

The quotation has been given at length because it points to a clear contrast with the situation in Scotland.

All the evidence then suggests that in Scotland the influence of the Canon law on the law of obligations was positive and direct. All the matters particularly mentioned by Coing as deriving from *obligatio naturalis* – naked pactions, simple promise, *jus quaesitum tertio* and the recognition of the principle of unjust enrichment – are to be found in Stair's *Institutions*.[76] This can surely be no accident. Stair declared his exposition of the law to be based on Scottish practice, and believed this practice, in turn, to owe much to Canon law. There is evidently a paradox here. A very conservative approach towards legal change led to the pre-Reformation jurisdiction of the Church courts in Scotland over promise and contract continuing little altered under the new commissary courts and thus to a further and very significant fusion of Canon law and Scots common law. A century later Stair's expository genius gave this area of law a distinctly modern appearance.

## F. THE TERM "POLLICITATION" – A DIGRESSION

Although Stair's division of voluntary obligations into promise and contract is quite clear, his inclusion of the term "pollicitation" in the phrase "promise, pollicitation or offer, paction, convention or contract" has given rise to much

---

75 Helmholz (n 37), at 62.
76 For the argument that the recognition of the principle of unjust enrichment in Scots law can be traced back to Stair, see H L MacQueen and W D H Sellar, "Unjust enrichment in Scots law", in E J H Schrage (ed), *Unjust Enrichment: The Comparative Legal History of the Law of Restitution* (1995) 289; also W D H Sellar, "Unjust enrichment", in *SME*, vol 15 (1996) at paras 73–86.

debate.[77] Only a brief account of that debate can be given here. In 1956 Sir Thomas Smith, influenced by Roman law, stated that promise was "a pollicitation as contrasted with an offer".[78] In 1957 Ashton-Cross disagreed, linking Stair's use of "pollicitation" with offer.[79] In 1958 Sir Thomas set out his views more fully: the term "pollicitation" denoted a unilateral juristic act, binding without acceptance; Stair's terminology was misleading.[80] Smith was, however, entirely at one with Stair's analysis: "Stair rightly distinguished, it is thought, between promise and offer, and between promise and contract."[81] As a result of Smith's writings and teaching, the term "pollicitation", used as a synonym for promise, acquired a renewed currency in modern Scots law.[82] Alan Rodger, writing on *jus quaesitum tertio*, also linked Stair's use of "pollicitation" with "promise" in the above sense, and made a distinction between "pollicitation promise" and "offer promise".[83] As a plank in his argument Rodger noted that in the first edition of Stair's *Institutions*, unlike the second, "pollicitation" is separated from "or offer" by a comma. He concluded from this that Stair regarded "pollicitation" and "promise" as synonymous, and that Stair had overlooked the removal of the comma, and the implied linking of "pollicitation" and "offer" in the relevant paragraph heading of the second edition. No jurist of Stair's eminence, he thought, could have linked "pollicitation" and "offer" intentionally.[84] In passing, it may be noted that any argument based on alterations in punctuation in different editions of early printed books must be regarded as extremely slender.[85]

---

77 Stair, *Inst*, 1.10.3.
78 T B Smith, "Jus quaesitum tertio: remedies of the "tertius" in Scottish law", 1956 *JR* 3 at 15 (reprinted in T B Smith, *Studies Critical and Comparative* (1962) 183).
79 D I C Ashton Cross, "Bare promise in Scots law", 1957 *JR* 138.
80 T B Smith, "Pollicitatio – promise and offer: Stair v Grotius", 1958 *Acta Juridica* 141, reprinted in Smith, *Studies* (n 78) 168: "Stair . . . is somewhat ambiguous and inconsistent in his terminology" (at 175); and see also T B Smith, *A Short Commentary on the Law of Scotland* (1962) ch 32 ("Unilateral promise (pollicitatio)").
81 Smith, *Short Commentary* (n 80), at 746.
82 Smith's chapter on "Unilateral promise (pollicitatio)" in his *Short Commentary* remains a valuable contribution. See further on Smith's work on promise H L MacQueen, "Glory with Gloag or the stake with Stair? T B Smith and the Scots law of contract", in D L Carey Miller and E C Reid (eds), *A Mixed Legal System in Transition: T B Smith and the Progress of Scots Law* (2005) 138 at 147–150, 159–160, 162, 166–167, 170.
83 Rodger (n 30).
84 Rodger (n 30) at 130–132.
85 For the general proposition, and for 17th-century Scottish legal works in particular, see J W Cairns, "The moveable text of Mackenzie: bibliographical problems for the concept of institutional writing", in J W Cairns and O F Robinson (eds), *Studies in Ancient Law, Comparative Law, and Legal History* (2000), 235 (reprinted in J W Cairns, *Law, Lawyers and Humanism: Selected Essays on the History of Scots Law, Volume 1* (2015) 498).

Responding to Rodger, Geoffrey MacCormack believed that Stair had linked pollicitation and offer quite deliberately, and pointed to a respectable intellectual tradition (including Grotius) which distinguished between pollicitation and promise.[86] MacCormack also pointed to the leading case of *Reoch v Young* in 1712, in which the defender cited Stair and distinguished between promise and pollicitation: "That it was no positive promise, but a mere pollicitation and offer . . . And Stair, B. I Tit. 10 s.3. makes a plain distinction betwixt a pollicitation and promise . . ."[87] More recently, Zimmermann and Hellwege have suggested that Stair may have intended, when using the term "pollicitation", to describe a promise *sub conditione*.[88]

In view of this debate it is worth emphasising that whether Stair intended to link "pollicitation" with "promise" or with "offer", or indeed with neither, is quite immaterial to his exposition of the law, and to its subsequent development. If the reference to "pollicitation" is deleted from Stair's account, the effect is exactly the same. Stair uses the term "pollicitation" once, and once only, in his *Institutions*. Of later writers, Bankton, Erskine, and Bell use the word not at all, although Baron Hume, in an off-hand remark, indicates that he believed that Stair equated pollicitation and promise: "pure promise or 'pollicitation' (as Lord Stair calls it)".[89] Although the term "pollicitation" does occasionally resurface, as in *Reoch* in 1712, and in *Macfarlane v Johnstone* in 1864, in which Lord President Inglis refers directly to Stair, the regular term in use in Scots law for a unilateral binding act of will, then and now, is "promise".[90] Thus "pollicitation" does not appear as an entry in either the first or the second edition of *Green's Encyclopaedia of Scots Law*.[91] Why Stair inserted "pollicitation" between "promise" and "offer" will probably never be satisfactorily explained. The arguments in favour of a link with "offer", as put forward by Geoffrey MacCormack, appear more convincing than those which suggest a link with "promise". It may be, however, that Stair did not intend a specific link with either, but merely wished to indicate

---

86 MacCormack (n 43) at 121–126.
87 MacCormack (n 43) at 122. For *Reoch v Young* (1712) Mor 9439, see below text accompanying nn 90 and 112.
88 Zimmermann and Hellwege (n 4) at 138–139.
89 Hume, *Lectures*, vol 2 at 23. The term *pollicitatio* does, of course, appear in the Romano-canonical passage in *Regiam Majestatem* borrowed from Goffredus de Trano (above, n 67); and Erskine refers to the Roman law *de pollicitationibus* (below text accompanying nn 101–102).
90 *Reoch v Young* (1712) Mor 9439; *Macfarlane v Johnston* (1864) 2 M 1210 (for which, see below text accompanying n 118). For the conventional usage see, for example, *Ferguson v Paterson* (1748) Mor 8440.
91 J Chisholm (ed), *Green's Encyclopaedia of Scots Law* (1896–1904); J L Wark (ed), *Green's "Dunedin" Encyclopaedia of Scots Law* (1926–35).

that he was familiar with the term *pollicitatio* and had it within his general purview.

## G. LATER WRITERS: MACKENZIE; BANKTON; ERSKINE; BELL; HUME

As noted in the introduction, the history of the doctrine of promise in Scots law from Stair to the present day can shortly be told: the law remained essentially the same until the Requirements of Writing (Scotland) Act 1995. Stair's contemporary, Sir George Mackenzie (1636–1691), inclined towards the Civil law more than did Stair, and his classification of obligations in his own, much shorter *Institutions*, published in 1684, three years after the first edition of Stair, is broadly in conformity with that of the Civil law. His treatment of promise, however, although brief, is quite in line with Stair:

> Though *verbal promises* do by our Law bind the *Promiser*, yet because the *Position* and Import of Words may be easily mistaken by the *Hearers*, therefore verbal *Obligations* or *Promises* can only be proven by *Oath* of Party, and not by *Witnesses*, though the Sum be never so small.[92]

Later writers lacked Stair's clarity of analysis and added little but confusion to this area of law. None was so deeply imbued in the tradition of the *jus commune* as Stair had been. Andrew M'Douall, Lord Bankton (1685–1760), defines "paction or compact" as "the agreement of one or more persons to pay or perform something to another person, or persons".[93] He further classifies this into "promise" and "contract" (thereby, incidentally differing from Stair, who considered paction and contract to be effectively the same thing).[94] Promise, according to Bankton, is that "whereby one obliges himself to another, without any *mutual obligation* or *valuable consideration*".[95] In this sense, writes Bankton, promise may be called a "gratuitous" obligation. He also notes, citing the *Digest* and *Regiam Majestatem*, that a promise may be real or personal, depending on whether it is made to the world at large, or to a particular person. Bankton then states, "[i]n a general acceptation, Promise may be applied to all contracts that are binding upon the part of one of the contracters only, which is called by the Greeks μονοπλευρος|, i.e. unilateral, or binding upon one side only". The occurrence of the word

---

92 G Mackenzie, *The Institutions of the Law of Scotland* (1684) 3.2 ("Of obligations by word or writ").
93 Bankton, *Inst*, 1.11 (at 323–324).
94 Above text accompanying n 35.
95 The italics are Bankton's.

μονοπλευρος| shows that Bankton had Stair in front of him, as Stair had also used and, indeed, perhaps invented this Greek word.[96] Bankton's account is confusing, however, in that his definition of promise might be thought to include a contract in which the obligation to perform is all upon one side, that is, one which is not for a "valuable consideration" and which might therefore be termed "nude" or "gratuitous".[97] As regards proof, Bankton notes that a "gratuitous promise" binds without writing, although writing may be necessary by way of proof. In his *Observations on the Law of England* at the end of the title, Bankton notes that, "a nude contract, or naked promise, without any consideration of interest," is not binding in English law, although it is in Scots.[98]

John Erskine of Carnock (1695–1768), unlike Stair, was attracted by the classification of obligations in Roman law: "We now proceed, according to the order of the Roman law, to explain the nature of contracts perfected by word ..."[99] Like Bankton, Erskine does not distinguish clearly between promise and gratuitous contract. In his *Principles*, first published in 1754, he writes:

> Where nothing is to be given or performed, but on the one part, it is properly called a promise, which, as it is gratuitous, does not require the acceptance of him to whom the promise is made. An offer, which must be distinguished from a promise, implies something to be done by the other party; and consequently is not binding on the offerer, till it be accepted ..."[100]

On the one hand, this seems to follow Stair's distinction between promise and contract, but on the other, it appears to rule out the possibility of a gratuitous contract: "an offer ... implies something to be done by the other party".

This impression is confirmed in Erskine's *Institutes*, published posthumously in 1773. Erskine adopts the term "verbal obligations" to apply to

---

96 T Mersinis, "Stair, *Institutions*, 1.10.5: a linguistic note" (1997) 1 *Edin LR* 368.
97 Too much emphasis should probably not be placed on Bankton's use of the word "consideration". He may not have had English law particularly in mind and, even if he did, there is no reason to believe that he wished to import the technicalities of English law. The passage from Stair, it must be admitted, is not particularly helpful: "Hence is our vulgar distinction betwixt obligations and contracts, the former being only where the obligation is μονοπλευρος|, on the one part; the other where the obligation is δευπλευρος|, obligatory on both parts, whereby both parties are obliged to mutual prestations."
98 Bankton, *Inst*, 1.11, at 324 and 345.
99 Erskine, *Inst*, 3.2.1.
100 Erskine, *Principles*, 3.2.1. The quotation is taken from the last edition revised by Erskine himself, the 3rd edition of 1764, but the words remained unchanged until the very last editions, edited by Sir John Rankine.

such obligations "as have no special name to distinguish them by".[101] He then divides "verbal obligations" into two classes: "*first*, promises, where nothing is to be given or performed but upon one part, and which are therefore always gratuitous"; and "*2dly*, verbal agreements (so called in contradistinction to promises), which require the intervention of two different persons at least, who come under mutual obligations to one another". "For these two," he continues, "are in this manner distinguished by the Roman law (L.3, *de pollicit.*), where *pacta*, or verbal agreements are said to be formed by the mutual consent of two persons, but promises to be the sole act of the promiser." Then follows his opinion, discussed above, that Stair's reference to the 1592 Act of Sederunt was mistaken. Rather he believes that the obvious reason why all verbal agreements and promises must be "obligatory in every nation" is that "by a common rule of law every agreement in a lawful matter, though constituted only verbally, induces a full or proper obligation". Elsewhere Erskine defines contract as "a voluntary agreement of two or more persons by which something is to be given or performed upon one part for valuable consideration, either present or future, on the other part".[102] Here again, he appears to rule out the possibility of a gratuitous contract.

Erskine returns to promise when he discusses "the doctrine of gratuitous obligations, otherwise called donations".[103] He defines donation as "that obligation which arises from the mere liberality of the giver". Erskine notes that a verbal obligation to gift moveable property, "which is usually called a promise", is as effective as a written one, save that it may have to be proven by oath. He contrasts Stair's view that promises are binding without acceptance with that of Grotius and Pufendorf: "Grotius, on the contrary (*De. jur. bell. et pac.* lib.2, c.11, 14), and Puffendorf (*De jur. nat. et gent.* lib.3, c.6, s.15), affirm that the most absolute promises require acceptance, because no obligation can be formed without the joint consent or concurrence of both parties." Erskine then tries to square the circle through a doctrine of presumed acceptance: "But acceptance, admitting that it is necessary towards constituting an obligation, may be reasonably presumed, without any formal act, in pure and simple donations, which imply no burden upon the donee; and Stair's opinion is agreeable to our practice."[104] Stair, however, had been quite clear that no acceptance was necessary, presumed or

---

101 Erskine, *Inst*, 3.2.1.
102 Erskine, *Inst*, 3.1.16. For the use of the word "consideration", see nn 41 and 97 above.
103 Erskine, *Inst*, 3.3.88.
104 Erskine, *Inst*, 3.3.88.

otherwise. Erskine's views on presumed acceptance in relation to promise may explain his restriction of "verbal agreements" as contrasted with "promises" to those agreements in which two or more parties come under "mutual obligations": the doctrine of presumed acceptance would tend to elide the difference between "promise" on the one hand, and "offer" requiring no counter-prestation, but only acceptance, on the other. In sum, it cannot be pretended that either Bankton or Erskine's treatment of the subject is in the least helpful.

George Joseph Bell (1770–1843) follows Erskine in this doctrine of presumed acceptance: "A promise", he writes in his *Principles*, "differs from an offer, as being a unilateral engagement, to which acceptance is presumed; while an offer is always and *in terminis* conditional, raised into an obligation only by acceptance."[105] Again, this is hardly helpful. Nevertheless, Bell's definition or something very similar, found its way into the first two editions of *Green's Encyclopaedia*.[106] In truth, Bell does not seem to have been interested in this type of analysis, or to have considered it of great practical importance, as he omits all reference to promise in this sense in his *Commentaries*.

Baron David Hume (1756–1838) also appears to have found this type of analysis uncongenial. In his lectures in 1796–97 Hume included some material on the classification of obligations, and acknowledged that Scots law allowed *pacta nuda* ("by our practice an agreement to lend money or perform any stipulation is actionable though *in nudis finibus*") but later he appears to have dropped this entire section from his lectures.[107] In his treatment of sale, however, Hume notes as an aside that there may be cases of "pure promise or 'pollicitation' (as Lord Stair calls it)", "where a writing on one part only shall bind the writer to a certain effect, without any return on the other part, written or verbal".[108] It is not clear whether Hume followed Erskine's suggestion of presumed acceptance: he notes that a promise "may be done away by express dissent or rejection".

The verdict on Stair's successors up to and including Hume and Bell, so far as this area of law is concerned, must be one of disappointment. Stair's work was not built on as it might have been. Instead, the clear distinction

---

105 Bell, *Principles*, § 9.
106 Thus *Green's Encyclopaedia*, vol 10 (n 91), sv "Promise": "A promise, as distinguished from an offer, is a unilateral obligation to which acceptance is presumed."
107 Hume, *Lectures*, vol 2, at 276–278 (Appendix A).
108 Hume, *Lectures*, vol 2, at 23. As to what Stair intended by the word "pollicitation", see above section F.

which Stair had made between *promise* following on a unilateral act of the will, and *contract* resulting from offer and acceptance was in danger of being obscured or even subverted, although more through inadvertence than by deliberate intent.

Traces of this confusion can still be detected in that long-standing textbook, *Gloag and Henderson*, and indeed beyond.[109] Every edition of the chapter on formation of contract in *Gloag and Henderson* begins by distinguishing "promise" from "mutual contract", and contrasting Scots law with that of England. An undertaking to keep an offer open for a certain period of time is given as the prime example of unilateral binding promise.[110] "Gratuitous promise" and "mutual contract" are then contrasted in relation to proof. The rule regarding "gratuitous promise" being subject to proof by writ or oath is set out and contrasted with the position regarding "onerous contract". Later the distinction is expressed as being between "gratuitous obligations" and "onerous obligations", as if these were the same as those obligations previously contrasted. Yet "gratuitous promise" and "gratuitous obligations" are not coterminous in Scots law, even if "mutual" and "onerous" contracts may sometimes be. A contract involving no counter-prestation or consideration may well be termed a "gratuitous contract" and, therefore a "gratuitous obligation", but it is not a gratuitous promise. The term "mutual contract" is not defined, but is contrasted first with "gratuitous promise", and thus would seem to refer to contract in general, resulting from offer and acceptance; later however, "mutual contract" appears to be equated with "onerous contract", a rather different proposition. This lack of clarity in analysis derives from Bankton, Erskine, and Bell rather than from Stair. In fact, it appears that the rule regarding proof by writ or oath applied to both promise and gratuitous contract, and included a promise with a suspensive condition attached.[111]

## H. EIGHTEENTH- AND NINETEENTH-CENTURY CASE LAW

The distinction drawn between obligations arising from promise as contrasted with those arising from offer followed by acceptance is sharp in

---

109  W M Gloag and R C Henderson, *Introduction to the Law of Scotland* (1st edn, 1927, and subsequent editions). For continuing confusion as to the meaning of the terms "gratuitous" and "unilateral" see below text accompanying nn 144–148.

110  *Gloag and Henderson* (n 109) ch 4 ("Law of contract: formation of contract") (in 14th edn (2017) ch 5).

111  For discussion of the rule in relation to gratuitous obligations, see Scottish Law Commission Memoranda Nos 39 and 66 (n 15). See also below text accompanying nn 144–148.

theory, but often blurred or of little consequence in practice. As a result, case law in this area is relatively slight, the more so given that the strict rule regarding the proof of gratuitous obligations militated against actions raised on the ground of promise. Such cases as there are, however, fully support the law as expounded by Stair.

The legal consequences of promise were raised sharply in *Reoch v Young* in 1712.[112] The facts are memorable and affecting. Jean Telfer "Madam Stewart" lay dying in her lodgings in Edinburgh. She indicated to her landlady, Catharine Young or Crawfurd, that she had banknotes and gold which she wished to distribute among her friends. She wished, in particular, to give Thomas Mackie, who had come to visit her, a note for £20 sterling (a considerable sum in 1712) which she had kept wrapped up in a napkin "as a token of her kindness". Crawfurd reported, however, that the note was not to be found in the napkin. Stewart then became very agitated, and Crawfurd to pacify her said that she would make up the sum to Mackie if it was not made up in some other way. Later Mackie assigned such claim as he might have to William Reoch who pursued Crawfurd for the full amount. Crawfurd acknowledged under oath that she had said words to the effect alleged but denied that she was bound to pay. Her main defence was that what she said "was no positive promise, but a mere pollicitation or offer, noways made *animo deliberato*, but by surprise, on a sudden emotion of the affections, to prevent and compose the passion and trouble her dying lodger was in, and so was not obligatory without immediate acceptance".[113] She cited Stair (who she alleged "makes a plain difference between a pollicitation and promise"), Grotius, Pufendorf, Cujas and the *Digest* in support, and denied that the Canon law maxim *omne verbum de ore fidei prolatum cadit in debitum* should apply.[114] The pursuer answered that, "That distinction of pollicitations and promises was but a nicety of the Roman law; but here is as positive as could be." The court found against Crawfurd, declaring "that though there was *locus poenitentiae* in synallagmas, yet there was none in simple and absolute promises." The case provides as clear a confirmation as one could wish of the law of promise as set out by Stair.

*Marshall v Blackwood* in 1747 concerned the effect of a promise to keep an offer open for a certain period of time.[115] Blackwood offered to sell barley to Marshall at a set price, indicating that the offer would remain open

---
112 *Reoch v Young* (1712) Mor 9439.
113 I follow here Fountainhall's Report at Mor 9440.
114 For the use of the term *pollicitatio*, see above section F.
115 *Marshall & M'Kell v Blackwood of Pitreavie* (1747) Elchies, "Sale", no 6.

for acceptance for a fortnight. Marshall accepted within the fortnight, meeting the conditions laid down in the offer, but was informed that the goods had already been sold. He sued successfully for damages, the decision turning on the casting vote of the President.

*Sir James Ferguson of Kilkerran v Paterson* in 1748 concerned a promise made by Paterson, confirmed by missive letter, to convey some rights in land if he was allowed to purchase his father's debts.[116] Paterson was allowed to purchase the debts, but declined to convey the property rights. He claimed that "this is a mutual contract by which Sir James is not bound, and therefore the defender cannot be bound". The pursuer took his stand on Stair, distinguishing between "three different forms by which men bind themselves to each other . . . all of them equally productive of actions at common law": promise, offer and "mutual contract". A promise, unlike an offer, required no acceptance. If the facts disclosed a promise, then Paterson was bound, "and it is no objection that the pursuer is not bound, because such was the intention of parties"; if they disclosed an offer, then the pursuer had accepted it, and so again the defender was bound. The court held Paterson to be bound by the missive letter to convey the property, although the report does not disclose whether the obligation was regarded as founded on promise or on offer and acceptance. The interest in the case lies in the analysis of voluntary obligations put forward by the pursuer in explicit reliance on Stair, and in the apparent acceptance of this by the court.

The Second Division case of *Petrie v Earl of Airlie* in 1834 concerned a promise or offer of reward.[117] The earl of Airlie offered a reward for information leading to the detection of the author of a placard which he regarded as false and scandalous: "a reward of one hundred guineas is hereby offered to any person who will give such information as may lead to the detection of the author and printer. The reward will be paid on conviction . . ." Petrie gave the desired information, but the Lord Advocate declined to prosecute. Lord Airlie also declined to raise a private prosecution or a civil action for damages. Petrie claimed his reward, but Airlie refused to pay on the ground that there had been no conviction. The sheriff, at first instance, assoilzied Airlie. The case was advocated to Lord Corehouse who found for Petrie: "The reclaimer having obtained from the advocator [Petrie] all that he stipulated for, he is not entitled to evade payment of the price which he offered for it, because it does not answer the purpose which he had in view."

---

116 *Ferguson v Paterson* (1748) Mor 8440.
117 *Petrie v Earl of Airlie* (1834) 13 S 68.

The Division adhered. The report of the case contains little by way of analysis. The decision may have been based on promise, but the word does not appear. In the circumstances, there being a writ running in the name of the defender, and so clear proof of promise, it would have made little difference whether the offer of reward was construed as a binding promise or as an offer followed by acceptance.

In *Macfarlane v Johnston* in 1864 Lord Justice-Clerk Inglis founded his opinion on Stair:

> There is a philosophical and practical distinction between a promise and an obligation [of a different kind], which is nowhere better stated than by Lord Stair (i. 10, 3). A promise is a pure and simple expression of the will of the party undertaking the obligation, requiring no acceptance, and still less requiring mutual consent. A promise is distinguished by Lord Stair from a pollicitation or offer which requires acceptance to make it binding, and still more from a paction which, in order to be binding, requires the mutual consent of the parties.[118]

Lord Inglis is quite explicit that promise requires no acceptance to be binding. He also emphasised, as did Lord Neaves, that no particular words were required in order to constitute a promise: "the distinction between a promise and an obligation of a different kind does not consist in the use of the word promise." Thus, depending on the circumstances, the word "agree" might be just as apt as "promise".

In *Morton's Trustees v Aged Christian Friend Society* in 1899, a leading case on *jus quaesitum tertio*, the basic Scottish position was reaffirmed by Lord Kinnear:

> It is a familiar doctrine in the law of Scotland, differing in that respect from the law of England, that an obligation is binding although it may not proceed on a valuable consideration, or may not be expressed in a solemn form, such as a deed under seal. What is necessary is that the pursuer should intend to bind himself in an enforceable obligation and should express that intention in clear words.[119]

## I. *CARLILL v CARBOLIC SMOKE BALL COMPANY* AND THE INFLUENCE OF ENGLISH LAW

The English case of *Carlill v Carbolic Smoke Ball Company*, decided by the Court of Appeal in 1893, opened up to Scots lawyers the prospect of an alternative analysis of cases which might previously have been considered

---

118 *Macfarlane v Johnston* (1864) 2 M 1210, 1213; for the meaning to be attached to the term "pollicitation", see above section F.
119 *Morton's Trs v Aged Christian Friend Society* (1899) 2 F 82, Lord Kinnear at 85.

under the head of "promise"; an analysis, moreover, which avoided some of the difficulties concerning proof.[120] English law did not recognise the doctrine of binding promise, save where a promise was constituted by a "deed under seal". In *Carlill*, however, as is well known, the performance of actions stipulated for in an offer of reward addressed to the world in general – in this instance the sniffing of the defendant's carbolic smoke ball – was construed as the acceptance of that offer, and held to result in a binding contract.

Scots lawyers soon followed suit, although *Petrie v Earl of Airlie*, if not based on promise, might also have been appealed to as a precedent. *Carlill* was cited in *Law v Newnes*, only a year later.[121] An advertisement in *Tit-Bits* promised payment of £100 to the person whom the proprietors of the newspaper "may decide to be the next of kin of anyone killed in a railway accident", provided that a current issue of *Tit-Bits* was found upon the deceased and he or she was a regular subscriber. The case, which went to the Inner House, concerned the proper identification of the next of kin. Both parties assumed that there was a valid contract, and that question was not argued in court. Alone among the judges, Lord Young said that he doubted whether a valid contract had in fact been constituted: "My own strong inclination is that the only sanction of their undertaking was the credit of the paper."[122] There seems to have been no discussion of promise. The facts in *Hunter v Hunter* in 1904 were very similar, down to a disclaimer by Lord Young.[123] Again the possibility of promise does not appear to have been canvassed. In the later House of Lords case of *Hunter v General Accident Company* a similar situation arose, once more involving a railway accident, and turning on the timeous registration of a coupon policy of insurance by the deceased. Again the nature of the obligation was not at issue, and the possibility of promise does not appear to have been canvassed.[124] In this case, however, there can be no doubt that the House of Lords believed that a valid contract of insurance had been constituted.

In *Paterson v Highland Railway* the question was whether an initial offer had been accepted.[125] The Railway had indicated that it was prepared to continue to accept an exceptional wartime rate for the carriage of pitwood for a further period of time. Before the period of time had elapsed, however,

120 *Carlill v Carbolic Smoke Ball Co* [1893] 1 QB 256.
121 *Law v Newnes* (1894) 21 R 1027.
122 *Law*, at 1031–1032.
123 *Hunter v Hunter* (1904) 7 F 136, 141–142.
124 *Hunter v General Accident Co* 1909 SC (HL) 30.
125 *A & G Paterson v Highland Railway Co* 1927 SC (HL) 32.

charges were increased. The pursuers objected, claiming that the offer to maintain the lower charges had been accepted. The balance of opinion in the Court of Session was in favour of a contract having been formed, but the House of Lords held otherwise, Lord Shaw of Dunfermline dissenting. Lord Dunedin, who gave the leading opinion, noted the difference between Scots and English law as regards consideration, and approved earlier statements as to the binding nature of a promise to keep an offer open in Scots law.[126] There was, however, he thought, no such promise to keep the offer open in the instant case. Lord Shaw believed, on the other hand, that an offer had been made and accepted. He appears to have considered the possibility of promise: "It appears unnecessary and insufficient to rest the rights of Messrs. Paterson solely upon a promise to which the railway companies were committed. In my opinion this was a case of contract, constituted by offer and acceptance."[127]

The most vigorous modern exponent of the doctrine of promise (or "pollicitation", as he was wont to describe it), the late Sir Thomas Smith, made some play of the four cases just discussed.[128] He considered that in their eagerness to follow *Carlill* Scots lawyers appeared to have overlooked the possibility of resting a case on promise, rather than on offer and acceptance. Looking to the matter of proof, Smith considered that in *Paterson's* case, in particular, reliance might have been placed on promise. As against this argument, standing the case of *Petrie v Earl of Airlie*, it is not clear that Scots law could not have arrived independently at the construction of a *Carlill-type* situation as one of offer and acceptance. Also, it would appear that in *Paterson's* case, at least, the possibility of promise was, in fact, considered by Lords Dunedin and Shaw, but rejected. Nevertheless, Smith's general point holds good: the fact that Scottish cases following after *Carlill* were considered on the basis of offer and acceptance should not be allowed to obscure the continuing usefulness of the doctrine of promise.

There are a number of situations in which the doctrine of promise can still be a useful weapon in the Scottish legal armoury. As Smith considered these in some detail, and others have elaborated on them since, there is no need to consider them at any length here.[129] The most frequently

---

126 Lord Dunedin at 38.
127 Lord Shaw at 45.
128 Smith, *Short Commentary* (n 80) at 748–751; for the use of the term "pollicitation", see above section F.
129 Apart from Smith, *Short Commentary* (n 80) ch 32, and the Scottish Law Commission Memoranda noted below, the most useful discussions are to be found in McBryde (n 3); Black

encountered in practice is a promise to keep an offer open for a period of time: the promisor is held bound by his unilateral declaration of will, and cannot withdraw the promise as he might if it were a mere offer.[130] Related to this is a *promise* of reward: again the promisor is not free to withdraw his promise, and thus many of the difficulties, real or imaginary, which have been posited in relation to *offers* of reward are wholly avoided. Related again and, as MacQueen has pointed out, of considerable potential commercial significance, are promises made in relation to options.[131] Another situation already discussed, in which the doctrine of promise has proved useful, is in relation to *jus quaesitum tertio*.[132] In addition, there are other situations, like that in the leading eighteenth-century case of *Reoch*, discussed above, which cannot be categorised so easily.[133]

The cases of *Bathgate v Rosie* and *Stone v Macdonald* illustrate the continuing application of the doctrine.[134] *Stone*, decided in 1979, concerned an option to purchase, open for ten years, the question being whether the option had been validly exercised. It was held that it had, and it was emphasised that the option was a promise as distinct from an offer. In *Bathgate*, decided in 1976, the mother of a boy who had broken a shop window promised the wife of the owner of the shop that she would pay for a new window. She later refused to pay. She did not deny that she had made the promise, but claimed that she had done so under the erroneous impression that she was legally bound to pay. The court held that the promise had not been motivated by error, and that the defenders were therefore bound to pay.

The great drawback of the doctrine of promise remained, until the Requirements of Writing (Scotland) Act 1995, that proof of the promise was limited to writ or oath. This disadvantage was fully recognised by Sir Thomas Smith and others as taking away many of the potential advantages of the doctrine.[135] In a much quoted passage, Lord Normand pointed out the disadvantages of proof by writ or oath, comparing the situation in Scots law unfavourably with English law concerning "consideration":

(n 3); H L MacQueen, "Offers, promises and options", 1985 *SLT (News)* 187; H L MacQueen, "Constitution and proof of gratuitous obligations: a comment on Scottish Law Commission Memorandum No 66", 1986 *SLT (News)* 1; and Zimmermann and Hellwege (n 4). MacQueen's articles are discussed further below, text accompanying nn 144–150.
130 See, for example, *Marshall v Blackwood*, above text accompanying n 115.
131 MacQueen, "Offers" (n 129).
132 Above text accompanying n 28.
133 *Reoch v Young* (1712) Mor 9439, above text accompanying n 112.
134 *Bathgate v Rosie* 1976 SLT (Sh Ct) 16; *Stone v Macdonald* 1979 SC 363.
135 Smith, *Short Commentary* (n 80) at 751–753.

There are probably few cases (or perhaps none) where an English court would hold that there was no consideration and a Scottish court would permit proof by witnesses, but there are probably many in which the English courts would hold that there was consideration and yet the Scottish courts would insist on proof scripto vel iuramento.[136]

The strongest attack on proof by writ and oath came from J J Gow, but there can be little doubt that he overstated the case.[137] This is not the place to enter into that debate, but it is worth noticing that in both *Reoch* in 1712 and *Bathgate* in 1976, although liability was denied, the fact of the promise was not.[138] Also, even though the fact that a promise had been made might initially be denied, it might be possible to shame the defender into an admission in open court if those who had heard the original promise were sitting on the public benches![139]

Smith believed that the distinction between promise *sub conditione* and contract through offer and acceptance might sometimes be narrow.[140] Perhaps one should frankly admit that the distinction may be so narrow on some facts as to be virtually invisible. The possibility of pleading an alternative case on promise, or on offer and acceptance, may seem illogical, yet still be useful in practice and serve the interests of justice.

## J. THE REQUIREMENTS OF WRITING (SCOTLAND) ACT 1995

It had long been evident that reform of the law on the constitution and proof of voluntary obligations was desirable. The law as it existed before 1995 was, as was widely recognised, obscure, illogical, and indefensible. As noted above, as early as 1580, the requirements of proof by writ or oath could be regarded as contrary to the *jus commune* and repugnant to common sense.[141] Gow's more recent caustic assessment of the value of the doctrine of proof by writ or oath has also been referred to.[142] It is relevant only to notice here the changes made to the long-standing rule of law that promises, and gratuitous obligations generally, while requiring no particular formalities for their constitution, could only be proved by writ or oath. Scottish

---

136 Lord Normand, "Consideration in the law of Scotland" (1939) 55 *LQR* 358 at 365.
137 Gow (n 27); and see Lubbe (n 6) at n 221. See also Scottish Law Commission Report No 112 on Requirements of Writing (1988) at para 3.14.
138 See above text accompanying nn 112 and 134.
139 As Robert Black points out to me.
140 Smith, *Short Commentary* (n 80) at 750, citing *Hunter v General Accident* (n 124) in particular.
141 Above text accompanying nn 18 and 19.
142 Above text accompanying n 137.

Law Commission Memorandum No 39 on *The Constitution and Proof of Gratuitous Obligations* (1977), prepared under the direction of Sir Thomas Smith, recommended the restriction of proof by writ or oath, in the absence of admission on record, to proof by writ only. No immediate action followed, but eight years later a further Memorandum (No 66, 1985) entitled *The Constitution and Proof of Voluntary Obligations and the Authentication of Writings* proposed the complete abolition of proof by writ or oath from Scots law.[143] Gratuitous obligations, it was proposed, should in future be *constituted* by writ. These proposals marked a radical change from the past, not only as regards the proof of gratuitous obligations, including promise, but also as regards their constitution.

The 1985 proposals were criticised by Hector MacQueen as being misguided as regards gratuitous obligations.[144] He welcomed the end of proof by writ or oath, but not the proposed introduction of a requirement that gratuitous obligations should be constituted in formal writing. He pointed out that, unlike most of the other proposals for reform, this represented "a tightening up of the law, rather than a relaxation of present proposals", and he believed that it would have deleterious effects on certain commercial transactions in which the doctrine of promise had played or might play a useful part. He noted that the earlier Memorandum of 1977 had proposed a general exception for commercial transactions from the rule requiring constitution by writing. He suggested that it would indeed be better to provide for such an exception. Alternatively, the proposed requirement of writing in the case of gratuitous obligations should be abandoned, save for some set exceptions. Less happily, as it turned out, he suggested that there might be less possibility of confusion if the term "unilateral obligations" were to be employed rather than "gratuitous obligations".

MacQueen's arguments were heeded, at least in part. The Requirements of Writing (Scotland) Act 1995 abolished proof by writ or oath, and prescribed constitution in writing, but made an exception in the case of obligations "undertaken in the course of business". Unfortunately, it confused the issue quite unnecessarily by referring to a "gratuitous unilateral obligation" but providing no definition of what was meant by this. It also referred to a "contract, unilateral obligation or trust". The Act begins:

---

143 To these two Memoranda should be added the succeeding Report: Scottish Law Commission (n 137).
144 MacQueen, "Constitution" (n 129).

1. (1) Subject to subsection (2) below and any other enactment, writing shall not be required for the constitution of a contract, unilateral obligation or trust.
(2) Subject to subsection (3) below, a written document complying with section 2 of this Act shall be required for—
   (a) the constitution of—
      (i) a contract or unilateral obligation for the creation, transfer, variation or extinction of an interest in land;
      (ii) a gratuitous unilateral obligation except an obligation undertaken in the course of business; . . .

It is not clear, in the absence of definition, how the phrase "gratuitous unilateral obligation" is to be interpreted.[145] If one looks to the historic role of proof by writ or oath in relation to "gratuitous obligations", and the understanding of the term "gratuitous obligations" set out in the Scottish Law Commission Memoranda which proposed the abolition of this rule of proof, then one might interpret the phrase as covering promise and gratuitous contract as these terms have been used in this chapter. However, the phrase "contract, unilateral obligation or trust" might be thought to suggest that a unilateral obligation must be distinct from a contract, at least in the context of this Act, notwithstanding the well-established use of the term "unilateral contract" south of the Border (to look no further). In that case, "gratuitous unilateral obligation" might be thought to apply to promise alone, and not to gratuitous contract. This indeed is the sense in which "gratuitous unilateral obligation" is glossed by Kenneth Reid in *Current Law Statutes Annotated*. This leads in turn to a result which seems odd and illogical: why should a promise to make a donation of £100 have to be constituted in writing, but not an offer (requiring only acceptance) to pay the same sum?

Even less desirable consequences would seem to flow from the interpretation of "gratuitous unilateral contract" put forward by Joe Thomson.[146] He suggests that, in the absence of statutory definition, the word "gratuitous" should be given "its ordinary meaning", which he takes to be where "something is done or given for nothing". Thomson therefore rejects – although with minimal discussion – the interpretation given to "gratuitous" in the relevant Law Commission Memoranda and, for that matter, by Robert Black and Hector MacQueen.[147] According to this more traditional interpretation,

---

145 See further on these terms M Hogg, *Obligations: Law and Language* (2017) chs 3 and 4.
146 J Thomson, "Promises and the requirement of writing", 1997 *SLT (News)* 284.
147 Note particularly Scottish Law Commission Memorandum No. 39 (n 15), at 41: "Whether an obligation is gratuitous or onerous is determined at the time when the obligation is constituted and while matters are still entire; if at that stage there is no counter-stipulation prestable

the quality of the obligation is determined when it is first formed, depending on whether or not the obligee is bound to do anything. Thus promise is always "gratuitous", whether subject to the fulfilment of a condition or not.[148] For Thomson, by contrast, a promise made subject to a condition may sometimes be "gratuitous" and sometimes not. Thus, to take examples which he himself gives, a promise to pay B £100 if he finds A's dog "cannot be regarded as gratuitous", whereas a promise to pay B £100 when he reaches 18 years may be so regarded. Thomson's argument, if accepted, would introduce a new and, it is suggested, unhelpful distinction into the law. Thomson does not focus on the meaning of "unilateral", nor does he consider whether gratuitous contracts come under the heading of "gratuitous unilateral obligations". If they do, presumably a distinction parallel to that which he suggests for promise would have to be made in that category also.[149]

As noted earlier in this chapter this entire area of law has been bedevilled by ambiguous and confusing terminology, exacerbated further in Scotland when the clarity of Stair was followed by the confusion of later writers. It is particularly unfortunate that the 1995 Act, although introducing some much-needed reform, should have added a new dimension to this confusion. It is also unfortunate that MacQueen's alternative suggestion as to the 1987 proposals was not acted upon: that the proposed requirement of writing in the case of gratuitous obligations should be abandoned, save for set exceptions. As matters stand, the exception in favour of commerce may well be thought to continue an anomaly. Why for example should a businessman to whom a promise has been made be favoured over an ordinary member of the public to whom a promise may have been solemnly made in the presence of a roomful of interested parties? In the past there was at least the possibility of shaming the promisor into admitting his promise in open court. With the requirement of constitution by writ this safeguard has in great measure disappeared. There was also the possibility of producing a subsequent writ under the promisor's hand. That too has ceased to be the case.

against the creditor the obligation is gratuitous, parole proof is excluded and nothing done by the promisee thereafter can convert the transaction into an onerous one." See also Black (n 3); MacQueen, "Constitution" (n 129); also MacQueen, "Offers" (n 129).

148 For a reply to Thomson, see M Hogg, "A few tricky problems surrounding unilateral promises", 1998 *SLT (News)* 25. Hogg also considers and seeks to explain McBryde's (n 3) statement that "not all promises are gratuitous" (at 48) as too, by implication, does MacQueen in the articles cited n 129. MacQueen and Thomson, *Contract Law* (n 3) para 3.21, agree to disagree.

149 This chapter has not considered the terminology of English law, particularly in regards to "unilateral contracts". For an account of the differences between Scots law and English law in this area, and consideration of recent English authority, see MacQueen and Hogg in the articles cited in n 148.

The 1995 Act does, however, allow for the possibility of subsequent actings conferring validity on an obligation defective in form.[150] Welcome though this is, it is difficult not to consider the introduction of the requirement of writing in the constitution of promise and, it may be, gratuitous contract to be a retrograde step. It is no longer possible to say with Stair that in the law of Scotland, "every paction produceth action".[151]

---

150 Section 1(3) and (4), which take the place of *rei interventus* and homologation.
151 Stair, *Inst*, 1.10.7; and above text accompanying nn 26 and 33.

# 16 Presumptions*

The history of Scots law as an independent system can be traced back at least as far as the thirteenth century when the notion of a "common law" of Scotland first appears. Scots law is generally recognised to be a "mixed" system, influenced by both the *jus commune* and by the Common law of England. On one view Scots law has been mixed from the very beginning, always open to both Civilian and to Common law influence, although to a varying extent in different centuries and in different branches of the law.[1] At all events the mix is a remarkably complex one. The history of presumptions in Scots law, indeed the history of evidence and proof generally, has been little studied, but it is evident that this area of Scots law has been influenced by both great European legal traditions, with Civilian influence undoubtedly predominant.

The original proposal to set up a Gerda Henkel working group on the comparative history of the law relating to presumptions and circumstantial evidence included a quotation from J B Thayer's *Preliminary Treatise on Evidence*, published in 1898. Thayer wrote that

> The quite modern facility in using the contrasted phrases, presumption of law and presumption of fact, has been attended with some attempt to introduce into our laws the niceties of the continental classification of the thousand and one assumptions, positions, presumptions – on innumerable subjects, – which have a place among the civilians. It has been the old mistake of pouring new wine into old bottles, and old wine into new.
> 
> . . .
> 
> At common law our principal triers of fact are that changing, untrained body of men the jury, to whom it would be idle to address such speculation on this subject as fill the books of the civilians . . .[2]

The drafter of the proposal, Michael Macnair, noted that Thayer's belief that Civilian influence on the Anglo-American law of presumptions was relatively late – "an eighteenth and nineteenth century novelty" – although shared by some later legal historians such as J H Langbein, had been questioned by

---

\* Originally published as "Presumptions in Scots law", in W D H Sellar and R H Helmholz (eds), *The Law of Presumptions: Essays in Comparative Legal History* (2009) 203–226.
1 For debate on the history of Scots law see ch 8 above.
2 J B Thayer, *Preliminary Treatise on Evidence at the Common Law* (1898) at 341, 343.

Barbara Shapiro in her *"Beyond Reasonable Doubt" and "Probable Cause"*, and by Macnair himself in his *The Law of Proof in Early Modern Equity*.[3] It has been further questioned, if not completely undermined, by the contributors to this volume. But it is Thayer's assertion that, "it would be idle to address that changing, untrained body of men the jury with the speculations on this subject that fill the books of the civilians", that strikes the Scots lawyer as the more surprising. The criminal jury, originally borrowed from England, has had a continuous history in Scots law since the thirteenth century, yet that does not seem to have prevented the reception of Civilian learning on procedure and presumptions. Nor has the re-introduction of the civil jury into Scots law early in the nineteenth century, again influenced by the English model, proved incompatible with the well-established law regarding presumptions.[4]

## A. THE INSTITUTIONAL WRITERS

The first considered treatment of the role of presumptions in Scots law is found in the late seventeenth century in the works of the "institutional" writers James Dalrymple, Viscount of Stair (1619–1695), writing on private law, and Sir George Mackenzie of Rosehaugh (1636–1691) writing on both private and criminal law. It is clear, however, that Scots law had received Civilian learning on proof and presumptions at an earlier date. Thus procedure before the Court of Session, Scotland's supreme court in civil matters, had been Romano-canonical since its establishment as a College of Justice in 1532. Early in the seventeenth century Lord Advocate Sir Thomas Hope (c 1580–1646), writing in his *Major Practicks* in a curious mixture of Latin and Scots, noted that a presumption *juris* alters the onus of proof, giving as examples Acts of the Scottish Parliament passed in 1503 and 1621:

> Praesumptio juris relevat ab onere probandi eum pro quo praesumitur, et rejecit illud onus in adversarium. Exemplum presumptionis juris habet lex 1503 c.77, viz: that a widdow who wes repute and haulden as wife to her husband defunct during his lyfetym non tenetur probare matrimonium legitimum, bot aucht to enjoy the benefit of ane tearce as laufull wife, ay and quhill it be found wtherwayes be the sentence of ane judge.[5]

---

3 B J Shapiro, *"Beyond Reasonable Doubt" and "Probable Cause": Historical Perspectives on the Anglo-American Law of Evidence* (1991); M R T Macnair, *The Law of Proof in Early Modern Equity* (1999) ch 9.
4 For the history of the jury in Scotland, see I D Willock, *The Origins and Development of the Jury in Scotland* (SS vol 23, 1966).
5 Hope, *Practicks*, 7.10 ("Of Probation in Generall"), at 45 ("A *praesumptio juris* lifts the burden

>     Aliud exemplum praesumptionis juris habet lex 1621 c.18; that all dispositions mad be ane bankrupt to a conjunct or confident persone, without any true just and neccessarie cause or a competent pryce, ar presumed to be in fraudem creditorum . . .[6]

The references are to the Act of 1504 concerning widows' terce and the Bankruptcy Act of 1621.[7]

On the criminal side, Sheriff Irvine Smith, discussing the state of Scots criminal law in the first half of the seventeenth century, notes the frequent use of the word "presumption", commenting that, "On what would now be described as circumstantial evidence and was then referred to as 'presumptions', no limits were set."[8]

In his *Institutions of the Law of Scotland*, first published in 1681, Lord Stair set out the law of Scotland on presumptions with his customary lucidity.[9] Stair's treatment is firmly rooted in the tradition of the *jus commune*. Under the heading of probation Stair deals first with "ordinary" probation, which he divides into probation by writ, by witnesses, or by the oath of parties. He then moves on to "extraordinary" probation, using also the terms "inartificial" to describe ordinary probation, and "artificial" to describe extraordinary probation. "The former three ways of probation," he says, referring to probation by writ, witness and oath, "are called inartificial; because they prove points expressly, directly and *in terminis*, and so require no art or skill to make parties understand, that the point found relevant is proven . . .". "But," he continues, "when the probation is not direct and express, but consequential and indirect, where the point to be proven is inferred to be true by consequence, it is not equally obvious to all capacities, whether that consequence be valid or not: and therefore it is called an artificial probation . . .".[10]

"Presumptions," writes Stair, "are the most important extraordinary probations."[11] Following the *jus commune* – "the so large treatises of law-

---

   of proof from the one in favour of whom it is presumed, and places that onus on the other side. The law of 1503 provides an example of a *praesumptio juris*, viz: that a widow who was reputed and held to be the wife of her deceased husband during his lifetime does not have to prove that the marriage was lawful, but ought to enjoy the benefit of a terce as a lawful wife, always until it be found otherwise by the sentence of a judge.") The law of 1503 is rightly of 1504: see ch 9 n 8.
6  Hope, *Practicks*, 7.10.47. ("The law of 1621 provides another example of a *praesumptio juris*; that all dispositions made by a bankrupt to a conjunct or confident person, without any true just or necessary cause or a competent price, are presumed to be in fraud of creditors . . .").
7  RPS 1504/3/42; 1621/6/30. The Acts of 1504 and 1621 are referred to again briefly below, text accompanying nn 110–112.
8  *Justiciary Cases* II, introduction at liii.
9  Stair, *Inst*, 4.45.9–24.
10 Stair, *Inst*, 4.45.2.
11 Stair, *Inst*, 4.45.9.

yers" – Stair notes that presumptions can be divided into three categories: *praesumptio judicis*; *praesumptio juris*; and *praesumptio juris et de jure*.[12] "*Praesumptio judicis*," he says, "is when the judge finds the probability of a point (wherein ordinary probations are not competent) to be eminently probable to be true; unless the contrary be proven by a more positive presumption."[13] "*Praesumptio juris*," on the other hand, "is where the law hath so presumed, but hath not statute, nor declared it for a rule." This is a stronger presumption than the presumption of a judge alone. "Of these presumptions," Stair continues, referring to presumptions *juris*, "there are multitudes in the Roman law, which swell the treatises of presumptions to a great measure", adding dryly that, "There are not wanting such presumptions in our law." He then observes that, "though presumptions be said to *transferre onus probandi*, rather than to prove, yet they do prove unless the contrary can be proven."[14] Stair notes that "presumptions of law" may derive from custom, by which he means judicial decisions, as well as from statute, the former, however, constituting by far the majority.[15] The third category, *praesumptio juris et de jure*, "is, when the statutory or declaratory part of the written law does statute or declare such a point to be true, without further probation." This presumption," he observes, "is not only a presumption in the law, but a presumption which becometh a law; and therefore admits no contrary probation."[16] That is to say, it is irrebuttable.

Stair takes care to distinguish presumptions *juris et de jure* from legal fictions: "Fiction of law is no presumption; for thereby the law-giver makes that which he knows not to be true, to be esteemed and held as if it were true." As an example of a legal fiction he gives the maxim that the heir is regarded in law as *eadem persona cum defuncto*.[17] Distinguishing between a presumption and a legal fiction on these lines is a recurring theme among later writers.[18]

Stair also divides presumptions into general and particular, the latter referring to particular areas of law, such as marriage, legitimacy and trusts. He gives many examples, most of them generally familiar in the Civilian

---

12 Stair, *Inst*, 4.45.12.
13 Stair, *Inst*, 4.45.12.
14 Stair, *Inst*, 4.45.13.
15 Stair, *Inst*, 4.45.13; also 4.45.16 where Stair uses the phrase "presumptions of law".
16 Stair, *Inst*, 4.45.14.
17 "The same person as the deceased": Stair, *Inst*, 4.45.15.
18 For an example, see W A Wilson, *Introductory Essays on Scots Law* (2nd edn, 1984) at 7, discussing provisions in the Succession (Scotland) Act 1964 concerning death in a common calamity. The relevant law is now contained in the Succession (Scotland) Act 2016 ss 9 and 10.

tradition. First among general presumptions is that liberty is presumed in opposition to slavery.[19] Other examples given relate to possession: that all possession is presumed to be lawful – described by Star as a presumption *juris* – and that possession of moveable goods presumes the property thereof (also *juris*).[20] Further general presumptions include the presumption against donation, the related *debitor non praesumitur donare*, and the presumption of life:

> Life is presumed. This some do extend to an hundred years of age, but others only to fourscore, which is confirmed by that of the Psalmist, that the age of man is threescore ten, unless by the strength of nature he come to fourscore.[21]

Although Stair was familiar with the Civilian division of proof into *plena* and *semi-plena*, there is no hint in his treatment of the elaborate counting of points referred to by Thayer which caused the system to fall into disrepute. Stair's experience, it may be noted, was practical as well as academic: he had been a Cromwellian judge in the 1650s, and was later twice Lord President of the Court of Session.

Sir George Mackenzie also had experience of practice at the highest level, rising to the post of Lord Advocate. He had a strong admiration for the Civilian tradition and his work is full of references to Civilian authority. His brief *Institutions of the Law of Scotland* appeared three years after Stair's great work. "Presumptions are a Kind of Probation," he writes, then divides them into "Praesumptiones juris, which though they be strong, yet they may be taken off by a contrary Probation . . . and praesumptiones juris & de jure", against which no probation can be admitted.[22]

Mackenzie's better-known *Laws and Customs of Scotland in Matters Criminal*, the earliest institutional work on Scots criminal law, was published in 1674. Treating of probation generally, Mackenzie remarks that because, "Probation is so fully treated by the Civilians and Canonists, and we differ so little from them, I shall only treat of it here in relation to our own Law."[23] He then considers four categories of probation: the standard probation by confession, by oath, and by writ, followed by probation by presumptions. "Presumptions," he writes, "are divided into presumptions that are violent (for strong Presumptions are so called) and these that are not violent; they

---

19 Stair, *Inst*, 4.45.17, 1.
20 Stair, *Inst*, 4.45.17, 7 and 8.
21 Stair, *Inst*, 4.45.17, 19.See below, text accompanying nn 109 and 110.
22 Mackenzie, *Inst*, 4.2.
23 Mackenzie, *Matters Criminal*, 2.24 proemium (Robinson edn at 369).

are likewise divided *in praesumptiones juris, & praesumptiones juris & de jure.*"²⁴ Once again, he does not mention presumptions *judicis*. Mackenzie refers to the ongoing controversy among the Civilians, both in writing and in practice, as to whether crimes may be proved by presumptions, but clearly believes that in practice they are, adding that, "This Difficulty hath favoured some of the Doctors to conclude, that this Case is arbitrary, and others to conclude, that Presumptions may infer *poena extraordinaria, sed non ordinaria.*"²⁵

Mackenzie's admiration for the *jus commune* even led him to argue for the abolition of the criminal jury in Scotland:

> Though of old, when Judges and Assizers [*that is, jurymen*] were equally ignorant, Assizers were appointed, yet now when Law is formed to a Science and that Judges are presumed to be learned, and Assizers not, it seems reasonable they should be supprest, as well in criminal Cases as in Civil . . .²⁶

Despite this plea, the criminal jury remains in Scotland to this day, and few are calling for its abolition. Mackenzie also comments that,

> Albeit it be a received Principle in our law, that the Justices are only Judges to the Relevancy, and Assizers to the Probation; yet to distinguish the Limits of their different Cognitions, becomes very oft difficult . . .²⁷

Like other writers on criminal law, Mackenzie emphasises the importance of an Act of the Scottish Parliament of 1587, to the effect that all proof should be led in the presence of the assize and the accused, noting that, "By the Civil Law, and the opinion of almost all Divines and Nations, *judices debent secundum allegata & probata.*"²⁸ Despite this, it is evident from other sources that the jury was still in a stage of transition in the seventeenth century, and that it had not then "entirely abandoned its original function of declaring facts within its own knowledge."²⁹

Andrew M'Douall, Lord Bankton (1685–1760), whose *Institute of the Laws of Scotland* was published between 1751 and 1753, considers presumptions under the heading of "Proof, or Evidence in general".³⁰ It is

---

24 Mackenzie, *Matters Criminal*, 2.25.4 (Robinson edn at 377–378). For the division into violent, probable and light presumptions, see Shapiro, *"Beyond Reasonable Doubt"* (n 3) at 165. Also, below, text accompanying n 37.
25 For these Civilian expressions, see Shapiro, *"Beyond Reasonable Doubt"* (n 3) at 157.
26 Mackenzie, *Matters Criminal*, 2.23.4 (Robinson edn at 359).
27 Mackenzie, *Matters Criminal*, 2.23.4 (Robinson edn at 356).
28 Mackenzie, *Matters Criminal*, 2.23.8 (Robinson edn at 363); *RPS* 1587/7/67.
29 Irvine Smith (ed) (n 9), introduction, at xlv.
30 M'Douall adopted the judicial title of Lord Bankton on his elevation to the Court of Session bench in 1755.

interesting to note the equation here of the terms "proof" and "evidence", in view of the rather different use of these terms in English law as outlined by Barbara Shapiro.[31] Following Stair and the *jus commune*, Bankton divides proof into "artificial" and "inartificial", as also into "ordinary" and "extraordinary". "To this last kind of probation," he continues, referring to extraordinary, "Presumptions may be referred."[32] Later, he writes,

> I therefore proceed to the other kind of proof, called artificial; because it arises from the circumstances of the parties and the cause [i.e. the case], which may be deemed a Circumstantial evidence. The grounds whereupon this artificial proof is founded are presumptions.[33]

Here Stair's "consequential and indirect" probation has become the more familiar "circumstantial evidence".[34]

Bankton then defines presumptions as "Probable evidence concerning the truth of a fact", before following the standard Civilian division into presumptions *hominis vel judicis; juris;* and *juris et de jure*.[35] "A presumption of the judge, or *praesumptio hominis*," he remarks, "arises from the nature and circumstances of the fact, whence the judge presumes in favour of the one or the other party." "*Praesumptio juris* or presumption of law," on the other hand, "is that which the law has introduced." Bankton notes that there are "a vast number" of these in the law. Presumptions *juris et de jure* are, "That which the law not only presumes to be true, but ordains it to be taken as such, without liberty to traverse it or prove the contrary."[36] He then, like Stair, distinguishes presumptions from fictions of law. Bankton concludes the chapter, in accordance with his general scheme, with observations on the law of England. Citing Sir Edward Coke, he writes that there are three sorts of presumptions in English law: "Violent, Probable and Light. Violent Presumption stands often in place of a clear proof. Probable moveth little; and Light Presumptions move not at all."[37]

Although repeating the old learning on presumptions, Bankton also writes, in a passage that seems remarkably modern:

---

31 The equation between "proof" and "evidence" can also be found in the contemporary index to Bankton, *Inst*.
32 Bankton, *Inst*, 4.26 at 629.
33 Bankton, *Inst*, 4.34 ("Presumptions. Fictions of Law") at 667–671.
34 Above, text accompanying n 10.
35 The definition appears in quotation marks, but without attribution. "Probable" here means proveable.
36 Bankton, *Inst*, 4.34 (at 668–669).
37 Bankton, *Inst*, 4.34 (at 668–669).

> Evidence is multifarious, and what degree of it shall be sufficient, cannot be defined by any rule of law; for it must be adapted to the cases respectively that come before the judges, or if the trial is by a jury, before them. And such evidence, whether direct proof, or a presumptive one (which I may call a Probable [*that is, provable*] Evidence), as convinces the conscience of the judges, is sufficient . . . That no certain rule can be given, as to what kind or degree of evidence is necessary in every case that may occur, that therefore the judge should not restrict himself to any one kind of it; but according to the nature and circumstances of the case, to consider in his own conscience what is sufficiently proved to the conviction of his mind, or what is defective in that respect, and to give judgment accordingly. An advice which all judges and juries ought to follow, as the variety of cases admits of a different consideration, as to the proof requisite to find out the truth of the same.[38]

Very much the voice of the Age of Reason.

John Erskine of Carnock (1695–1768), whose *Institute of the Law of Scotland* was published posthumously in 1773, considers presumptions under the general heading of "Probation". He notes first that proof may be direct, as in proof by writings, by oath and by witnesses. However, he continues:

> Where facts do not admit of a direct proof the laws of all nations allow of a proof by circumstances and presumptions, which in many cases carries as high a degree of conviction as the direct. Presumptions are consequences drawn from facts notorious or already proved, which infer the certainty, or at least a strong probability, of other facts to be proved; and hence presumptive evidence is by Aristotle, and after him by Tully, called artificial . . .[39]

This passage looks back to Stair on "consequential and indirect" probation, and to Bankton on "circumstantial evidence", as well as giving a useful working definition of presumptions.[40]

Erskine then gives the threefold division into *juris et de jure*, *juris* and *hominis vel judicis*.[41] He distinguished presumptions *juris* into two kinds, "proper presumptions arising from the supposition of certain facts", examples given being the presumption in favour of property which arises from the possession of moveables, and the maxim *debitor non praesumitur donare*; and, secondly, presumptions grounded not –

> on positive facts, but rather on general rules, which, though they are in the form of words positive, may easily be converted into negative propositions, and derive

---

38 Bankton, *Inst*, 4.34 (at 631). The reference to a jury is likely to be to the criminal jury.
39 Erskine, *Inst*, 4.2.34. "Tully" is Cicero.
40 Above, text accompanying nn 10 and 37.
41 Erskine, *Inst*, 4.2.35–37. I have generally referred to presumptions *juris* etc, rather than *iuris*, as this reflects the spelling of most Scottish writers.

their force entirely from the want of contrary proof. Thus the rules, that every man is presumed honest, that immunity from servitude is presumed, that life is presumed, with many others of the same kind, are, in other words, that guilt is not presumed, nor servitude, nor death.[42]

Erskine suggests that presumptions *hominis vel judicis* differ from presumptions *juris* "only in this", that presumptions *juris* are founded on statute, customs or decisions. Like Stair and Bankton, he carefully distinguishes a presumption from a legal fiction.

The second great writer on Scots criminal law, Baron David Hume (1756–1838), namesake and nephew of the famous philosopher, says little about presumptions as such in his *Commentaries on Crimes*, but does consider the role of circumstantial evidence. In principle, Scots law adhered to the Civilian rule requiring two witnesses to corroborate each other. Hume notes that "circumstantial evidence" could supply the lack of a second witness. He then poses the question whether it is lawful to convict on circumstantial evidence alone. He concludes that it is, writing that it "is not only vouched by the whole series of our criminal records, but is grounded also in reason and necessity, and the law and practice of all other civilized nations." In cases like this, however, Hume thought it necessary, "to recommend to jurymen the propriety of caution and reserve, in which indeed they are seldom wanting, as to the sufficiency of the presumptions of guilt on which they are to condemn."[43]

The last of the great institutional writers on Scots private law, George Joseph Bell (1770–1843), deals quite shortly with presumptions in his *Principles of the Law of Scotland* under the heading of "Presumptive Evidence".[44] The main features of Bell's treatment are attention to the role of the (civil) jury, re-established in Scotland in 1815, and the omission of the presumption *hominis vel judicis*:

> There are some cases in which the law has settled certain presumptions, of force sufficient to guide the jury in weighing evidence. And, 1. Presumptio juris and de jure is absolute, and must be so received by the jury... [*various examples follow*] 2. Presumptio juris is not an absolute but prima facie proof, yielding to evidence.[45]

---

42 Erskine, *Inst*, 4.2.36.
43 Hume, *Commentaries*, vol 1, at 237. Compare Mackenzie, above text accompanying nn 26 and 27. Hume also gave lectures on Scots private law, printed posthumously in the twentieth century in six volumes by the Stair Society, but there did not discuss presumptions as such.
44 G J Bell, *Principles of the Law of Scotland* (2nd edn, 1830) at para 2319; and (3rd edn, 1833) at para 2320. There is no general treatment of presumptions in Bell's first edition of 1829.
45 See n 44 above.

In the edition of 1839, however, the last to be edited by Bell himself, the section on presumptive evidence begins as follows:

> Circumstantial evidence is not the same with presumptive proof, except in so far as an inference may be called a presumption. Presumptions are legal rules to exclude, or to abridge, or to aid the inquiry, by regulating the onus probandi. A presumption of fact, is an inference from circumstances; a presumption of law, is a rule of exclusive, or inclusive, or prima facie proof. There are some cases in which the law has settled certain presumptions of force sufficient to guide the jury in weighing evidence . . .[46]

There are some points of interest here: the treatment of presumptions *hominis vel judicis*, now effectively re-labelled "presumptions of fact", as merely an example of circumstantial evidence; and the contrasting of "presumptions of law", that is, presumptions *juris et de jure* and presumptions *juris*, with "presumptions of fact".

It is also worth noting that in Bell's "General View" of parole and presumptive evidence, he pays particular attention to jury trial:

> One great benefit of jury trial is, that it requires less the exclusion of any kind of evidence; leaving the collected materials to be disposed of on the footing of credibility, by an impartial tribunal of men accustomed to judge of the ordinary transactions of life. But still there are certain technical rules of exclusion of testimony, in which what may be called the *law* of parole evidence consists. The questions on all such matters are two: 1. What is *admissible* testimony? 2. What is sufficient evidence? – the former being matter of law for the Court; the latter being matter of deliberation and decision for the jury, but still with some aid from the law as to what shall not in particular cases be held sufficient evidence.[47]

## B. TEXTBOOK WRITERS

The earliest monographs on the law of evidence in Scotland, by James Glassford and George Tait respectively, both antedated Bell's *Principles*. As Shapiro suggests, Glassford's *Essay on the Principles of Evidence*, published in 1820, is an example of the overlap between legal and philosophical writing.[48] In his Advertisement Glassford writes that his aim is to analyse and illustrate the principles from which the legal rules of evidence are drawn. The second part of his Essay, "Of Legal Evidence", considers evidence

---

46 Bell, *Principles* (4th edn, 1839) at para 2260. The text then continues as in the previous editions. This text remains in what became the standard edition of Bell's *Principles*, the 10th by W Guthrie (1899).
47 Bell, *Principles*, 4th edn (n 46) at para 2236.
48 J Glassford, *Essay on the Principles of Evidence and their Applications to Subjects of Judicial Inquiry* (1820). See Shapiro, "*Beyond Reasonable Doubt*" (n 3) at 179–180.

in courts of law, the courts in question being Scottish, although English authority is sometimes cited. In a section headed "Argumentative Evidence, or Evidence from Facts and Circumstances", Glassford notes that circumstantial proof is daily received in the civil courts, and that "even in questions strictly of a Criminal kind, it is equally established . . . that the evidence from facts and circumstances . . . may afford a proof sufficient either for acquittal or conviction."[49] In the following section, "Of Presumptions", Glassford notes that presumptions are similar to circumstantial evidence in being both indirect and secondary; but that presumptions "are conclusions drawn without regard to the circumstances of an individual case."[50] Although the Civilians divide presumptions into various classes, the real difference between them, he says, lies in their comparative strength or weakness.[51] He does not list the standard Civilian categories, but observes that, "Although Presumptions are commonly distinguished into those of law and those of fact . . . all . . . are founded at bottom on the principles of reason."[52] It is worth noting that Glassford's definition of presumptions given above, by excluding the circumstances of an individual case, must necessarily exclude presumptions *hominis vel judicis*.

George Tait's *Treatise on the Law of Evidence in Scotland* first appeared in 1824 with further editions in 1827 and 1834.[53] In his preface he mentions that Glassford's *Essay* had appeared while he was preparing his own work, but that he believes there still to be room for his own more practical treatment. Tait distinguishes clearly between circumstantial proof and proof from presumptions *juris*. The former applies, "where the fact to be established is inferred from other facts proved or admitted, having a special relation to the particular point at issue, and being of such a nature to lead by necessary or legitimate inference to a belief in the truth of the principal fact sought to be established"; whereas presumptions *juris* apply, "where the fact to be established is inferred from certain general conclusions of law, applicable to the point at issue, without reference to the particular

---

49  Glassford, *Essay* (n 48) section 2, at 563, 569 and 572. Compare Hume's remarks, text accompanying n 43; also Mackenzie, text accompanying n 25.
50  Glassford, *Essay* (n 48) section 2, at 582–592.
51  J S More makes much the same point in his authoritative edition of Stair's *Institutions* (1832) when he comments that, "Proof by presumption or inference admits of all degrees, and is so liable to be modified and affected by the peculiar circumstances of each case, that it cannot be reduced within definite rules." (Vol 2, notes, at ccccxix.)
52  Glassford, *Essay* (n 48) section 2, at 583–584.
53  I have used G Tait, *Treatise on the Law of Evidence in Scotland* (3rd edn, 1834).

circumstances of the individual case."⁵⁴ Consonant with this view, Tait, like Glassford, omits all mention of presumptions *hominis vel judicis*. Tait notes of presumptions *juris et de jure* that they are "not properly presumptions of fact, but rather legal doctrines established from expediency upon an unchallengeable assumption of facts."⁵⁵ His examples of presumptions *juris*, although largely conventional, include a category on prescription.

In 1855, a few years after Bell's death, W G Dickson published his *Treatise on the Law of Evidence in Scotland*, a work which was to hold the field for over a hundred years.⁵⁶ Bell, Glassford and Tait had cited relatively little English authority in their treatment of evidence and presumptions. Dickson, however, made full use of English writing, citing Starkie, Bentham, Mill, and Best, as also Mr Justice Wills' "Essay on Circumstantial Evidence".⁵⁷ Dickson also drew on Civilian authors such as Mascardi and Menochio, as well as on Scottish authority.⁵⁸ He was concerned to distinguish between circumstantial and presumptive evidence, his first title on evidence being, "Of Evidence as divided into Direct and Indirect, and of the difference between Circumstantial and Presumptive Evidence."⁵⁹ He notes that the terms circumstantial and presumptive were "often used synonymously", but believes them to be "different species of the genus 'indirect' evidence."⁶⁰ He writes that,

> In this view, presumptive evidence consists of a single fact or a small group of facts, from which another fact is inferred, on account of the general experience of mankind having found them to be frequently coincident.⁶¹

In the third edition of Dickson this becomes,

> A presumption is an inference as to the existence of one fact from a knowledge of the existence of some other fact, drawn solely by virtue of previous experience of the ordinary connection between known and inferred facts, and independently of any process of reason in the particular case.

---

54 Tait, *Treatise* (n 53) at 439; also at 447.
55 Tait, *Treatise* (n 53) at 447.
56 W G Dickson, *A Treatise on the Law of Evidence in Scotland* (2 vols, 1855).
57 Dickson, *Treatise* (n 56) at para 248, note (a). For Starkie, see below. Best is added to the list in the third edition of Dickson, ed P J Hamilton Grierson (1887) at para 65.
58 J Mascardus, *Conclusiones probationum omnium quae in foro quotidie versantur* (1584). For Menochio see below n 115, and A Giuliani, "Civilian treatises on presumptions, 1580–1620", in Helmholz and Sellar (eds), *Presumptions* (n °), *passim*.
59 Dickson, *Treatise* (n 56) at 144.
60 Dickson, *Treatise* (n 56) at para 247.
61 Dickson, *Treatise* (n 56) at para 247.

"An inference from circumstantial evidence," on the other hand, "is the result of reason exercised upon the facts, or of reason and experience conjoined . . .".[62] The footnotes refer to the English writer Thomas Starkie whose "immensely influential" treatise on the English law of evidence was first published in 1824.[63] In fact, as will be seen, Dickson's definition follows Starkie virtually to the letter.[64]

It is worth noting, however, that if Dickson had read Starkie and other English authors, Starkie in his turn had read Pothier and Heineccius, and was familiar with the Civilian division into presumptions *juris et de jure* and presumptions *juris*.[65] Confusingly, Starkie distinguishes between these two presumptions (or their English equivalents), and what he terms "presumptive or circumstantial evidence". "Circumstantial, or, as it is frequently termed, presumptive evidence," he writes, "is any which is not direct and positive."[66] Then follows the definition of a presumption copied by Dickson:

> A presumption in strictness is an inference as to the existence of one fact, from the existence of some other fact, made solely by virtue of previous experience of the ordinary connection between known and inferred facts, and independently of any process of reason in the particular instance.[67]

Starkie avoids the term presumption *hominis vel judicis* altogether, although he does refer to "presumptions of mere fact". His use of the phrase "presumptive evidence" as contrasted with "presumptions" is thoroughly confusing, the more so given Dickson's contrast between "circumstantial" and "presumptive" evidence, and Bell's treatment of presumptions generally under the heading "Presumptive Evidence".

It might have been expected that Dickson would have followed Tait and Bell in avoiding the expression presumption *hominis vel judicis* altogether and referring only to circumstantial evidence. However, he does not do so, but repeats the time-honoured division into presumptions *juris et de jure;*

---

62 Dickson, *Treatise*, 3rd edn (n 57) at para 64.
63 T Starkie, *Practical Treatise of the Law of Evidence* (1820). The phrase "immensely influential" is Shapiro's "*Beyond Reasonable Doubt*" (n 3) at 180. I have used the second edition (1833).
64 Dickson, *Treatise* (n 56) at para 292 also defines a presumption as, "an inference as to the existence of one fact, drawn from the existence of another fact, and manifest to most persons of ordinary intelligence."
65 Starkie, *Practical Treatise* (n 63) vol 2, at 679ff.
66 Starkie, *Practical Treatise* (n 63) vol 1, at 494.
67 Starkie, *Practical Treatise* (n 63) vol 1, at 494. In his second volume Starkie defines a presumption in similar terms: "A presumption may be defined to be an inference as to the existence of one fact, from the existence of some other fact, founded upon a previous experience of their connection" (Starkie, *Practical Treatise* (n 63) vol 2, at 679–680).

*juris (tantum)*; and *hominis vel judicis*.[68] Dickson also reacted unfavourably, at least at first, to the contrast between the terms "presumption of law" and "presumption of fact". In his first edition, he wrote, "The division sometimes adopted into *presumptiones juris* and *presumptiones facti* is thought to be erroneous. All presumptions are *facti*; both the evidentiary matter and the inference being facts."[69] This statement, however, does not re-appear in the third edition in 1887.[70]

In fact, the Court of Session in the Full Court case of *Millar v Mitchell, Cadell & Co* in 1860 had given judicial approval to the use of the terms "presumption of law" and "presumption of fact".[71] The question was whether a particular mercantile usage was a presumption *juris* or a presumption of fact. In finding it to be the latter, eight of the consulted judges use the phrase, "a mere presumption of fact, or, as the institutional writers express it, *praesumptio hominis*".[72] Looking to Erskine, they stated that, "A *praesumptio juris* may be introduced, either by statute or by custom", noting further that before a presumption "can have the authority of a proper *praesumptio juris*, it must be recognised, and take its place as a part of the system to which it belongs. Till it has been so recognised it is fact and not law."[73]

Dickson on *Evidence* was not superseded until the appearance in 1964 of the *Law of Evidence in Scotland* by Sheriffs A G and N M L Walker.[74] Although the authors avowedly set out to treat the subject *de novo*, they naturally draw on Dickson's work. Thus they define a presumption as follows, citing Dickson:

> A presumption has been said to be an inference as to the existence of one fact from a knowledge of the existence of another fact, drawn solely by the virtue of previous experience of the ordinary connection between the known and inferred facts, and independent of any process of reasoning in the particular case.[75]

Ironically, as already noted, this is pure Starkie. The authors also note Dickson's distinction between presumptions and circumstantial evidence, but write later that presumptions *hominis vel judicis*, "are frequently difficult

---

68 Dickson, *Treatise* (n 57) at para 294.
69 Dickson, *Treatise* (n 57) at para 294, n (r).
70 Dickson, *Treatise*, 3rd edn (n 58).
71 *Millar v Mitchell, Cadell and Co* (1860) 22 D 833.
72 *Millar* at 843.
73 *Millar* at 844.
74 A G Walker and N M L Walker, *The Law of Evidence in Scotland* (1964) at para 54.
75 Walkers, *Evidence* (n 74) at para 54.

to distinguish from circumstantial evidence", citing the case of *Millar v Mitchell, Cadell & Co*.[76]

Although declaring that none of the standard classifications of presumptions had proved to be "entirely satisfactory or particularly useful", the authors adopt the familiar threefold division into presumptions *juris et de jure, juris tantum* and *hominis vel judicis*, while noting that presumptions *hominis vel judicis* are sometimes termed "presumptions of fact".[77] Presumptions *juris et de jure* they regard as rules of substantive law which have little place in a work on evidence. Presumptions *juris tantum* and *hominis vel judicis*, on the other hand, do have a place in the law of evidence and affect the burden of proof, "one of their principal uses being to establish facts which, by their nature, are incapable of proof by direct evidence."[78] They then consider presumptions under the headings "Irrebuttable Presumptions Juris et De Jure", and "Rebuttable Presumptions – Juris tantum and Hominis vel Judicis".[79] They refer back to Dickson and the institutional writers and to Scottish statutes and cases, but seldom cite English authority. Following the institutional writers and the case of *Millar*, a presumption *juris* is said to differ from a presumption *hominis vel judicis* in that it has been recognised by statute, custom or judicial decision. A presumption *hominis vel judicis*, on the other hand, emerges only after consideration of the circumstances of each particular case.[80]

A second edition of the Walkers on *Evidence* appeared in 2000, edited by Margaret Ross and James Chalmers.[81] This generally follows the first edition, save that the preferred terminology is for "presumptions of law" and "presumptions of fact", rather than presumptions *juris et de jure, juris tantum* and *hominis vel judicis*. A section on "Irrebuttable Presumptions of Law" precedes one on "Rebuttable Presumptions of Law and Fact".[82] A reference to Erskine cited in the first edition for the distinction between presumptions *juris* and presumptions *hominis vel judicis* now becomes authority for the distinction between presumptions of law and presumptions of fact.[83]

---

76 *Millar* (n 71) at 844–845.
77 Walkers, *Evidence* (n 74) at para 56.
78 Walkers, *Evidence* (n 74) at para 54.
79 Walkers, *Evidence* (n 74) at paras 55 and 56.
80 Walkers, *Evidence* (n 74) at para 56.
81 M L Ross and J Chalmers (eds), Walker and Walker, *The Law of Evidence in Scotland* (2nd edn, 2000). The 3rd (2009), 4th (2017) and 5th (2020) editions of this work appeared after the first publication of this chapter. I Callendar joins the editorial team in the 5th edition.
82 Ross and Chalmers (eds) (n 81) at paras 3.2.1 and 3.2.2.
83 Erskine, *Inst*, 4.2.37.

Some further treatments of the law of evidence in Scotland appeared between the two editions of Walkers on *Evidence*, notably Sheriff A B Wilkinson's *Scottish Law of Evidence* in 1986, and Sheriff, later Lord Macphail, and Sheriff Linda Ruxton's contribution on evidence in the *Stair Memorial Encyclopaedia* in 1990.[84] In his preface Wilkinson writes that, "particular attention has been paid to distinctive Scottish characteristics (of the law)." In keeping with this he cites little English authority. However, he does suggest in a brief historical outline that, "From the early nineteenth century onwards the main external source for the development of the Scottish rules of evidence has . . . been English law."[85] Rather surprisingly, in view of his attachment to Scots law, Wilkinson adopts the American writer Thayer's definition of presumptions:

> Presumptions are aids to reasoning and argumentation which assume the truth of certain matters for the purpose of some given enquiry. They may be grounded in general experience, or probability of any kind; or merely on policy or convenience. On whatever basis they rest, they operate in advance of argument or evidence, or irrespective of it, by taking something for granted; by assuming its existence.[86]

Wilkinson then classifies presumptions into "conclusive presumptions of law (presumptions *juris et de jure*); rebuttable presumptions of law (presumptions *juris* or *juris tantum*); and rebuttable presumptions of fact (presumptions *judicis* or *hominis* or *facti*)." This last category he describes as "something of a misnomer", as presumptions of fact "are really ways of describing the operation of inferences based on circumstantial evidence."[87] He accepts that there is an argument that presumptions of fact should not be called presumptions at all, but believes the terminology to be useful. Rebuttable presumptions of law, he believes, can be divided into two different categories: presumptions which depend on the proof of basic facts for their operation, and presumptions, such as the presumption of sanity – and, one assumes, the presumption of innocence, although this is not specifically mentioned – which require no proof in themselves but indicate where the legal onus probandi lies.[88] As already noted, the same point had been taken by Erskine.

---

84 A B Wilkinson, *The Scottish Law of Evidence* (1986); I D Macphail and L M Ruxton, "Evidence", in *SME*, vol 10 (1990). The re-issue of the latter in 2006, edited by Sheriff A Stewart, contains no substantial changes as regards presumptions.
85 Wilkinson, *Evidence* (n 84) at 4.
86 Wilkinson, *Evidence* (n 84) at 191–192, citing Thayer (n. 2) p. 314.
87 Wilkinson, *Evidence* (n 84) at 193.
88 Wilkinson, *Evidence* (n 84) at 192–193.

Macphail and Ruxton also adopt the classification into irrebuttable presumptions of law, rebuttable presumptions of law and rebuttable presumptions of fact, relegating the older terminology to a footnote.[89] Like other writers from Stair onwards, they observe that the notion of irrebuttable presumptions is a contradiction in terms. Presumptions of fact, they consider to be, "another misleading term signifying inferences which may or may not be drawn from circumstantial evidence without infringing any rule of law", a view again comparable to that of many earlier writers.[90] A rebuttable presumption of law they define as, "an assumption, prescribed by statute or defined by authoritative judicial decision, which must be made unless overcome by contrary evidence."[91]

Macphail and Ruxton also discuss presumptions in the context of the criminal law. They note that rebuttable presumptions of law rarely feature in a criminal trial, adding that, "It is thought that the court would take very great care in applying any such presumptions in favour of the prosecution."[92] They also comment that the use of the terms "presumption of innocence" or "presumption of sanity" in criminal cases is a misleading way "of expressing rules of fundamental importance as to the incidence of the burden of proof." Unlike Erskine and Wilkinson, they suggest that these are not presumptions at all, "because they do not depend on an inference from proof of a basic or preliminary fact".[93]

Three further recent works on evidence may be briefly noted. Field on *The Law of Evidence in Scotland* (1988) reached a third edition as Raitt on *Evidence* in 2001.[94] Raitt divides presumptions into irrebuttable presumptions of law, rebuttable presumptions of law, and rebuttable presumptions of fact.[95] Irrebuttable presumptions of law are said to amount on some occasions to a legal fiction. Examples included within this category include prescription. Rebuttable presumptions of fact are distinguished from circumstantial evidence, although not altogether convincingly. The use of the

---

89 Macphail and Ruxton (n 84) at para 750, n 3.
90 Macphail and Ruxton (n 84) at para 750. Elsewhere they define presumptions of fact as, "no more than inferences, suggested by ordinary experience, which may be drawn from facts which have been proved in any individual case" (at para 751).
91 Macphail and Ruxton (n 84) at para 750.
92 Macphail and Ruxton (n 84) at para 754.
93 Macphail and Ruxton (n 84) at para 754. See above, text accompanying nn 42 and 88.
94 D Field, *The Law of Evidence in Scotland* (1988); D Field and F E Raitt, *The Law of Evidence in Scotland* (2nd edn, 1996); and F E Raitt, *Evidence* (3rd edn, 2001). F E Raitt with E H Keane, *Evidence: Principles, Policy and Practice* (2013) appeared after the first publication of this chapter.
95 Raitt, *Evidence* (3rd edn) (n 94) at para 3.02.

terms "presumption of innocence" and "presumptions of sanity" are highlighted as "common misuses of the word presumption".[96]

Sheldon on *Evidence* (1998) and Chalmers on *Evidence* (2006) are more of the nature of primers. They too divide presumptions into irrebuttable presumptions of law, rebuttable presumptions of law, and rebuttable presumptions of fact, with no mention of traditional Civilian terminology. Neither, however, includes prescription as an example of an irrebuttable presumption of law. Chalmers suggests that rebuttable presumptions of fact are less easy to identify than presumptions of law, "probably because it is difficult to differentiate such presumptions from the everyday process of inferring certain facts from other facts where this seems reasonable to do."[97]

## C. OVERVIEW

The story of presumptions in Scots law over the last three or four hundred years is relatively unproblematic. The treatment of the subject by Stair and other institutional writers is firmly based on the *jus commune* division into presumptions *juris et de jure*, presumptions *juris tantum*, and presumptions *judicis vel hominis*. In criminal law the Civilian division of presumptions into violent, probable and light is also found. In the field of presumptions, as in other areas of law, Civilian learning has been integrated into the common law of Scotland without apparent difficulty. There is little sign that the existence of the criminal jury in Scotland since the early thirteenth century and the revival of the civil jury in the early nineteenth have caused any problems. This may be so, at least in part, because the more elaborate calculus of Civilian theory on evidence and presumptions so castigated by Thayer does not seem to have taken root in the Scottish law of evidence.

If the story of presumptions has been relatively unproblematic it has also been one of remarkably little change; and this despite the influence of English law from the beginning of the nineteenth century onwards. Stair and Erskine on presumptions are still cited in the courts as authoritative statements of the law. Indeed, there is little to differentiate their account of the law from that of the Walkers on *Evidence* in the later twentieth century. Even the Latin names attached to many presumptions, such as the *praepositura rebus domesticis* of a married woman, survived well into the twentieth century; and some, such as the *apocha trium annorum*, are

---

96 Raitt, *Evidence* (3rd edn) (n 94) at para 3.23.
97 D Sheldon, *Evidence* (1998) at 10–13; J Chalmers, *Evidence* (2006) at 17–20.

still current.[98] Several themes recur regularly over the centuries: the fact that the so-called presumptions *juris et de jure* are truly rules of law; the distinction between presumptions and legal fictions; the different status to be accorded the presumption of innocence and the presumption of sanity, if indeed these should be termed presumptions; and the running debate as to whether it is possible to distinguish meaningfully between presumptions *judicis vel hominis*, now generally termed presumptions of fact, and circumstantial evidence. The term "circumstantial evidence" itself appears in regular use from the time of Bankton and Erskine in the mid-eighteenth century. It does not appear in Stair, who writes more in terms of "consequential and indirect" probation. On the criminal side the question whether circumstantial evidence alone can be enough to secure a conviction has been regularly addressed; the answer, albeit hesitant, has regularly been in the affirmative.

On the face of it, the greatest difference over the centuries has been the change in terminology from presumptions *juris et de jure, juris tantum*, and *judicis vel hominis* to "presumptions of law" and "presumptions of fact". This change has been very gradual, taking place from the beginning of the nineteenth century to the present day. It is clear that, in Scots law at least, the change has been one in name only and not of substance. The term "presumption of law", already found in Stair, is a straightforward translation of *praesumptio juris*; the term "presumption of fact", ambiguous and uncertain at first, has come into regular use as the equivalent of *praesumptio hominis vel judicis*. It is only in the last 20 years or so that the Civilian terminology has begun to fade out of use altogether. This is as likely to be due to decreased Latinity as to English influence. Yet it may be suggested that there is a danger that the now well accepted division into law and fact might suggest to those unaware of the historical background that there is a difference in kind between these two types of presumptions when it is certainly arguable that there is only a difference of degree. Despite the apparent difference in kind there was, and still is, a sliding scale according to the strength of the presumption, and the borderline between presumptions *juris* and presumptions *hominis vel judicis* is permeable. The true difference in kind was between presumptions *juris et de jure*, which are not truly presumptions at all, and the other categories.

98 A married woman, living with her husband, was presumed to have the *praepositura rebus domesticis*, and, as such, to be able to pledge her husband's credit for household necessities. The term *apocha trium annorum* describes the presumption that three consecutive receipts for a regular payment indicate that all previous instalments have been paid.

How does one explain the fact that there has been so little change in the law regarding presumptions over the centuries? The clue probably lies in the quotation noted above from Bankton in the mid-eighteenth century.[99] The old learning on presumptions, although dutifully repeated, was rapidly giving way in practice to a more *ad hoc* appraisal of the evidence in the light of the facts and circumstances of each individual case. This may go some way to explain the sometimes sterile and repetitious debates about presumptions in the textbooks over the centuries: had presumptions been crucially important in practice, the focus on them would have been much sharper.

Another question which might be asked is why the influence of the Anglo-American Common law did not cause more change. Although Scottish authority has generally been preferred, the fact that English writers and authority have been regularly cited by Scottish courts and writers for well on two hundred years, and occasionally cited for much longer, is not in doubt. Dickson's reliance on Starkie, Wills and Best in the nineteenth century has been replaced towards the end of the twentieth by the citation of Cross on *Evidence* and Lord Denning on presumptions and the burden of proof.[100] As has been observed, even the definition of a presumption has been copied from English or American writers, Dickson following Starkie, the Walkers following Dickson, and Wilkinson citing Thayer. There is a parallel to be made as regards English influence on Scots law with the experience of another "mixed" system, that of South Africa, as set out by Jacques du Plessis elsewhere.[101] The parallel, admittedly, is not exact, as English law was imposed in South Africa, whereas, in Scotland, it was followed willingly. However, the reason why the influence of English law did not cause a fundamental deviation in the course of either Scots or South African law on presumptions is likely to be the same: English law on presumptions, as it came to be expounded in the nineteenth century, was itself heavily influenced by the Civil law. This is well set out by du Plessis who comments on the irony of the law on presumptions in South Africa becoming detached from its Roman-Dutch roots, only to receive the tradition of the *jus commune* anew through the medium of English law and the distinction between law and fact.[102]

---

99 Above, text accompanying n 38.
100 Sir R Cross, *Evidence* (1st edn, 1958). Lord Denning's article has been much cited: A T Denning, "Presumptions and burdens" (1945) 61 *LQR* 379.
101 J du Plessis, "Presumptions in South African law: an historical perspective", in Helmholz and Sellar, *Presumptions* (n °) at 227.
102 Du Plessis (n 102), at 239. See also Shapiro, *"Beyond Reasonable Doubt"* (n 3), at 184.

## D. FURTHER AVENUES FOR RESEARCH?

Although the main story is relatively uneventful there are some other points of interest which suggest possibilities for further historical and comparative study. These can only be touched on lightly here. One is the way in which particular presumptions can move from one category to another, from a presumption *judicis*, for example, to a presumption *juris*, or vice-versa. Thus, there has been continuing uncertainty as to whether the presumption of ownership arising from the possession of moveables should be classed as a presumption of law (*juris tantum*) or a presumption of fact (*judicis vel hominis*), Stair and the older authorities opting for the former, but more recent authority tending towards the latter.[103] Sometimes a presumption can even move from being a rule *juris et de jure* to becoming a presumption *juris tantum*. This appears to have happened in relation to marriage *per verba de futuro subsequente copula* in Scots law. This form of valid though irregular marriage originated in the medieval Canon law, and remained part of Scottish marriage law until abolished by Act of Parliament in 1939.[104] Marriage was constituted by the operation of a presumption that intercourse following on an engagement to marry took place on the faith of the promise of marriage and indicated present consent to that marriage. In Canon law and, it would seem, at first in Scots law, this was a presumption *juris et de jure* and was irrebuttable.[105] Latterly, however, the presumption appears to have been regarded as a rebuttable presumption *juris* only.[106] Sometimes there is uncertainty whether to label well-accepted doctrines of law as presumptions or not: this has been the case with prescription and, separately, with presumptions of innocence and sanity.[107] Sometimes a presumption can simply disappear, as in the case of the superstition or presumption attached to touching a corpse, discussed below.

---

103 For this debate see D L Carey Miller, *Corporeal Moveables in Scots Law* (2nd edn, 2005) para 1.19, and "Title to moveables: Mr Sharp's Porsche" (2003) 7 *Edin LR* 221, commenting on the case of *Chief Constable of Strathclyde Police v Sharp* 2002 SLT (Sh Ct) 95. In the earlier case of *George Hopkinson v Napier & Son* 1953 SC 139 at 147, Lord President Cooper said in terms, "if the circumstances do not raise the plea of bar . . . the possession of the moveables can create no more than a presumption of fact, more or less strong according to the circumstances, but capable of being redargued."
104 Marriage (Scotland) Act 1939 s 5. See chs 9 and 10 above.
105 Stair and Erskine both seem to suggest that the presumption was irrebuttable.
106 *Mackie v Mackie* 1917 SC 276; and see E M Clive, *Husband and Wife* (4th edn, 1997) at para 05.014.
107 Above, text accompanying nn 42, 88 and 93.

Another point of interest lies in the counterpoint between the common law of Scotland (that is, custom, case law or precedent) and statute in the recognition and management of presumptions. A good example of this in Scots law is the presumption of life and its *alter ego*, the presumption of death. At common law there was a well tried presumption of life (a presumption *juris*) to the effect that a man or woman should be presumed to live for eighty years or even more before his or her death could be assumed, although no doubt the force of the presumption lessened as the years advanced.[108] Such a long presumption of life proved highly inconvenient, and a statutory presumption of death was introduced for some purposes in 1881, and again as regards death in a common calamity in 1964, but the presumption of death at common law remained until it, together with the provisions of the 1881 and 1964 Acts, were replaced by the Presumption of Death (Scotland) Act of 1977 which consolidated the law, and set a more practical limit of seven years.[109] Another area of law in which an original common law presumption became much overlaid by statute was the law of deathbed which is considered separately below.

Sometimes it is difficult to tell whether a statutory presumption marked a change in the law, or merely confirmed existing practice. The Acts of 1504 and 1621 cited by Sir Thomas Hope in his seventeenth-century *Major Practicks* as examples of presumptions *juris* which affected the onus of proof are cases in point.[110] The Act of 1504 concerned the situation where a widow who claimed her terce (that is, her liferent of a third part of her husband's heritable estate) in a secular court after his death and was met with the objection that she had not been the lawful wedded wife of the deceased. The statute enacted that if it could be shown that she had been generally held and reputed to be the widow of the deceased during his lifetime, then that was sufficient proof of marriage unless and until a judgement of an ecclesiastical court held otherwise – in other words, it raised a presumption of marriage. Curiously, a misunderstanding of the purport of the 1504 Act led to the eventual recognition in Scots law of a type of irregular marriage known as "marriage by cohabitation with habit and repute".[111] The Bankruptcy Act of 1621 cited by Hope was concerned with the gratuitous alienation of property by someone verging on bankruptcy to "conjunct and confident" persons.

---

108 For Stair on this, see above, text accompanying n 21.
109 Presumption of Life Limitation (Scotland) Act 1881; Succession (Scotland) Act 1964 s 31. The latter has been replaced by the Succession (Scotland) Act 2016 s 9.
110 Above, text accompanying nn 5–7.
111 See chs 9 and 10 above.

Such alienations were presumed to be in defraud of creditors (again a presumption *juris*) and struck down. This statute remained in force for over 350 years until it was repealed and replaced by the Bankruptcy (Scotland) Act 1985.[112]

In the criminal law an Act of 1690 was passed to settle doubts which had arisen as to what evidence could properly be admitted to secure a conviction in cases of child murder, given that the evidence in question was likely to be circumstantial. It was enacted that a woman who had given birth to a child would be presumed guilty of child murder (a presumption *juris*) if she had concealed the pregnancy, sought no help at the time of delivery, and the child had subsequently been found dead or had gone missing.[113] Although the statute was intended to make it easier to convict the guilty, it also opened the possibility of condemning the innocent. In his novel *The Heart of Midlothian* Sir Walter Scott made the most of its dramatic potential. The heroine of the novel, Effie Deans, although innocent of the offence, is found guilty of child murder under the statute of 1690 and sentenced to death with the full panoply of the law by the doomster of the High Court of Justiciary. Scott's description of the legal proceedings leading to Effie's conviction gives an insight into Scottish criminal justice and emphasises the influence of the Civil law.[114]

Another way of approaching presumptions is to consider the historical source from which presumptions spring: is the origin of a presumption to be found in the Civil law, the Canon law, Feudal law, or in Scottish statutory or common law? The bulk of presumptions found in Scots law, as in the western legal tradition generally, undoubtedly come from the *jus commune*, the authoritative statement of which is to be found in the *De Praesumptionibus* of Giacomo Menochio (Menochius) (1532–1607).[115] Some of the best-known presumptions come more specifically from medieval Canon law, such as the presumption relating to marriage *per verba de futuro subsequente copula* noted above. Another example is the presumption *pater est quem nuptiae demonstrant*, by which it is presumed (a presumption *juris*) that the father of a child born to a married woman is her husband. This

---

112 Bankruptcy (Scotland) Act 1985 ss 75(2) and 34, have themselves been replaced by Bankruptcy (Scotland) Act 2016 s 98.
113 RPS 1690/4/111. The Act was repealed in 1809. Glassford, *Essay* (n 48) at 581, discusses this Act and notes earlier legislation addressing the same problem in England and France.
114 Sir W Scott, *The Heart of Midlothian*, ch 23. For the significance of the incident as a Celtic survival in Scots law see chs 1 and 2 above. The account is of course fictional, but Scott was familiar with legal practice as an advocate and, as sheriff of Selkirk, a judge.
115 J Menochius, *De Praesumptionibus, conjecturis signis & indiciis* (1st edn, 1587; 2nd edn, 1686).

was the subject of the controversial First Division case of *Imre v Mitchell* decided in 1958.[116] In *Imre* a pregnant woman had persuaded a man to marry her on the basis that he was the father of the unborn child. The child was born prematurely, a month before the marriage actually took place. The couple later split up and the man – unusually at that time – was awarded custody of the child. The woman then claimed that her husband was not the father of the child and brought an action for declarator of bastardy (as it was then termed). Blood test evidence, then a relative novelty, indicated that the chance of the husband being the father of the child was of the order of one in 100,000. Nevertheless the Court held that the presumption *pater est* still applied, Lord President Clyde looking to Bankton, Erskine and the Decretals of Pope Gregory IX, and referring to "this almost irrebuttable presumption".[117]

Richard Helmholz has noted the debate in the *jus commune* as to what circumstances were enough to infer adultery given that direct evidence was rarely available. Was it enough that the parties had been found in compromising circumstances – *solus cum sola, nudus cum nuda*? "The learned law," he concludes, "did authorize a presumption from such facts."[118] Jacques du Plessis has noted that in Roman-Dutch law a young man and woman being found together naked in bed raised "a *violente* presumption of adultery and *hoererije*".[119] The same question arose in a memorable Scottish case heard by the commissary court in 1708.

In a process of divorce for adultery, it was libelled that the defender on one or other of the days specified –

> received John Lord Belhaven, naked or undressed, at unseasonable hours of the night or day, in to her bed-chamber, where she was then lying in naked-bed, and that they staid together alone, with close doors, until the next morning. *Objected*, the circumstances libelled are not sufficient in this cold climate, to infer adultery. *Answered*, they would be sufficient even in a criminal pursuit, much more in a civil action of divorce.

The commissaries repelled the objection, and found the qualifications in the libel relevant to infer adultery.[120]

---

116 *Imre v Mitchell* 1958 SC 439. This presumption, based on common law at the time of *Imre*, is now statutory: Law Reform (Parent and Child) (Scotland) Act 1986 s 5.
117 *Imre* at 462.
118 R H Helmholz, "The law of presumptions and the English ecclesiastical courts", in Helmholz and Sellar, *Presumptions* (n °) 137, at 145.
119 Du Plessis (n 102), at 231.
120 *Earl of Wigton v Lady Margaret Lindsay* (1708), in F P Walton (ed), *Lord Hermand's Consistorial Decisions 1684–1777* (SS vol 6, 1940) at 45.

The Feudal law lies at the root of the law of deathbed in which presumptions played a major part. In Scotland the law of deathbed can be traced back to the fourteenth-century legal treatise *Regiam Majestatem*, here following the English treatise *Glanvill*.[121] The developed law is set out by the institutional writers and gave rise to much litigation. By the law of deathbed the "heir-at-law", that is the heir entitled to succeed to the heritable, or landed estate, was entitled to set aside all deeds granted to his prejudice on deathbed (*in lecto*). For a grant to be valid the grantor had to have been in full possession of his faculties, or, as it was expressed, in *liege poustie*, or *in legitimam potestatem*. But how could it be shown that a grantor had been in *liege poustie* if he died not long after executing the deed? Various presumptions were recognised by the common law. Notably, any presumption that the grantor had not been in *liege poustie* could be elided if it could be shown that after the date of the gift he had been seen going to kirk [that is, to church] or to market freely and unsupported. Further ancillary questions arose. What counted as support? What if there had been "no convention or congregation" at kirk or market at the time? Did any equivalent acts suffice? Stair was uncertain whether going to kirk or market raised a presumption *juris et de jure*, or merely *juris*.[122] In 1692 the Court of Session declared by Act of Sederunt that going to kirk or market must be performed in daytime and when people were gathered together;[123] while in 1696 the Scots Parliament enacted that it should be a sufficient defence against the objection of deathbed that the grantor had lived for sixty days after executing the deed, even if he had never gone to kirk or market during that time.[124] Questions about deathbed, however, continued to cause uncertainty in the law until eventual abolition in 1871.[125]

Finally, there was a presumption, born of ancient superstition, which disfigured the law of Europe, Scotland included, for many centuries. It was once an important adminicle of evidence, which raised a presumption of guilt, if the corpse of someone who had been killed or had died in suspicious circumstances, were to bleed at the touch, or in the presence of, somebody suspected in the death. The superstition is immemorially old and has clear

---

121 *RM (Cooper)*, 2.18, following *Glanvill*, 7.1.
122 Stair, *Inst*, 3.4.28.
123 Act anent persons going to Church and Mercate after granting of dispositions, 29 Feb 1692, in *An Abridgement of the Acts of Sederunt of the Lords of Council and Session from January 1553, to February 1794* (1794) at 138–139 (no 181).
124 *RPS* 1696/9/56.
125 34 & 35 Victoria, c 81.

links with trial by ordeal and the *judicium dei*. It is used to dramatic effect in the *Nibelungenlied* when Siegfried's corpse bleeds in the presence of his murderer Hagen; it surfaced after the death of Henry II Plantagenet in 1189 when it was whispered that Henry's corpse had bled in the presence of his son and successor Richard "Coeur de Lion" who had just defeated his father in battle; and it is to be found in the sixteenth century in Menochio's famous treatise on presumptions.[126] In Scotland, the presumption was still active in the sixteenth and seventeenth centuries. It is attested to by King James VI, no less, who wrote in his *Daemonologie* that, "In a secret murther, if the dead carcase be at any time thereafter handled by the murtherer, it wil gush out of bloud; as if the blud wer crying to the heaven for revenge of the murtherer, God having appointed that secret super-naturall signe, for tryall of that secret unnaturall crime . . .".[127] The superstition was alluded to in the trial of the Mures of Auchindrain in 1611.[128] The custom of touching the corpse was referred to again in 1636 when Andrew Smeaton was accused before the justice-depute of the homicide of George Shaw, whose body had been found in a moss in the parish of Foulis Wester in Perthshire. In his defence Smeaton produced a testimonial subscribed by the minister and landowners of the parish. This narrated that Shaw's body had been taken to the churchyard of Foulis Wester where a large number of people had assembled. There, "Accoirding to ancient custome he was tuiched and handled be ane and uther thair present Giff [if] the bleiding as ane infallible signe and taikin [token] the said murthour mycht be cognosced." Among others Smeaton had touched and even embraced the body, but, the testimonial continued, "We could persive [perceive] nor find na appearance nor argument of ony guiltines in him thairof." The charges were dropped.[129] A late example is noted by David Hume who refers in his *Commentaries on Crime* to the case of Philip Stansfield, convicted of parricide in 1688.[130] Hume writes that,

---

126 "Now it is a great marvel and frequently happens today that whenever a blood-guilty murderer is seen beside the corpse the wounds begin to bleed" (A T Hatto (trans), *The Nibelungenlied* (1965) at 137). Menochius, *De Praesumptionibus* (n 115), I, qu 89, n 128, at 117: "The thirtieth indication emerges from this, when the investigated or accused person is brought to the corpse, and the corpse bleeds."
127 King James VI, *Daemonologie, in Forme of a Dialogue* (1597) at 80–81; reprinted in J Craigie (ed), *Minor Prose Works of King James VI and I* (Scottish Text Society, 1982).
128 R Pitcairn, *Criminal Trials in Scotland, 1488–1624* (3 vols, 1833) vol 3, at 143; see also at 182–199.
129 *Justiciary Cases* I, at 264–267.
130 For the trial, conviction and gruesome execution of the wayward Philip for treason and cursing his father as well as parricide, see T B Howell, *A Complete Collection of State Trials* XI (1811) no 354; W Roughead, *Twelve Scots Trials* (1913) at 63ff. For a contemporary account edited

"One of the circumstances stated in the libel, and given in evidence, in the case of Standsfield, as a presumption of his guilt, was that the dead body of his father bled afresh when the panel [the accused] touched it."[131] Hume adds: "He was, however, convicted on very strong presumptions."

by Sir Walter Scott, see J Lauder of Fountainhall, *Chronological Notes of Scottish Affairs, from 1680 to 1701* (1822) at 234–236.
131 Hume, *Commentaries*, vol 1, at 462.

# Index

Note: References to footnotes are represented as page number followed by note number (55n11). Page numbers for figures appear in italics.

Aberdeen, University of, 160, 236
Act of Union *see* Treaty and Acts of Union
Adam, Frank, 107–8, 115
Adomnan's Law, 19
Adrian IV, Pope, 91
adultery, 4, 227–9, 231–2, 233, 369
affinity, 232–3, 236, 237; *see also* incest
Ailes, Adrian, 120, 121
Ailred of Rievaulx, 94
Alexander II, King of Scots, 72, 78
Alexander III, King of Scots, 24, 57–8, 108–16, *112, 113*, 117–19, 120
Alexander III, Pope, 91, 197–198, 200
Angles, law of, 17–18
Anglo-Norman feudalism *see under* Feudal law
Anselm, Saint, 90–91
Anton, A E, 85–6, 87, 204, 288–9, 291
arbitration, 165
Ardwall, Lord, 210, *210*–211
army service, 25, 62, 77–9
Arran, earls of, 13
Arran, James Hamilton, 3rd earl of, 182
Ashton-Cross, D I C, 204–5, 208, 328
Asso y del Río, Ignacio Jordán de, 39
assythment, 55, 68–9, 117, 164, 243–4
Atholl, earldom of, 96
Atholl, John, earl of, 111–13
Atholl, Walter Stewart, earl of, 308–9, *310*
Auchinleck Chronicle, 259, 260
Ault, W O, 135–6, 137, 141

Baillie, James, 14
Baird Smith, David, 5n14
bairns' part *see* legitim
Baker, Sir John H, 242, 254, 286n41
Balfour, Sir James, of Denmilne, 119

Balfour, Sir James, of Pittendreich
  judicial career, 324
  *Practicks*, 40, 76, 128, 251, 256n65, 324
Balliol, John, King of Scots, 111, 120, 121
bankruptcy, 37–8, 151, 348, 367–8
Bankton, Lord *see* M'Douall, Andrew
Bannerman, J W M, 55n11, 63n53, 73, 79, 114, 117, 117–19, 122
Barclay, Margaret, 308–9, *310*
barony courts, 10–11, 26–7, 44–5, 74–7, 124–5
Barrow, G W S
  importance to Sellar, 6, 11, 53, 116
  on Anglo-Saxon influence, 60, 61
  on the *breitheamh*, 56, 117
  on "Couthal" as type of birlaw, 141
  on the Great Cause, 72–3
  on importations from English law, 182–3
  on office of justiciar, 23n20, 28n36, 175
  on pre-feudal courts, 76
  on rendering of army service, 78
  on Robert Bruce, 258
  on Scone seal, 110–11, 113
  on Scottish common law, 55
  on tanistry, 72n91
Bartolus de Saxoferrato, 326
Beaton (alias MacBeth) physicians, 63, 73, 117
Beaton, Archibald, 324
Bede Ferdan, 29
Bell, George Joseph
  *Commentaries*, 45, 47
  *Principles*, 333, 354–5, 357
Bernard of Pavia, 257

Bible
  Exodus, 247, 257
  Leviticus, 30, 179, 234, 236–7
  Numbers, 282–3
Binchy, D A, 54, 58, 60n34, 89
Birks, Peter, 174, 186–7, 189
birlaw, 123–141
  and barony courts, 124–5
  etymology, 125, 127, 129, 133, 134–5, 139
  examples in Scotland, 124, 125–33
  operation in England, 134, 135–8
  origins in Danelaw, 135, 139–41
  reasons for decline, 138
  reference in *Regiam Majestatem*, 125–7
  role, 124
  Scandinavian provenance, 139–41
Bisset, Thomas, of Balwillo, 308–9
Black, Robert, 68, 311, 343
blench ferme, 25
blood feuds, 243
Bonet, Honoré, 248–9, 256, 261
Borbone, Carlo Ferdinando, Prince of Capua, 226
Boswell, James, 21, 46, 71
Bourgogne, Sir Robert, 62, 76
Bower, Walter, 109, 110, *112*
*breitheamh*, 21–2, 22, 56–7, 82, 96–7, 97
Brexit, 52
brieves of right, 302–3, 304–6, 307
Brink, Stefan, 140
Britons, law of, 17–18
Brougham, (Henry) Lord, 46, 221, 225
Broun, Dauvit, 116
Bruce, Robert (Robert I, King of Scots), 70, 158, 258–9, 263–4, 281
Bruce, Robert (the Competitor), 72–3
Brus, Robert de, 244
Buchanan, George, 80, 81, 167, 186n62
Buchanan, William, of Auchmar, 73
burlaw *see* birlaw
Byrne, F J, 59, 60

cain, 21, 62, 77, 81, 164
Cairns, J W, 9, 46n103, 189, 189n79, 189n80, 216n2
Callendar, Isla, 360n81
calp, taking of, 264
Cameron, John, 5n14, 54

Campbell, A H, 280
Campbell, Archibald, 5th earl of Argyll, 229
Campbell chiefs, 70–1
Campbell, Elizabeth, 103
Campbell, Gillespic, 265
Campbells of Kilmun, 25
Canon law
  and Celtic secular marriage, 70, 88, 92–3, 97–8
  connection with Roman law, 20
  as living law, 164
  of marriage, 193, 195–8, 202, 227
Canon law influence
  on English law, 28, 326–7
  on Scots law, 28–32, 164–5, 187–8
  contract, 318–9
  Court of Session, 31–2, 165, 166, 323, 347
  homicide, 247, 257–8
  incest, 234–8
  legitimation, 193–4
  marriage, 29–30, 193, 195–8, 218–19, 221–3, 232
  obligations, 313, 317, 318–19, 322–6, 327
  in *Regiam Majestatem*, 165, 325, 329n89
  Sellar's approach to, 7–8, 10
  sheriff courts, 31–2, 165
  succession, 165
  writings of Craig, 29, 188, 195, 218, 323
  writings of Stair, 8, 198, 218, 323
Cant, R G, 80, 81
Carey Miller, D L, 182
Carpenter, David, 156n2
Carrick, earldom of, 67
Carrick, Niall, earl of, 64, 263–4
Carrick, Roland of, 64
Caupeny (Capigny), James or Jack, 120, 120–1
célsine, 60, 63
Celtic law, surviving traces, 53–83
  overviews, 21–2, 163–4
  in courts and court procedure, 74–7
  culrath, 74–6, 117, 164
  MacDuff, Law of Clan, 76
  *maor* (mair) and serjeant, 64, 82

in criminal law, 68–9
  assythment, 55, 68–9, 117, 164,
    243–4
  letter of slains (*sláinte*), 68–9, 117,
    164
land law burdens
  cain, 21, 62, 77, 81, 164
  military service (*fecht* and *slúagad*),
    25, 62, 77–9
in law of persons
  Celtic secular marriage *see* Celtic
    secular marriage
  fosterage, 21, 70–1
  tocher, 71
in law of succession, 71–4
  tanistry, 71–4, 82, 107
moot (*mót, mòd*), 60–1
offices and titles
  *breitheamh* (brieve), 21–2, 22, 56–7,
    82, 96–7, 97
  *deòradh* (dewar), 64–5
  *kenkynolle* (*cenn cineóil, ceann
    cinéil*), 64, 264
  *maor* (mair) and serjeant, 64, 82
  mormaor, 63–4
  *seanchaidh* (sennachie) *see*
    seanchaidh
  *tòiseach* (head of kindred), 64
  toiseachdeor, 65–8
in royal prerogative, 79–81
scholarship surrounding, 54–5
Sellar's approach to, 5–6, 12
taking of calp, 264
*see also célsine; coigreach;* monarchy
  and kingship
Celtic secular marriage, 84–106
  overview, 69–70
  and Canon law, 70, 88, 92–3, 97–8
  in early Irish law and custom, 87–93, 94
  in Gaelic Scotland, 93–106, 217
  position of children, 84, 85, 89
  trial marriage (handfasting), 84–6, 89
Chalmers, James, 360, 363
Charles I, King of England, 108
*chaudemellee*, 241–2, 245–262 *passim*
child murder, 368
children
  age of capacity, 221–2, 277
  of Celtic secular marriage, 84, 85, 89

fosterage, 21, 70–1
*legitim* (bairns' part), 37, 149, 163, 178,
  266, 271–2, 290, 294
legitimation, 30, 165, 193–4, 293
succession where adopted or
  illegitimate, 293
chivalry, court of, 303–4; *see also* judicial
  duels
Church court jurisdiction
  marriage, 193, 194, 196–7, 228
  obligations, 318–319, 322–3, 324–5
  succession, 288, 291
circumstantial evidence, 352, 354, 357–8,
  364; *see also* presumptions
civil procedure, 31, 165
Civilian law *see* Roman law
Clanchy, M T, 161–2
Clanrickard, Richard Burke, 2nd earl of,
  92
Clerk, Sir John, of Penicuik, 80n140
Clive, E M, 191, 193, 201, 202, 205–7,
  213, 216n2, 224
Clyde, J A, Lord President, 34, 145n15,
  179n29
Clyde, J L, Lord President, 51, 369
codification of law, 46
cohabitation with habit and repute
  (MCHR) *see under* marriage
*coigreach*, 24, 65
Coing, Helmut, 326–7
Coke, Sir Edward, 145, 154, 256n65, 352
Colonsay, Lord, 203; *see also* M'Neill,
  Duncan
Colquhoun, Lady Helen, of Luss, 21, 77
Columba, Saint, 79
Colville, John, 132
commissary courts, 35, 195, 218, 228, 267,
  278, 288, 291, 323–5
common law, terminology, 20–1, 148,
  157
Comrie family, 82
Comrie, Jean, 82
Comyn, John, 95, 258–9
Connanus, Franciscus, 319–20
conquest, law of, 162–3, 284
consanguinity, 232–3; *see also* incest
Constantine, Emperor, 295
contract *see* promise
conveyancing *see* land law

Cooper, Thomas Mackay, Lord President
  on Canon law, 7, 228
  and Celtic law, 5
  on early statutes, 37
  on history of Scots law ("false starts and rejected experiments"), 2, 16–17, 54, 55, 161, 175, 176–7
  on influence of English Common law, 16–17, 161
  on influence of Roman law on succession, 295–6
  inspired leadership of, 51
  on late 15th century central courts, 34
  as Lord Advocate, 4n8
  on modern law, 47–51
  parentage, 5n16
  on presumptions, 366n103
  on royal justice, 6
  on sovereignty of Parliament, 44
  on Stair's *Institutions*, 40–1, 142, 144
  *Regiam Majestatem*, 14, 27, 247, 249–50, 289–90
  *Register of Brieves*, 14
  *Scottish Legal Tradition*, 16, 40–1, 47
Coopland, G W, 248n38
Coquille, Guy, 39
Corehouse, Lord, 336–7
*Corpus Iuris Canonici*, 28
Cottingham, Robert de, 258
Council of the Isles, 96; *see also* Lordship of the Isles
Court of Session
  appeals from, 43
  Canon law influence, 31–2, 165, 166, 323, 347
  citation of decisions, 41, 150–4, 174
  ecclesiastical court appeals, 35, 195
  foundation and development, 7, 33–5, 47
  as "the King's Great Consistory", 165, 218, 325
courtesy, 3, 26, 149, 163, 265, 284–6, 292, 295, 301–2, 304–6
  early cases concerning, 297–309, 299, 310
Craig, Thomas, of Riccarton
  editions of *Jus Feudale*, 13–14
  importance as writer, 10, 11, 38, 39, 45
  importance of *Jus Feudale*, 38, 39
  on Canon law, 29, 188, 195, 218, 323
  and English law, 144–8, 168–70, 181
  on hierarchy of sources, 8, 170–2
  influence on Stair, 41, 144, 145, 149, 151–2
  Lord Kames' comment regarding, 191n2
  on *Regiam Majestatem*, 147–8
  on registration of sasine, 178–9
  on Roman law, 41–2, 169–70, 185
  on terce and courtesy, 149, 194
Cranworth, Lord Chancellor, 49–50, 203 210
Crawford, Barbara, 139n75
Crichton, Robert, 69
Croft Dickinson *see* Dickinson, W C
Cross, Sir Rupert, *Evidence*, 365
Crown Prosecution Service, 50
croy, 69
culrath, 74–6, 117, 164

Dalriada, kingdom of, 17, 18–19
Danelaw, 135, 139–41
David, Hélène, 142, 153
David I, King of Scots, 25, 61–2, 72, 157
David II, King of Scots, 25, 67, 249–50, 265, 285, 297, 300–1, 308
Davidson, Lord, 211
Davies, John Reuben, 14
Deas, Lord, 269
deathbed, law of, 162, 277, 282, 370
Declaration of Arbroath, 80, 81
delegated legislation, growth of, 47, 48
delict, 9, 47–8, 188
Denning, (A T) Lord, 365
desertion, 4, 227–8, 229–32
detention without trial, 42
devolution, 50
Dewar, Finlay, 24
dewar, title of, 64–5
Dicey, A V, 44
Dickinson, W C, 2n4, 55, 61, 64, 65–7, 76, 82, 108, 123–5
Dickson, W G, *Treatise on Evidence*, 357–9
diminished responsibility, 48
divorce, 4, 5, 89, 93, 195, 227–32, 369
Dodd, Leslie, 13, 145n15, 169n65, 179n29

Dolezalek, Gero, 38n75
Donald III (Donald Ban), King of Scots, 94–5
Donald of Isla, Lord of the Isles, 73
Donaldson, Gordon, 322–3
donations *mortis causa*, 183, 274, 295, 295n92
doomster, 21–2, 56
Douglas, Sir Archibald, 299–301
Douglas, James, 9th earl of Douglas, 260
Douglas, Sir James, of Dalkeith, 26, 297–309 *passim*, *299*, *310*
Douglas, Margaret, of Galloway, 260
Douglas, Mary, 298, *299*, 300, *310*
Douglas, William, 1st earl of Douglas, 298
Douglas, William, 8th earl of Douglas, 259–61
Douglas, Sir William, of Liddesdale, 298, *299*
Dove Wilson, John, 54
Du Plessis, Jacques, 365, 369
duels *see* judicial duels
Dunbar, Agnes, 308
Dunbar, William, 303
Duncan, A A M, 7n29, 11n48, 14, 55n11, 60, 94n42, 110–1, 116, 125, 246n32, 259
Duncan I, King of Scots, 94–5
Duncan II, King of Scots, 95–6, 157
Dundas, Lord President, 172
Dunedin, Lord President, 228, 315, 339
Dunlop, Annie, 260, 260–1
Durantis, William, *Speculum Judiciale*, 164
Durkan, John, 145n15

ecclesiastical courts *see* Church courts
Edgar, King of Scots, 157
Edinburgh, University of, 175, 189, 221
Edmondson, Joseph, 108, 120
Edward I, King of England, 25, 120, 121, 158, 159
Edward III, King of England, 297
Elizabeth I, Queen of England, 146, 182
Elizabeth II, Queen of Great Britain, 57
Elphinstone, Bishop William, 31, 160, 166, 323n59
Elphinstone, William senior, 159
Elton, Sir Geoffrey, 54n2

Emslie, George, Lord Justice General, 239
English Common law
  birlaw, 134, 135–8
  Canon law influence, 28, 326–7
  divorce, 231–2
  homicide and murder, 239–42, 254, 257, 262
  judicial duels and writs of right, 302–3
  legitimation, 30, 194
  marriage laws, 179, 219, 233
  obligations, 313n12, 318–19, 331, 337–8, 344n149
  presumptions, 352
  procedure by writ and inquest, 24
  research on juries, 243
  Roman law influence, 36, 346–7
  succession, 280, 283, 284, 288, 290, 291, 293
    rights of dower and curtesy, 194, 195n12, 285, 286, 301n12, 302, 304–5
English law influence
  on Scottish Common law, 160–3, 176–8
    Anglo-Norman imports, 23–6, 60–3
    debate in 1990s, 173–4
    evidence, 361, 365
    homicide, 243, 255–7
    House of Lords decisions, 48–51
    juries, 347
    role of *Glanvill see* Glanvill, Ranulf de
    Sellar's approach to, 6–7
    succession, 162–3, 283–4, 293, 294
    terminology of "common law", 148–9, 157
  views of writers
    Craig, 144–8, 168–70, 181
    Pont, 181–2
    Skene, 167–8, 181
    Stair, 6–7, 142–55, 162, 176
  on Scottish legislation
    borrowings from England, 178–80
    drafting by English lawyers, 48–9
entails, 268–9, 271, 272, 274, 281
Erskine, John, of Carnock
  importance as writer, 45
  on birleymen, 128
  on law of deathbed, 282
  on marriage, 191–2, 200

Erskine, John, of Carnock (*cont.*)
  on obligations, 321
  on presumptions, 353–4, 360
  on promise, 329n89, 331–3
Erskine, Sir Robert, 299–301
Erskine, Sir Thomas, 26, 297–309 *passim*, 299, *310*
Erskine, (Thomas) Lord, 225
Ethelred II, King of England, 141
Eugenius IV, Pope, 99
Evans-Jones, Robin, 182, 183, 189n76, 190n82
evidence *see* presumptions

Faculty of Advocates, 3, 45–6
*fecht*, 62, 77–9
Ferdinand II, King of Naples, 226
Fergus Mor mac Erc, King of Scots, 57
Fergusson, Sir James, of Kilkerran, 197n24
feu ferme, 25
Feudal law
  arrival in Scotland, 60–3, 147
  land ownership, 3, 4–5, 25, 62, 78
  *Libri Feudorum*, 20, 161
  Sellar's approach to, 11
  in Western Europe, 20, 161
Field, David, *Law of Evidence*, 362
Fife, Constantine, earl of, 62
Fife, Duncan, earl of, 62
Fife, earls of, 62n46, 76
Fife, Malcolm, earl of, 108, 110, 111, 113
FitzPatrick, Elizabeth, 115
Fordun, John of, 58, 61, 87, 95, 108, 115–16, 121, 297, 298–300, 304
forethocht felony, 241–2, 245–62 *passim*
Forrester, Thomas, 75
fosterage, 21, 70–1
franchise courts *see* barony courts; regality courts
Fraser, Lord, of Tullybelton, 51
Fraser, Patrick, Lord, 192–3, 199, 222n26, 223
Fraser, Sir William, 77
French law, 15, 46, 143

galley service, 79
Gallich, Donald, 100
Gane, C H W, 68

George Heriot's Hospital, 180–1
German law, 15, 35, 46, 143
*Gesta Annalia*, 108–9, 115, 116, 121
Glanvill, Ranulf de, *De Legibus*
  as source for *Regiam Majestatem*
    generally, 27, 147, 149, 162, 176, 280
  on homicide, 245
  on law of deathbed, 282, 370
  on leaving heritage by will, 281
  on legal rights, 163, 194–5, 266, 289–90, 301
Glasgow, University of, 98n56
Glassford, James, *Principles of Evidence*, 355–6, 357
Glenlee, Lord, 208, 211, 213
*Gloag and Henderson*, 45, 317n34, 334
Godfrey, A M, 34n57, 34n61
Goff, (Robert) Lord, 239
Goffredus de Trano, 165n50, 325, 329n89
Goodare, Julian, 180n36
Goody, Jack, 236
Gordon, Sir Gerald, 240, 250, 262
Gordon, Sir Robert, 67, 102
Gordon, W M, 183
Gormlaith, Irish Queen, 90
Gow, J J, 311n1, 316n27, 341
Grant, Alexander, 78, 301n9
Gratian, Emperor, 28
gratuitous obligations, 330, 332, 334, 341, 341–5
Gray, Sir Thomas, 258
Great Cause, 72–3, 158, 283
Green, T A, 240, 242, 243, 256
Greene, David, 69
*Green's Encyclopaedia of Scots Law*, 329, 333
Gregory, Donald, 84–5, 86, 98, 99, 106
Gregory VII, Pope, 90
Gregory IX, Pope, *Decretals*, 28, 164, 196, 197, 257–8
Gretton, G L, 180n39, 295n87
Grieve, Henry, 120
Grimble, Ian, 102
Groenewegen van der Made, Simon à, 320
Grotius, Hugo, 294, 313, 318, 319, 320, 332
Gruamach, Donald, 100–1
Gruoch, Queen, 19

Gudelinus, Petrus, 318
Gulathing Code, 32
Gunn, Elizabeth, 100
Guthrie, Lord, 209, 213, 214

Haddington, Sir Thomas Hamilton, 1st earl of, 326
  Haddington's Decisions, 316n31
Hailes, Lord, Reports, 31, 219, 315
Hamilton, Robert, 34
handfasting, 84–86, 89
Hannay, R K, 7n29
Harald Maddadsson, 96n49
Harding, Alan, 6, 175
Hardwicke, Philip Yorke, 1st earl of, 219, 225
Hay, Sir Gilbert, 248–9, 260, 261
Hay, William, 193, 196, 236
Heineccius, Johann Gottlieb, 358
Hellwege, Phillip, 311, 329
Helmholz, R H, 29n37, 318–19, 326–7, 369
Henry of Scotland, 72
Henry II, King of England, 91, 371
Henry VIII, King of England, 179, 216n89
Heriot, George, 180–1
heritage *see under* succession
Hermand, Lord, 230
hierarchy of sources, 8, 170–2
High Court of Justiciary, 6, 22, 43, 48, 56
Hodge, (Patrick) Lord, 51
Home, Henry, Lord Kames
  importance as writer, 46
  comment regarding Craig, 191n2
  on harmonisation of laws, 146
  on marriage, 199, 222n26
  on murder, 254
  on repledging to franchise courts, 76
  Sellar's interest in, 9n42, 55
  on Stair's *Institutions*, 152
  style letter of slains, 164
homicide, 239–62
  and assythment, 243–4
  bleeding as presumption of guilt, 370–2
  casual homicide, 251, 252–4, 257
  child murder, 368
  debate in England, 239–40, 241–2

forethocht felony/*chaudemellee* distinction, 241–2, 245–62 *passim*
  killing of John Comyn, 258–9
  killing of William, earl of Douglas, 259–61
  murder as secret killing, 244
Hope, (David) Lord, of Craighead, 40n81, 51, 286–7
Hope, Sir Thomas, Lord Kerse, 322
Hope, Sir Thomas, *Major Practicks*, 40, 322, 325, 347–8, 347n5, 348n6, 367
House of Lords, 43, 49–50, 50–1
Hume, Baron David
  importance as writer, 45, 47, 354
  on circumstantial evidence, 354
  on homicide and murder, 250, 255, 257, 371–2
  on incest cases, 235
  on marriage, 200–1
  on promise, 329, 333
  on succession, 290, 291, 293–4, 295
Hywel Dda (South Welsh king), 18

Iceland, 32n50, 96n49
incest, 30, 37, 232–8
Ine, West Saxon king, 141
Ingibjorg Finnsdottir, 95–6
Inglis, John, Lord Justice-Clerk/Lord President, 183n51, 202, 205, 206, 274, 329, 337
Innes, Cosmo, 11n48, 14, 37, 86–7, 129, 133–4, 196
Innes, Sir Thomas, of Learney, 58, 107–8, 115, 116, 120, 122
institutional writers, 3, 39, 45
  *see also* Bell, George Joseph; Craig, Thomas; Erskine, John; Hume, Baron David; Mackenzie, Sir George, of Rosehaugh; M'Douall, Andrew, Lord Bankton; Stair, James Dalrymple, Viscount
intestate succession, 177–8, 282–7, 288, 292
Ireland
  early law, 18, 19, 60
  kings of, 58–9, 87–8
  marriage law and customs, 87–93, 94, 220, 225, 226, 232
Ireland, R D, 193

Irnerius, 19–20
Irvine Smith, James, 234, 348
Isabelle of Vermandois, 60

James I, King of Scots, 308
James II, King of Scots, 76, 259–1
James III, King of Scots, 65, 159–60
James IV, King of Scots, 159, 160
James V, King of Scots, 54, 229
James VI, King of Scots, 43, 63, 145, 166–7, 371
James VII, King of Scots, 80
Johnson, Samuel, 21, 71
Jolowicz, J A, 85
Jones, Michael, 140
judicial duels, 297–301, 302–4, 306, 309
judicial review, 48
judicial torture, 180
juries, 24, 163, 243, 262, 346–7, 351, 354–5, 363
*jus commune*, 21, 318–20, 368
*jus quaesitum tertio*, 316–17, 327
*jus relictae*, 149, 163, 178, 266, 271–2, 290, 294
*jus relicti*, 271–2, 290, 294
justiciar, 6, 23, 26, 62, 163
Justinian, *Corpus Iuris Civilis*, 16, 19–20, 36, 161, 185, 294

Kames, Lord *see* Home, Henry
Kaye, J M, 240, 241–2, 255–6
Keane, E H, 362n94
Keith, Janet, 306, *310*
Keith, Sir Robert, 281
*kenkynolle* (*cenn cineóil*, *ceann cinéil*), 64, 264
Kennedy chiefs, 64
Kenneth mac Alpin, King, 17, 57, 122n66, 163
king's poet (*ollamh*), 117–19
kingship *see* monarchy and kingship
Kinloch, Lord, 286
Kinnear, Lord, 337
Knox, Jean, 30, 235, 237
Kötz, Hein, 154
Kyllachy, Lord, 315

Lamberton, Bishop William, 258, 259

land
  burdens and servitudes, 21, 25, 62, 77–9, 81, 130n30, 164
  feudal tenure, 3, 4–5, 25, 62, 78
  leases, 38
  registration of title, 3, 5, 38, 178–9
  trust disposition and settlement, 276, 281–2
  udal ownership, 32
  *see also* succession
Lanfranc, Archbishop, 90
Langbein, J H, 346
Law Society of Scotland, 51
leases, law of, 38
Lee, R W, 294
legal profession, 3, 26, 31, 45–6
legal rights *see* courtesy; *jus relictae*; *jus relicti*; *legitim*; terce
*legitim*, 37, 149, 163, 178, 266, 271–2, 290, 292, 294
legitimation, 30, 165, 193–4, 293
Leneman, Leah, 216n2
Lennox, earldom of, 67
Leslie, Bishop John, 36, 181, 185–6
Leuven, University of, 159
Levack, B P, 180
*Libri Feudorum*, 20, 161
liferent and fee, 270, 272–3
Lindsay, Sir Jerome, of Annatland, 108, 119
Lord Lyon King of Arms, 6, 12–13, 58, 107–8, 119–22; *see also* Innes, Sir Thomas, of Learney; Lyon Court
Lordship of the Isles, 22, 56, 56–7, 63, 73, 96–7
  inauguration ceremonies, 58, 114–15, 118–19
Luig, Klaus, 153, 154
Lyall, R J, 119
Lyon Court, 12–13, 107, 108, 264; *see also* Lord Lyon King of Arms

McAndrew, Bruce, 111
MacAulay, Aulay, of Ardincaple, 264
MacBeth, Fergus, 63; *see also* Beaton physicians
Macbeth, King of Scots, 19
McBryde, W W, 311
M'Caig, Catherine, 268

M'Caig, John Stuart, 268
MacCormack, Geoffrey, 320n43, 329
MacDonald, Alexander, Lord of the Isles, 99
MacDonald, Alexander, of Dunnyveg, 102
MacDonald, Alexander, of Glengarry, 100
MacDonald, Alexander, of Lochalsh, 100
MacDonald, Angus Og, 97, 101
MacDonald, Celestine (Gillespic), of Lochalsh, 84, 99, 99–100
MacDonald, Donald Dubh, 101
MacDonald, Elizabeth (wife of Alexander, Lord of the Isles), 99
MacDonald, Flora, 106, 217
MacDonald, Hugh (Uisdean) (ascribed to), 114–15, 118, 121
MacDonald, Hugh (Uisdean, Austin), of Sleat, 84, 99, 100, 104
Macdonald, J H A, Lord Justice-Clerk, 240
MacDonald, John, Lord of the Isles, 99, 100, 101
MacDonald, John Móideartach, 101
MacDonald, John Mor ("the Tanist"), 73
MacDonald, John Mor, of Dunivaig, 101–2
MacDonald, Margaret, 102
MacDonald, Ranald Mor, of Benbecula, 70, 101, 104, 105–6, 217
MacDonald, Ranald Og, of Benbecula, 106
MacDonald, Ranald (son of Somerled), 97
MacDonald, Somhairle, 92
MacDonalds
  of Clanranald, 81, 103–4
  of Dunivaig and the Glens, 97
  of Keppoch, 81, 101–2
  of Sleat, 103–4
  *see also* Lordship of the Isles
M'Douall, Andrew, Lord Bankton, *Institutes*, 45, 142, 274, 330–1, 351–3
MacDougall, Ewen, lord of Argyll, 77
MacDuff, Law of Clan, 76
McEwan, R G, 212
McGladdery, Christine, 260, 260–1
MacGregor, Alexander, of Glenstrae, 264
MacGregor chiefs, 274
Mackay, Aeneas, 54
MacKay, Donald, 102

Mackay, (J P H) Lord, of Clashfern, 51
MacKay, John, 102
McKechnie, Hector, 175
Mackenzie, Sir George, of Rosehaugh
  career and works, 14, 42, 45, 350
  on homicide and murder, 253–4, 257, 258n73
  on passing of risk, 152n48
  on presumptions, 347, 350–1
  on promise, 330
  on *Regiam Majestatem*, 149
  on statutes and cases, 153
MacKenzie, Hector Roy, of Gairloch, 102
MacKenzie, Janet, 103
MacKenzie, John, of Killin, 102
MacKenzie, Kenneth, Lord Kintail, 103
MacKenzie, Kenneth, of Kintail, 102
Mackenzie Stuart, Lord, 321–2, 326
Mackintosh, Lord, 208
MacLaide, Christiana, 99
Maclean, Alasdair, 106
MacLean, Catherine, 102
MacLean, Lachlan Cattanach, of Duart, 102–3
MacLeans, genealogy, 110
MacLeod, Alexander, of Harris, 102
MacLeod, Mary, of Dunvegan, 74, 98
MacLeod, Rachael, 82n154
MacLeod, Ruairi, 103
MacLeod, Torquil, of Lewis, 100–1
MacLeod, Torquil Conanach, 103
MacLeods of Assynt, 25, 98
MacLeods of Lewis, 98, 103
Macmillan, (H P) Lord, 283
MacMurrough, Dermot, king of Leinster, 91
Macnair, Michael, 346–7
MacNeil, Hector Og, of Ersary, 82
Macneil, Ruairi, of Barra, 70, 104–5
M'Neill, Duncan, Lord Advocate, 220–1, 230–1; *see also* Colonsay, Lord
MacNeills of Gigha, 73
Macneils of Barra, 98
MacNiocaill, Gearoid, 88
Macphail and Ruxton, "Evidence", 361, 362
MacPhail, J R N, 100
MacPherson, James, 75
MacPherson, John, 74

MacQueen, H L, 158, 173, 174, 177, 186n61, 187n69, 189, 340, 342, 343, 344
MacQueen, Tadhg, 82
MacRae, Reverend Farquhar, 103
McRoberts, David, 160
MacRuairi, Christiana, 98
MacRuairi, Dugald, king of Innse Gall, 97
MacVurich, Lachlan, 114
Maine, Sir Henry, 88
Maitland, F W, 11n48, 12, 28, 159, 163, 233, 238, 241, 255–6, 283, 287, 289–90, 302, 306
Major, John, 80, 81
Malcolm II, King of Scots, 61
Malcolm III (Malcolm Canmore), King of Scots, 57, 87, 94, 94–6
Malcolm IV, King of Scots, 59–60, 72, 157
malice aforethought, 241–2, 245–62 *passim*
manrent, 63, 260
Manuel y Rodríguez, Miguel de, 39
*maor* (mair), 64, 82
Mapstone, Sally, 261n90
Mar, earldom of, 63, 67, 96, 306–7
Margaret, Queen of Scots (wife of James III), 32
Margaret, Saint, Queen of Scots (wife of Malcolm Canmore), 94, 95
marriage
  overview, 4, 5
  Canon law influence, 29–30, 193, 195–8, 218–19, 221–3, 232
  Celtic secular marriage *see* Celtic secular marriage
  clandestine, 225–226
  by cohabitation with habit and repute (MCHR), 191–215, 223–4
    under 1939 Act, 203–7
    case law, 202–3, 207–13, 229
    institutional writers on, 191–2, 199–201
    origins, 165, 191–8, 367
  constitution of, 217–26
  contracts of, 273–4
  dissolution of, 4, 5, 195, 227–32
  jurisdiction of courts, 35, 193, 195, 217–18, 228, 323–5

  prohibited degrees and incest, 30, 37, 179, 232–8
  scholarship on, 216–7
Martin, Martin, 84, 89, 106, 114, 120
Martin, Olaus, 71
Mascardus, Jacobus, 357
Matheson, William, 71
Maule, Sir Thomas, of Panmure, 308–9, *310*
Mayfield, Lord, 211
Medwyn, Lord, 287
Megaw, Basil, 57n21
Menochio, Giacome (Menochius), 357, 368, 371n126
Menteith, earldom of, 96
Menzies, Archibald, 324
Meyer, Poul, 140
military service, 25, 62, 77–9
Millar, Thomas, 254–5
Mitchell, J D B, 44, 175
Mitchell, J G, 212
Mitchison, Rosalind, 216n2
Modestinus, 202–3
Molina, Luis de, 316, 318, 320
monarchy and kingship
  differences in royal prerogative, 79–81
  early kingship, 58–60
  inauguration ceremonies, 57–8, 108–16, *112, 113*, 117–22
  royal charters, 157
  royal succession, 17–18, 81, 274
  symbolism, 160
  *see also* tanistry
Moncreiffe, Sir Iain, of that Ilk, 111
Monro, Donald, 97
moot (*mót, mòd*), 60–1
Moray, James Stewart, 1st earl of, 234
More, J S, 201, 356n51
Morison, Lord, 203
mormaor, 63–4
mortancestry, brieve of, 302–3, 304–6, 307
Morton, James Douglas, 4th earl of, 186
Morton, Lord, of Shuna, 239
moveables *see under* succession
murder *see* homicide
Mure, Lord, 202, 205, 206
Murray, A L, 69n77, 128
Murray, David, 5n14

Murray, Lord, 211–12
Murray, William, Lord Mansfield, 46

Neaves, Lord, 202, 205, 206, 337
Neilson, George, 5n14, 11n48, 55, 183–4, 297, 303–4
Nicholls, Kenneth, 68–9, 70, 88, 91–2, 116
Nicholson, Ranald, 260, 300n9
Normand, Lord, 340–1
"notour" adultery, 228, 233
novel dissasine, brieve of, 302–3, 304–6

Ó Corráin, Donnchadh, 59, 60, 88, 118
Ó Maol-Chonaire, 118
Obertus de Orto, 20, 161
O'Brien kings of Munster, 59, 90–1
O'Cathan, Aine, 97
O'Connor, Aedh, king of Connacht, 97
O'Connor, Cablaigh Mor, 92
O'Connor kings of Ireland, 118
O'Connor, Ruairi (Roderic), High King of Ireland, 87, 91, 103
O'Connor, Tadg, 92
O'Connor, Turlough, king of Connacht, 91, 92
O'Donnell, Calvagh, 102
O'Donnell, Charles James, 53
O'Donnell, Frank Hugh, 53
O'Donnell, Niall, king of Tirconell, 92
Ogilvie, (James) Lord, 75
Ollivant, Simon, 193, 323
O'Neill, Shane, 102
Orkney, 4, 32, 139
Orkney, William Sinclair, earl of, 261
O'Rourke, Aedh, king of Brefne and Cathal, 92
O'Rourke, Devorgilla, 91
outlawry, 273

Pálsson, Hermann, 96n49
Panormitanus (Niccolo de Tudeschis), 198
parliamentary practice, 180
Paschal II, Pope, 94
Paton, G C H, 201
Patrick, Lord, 208
Peake, Frederick G (Peake Pasha), 133
Peel, John, 226

Petrus de Palude, 236
Philipp, Karl (Charles), Prince of Schwarzenberg, 111
Picts, 17–18
"pit and gallows", right of, 26
Pitcairn, Robert, *Criminal Trials*, 250
Plucknett, T F T, 284
Pocock, J G A, 145, 148
pollicitation, 327–30
Pollock, Sir Frederick, 283
Pont, Reverend Robert, 181–2
Pothier, R J, 358
Practicks, 39–40; *see also* Balfour, Sir James, of Pittendreich; Hope, Sir Thomas; Spotiswoode, R,
Prestwich, Michael, 259
presumptions, 346–72
  overview of law, 363–5
  possibilities for further study, 366–72
  treatment by institutional writers, 347–55
  treatment by textbook writers, 355–63
prior rights, 292
promise, 311–45
  case law, 334–41
  in *jus commune*, 318–20
  Requirements of Writing (Scotland) Act, 341–5
  in Scottish common law and practice, 320–2, 325–6, 327
  in Stair's *Institutions*, 30–1, 311, 312–17, 327–30, 331
  treatment by later writers, 330–4
Protectorate, 15, 144
public prosecutions, 69
Pufendorf, Samuel, 320, 332

Raitt, F E, *Evidence*, 362–3
Ramsay, Allan (poet), 132
Ranulf de Glanvill, 27
Raymond of Peñafort, Saint, 164, 257–8
Reed, (Robert) Lord, of Allermuir, 51
Reformation, 7, 10, 35, 164, 195, 323
regality courts, 10–11, 26, 44–5, 74–7
*Regiam Majestatem*
  Canon law imports, 165, 325, 329n89
  controversy surrounding, 14, 27, 147
  date of, 27, 244–5
  importance of, 27

*Regiam Majestatem (cont.)*
  as source of Stair's ancient customs, 149, 162, 176, 280
  on birlaw, 124, 125–7
  on homicide and murder, 244–5, 251–2
  on law of deathbed, 282, 370
  on leaving heritage by will, 281
  on legal rights, 163, 194–5, 266, 289–90, 301
  on obligations, 329n89
  Cooper edition, 14, 27, 247, 249–50, 289–90
  Skene editions, 14n61, 39, 67, 126, 127, 154, 166–8, 181, 290
  new edition, 14
Register of Sasines, 3, 5, 38, 178–9
Reid, K G C, 343
Reid, Lord, of Drem, 51, 309n42
Richard I, King of England, 371
Richter, Thomas, 316n30
Robert I, King of Scots *see* Bruce, Robert
Robert II, King of Scots, 119, 300–1
Robert III, King of Scots, 30, 306
Robertson, David, 131n32, 138
Robertson, J J, 175
Robertson, Lord, 209–10, 210
Robinson, Olivia, 14
Rodger, Alan (Lord Rodger of Earlsferry), 51, 316n29, 316n30, 316n31, 328–9
Roman (Civilian) law
  connection with Canon law, 20
  definition of Civilian system, 185
  intestate succession, 282
  naked pactions (*pacta nuda*), 315–16, 317, 319–20
Roman law influence
  on English law, 36, 346–7
  on Scots law
    corroboration in evidence, 354
    homicide, 258
    issues of independence, 159
    presumptions, 346, 349, 350, 363
    Reception in Scotland, 36–7, 172, 182–7
    role of church and judges, 10, 166
    Sellar's approach to, 8–10
    succession, 184–5, 293–6
    views of Craig, 41–2, 169–70, 185
    views of Stair, 8, 143, 185, 188–9

Ross, Donald, Lord Justice-Clerk, 210
Ross, Margaret, 360
royal justice, 6
royalty *see* monarchy and kingship
Russell, John, 182n46
Ruxton, L M, 361, 362

sale of goods, 152n48
Sánchez, Tomás, 228
Scone Abbey seal, 110–14, *113*, 122n66
Scotia, kingdom of, 17, 156–7
Scots of Dalriada, 17, 18–19
Scott, John, Lord Eldon, 225
Scott, Sir Walter, 22, 46, 56, 85, 132, 216n2, 368, 372n130
Scottish Enlightenment, 45–6
Scottish Land Court, 12
Scottish Law Commission, 51, 215, 224, 341–2, 343
Scottish Universities Law Institute, 51
Scrope, John, 80n140
sea law, 38
Seafield, Lord, 52
*seanchaidh* (sennachie)
  appearance and status, 109n11, 117, 118
  and Lord Lyon King of Arms, 58, 107–8, 119–22
  role and duties, 58, 107, 113–14, 115, 118–19
Selchow, Johann Heinrich Christian von, 39
Sellar, W D H
  approach to legal history, 1–2, 5–14
  as Lord Lyon King of Arms, 6, 12–13
  studies and legal training, 2–3, 81
*Senchus Fer nAlban*, 18–19, 79
serjeant, 64, 82
Seton, Sir Alexander, 309, *310*
Shapiro, Barbara, 346–7, 352, 355
Shaw, Lord, of Dunfermline, 339
Sheills, Thomas, 132
Sheldon, David, *Evidence*, 363
Shelley, Percy Bysshe, 226
sheriff courts, 31–2, 165
sheriff, office of, 23, 26, 32, 163
sheriffdoms, 61
Shetland, 4, 32, 139
Simms, Katherine, 91, 92, 93, 99

Simpson, A W B, 269
Sinclair, John, 39–40
Skene family, 73–4
Skene, Sir John
  parentage, 73–4
  studies abroad, 166
  views on Scottish Common law, 166–8
  on early marriage customs, 85, 86, 89, 98, 106
  *Of Crimes and Judges in Criminall Causes*, 251
  *Regiam Majestatem*, 14n61, 39, 67, 126, 127, 154, 181, 290
  *De Verborum Significatione*, 39, 74–5, 76, 124, 127, 251, 285–6, 301–2
Skene, W F, 55, 115–16, 297
slains (*sláinte*), letter of, 68–9, 117, 164
*slúagad*, 62, 77–9
Smith, D B, 228
Smith, Sir Thomas (T B), 3, 51, 183n54, 193, 204, 205, 311, 316n29, 328, 339, 340, 341, 342
Smyth, A P, 18n4
Smythe, Penelope Caroline, 226
Somerville, Marion, 82n152, 104–5
Sophia, Electress of Hanover, 274
Sorn, Lord, 228n53
Spens, John of, 24
Spotiswoode, Robert, *Practicks*, 326
Stair, James Dalrymple, Viscount
  importance as writer, 10, 40–1, 45
  role as judge, 144, 350
  *Decisions of the Court of Session*, 152
  *Institutions*
    authorial approach, 41, 41–2, 150–4, 174
    and Canon law, 8, 198, 218, 323
    on classification of obligations, 188–9
    on commissary courts, 325
    on contract law, 30–1
    on customary law, 7, 8, 148–50, 176, 177
    and definition/meaning of words, 143–4
    and hierarchy of sources, 8
    importance of work, 2, 40–1
    influence of English law, 6–7, 142–55, 162, 175–6
    on marriage, 199–200, 236
    More 1832 edition, 356n51
    on presumptions, 347, 348–50
    on promise, 30–1, 311, 312–18, 319–22, 327–30
    on quality of Scots law, 172
    and Roman law, 8, 143, 185, 188–9
    on succession, 177, 269, 280, 280–1, 282, 283, 287, 290, 295, 296
    on testamentary writings, 277
    on unjust enrichment, 143, 188–9
*Stair Memorial Encyclopaedia*, 51, 311, 361
Starkie, Thomas, 358
statute law
  borrowings from England, 178–80
  drafting by English lawyers, 48–9
  growth of, 47, 48
Stein, P G, 167, 182, 183n54, 184
Stevenson, Robert Louis, 254
Stewart, Alistair, 361n84
Stewart, Lady Jane, 229
Stewart, Sir Robert, 309, *310*
Stott, Lord, 210–11, 212, 213
Strathearn, Malise, earl of, 108, 110, 113
Stubbs, William, 28
succession, 279–96
  overview, 3–4, 279–80
  adopted children, 293
  Canon law influence, 165
  Celtic law traces, 71–4
    tanistry, 71–4, 82, 107
  and Celtic secular marriage, 85, 89
  Common law rules
    heritage, 25–6, 162–3, 267, 271, 280–7
    moveables, 178, 267, 280–1, 287–91
  English law influence, 6–7, 162–3, 177–8, 283–4, 293, 294
  and illegitimacy, 165, 193–4, 293
  on intestacy, 177–8, 282–7, 288, 292, 293
  law of conquest, 162–3, 284
  law of deathbed, 162, 277, 282, 370
  legal rights *see* courtesy; *jus relictae*; *jus relicti*; *legitim*; terce
  reforms under Succession (Scotland) Act 1964, 4, 267, 290, 292–3

Succession (cont.)
  Roman law influence, 184–5, 293–6
  see also testamentary writings
Supreme Court, 51

Tacitus, Germania, 141
tailzies, 268–9, 271, 272, 274, 281
Tait, George, Treatise on Evidence, 356–7
tanistry, 71–4, 82, 107
Taylor, Alice, 13, 14
terce, 3, 163, 165, 192, 194–5, 265, 271–2, 284–5, 292, 347–8, 367
testamentary writings
  corporeal and incorporeal property rights, 270–1
  form and character, 273–6
  historical summary, 267
  incapacity, 277
  limitations on acts, 271–3
  under medieval law, 263–6
  reasons for, 268–9
  and succession to heritage, 267, 271, 281–2
  and succession to moveables, 289–91
  taking of calp, 264
  unenforceable bequests, 268
  see also succession; trusts
Thayer, J B, Evidence, 346–7, 350, 361
Thomson, Derick, 55n11, 116–17
Thomson, J Maitland, 119
Thomson, Joseph M, 343–4
Thomson, Lord Justice-Clerk, 208, 213
Thomson, Thomas, 14
Thorfinn the Mighty, 95–6
tocher, 71
tòiseach, 64
toiseachdeor, 65–8, 66
Treaty and Acts of Union, 2, 43–4, 274
Trevor-Roper, Hugh, Lord Dacre, 54n2
trial by combat, 55
trial by jury, 163
  see also juries
trusts, 180–1, 295; see also testamentary writings
Tynwald court, Isle of Man, 77

Udal law, 4, 5–6, 32
Ullmann, Walter, 164

unjust enrichment, 9, 47–8, 143, 187, 188–9, 326, 327

Vatican archives, 97–8
Vinogradoff, Sir Paul, 85, 135

Walker, D M, 50, 54, 183n54, 193
Walkers on Evidence, 359–60
Walter of Guisborough, 258
Walton, F P, 193, 201–2, 205
ward holding, 25; see also military service
Watson, Alan, 36n67, 185
Watt, D E R, 109
Wedderburn, Alexander, 46
Weir, John, 30, 235
Welsh law, medieval, 18
Welwood, William, 38
Wesenbecius, Matthaeus, 319
Westbury, Lord, 202–3, 210
Westermarck, Edvard, 85
Whitelaw, Archibald, 159
Whitty, N R, 174
Wilkinson, A B, Evidence, 361
William fitz Duncan, 96
William I, King of Scots, 25, 49–60, 72, 157
William of Malmesbury, 95
wills see testamentary writings
Wills, Justice, 357
Wilson, J G, 193, 201n49, 205
Winchester, Angus, 137, 138, 141
Winton, Robert Seton, 1st earl of, 180
Wishart, Bishop Robert, 259
Witte, John, jr, 234n83
Wormald, Jenny, 55n11, 68
Wormald, Patrick, 55n11, 58–9
writ and inquest, procedure by, 23–4
writ or oath, proof by, 314–16, 340–1, 342
Wyntoun, Andrew of, 94–5

Young, Alan, 259
Young, Lord, 338

Zimmermann, Reinhard, 182, 291, 311, 329
Zweigert, Konrad, 154

EU representative:
Easy Access System Europe
Mustamäe tee 50, 10621 Tallinn, Estonia
Gpsr.requests@easproject.com

www.ingramcontent.com/pod-product-compliance
Lightning Source LLC
Chambersburg PA
CBHW070805300426
44111CB00014B/2433